R.S.LS

UNDERSTANDING INTERDEPENDENCE

THE MACROECONOMICS OF THE OPEN ECONOMY

UNDERSTANDING INTERDEPENDENCE

THE MACROECONOMICS
OF THE OPEN ECONOMY

Peter B. Kenen, Editor

Papers Presented at a Conference Honoring the
Fiftieth Anniversary of Essays in International Finance

PRINCETON UNIVERSITY PRESS   PRINCETON, NEW JERSEY

Copyright © 1995 by Princeton University Press
Published by Princeton University Press, 41 William Street,
Princeton, New Jersey 08540
In the United Kingdom: Princeton University Press, Chichester, West Sussex
All Rights Reserved

Library of Congress Cataloging-in-Publication Data

Understanding interdependence : the macroeconomics of the open
  economy / edited by Peter B. Kenen.
        p.   cm.
    "Papers presented at a conference honoring the fiftieth anniversary of
  Essays in international finance."
    Includes bibliographical references and index.
    ISBN 0-691-03408-7
    1. International finance—Congresses.   2. Foreign exchange rates—
  Congresses.   3. Monetary policy—Congresses.   I. Kenen, Peter B.,
  1932–   .
  HG205.U53   1995
  332\.042—dc20   94-36531
                                                             CIP

This book has been composed in Times Roman

Princeton University Press books are printed on acid-free paper
and meet the guidelines for permanence and durability of the
Committee on Production Guidelines for Book Longevity of the
Council on Library Resources

Printed in the United States of America

10 9 8 7 6 5 4 3 2

Contents

Figures

Tables _____

Introduction

IN JUNE 1943, the International Finance Section at Princeton University published the first of its *Essays in International Finance*. It was written by Friedrich A. Lutz and compared the Keynes and White plans for organizing the international monetary system after the Second World War. Soon thereafter, the Section published three more *Essays* concerned with postwar monetary problems, including Ragnar Nurkse's celebrated paper, *Conditions of International Monetary Equilibrium*.

In April 1993, the International Finance Section celebrated the fiftieth birthday of its *Essays* by convening a conference at Princeton. The conference reviewed recent research on international monetary issues but also examined policy problems that call for more research. Five sessions were devoted to surveys and assessments of recent research, two panels examined key policy problems, and Paul Krugman concluded the conference with a lecture in which he asked what we know and need to know about the international monetary system. The papers and panelists' presentations are published in this volume.

The first of the five sessions on recent research was concerned with exchange-rate behavior and the evolution of exchange-rate arrangements. The second examined recent work on the dynamics of current-account adjustment. The third examined research on capital mobility and international debt. The fourth session dealt with stabilization and liberalization in open economies. The fifth was devoted to research on international policy coordination and on monetary unification. There were discussants at each session, but their comments are not published in this book, because the conference papers have been revised extensively to take account of the discussants' comments. The first of the two panel discussions, led by Charles Kindleberger, debated the case for reforming the exchange-rate regime. The second panel, led by Paul Volcker, examined the outlook for stabilization and reform in the countries of Central Europe and the former Soviet Union.

The International Finance Section was founded in 1929 as an affiliate of the Department of Economics. It was funded initially by a gift in memory of James Theodore Walker, who died in an airplane accident two days after graduating from Princeton in 1927. The income from that gift has been used to finance the Walker Professorship of Economics and International Finance, as well as the work of the International Finance Section. The first Walker Professor, Edwin Kemmerer, also served as the first director of the Section. The research facilities of the Section were greatly strengthened by the collection of books and documents donated by Benjamin Strong, president of the Federal Reserve Bank of New York. The Section's present offices were provided by a generous grant from Merrill Lynch & Company.

In its early years, the Section financed and published research by faculty and staff at Princeton, including works by Frank Graham, Frank Fetter, and Richard Lester. The first few *Essays* were likewise written by economists associated with the Section. (Ragnar Nurkse was affiliated with the secretariat of the League of Nations, which had its home in Princeton during the Second World War.) In the late 1940s, however, the Section started to publish *Essays* by other economists, including Sir Roy Harrod, Raymond Vernon, Thomas Schelling, and James Meade. In 1950, moreover, the Section began to publish a new series, *Princeton Studies in International Finance*, and in 1995, it introduced a third, *Special Papers in International Economics*.[1]

Frank Graham became Walker Professor in 1945, followed by Jacob Viner in 1950, but they did not wish to assume the directorship of the Section. That position was filled by Gardner Patterson, who served from 1949 to 1958, and by Lester Chandler, who served from 1958 to 1960. The two positions were reunited in 1960, when Fritz Machlup became Walker Professor, and I have held both of them since 1971. The Section continues to support research by faculty and students at Princeton and has sponsored many conferences and meetings, including those of the "Bellagio Group" of officials and academics, which met periodically for ten years, starting in 1964. The Section is best known for its publications, however, having issued 190 *Essays*, 74 *Studies*, and 18 *Special Papers* as of the end of 1993.

Coincidentally, the conference on which this volume is based took place exactly twenty years after a similar conference sponsored by the Section, although the scope of the earlier conference was wider in one way and narrower in another.[2] It dealt with trade and trade policy, as well as monetary issues, but concentrated on empirical research, whereas the papers in this volume deal also with theoretical work. It is instructive, however, to compare the ways in which the two sets of conference papers cover common ground.

Both conferences heard papers on the roles of price and income changes in current-account adjustment, but the paper presented in 1973 devoted much attention to the sizes of the long-run price and income effects, whereas the paper presented in 1993 focused far more heavily on the short-run price effects and on factors affecting the pass-through of exchange-rate changes into import prices. Both conferences heard papers on capital mobility, but the 1973 paper was largely concerned with the modeling of capital flows, whereas the 1993

[1] A complete list of the Section's publications and a longer history of the Section itself can be found in another volume, *The International Monetary System: Highlights from Fifty Years of Princeton's Essays in International Finance* (Boulder, Colo., Westview Press, 1993), which was published on the eve of the conference to which this volume is devoted. It contains a dozen *Essays* chosen by a panel of economists who were asked to select those *Essays* that have had "a lasting impact on the way we think about the international monetary system."

[2] The papers presented at that conference appeared in *International Trade and Finance: Frontiers for Research* (Cambridge, Cambridge University Press, 1975).

paper made no use whatsoever of capital-flow data; it focused instead on indirect ways to measure capital mobility, using tests suggested by arbitrage conditions and by recent theoretical work on the implications of risk pooling and intertemporal optimization.

The earlier conference volume contained two papers that used large, multi-country models to analyze balance-of-payments adjustment under floating and pegged exchange rates, and it included a paper on reserves and liquidity, but there are no such papers in this volume. Conversely, this volume contains papers on exchange-rate behavior, intertemporal models of the current account, stabilization and reform in developing countries, the resolution of the international debt crisis, experience with international policy coordination, and the political economy of monetary union, but there were no such papers in the earlier volume. Clearly, the world has changed greatly, and so has our research agenda.

There is another difference between the two volumes. All of the papers in the earlier volume surveyed and synthesized large bodies of research, and some of the papers in this volume do that once again. The paper by Mark Taylor, for example, reviews research on exchange-rate behavior under various exchange-rate regimes, and the paper by Peter Hooper and Jaime Marquez reviews research on the roles of exchange rates and prices in the international adjustment process, although it reports original research as well. But several papers break new ground. Barry Eichengreen seeks to explain *why* countries switch between pegged and floating exchange rates. Michael Bruno provides a general framework for comparing experience across countries with inflation, growth, and stabilization. Charles Goodhart examines the political and economic obstacles to monetary union. I tried at first to insist that all of the authors produce comprehensive survey papers, but some of them fought for more freedom, and I am glad that I gave in.

Several people worked hard on this book. Giuseppe Bertola, assistant director of the International Finance Section, helped to plan the conference and worked closely with several authors on the revisions of their papers. Margaret Riccardi, the Section's own editor, edited all of the papers and prepared the manuscript for publication. Lillian Spais managed the flow of papers and people before, during, and after the conference. I am deeply grateful to them. I am likewise grateful to the authors of this book. They were remarkably attentive to deadlines and equally attentive to the comments and suggestions made by me and their discussants.

Peter B. Kenen

I

APPRAISING EXCHANGE-RATE ARRANGEMENTS

1

The Endogeneity of Exchange-Rate Regimes

BARRY EICHENGREEN

THE INTERNATIONAL monetary system has passed through a succession of phases characterized by the dominance of alternatively fixed or flexible exchange rates. Indeed, one of the more remarkable features of the last hundred years of international monetary experience is the regularity with which one regime has superseded another.[1] The quarter century leading up to World War I was the heyday of the classical gold standard, when exchange rates were pegged to gold and to one another over an increasing portion of the industrial and developing world. The war provoked the breakdown of the gold standard and was followed by an interlude of floating rates. Countries returned to gold in the second half of the 1920s, only to see their laboriously constructed fixed-rate system give way to renewed floating in the 1930s. The Bretton Woods Agreement of 1944 inaugurated another quarter century of exchange-rate stability. The next episode of floating began in the early 1970s and now seems to be in the process of being supplanted, mainly in Europe, by a move back toward fixed rates.

How are these repeated shifts between fixed and flexible exchange rates to be understood? Although the literature contains many illuminating studies of particular episodes in the history of the international monetary system (the rise of the gold standard or the breakdown of Bretton Woods, for example), it shows few attempts to develop general explanations for shifts between fixed-

This paper develops further some ideas sketched in an article contributed to a forthcoming festschrift in honor of Luigi De Rosa, edited by Elio D'Auria, Ennio Di Nolfo, and Renato Grispo. It draws on an ongoing collaboration with Beth Simmons of Duke University. I thank Luisa Lambertini, Graham Schindler, David Takaichi, and Pablo Vasquez for research assistance, and Jeffrey Frieden, Stanley Black, and Jacob Frenkel for comments. Financial support was provided by the Center for German and European Studies and the Center for International and Development Economics Research of the University of California at Berkeley. Much of the research for this paper was completed during a visit to the Wissenschaftskolleg zu Berlin, the hospitality and support of which are acknowledged with thanks.

[1] Readers dissatisfied by this capsule account will find remarkably few histories of this century of international monetary experience. Yeager (1966) gives a now dated, but still useful, account; Eichengreen (1985) provides a very brief overview that brings the story up to the early 1980s; and Bordo (1993) presents a more recent survey, focusing mainly on the macroeconomic characteristics of these different regimes.

and flexible-rate regimes.[2] Similarly, although the discipline of international economics contains many models of the collapse of fixed-rate regimes and of the transition from floating to pegged rates, few of the models attempt to endogenize the factors responsible for these shifts.[3] That is my goal here. I advance six hypotheses with the capacity to explain the alternating phases of fixed and flexible exchange rates into which the last century can be partitioned.

Before proceeding, some caveats are in order. First, I shall limit my attention to the dominant exchange-rate regime prevailing in the industrial countries at a given time. Thus, I treat the 1950s and 1960s as a period of fixed rates and the 1970s and 1980s as a period of floating, despite the fact that certain countries allowed their exchange rates to float in the first period or pegged them in the second. The hypotheses considered here are designed to shed light on changes over time in the dominant exchange-rate regime, not to illuminate cross-country variations.

Second, I make no claim for the novelty of the hypotheses considered here. All of them may be found in the literatures that have grown up around particular episodes in the history of international money and finance. The contribution of this discussion is rather to show how these hypotheses might be developed into a unified framework for studying the endogeneity of exchange-rate regimes.

Third, I make no pretense of systematically testing theory against evidence. Doing so would require more space than is afforded by one essay. But an important property of a satisfactory explanation for the endogeneity of exchange-rate regimes is that it can be empirically validated or rejected. The evidence presented here is intended to illustrate whether—and if so how—subsequent investigations might go about this task.

Fourth and finally, there is nothing necessarily incompatible about the six perspectives considered. It will be clear as we proceed that the overlap among competing hypotheses is considerable. An adequate account of the endogeneity of exchange-rate regimes will have to incorporate several explanations.

---

[2] For examples of episodic studies, see Gowa (1983), Cairncross and Eichengreen (1983), and Kunz (1987).

[3] The now-classic model of the collapse of fixed-exchange-rate regimes, building on Salant and Henderson (1978), is Krugman (1979). In most of this literature, switches from fixed to flexible rates are modeled as the consequence of incompatible monetary-fiscal and exchange-rate policies, with no attempt to endogenize the policies responsible for this outcome (a few important, if isolated, exceptions to this generalization are mentioned below). Similar statements apply to models of switches from flexible to fixed rates (Smith and Smith, 1990; Miller and Sutherland, 1990).

1 Leadership

A first perspective associates the maintenance of fixed exchange rates with the exercise of international economic leadership by a dominant power. This application of "the theory of hegemonic stability," associated with the work of Charles Kindleberger (1986), regards exchange-rate stability as an international public good from which all participants in the international monetary system benefit. But the public-good nature of exchange-rate stability means that the benefits of any one nation's contribution to the maintenance of the fixed-rate system accrue not just to its residents but to foreigners as well. This gives rise to a problem of collective action in which this stabilizing influence tends to be undersupplied. Countries may fail to refrain from actions that destabilize the fixed-rate regime if the benefits of those actions accrue to them alone but the costs are shared with their neighbors.

Hence, there is need for a "hegemon," or dominant power, to internalize these international externalities. If one country is large enough to reap the lion's share of the benefits of international monetary stability, it will willingly bear a disproportionate share of the burden of stabilizing the system. Alternatively, an unusually powerful nation may be able to compel other countries to contribute their fair shares to regime maintenance. The analogy is with a dominant firm in an imperfectly collusive cartel. The dominant supplier—Saudi Arabia in the Organization of Petroleum Exporting Countries (OPEC), for example—may willingly adjust its production to maintain cartel stability in the face of defection by one or more of its rivals, because it reaps the largest absolute benefits from the collective restriction of output. Alternatively, it may threaten to apply sanctions against potential defectors in order to compel their cooperation.

Variants of this interpretation of the preconditions for international monetary stability are found in Viner (1932), Gayer (1937), Brown (1940), and Nevin (1955), all of whom suggest that the troubled life and early demise of the interwar gold standard reflected inadequate leadership. The interwar gold standard, they allege, was destabilized by the absence of a dominant economic power to oversee its operation. By implication, the superior operation of the nineteenth-century gold standard was attributable to the leadership exercised by the British nation and its monetary agent, the Bank of England. Kindleberger's contribution was to frame the argument more analytically and to generalize it, suggesting that the return to fixed exchange rates after World War II and the relatively smooth operation of the Bretton Woods system for a quarter century thereafter were attributable to the beneficent influence of U.S. hegemony.

Two objections can be raised to this interpretation. First, the public-good characterization of fixed exchange rates, however appealing, is of questionable validity. In 1992, for example, Argentina stabilized its exchange rate against the dollar. Is it not accurate to say that essentially all the benefits of this action accrued to the Argentine Republic? Similarly, the members of the European Monetary System (EMS) have pegged their currencies to one another without the support of the world's leading economic power, the United States. Is it not also accurate to say that the benefits accrue to EMS participants and not to other countries, including the United States?

Second, the association of hegemony with international monetary stability may be a misreading of the evidence. As I have argued elsewhere (Eichengreen, 1989, 1992), the picture of Britain's having single-handedly operated the classical gold standard tends to be overdrawn. London may have been the leading international financial center prior to World War I, but it had significant rivals, notably Paris and Berlin, both of which possessed their own spheres of influence. The prewar gold standard was a decentralized, multipolar system, the smooth operation of which was hardly attributable to stabilizing intervention by a dominant economic power. Similarly, given the perspective afforded by distance, neither the design nor the maintenance of the Bretton Woods system seems solely attributable to the stabilizing influence exercised by the United States.[4] Great Britain succeeded in securing extensive concessions in the design of Bretton Woods, notably the right to maintain exchange controls on capital-account transactions (for a transitional period of perhaps five years) and current-account transactions (for an indefinite period) and to alter the exchange-rate peg unilaterally in the event of fundamental disequilibrium. When exchange-rate stability was threatened in the 1960s, rescue operations were mounted not by the United States but collectively by the Group of 7 (G-7). Effective leadership by a dominant economic power may have been absent in the 1930s and following the collapse of Bretton Woods, but it is far from clear that the surrounding intervals of exchange-rate stability were predicated on its presence.

How might one test more systematically for differences over time in the prevalence of international economic leadership that are sufficient to explain changes in the adequacy with which different fixed-exchange-rate regimes worked? Kindleberger (1986) has sought to operationalize the concept of economic leadership by suggesting five functions that the hegemon must undertake to stabilize the operation of the international economic system: it must (1) maintain a relatively open market for distress goods, (2) provide countercyclical, or at least stable, long-term lending, (3) police a relatively stable system of exchange rates, (4) ensure the coordination of macroeconomic policies, and (5) act as lender of last resort by discounting or otherwise providing liquidity in financial crisis. The extent to which the presumptive leader has

---

[4] Bordo and Eichengreen (1993) contain a recent collection of studies of Bretton Woods experience.

carried out these functions in different periods might be studied by measuring, for example, the openness of its market to distress goods, or fluctuations in the time profile of its long-term lending.

A problem in this approach is that a stable "international economic system," the dependent variable with which Kindleberger is concerned, is not the same as a stable system of (fixed) exchange rates. Whether the latter is a necessary condition for the former is unclear. Conversely, it is questionable whether functions (1), (2), (4), and (5) are necessary conditions for carrying out function (3). Might not a hegemon support a system of fixed exchange rates without at the same time, for example, engaging in stable long-term lending? Even if countercyclical lending by the leading creditor country contributes positively to the maintenance of fixed rates, it need not be essential.

Our discussion has skipped glibly over the difficulty of measuring the concepts associated with this view. How open must a market be to be "relatively open" to distress goods? How does one distinguish "distress goods" from other exports? Only in the financial realm has some progress been made in operationalizing such notions. Eichengreen (1987) used time-series methods to investigate whether the Bank of England's discount rate exercised a disproportionate influence over discount rates worldwide under the gold standard. Employing Granger causality tests to investigate the bivariate relation between the Bank of England's discount rate and rates of the Bank of France and the German Reichsbank, he found that changes in the Bank of England's rate had a strong tendency to provoke subsequent adjustments in the other rates, although evidence of reverse causality was weaker. For the EMS period, Giovannini (1989) and Cohen and Wyplosz (1989) report similarly that changes in German interest rates have had a much stronger tendency to prompt changes in interest rates in other EMS countries than is conversely true.[5]

Even for those inclined to uncritically accept this evidence, inferring the validity of the leadership hypothesis from the timing of interest-rate changes nonetheless remains problematic. Even if changes in the Bank of England's rate led (and led to) changes in the rates of other central banks during the gold-standard years, and, even if changes in German rates have done the same under the EMS, this speaks only obliquely to the importance of leadership—as the concept is formulated above—in the operation of these systems. It says nothing about the willingness of Britain or Germany to bear a disproportionate share of the burden of stabilizing the system or to compel other countries to contribute their fair shares to regime maintenance. And it fails to distinguish an alternative hypothesis: that the discount rates of these so-called "center"

[5] Fratianni and von Hagen (1992) dispute this conclusion. To capture the "German dominance hypothesis," they specify and reject a stronger null hypothesis, that is, that the monetary policies of the EMS countries other than Germany do not respond to monetary-policy changes outside the EMS, and that Germany makes absolutely no response to monetary-policy changes in other EMS countries.

countries were only serving as focal points for the international cooperation that really was critical for regime maintenance.

2 Cooperation

Thus, a second explanation, formulated in reaction to the first, emphasizes international cooperation. In this view, international monetary stability, of which fixed exchange rates are one aspect, requires collective management. The stability of exchange rates under the classical gold standard, in the second half of the 1920s, for a quarter of a century after World War II, and in Europe in the 1980s, is attributed in this view to systematic and regular cooperation among countries and their central banks. This hypothesis does not question the public-good character of international monetary stability, only the contention that its provision has required hegemonic dominance.

Under the classical gold standard, minor problems were dispatched by tacit cooperation, generally achieved without open communication among the parties involved. When global credit conditions were overly restrictive and a loosening was required, the requisite adjustments had to be undertaken simultaneously by several central banks. Unilateral action was risky; if one central bank reduced its discount rate but others failed to follow, that bank would suffer reserve losses and might be forced to reverse course. Under such circumstances, the most prominent central bank, the Bank of England, signaled the need for cooperative action by lowering its discount rate, and other central banks responded in kind. By playing follow-the-leader, the central banks of different countries coordinated the necessary adjustments.

Balance-of-payments crises, in contrast, required different responses of different countries. With the central bank experiencing the crisis having to stem its loss of reserves, other central banks could help the most by encouraging reserves to flow out of their coffers. Contrary movements in discount rates were needed. Because the follow-the-leader approach did not suffice, overt, conscious cooperation was required. Foreign central banks and governments also discounted bills on behalf of the weak-currency country and lent gold to its central bank. Consequently, the resources on which any one country could draw when its gold parity was under attack far exceeded its own reserves; they included the resources of the other gold-standard countries. This provided countries with additional ammunition for defending their gold parities, a form of cooperation that was crucial to the maintenance of the gold-standard system.

In advancing this view, my own work (Eichengreen, 1992) has relied on narrative evidence. For example, I described the response of European central banks to the Baring Crisis of 1890. The solvency of the House of Baring, which had borrowed to purchase Argentine central and local government bonds, was threatened by the collapse of the market in these securities following the arrival in London of news of the Argentine revolution. Confidence in other British financial institutions was disturbed, especially those from which Baring Brothers had borrowed. Foreign deposits were liquidated, and gold drained from the Bank of England as residents shifted out of deposits. In November 1890, at the height of the crisis, the bank's reserve fell to less than £11 million. Baring Brothers alone required an infusion of £4 million to avoid having to close its doors.

Committing such a large share of the Bank of England's remaining reserve to domestic uses threatened to undermine confidence in the convertibility of sterling. Fortunately, the dilemma was resolved through international cooperation. The Bank of England solicited a loan of £2 million in gold from the Bank of France and obtained £1.5 million in gold coin from Russia. Within days, the Bank of France made another £1 million in gold available. The news, as much as the fact, of these loans did much to restore confidence; it was not even necessary for the second tranche of French gold to cross the English channel.

Like the Baring Crisis, the 1907 financial crisis culminated more than a year of financial turbulence. In 1906, frantic expansion in the United States led to extensive American borrowing in London and to a drain of coin and bullion from the Bank of England. The bank responded by raising its discount rate repeatedly. But, with interest rates also high on the Continent, the measure attracted little gold. As in 1890, the threat to sterling was contained through international cooperation. The Bank of France repeatedly offered a loan to the Bank of England. The latter preferred instead, however, to have the Bank of France purchase sterling bills. The entry for foreign bills on the asset side of the balance sheet of the Bank of France rose from zero at the beginning of December 1906 to more than F65 million in November 1907 (roughly £3 million). Gold flowed out from the Bank of France, relieving the pressure on the Bank of England.

In addition to taking these steps, the Bank of England made clear to British investors holding American paper that their excessive holdings of such bills threatened the stability of the London market. In response to this pressure, British investors allowed 90 percent of this paper to run off in the early months of 1907. Credit conditions tightened in the United States, bursting the financial bubble.

As business in the United States turned down, nonperforming loans turned up, and a wave of bank failures broke out. These provoked a shift out of deposits and into currency, a surge in the demand for gold in the United States, and a drain from the Bank of England. Again, the key to containing the crisis was international cooperation. Both the Bank of France and the Reichsbank allowed their reserves to decline and transferred gold to England to finance England's transfer of gold to the United States. This willingness of other countries to part with gold was indispensable to the defense of the sterling parity.

The techniques developed in response to the difficulties of 1906 and 1907 were used regularly in subsequent years. In 1909 and 1910 the Bank of France again discounted sterling bills to ease seasonal strain on the Bank of England. The Italian financial expert Luigi Luzzatti recommended institutionalizing the practice through the establishment of an agency on the order of the Bank for International Settlements.

The reconstructed gold standard of the 1920s was similarly predicated on extensive international cooperation. Virtually every country that pegged its exchange rate in the mid-1920s received stabilization loans from the League of Nations or from foreign governments and central banks. American, British, French, and German central bankers consulted one another regularly and in July of 1927 held a summit on Long Island to coordinate adjustments in their discount rates. Prior to the death in 1928 of Benjamin Strong, the governor of the Federal Reserve Bank of New York, the record of international cooperation had shown "considerable merit."[6] Thereafter, declining cooperation coincided with the growing difficulties of operating the fixed-rate system.[7] The collective support operations and coordinated adjustments in domestic policies needed to sustain the system in 1931 were not sufficiently forthcoming.

This hypothesis also fits post–World War II experience with Bretton Woods. Monetary cooperation in Europe was extensive, starting with the European Payments Union, which provided balance-of-payments financing and a venue for ongoing consultation. New institutions, such as the Organisation for Economic Co-operation and Development (OECD) and the International Monetary Fund (IMF), were constructed to mobilize and monitor cooperative ventures over a wider area. Countries as prominent as the United Kingdom borrowed from the IMF to support their fixed exchange rates. As the period drew to a close, the IMF gave promise of becoming an important source of international liquidity in its role as the creator of Special Drawing Rights.

Finally, the hypothesis is consistent with one interpretation of the success of the EMS. The EMS is seen as a symmetric agreement sustained by, and in turn sustaining, reciprocal cooperation among the participating countries (Fratianni and von Hagen, 1992). The system is supported by institutional arrangements to systematize international cooperation. The EMS Act of Foundation explicitly requires strong-currency countries to provide unlimited support to their weak-currency counterparts. Participating central banks may also draw on the system's Very Short Term Credit Facility for up to seventy-five days. At the same time, the 1992 EMS crisis is a reminder that, even

[6] The quotation is from Clarke (1967, p. 20), who provides the definitive account of central-bank cooperation in the 1920s.

[7] I return in the next section to the inadequacies of international cooperation in the 1920s and consider explanations for the reason why it was not forthcoming.

when institutionalized—in this case by a European Council resolution—international cooperation cannot be taken for granted: an interpretation of the different fates of the Italian lira and British pound (both of which were forcibly devalued) and the French franc and Danish krone (which were successfully defended) is that the principal strong-currency country, Germany, cooperated more extensively with the first set of countries than with the second (Eichengreen and Wyplosz, 1993).

A limitation of this general approach, implied by the conclusion to the preceding section, is the difficulty of drawing the line between leadership and cooperation. A leader is often required to organize cooperative ventures. Much of the evidence consistent with international cooperation is also consistent with one country's taking a leadership role in cooperative arrangements.[8] A second limitation is the difficulty of measuring the actual extent of international cooperation. Econometric models have been widely used to assess the advantages and prevalence of cooperation. Broadberry (1989) calibrated a simple two-country model of monetary policy that can be used to estimate the advantages of cooperative monetary-policy responses between the wars. Foreman-Peck, Hughes Hallett, and Ma (1992) estimated an even more ambitious monthly econometric model of the transmission of the Great Depression among the principal industrial countries and applied it to this same question. Fratianni and von Hagen (1992) similarly used an empirical model of the EMS countries to demonstrate that monetary-policy cooperation is welfare enhancing relative to noncooperative policies and that an exchange-rate rule can in some cases move countries toward the cooperative solution. In all these simulations, cooperative solutions differ from observed outcomes, indicating that, in practice, international cooperation remains incomplete. This does not imply, however, that cooperation is absent or unimportant. Moreover, cooperative and noncooperative policies are typically judged in terms of their ability to stabilize output and prices, not their success in maintaining a fixed-rate regime. Although policies that stabilize output and prices are often compatible with maintenance of a fixed-exchange-rate regime, this need not be the case.[9]

3 Intellectual Consensus

A third explanation emphasizes intellectual consensus as a prerequisite for fixed-rate regimes. This explanation is directly related to the preceding perspective stressing international cooperation. If collaboration among countries

---

[8] This observation is implicit in the preceding discussion of day-to-day cooperation under the classical gold standard, which was organized on a follow-the-leader basis. In recognition of the importance of leadership to cooperative regimes, Keohane (1984) has suggested the concept of "hegemonic cooperation."

[9] A conflict is likely to arise when the incidence of macroeconomic disturbances differs across countries. This, of course, is the classic point of Mundell (1961). I return to it in the next section.

is required for the maintenance of a fixed-rate system, policymakers must be able to agree on the measures to be taken collaboratively. As Frankel and Rockett (1988) show, it is only by the sheerest coincidence that national policymakers who subscribe to different models of the economy will agree on what policy adjustments are needed to respond to economic problems threatening the stability of the exchange-rate system. A common model thus facilitates "regime-preserving cooperation."[10]

An illustration of this point is the troubled efforts at cooperation that plagued the interwar gold standard.[11] Before World War I, the acquisition over many years of a common conceptual approach to financial management had provided a framework conducive to international monetary cooperation. But different national experiences with inflation and deflation after the war and differences across countries in the severity of the early phases of the depression shattered this consensus and disrupted cooperation between countries such as Britain and France.[12] In Britain, deflation was recognized as a persistent problem even before the depression struck. Britain's slump resulted, in the dominant view, from a deflationary shock imported from abroad. World prices had started to collapse with the onset of the global depression, and the decline in international prices had not reduced domestic prices commensurately. Instead, rigidities in the domestic wage-price structure had priced British goods out of international markets, producing the macroeconomic slump. This interpretation of the crisis pointed to a policy response, that is, that monetary policy should be used to stabilize prices and to restore them to 1929 levels.

This conceptual framework had direct implications for the international monetary system. If the exchange rate was fixed, it was impossible for any one central bank to pursue reflationary initiatives. Unless reflationary policies were coordinated internationally, currency depreciation was a necessary concomitant. Absent a French commitment to reflate, the British saw themselves with no choice but to abandon the fixed-rate system.

The French refused to support British efforts to reconcile regime maintenance with monetary reflation because they subscribed to a different concep-

---

[10] The phrase in quotation marks paraphrases Kenen (1990). The relevance of these considerations to the recent evolution of Europe's exchange-rate regime should be obvious. It can be argued, for example, that the stagflation of the 1970s led to the emergence of a consensus that discretionary monetary policy is a blunt instrument for addressing problems of unemployment and is best directed toward price stability; this was a precondition for the establishment of the EMS. Similarly, the solidification of this view facilitated the successful negotiation in 1991 of the Maastricht Treaty on Economic and Monetary Union (although continued resistance to the Treaty's provisions in Britain and other countries indicates that consensus remains incomplete).

[11] The paragraphs that follow summarize the argument of Eichengreen and Uzan (1993).

[12] Although the brief summary here emphasizes the scope for cooperation between Britain and France, the complete story, as recounted in Eichengreen and Uzan (1993), must consider also cooperation between those countries and the United States.

tual model.[13] French policymakers looking backward from the vantage point of the 1930s saw inflation as the real and present danger, even when prices had already begun to collapse as the global slump spread. French policymakers attributed the crisis not to deflation and the passivity of policymakers but to monetary instability. In the prevailing French view, growing reliance on foreign-exchange reserves had fatally loosened the gold-standard constraints. Central banks had willingly accumulated sterling and dollar balances over the second half of the 1920s, allowing the Bank of England and the Federal Reserve System to pursue excessively expansionary policies. Between 1913 and 1929, productive capacity worldwide had expanded more rapidly than the supply of monetary gold. Because the demand for money rose with the level of activity, lower prices were necessary to provide a matching increase in the supply of real balances. Under the gold standard, a smooth deflation, such as that from 1873 to 1893, was the normal response. But in the 1920s, central banks used their discretionary power to block the downward adjustment of prices. They pyramided domestic credit on foreign-exchange reserves. Liberal supplies of credit had fueled speculation, raising asset prices to unsustainable heights and setting the stage for the stock market crash. Following that shock, central banks rushed to liquidate exchange reserves and prices fell abruptly. The consequent insufficiency of investment was the immediate cause of the slump.

In France, then, the crisis of the 1930s was seen as an inevitable consequence of the unrealistic policies pursued by central banks in the 1920s. To prevent deflation at that point from running its course would inaugurate another era of speculative excess and, ultimately, another depression. It was better to allow excess liquidity to be purged and prices to drop to sustainable levels. Only then would investor confidence be restored and sustainable recovery commence.

For the French, nothing more dramatically symbolized the problem of financial instability than disarray in the international monetary sphere. Exchange-rate instability discouraged investment and international trade. Maintaining the gold standard and respecting the constraints it imposed on inflation were regarded as the most important steps policymakers could take to promote confidence and recovery.

Thus, disagreement over the appropriate model of the economy prevented policymakers in different countries from agreeing on a coordinated response. Where unemployment was quickest to scale high levels, policymakers came

---

[13] To minimize confusion, I should emphasize that the remainder of this paragraph is entirely a characterization of the dominant French perspective in the 1930s. There is an intriguing parallel here with the 1960s, when the French again subscribed to a model of the international monetary economy different from the one followed by other leading countries. This again created problems for the organization of a collective response to systemic strains. On the French model and policy objectives, see Bordo, Simard, and White (1993).

under pressure to resist deflationary impulses imported from abroad and to initiate reflation. But the expansion of domestic credit was compatible with the maintenance of fixed exchange rates only if it was coordinated internationally. The British were forced to pursue monetary reflation unilaterally, and the fixed-exchange-rate system was an immediate casualty. Thus, the absence of a common conceptual framework was ultimately responsible for the collapse of the fixed-rate system.

Another variant of this hypothesis is concerned with regime design rather than regime maintenance. Although early fixed-rate systems, such as the classical gold standard, seem to have sprung up spontaneously, more recent regimes, such as Bretton Woods and the European Monetary System, are products of international negotiations. Here, an international consensus on the design of such a system can be a critical precondition for success. Ikenberry (1993, p. 157) emphasizes the importance of transnational consensus for the successful conclusion and ratification of the Bretton Woods Agreement. A set of policy ideas inspired by the Keynesian revolution and embraced by prominent British and American economists and policymakers was crucial, he argues, for "defining government conceptions of postwar interests, building coalitions in support of the postwar settlement, and legitimating the exercise of American power."

At the outset of negotiations, divergent views within and between the British and American political establishments posed obstacles to reaching a transnational agreement on how to structure the postwar international economic order. State Department officials in particular and American policymakers in general attributed the severity of the depression of the 1930s to the collapse of international transactions. Hence, they attached priority to the restoration of free trade. Britain's wartime cabinet, by contrast, identified the crisis of the 1930s with deflationary pressures imported from abroad. They thus sought to structure international monetary institutions so as to free Britain from external constraints and to temper trade arrangements with measures that would allow the government to maintain a high pressure of domestic demand as a way of guaranteeing full employment. Reinforcing this disagreement over trade was the British desire to continue cultivating commercial ties with its Commonwealth through the extension of tariff preferences versus the desire of American policymakers to obtain equal access to Commonwealth markets through the global adoption of policies of nondiscrimination.

A community of economic and policy specialists in both governments played a critical role in shifting the focus of discussions from these contentious issues of trade to the monetary arena. There, emerging Keynesian ideas had already begun to define a common ground on which officials from both countries could agree. Experts from the two countries were heavily influenced by Keynesian ideas and shared a common model of the role of monetary policy in economic management. This led them to compatible views about the way international monetary arrangements should be structured to facilitate the pursuit of stabilizing domestic policies. Compared to their disagreements over trade, differences of opinion in the monetary arena were minor. Negotiators differed only over how much international liquidity should be provided by the newly created IMF, not over whether such liquidity should be provided at all. They disagreed only over the extent to which capital controls could be used to reconcile domestic monetary autonomy with exchange-rate stability, not over whether such controls were permissible. The degree of consensus is attributable, in this view, to agreement over the role for monetary management in the postwar world.

In 1933, by contrast, an absence of consensus blocked the successful conclusion of negotiations over reform and reconstruction of the international monetary system.[14] The French wanted the British and, after April 1933, the Americans to restore fixed exchange rates on a basis that would have severely limited the options available to policymakers. The British, in contrast, would accept exchange-rate stabilization only if it were coupled with an agreement for coordinated monetary reflation. Disagreements over the appropriate conceptual model of the economy thus proved to be an insurmountable obstacle to regime design as well as regime maintenance.

4 Behavior of the Macroeconomy

A fourth explanation for differences over time in the prevalence of fixed-rate systems is the stability of the macroeconomy. When macroeconomic disturbances are large, countries find it costly to maintain stable exchange rates.[15] Draconian adjustments in domestic policies may be required to defend the exchange-rate peg, exacerbating already serious problems of unemployment. From this perspective, it is no coincidence that the interwar gold standard collapsed following the onset of the depression of the 1930s, or that the final demise of the Bretton Woods system in 1973 coincided with the first OPEC oil-price shock.

Yet, systematic comparisons of fixed- and flexible-exchange-rate regimes fail to confirm that output is less volatile in fixed-rate periods. Using data for various samples of countries, Bordo (1993) and Eichengreen (1994) show that the standard deviation of detrended national output was more volatile during

[14] On this view of the 1933 London Economic Conference, see O'Dell (1988) and Eichengreen and Uzan (1993).

[15] See, for example, Giovannini (1993) for an instance of this argument. Statements like this obviously raise important issues of simultaneity (of how the exchange-rate regime affects the nature of the shocks), to which I return below.

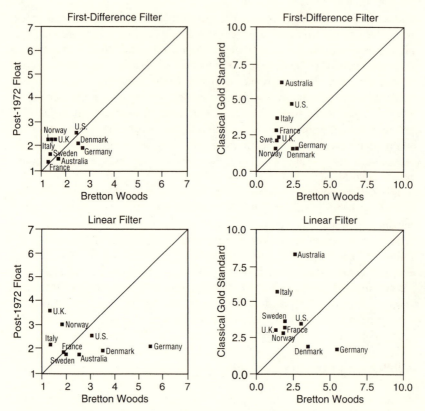

Figure 1.1 Standard Deviation of GDP under Different Exchange-Rate Regimes

the Bretton Woods quarter century (1945 to 1970) than during the flexible-rate period that followed. Output was more volatile still during the classical gold-standard years.

Figure 1.1 displays two measures of output variability under (1) the post-1972 float, (2) the Bretton Woods system, and (3) the classical gold standard.[16] The raw time series are filtered by removing a linear trend from the logarithm of the variable and, alternatively, by first-differencing the logarithm of the variable. The first-difference filter provides more information on high-frequency business-cycle movements in the underlying variable; the linear filter provides more information on low-frequency shifts. The standard deviations shown are in percentage points per year. A point on the 45 degree line indicates no difference in the volatility of GDP across periods. On the left-hand side of the figure, the Bretton Woods years (1950 to 1970) are dis-

---

[16] The data underlying these figures are described in detail in Eichengreen (1994).

played on the horizontal axis; the floating years (1973 to 1990), on the vertical one. The observations in the top left-hand panel, where the first-difference filter is used, cluster around the 45 degree line, suggesting little change in output volatility at business-cycle frequencies. The unweighted average across countries of standard deviations indicates that output volatility rose slightly following the shift from fixed to floating rates (from 1.72 to 1.98), but that this change is statistically insignificant at standard confidence levels. The bottom left-hand panel, where the linear filter is used, suggests, if anything, a slight reduction in output volatility at lower frequencies in the post-Bretton Woods period.

The conclusion that output volatility was no greater under floating than under fixed rates is reinforced by the right-hand side of the figure, which compares Bretton Woods, again on the horizontal axis, with the classical gold-standard years (1880 to 1913) on the vertical axis. The simple arithmetic average of standard deviations of detrended GDP is some 50 percent larger under the gold standard than under Bretton Woods (or than under the post–Bretton Woods float). This is true regardless of which filter is used.[17]

Output variability is an imperfect measure of the magnitude of disturbances, of course, because it conflates impulses and responses. Bayoumi and Eichengreen (1992) have therefore used time-series methods to estimate the magnitude of the disturbances themselves. They apply to data on output and prices a procedure proposed by Blanchard and Quah (1989) for distinguishing temporary from permanent disturbances. Temporary disturbances are those that have only a transitory effect on output but that permanently alter prices. Insofar as they have a positive impact on prices, they are interpretable as demand shocks. Permanent disturbances alter both output and long- and short-run prices. Insofar as they have a negative impact on prices, it is tempting to interpret them as supply shocks.

Bayoumi and Eichengreen find that supply-and-demand shocks were essentially the same size following the collapse of Bretton Woods as during it. (Supply shocks in these respective regimes are shown in the left panel of Figure 1.2; demand shocks, in the right panel.) In contrast, the average magnitude of supply shocks was three times as large under the classical gold standard as under either Bretton Woods or the post–Bretton Woods float, whereas demand shocks were roughly twice as large under the classical gold standard. Thus, it is not possible to explain the smooth operation of the pre-1914 gold standard or the permanence of the post-1972 transition to floating on the basis of differences in the stability of the economic environment.

What may matter more than the magnitude of disturbances is their correlation across countries. If countries experience common disturbances, a

---

[17] This also remains true when Romer's (1989) cyclical corrected estimates of U.S. output are substituted for the standard series.

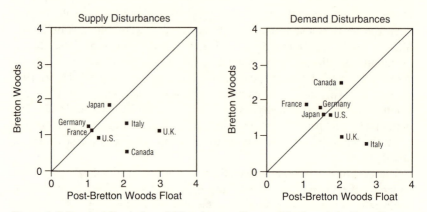

Figure 1.2 Standard Deviation of Disturbances: Bretton Woods and the Post–Bretton Woods Float

common policy response may suffice, and no threat will be posed to a fixed-rate system. Only when different disturbances impinge on different countries will different policy responses be called for and fixed exchange rates be threatened.

With this insight in mind, Floyd (1985) examined the behavior of countries' terms of trade as an indicator of the asymmetry of disturbances. His assumption was that when the terms of trade are highly variable (demand and supply disturbances in different countries cause the relative prices of the goods they produce to move in different directions), fixed rates will be difficult to maintain. He found that relative national price levels were much more stable under the classical gold standard and Bretton Woods than between the wars or after 1971.

Figure 1.3 looks at the cross-country correlation of output movements directly (with output first detrended as described above). The results for the post–World War II period, for which the correlation of output in each country with output in the United States is computed, are sensitive to the choice of filter: first-differencing indicates a rise in the correlation after 1972, although the linear filter shows little evidence of change. The results for the pre–World War I gold standard show a lower correlation than during either the Bretton Woods years or the post–Bretton Woods float.[18] Thus, there does not appear to be a direct correlation between the cross-country dispersion of output movements and the exchange-rate regime.

Output and terms-of-trade fluctuations are imperfect indicators for the sym-

[18] Because the United States played a less dominant role in the world economy before World War I than after World War II, the right-hand side of Figure 1.3 presents correlations of GDP growth rates with the United Kingdom rather than with the United States.

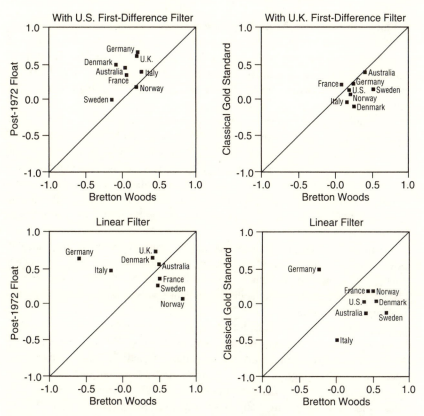

Figure 1.3 Cross-Country Correlations of GDP under Different Exchange-Rate Regimes

metry of disturbances, reflecting as they do both shocks and macroeconomic responses. Bayoumi and Eichengreen (1992) have therefore examined the covariation across countries of estimated supply-and-demand disturbances. They find no clear ordering of fixed- and flexible-rate regimes. For example, the dispersion of supply-and-demand shocks across countries was larger under the gold standard than under the post–Bretton Woods float. It hardly seems possible, therefore, to explain the successful maintenance of fixed-rate regimes such as the classical gold standard on the basis of an unusually symmetrical distribution of shocks. Similarly, the share of the variance in both supply-and-demand shocks to the G-7 countries explained by the first principal component actually rises between the Bretton Woods years from 1955 to 1970 and the floating-rate years from 1973 to 1988. Again, it does not seem possible to explain the transition from fixed to flexible exchange rates after 1971 on the basis of a greater cross-country dispersion of shocks.

5 Fiscal Policy and Monetary Rules

A fifth explanation emphasizes the role of a fixed-rate regime as an anti-inflationary rule or commitment mechanism. Shifts between fixed and flexible rates then reflect changes in the balance of costs and benefits of adhering to such a rule.

The literature in which this approach is discussed sees fixed exchange rates as a solution to the time-consistency problem analyzed by Kydland and Prescott (1977). A government with complete discretion over the formulation of monetary policy will have an incentive to engineer a surprise inflation as a way of imposing a levy on money balances. Agents will reduce their money holdings to protect themselves. In the resulting equilibrium, as Barro and Gordon (1983) show, money holdings will be inefficiently low and inflation inefficiently high.

Fixing the exchange rate against a country committed to the maintenance of price stability can be viewed as a pledge not to use the seigniorage tax. This enables policymakers to reduce actual and expected inflation to zero and to raise real-money balances to socially efficient levels at the cost of relinquishing seigniorage altogether.

From this perspective, it is not possible to say in general whether fixed or flexible exchange rates will be preferred. Flexibility will be more attractive the lower is the government expenditure share of GNP (because high average spending implies high expected inflation under floating rates and hence greater gains from fixity) and the more variable is government spending (because the authorities will want to smooth the time profile of distortionary taxes, and one way of doing so is through the use of seigniorage).[19]

Table 1.1 compares the level and variability of government spending in the G-7 countries under alternative exchange-rate regimes. The Bretton Woods period stands out as an era of unusual stability in government spending, whether measured by the standard deviation or the coefficient of variation of the public expenditure-to-GNP ratio. This is consistent with the notion that the absence of a need to resort to seigniorage to smooth the time profile of distortionary taxes was associated with the maintenance of fixed rates. The rise of both measures of variability following the transition to the post–Bretton Woods float is similarly consistent with this view, as is the relatively high level of both ratios during the period of exchange-rate instability between the wars.

In other respects, however, the results in the table are more difficult to reconcile with the tax-smoothing theory. Rather than varying in concert with the exchange-rate regime, government spending ratios rise steadily with time.

---

[19] In addition, de Kock and Grilli (1989) show that floating is more desirable the greater the revenue from fully anticipated inflation, the smaller the liquidity cost of inflation, and the greater the revenue from surprise inflation.

TABLE 1.1

Level and Variability of Government Spending Ratios (all variables as percent of GNP)

	Mean	Standard Deviation	Coefficient of Variation
Gold standard (1881–1913)	9.1	2.4	.2115
Interwar period (1919–38)	16.6	4.1	.3181
Bretton Woods (1945–70)	22.9	1.7	.0758
Post-Bretton Woods float (1974–89)	27.6	2.5	.1130

Sources: Government-spending data are from Eichengreen, 1993; GNP estimates are from Bordo, 1993.

Note: All figures are arithmetic averages of annual data for Canada, France, Germany, Japan, the United Kingdom, and the United States.

The gold-standard era is particularly problematic for the theory. Spending ratios were historically low but relatively variable during the gold-standard years, but both conditions should have been associated with floating rates. These findings do not imply that the tax-smoothing theory is necessarily wrong, only that, as an explanation for shifts between exchange-rate regimes, it is incomplete and sometimes dominated by other factors.

More generally, both fixed and flexible exchange rates can be seen as elements of a single contingent rule under which governments refrain from engaging in inflationary finance except in the event of well-defined contingencies, such as wars and financial crises (see de Kock and Grilli, 1989; Bordo and Kydland, 1991). If certain conditions are met, the public will regard their governments' commitments as credible; in normal times, expected and actual inflation are zero, and, in exceptional circumstances, the government is permitted to resort to the inflation tax without undermining the credibility of its subsequent commitment to price stability.

Empirical testing of this explanation against historical evidence has scarcely begun. Using more than a hundred years of data for Britain, de Kock and Grilli (1989) show that shifts from fixed to flexible exchange rates have typically coincided with sudden increases in government spending and in the magnitude of seigniorage revenues, whereas the restoration of fixed rates has coincided with the return of expenditure to normal levels. Their data are reproduced as Figure 1.4.[20] Government spending on goods and services and seigniorage are both expressed as shares of GDP. The two pronounced peaks in both series occur at the same time, and in each instance, they coincide with

---

[20] Actually, I have measured seigniorage slightly differently, as the change in the money base expressed as a ratio to GDP. Data are from Mitchell (1988) and Capie and Webber (1985).

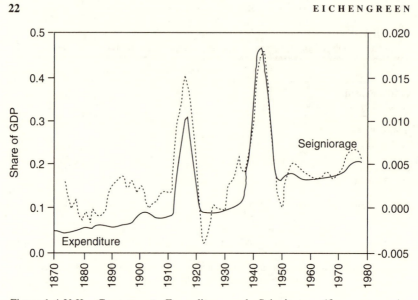

Figure 1.4 U.K. Government Expenditure and Seigniorage (*five-year moving averages*)

the suspension of fixed-rate systems. The temporal coincidence of the breakdown of the interwar gold standard with the budgetary difficulties of the depression is also consistent with this view—Figure 1.4 shows a noticeable rise in the seigniorage share of GDP coincident with these events. So is the concurrence of growing U.S. fiscal deficits with the breakdown of Bretton Woods, although these trends find no echo in analogous series for the United Kingdom.

Fixed exchange rates have been interpreted as a commitment technology in the literature on the EMS as well. But, as contributors to that literature have pointed out, it is not clear why an indirect commitment to stabilize the price level by stabilizing the exchange rate should be more credible than a direct commitment to stabilize prices.[21] Neither is it clear what enables some governments but not others to commit credibly to an exchange-rate rule. Perhaps rules can be sustained only by governments that care enough about the future to value their reputation for respecting them. Governments with a low probability of survival care relatively little about the future and may therefore have little interest in cultivating the credibility of their commitment to a fixed-rate rule. Political stability may thus influence the choice of an exchange-rate re-

[21] See, for example, Fratianni and von Hagen (1992). One possible answer is that the exchange rate is a more transparent indicator of policy. Data on the exchange rate are available continuously, rather than each month or quarter when price-index reports are released. See Melitz (1988) and Kenen (1992) for further discussion along these lines.

TABLE 1.2
Political Determinants of the Rate of Exchange-Rate
Depreciation, 1921–26 (dependent variable is percent
change in domestic currency units per dollar)

Explanatory Variable	(1)	(2)	(3)
Constant	−0.97	−1.11	2.04
	(4.36)	(4.59)	(5.00)
Government instability	−0.07	−0.07	−0.10
	(2.12)	(1.85)	(2.57)
Central-bank independence	0.12	0.12	0.15
	(5.22)	(5.31)	(5.94)
Governing majority		0.01	0.01
		(1.13)	(0.67)
Percent Left			0.02
			(2.51)
Lagged output growth			0.30
			(1.90)
N	103	93	76
Standard error	0.199	0.196	0.184

Source: For details on data sources, see Eichengreen and Simmons,
1993.
Note: t-statistics are in parentheses. All equations include dummy variables for country and year.

gime. There has been some research documenting the positive association of
government turnover with inflation (Grilli et al., 1991), but no historical work
has as yet been done tracing the association between political stability and the
exchange-rate regime.

Table 1.2 relates one measure of government instability to the percentage
change in dollar exchange rates in the first half of the 1920s. The 1920s would
seem to be a fertile testing ground for theories that relate the choice of
exchange-rate regime to government durability and consequent incentives, for
government stability and exchange-rate policy varied widely across countries
in the aftermath of World War I. Some countries, led by Britain, forced their
exchange rates to appreciate until the prewar gold-standard parity against the
dollar had been restored. Others, such as Germany, saw their exchange rates
collapse as a result of hyperinflation. Still others, such as France and Belgium, followed a middle course, permitting depreciation to persist before restoring a fixed exchange rate at a depreciated value against the dollar. The
question is whether differing degrees of government stability help to explain
these choices.

Results of a pooled time-series cross-section analysis for the countries of Europe, plus the United States and Japan, are shown in Table 1.2.[22] Because exchange rates are measured in domestic currency units per U.S. dollar, a negative sign indicates that a factor is associated with depreciation. The first column shows that exchange rates depreciated more quickly in countries with unstable governments (measured as the number of cabinet changes per year), consistent with the view that such governments have less reason to value their reputations and are hence more inclined to follow policies leading to depreciation (and, in this context, less likely to value the reputational advantages of restoring the prewar parity). In addition, countries with more politically independent central banks were more successful at resisting these pressures.

The next column adds an additional political variable: the share of parliamentary seats held by the governing party or coalition. If the rate of cabinet turnover is a measure of the current durability of the government, the size of its majority might be regarded as a leading indicator of its expected future durability. Larger majorities seem to have been associated with policies of exchange-rate stability, although this coefficient does not differ significantly from zero at standard confidence levels.[23]

The final column adds a measure of the political orientation of elected representatives (share of parliamentary seats held by left-wing parties) and a measure of economic conditions (the rate of growth of industrial production lagged one year). It shows that faster-growing countries succeeded in maintaining stronger exchange rates. Political orientation also enters as a significant determinant of exchange-rate policy, although, in this period, the presumption that left-wing governments are more inflation prone is not supported. Perhaps left-wing governments entered office with inferior financial reputations and stood to gain more from maintenance of the gold standard. This is consistent with Simmons's (1991) finding for the post-1925 period that countries with greater left representation in parliament stayed on the gold standard longer.[24]

Simmons (1991) provides a more comprehensive analysis of these issues using data for the 1930s, when countries once again chose between the gold standard and floating rates. Her regressions control for a wider variety of political and economic correlates of the exchange rate. She, too, finds that

---

[22] Observations for nondemocratic governments are excluded. The countries included are Austria, Belgium, Bulgaria, Czechoslovakia, Denmark, Finland, France, Germany, Hungary, Italy, Japan, the Netherlands, Norway, Poland, Romania, Spain, Sweden, Switzerland, the United Kingdom, and the United States. The number of observations varies because of missing data. The results were virtually identical when the United States and Japan were excluded, leaving an entirely European sample.

[23] In part, this reflects the relatively high correlation between majority size and cabinet turnover.

[24] She also finds that countries with higher Left representation devalued more frequently in the 1930s.

more unstable governments had a greater tendency to leave the gold standard and to depreciate their currencies.

This line of research is not without limitations. In particular, there is the danger that empirical results are significantly contaminated by simultaneity bias. In addition to the tendency for unstable governments to pursue policies associated with exchange-rate instability, disturbances that destabilize exchange rates and other related variables may heighten dissatisfaction with domestic policy, thereby leading to the fall of the government. Properly sorting out cause and effect will require estimation of a full structural model of these relationships.

6 Distributional Politics

Neither explanations emphasizing interactions between domestic and foreign governments nor those concerned with interactions between government and the private sector explicitly disaggregate the polity into competing interest groups. A sixth explanation for shifts between fixed- and flexible-exchange-rate regimes therefore focuses on the changing balance of political power between interest groups favoring a particular regime and those opposed to it.

Consider the decision of whether to devalue or revalue the currency. Devaluation increases the prices of traded goods relative to those of nontraded goods and services, enhancing profitability in sectors producing tradables and raising the incomes of factors of production employed there. We should expect devaluation to be favored by producers of tradables and opposed by producers of nontradables. The intensity with which these groups lobby should increase with the extent of their competitive difficulties.

Frieden (1991) has shown how several critical episodes in the history of American exchange-rate policy can be interpreted in this light. Dollar devaluation was championed in the 1890s by farmers and other producers of traded goods who suffered from slumping prices in the face of an expansion of foreign supplies. In 1933, devaluation was favored by farmers, silver miners, and other producers of traded goods whose prices had collapsed after 1929 but was opposed by the service sector. In 1971, pressure for devaluation from the sector producing traded goods was intensified by the fact that nontradables prices increased more than twice as fast as tradables prices between 1967 and 1970.

The level of the exchange rate is not the same thing, of course, as the choice of an exchange-rate regime. Producers of tradables and nontradables may agree on the desirability of either fixed or floating rates but disagree about the appropriate level for those rates. Conversely, other distributional interests may care more about the stability or flexibility of the exchange rate than about its average level. Frieden argues, for example, that those heavily involved in international trade, finance, and investment favor fixed-rate regimes that minimize the uncertainties associated with transacting across borders and that thereby promote the expansion of international commerce. These groups may thus care more about the stability of the exchange rate than about its average level.[25]

The strength of this approach is that it injects domestic politics into the history of international money and finance. A limitation is the difficulty of testing this explanation against the alternatives. Although it is always possible to identify interest groups or coalitions favoring and opposing the exchange-rate regime that is adopted, it need not follow that lobbying by special-interest groups was central to the choice of regime. Ikenberry's (1993) work on the importance of expert opinion reminds us that the general public often regards decisions over exchange-rate policy as abstruse, leaving officials considerable leeway for independent action motivated on other grounds.

Thus, the question is whether it is possible empirically to identify the effect of interest-group pressure on the choice of exchange-rate regime. Remarkably little literature actually addresses this issue, which takes as its dependent variable either electoral outcomes of campaigns in which the exchange-rate regime was prominent or voting outcomes of parliamentary or congressional debates in which the issue figured.

To illustrate the point, I consider voting patterns in the 1896 U.S. presidential election. In this more than any other nationwide election, the exchange-rate regime was the central issue (see Jones, 1964, p. 6). On one side was William McKinley, who supported the existing gold standard. On the other was William Jennings Bryan, who proposed supplementing gold coinage with that of silver, raising the price level, and allowing the dollar to depreciate against foreign currencies if necessary to achieve his other aims. Bryan and the Democrats rejected as impractical international bimetallism (which would have maintained the dollar's stability against foreign currencies through an agreement under which all gold-standard countries would coin gold and silver in common proportions); thus, the Democrats' position would have committed the United States to silver monometallism and a fluctuating exchange rate.

Standard accounts of the campaign (Williams, 1936) argue that free silver was the dominant issue. Next in importance was the tariff, which protected eastern manufacturers against import competition, and to which the Republican candidate, William McKinley, had "devoted his career . . . with a singular concentration" (Jones, 1964, p. 105). This suggests that the election should be seen as a conflict between export interests (mainly agriculture), who would have benefited from depreciation, and producers of importables (mainly manufactures), who benefited more from the tariff. In addition, it can be thought of as setting debtors, who suffered from deflation and high interest rates, and silver producers, who suffered from the slump in silver prices,

---

[25] Note that producers of tradables and exporters may, but need not, be one and the same.

against the railways and financial interests, who benefited from U.S. adherence to the gold standard.

Table 1.3 reports logit estimates of the determinants of Bryan's share of the vote by state in the 1896 election (logit estimates are reported because the dependent variable is bounded by zero and one). The first column shows the

TABLE 1.3

Determinants of Bryan's Share of the 1896 Presidential Vote (dependent variable is Bryan's share of the vote)

Explanatory Variable	(1)	(2)	(3)	(4)	(5)
Constant	−0.05	−0.22	0.33	−1.51	−0.58
	(0.23)	(1.15)	(0.94)	(2.33)	(1.97)
Employment in agriculture	1.23			2.71	1.12
	(1.75)			(2.48)	(1.89)
Employment in manufacturing	−1.02			−1.55	−1.03
	(1.77)			(2.89)	(2.38)
Density of rail lines		−1.59			
		(2.03)			
Inverse of density of banks		0.04		0.02	0.03
		(3.72)		(1.56)	(2.65)
Silver output per capita		0.01		0.01	0.01
		(3.87)		(1.83)	(1.91)
Mortgage debt per acre		0.07		0.08	0.11
		(2.11)		(2.41)	(3.61)
Employment in mining				10.48	9.18
				(2.45)	(2.55)
Urbanization			−1.55	3.76	
			(1.95)	(3.19)	
Average value of farms			0.01		
			(1.42)		
Employment in railroads			−2.09		
			(0.18)		
R^2	0.19	0.46	0.10	0.64	0.62

Sources: All explanatory variables are drawn from the 1896 U.S. *Statistical Abstract*, the 1890 *Census*, and the report of the National Monetary Commission (Andrew, 1910). Votes for the Populist party are added to Bryan's votes on the grounds that the two parties' positions on international economic issues were essentially the same. The results are virtually identical when Bryan's votes alone are considered.

Note: All equations are estimated by logit methods; *t*-statistics are in parentheses. All employment numbers are expressed as a share of the gainfully employed.

results of estimating the simplest model, in which the explanatory variables are the shares of gainful employees in the export- and import-competing sectors (agriculture and manufacturing, respectively). Both variables have their expected signs and differ significantly from zero at the 90 percent confidence level; Bryan's vote increased with employment in agriculture but fell with employment in manufacturing.

An alternative is to model the incidence of specific grievances that gave rise to dissatisfaction with the prevailing economic and monetary order. Farmers complained about exorbitant railroad rates; debtors, about exorbitant mortgage interest rates; and miners, about slumping silver prices. The second equation therefore regresses the electoral outcome on average railroad mileage per square acre as a measure of the competitiveness of the transportation-services industry, the number of inhabitants per commercial bank as a measure of the competitiveness of the financial-services industry, the per capita silver production in 1895, and the value of mortgage debt per acre.[26] Again, all variables have the expected sign and differ significantly from zero at the 90 percent confidence level or better. States where banking was more concentrated, where there were fewest competing railway lines, where silver production was most important, and where the burden of agricultural mortgage debt was heaviest tended to go with Bryan.

Hollingsworth (1963) and other historians emphasize still a third set of factors, arguing that the fundamental electoral cleavage in 1896 ran along urban/rural lines. Whereas farmers embraced the devaluationist cause, urban workers were unsympathetic. The intensity with which farmers opposed deflation depended on the value of their farms and, hence, the burden of mortgage debts. In addition, these historians emphasize that the railways lobbied their employees intensively to vote against Bryan, a fact that may have played a role in the outcome (Jones, 1964, p. 334). The third equation therefore regresses the voting pattern on the share of urban population (the share living in cities with at least eight thousand residents), the share of the gainfully employed working on the railroads, and the average value of owned and encumbered farms. Urbanization has its expected negative sign and differs from zero at the 90 percent level. The other two variables, although correctly signed, are statistically insignificant.

The final two columns report hybrid equations that include employment shares in agriculture and manufacturing, two measures of mining as a special-interest group (employment in mining and per capita silver output), urban-

---

[26] Trojanowski (1980) shows that the density of railways is a good measure of the competitiveness of the transport industry, and James (1976) provides analogous evidence for the banking industry. The 1890 *Census* distinguishes mortgages on acres from mortgages on (urban) lots; I scale the former by the acreage of each state. The results are unchanged when employment in mining is used in place of silver production; I discuss below an equation in which this variable is also included.

ization, mortgage debt, and inhabitants per bank.[27] The coefficients on all variables but the last differ from zero at the 90 percent level or better.

The only surprising sign is that on urbanization. Upon controlling for the sectoral composition of employment, one finds that urbanization is positively, not negatively, related to Bryan's share of the vote.[28] In the final equation, I therefore exclude this variable. The remaining coefficients all now display their expected signs and differ significantly from zero at the 90 percent level.[29]

7 Conclusion

Scholars attempting to account for changes over time in the structure of the international monetary system suffer from an embarrassment of riches. The historical record shows a profusion of potential explanations for the shifts between fixed- and flexible-exchange-rate regimes. The problem is not to frame hypotheses, of which there are an abundance, but to gauge the explanatory power of the hypotheses against the evidence. Case studies of particular historical junctures in which the international monetary system was transformed should be supplemented with quantitative studies using data over time and across countries to analyze the choice of exchange-rate regime. One cannot help but be struck by how little progress has yet been made in pursuit of this agenda.

The evidence reported here supports a number of the different hypotheses considered. In this sense, it confirms that monocausal explanations are unlikely to provide an adequate account of the endogeneity of exchange-rate regimes. Blending the competing theories thus becomes an important task for subsequent research. For example, external pressures to adapt policies to facilitate international cooperation could be imported into approaches emphasizing the primacy of domestic politics. Interactions between governmental stability and distributional outcomes need to be explicitly recognized, as do the distributional consequences of the fiscal shocks seemingly associated with shifts from fixed to floating rates.

Finally, a comprehensively endogenous approach to the choice of exchange-rate regime would have to explain how the evolution of the regime in place can itself alter the balance of costs and benefits and lead to a shift to alternative arrangements. An example of endogenous regime dynamics is the Triffin

[27] Coal mining and kindred sectors are excluded from the employment-in-mining variable.

[28] Jones (1964, p. 344), in fact, notes that Bryan did better in the urban than in the rural portions of New England and the Middle Atlantic regions, and that he won an absolute majority of the urban vote in the Rocky Mountain states.

[29] That the significance of bank density is affected by the inclusion or exclusion of urbanization is not surprising, because bank density is so different in urban and rural areas.

paradox. Triffin (1960) argued that under a gold-exchange standard, the system's demand for international liquidity tends to be met by an increase in the supply of foreign-exchange reserves relative to gold, thereby reducing confidence in the reserve currency and ultimately provoking a shift to floating rates. Another example, under an adjustable peg system, such as Bretton Woods or the EMS, is the desire of policymakers to convince the markets of their commitment to that peg by resisting exchange-rate changes at all cost, and thereby leading to rigidity, crisis, and ultimately to a shift to flexible rates. Finally, there is the notion that fixed-rate regimes based on hegemonic dominance so heighten the burden on the hegemon that they lead to hegemonic decline and to a shift away from the regime superintended by the hegemon (Cowhey and Long, 1983). A truly satisfactory approach would have to follow these pioneering efforts by endogenizing the costs and benefits of alternative regimes along with the choice of the regime itself.

References

Andrew, A. Piatt, *Monetary Statistics of the United States*, Washington, D.C., National Monetary Commission, 1910.

Barro, Robert J., and David Gordon, "Rules, Discretion and Reputation in a Model of Monetary Policy," *Journal of Monetary Economics*, 12 (July 1983), pp. 101–121.

Bayoumi, Tamim A., and Barry Eichengreen, "How Exchange Rate Regimes Differ: Some Historical Evidence," paper presented at the Banca d'Italia Conference, Perugia, July 1992.

Blanchard, Olivier, and Danny Quah, "The Dynamic Effects of Aggregate Demand and Supply Disturbances," *American Economic Review*, 79 (September 1989), pp. 655–673.

Bordo, Michael D., "The Bretton Woods International Monetary System: An Historical Overview," in Bordo and Eichengreen, *A Retrospective on the Bretton Woods System*, 1993, pp. 3–108.

Bordo, Michael D., and Barry Eichengreen, eds., *A Retrospective on the Bretton Woods System*, Chicago, University of Chicago Press, 1993.

Bordo, Michael D., and Finn E. Kydland, "The Gold Standard as a Rule," Rutgers University, New Brunswick, and Carnegie-Mellon University, 1991, processed.

Bordo, Michael D., Dominique Simard, and Eugene White, "France and the Bretton Woods International Monetary System," Rutgers University, New Brunswick, N.J., 1993, processed.

Broadberry, Steven, "Monetary Interdependence and Deflation in Britain and the United States between the Wars," in Marcus H. Miller, Barry Eichengreen, and Richard Portes, eds., *Blueprints for Exchange Rate Management*, New York, Academic Press, 1989, pp. 47–70.

Brown, William Adams, *The International Gold Standard Reinterpreted, 1914–1934*, New York, National Bureau of Economic Research, 1940.

Cairncross, Alec, and Barry Eichengreen, *Sterling in Decline: The Devaluations of 1931, 1949 and 1967*, Oxford, Blackwell, 1983.

Capie, Forrest, and Alan Webber, *A Monetary History of the United Kingdom, 1870–1982*, London, Allen and Unwin, 1985.

Clarke, Stephen V. O., *Central Bank Cooperation, 1924–1931*, New York, Federal Reserve Bank of New York, 1967.

Cohen, Daniel, and Charles Wyplosz, "The European Monetary Union: An Agnostic Evaluation," in Ralph C. Bryant, David A. Currie, Jacob A. Frenkel, Paul R. Masson, and Richard Portes, eds., *Macroeconomic Policies in an Interdependent World*, Washington D.C., Brookings Institution, 1989, pp. 311–337.

Cowhey, Peter F., and Edward Long, "Testing Theories of Regime Change: Hegemonic Decline or Surplus Capacity?" *International Organization*, 37 (Spring 1983), pp. 157–188.

de Kock, Gabriel, and Vittorio Grilli, "Endogenous Exchange Rate Regime Switches," National Bureau of Economic Research Working Paper No. 3066, Cambridge, Mass., National Bureau of Economic Research, 1989.

Eichengreen, Barry, "Introduction," in Barry Eichengreen, ed., *The Gold Standard in Theory and History*, London, Methuen, 1985.

———, "Conducting the International Orchestra: Bank of England Leadership Under the Classical Gold Standard," *Journal of International Money and Finance*, 6 (June 1987), pp. 5–29.

———, "Hegemonic Stability Theories of the International Monetary System," in Richard N. Cooper, Barry Eichengreen, Gerald Holtham, Robert Putnam, and Randall Henning, *Can Nations Agree? Issues in International Economic Cooperation*, Washington, D.C., Brookings Institution, 1989, pp. 255–298.

———, *Golden Fetters: The Gold Standard and the Great Depression, 1919–1939*, New York, Oxford University Press, 1992.

———, "Three Perspectives on the Bretton Woods System," in Bordo and Eichengreen, *A Retrospective on the Bretton Woods System*, 1993, pp. 621–658.

———, "History of the International Monetary System: Implications for Research in International Macroeconomics and Finance," in Frederick van der Ploeg, ed., *Handbook of International Macroeconomics*, Oxford, Blackwell, forthcoming 1994.

Eichengreen, Barry, and Beth A. Simmons, "International Economics and Domestic Politics: Notes from the 1920s," in Charles Feinstein, ed., *Banking and Finance Between the Wars*, Oxford, Oxford University Press, 1993.

Eichengreen, Barry, and Marc Uzan, "The 1933 World Economic Conference as an Instance of Failed International Cooperation," in Peter B. Evans, Harold K. Jacobson, and Robert D. Putnam, eds., *Double-Edged Diplomacy*, Berkeley, University of California Press, 1993, pp. 171–206.

Eichengreen, Barry, and Charles Wyplosz, "The Unstable EMS," *Brookings Papers on Economic Activity*, No. 1 (1993), pp. 51–124.

Floyd, John E., *World Monetary Equilibrium*, Philadelphia, University of Pennsylvania Press, 1985.

Foreman-Peck, James, Andrew Hughes Hallett, and Yue Ma, "A Monthly Econometric Model of the Transmission of the Great Depression between the Principal Industrial Economies," St. Anthony's College, Oxford, and Strathclyde University, 1992, processed.

Frankel, Jeffrey A., and Katharine E. Rockett, "International Macroeconomic Policy Coordination: When Policymakers Do Not Agree on the True Model," *American Economic Review*, 78 (June 1988), pp. 318–340.

Fratianni, Michele, and Jürgen von Hagen, *The European Monetary System and European Monetary Union*, Boulder, Colo., Westview Press, 1992.

Frieden, Jeffry A., "Greenbacks, Gold and Silver: The Politics of American Exchange Rate Policy, 1870–1973," CIBER Working Paper 91–04, Anderson School of Management, University of California, Los Angeles, 1991.

Gayer, Arthur D., *Monetary Policy and Economic Stabilization*, London, Black, 1937.

Giovannini, Alberto, "How Do Fixed-Exchange-Rate Regimes Work? Evidence from the Gold Standard, Bretton Woods and the EMS," in Marcus H. Miller, Barry Eichengreen, and Richard Portes, eds., *Blueprints for Exchange Rate Management*, New York, Academic Press, 1989, pp. 13–41.

———, "Bretton Woods and its Precursors: Rules Versus Discretion in the History of International Monetary Regimes," in Bordo and Eichengreen, *A Retrospective on the Bretton Woods System*, 1993, pp. 109–154.

Gowa, JoAnne, *Closing the Gold Window*, Ithaca, N.Y., Cornell University Press, 1983.

Hollingsworth, J. Rogers, *The Whirligig of Politics: The Democracy of Cleveland and Bryan*, Chicago, University of Chicago Press, 1963.

Ikenberry, John, "The Political Origins of Bretton Woods," in Bordo and Eichengreen, *A Retrospective on the Bretton Woods System*, 1993, pp. 155–200.

James, John, "Banking Market Structure, Risk and the Pattern of Local Interest Rates in the United States, 1893–1911," *Review of Economics and Statistics*, 58 (November 1976), pp. 453–462.

Jones, Stanley L., *The Election of 1896*, Madison, University of Wisconsin Press, 1964.

Kenen, Peter B., "The Coordination of Macroeconomic Policies," in William H. Branson, Jacob A. Frenkel, and Morris Goldstein, eds., *International Policy Coordination and Exchange Rate Fluctuations*, Chicago, University of Chicago Press, 1990, pp. 63–108.

———, "Floating Exchange Rates Reconsidered: The Influence of New Ideas, Priorities and Problems," Princeton University, 1992, processed.

Keohane, Robert, *After Hegemony*, Princeton, N.J., Princeton University Press, 1984.

Kindleberger, Charles P., *The World in Depression, 1929–1939*, Berkeley, University of California Press, 1973; rev. enl. ed., 1986.

Krugman, Paul R., "A Model of Balance of Payments Crises," *Journal of Money, Credit and Banking*, 11 (August 1979), pp. 311–325.

Kunz, Diane, *The Battle for Britain's Gold Standard in 1931*, London, Croom Helm, 1987.

Kydland, Finn E., and Edward C. Prescott, "Rules Rather than Discretion: The Inconsistency of Optimal Plans," *Journal of Political Economy*, 85 (June 1977), pp. 473–491.

Melitz, Jacques, "Monetary Discipline, Germany, and the European Monetary System:

A Synthesis," in Francesco Giavazzi, Stefano Micossi, and Marcus H. Miller, eds., *The European Monetary System*, Cambridge and New York, Cambridge University Press, 1988, pp. 50–84.

Miller, Marcus H., and Alan Sutherland, "Britain's Return to Gold and Entry into the EMS: Expectations, Joining Conditions and Credibility," CEPR Discussion Paper No. 465, London, Centre for Economic Policy Research, October 1990.

Mitchell, Brian R., *British Historical Statistics*, Cambridge and New York, Cambridge University Press, 1988.

Mundell, Robert A., "A Theory of Optimum Currency Areas," *American Economic Review*, 51 (September 1961), pp. 657–664.

Nevin, Edward, *The Mechanism of Cheap Money*, Cardiff, University of Wales Press, 1955.

O'Dell, John S., "From London to Bretton Woods: Sources of Change in Bargaining Strategies and Outcomes," *Journal of Public Policy*, 8 (July–December 1988), pp. 287–316.

Romer, Christina, "The Prewar Business Cycle Reconsidered: New Estimates of Gross National Product, 1869–1908," *Journal of Political Economy*, 97 (February 1989), pp. 1–37.

Salant, Stephen W., and Dale W. Henderson, "Market Anticipations of Government Policies and the Price of Gold," *Journal of Political Economy*, 86 (August 1978), pp. 627–648.

Simmons, Beth A., "Who Adjusts? Domestic Sources of Foreign Economic Policy During the Interwar Years," Ph.D. diss., Harvard University, 1991.

Smith, Gregor W., and R. Todd Smith, "Stochastic Process Switching and the Return to Gold, 1925," *Economic Journal* (London), 100 (March 1990), pp. 164–175.

Triffin, Robert, *Gold and the Dollar Crisis*, New Haven, Yale University Press, 1960.

Trojanowski, Joseph, "The Stability of Freight Rate Agreements at Minor Railroad Junctions in Iowa and Kansas 1880–1910," Ph.D. diss., Yale University, 1980.

U.S. Department of Commerce, *Statistical Abstract of the United States*, Washington, D.C., Government Printing Office, 1896.

U.S. Department of Commerce, Bureau of the Census, *11th Census of the United States*, Washington, D.C., Government Printing Office, 1891.

Viner, Jacob, "International Aspects of the Gold Standard," in Quincy Wright, ed., *Gold and Monetary Stabilization*, Chicago, University of Chicago Press, 1932, pp. 3–39.

Williams, Wayne C., *William Jennings Bryan*, New York, Putnam's, 1936.

Yeager, Leland, *International Monetary Relations*, New York, Harper and Row, 1966.

2

Exchange-Rate Behavior under Alternative Exchange-Rate Arrangements

MARK P. TAYLOR

1 Introduction

Over the last fifty years, exchange rates between the national currencies of the major industrialized countries have been subject to broadly three types of arrangements. Until the early 1970s, most of these countries participated in the system of pegged exchange rates designed at the Bretton Woods Conference in 1944. The breakdown of that system in the early 1970s gave way to a period of generalized floating that, by and large, is still in force. During the recent period of managed floating, however, the authorities of the major industrialized economies have occasionally agreed, overtly or covertly, to hold their exchange rates against certain currencies within prearranged bounds. The most obvious example of such a target zone is the European Monetary System (EMS); less formal target-zone arrangements are exemplified by the covert (and now forgotten) "reference ranges" adopted by the G-7 countries under the 1987 Louvre Accord.

These shifts in exchange-rate arrangements since World War II have profoundly influenced research on the behavior of nominal exchange rates. The monetary- and portfolio-balance models of exchange-rate behavior, developed in the recent period of floating, can be seen as the direct descendants of models of balance-of-payments adjustment developed during the Bretton Woods era. Furthermore, the literatures on exchange-rate intervention and target zones were developed as direct responses to shifting official attitudes toward exchange-rate management and the establishment of pegged-exchange-rate systems such as the EMS.

I attempt here to provide an overview and interpretation of this research but

Detailed and constructive comments on a previous draft of this paper were provided by conference discussants Stanley Black and Kenneth Froot. I am also grateful for comments from Andrew Atkeson, Leonardo Bartolini, Tamim Bayoumi, Giuseppe Bertola, William Branson, Guillermo Calvo, Robert Flood, Jeffrey Frankel, Peter Garber, Maurice Obstfeld, Kenneth Rogoff, Alan Stockman, and John Williamson. Responsibility for any remaining errors of omission or interpretation remains with the author. The views represented in the paper are those of the author and are not necessarily those of the International Monetary Fund or of its member authorities.

not an exhaustive review.[1] To contain such a vast literature within the confines of a single article would be an ambitious aim, and I can hope only to brush out the salient aspects and provide a personal interpretation. The present contribution, moreover, may be viewed as an extension and update of several previous exchange-rate surveys and as a simplification and synthesis of more specialized papers.[2]

I begin in Section 2 by outlining the theoretical literature on exchange-rate determination when the rate is assumed to float freely. Section 3 discusses the empirical evidence on these theoretical models, and Section 4 considers the theory and evidence relating to the efficiency of foreign-exchange markets. The nature, role, and effectiveness of official intervention in foreign-exchange markets is reviewed in Section 5. Section 6 considers the literature on target zones, and Section 7 attempts to draw some overall conclusions and to provide suggestions for likely or desirable future research developments.

2 Theories of Exchange-Rate Determination under a Free Float

The Literature before 1970[3]

Notable early contributions of the postwar period include Nurkse (1944) and Friedman (1953). Nurkse's work, warning that the dangers of "bandwagon effects" may generate market instability, is representative of the immediate postwar consensus favoring fixed exchange rates. Friedman, in his classic apologia of floating exchange rates, argued that speculation would, in fact, be stabilizing. Roughly midway between Nurkse and Friedman, in both time and point of view, is Meade (1951). Indeed, the highly influential work of Mundell (1961, 1962, 1963) and Fleming (1962) can be seen as deriving in many important ways from Meade's work, which essentially opened up the Keynesian model that formed the cornerstone of postwar macroeconomic analysis. In the verbal exposition of his capital-account theory, Meade had worked through the stock-equilibrium implications of a movement in international interest-rate differentials, but he did not faithfully represent this feature in the

[1] In particular, this chapter does not explicitly consider models of the real exchange rate (see Obstfeld [1985] for more attention to real factors). Neither does it explicitly discuss the related theoretical literature on general-equilibrium models of exchange-rate determination (Stockman, 1980; Lucas, 1982; Backus, Kehoe, and Kydland, 1992). Some of this literature is surveyed nontechnically in Stockman (1987).

[2] See, for example, the general survey of MacDonald and Taylor (1992), earlier empirical work surveys by Kohlhagen (1978), Levich (1985), and Isard (1988), and the exchange-rate-theory surveys of Mussa (1984), Branson and Henderson (1985), Frenkel and Mussa (1985), Kenen (1985), and Obstfeld and Stockman (1985).

[3] Kenen (1985) provides a detailed discussion of the evolution of postwar economic thought on international macroeconomics. See Taylor (1990) for a more general discussion of economic thought on the open economy since the mercantilists.

mathematical appendix to his volume. Because Mundell and Fleming based
their models on Meade's mathematical appendix, they ignored the stock-flow
implications of changes in interest-rate differentials. Thus, the integration of
asset markets and capital mobility into open-economy macroeconomics, although an important contribution of the Mundell-Fleming model, employed
an inadequate treatment of asset-market equilibrium. Many of the more recent
exchange-rate models, however, such as the portfolio-balance model, can be
viewed as attempts to repair this fault in the Mundell-Fleming model. Polak
(1957) and Johnson (1958) had also stressed the distinction between stock and
flow equilibria in the open-economy context, and subsequent work done in the
late 1960s by Ott and Ott (1965), McKinnon and Oates (1966), and others
began to integrate open-economy macroeconomic analysis with financial
portfolio-balance analysis by imposing explicit stock-equilibrium constraints.
Slightly later work by Branson (1968) and others built on this work by incorporating other features of the theory of financial-portfolio choice.

The Flexible-Price Monetary Model

The monetary approach to the exchange rate, which emerged as the dominant
exchange-rate model when the recent float began in the early 1970s (Frenkel,
1976; Mussa, 1976, 1979), starts from the definition of the exchange rate as
the relative price of two monies and attempts to model that relative price in
terms of the relative supply of and demand for those monies. The algebra of
the basic flexible-price monetary model (FLPM) is straightforward. Its building blocks include equations describing domestic and foreign money-market
equilibrium and imposing continuous purchasing-power parity. The demand
for money is assumed to depend on real income (y), the price level (p), and
the level of the nominal interest rate (r); foreign variables are denoted by an
asterisk. With all variables except interest rates expressed in logarithms, monetary equilibria in the domestic and foreign country, respectively, are given by

$$m_t^s = p_t + \phi y_t - \lambda r_t , \tag{1}$$

$$m_t^{s*} = p_t^* + \phi^* y_t^* - \lambda^* r_t^* . \tag{2}$$

In the simplest formulation, all goods are assumed tradable, and equilibrium in the traded-goods market ensues when there are no further profitable
incentives for trade flows to occur—that is, when prices in a common currency are equalized and purchasing-power parity holds. The purchasing-
power-parity condition is

$$s_t = p_t - p_t^* , \tag{3}$$

where s_t is the (logarithm of the) nominal exchange rate (the domestic price of foreign currency). The domestic money supply determines the domestic price level, and the exchange rate is therefore determined by relative money supplies. Algebraically, solving (1), (2), and (3) for the exchange rate gives

$$s_t = (m^s - m^{s*})_t - \phi y_t + \phi^* y_t + \lambda r_t - \lambda^* r_t^* , \tag{4}$$

which is the basic flexible-price monetary equation. From (4), we can see that an increase in the domestic money supply, relative to the foreign money stock, will lead to a rise in s_t, that is, a depreciation of the domestic currency in terms of the foreign currency. This seems intuitively plausible, but a rise in the domestic interest rate causes the domestic currency to depreciate (raises s_t), despite the fact that the higher interest rate makes domestic assets more attractive to foreign investors. To understand this, one has to remember the fundamental role of the domestic and foreign demands for money in the flexible-price monetary model. A rise in domestic real income, for example, creates an excess demand for the domestic money stock. As agents try to increase their (real) money balances, they reduce expenditure, and prices fall until money-market equilibrium is achieved. As prices fall, purchasing-power parity ensures an appreciation of the domestic currency. An exactly converse analysis explains the response of the exchange rate to the interest rate, that is, an increase in the domestic interest rate reduces the domestic demand for money and so leads to a depreciation. Because the domestic interest rate is endogenous in the flexible-price monetary model, however, it is, in fact, not completely logical to consider increases in r that are independent of movements in r^* or in domestic or foreign incomes or money supplies.

In practice, researchers often simplify the model by assuming that the domestic and foreign money-demand coefficients are equal ($\phi = \phi^*$ and $\lambda = \lambda^*$). By invoking the uncovered interest-parity condition, that the domestic-foreign interest differential is just equal to the expected rate of depreciation of the domestic currency (Δs_{t+1}^e), the latter can be substituted for $(r - r^*)_t$ (where the superscript e denotes agents' expectations formed at time t). This substitution gives

$$s_t = (m - m^*)_t - \phi(y - y^*)_t + \lambda \Delta s_{t+1}^e , \tag{5}$$

which brings out very clearly the forward-looking nature of the model. In estimating equations like (5), researchers often use the forward premium to replace the interest differential, implicitly assuming covered interest parity.

The rational-expectations solution[4] to (5) is

$$s_t = (1 + \lambda)^{-1} \sum_{i=0}^{\infty} \left(\frac{\lambda}{1 + \lambda}\right)^i [(m - m^*)^e_{t+i} + \phi(y - y^*)^e_{t+i}] , \qquad (6)$$

where it is understood that expectations are conditioned on information at time t. It is well known from the rational-expectations literature, however, that equation (6) is only one solution to (5) and comes from a potentially infinite set. If we denote the exchange rate given by (6) as $\hat{s}_t$, it is straightforward to demonstrate that equation (5) has multiple rational-expectations solutions, each of which may be written in the form

$$s_t = \hat{s}_t + b_t , \qquad (7)$$

where b_t, the "rational-bubble" term, satisfies

$$b^e_{t+1} = \lambda^{-1}(1 + \lambda)b_t , \qquad (8)$$

and $\hat{s}_t^*$ is the solution to (6) in the absence of bubbles. Testing for the presence of bubbles can be interpreted as an important specification test of the model, because bubbles represent significant departures from the fundamentals of the model that would not be detected using a specification of the form (4).

Although the elegant simplicity of the flexible-price monetary model is seductive, it should be noted that a large number of assumptions—in addition to those of continuous purchasing-power parity and stable money-market equilibria—are made implicitly in order to achieve this simplicity. Open-economy macroeconomics is essentially about six aggregate markets: goods, labor, money, foreign exchange, and domestic and foreign bonds (that is, nonmonetary assets). But the flexible-price monetary model concentrates directly on equilibrium conditions in only one of these markets, the money market. This is implicitly achieved in the following fashion. First, domestic and foreign assets are assumed to be perfectly substitutable, so that the domestic and foreign bond markets are joined as a single market. Next, it is assumed that the exchange rate adjusts freely to equilibrate supply and demand in the foreign-exchange market, that equilibrium in the goods market is maintained by perfectly flexible prices, and that equilibrium in the labor market is maintained by flexible wages. These assumptions impose equilibrium on three of the five remaining markets. Hence, by Walras's law (the principle that equilibrium in $n - 1$ markets of an n-market system implies equilibrium in the nth market), the equilibrium of the full system is then determined by the equilibrium conditions for the money market. Many of these underlying assumptions are highly debatable, however, and some of them—notably the

---

[4] The application of rational expectations to exchange rates was pioneered by Black (1973).

assumptions of perfect price flexibility and full employment—seriously impair the usefulness of the model for real-world policy analysis.

The Sticky-Price Monetary Model

A further problem with the flexible-price variant of the monetary approach is that it assumes *continuous* purchasing-power parity (equation [3]). The detailed discussion below, however, indicates that there is substantial empirical evidence that purchasing-power parity does not hold continuously, and there is even some debate as to whether it holds in the long run. An attempt to accommodate this evidence led to the development of a second generation of monetary models, first by Dornbusch (1976). The sticky-price monetary model allows for substantial overshooting of the nominal and real (price-adjusted) exchange rate above the long-run equilibrium level implied by purchasing-power parity, because the "jump variables" in the system— exchange rates and interest rates—compensate for stickiness in other variables, notably goods prices.

The intuition underlying the overshooting result in the sticky-price monetary model is relatively straightforward. Consider the effects of a cut in the nominal domestic money supply. Because prices are sticky in the short run, a cut in the nominal money supply implies an initial fall in the real money supply and a consequent rise in the interest rate in order to clear the money market. The rise in the domestic interest rate then leads to a capital inflow and an appreciation of the nominal exchange rate (that is, a rise in the value of domestic currency in terms of foreign currency). Foreign investors are aware that they are artificially forcing up the exchange rate and that they may therefore suffer a foreign-exchange loss when the proceeds of their investment are reconverted into their local currency. However, for as long as the *expected* foreign-exchange loss (expected rate of depreciation) is less than the *known* capital-market gain (the interest differential), risk-neutral investors will continue to buy domestic assets. A short-run equilibrium is achieved when the expected rate of depreciation is just equal to the interest differential (uncovered interest parity holds). Because the expected rate of depreciation must then be nonzero for a nonzero interest differential, the exchange rate must have overshot its long-run equilibrium level. In the medium run, however, domestic prices begin to fall in response to the fall in money supply. This alleviates pressure in the money market (the real money supply rises), and the domestic interest rate begins to decline. The exchange rate then depreciates slowly in order to converge on the long-run purchasing-power-parity level.

The essential characteristics of the sticky-price monetary model can be seen in a three-equation continuous-time structural model, holding foreign variables and domestic income constant (these are simplifying rather than necessary assumptions):

$$\dot{s} = r - r^* , \tag{9}$$

$$m^s = p + \phi\bar{y} - \lambda r , \tag{10}$$

$$\dot{p} = \pi[\alpha + \delta(s - p) - \sigma r - \bar{y}] . \tag{11}$$

Equation (9) is the uncovered interest-parity condition expressed in continuous time and using certainty equivalence because of the linearity of the model. Equation (10) is a domestic-money-market equilibrium condition, and equation (11) is a Phillips-curve relationship, connecting domestic price movements to excess aggregate demand, where aggregate demand has an autonomous component that depends upon international competitiveness, and a component that is interest-rate sensitive. Using a bar to denote a variable in long-run (noninflationary) equilibrium, we can reduce this system to a two-equation differential-equation system:

$$\begin{bmatrix} \dot{s} \\ \dot{p} \end{bmatrix} = \begin{bmatrix} 0 & 1/\lambda \\ \pi\delta & -\pi/\delta + \sigma/\lambda \end{bmatrix} \begin{bmatrix} s - \bar{s} \\ p - \bar{p} \end{bmatrix} . \tag{12}$$

The coefficient matrix in (12) has a negative determinant, so the system has a unique convergent saddle path. The qualitative solution to (12) is shown in Figure 2.1, where the saddle path slopes down from left to right in (s,p) space.

Now consider again the effects of a cut in the money supply. In the long run, the price level will be lower, at $\bar{p}_1$ instead of the initial level $\bar{p}_0$ in Figure 2.2, because of the neutrality of money in this model. Because long-run purchasing-power parity also holds in the model, and foreign prices are held constant, the long-run exchange rate will appreciate proportionately (that is, s will be lower), moving from $\bar{s}_0$ to $\bar{s}_1$ along the 45 degree ray. The stable saddle path, which originally went through point A, must now go through the new long-run equilibrium, B. Because prices take time to adjust, however, the economy cannot jump directly from A to B. Instead, prices remain fixed instantaneously and the exchange rate jumps to s_2 in order to get onto the new saddle path. Prices then adjust slowly, and the economy moves along the saddle path from C to the new long-run equilibrium, B. The net effect of the cut in the money supply is a long-run appreciation of $\bar{s}_0 - \bar{s}_1$, with an initial overshoot of $s_2 - \bar{s}_1$.

Frankel (1979) argues that the sticky-price monetary model should allow a role for secular differences between inflation rates. In his real-interest-differential variant of the sticky-price monetary model, he includes the long-term interest-rate differential as a proxy for the long-term inflation-rate differential.

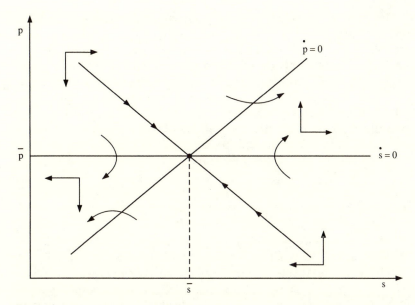

Figure 2.1 The Qualitative Saddle-Path Solution to the Sticky-Price Monetary Model

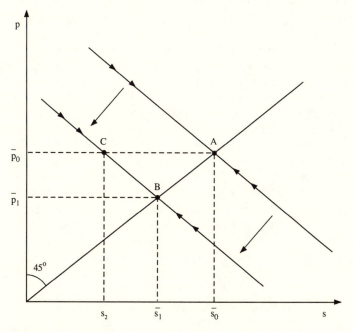

Figure 2.2 Overshooting in the Sticky-Price Monetary Model

The sticky-price monetary model is clearly an advance over the simple monetary model with continuous purchasing-power parity. It is still fundamentally monetary, however, in that attention is focused on equilibrium conditions in the money market. As noted above, a number of assumptions are implicitly involved, including perfect substitutability between domestic and foreign nonmonetary assets (but *non*substitutability of monies[5]). This perfect-substitutability assumption is relaxed in the portfolio-balance model of exchange-rate determination. In addition, the portfolio-balance model is stock-flow consistent, in that it allows current-account imbalances to have a feedback effect on wealth and, hence, on long-run equilibrium.

The Portfolio-Balance Model

The portfolio-balance model of exchange-rate determination was developed in the 1970s and 1980s by a number of authors, including Black (1973), Branson (1977, 1984), and Allen and Kenen (1980); a comprehensive treatment is given in Branson and Henderson (1985). In common with the flexible-price and sticky-price monetary models, the level of the exchange rate in the portfolio-balance model is determined by supply and demand in the markets for financial assets. The exchange rate, however, is a principal determinant of the current account of the balance of payments. A surplus (deficit) on the current account represents a rise (fall) in net domestic holdings of foreign assets, which in turn affects the level of wealth, which in turn affects asset demands, and these affect the exchange rate. The portfolio-balance model is, therefore, an inherently dynamic model of exchange-rate adjustment that encompasses asset markets, the current account, the price level, and the rate of asset accumulation. Another feature of the portfolio-balance model is that it allows a distinction between short-run equilibrium (supply and demand are equated in asset markets but stocks are not yet affected by flows) and dynamic adjustment to long-run equilibrium (in which the level of wealth is static and there is no tendency for the system to move over time). Although this is also a characteristic of the sticky-price monetary model, the latter does not attempt to allow for the full interaction among the exchange rate, the balance of payments, the level of wealth, and stock equilibrium.

In its simplest form, the portfolio-balance model divides the net financial wealth of the private sector (W) into three components: money (M), domestically issued bonds (B), and foreign bonds denominated in foreign currency (F). The stock of domestically issued bonds (B) can be thought of as government debt held by the domestic private sector; the stock of foreign bonds

---

[5] See Calvo and Rodriguez (1977) and Girton and Roper (1981) for a relaxation of this assumption of nonsubstitutability of monies.

denominated in foreign currency (F) is the level of net claims on foreigners held by the private sector. Because a current-account surplus must be exactly matched by a capital-account deficit under a free float (that is, a capital out-flow and, hence, an increase in net foreign indebtedness to the domestic econ-omy), the current account must define the rate of accumulation of F over time. With foreign and domestic interest rates given by r and r^*, as before, we can write the definition of wealth and simple domestic-demand functions for its components as follows:[6]

$$W \equiv M + B + SF ,$$ (13)

$$M = M(r, r^*)W \quad M_r < 0, M_r^* < 0 ,$$ (14)

$$B = B(r, r^*)W \quad B_r > 0, B_r^* < 0 ,$$ (15)

$$SF = F(r, r^*)W \quad F_r < 0, F_r^* > 0 ,$$ (16)

$$\dot{F} = N(S/P) + r^*F \quad N_{S/P} > 0 .$$ (17)

Relation (13) is an identity defining wealth. The major noteworthy charac-teristics of (14) to (16) are that the scale variable is the level of wealth (W), as is standard in most expositions of the portfolio-balance model, and the de-mand functions are homogeneous in wealth; this allows them to be written in nominal terms (prices are made to cancel out by assuming homogeneity in prices and real wealth). Equation (17) makes the rate of change of F, the capital account, equal to the current account, which is in turn equal to the sum of the trade balance ($N[.]$) and net debt-service receipts (r^*F). The trade bal-ance depends positively on the level of the real exchange rate (a devaluation improves the trade balance).

Consider first the immediate effects of monetary and fiscal policy on the exchange rate in this framework. A contractionary monetary policy (M down) reduces nominal financial wealth (through [13]) and so reduces the demands for both domestic and foreign bonds (through [15] and [16]). As foreign bonds are sold and the proceeds converted into domestic currency, the immediate effect is an exchange-rate appreciation.

In reality, of course, the authorities will alter the supply of domestic bonds by open-market operations—for example, by printing money and using it to purchase domestic bonds, a so-called open-market purchase. In order to in-duce agents to hold more money and fewer bonds during an open-market purchase, the domestic interest rate must fall. As agents buy foreign bonds in an attempt to compensate for the reduction in their holdings of domestic bonds, the exchange rate will depreciate, driving up the domestic value of

---

[6] We use the notation $X_w = \partial X / \partial w$. Note that all of the variables are now in levels rather than logarithms, so that S (upper case), for example, denotes the domestic price of foreign currency.

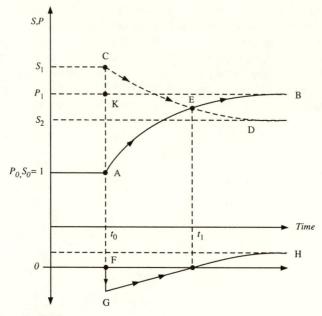

Figure 2.3 Dynamic Adjustment in the Portfolio-Balance Model:
An Open-Market Purchase of Domestic Bonds

foreign bonds. The net impact effect is a lower domestic interest rate and a
depreciated currency.

Now consider the full dynamics of an open-market purchase. Suppose that
the economy was initially in equilibrium with a zero trade balance and no net
foreign assets (hence, a zero current account). This is depicted in Figure 2.3 at
the point corresponding to time t_0. Figure 2.3 is drawn so that the initial (t_0)
values of the price level and the exchange rate are normalized to unity. The
impact effect of an open-market purchase is a depreciation of the exchange
rate, say from S_0 to S_1 (AC). If we assume that the Marshall-Lerner condition
holds and ignore any "J-curve" effects, the improvement in competitiveness
will improve the trade balance from zero to a positive amount (FG). This
means that the current account goes into surplus, and domestic residents begin
to acquire wealth in the form of net foreign assets (equation [17]). Other
things being equal, however, a rise in wealth will raise the demand for domestic bonds, so agents will sell some foreign bonds, and the exchange rate will
begin to appreciate, from point C along CD in the diagram. This erosion of
competitiveness will lead to a deterioration of the trade balance along GH.
Meanwhile, the increase in the money supply will have begun to increase
goods prices along the path AB toward the new long-run equilibrium price
level, P_1; this amplifies the deterioration of competitiveness and, hence, of the

trade balance.[7] At point E (time t_1), the exchange rate and the price level are equal in value, so their ratio is unity—the same as the initial ratio at time t_0. Because we have implicitly held foreign prices constant, the real exchange rate is back to its original level, so the trade balance must be back to its original level, that is, zero. This is no longer enough to restore long-run equilibrium, however, because domestic residents have acquired a positive level of net foreign assets and will be receiving a stream of interest income (r^*F) from abroad. Therefore, they will still be acquiring foreign assets, so the exchange rate will still be appreciating. In order for the current-account balance to be zero, the trade balance must actually go into deficit. This requires a further appreciation of the exchange rate to its long-run equilibrium level (S_2), by which time the price level has reached its long-run equilibrium level (P_1), and the current account just balances ($-N[S_2/P_1] = r^*F$), so that there is no further net accumulation of foreign assets. The overall effect of the open-market purchase on the exchange rate is a long-run depreciation from S_0 to S_2, with an initial overshoot of $S_1 - S_2$.

This exposition of the portfolio-balance model has assumed that exchange-rate expectations are static, so that the expected rate of depreciation is zero. Technically, expectations could be introduced into this simple formulation by adding the expected rate of depreciation to the foreign interest rate in each of the asset-demand equations (14) to (16), so that the resulting argument becomes the expected return to holding foreign bonds. There is not space here to develop the model more fully in that direction; the reader is referred to Branson (1984) and Branson and Henderson (1985).[8] In fact, most of the properties of the model remain intact when rational expectations are introduced, but impact effects become much more pronounced, and a key distinction must now be drawn between anticipated disturbances (the effect of which will already be discounted into the current exchange-rate level) and unanticipated disturbances (which require an initial jump in the exchange rate and then a slow adjustment to the new equilibrium). A more completely specified model would also allow for interaction among production, consumption, saving, and the level of wealth; on this, see, in particular, Allen and Kenen (1980).

3 Empirical Evidence on Asset-Approach Exchange-Rate Models

Tests of the Monetary Models

At the outset of the recent float, the flexible-price monetary model was the dominant theoretical model of exchange-rate determination, and the earliest

[7] We are implicitly assuming an extra mechanism whereby an increase in the money supply raises goods prices. This is uncontroversial, however.

[8] Branson and Henderson (1985) also examine the properties of the portfolio-balance model when net domestic holdings of foreign nonmonetary assets are negative.

tests of exchange-rate models therefore relate to that approach. Lacking a run of data for the new period that was sufficiently long for econometric purposes, however, researchers looked initially to the 1920s float as a testing ground. The already well-researched German hyperinflation of the 1920s provided a particularly suitable laboratory for studying the monetary model, because the movements in real, compared to nominal, macroeconomic variables were relatively unimportant during that episode. Frenkel (1976) found evidence strongly supportive of the flexible-price monetary model for the dollar-mark exchange rate over the first four years of the 1920s.

The further passage of time and accumulation of floating-period data allowed estimation of the flexible-price monetary model for the 1970s float, and these early studies were also broadly supportive of the flexible-price monetary model (for example, Bilson, 1978; Dornbusch, 1979). Hence, this first round of studies concluded that the monetary model provided a reasonable guide to the behavior of floating exchange rates. Beyond the late 1970s, however, the flexible-price monetary model (and its real-interest-differential variant) ceased to provide a good explanation of variations in exchange rates. The estimated equations broke down, providing poor fits, exhibiting incorrectly signed coefficients, and failing general equation diagnostics (Frankel, 1984). In particular, estimates of equations for the dollar-mark rate often produced coefficients implying that increases in Germany's money supply caused its currency to appreciate. Frankel (1982a) called this the "mystery of the multiplying marks."

Some authors have sought to explain this breakdown as resulting from the inappropriateness of coefficient restrictions derived from the assumption of identical parameters in the domestic and foreign money-demand functions; others have argued that the monetary model is more crucially misspecified. Frankel (1982a), for example, argues that German current-account surpluses during the late 1970s may have led to a relative rise in German wealth, which does not figure in the usual flexible-price monetary formulation. By adding proxies for U.S. and German wealth (cumulated current-account surpluses plus government debt) to the flexible-price monetary equation, Frankel greatly improves its performance. A further explanation for the failure of the monetary-approach equations may be the relative instability of the underlying money-demand functions and the simplistic functional forms that are implicitly used to represent money demand (Frankel, 1984).

Other authors have pointed out that having the expected rate of depreciation (or, under uncovered or covered interest parity, the interest differential or the forward premium) on the right-hand side of the equation may impart an important simultaneity to the equation (see equation [5]). One way of dealing with such simultaneity is offered by the rational-expectations solution of the monetary model, which effectively gives an equation purged of this expectational term (equation [6]), but it requires additional assumptions in order to arrive at a closed-form solution. Although some researchers have found that the rational-expectations flexible-price monetary model works reasonably well for the 1980s (Hoffman and Schlagenhauf, 1983), a recent treatment by MacDonald and Taylor (1993a) for the dollar-mark exchange rate decisively rejects the rational-expectations restrictions.

More recently, MacDonald and Taylor (1991a, 1993a, 1994) have tested the monetary model by viewing it as defining a long-run equilibrium toward which the exchange rate converges while also allowing for complicated short-run dynamics. They apply dynamic modeling techniques and multivariate co-integration analysis, following, for example, Engle and Granger (1987) and Johansen (1988). MacDonald and Taylor find some evidence to support use of the monetary model as a long-run equilibrium model. It should be noted, however, that all of the monetary models collapse to an equilibrium condition of the form (4) in the long run, so that these tests have no power to discriminate between alternative varieties.

Meese (1986) tests for rational bubbles in the framework of the monetary model, a form of specification test, by estimating both a version of equation (4), which produces consistent coefficient estimates regardless of the presence or absence of rational bubbles, and a closed-form version of (6), which produces consistent coefficient estimates only in the absence of bubbles. For three major exchange rates, Meese finds that the two sets of coefficient estimates are significantly different and so rejects the no-bubbles hypothesis. An alternative way of testing for bubbles is to test for the "excess volatility" that bubbles would create—volatility additional to that generated by the expected fundamentals. Tests of this kind have generally found evidence of excess volatility in the foreign-exchange market (Huang, 1981). There are, however, a number of technical problems with this approach. For example, the excess-volatility finding may be due to measurement error, to inappropriate stationary-inducing transformations, or to small-sample bias.[9]

Flood and Rose (1992) have constructed a new set of very general excess-volatility tests based on the monetary class of models. They compare the volatility of what they call "traditional fundamentals" and "virtual fundamentals." Their measure of virtual fundamentals (VF_t) is backed out of an equation such as (4):

$$VF_t = s_t - \lambda(r - r^*)_t . \qquad (18)$$

The traditional fundamentals (TF_t) implied, for example, by the flexible-price monetary model are:

---

[9] MacDonald and Taylor (1993a) test for bubbles by testing for cointegration of the exchange rate and the fundamentals, although the Monte Carlo evidence of Evans (1991) questions the power of tests of this kind.

$$TF_t = (m - m^*)_t - \phi(y - y^*)_t \, . \tag{19}$$

Observing the increased volatility of exchange rates under the floating-rate regime, Flood and Rose argue that any tentatively adequate exchange-rate model should have traditional fundamentals that are also much more volatile during a floating-rate regime. Working with a number of OECD exchange rates, however, they find little shift in the volatility of the traditional fundamentals in flexible- or sticky-price monetary models across regimes, whereas there is extremely strong evidence of a rise in the volatility of the virtual fundamentals with a shift to a floating-rate regime. A problem with the study by Flood and Rose is that their measure of the virtual fundamentals may include a risk premium, the deviation from uncovered interest parity (see Section 4), which might well be more volatile under a floating-rate regime. It seems unlikely, however, that the behavior of the risk premium can entirely account for the difference in volatility across regimes. Similar evidence is reported by Baxter and Stockman (1989), who examine the time-series behavior of a number of key macroeconomic aggregates for forty-nine countries over the postwar period. Although they detect evidence of greater variability in the real exchange rate when the nominal exchange rate is floating than when it is pegged, Baxter and Stockman find no systematic differences in the behavior of the macroeconomic aggregates under alternative exchange-rate arrangements. Again, this suggests that speculative forces at work in the foreign-exchange market are not reflected in the usual menu of macroeconomic fundamentals.

Tests of the Portfolio-Balance Model

The portfolio-balance approach to the exchange rate has attracted much less empirical work than the monetary approach, presumably because researchers have encountered problems in mapping theoretical portfolio-balance models into real-world financial data. There are difficult methodological issues, such as which nonmonetary assets to include in the empirical model, and the relevant data are not always available, especially on a bilateral basis.

Log-linear versions of a reduced-form exchange-rate equation derived from a system such as (13) through (17), using cumulated current accounts for the stock of foreign assets, have been estimated for many of the major exchange rates in the 1970s, with relatively poor results. The estimated coefficients are generally insignificant and there is a persistent problem of residual autocorrelation (Branson, Halttunen, and Masson, 1977, 1979; Bisignano and Hoover, 1982).

The imperfect substitutability of domestic and foreign assets that is assumed in the portfolio-balance model is equivalent to assuming that there is a risk premium separating expected depreciation and the domestic-foreign interest-rate differential. In the portfolio-balance model, this risk premium will be a function of relative domestic and foreign debts outstanding. An indirect method of testing the portfolio-balance model is therefore to test for empirical relationships between the risk premium and the stocks of debt outstanding. Investigations have usually reported statistically insignificant relationships (Frankel, 1982b; Rogoff, 1984). In a recent study of the effectiveness of exchange-rate intervention for the dollar-mark and dollar–Swiss franc rates during the 1980s, Dominguez and Frankel (1993a) measure the risk premium using survey data. They show that the resulting measure can in fact be explained by an empirical model that is consistent with the portfolio-balance model in which investors engage in mean-variance optimization on the part of investors; a similar result for the dollar-mark rate is reported by Black (1993). In some ways, the relative success of the Dominguez and Frankel (1993a) and Black (1993) studies is consistent with the recent empirical literature on the efficiency of foreign-exchange markets. This literature, discussed in the next section, suggests the existence of significant foreign-exchange risk premia and nonrational expectations. Evidence of risk premia is tantamount to evidence for the imperfect substitutability of domestic and foreign assets in investors' portfolios; evidence of nonrational expectations may explain why tests of the portfolio-balance model assuming rational expectations have met with mixed success, whereas those employing survey data appear to perform better empirically. This is an avenue that warrants further research.

The Out-of-Sample Forecasting Performance of Asset-Approach Exchange-Rate Models

Another way of examining the empirical content of exchange-rate theories is to examine their *out-of-sample* forecasting performance. In a landmark paper, Meese and Rogoff (1983a) compare the out-of-sample forecasts produced by various exchange-rate models with forecasts produced by a random-walk model, by the forward exchange rate, by a univariate regression of the spot rate, and by a vector autoregression. They use rolling regressions to generate a succession of out-of-sample forecasts for each model and for various time horizons. Some of their results are summarized in Table 2.1, which lists the root-mean-squared error (RMSE) for the six-month time horizon and compares the forecasts produced by the random-walk model with those produced by the flexible-price monetary model, by Frankel's (1979) real-interest-rate-differential (RID) variant of the monetary model, and by a synthesis of the monetary and portfolio-balance models suggested by Hooper and Morton (1982). These results suggest that none of the asset-market approaches outper-

TABLE 2.1
Root-Mean-Squared Forecast Errors for Selected Exchange-Rate Equations

Exchange Rate	Random Walk	FLPM	RID	Monetary-Portfolio Synthesis
Dollar-mark	8.71	9.64	12.03	9.95
Dollar-yen	11.58	13.38	13.94	11.94
Dollar-sterling	6.45	8.90	8.88	9.08
Effective dollar rate	6.09	7.07	6.49	7.11

Source: Meese and Rogoff (1983a).

forms the simple random walk, even though the models are allowed to employ *actual* future values of the various independent variables.

Further work by the same authors (Meese and Rogoff, 1983b) suggests that the estimated models may have been affected by simultaneity bias. Imposing coefficient constraints taken from the empirical literature on money demand, Meese and Rogoff find that, although the coefficient-constrained reduced forms of the asset models still fail to outperform the random-walk model for most horizons up to a year, parameter constraints can be combined to suggest that the asset models do outperform the random-walk model for horizons beyond twelve months. Even at these longer horizons, however, the models are unstable in that the minimum RMSE models have different coefficient values at different horizons.

Although beating the random walk still remains the standard metric by which to judge empirical exchange-rate models, researchers have found that one key to improving forecast performance lies in the introduction of equation dynamics. This has been done in various ways: by using dynamic forecasting equations for the forcing variables in the forward-looking, rational-expectations version of the flexible-price monetary model, by incorporating dynamic partial-adjustment terms into the estimating equation, by using time-varying parameter-estimation techniques, and—most recently—by using dynamic error-correction forms (Pentecost, 1991).[10]

Short-Run Noise: The Influence of Technical Analysis

A broad conclusion that emerges from our discussion is that the asset-approach models have performed well for some time periods, such as the

---

[10] Other intriguing evidence on this issue is provided in a recent paper by Black (1993). Black simulates a weekly portfolio-balance model of the dollar-mark exchange rate, in which short-run rationality of expectations is relaxed (although long-run model consistency is imposed). Working with a twelve-week out-of-sample period in 1988, he finds that the one-step-ahead forecasts are superior to those of a random walk.

interwar period and the first part of the recent float (1973 to 1978), but have not provided an adequate explanation for the behavior of the major exchange rates during the latter part of the recent float. One suggested explanation for this breakdown is that the foreign-exchange market has become increasingly dominated by analysts who base their predictions not on economic theory— the "fundamentals"—but on the identification of supposedly recurring patterns in graphs of exchange-rate movements—that is, "technical" or "chartist" analysts (Allen and Taylor, 1993).

In a survey conducted by the Group of Thirty (Goedhuys, 1985), it was found that 97 percent of banks and 87 percent of securities houses believed that the use of technical analysis has a significant impact on the foreign-exchange market. In an analysis of survey questionnaires sent to chief foreign-exchange dealers in the London market in 1988, Taylor and Allen (1992) found that at time horizons of intraday to one week, approximately 90 percent of survey respondents used some chartist input when forming their exchange-rate expectations, with 60 percent judging charts to be at least as important as fundamentals; at longer forecast horizons, however, the weight given to economic fundamentals increases markedly. Analyzing the accuracy of a number of individual technical analysts' one-week-ahead and four-week-ahead forecasts for three major exchange rates, Allen and Taylor (1990) found that some individuals were consistently able to outperform a range of alternative forecasting procedures. Earlier studies by Goodman (1979, 1980) of the profitability of exchange-rate forecasts provided both by chartist and by fundamentals-based services found that the forecasts of the services that used chartist methods outperformed forward-rate forecasts in qualitative tests, whereas forward-rate forecasts outperformed the forecasts of the services that used fundamentals.

Theoretical analyses of the interaction between fundamental and nonfundamental advice in the foreign-exchange market have been relatively few. Goodhart (1988) shows how exchange-rate misalignments might occur by considering the possibility that the exchange rate is determined by the balance between chartist and fundamentalist predictions.[11] A similar approach is developed more formally by Frankel and Froot (1986, 1990), who explain the sharp rise in the demand for the U.S. dollar over the 1981–85 period as a shift in the weight of market opinion away from fundamentalists and toward chartists. This shift is modeled as a Bayesian response to the inferior forecasting performance of the economic fundamentalists. De Grauwe, Dewachter, and Embrechts (1993), using chaos theory, simulate a number of exchange-rate models involving fundamentalist and chartist expectations and find that the simulated series mimic a number of properties of actual exchange-rate data, such as long swings, near-unit roots, and sometimes perverse short-term reactions to movements in the fundamentals.

[11] This is in some ways similar to the simple model of the stock market suggested by Shiller (1984), in which the equilibrium price depends on the balance between fundamentalists (smart money) and ordinary investors who subscribe to popular models.

4 The Efficient-Markets Hypothesis

Testing the Efficiency of the Foreign-Exchange Market

Much of the work on exchange-rate determination is implicitly based on the assumption of foreign-exchange-market efficiency, under which market exchange rates reflect the underlying economic fundamentals. If a speculative market is efficient, then prices in that market should fully reflect information available to market participants, and it should be impossible for a speculator to earn excess returns. In its simplest form, the efficient-markets hypothesis can be reduced to a joint hypothesis that market participants are, in an aggregate sense, endowed with rational expectations and are risk neutral.[12] It is possible to modify the definition to adjust for risk, so that the hypothesis of market efficiency is then a joint hypothesis derived from a model of equilibrium returns (which may admit risk premia) and rational expectations.

If the risk-neutral efficient-markets hypothesis holds, the expected foreign-exchange gain from holding one currency rather than another (the expected rate of appreciation) must be just offset by the opportunity cost (the interest-rate differential) of holding funds in that currency rather than the other. This is the uncovered interest-parity condition. It is the cornerstone for tests of efficiency in the foreign-exchange market:

$$\Delta s_{t+k}^e = (r - r^*)_t \; . \tag{20}$$

Early tests of efficiency that tested for the randomness of exchange-rate changes (Poole, 1967) are based on a misconception. If the nominal interest differential is identically equal to a constant, and expectations are rational, equation (20) implies that the log-level of the exchange rate does indeed follow a random walk (with drift if the constant is nonzero). Generally, however, the random-walk model is inconsistent with the uncovered interest-parity condition (20). The analysis of Cumby and Obstfeld (1981) can be seen as a logical, and theoretically correct, extension of the literature on the randomness of exchange-rate changes, because it tests for randomness of deviations from uncovered interest parity.

Another method of testing market efficiency is to test for the profitability of filter rules. A simple x percent filter rule instructs a trader to buy a currency whenever it rises x percent above its most recent trough and to sell it whenever it falls x percent below its most recent peak. If the market is efficient and uncovered interest parity holds, the interest costs of such a strategy should, on average, eliminate any profit. An analysis by Dooley and Shafer (1984) not

[12] Rational expectations are required only in the sense that the market achieves the rational-expectations equilibrium. This might be reached in a market in which only a very few rational speculators police this equilibrium.

only inciudes interest costs but also allows for transactions costs by using bid-and-asked exchange-rate quotations. After applying a number of filter rules to daily data for nine exchange rates in the 1970s, they report that small filters—1, 2, and 3 percent—would have systematically generated profits for all exchange rates over the sample period. It is not clear, however, that the optimal filter rule could have been chosen *ex ante*, and there appears also to be an important element of riskiness, in that substantial losses are generated in many subperiods.

More usually, the literature on foreign-exchange-market efficiency has involved regression-based analyses of spot and forward exchange rates. Under covered interest parity, the interest-rate differential should be just equal to the forward premium. Under rational expectations, moreover, the expected change in the exchange rate should differ from the actual change only by a rational-expectations forecast error. Hence, the uncovered interest-parity condition (20) can be tested by estimating a regression relationship of the form

$$\Delta s_{t+k} = \alpha + \beta \, (f - s)_t + u_{t+k} \, , \tag{21}$$

where f is the logarithm of the forward rate for maturity k periods ahead.[13] If agents are risk neutral and have rational expectations, we should expect the slope parameter (β) to be equal to 1, and the disturbance term, the rational-expectations forecast error under the null hypothesis, to be uncorrelated with information available at time t. Empirical studies of (21) for a large variety of currencies and time periods within the recent float generally report results that are unfavorable to the efficient-markets hypothesis (Fama [1984], Mc-Callum [1992], and Clarida and Taylor [1993] are recent examples). Froot (1990) reports that, across seventy-five published estimates of (21), the average estimated value of the slope parameter is -0.88; and, indeed, it seems to be generally accepted that estimates of β in equations such as (21) are closer to minus unity than plus unity. A typical example of the result obtained by researchers is reported here as equation (22), from Fama (1984), estimated on monthly data for the dollar-mark exchange rates from 1973 to 1982, with standard errors in parentheses:

$$\Delta s_{t+1} = 0.36 - 1.32 \, (f - s)_t \, . \tag{22}$$
$$(0.44) \quad (0.66)$$

---

[13] Regression relationships involving exchange rates are normally expressed in logarithms in order to circumvent the so-called Siegel paradox (Siegel, 1972): because of Jensen's inequality, one cannot simultaneously have an unbiased expectation of, say, the mark-dollar exchange rate (marks per dollar) and of the dollar-mark exchange rate (dollars per mark) because $1/E(S) \neq E(1/S)$. Although the problem seems to be avoided if exchange rates are expressed in logarithms, because $E(-s) = -E(s)$, agents must still form expectations of final payoffs S and $1/S$, so it is not clear that taking logarithms avoids the problem. McCulloch (1975), using 1920s data, demonstrates that the operational importance of the Siegel paradox is slight.

Note that this stylized result, the so-called forward-discount bias, does not necessarily imply that the forward rate contains no information relevant to forecasting the future spot exchange rate, as some researchers have claimed.[14] As demonstrated by Clarida and Taylor (1993), the forward-discount bias may be the result of departures from the simple efficient-markets hypothesis; the information content of forward premia remains high.

Alternatively, researchers have tested the orthogonality of the forward-rate forecast error to a given information set by imposing the restriction $\beta = 1$ in (21) and testing the null hypothesis that $\Psi = 0$ in regressions of the form

$$s_{t+k} - f_t = \Psi X_t + u_{t+k} , \qquad (23)$$

where X_t is a vector of variables known at time t. Orthogonality tests of this kind, in which lagged forecast errors of the exchange rate in question are included in X_t, have generally rejected the simple, risk-neutral efficient-markets hypothesis; even stronger rejections are usually obtained when additional information, such as lagged forecast errors for other exchange rates, is included in X_t (Hansen and Hodrick, 1980; Boothe and Longworth, 1986; Hodrick, 1987).

Rationalizing the Inefficiency Finding

The rejection of the simple, risk-neutral efficient-markets hypothesis, the "inefficiency finding," may be due to risk aversion on the part of market participants or to a departure from the pure rational-expectations hypothesis, or both. If foreign-exchange-market participants are risk averse, the uncovered interest-parity condition (16) may be distorted by a risk premium that is time-varying and correlated with the forward premium or with the interest-rate differential; this would confound efficiency tests of the kind outlined above (Fama, 1984). This reasoning has led to a search for stable empirical models of the risk premium under the assumption of rational expectations. Hansen and Hodrick (1983), for example, test the restrictions implied by an intertemporal asset-pricing model of the risk premium by using a latent-variables approach and testing the overidentifying restrictions in an econometric model where the latent variables driving the risk premium are instrumented on past forecast errors. Although Hansen and Hodrick are unable to reject the model's restrictions, Hodrick and Srivastava (1986), using an extended data set and instrumenting the forward premium, are easily able to reject the implied orthogonality conditions.

---

[14] Cumby and Obstfeld (1984, p. 139), for example, write that "forward premia contain little information regarding subsequent exchange-rate fluctuations . . . exchange-rate changes over the recent period of floating seem to have been largely unanticipated."

Because of the theoretical relation between risk and the second moments of asset-price distributions, researchers have often asked whether the risk premium can be treated as a function of the variance of forecast errors or exchange-rate movements. Frankel (1982b), for example, derives asset-demand functions for six currencies, using a mean-variance optimization framework. This yields risk premia that are functions of the covariance matrix of expected rates of depreciation across the exchange rates of the currencies involved. Estimation of these parameterizations, however, does not lead Frankel to reject the hypothesis of risk neutrality. Giovannini and Jorion (1989) effectively extend Frankel's analysis by employing an autoregressive conditional heteroscedasticity (ARCH) parameterization of the second moments, so that the covariance matrix of returns is allowed to vary over time. They find that the time-varying second moments are in fact significant in explaining the *ex ante* risk premium, although they reject the overidentifying restrictions implied by the international capital-asset-pricing model under rational expectations.[15]

An alternative explanation for the rejection of the simple efficient-markets hypothesis is that exchange-rate expectations have not been modeled adequately. Arguments in this group invoke the "peso problem" (originally suggested by Rogoff [1979]), rational bubbles, learning about regime shifts (Lewis, 1989), and inefficient information processing (as suggested, for example, by Bilson [1981]). The "peso problem" refers to a situation in which agents attach a small probability to a large change in the economic fundamentals that does not actually occur in sample. Under these circumstances, the distribution of forecast errors may be skewed even if agents' expectations are rational, and econometric estimates may thus generate evidence of nonzero excess returns from forward speculation. The rational-bubbles explanation is discussed above in the context of empirical tests of models of exchange-rate determination. In common with the peso problem, rational bubbles may produce nonzero excess returns even when agents are risk neutral. Similarly, when agents are learning about their environment, they may be unable fully to exploit arbitrage opportunities that are apparent in the *ex post* data. A problem with invoking peso problems, bubbles, or learning as explanations for the forward-discount bias is that, as noted above, a very large number of econometric studies, encompassing an even larger range of exchange rates and sample periods, have found that the direction of bias is the same; the estimated uncovered interest-parity slope parameter, β in (16), is negative and closer to minus unity than plus unity. For example, Lewis (1989) has studied the relation between dollar appreciation in the early 1980s and learning about the U.S. money-supply process and has noted a persistence in the forward-rate

---

[15] MacDonald and Taylor (1991b) find that a generalized ARCH paramaterization of the risk premium is reasonably successful in explaining the risk premium for franc-sterling and franc-dollar exchange rates during the interwar float.

errors that, in itself, is *prima facie* evidence against the learning explanation; agents cannot forever be learning about a one-time regime shift. Similarly, the peso problem is essentially a small-sample phenomenon; it cannot explain the *overall* stylized fact that estimates of β are negative.[16]

A problem with much of the empirical work on the possible rationalizations of the inefficiency finding is that in testing one leg of the joint hypothesis, researchers have typically assumed that the other leg is true. For example, the search for a stable empirical risk-premium model has generally been conditioned on the assumption of rational expectations. Clearly, one would like to be able to test both components of the joint hypothesis in order to discern which component is at fault. The recent availability of survey data on exchange-rate expectations has allowed researchers to do just that. One emerging conclusion is that measured risk premia, defined as the forward rate minus the average (usually median) exchange-rate-survey expectation, do appear to be statistically related to the second moments of exchange-rate changes (Dominguez and Frankel, 1993a; Black, 1993) or to the conditional second moments of the survey forecast errors (MacDonald and Taylor, 1993b). Moreover, although Froot and Frankel (1989) cannot reject the hypothesis that the bias is entirely due to systematic expectational errors, the overall conclusion appears to be that both risk aversion and departures from rational expectations are responsible for rejection of the simple efficient-markets hypothesis (see Takagi [1991] for a review of survey-data studies).

Once nonrational expectations on the part of at least some agents in the foreign-exchange market are admitted as a possibility, the class of alternative hypotheses becomes very large indeed. One such hypothesis is that traders are heavily influenced by nonfundamental, chartist analysis, as noted above. Moreover, the analysis of survey data by Frankel and Froot (1990) indicates that at short horizons, agents tend to forecast by extrapolating recent trends, whereas at longer horizons, they tend to incorporate into their forecasts a long-run equilibrium condition, such as purchasing-power parity; this is consistent with the evidence presented by Taylor and Allen (1992) that foreign-exchange traders give more weight to fundamentals than to chartist analysis at long forecast horizons.

Other Arbitrage Conditions

Although uncovered interest parity is the basic arbitrage condition for assessing the efficiency of the foreign-exchange market, two other arbitrage

---

[16] In a recent paper, Kaminsky (1993) develops a model that combines the effect of the peso problem with learning about switching regimes (a combination she terms the "generalized peso problem"). Using monthly spot, forward, and survey data on the dollar-sterling exchange rate for the period from 1976 to 1987, she argues that such a model can explain a high proportion of survey and forward-rate error.

conditions, covered interest parity and purchasing-power parity, receive considerable attention in the literature.

COVERED INTEREST PARITY[17]

If foreign-exchange markets are operating efficiently, arbitrage should ensure that the covered interest differential on similar assets is continuously equal to zero, so that covered interest parity should hold:

$$(r - r^*)_t - (f - s)_t = 0 \ . \tag{24}$$

It is clearly important in this connection to consider domestic and foreign assets that are comparable in terms of maturity and also in terms of other characteristics such as default and political risk. Most often, researchers have used offshore (Euro-currency) interest rates to test covered interest parity.[18]

Frenkel and Levich (1975, 1977) have tested for departures from (24) for a number of major exchange rates during the 1970s, allowing for transactions costs, and they find very few departures when Euro-deposit rates are used but significantly more (some 20 percent) when Treasury-bill rates are used. Further evidence supportive of covered interest parity is provided by Clinton (1988) for several major exchange rates during the recent float.

Some authors have stressed the importance of data quality in testing covered interest parity. For example, in a comment on the Frenkel-Levich papers, McCormick (1979), using higher-quality data for U.K.-U.S. Treasury-bill rates, finds that most of the deviations from covered interest parity (70 to 80 percent) are larger than can be explained by transactions costs alone. Taylor (1987, 1989) goes further and argues that, in order to provide a true test of covered interest parity, it is important to have contemporaneous data on the appropriate exchange rates and interest rates—those at which a dealer could actually have dealt. Using very high-quality, high-frequency, contemporaneously sampled data for spot and forward dollar-sterling and dollar-mark exchange rates and the corresponding Euro-deposit interest rates for a number of maturities, Taylor finds, *inter alia*, that there are few profitable violations of covered interest parity, even in periods of market uncertainty and turbulence. One interesting feature of this work is the finding of a maturity effect; the frequency, size, and persistence of arbitrage opportunities appear to be an increasing function of the length of maturity of the underlying financial instruments. A rationale is offered for this in terms of banks' prudential credit limits.

[17] See Taylor (1992a) for a survey essay on covered interest parity.

[18] Movements in the offshore-onshore interest differential, such as the difference between the Euro-deposit rate and the rate offered for deposits in the same currency and at the same maturity in the domestic interbank market, are often interpreted as an indicator of the level of capital mobility or the effectiveness of capital controls.

Another way of testing covered interest parity, in which the forward premium is regressed on the interest differential, has also been strongly supportive of this parity condition (Branson, 1969). It is not clear, however, what regression-based analyses of covered interest parity are actually being tested. A researcher may be unable to reject the hypothesis that the intercept and slope coefficients are respectively zero and unity, but the fitted residuals may themselves represent substantial arbitrage opportunities.

PURCHASING-POWER PARITY

Under purchasing-power parity, the exchange rate should reflect relative prices in the countries concerned. Absolute purchasing-power parity implies that the exchange rate is equal to the ratio of the two relevant national price levels. Relative purchasing-power parity holds that changes in the exchange rate are equal to changes in relative national prices. Purchasing-power parity has been viewed as a theory of exchange-rate determination, as a short- or long-run equilibrium condition in more general exchange-rate models, and as an arbitrage condition in either goods or asset markets (Frenkel, 1976, 1978; Officer, 1976; Dornbusch, 1992). Roll (1979), for example, argues that if international goods arbitrage is efficient, the expected return to holding foreign goods (that is, the expected change in the real exchange rate) should be zero:

$$(\Delta s - \Delta p + \Delta p^*)^e_{t+1} = 0 \,, \tag{25}$$

which is a form of *ex ante* relative purchasing-power parity. Clearly, if expectations are rational, equation (25) implies that the real exchange rate, $q_t \equiv s_t - p_t + p_t$, will follow a random walk. Adler and Lehmann (1983) derive a similar condition by considering efficient cross-border arbitrage in financial assets and invoking a number of auxiliary assumptions including the Fisher condition relating real and nominal rates of return, the uncovered-interest-parity condition, and real-interest-rate parity.[19] Both of these studies, and others as well, such as Darby (1980) and Cumby and Obstfeld (1984), find difficulty in rejecting the hypothesis that changes in the real exchange rate are random in the recent floating-rate period. In other words, they cast doubt on the validity of purchasing-power parity.

More general tests of purchasing-power parity have often involved estimates of the equations:

---

[19] In Roll's derivation, the real exchange rate is defined with respect to the prices of tradable goods, whereas, in the Adler and Lehmann derivation, the real exchange rate is defined with respect to relative consumer prices (or whatever price series are assumed to be used to calculate expected inflation in the Fisher equations).

$$s_t = \alpha + \beta p_t - \beta^* p_t^* + u_t \,, \qquad\qquad (26)$$

$$\Delta s_t = \beta \Delta p_t - \beta^* \Delta p_t^* + u_t \,. \qquad\qquad (27)$$

A test of the restrictions $\beta = \beta^* = 1$ in (26) can be interpreted as a test of absolute purchasing-power parity; a test of the same restrictions applied to (27) can be interpreted as a test of relative purchasing-power parity. Frenkel has estimated these equations using interwar floating-rate data (Frenkel, 1978) and data for the recent floating experience (Frenkel, 1981). The results for the interwar period are highly supportive of purchasing-power parity, but purchasing-power parity in both its absolute and relative forms is resoundingly rejected by the data for the recent float. In further tests of purchasing-power parity for the interwar and recent floating periods, Krugman (1978) reports estimates of (30) and (31) that are largely unfavorable to purchasing-power parity.[20]

More recently, researchers have tested for cointegration among nominal exchange rates and prices by testing for mean reversion in the real exchange rate or in the residual of an equation such as (26). Earlier cointegration studies generally failed to find a significant mean reversion of the exchange rate toward purchasing-power parity in the recent floating experience (Taylor, 1988; Mark, 1990) but were supportive of reversion in the interwar float (Taylor and McMahon, 1988). Very recent applied work on long-run purchasing-power parity among the major industrialized economies has, however, been more favorable to the long-run purchasing-power-parity hypothesis for the recent float (Cheung and Lai, 1993). Lothian and Taylor (1993) have used Monte Carlo methods to show that the period covered by the recent float may simply be too short to give much power to the normal statistical tests. Finally, these authors also apply standard unit-root tests to data for the dollar-sterling and sterling-franc exchange rates spanning almost two centuries and find strong evidence of long-run reversion toward purchasing-power parity. Abuaf and Jorion (1990) increase the power of their tests by using longer time series and by using systems-estimation methods in which the first-order autoregressive coefficient of the real exchange rate is constrained to be equal across a range of real exchange rates. They are thus able to reject the unit-root (random-walk) hypothesis for the real exchange rate. Diebold, Husted, and Rush (1991) apply fractional-integration techniques to nineteenth-century data and find evidence of long-run purchasing-power parity.

5 Official Intervention

Official intervention in foreign-exchange markets occurs when the authorities buy or sell foreign exchange, normally against their own currency and in

---

[20] Krugman uses a longer sample than Frenkel (1978) for the interwar period.

order to affect the exchange rate. Sterilized intervention occurs when the authorities, simultaneously or with a very short lag, take action to offset or "sterilize" the effects of the resulting change in official foreign-asset holdings on the domestic monetary base. The exchange-rate effects of intervention—in particular, sterilized intervention—have been debated in the literature. Indeed, as noted by Kenen (1982), the views of both policymakers and researchers about the effects of intervention appear to be even more volatile than exchange rates themselves. At the outset of the current float in the early 1970s, a "clean" rather than "dirty," or managed, float was favored. Then, in the late 1970s, the United States was frequently criticized for its reluctance to intervene in support of the dollar. By the early 1980s, however, the prevailing consensus among economists, policymakers, and market practitioners was that intervention, particularly sterilized intervention, could have only small and transitory effects on the exchange rate. This view was enshrined in the conclusions of the Jurgensen Report (1983), commissioned by the 1982 G-7 Economic Summit of Heads of Government at Versailles. After the September 1985 G-5 meeting at the Plaza Hotel in New York, however, official views on the usefulness of intervention appeared to switch again. Since that time, intervention in the markets for the major currencies has been regular and, at times, heavy.[21] Although a theoretical case for the effectiveness of sterilized intervention can be derived from the portfolio-balance model, the empirical evidence has been relatively mixed.

The Channels of Influence

Sterilized intervention may influence the exchange rate through two channels: by changing the relative supplies of assets, and by signaling policy intentions. Its effects through the first channel can be analyzed within the framework of the portfolio-balance model. Suppose, for example, that the authorities purchase foreign exchange and make an open-market sale of domestic bonds in order to sterilize the effect on the money supply. If domestic and foreign bonds are perfect substitutes in private agents' portfolios and agents are initially in stock equilibrium, they will sell foreign bonds one for one with the increase in their holdings of domestic bonds. They will then sell the same amount of foreign currency that the authorities purchased, and there will be no net effect on the level of the exchange rate.[22] If domestic and foreign bonds are less than perfect substitutes, however, private sales of foreign bonds will be less than the increase in private holdings of domestic bonds, and intervention will affect the level of the exchange rate.

---

[21] Dominguez and Frankel (1993b) provide an up-to-date account of the history of official intervention during the recent float.

[22] See Kenen (1982) for a thorough analysis of the long- and short-run effects of intervention in the framework of the portfolio-balance model.

The second channel of influence, the signaling, or expectations, channel (Mussa, 1981), allows for intervention to affect exchange rates by providing the market with relevant information that was previously not known or incorporated into the current exchange rate. This line of argument presumes that the authorities have information not otherwise available to market participants and that they are willing to reveal this information through their actions in the foreign-exchange market. Even in a simple flexible-price monetary model, sterilized intervention can affect exchange rates through the signaling channel by altering agents' expectations about future movements in relative money supplies or incomes, a change that then feeds back into the current exchange rate (see equation [6]).

The Empirical Evidence on the Effectiveness of Intervention[23]

Empirical work on the effectiveness of intervention through the portfolio-balance channel has generally taken one of three forms. First, researchers have estimated the structural asset-demand equations of portfolio-balance models (Obstfeld, 1983; Lewis, 1988). Second, researchers have estimated *inverted* asset-demand equations in which the *ex post* difference in rates of return between domestic and foreign assets is regressed on a range of variables: under the joint null hypothesis of perfect substitutability and rational expectations, the estimated regression coefficients should be insignificantly different from zero (Rogoff, 1984; Danker et al., 1987). A third approach involves estimating asset-demand equations derived in a specific optimization framework, such as mean-variance analysis (Frankel, 1982b). Much of the literature using these three approaches has found difficulty in rejecting the hypothesis that intervention acting through the portfolio-balance channel cannot strongly affect exchange rates. A recent treatment by Obstfeld (1990), for example, argues that sterilized intervention in itself has not played an important role in altering exchange rates since the 1985 Plaza Accord, but rather that realignments of external rates have occurred as the result of appropriate macroeconomic policy coordination. This conventional wisdom has been challenged in several recent papers, however. Dominguez and Frankel (1993a), for example, use survey data on dollar-mark and dollar–Swiss franc exchange-rate expectations to construct measures of the risk premium, gauged as the deviation from uncovered interest parity, and they find that intervention is a significant explanatory variable for the risk premium (see also Black, 1993).[24]

Assessing the influence of sterilized intervention through the signaling

[23] Recent surveys of the empirical literature on foreign-exchange-market intervention include Almekinders and Eijffinger (1991), Edison (1992), and Taylor (1992b).

[24] Ghosh (1992, p. 219) also finds evidence of a statistically significant portfolio-balance effect on the dollar-mark exchange rate during the 1980s but argues that the effect is so small empirically as to be "a theoretical curiosum rather than a practical policy tool."

channel involves testing for the significance of intervention variables in equations explaining exchange-rate expectations. Tests of this sort have typically produced very mixed results (for example, Dominguez, 1986; Humpage, 1989). Nevertheless, Dominguez and Frankel (1993c), again using survey data on dollar-mark exchange-rate expectations, find that official announcements of exchange-rate policy and reported intervention significantly affect exchange-rate expectations and that, overall, the effectiveness of intervention is very much enhanced if it is publicly announced.

Although Dominguez and Frankel (1993a, 1993c) offer no explanation for the difference between their results and those in much of the earlier literature, Edison (1992) points out that the more obvious distinguishing factors include the use of survey data rather than a reliance on rational expectations, the use of a bilateral model rather than a multicurrency model, and the use of data limited exclusively to the 1980s.

Each of the Dominguez and Frankel studies cited above employs daily intervention data obtained from the U.S. and German authorities. Catte, Galli, and Rebecchini (1992) employ, in addition, daily data on intervention by the Japanese authorities and also conduct a statistical analysis of coordinated G-3 intervention in the period from 1985 to 1991. They identify seventeen episodes of coordinated intervention and claim that all were successful in the sense of reversing the trend in the value of the dollar and, in the case of the Plaza episode (late 1985), making it resume its fall. They also identify ten major turning points in the dollar-mark exchange rate over the period under study and find that nine coincide exactly with periods of concerted intervention. Note that Catte, Galli, and Rebecchini make no attempt to disentangle sterilized from unsterilized intervention; neither do they attempt to disentangle the portfolio-balance and signaling effects. In interpreting their own results, however, they seem to favor the signaling-channel explanation. They suggest that, given the magnitude of uncertainty about the link between exchange rates and fundamentals, the signals provided by intervention may help coordinate agents' expectations; the signals may induce agents to converge on a particular model of the economy and thus to pick a value for the exchange rate similar to that targeted by the authorities.

Although the empirical evidence is still somewhat mixed, policymakers and researchers may be reaching a new consensus that intervention is effective. This should not be interpreted, however, to imply that the authorities can divorce exchange-rate policy from domestic monetary and fiscal policies. Stock adjustments made through the portfolio-balance channel cannot be used indefinitely to offset flow disequilibria, such as large current-account imbalances, that reflect economic fundamentals. Furthermore, use of the signaling channel can be effective in the long run only if the signals given are seen as consistent with the underlying monetary and fiscal policies and with other economic fundamentals. Otherwise, the authorities will lose credibility and thus damage the power of the signaling effects. They may even provoke a speculative attack on the currency as forward-looking agents attempt to solve a system for which there is no consistent solution. Other asset-market instabilities may also ensue.[25]

6 Target Zones

A "target zone" is a range within which the authorities are committed to containing the exchange rate. The clearest example of a target zone is the Exchange Rate Mechanism of the EMS. Following an original paper by Krugman, circulated in 1987 and published in 1991, a literature on this topic has grown with remarkable speed. Undoubtedly, much of the appeal of researching target zones lies in the elegant mathematics employed and the application of tools such as stochastic calculus, previously applied mainly in financial economics. Beyond this, however, the target-zone literature has provided important insights into how actual target zones do, and do not, behave.[26]

The Basic Target-Zone Model

Consider a stylized monetary model of the exchange rate expressed in continuous time:

$$s = m + v + \lambda E(ds)/dt . \tag{28}$$

Equation (28) is the continuous-time analog of equation (5), where v lumps together all of the right-hand fundamentals in (5) apart from domestic money and the expected exchange-rate change. Thus, v is a general-purpose term encompassing changes in real output, foreign variables, and so on. The money supply is assumed to be a policy variable under the control of the authorities. The shift variable, v, is assumed to follow a Brownian motion without drift, which is the continuous time-analog of a random walk:[27]

$$dv = \sigma dz , \tag{29}$$

where dz is a standard Wiener process satisfying $E(dz) = 0$ and $\mathrm{Var}(dz) = dt$.

---

[25] An example is afforded by the attempt of the United Kingdom to "shadow" the German mark in late 1987 and early 1988. Because the U.K. authorities were unwilling to coordinate their monetary policy with that of Germany (in particular, to bring interest rates down), sterling experienced strong upward pressure, which the authorities were ultimately unable to resist.

[26] Comprehensive surveys of the target-zone literature can be found in Bertola (1994) and Svensson (1992). Another useful reference is Krugman and Miller (1992).

[27] The zero-drift assumption is made for expositional expediency only. Most of the target-zone literature allows for drift in the fundamentals.

Under a *free float*, in which the authorities allow the exchange rate to wander while keeping m fixed, the assumption that v follows a Brownian-motion process implies that s itself follows a Brownian-motion process and, in particular, that the expected change in the exchange rate is zero:

$$E(ds)/dt = 0 . \tag{30}$$

From (28) and (30) we can see that in a plot of the exchange rate against the fundamentals $(m + v)$, s would lie on a 45 degree ray passing through a point the coordinates of which are the central parity and the initial value of $m + v$ (*FF* in Figure 2.4).

Under a *fixed-rate* regime, the authorities alter m in order to offset movements in v; the expected exchange-rate change would still be zero, but a plot of s against $m + v$ would collapse to a single point. In the *basic target-zone model*, the authorities stand ready to intervene at the upper (s_{max}) and lower (s_{min}) edges of the band, where they will alter the level of the fundamentals (the level of m) by just enough to keep the exchange rate within the band.[28] Technically, the solution to the basic target-zone model implies that the relation between the exchange rate and the fundamentals is described by a nonlinear, S-shaped curve (*TZ* in Figure 2.4). This characteristic S-shape is the graphical representation of the two main features of the Krugman model: the "honeymoon" effect and the "smooth-pasting" conditions.

The honeymoon effect refers to the fact that, in a plot of s against $m + v$ under a fully credible target-zone arrangement, s will lie on a curve less steep than the 45 degree line (if $m + v$ is on the horizontal axis). The intuition behind this assertion is that if s is near the top of the band, the authorities are likely to reduce m in order to keep s within the band. Hence, the expected future value of m is lower, and the current value of s must therefore be lower than it would be under a free float, given the current level of $m + v$. Accordingly, s must lie below the 45 degree "free-float line." By a symmetric argument, if s is near the lower edge of the band, it must be above the free-float line. The honeymoon effect is thus a way to say that a perfectly credible target zone is inherently stabilizing. The belief that the authorities will intervene makes the exchange rate more stable within the band than it would be under a free float; the range of variation in the exchange rate will be smaller for any given range of variation in the fundamentals.

The smooth-pasting conditions are boundary conditions for the solution of the basic target-zone model. These conditions assert that the permissible exchange-rate path plotted against $m + v$ must "paste" smoothly onto the upper and lower edges of the band, so that the relation between the exchange

---

[28] Clearly, intervention is assumed to be unsterilized, because it affects the exchange rate through changes in the money supply.

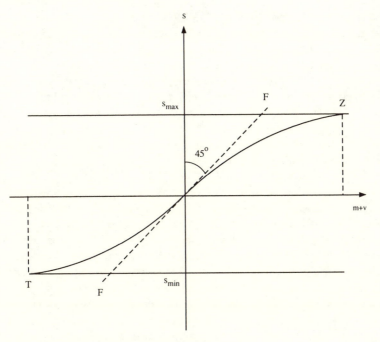

Figure 2.4 The Basic Target-Zone Model

rate and the fundamentals becomes increasingly bent as the rate approaches the edges of the band. In mathematical terms, the slope of the path must tend toward zero as it nears the edges of the band. An intuitive interpretation of the smooth-pasting conditions was put forward originally by Flood and Garber (1991).

First, for notational convenience, bundle the underlying fundamentals into one variable, say, κ, by writing $m + v = \kappa$. Second, write the solution to (28) and (29) as a very general continuous function, for example, $g(.)$:

$$s = g(\kappa) . \tag{31}$$

Obvious boundary conditions on $g(.)$ are that s_{max} and s_{min} should lie in its range:

$$g(\kappa^u) = s_{max} , \tag{32}$$

$$g(\kappa^\ell) = s_{min} , \tag{33}$$

where κ^u and κ^ℓ are associated values of the fundamentals.

Now consider intervention by the authorities in defense of the upper limit of the target zone. Specifically, consider a point κ^* in the neighborhood of κ^u at which the authorities intervene, and reduce m so that κ falls by a discrete amount, $\Delta\kappa$. Whenever the exchange rate gets to $g(\kappa^*)$, therefore, the authorities intervene by a discrete amount, $\Delta\kappa$, and return the exchange rate instantly to $g(\kappa^* - \Delta\kappa)$. As soon as s touches $g(\kappa^*)$, then, traders are offered a riskless arbitrage opportunity: they can sell foreign currency just before the intervention, buy it back just after the intervention, and make a percentage profit equal to $g(\kappa^*) - g(\kappa^* - \Delta\kappa)$. This arbitrage opportunity will be eliminated, however, if agents know the size of the discrete intervention and the market is efficient. Therefore,

$$g(\kappa^*) = g(\kappa^* - \Delta\kappa) . \tag{34}$$

This condition is depicted in the top panel of Figure 2.5. Now suppose that intervention is not discrete but infinitesimal. That is to say, the authorities intervene at κ^u so that s moves, not by a discrete jump, but by an infinitesimally small amount, just large enough to keep s within the band. Formally, we can let $\Delta\kappa$, the size of the intervention, tend toward zero. Rearranging the arbitrage condition, (32), dividing by $\Delta\kappa$, and taking this limit, we have[29]

$$\lim_{\Delta\kappa \to 0} [g(\kappa^*) - g(\kappa^* - \Delta\kappa)]/\Delta\kappa = 0 , \tag{35}$$

which is just the boundary condition on the first derivative of $g(\kappa)$, that is, the smooth-pasting condition:

$$g'(\kappa^u) = 0 , \tag{36}$$

where we have used the fact that $k^* = k^u$ when intervention is infinitesimal; because the authorities will only intervene by an amount just enough to keep s within the zone, they will thus do so only at the edge of the band. This is depicted in the bottom panel of Figure 2.5.

By a symmetric argument concerning intervention in support of the lower edge of the target zone, we have

$$g'(\kappa^\ell) = 0 . \tag{37}$$

Thus, the basic Krugman target-zone model predicts that a plot of the exchange rate against the fundamentals will produce an S-shaped curve pasted smoothly onto the upper and lower edges of the target zone (as in Figure 2.4). The smooth-pasting conditions are important for a number of reasons.

---

[29] It is important to note that κ^* is not held fixed as $\Delta\kappa$ tends to zero. Indeed, if the authorities intervene just sufficiently to keep the rate within the band, then clearly κ^* tends to κ^u as $\Delta\kappa$ tends to zero.

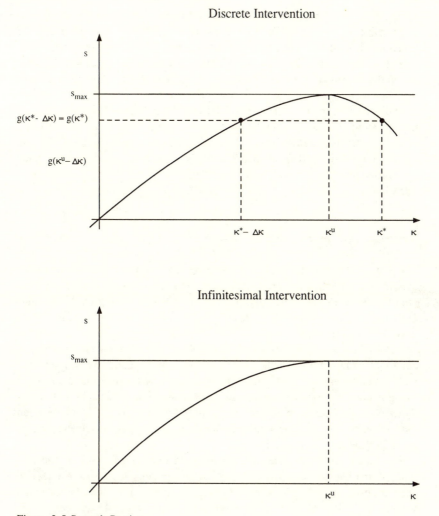

Figure 2.5 Smooth Pasting

First, the solution to equations (28) and (29) within a symmetric target zone (that is, $g[\kappa]$) is a family of S-shaped functions of the form

$$s = m + v + A[e^{\alpha(m+v)} - e^{-\alpha(m+v)}] \, , \qquad (38)$$

where $\alpha = (2/\lambda\sigma^2)^{1/2}$ and A is an undetermined coefficient.[30] Within this family, however, there is a unique value of A and thus a unique curve that

[30] Note that the solution would be slightly more complicated if we had allowed for nonzero drift in the fundamentals. This is of no qualitative importance.

satisfies the smooth-pasting conditions, (36) and (37). Hence, those conditions define a unique arbitrage-free relation between the exchange rate and the fundamentals within a fully credible target zone. Second, smooth pasting implies a nonzero value of A in (38) and hence a nonlinear relation ($g[\kappa]$) between the exchange rate and the fundamentals. Potentially, this might explain why linear or log-linear exchange-rate models have performed so poorly empirically, as was noted. Third, smooth pasting confers testable implications on the target-zone model. It implies not only a nonlinear relation between the exchange rate and the fundamentals—which can be tested—but also that the exchange rate will tend to stay near the edges of the band, because movements in the fundamentals near the center of the band will produce larger exchange-rate changes.

Empirical Tests of the Basic Target-Zone Model

The empirical implications of the basic target-zone model have been tested on data from the EMS, the Nordic countries, the Bretton Woods system, and the gold standard (Flood, Rose, and Mathieson, 1991; Lindberg and Söderlind, 1991, 1992; Bertola and Caballero, 1992). Without exception, these tests have rejected the basic model.

Empirical examination of the behavior of exchange rates within actual target zones shows, for example, that the rates do not spend most of their time near the edges of the band. Similarly, plots of the exchange rate against the fundamentals, variously defined,[31] do not reveal anything resembling the predicted S-shape, and more general tests for nonlinearity in the relation between the exchange rate and the fundamentals have found little evidence of nonlinearity (Meese and Rose, 1990).

A possible reason for the lack of observed nonlinearity may be the myopia of market participants. If expected movements in the exchange rate are extremely heavily discounted, the smooth-pasting effect becomes much weaker. Formally, this occurs as λ tends to zero and the 45 degree line reemerges. Nevertheless, such small values of λ, the interest semi-elasticity of the demand for money, are not found in empirical work on money-demand functions.

If the assumptions of the basic target-zone model are correct (that the target zone is fully credible, expectations are rational, and a simple monetary model holds), uncovered interest parity implies that the interest differential will reflect the expected rate of depreciation.[32] Moreover, when the domestic cur-

---

[31] See equation (18) for a simple way of constructing a measure of the fundamentals.

[32] Rose and Svensson (1991) report regression results, using daily data on the mark-franc spot exchange rate and one-month Euromark and Eurofranc interest rates, which are supportive of uncovered interest parity (that is, the simple efficient-markets hypothesis) over the EMS period.

rency is weak, so that s is near the top of the band, there is only one way for s to go—down. Thus, high values of s should be associated with a negative expected rate of depreciation. If the expected rate of depreciation is equal to the interest differential, however, there should be a negative correlation between the interest differential and the level of the exchange rate. In fact, investigations of the relation between exchange rates and interest-rate differentials within target zones have found only very weak correlations, and these tend, if anything, to be positive rather than negative (Flood, Rose, and Mathieson, 1991; Svensson, 1991a).

A further worrying feature of the target-zone literature is the failure to obtain plausible, statistically significant estimates of the interest-rate semi-elasticity, λ in equation (28). Many studies assume a value of λ rather than estimate it. This suggests a fundamental problem with the approach.

Although it is often argued that theories should be judged by the usefulness and accuracy of their predictions rather than the realism of their assumptions, the crucial assumptions of the basic target-zone model—perfect credibility and intervention only at the edges of the band—have also been subject to investigation. It has been argued, for example, that existing target zones, such as the EMS, are not perfectly credible because very high interest differentials are often evident immediately before realignments, and these levels can be interpreted as reflecting a demand by investors for high interest rates to compensate them for holding currencies that are expected to be devalued. Equivalent evidence of imperfect credibility has been inferred from the fact that forward rates often lie outside the band (Svensson, 1991b; Flood, Rose, and Mathieson, 1991).

With respect to the assumption that interventions occur only at the edges of the band, rather than intramarginally, there is substantial evidence that intervention in the EMS has been predominantly intramarginal (Dominguez and Kenen, 1992; Lindberg and Söderlind, 1991). Moreover, it is clear that the stabilization of exchange rates in the EMS is accomplished partly by the general harmonization of monetary policies, rather than by adjustments specifically triggered when exchange rates hit the edges of the bands.

In its use of a simple monetary exchange-rate model, moreover, the target-zone literature may have been unduly naive. It was shown at length above that the empirical evidence on the monetary models is overwhelmingly negative, albeit for regimes closer to free floats than to target zones. Krugman and Miller (1993, p. 284) observe, for example, that "the target-zone literature has in effect given a new lease on life to an exchange-rate model that has otherwise been thoroughly discredited; this is unfortunate."

Yet, strong rejections of uncovered interest parity are reported by Artis and Taylor (1989), using monthly data on a range of exchange rates against the mark (including the mark-franc rate) over the EMS period.

The implicit assumption of market efficiency in the target-zone model, despite mounting evidence to the contrary, has also been criticized.[33] Krugman and Miller (1993), for example, argue that policymakers have in the past been willing to enter into target-zone arrangements precisely because of their skepticism about the efficiency of foreign-exchange markets and the rationality of market participants. If the resort to target zones is in fact largely motivated by the fear of irrational runs on a currency, it is ironic that the standard target-zone model rules this out by assumption.

Rehabilitating the Target-Zone Model

Faced with the evidence against the basic target-zone model, a number of authors have sought to rehabilitate the model by modifying its underlying assumptions.

If it is assumed that the target zone is not perfectly credible, a number of the empirical findings discussed above can be rationalized. For example, the target-zone model predicts that the level of the exchange rate will be negatively correlated with expected depreciation *within* the band. If agents perceive a nonzero probability of realignment, so that the target zone is not perfectly credible, total expected depreciation will be the sum of expected depreciation within the band *plus* the expected change in the central parity. There is then no reason why the exchange rate should be negatively correlated with the expected movement in the parity—in fact, quite the opposite. Hence, imperfect credibility might explain the lack of strong negative correlation between exchange rates within a target zone and the interest differential. Svensson (1993) estimates confidence intervals for expected depreciation within the band from simple linear regressions of the exchange rate on the lagged exchange rate. He uses these estimates to show that, although the credibility of the EMS grew significantly over its period of operation, it was never perfectly credible in the sense that there was insignificant realignment risk for the majority of member currencies.

Rose and Svensson (1991) have plotted exchange rates against estimates of a composite fundamental adjusted for the expected realignment in the central parity. Although they find evidence of the honeymoon effect (a slope less than unity), they do not observe evidence of smooth pasting.

Incorporating intramarginal intervention into the target-zone model substantially reduces the impact of the smooth-pasting conditions. This is because as *s* approaches the edge of the band, the authorities are already known

---

[33] Note that simple plots of the exchange rate against the fundamentals, as in Flood, Rose, and Mathieson (1991), are not conditioned on the assumption of rational expectations but are still not supportive of the model.

to be intervening. The perceived probability of hitting the edge of the band is therefore lower than with marginal intervention. Hence, the probability of a riskless arbitrage opportunity's occurring will likewise be lower, and the slope of the curve relating the exchange rate to the fundamentals will be closer to unity throughout its length (although still less than unity), with smooth pasting occurring only when the exchange rate is very close to the edge of the band. Thus, intramarginal intervention may explain why researchers have found little evidence of nonlinearity or the characteristic S-shaped curve. Estimation of a target-zone model incorporating intramarginal intervention for the Swedish krona has led to some improvement in empirical results for the target-zone model (Lindberg and Söderlind, 1991).

Although the empirical results in the target-zone literature are largely negative, this work has nevertheless yielded some insights into the behavior of exchange rates under such regimes. In particular, we have discovered that within target zones, the behavior of exchange rates is in many ways similar to their behavior under a managed float, with frequent intramarginal interventions generating mean reversion toward the parity. The search for nonlinearities prompted by the basic Krugman model—which Krugman in any case offered more as an example of the conditions under which target zones would be stable than as a description of actual target zones—is probably now at an end. The next phase of work in this area is likely to concentrate more on improving the realism of the underlying models—for example, by allowing for risk premia and perhaps for the presence of noise traders.[34] The allowance for currency substitutability would be another suitable extension of the imperfectly credible target-zone model with intramarginal intervention; a more ambitious project would be to develop a multilateral-target-zone model, as opposed to a bilateral-target-zone model. A realistic multilateral model, however, would have to come to grips with modeling the differing degrees of credibility of the bilateral target zones included in it. This appears to be a characteristic of the EMS. Examination of the different effects of various intervention policies and of macroeconomic policy harmonization are also clearly relevant topics for investigation.

7 Conclusion

Although the results of the research program surveyed above are largely negative, they are important. At the very least, they show us what is not viable and what new hypotheses need to be investigated. The world is a lot more complex than we would like it to be. A wide spectrum of fairly simple hypotheses and approaches—for example, the broad class of asset-market exchange-rate

---

[34] Miller and Weller (1991) have already extended the model to include price stickiness.

models, the simple efficient-markets hypothesis (that is, the joint hypothesis of risk neutrality and rational expectations), and the basic target-zone model —have either received poor support from the data or have been flatly rejected.

Nevertheless, recent research provides some support for certain long-run relationships suggested by economic theory, so further progress might be made by concentrating on the long-run determinants of exchange rates. Conversely, further attempts to explain short- to medium-term exchange-rate movements based *solely* on macroeconomic fundamentals may not prove successful.[35] The macroeconomic fundamentals are clearly not orthogonal to short-run exchange-rate behavior, but they do not appear to tell the whole story. An obvious avenue to explore, therefore, is the role of microeconomic fundamentals. Issues that might be examined include heterogeneities in behavior and in access to information across market participants, and the transmission of information among traders, which may lead to epidemics and herding behavior (see, for example, Froot and Thaler, 1990; Scharfstein and Stein, 1990). To examine the microeconomic fundamentals, however, may mean grasping the nettle of "nonrational" behavior more generally. A distinction should be made in this regard between irrationality and nonrational expectations, because agents may be rational maximizers but may not conform fully to the rational-expectations hypothesis. To avoid the charge of vacuousness, the realistic modeling of exchange-rate behavior should probably embody alternative, more realistic informational and transactional constraints on rational maximizing agents, some of whom may use "popular" models and rules of thumb rather than the "true" model when they form expectations. Admitting behavior of this kind into models of the foreign-exchange market is challenging, not least because it admits an "open-ended," potentially limitless set of behaviors.[36] One partial solution to this problem is to use survey data on exchange-rate expectations, and it is interesting that some tentative positive empirical evidence on the portfolio-balance model has recently been reported by researchers using such data (Black, 1993; Dominguez and Frankel, 1993a, 1993c). More general survey-based research, on agents' behavior as well as

[35] Not only has the search for macroeconomic fundamentals been extensive, but the results of Baxter and Stockman (1989), Flood and Rose (1992), and others, as noted above, suggest that the usual set of macroeconomic fundamentals is unlikely to be capable of explaining exchange-rate movements on its own. As Dornbusch (1987, p. 1) notes, "Research on exchange-rate economics has grown tired searching for risk premia determinants or for new macroeconomic models."

[36] Such concerns do not, however, seem to have presented much of a problem to a number of notable economists in the past. Indeed, Keynes's (1930, p. 237) views on this issue appear, if anything, unduly pessimistic: "[T]he vast majority of those who are concerned with the buying and selling of securities know almost nothing whatever about what they are doing. They do not possess even the rudiments of what is required for a valid judgment, and are the prey of hopes and fears easily aroused by transient events and as easily dispelled. This is one of the odd characteristics of the capitalist system under which we live, which, when we are dealing with the real world, is not to be overlooked."

their forecasts, might also yield insights into the day-to-day, or even trade-by-trade, behavior of market participants (see, for example, Taylor and Allen, 1992).

Some remarks are also appropriate concerning the relation between exchange-rate economics and the wider field of financial economics. Clearly, exchange-rate economics falls within the field of finance, although it has traditionally been treated more as a branch of macroeconomics. This to some extent explains the emphasis on macroeconomic fundamentals in most exchange-rate models, but, given the linkages of the international financial markets, it seems clear that the foreign-market exchange rates cannot be studied in isolation from other capital markets. Moreover, evidence of inefficiencies in the foreign-exchange market and the rejection of asset-market exchange-rate models parallels the evidence of anomalous behavior in capital markets and the rejection of the present-value model of stock prices. It is therefore not surprising that financial economists have made suggestions similar to those made in this section, calling for more emphasis on "popular models" and survey research, and they have begun to examine the interactions of heterogeneous market participants.[37]

As the macroeconomic fundamentals perform so poorly in explaining actual exchange-rate behavior, so that exchange rates appear to be excessively volatile and prone to sustained periods of misalignment, it may be more useful to treat the macroeconomic fundamentals as a normative guide for the assessment of the appropriateness of market rates than as a positive guide to their short-run behavior (see, for example, Frenkel and Goldstein, 1986). Although there is currently no consensus among economists concerning the appropriate measure of the desired or equilibrium exchange rate (Krugman, 1990), it seems clear that the *actual* course of the major exchange rates over the recent float has not followed closely *anyone's* desired or equilibrium path. Viewed from this perspective, the macroeconomic fundamentals provide at least a framework for policy discussion and analysis.

References

Abuaf, Niso, and Philippe Jorion, "Purchasing Power Parity in the Long Run," *Journal of Finance*, 45 (March 1990), pp. 157–174.

---

[37] See, for example, Shiller (1989) and Campbell and Kyle (1993) for discussions of the literature on the present-value model of stock prices, and Dimson (1988) on stock-market anomalies. Shiller (1990) and Shleifer and Summers (1990) provide nontechnical discussions of "noise trading" and "popular models," respectively. Shleifer and Summers (1990, p. 19) observe drily that "the stock in the efficient-markets hypothesis—at least as it has traditionally been formulated—crashed along with the rest of the market on October 19, 1987. Its recovery has been less dramatic than that of the rest of the market."

Adler, Michael, and Bruce Lehmann, "Deviations from Purchasing Power Parity in the Long Run," *Journal of Finance*, 38 (December 1983), pp. 1471–1478.

Allen, Helen L., and Mark P. Taylor, "Charts, Noise and Fundamentals in the Foreign Exchange Market," *Economic Journal* (London), 100 (March 1990), pp. 49–59.

———, "Chartist Analysis," in Peter Newman, Murray Milgate, and John Eatwell, eds., *The New Palgrave Dictionary of Money and Finance*, London, Macmillan; New York, Stockton, 1993, pp. 339–342.

Allen, Polly Reynolds, and Peter B. Kenen, *Asset Markets, Exchange Rates, and Economic Integration: A Synthesis*, Cambridge and New York, Cambridge University Press, 1980.

Almekinders, Geert J., and Sylvester C.W. Eijffinger, "Empirical Evidence on Foreign Exchange Market Intervention: Where Do We Stand?" *Weltwirtschaftliches Archiv*, 127 (December 1991), pp. 645–678.

Artis, Michael J., and Mark P. Taylor, "Some Issues Concerning the Long-Run Credibility of the European Monetary System," in Ronald MacDonald and Mark P. Taylor, eds., *Exchange Rates and Open Economy Macroeconomics*, Oxford, Blackwell, 1989, pp. 295–306.

Backus, David K., Patrick J. Kehoe, Finn E. Kydland, "International Real Business Cycles," *Journal of Political Economy*, 100 (August 1992), pp. 745–775.

Baxter, Marianne, and Alan C. Stockman, "Business Cycles and the Exchange Rate System," *Journal of Monetary Economics*, 23 (June 1989), pp. 377–400.

Bertola, Giuseppe, "Continuous-Time Models of Exchange Rates and Intervention," in Frederick van der Ploeg, ed., *Handbook of International Macroeconomics*, Oxford, Blackwell, forthcoming 1994.

Bertola, Giuseppe, and Ricardo J. Caballero, "Target Zones and Realignments," *American Economic Review*, 82 (June 1992), pp. 520–536.

Bilson, John F. O., "Rational Expectations and the Exchange Rate," in Jacob A. Frenkel and Harry G. Johnson, eds., *The Economics of Exchange Rates*, Reading, Mass., Addison-Wesley, 1978, pp. 75–96.

———, "The Speculative Efficiency Hypothesis," *Journal of Business*, 54 (October 1981), pp. 435–451.

Bilson, John F. O., and Richard C. Marston, eds., *Exchange Rate Theory and Practice*, Chicago, University of Chicago Press, 1984.

Bisignano, Joseph, and Kevin D. Hoover, "Some Suggested Improvements to a Simple Portfolio Balance Model of Exchange Rate Determination with Special Reference to the U.S. Dollar-Canadian Dollar Rate," *Weltwirtschaftliches Archiv*, 118 (January 1982), pp. 19–37.

Black, Stanley W., *International Money Markets and Flexible Exchange Rates*, Princeton Studies in International Finance No. 32, Princeton, N.J., Princeton University, International Finance Section, March 1973.

———, "The Relationship of the Exchange Risk Premium to Net Foreign Assets and Central Bank Intervention," Working Paper 93–01, Department of Economics, University of North Carolina, 1993.

Boothe, Paul, and David J. Longworth, "Foreign Exchange Market Efficiency Tests: Implications of Recent Empirical Findings," *Journal of International Money and Finance*, 5 (June 1986), pp. 135–152.

Branson, William H., *Financial Capital Flows in the U.S. Balance of Payments*, Amsterdam, North-Holland, 1968.

———, "The Minimum Covered Interest Differential Needed for International Arbitrage Activity," *Journal of Political Economy*, 77 (December 1969), pp. 1028–1035.

———, *Asset Markets and Relative Prices in Exchange Rate Determination*, Reprints in International Finance No. 20, Princeton, N.J., Princeton University, International Finance Section, June 1980; reprinted from *Sozialwissenschaftliche Annalen*, 1 (January 1977), pp. 69–89.

———, "Exchange Rate Policy after a Decade of 'Floating,' " in Bilson and Marston, *Exchange Rate Theory and Practice*, 1984, pp. 79–117.

Branson, William H., Hannu Halttunen, and Paul R. Masson, "Exchange Rates in the Short Run: The Dollar-Deutschemark Rate, *European Economic Review*, 10 (December 1977), pp. 303–324.

———, "Exchange Rates in the Short Run: Some Further Results," *European Economic Review*, 10 (October 1979), pp. 395–402.

Branson, William H., and Dale W. Henderson, "The Specification and Influence of Asset Markets," in Jones and Kenen, *Handbook of International Economics*, 1985, pp. 749–805.

Calvo, Guillermo A., and Carlos A. Rodriguez, "A Model of Exchange Rate Determination under Currency Substitution and Rational Expectations," *Journal of Political Economy*, 85 (June 1977), pp. 261–278.

Campbell, John Y., and Albert S. Kyle, "Smart Money, Noise Trading and Stock Price Behavior," *Review of Economic Studies*, 60 (January 1993), pp. 1–34.

Catte, Pietro, Giampaolo Galli, and Salvatore Rebecchini, "Concerted Interventions and the Dollar: An Analysis of Daily Data," paper presented at the Rinaldo Ossola Memorial Conference, Banca d'Italia, July 1992.

Cheung, Yin-Wong, and Kon S. Lai, "Long-Run Purchasing Power Parity During the Recent Float," *Journal of International Economics*, 34 (February 1993), pp. 181–192.

Clarida, Richard H., and Mark P. Taylor, "The Term Structure of Forward Exchange Premia and the Forecastability of Spot Exchange Rates: Correcting the Errors," CEPR Discussion Paper No. 773, London, Centre for Economic Policy Research, June 1993.

Clinton, Kevin, "Transactions Costs and Covered Interest Arbitrage: Theory and Evidence," *Journal of Political Economy*, 96 (April 1988), pp. 358–370.

Cumby, Robert E., and Maurice Obstfeld, "Exchange Rate Expectations and Nominal Interest Rates: A Test of the Fisher Hypothesis," *Journal of Finance*, 36 (June 1981), pp. 697–703.

———, "International Interest Rate and Price Level Linkages under Flexible Exchange Rates: A Review of Recent Evidence," in Bilson and Marston, *Exchange Rate Theory and Practice*, 1984, pp. 121–151.

Danker, Deborah, Richard D. Haas, Dale W. Henderson, Steven A. Symansky, and Ralph W. Tryon, "Small Empirical Models of Exchange Market Intervention: Application to Germany, Japan, and Canada," *Journal of Policy Modeling*, 9 (Spring 1987), pp. 143–173.

Darby, Michael, "Does Purchasing Power Parity Work?" National Bureau of Economic Research Working Paper No. 607, Cambridge, Mass., National Bureau of Economic Research, December 1980.

De Grauwe, Paul, Hans Dewachter, and Mark Embrechts, *Exchange Rate Theory: Chaotic Models of Foreign Exchange Markets*, Oxford, Blackwell, 1993.

Diebold, Francis X., Steven Husted, and Mark Rush, "Real Exchange Rates Under the Gold Standard," *Journal of Political Economy*, 99 (December 1991), pp. 1252–1271.

Dimson, Elroy, ed., *Stock Market Anomalies*, Cambridge, Cambridge University Press, 1988.

Dominguez, Kathryn M., "Does Sterilized Intervention Influence Exchange Rates? A Test of the Signalling Hypothesis," Harvard University, June 1986, processed.

Dominguez, Kathryn M., and Jeffrey A. Frankel, "Does Foreign Exchange Intervention Matter? The Portfolio Effect," *American Economic Review*, 83 (December 1993a), pp. 1356–1369.

———, *Does Foreign Exchange Intervention Work? Consequences for the Dollar*, Washington, D.C., Institute for International Economics, 1993b.

———, "Foreign Exchange Intervention: An Empirical Assessment," in Jeffrey A. Frankel, ed., *On Exchange Rates*, Cambridge, Mass., MIT Press, 1993c, pp. 12–27.

Dominguez, Kathryn M., and Peter B. Kenen, "Intramarginal Intervention in the EMS and the Target-Zone Model of Exchange-Rate Behavior," *European Economic Review*, 36 (December 1992), pp. 1523–1532

Dooley, Michael P., and Jeffrey R. Shafer, "Analysis of Short-Run Exchange Rate Behavior: March 1973 to November 1981," in David Bigman and Teizo Taya, eds., *Floating Exchange Rates and the State of World Trade Payments*, Cambridge, Mass., Ballinger, 1984, pp. 43–69.

Dornbusch, Rudiger, "Expectations and Exchange Rate Dynamics," *Journal of Political Economy*, 84 (December 1976), pp. 1161–1176.

———, "Monetary Policy Under Exchange Rate Flexibility," in Federal Reserve Bank of Boston, *Managed Exchange Rate Flexibility: The Recent Experience*, Boston, Federal Reserve Bank of Boston, 1979, pp. 90–122.

———, "Exchange Rate Economics: 1986," *Economic Journal* (London), 97 (March 1987), pp. 1–18.

———, "Purchasing Power Parity," in Peter Newman, Murray Milgate, and John Eatwell, eds., *The New Palgrave Dictionary of Money and Finance*, London, Macmillan; New York, Stockton, 1992, pp. 236–244.

Edison, Hali J., "The Effectiveness of Central Bank Intervention: A Survey of the Post-1982 Literature," Washington D.C., Board of Governors of the Federal Reserve System, June 1992, processed.

Engle, Robert F., and Clive W.J. Granger, "Cointegration and Error Correction: Representation, Estimation and Testing," *Econometrica*, 55 (March 1987), pp. 251–276.

Evans, George W., "Pitfalls in Testing for Explosive Bubbles in Asset Prices," *American Economic Review*, 81 (September 1991), pp. 922–930.

Fama, Eugene F., "Forward and Spot Exchange Rates," *Journal of Monetary Economics*, 14 (November 1984), pp. 319–338.

Fleming, J. Marcus, "Domestic Financial Policies under Fixed and Floating Exchange Rates," *International Monetary Fund Staff Papers*, 3 (November 1962), pp. 369–380.

Flood, Robert P., and Peter M. Garber, "The Linkage Between Speculative Attack and Target Zone Models of Exchange Rates," *Quarterly Journal of Economics*, 106 (December 1991), pp. 1367–1372.

Flood, Robert P., and Andrew K. Rose, "Fixing Exchange Rates: A Virtual Quest for Fundamentals?" Seminar Paper 529, Stockholm, Institute for International Economics, December 1992.

Flood, Robert P., Andrew K. Rose, and Donald J. Mathieson, "An Empirical Exploration of Exchange Rate Target Zones," *Carnegie-Rochester Conference Series on Public Policy*, 35 (Autumn 1991), pp. 7–65.

Frankel, Jeffrey A., "On the Mark: A Theory of Floating Exchange Rates Based on Real Interest Differentials," *American Economic Review*, 69 (September 1979), pp. 610–622.

————, "The Mystery of the Multiplying Marks: A Modification of the Monetary Model," *Review of Economics and Statistics*, 64 (August 1982a), pp. 515–519.

————, "In Search of the Exchange Risk Premium: A Six-Currency Test Assuming Mean-Variance Optimization," *Journal of International Money and Finance*, 1 (December 1982b), pp. 255–274.

————, "Tests of Monetary and Portfolio Balance Models of Exchange Rate Determination," in Bilson and Marston, *Exchange Rate Theory and Practice*, 1984, pp. 239–260.

Frankel, Jeffrey A., and Kenneth A. Froot, "Understanding the U.S. Dollar in the Eighties: The Expectations of Chartists and Fundamentalists," *Economic Record*, 12, Supplement (January 1986), pp. 24–38.

————, "Chartists, Fundamentalists and the Demand for Dollars," in Anthony S. Courakis and Mark P. Taylor, eds., *Private Behaviour and Government Policy in Interdependent Economies*, Oxford, Clarendon; New York, Oxford University Press, 1990, pp. 73–126.

Frenkel, Jacob A., "A Monetary Approach to the Exchange Rate: Doctrinal Aspects and Empirical Evidence," *Scandinavian Journal of Economics*, 78 (March 1976), pp. 200–224.

————, "Purchasing Power Parity Doctrinal Perspective and Evidence from the 1920's," *Journal of International Economics*, 8 (May 1978), pp. 169–191.

————, "Flexible Exchange Rates, Prices and the Role of "News": Lessons from the 1970s," *Journal of Political Economy*, 89 (August 1981), pp. 665–705.

Frenkel, Jacob A., and Morris Goldstein, "A Guide to Target Zones," *International Monetary Fund Staff Papers*, 33 (December 1986), pp. 633–673.

Frenkel, Jacob A., and Richard M. Levich, "Covered Interest Arbitrage: Unexploited Profits?" *Journal of Political Economy*, 83 (April 1975), pp. 325–338.

————, "Transactions Costs and Interest Arbitrage: Tranquil versus Turbulent Periods," *Journal of Political Economy*, 85 (December 1977), pp. 1207–1224.

Frenkel, Jacob A., and Michael L. Mussa, "Asset Markets, Exchange Rates, and the Balance of Payments," in Jones and Kenen, *Handbook of International Economics*, 1985, pp. 679–747.

Friedman, Milton, "The Case for Flexible Exchange Rates," in Milton Friedman, *Es-*

says in Positive Economics, Chicago, University of Chicago Press, 1953, pp. 157–203.

Froot, Kenneth A., "Short Rates and Expected Asset Returns," National Bureau of Economic Research Working Paper No. 3247, Cambridge, Mass., National Bureau of Economic Research, January 1990.

Froot, Kenneth A., and Jeffrey A. Frankel, "Forward Discount Bias: Is It an Exchange Risk Premium?" *Quarterly Journal of Economics*, 104 (February 1989), pp. 139–161.

Froot, Kenneth A., and Richard H. Thaler, "Anomalies: Foreign Exchange," *Journal of Economic Perspectives*, 4 (Summer 1990), pp. 179–192.

Ghosh, Atish R., "Is it Signalling? Exchange Intervention and the Dollar-Deutschemark Rate," *Journal of International Economics*, 32 (May 1992), pp. 201–220.

Giovannini, Alberto, and Philippe Jorion, "The Time Variation of Risk and Return in the Foreign Exchange and Stock Markets," *Journal of Finance*, 44 (June 1989), pp. 307–325.

Girton, Lance, and Don Roper, "Theory and Implications of Currency Substitution," *Journal of Money Credit and Banking*, 13 (February 1981), pp. 12–30.

Goedhuys, Diederik W., ed., *The Foreign Exchange Market in the 1980s: The Views of Market Participants*, New York, Group of Thirty, 1985.

Goodhart, Charles A.E., "The Foreign Exchange Market: A Random Walk with a Dragging Anchor," *Economica*, 55 (November 1988), pp. 437–460.

Goodman, Stephen H., "Foreign Exchange Rate Forecasting Techniques: Implications for Business and Policy," *Journal of Finance*, 34 (January 1979), pp. 415–427.

———, "Who's Better Than the Toss of a Coin?" *Euromoney* (September 1980), pp. 80–84.

Hansen, Lars P., and Robert J. Hodrick, "Forward Exchange Rates as Optimal Predictors of Future Spot Rates: An Econometric Analysis," *Journal of Political Economy*, 88 (October 1980), pp. 829–853.

———, "Risk Averse Speculation in the Forward Foreign Exchange Market: An Econometric Analysis of Linear Models," in Jacob A. Frenkel, ed., *Exchange Rates and International Macroeconomics*, Chicago, University of Chicago Press, 1983, pp. 113–152.

Hodrick, Robert J., *The Empirical Evidence on the Efficiency of Forward and Futures Foreign Exchange Markets*, London, Harwood, 1987.

Hodrick, Robert J., and Sanjay Srivastava, "The Covariation of Risk Premiums and Expected Future Spot Exchange Rates," *Journal of International Money and Finance*, 5, Supplement (March 1986), pp. S5–21.

Hoffman, Dennis, and Don E. Schlagenhauf, "Rational Expectations and Monetary Models of Exchange Rate Determination: An Empirical Examination," *Journal of Monetary Economics*, 11 (March 1983), pp. 247–260.

Hooper, Peter, and John Morton, "Fluctuations in the Dollar: A Model of Nominal and Real Exchange Rate Determination," *Journal of International Money and Finance*, 1 (April 1982), pp. 39–56.

Huang, Roger D., "The Monetary Approach to the Exchange Rate in an Efficient Foreign Exchange Market: Tests Based on Volatility," *Journal of Finance*, 36 (March 1981), pp. 31–41.

Humpage, Owen F., "On the Effectiveness of Exchange Market Intervention," Cleveland, Ohio, Federal Reserve Bank of Cleveland, June 1989, processed.

Isard, Peter, "Exchange Rate Modeling: An Assessment of Alternative Approaches," in Ralph C. Bryant, Dale W. Henderson, Gerald Holtham, Peter Hooper, and Steven A. Symansky, eds., *Empirical Macroeconomics for Interdependent Economies*, Washington, D.C., Brookings Institution, 1988, pp. 183–201.

Johansen, Soren, "Statistical Analysis of Cointegration Vectors," *Journal of Economic Dynamics and Control*, 12 (June-September 1988), pp. 231–254.

Johnson, Harry G., "Towards A General Theory of the Balance of Payments," in Harry G. Johnson, *International Trade and Economic Growth*, London and New York, Allen and Unwin, 1958, pp. 153–168.

Jones, Ronald W., and Peter B. Kenen, eds., *Handbook of International Economics*, Vol. 2, Amsterdam and New York, North-Holland, Elsevier, 1985.

Jurgensen, P. (Chairman), *Report of the Working Group on Exchange Market Intervention*, Washington, D.C., U.S. Treasury Department, 1983.

Kaminsky, Graciela, "Is there a Peso Problem? Evidence from the Dollar-Pound Exchange Rate, 1976–87," *American Economic Review*, 83 (June 1993) pp. 450–472.

Kenen, Peter B., "Effects of Intervention and Sterilization in the Short Run and the Long Run," in Richard N. Cooper, Peter B. Kenen, Jorge Braga de Macedo, and Jacques van Ypersele, eds., *The International Monetary System Under Flexible Exchange Rates*, Cambridge, Mass., Ballinger, 1982, pp. 51–68.

———, "Macroeconomic Theory and Policy: How the Closed Economy Was Opened," in Jones and Kenen, *Handbook of International Economics*, 1985, pp. 625–677.

Keynes, John Maynard, *A Treatise on Money*, London, Macmillan, 1930.

Kohlhagen, Steven W., *The Behavior of Foreign Exchange Markets—A Critical Survey*, Monograph 1978–3, Graduate School of Business Administration, New York University, June 1978.

Krugman, Paul R., "Purchasing Power Parity and Exchange Rates: Another Look at the Evidence," *Journal of International Economics*, 8 (August 1978), pp. 397–407.

———, "Equilibrium Exchange Rates," in William H. Branson, Jacob A. Frenkel, and Morris Goldstein, eds., *International Policy Coordination and Exchange Rate Fluctuations*, Chicago, University of Chicago Press, 1990, pp. 159–195.

———, "Target Zones and Exchange Rate Dynamics," *Quarterly Journal of Economics*, 106 (August 1991), pp. 669–682.

Krugman, Paul R., and Marcus H. Miller, *Exchange Rate Targets and Currency Bands*, Cambridge, Cambridge University Press, 1992.

———, "Why Have a Target Zone?," *Carnegie-Rochester Conference Series on Public Policy*, 38 (Summer 1993), pp. 279–314.

Levich, Richard M., "Empirical Studies of Exchange Rates: Price Behavior, Rate Determination, and Market Efficiency," in Jones and Kenen, *Handbook of International Economics*, 1985, pp. 979–1040.

Lewis, Karen K., "Testing the Portfolio Balance Model: A Multilateral Approach," *Journal of International Economics*, 24 (February 1988), pp. 133–150.

———, "Changing Beliefs and Systematic Rational Forecast Errors with Evidence from Foreign Exchange," *American Economic Review*, 79 (September 1989), pp. 621–636.

Lindberg, Hans, and Paul Söderlind, "Testing the Basic Target Zone Model on Swedish Data," Seminar Paper No. 488, Stockholm, Institute for International Economic Studies, May 1991.

———, "Target Zone Models and Intervention Policy: The Swedish Case," Seminar Paper No. 496, Stockholm, Institute for International Economic Studies, April 1992.

Lothian, James R., and Mark P. Taylor, "Real Exchange Rate Behavior: The Recent Float from the Perspective of the Past Two Centuries," Washington D.C., International Monetary Fund, 1993, processed.

Lucas, Robert E., Jr., "Interest-Rates and Currency Prices in a Two-Country World," *Journal of Monetary Economics*, 10 (November 1982), pp. 335–359.

McCallum, Bennett T., "A Reconsideration of the Uncovered Interest Parity Relationship," National Bureau of Economic Research Working Paper No. 4113, Cambridge, Mass., National Bureau of Economic Research, July 1992.

McCormick, Frank, "Covered Interest Arbitrage: Unexpected Profits? Comment," *Journal of Political Economy*, 87 (April 1979), pp. 171–186.

McCulloch, J. Huston, "Operational Aspects of the Siegel Paradox," *Quarterly Journal of Economics*, 89 (February 1975), pp. 170–172.

MacDonald, Ronald, and Mark P. Taylor, "The Monetary Approach to the Exchange Rate: Long-Run Relationships and Coefficient Restrictions," *Economics Letters*, 37 (October 1991a), pp. 179–185.

———, "Risk, Efficiency, and Speculation in the 1920s Foreign Exchange Market: An Overlapping Data Analysis," *Weltwirtschaftliches Archiv*, 127 (June 1991b), pp. 500–523.

———, "Exchange Rate Economics: A Survey," *International Monetary Fund Staff Papers*, 39 (March 1992), pp. 1–57.

———, "The Monetary Approach to the Exchange Rate: Rational Expectations, Long-Run Equilibrium, and Forecasting," *International Monetary Fund Staff Papers*, 40 (March 1993a), pp. 89–107.

———, "On the Foreign Exchange Risk Premium: Some New Survey-Based Results," Washington D.C., International Monetary Fund, 1993b, processed.

———, "The Monetary Model of the Exchange Rate: Long-Run Relationships, Short-Run Dynamics, and How to Beat a Random Walk," *Journal of International Money and Finance*, forthcoming 1994.

McKinnon, Ronald I., and Wallace E. Oates, *The Implications of International Economic Integration for Monetary, Fiscal, and Exchange-Rate Policy*, Princeton Studies in International Finance No. 16, Princeton, N.J., Princeton University, International Finance Section, March 1966.

Mark, Nelson C., "Real and Nominal Exchange Rates in the Long Run: An Empirical Investigation," *Journal of International Economics*, 28 (February 1990), pp. 115–136.

Meade, James E., *The Balance of Payments*, London, Oxford University Press, 1951.

Meese, Richard A., "Testing for Bubbles in Exchange Markets: A Case of Sparkling Rates?" *Journal of Political Economy*, 94 (April 1986), pp. 345–373.

Meese, Richard A., and Kenneth S. Rogoff, "Empirical Exchange Rate Models of the Seventies: Do They Fit Out of Sample?" *Journal of International Economics*, 14 (February 1983a), pp. 3–24.

————, "The Out-of-Sample Failure of Empirical Exchange Rate Models: Sampling Error or Misspecification?" in Jacob A. Frenkel, ed., *Exchange Rates and International Macroeconomics*, Chicago, University of Chicago Press, 1983b, pp. 67–112.

Meese, Richard A., and Andrew K. Rose, "Nonlinear, Nonparametric, Nonessential Exchange Rate Estimation," *American Economic Review*, Papers and Proceedings, 80 (May 1990), pp. 192–196.

Miller, Marcus H., and Paul Weller, "Exchange Rate Bands with Price Inertia," *Economic Journal* (London), 101 (November 1991), pp. 1380–1399.

Mundell, Robert A., "Flexible Exchange Rates and Employment Policy," *Canadian Journal of Economics and Political Science*, 27 (November 1961), pp. 509–517.

————, "The Appropriate Use of Monetary and Fiscal Policy for Internal and External Stability," *International Monetary Fund Staff Papers*, 9 (March 1962), pp. 70–79.

————, "Capital Mobility and Stabilization Policy under Fixed and Flexible Exchange Rates," *Canadian Journal of Economics and Political Science*, 29 (November 1963), pp. 475–485.

Mussa, Michael L., "The Exchange Rate, the Balance of Payments, and Monetary Policy Under a Regime of Controlled Floating," *Scandinavian Journal of Economics*, 78 (March 1976), pp. 229–248.

————, "Empirical Regularities in the Behavior of Exchange Rates and Theories of the Foreign Exchange Market," *Carnegie-Rochester Conference Series on Public Policy*, 11 (Spring 1979), pp. 9–57.

————, "The Role of Intervention," Occasional Paper No. 6, New York, Group of Thirty, 1981.

————, "The Theory of Exchange Rate Determination," in Bilson and Marston, *Exchange Rate Theory and Practice*, 1984, pp. 13–78.

Nurkse, Ragnar, *International Currency Experience*, Geneva, League of Nations, 1944.

Obstfeld, Maurice, "Exchange Rates, Inflation and the Sterilization Problem: Germany 1975–81," *European Economic Review*, 21 (March-April 1983), pp. 161–189.

————, "Floating Exchange Rates: Experience and Prospects," *Brookings Papers on Economic Activity*, No. 2 (1985), pp. 369–450.

————, "The Effectiveness of Foreign-Exchange Intervention: Recent Experience," in William H. Branson, Jacob A. Frenkel, and Morris Goldstein, eds., *International Policy Coordination and Exchange Rate Fluctuations*, Chicago, University of Chicago Press, 1990, pp. 197–246.

Obstfeld, Maurice, and Alan C. Stockman, "Exchange-Rate Dynamics," in Jones and Kenen, *Handbook of International Economics*, 1985, pp. 917–977.

Officer, Lawrence H., "The Purchasing Power Parity Theory of Exchange Rates: A Review Article," *International Monetary Fund Staff Papers*, 23 (March 1976), pp. 1–60.

Ott, David J., and Attiat F. Ott, "Budget Balance and Equilibrium Income," *Journal of Finance*, 20 (March 1965), pp. 71–77.

Pentecost, Eric J., "Econometric Approaches to Empirical Models of Exchange Rate Determination," *Journal of Economic Surveys*, 5 (January 1991), pp. 71–98.

Polak, Jacques J., "Monetary Analysis of Income Formation and Payments Problems," *International Monetary Fund Staff Papers*, 4 (November 1957), pp. 1–50.

Poole, Walter, "Speculative Prices as Random Walks: An Analysis of Ten Time Series of Flexible Exchange Rates," *Southern Economic Journal*, 33 (April 1967), pp. 468–478.

Rogoff, Kenneth S., "Expectations and Exchange Rate Volatility," Ph.D. diss., Massachusetts Institute of Technology, 1979.

———, "On the Effects of Sterilized Intervention: An Analysis of Weekly Data," *Journal of Monetary Economics*, 14 (September 1984), pp. 133–150.

Roll, Richard, "Violations of Purchasing Power Parity and Their Implications for Efficient International Commodity Markets," in Marshall Sarnat and Giorgio P. Szego, eds., *International Finance and Trade*, Cambridge, Mass., Ballinger, 1979, pp. 133–176.

Rose, Andrew K., and Lars E. O. Svensson, "Expected and Predicted Realignments: The FF-DM Exchange Rate During the EMS," Seminar Paper No. 485, Stockholm, Institute for International Economic Studies, July 1991.

Scharfstein, David S., and Jeremy C. Stein, "Herd Behavior and Investment," *American Economic Review*, 80 (June 1990), pp. 465–470.

Shiller, Robert J., "Stock Prices and Social Dynamics," *Brookings Papers on Economic Activity*, No. 2 (1984), pp. 457–498.

———, *Market Volatility*, Cambridge, Mass., MIT Press, 1989.

———, "Speculative Prices and Popular Models," *Journal of Economic Perspectives*, 4 (Spring 1990), pp. 55–65.

Shleifer, Andrei, and Lawrence H. Summers, "The Noise Trader Approach to Finance," *Journal of Economic Perspectives*, 4 (Spring 1990), pp. 19–33.

Siegel, Jeremy J., "Risk Interest Rates and the Forward Exchange," *Quarterly Journal of Economics*, 86 (May 1972), pp. 303–319.

Stockman, Alan C., "A Theory of Exchange Rate Determination," *Journal of Political Economy*, 88 (August 1980), pp. 673–698.

———, "The Equilibrium Approach to Exchange Rates," *Federal Reserve Bank of Richmond Review*, 73 (March-April 1987), pp. 12–30.

Svensson, Lars E. O., "The Term Structure of Interest Rates in a Target Zone: Theory and Swedish Data," *Journal of Monetary Economics*, 28 (August 1991a), pp. 87–116.

———, "The Simplest Test of Target Zone Credibility," *International Monetary Fund Staff Papers*, 38 (September 1991b), pp. 655–665.

———, "An Interpretation of Recent Research on Exchange Rate Target Zones," *Journal of Economic Perspectives*, 6 (Fall 1992), pp. 119–144.

———, "Assessing Target Zone Credibility: Mean Reversion and Devaluation Expectations in the ERM 1973–1992," *European Economic Review*, 37 (May 1993), pp. 763–802.

Takagi, Shinji, "Exchange Rate Expectations: A Survey of Survey Studies," *International Monetary Fund Staff Papers*, 38 (March 1991), pp. 156–183.

Taylor, Mark P., "Covered Interest Parity: A High-Frequency, High-Quality Data Study," *Economica*, 54 (November 1987), pp. 429–438.

———, "An Empirical Examination of Long-Run Purchasing Power Parity Using Cointegration Techniques," *Applied Economics*, 20 (October 1988), pp. 1369–1382.

———, "Covered Interest Arbitrage and Market Turbulence," *Economic Journal* (London), 99 (June 1989), pp. 376–391.

————, *The Balance of Payments: New Perspectives on Open-Economy Macro-economics*, Aldershot, Edward Elgar, 1990.

————, "Covered Interest Parity," in Peter Newman, Murray Milgate, and John Eat-well, eds., *The New Palgrave Dictionary of Money and Finance*, London, Mac-millan; New York, Stockton, 1992a, pp. 509–511.

————, "Sterilized Intervention," in Newman, Milgate, and Eatwell, *The New Pal-grave Dictionary of Money and Finance*, 1992b, pp. 546–549.

Taylor, Mark P., and Helen L. Allen, "The Use of Technical Analysis in the Foreign Exchange Market," *Journal of International Money and Finance*, 11 (April 1992), pp. 304–314.

Taylor, Mark P., and Patrick C. McMahon, "Long-Run Purchasing Power Parity in the 1920s," *European Economic Review*, 32 (January 1988), pp. 179–197.

3

Panel: One Money for How Many?

ALTHOUGH THE title given to this session of the conference deliberately evokes the title *One Market, One Money* used by the Commission of the European Communities for its study of Economic and Monetary Union (EMU) in Europe, the papers that follow deal with a broader subject: How should the international monetary system be organized? Should the leading industrial countries plan to move to fixed exchange rates in the years ahead? And, if they do not move in that direction, should they try to manage their exchange rates intensively or leave them primarily to market forces?

In other words, the papers deal with an old but open question about the comparative merits of fixed and floating exchange rates. But they take up this issue in the light of the new literature spawned by the debate about EMU, the recent history of exchange-rate management under the Plaza and Louvre agreements and the European Monetary System, and the striking shift of the debate about exchange-rate policy from a focus on the role of exchange-rate changes in balance-of-payments adjustment to a concern with the effect of exchange-rate pegging on the credibility of national policies.

The three economists contributing brief papers to this session were chosen because they have already made important contributions to the discussion. Richard Cooper has argued that the leading industrial countries should start to think about moving to a single currency managed by a single central bank. Ronald McKinnon has not gone that far but has argued that the leading industrial countries should conduct their national monetary policies in accordance with strict rules aimed at keeping exchange rates fixed while also achieving price stability—a regime he has described elsewhere as a "gold standard without gold." Michael Mussa continues to favor floating exchange rates, because the major industrial countries have neither the need nor the will to establish a world money. It is possible, he argues, for well-managed paper monies to deliver macroeconomic stability, and there is thus no reason to subordinate national monetary policies to some higher monetary sovereign.

RICHARD N. COOPER

A smoothly functioning international monetary system is not an end in itself. It should serve the broader aims of society and be instrumental in making life better for ordinary people. But what do ordinary people want from society and government? Traditionally, their objectives and reasonable expectations include physical and psychological security, high and preferably increasing material standards of living, and a sense of some control over their own destinies. For international economists, these objectives can be abbreviated as PPP—peace, prosperity, and participation.

Most analysis of international economic regimes focuses quite properly on their macroeconomic performance. If that goes badly wrong, a regime clearly fails to serve the objectives of ordinary people. But exchange-rate arrangements also have a microeconomic aspect that is too often neglected. I want to draw attention to two microeconomic disadvantages of the current arrangements of market-determined floating exchange rates, each from the perspective of the well-being of ordinary people.

The less important but more visible of these is the cost to travelers of having to convert currencies, usually at highly disadvantageous rates. The difference in London airport recently between the posted buy and sell rates between the U.S. dollar and British pound was 14 percent, a gross margin (before allowing for transactions fees) not much different from that for merchandise in an American supermarket. This amounts to a tremendous tax on travel. Fixing central rates within a wide band, as in the European Monetary System (EMS), does not help very much. Several years ago, *The Economist* ran the notional experiment of traveling from London to Athens through all twelve members of the European Community (EC), converting currencies on entering each new country. The traveler began with £100 and finished in Athens with less than £20 to spend, having done nothing but convert currencies.

These individual cash exchanges do not bulk large in international transactions as a whole, which typically can be done by bank transfers at wholesale rates. But it is worth keeping in mind that millions of ordinary people now travel outside their home countries (16 million Americans in 1990, 12 million Japanese), and currency conversion is the only direct contact they have with international monetary arrangements. This highly visible aspect of the current system does not serve them well.

More significant economically is the influence floating exchange rates have on the decisions of the ten to thirty thousand businesspeople whose collective investment choices will determine future standards of living throughout the world. The direct costs of currency conversion for corporations doing business *within* the European Community have been estimated at 0.5 percent of Community GDP (Commission, 1990). This is not a negligible amount, but I am more concerned here with the indirect, long-term costs and, in particular, with the influence of exchange-rate uncertainty on investment decisions.

Many industries today are oligopolistic in structure. This generally means that firms and their customers like and expect fixed, posted prices, at least as a starting point for negotiation of discounts. It also means that few of the firms will deviate far from their competitors in their strategies of pricing, product innovation, capacity creation, and marketing. For a host of reasons, oligo-polistic firms do not like to be far from the crowd. Making mistakes, even big mistakes, can be more easily justified to shareholders and other stakeholders if near competitors have made similar mistakes.

As international competition becomes more acute in oligopolistic indus-tries, exchange-rate fluctuations create a major problem for management. These fluctuations cannot be ignored, because profits amount to only about 5 percent of the selling price of many manufactured goods. Thus, an ordinary weekly swing of 5 percent in exchange rates can wipe out profits on an un-hedged transaction (or double them, but that possibility does not fully com-pensate risk-averting management); the reasons for these swings reside in the financial world and are largely beyond the ken of those whose specialty is manufacturing or marketing. It is increasingly easy to hedge any particular sale abroad through a variety of financial instruments, but it is not possible through financial instruments to hedge satisfactorily a capacity-increasing in-vestment aimed at foreign sales.

Allowing prices in foreign markets to fluctuate with exchange rates irritates customers and runs the risk of losing sales. But maintaining steady local prices in each of several national markets in the face of fluctuating exchange rates is impossible without creating the potential for arbitrage between those markets.

How are firms likely to respond to these difficulties? First and most benign, they will diversify their investments across currency areas where they have major markets. Japanese firms, for example, will want to "hedge" by invest-ing in productive facilities in the United States and in Europe. Although this practice is not undesirable in itself, it implies, insofar as it is motivated by currency uncertainty, that the hedging investments will have lower yields than they would if they could be made in the best location regardless of exchange-rate uncertainties. This diversion represents a loss to future generations.

Second, all other factors being equal, risk-averse firms will reduce their total level of investment under a regime of exchange-rate uncertainty. Al-though there is little systematic empirical evidence linking investment to exchange-rate uncertainty, there is a certain amount of circumstantial evi-dence. Caballero and Corbo (1989) find a strong negative impact of real-exchange-rate variability on the exports from six developing countries and, by inference, on investment for export. De Grauwe (1988), looking at variability in excess of one year, concludes that about 20 percent of the 5.7 percentage-point slowdown in the growth of world trade since 1973 can be explained by exchange-rate variability; if intra-EC trade is excluded, exchange-rate vari-ability accounts for nearly 30 percent of the 4.2 percentage-point slowdown. It is noteworthy that the ratio of investment to GDP in the industrialized (OECD) countries fell by 2 to 3 percentage points following the introduction of generalized floating exchange rates in 1973, from roughly 24 percent in the late 1960s to 22 percent in the second half of the 1970s, and to 21 percent in the 1980s. But the period following 1973 was subject to several major oil-price shocks, to a sharp rise followed by a fall in the rate of inflation in the OECD countries, and, in 1974–75 and 1981–82, to the two deepest post-1945 industrial recessions. Too many events took place to impute with any confidence the markedly lower investment rates to exchange-rate variability, but neither can its role be ruled out, particularly because the decline occurred more in tradable than in nontradable goods.

Third, in the face of exchange-rate variability, which greatly complicates pricing strategies, business firms will seek government assistance in separating markets, to discourage arbitrage from one currency area to another. In the mid-1980s, Japanese and European firms attempted to maintain their dollar prices in the U.S. market, as well as local currency prices in their home markets, despite wide movements in the dollar exchange rate. In the United States, a trade association was created to lobby for legislative and administrative action against "gray-market" goods, that is, goods that were (perfectly legally) shipped by brokers or dealers outside of normal channels to take advantage of the arbitrage possibilities. This response was carried to an absurd length when Duracell filed a trademark-violation complaint in the United States against Duracell batteries produced in a wholly Belgian-owned subsidiary and imported into the United States by independent importers. Duracell properly lost the case, but only after tying up the importer in court for some time. Antidumping laws, which make no provision for movements in exchange rates, offer a field day for competitors against imported products that remain priced to market even when the exporting country's currency appreciates. Successful protectionist action, or even harassing action, introduces microeconomic inefficiencies; even the possibility of such actions may discourage investment.

With respect to the efficiency gains from money, we are faced with serious deficiencies of conventional monetary theory, which accords no role to money in establishing and conveying to economic agents the proper *relative* prices that provide the signals for resource allocation in a market economy. I suspect that, as national economies become more open, frequent movements in nominal exchange rates cause more uncertainty with regard to the proper allocative signals than does moderate inflation. The same instincts that lead economists and others to attribute greater economic damage to inflation than is suggested by formal economic modeling should also lead them to be more skeptical of the net positive claims for exchange-rate flexibility.

These microeconomic considerations will not, and should not, be decisive in the choice of an exchange-rate regime, but neither should they be wholly neglected. The ultimate solution is to establish a single currency, at least among the major manufacturing regions—Japan, the United States, and the EC. Such an idea raises a host of management issues, for a single currency must have a single monetary policy, one that, in this case, would span many nations. That would be challenging but not impossible to arrange.

An assessment of such a single-currency area also raises a host of complex issues about the pattern of disturbances to which the participating economies are likely to be subject in the future, as well as questions about their capacity to adjust to these disturbances. I shall simply venture the opinion that, with monetary union, disturbances *between* these large and diverse economies, such as might call for exchange-rate adjustment, would likely be much smaller than the disturbances within them, where even today we do not rely on changes in exchange rates as part of the adjustment process. The main disturbances between these regions in the future are likely to be monetary in nature, creating complications for the real side of the economy such as those already discussed. With a common monetary regime and its accompanying integrated capital market, that type of disturbance would not be possible. Over time, the costs associated with flexible exchange rates among these three regions are likely to grow relative to the benefits of flexible rates, so it is not too early to begin thinking about alternative arrangements.

References

Caballero, Ricardo J., and Vittorio Corbo, "The Effects of Real Exchange Rate Uncertainty on Exports: Empirical Evidence," *World Bank Economic Review*, 3 (May 1989), pp. 263–278.

Commission of the European Communities, "One Market, One Money: An Evaluation of the Potential Benefits and Costs of Forming an Economic and Monetary Union," *European Economy*, No. 44 (October 1990), pp. 63–68.

De Grauwe, Paul, "Exchange Rate Variability and the Slowdown in the Growth of International Trade," *International Monetary Fund Staff Papers*, 35 (March 1988), pp. 63–84.

R O N A L D   I .   M C K I N N O N

1 The Fiscal Constraints

How extensive should be the domain of single currencies? This question is of obvious immediate concern to Europeans, but, before addressing it in the European context, I shall briefly update the old theory of optimum currency areas (OCA) to take fiscal constraints into account.

In open-economy macroeconomics, traditional theorizing typically ignores the fiscal constraints on monetary policies and the way the nature of the monetary regime limits what fiscal authorities can do. Instead, going back to Tinbergen (1952) and Meade (1951), textbooks still treat monetary and fiscal policies as if they were separable policy instruments.

The theory of optimum currency areas in the early 1960s (Mundell, 1961; McKinnon, 1963) is no exception. By failing to analyze interactions between fiscal and monetary policies, OCA theory could not distinguish between the case for fixed exchange rates (within narrow bands), on the one hand, and the case for nation-states joining together in common currency, on the other. In this brief note, I shall first describe this omission, and then spell out its implications for Maastricht and beyond.

2 Optimum Currency Areas Revisited

In the early 1960s, OCA theory was still dominated by the Keynesian idea of macroeconomic activism. National monetary autonomy was viewed positively in its own right and as part of a package for offsetting "shocks" emanating from the private sector. The problem of time inconsistency, resulting from the high degree of discretion allowed monetary authorities, had not yet been identified. Indeed, some writers (such as Johnson [1972]) believed discretionary monetary policy could be used to pick an optimal trade-off between inflation and unemployment along a stationary Phillips curve!

Embracing this professional enthusiasm for monetary activism, Mundell (1961) leaned toward making separate currency areas relatively small—thus maximizing the number of independent monetary authorities. Mundell maintained that the boundaries for an OCA should be sufficiently tightly drawn to ensure a high degree of labor and capital mobility within the "small" area.

Against the advantages of microeconomic monetary management, McKinnon (1963) argued that the efficiency of international trade and investment would suffer if trade had to take place across fluctuating exchange rates and that the national money would become less useful as a store of value and unit of account. Because very small economies tend to be more open on current account, they would do better to create a "large" currency area by fixing their exchange rates against the currency of a dominant trading partner. Fixing to a large, stable trading partner with an internationally usable currency could better anchor domestic monetary policy.

The balance of these two considerations, then, defined the currency area's optimum extent. As if frozen in time, modern textbooks still view the trade-offs this way. But, within whatever sized OCA one might pick, this old literature does not really say whether a common currency or "permanently" fixed exchange rates would be optimal. To understand this critical subproblem, we must appeal to the fiscal constraints on monetary policy and the monetary constraints on fiscal policy.

3 Fiscal Constraints on Moving to a Common Currency: Some European Illustrations

Suppose that the optimum currency area is well defined and that countries closely linked in investment and trade agree that exchange-rate stability is paramount. This was the consensus in Western Europe from the inception of the EMS in 1979 through September 1992, when Britain and Italy fell out of the European Exchange Rate Mechanism (ERM).

What, then, are the major arguments in favor of moving to a common currency, under which nations would yield autonomy in monetary policy, and the 2.25 percent exchange margins of the old ERM would be squeezed to zero? Europeans favoring such a move cite the strong political symbolism of a common currency, the reduction it would effect in long-run investment risk (without a common currency, exchange risk can never fully be eliminated), and the elimination of money-changing costs for tourists moving from one European country to another. In addition, perhaps the proposed European Central Bank (ECB) could ensure, on average, a more stable price level for the group as a whole than most European countries could guarantee by acting alone.

There are two sets of arguments against the move to a common currency. The first cites the well-recognized problem of "convergence." During the transition, countries with differing inflation rates might not be able to align their exchange and interest rates sufficiently to risk jumping to a common currency. Neither Britain nor Italy were in proper alignment with the rest of the group when they were forced to leave the ERM in September 1992. Nevertheless, if convergence were all that mattered for any one country to join a common currency system, waiting for the right moment to jump would be the only major issue. This transitional convergence problem is serious but surmountable.

The second constraint on moving to a common currency is fiscal, and it is more fundamental in the sense that it would continue to plague the putative monetary union even if initial "convergence" had been successfully achieved. Unlike the need for converging national rates of price inflation, the fiscal problem is not simply one of "convergence" of public debts and deficits to some common level. The issue is more basic. Because debt overhangs at the national level are simply too high in an absolute sense, European governments —whether among the core countries or not—could not afford to cede control of their national central banks to some pan-European authority, such as the ECB.

The overhang of national debt in European economies averaged over 60 percent of GDP in 1992 (see Table 3.1), the supposed target ceiling negotiated at Maastricht before any member country could enter the common-currency arrangement. But fiscal conditions among the member countries are very dif-

TABLE 3.1

European Countries: Convergence Indicators for 1993 and 1994 (percent)

	1992 GDP Weights		Consumer Price Inflation		General Government Balance/GDP		Gross Government Debt/GDP[a] 1992	Long-Term Interest Rates August 1993
	In EC	In World	1993	1994	1993	1994		
EC countries								
France	19.2	3.6	2.2	2.2	-6.0	-5.9	52.6	6.4
Germany	23.2	4.3	4.6	2.9	-4.8	-3.5	42.5	6.4
Italy	18.4	3.4	4.5	4.6	-10.3	-9.2	115.1	10.3
United Kingdom[b]	17.7	3.3	3.2	3.8	-8.6	-7.4	35.1	7.0
Largest four countries[c]	78.5	14.6	3.7	3.3	-7.3	-6.3	60.3	7.4
Belgium	3.1	0.6	2.8	2.9	-6.7	-5.6	121.0	7.1
Denmark[d]	1.7	0.3	1.1	1.8	-3.5	-4.2	71.3	6.7
Greece[e]	1.7	0.3	14.3	9.5	-12.9	-13.3	108.6	20.3
Ireland	0.7	0.1	2.0	3.0	-3.4	-3.8	95.9	7.6
Luxembourg	0.1	—	4.0	3.3	0.1	—	5.8	6.8
Netherlands	4.7	0.9	2.0	2.8	-3.9	-3.9	79.0	6.2
Portugal	1.5	0.3	6.3	5.6	-6.4	-5.4	63.7	10.5
Spain	8.1	1.5	4.7	4.1	-6.3	-7.1	47.9	9.2
Smallest eight countries[c]	21.5	4.0	4.3	3.9	-6.0	-6.2	74.3	8.9
All EC[c]	100.0	18.6	3.8	3.5	-7.0	-6.3	63.4	7.8

(continued)

TABLE 3.1 *(Continued)*

| | 1992 GDP Weights | | Consumer Price Inflation | | General Government Balance/GDP | | Gross Government Debt/GDP[a] | Long-Term Interest Rates |
	In EC	In World	1993	1994	1993	1994	1992	August 1993
Maastricht convergence criteria[f]	...	...	3.2	3.8	−3.0	−3.0	60.0	8.8
Non-EC countries								
Austria	...	0.4	3.7	2.5	−3.4	−3.0	49.4	6.5
Finland	...	0.3	2.8	4.1	−12.2	−9.5	39.5	7.7
Norway	...	0.3	2.5	2.3	−3.6	−3.4	43.0	6.2
Sweden	...	0.5	5.0	3.7	−13.5	−11.5	55.0	7.7
Switzerland	...	0.7	3.6	2.3	−2.4	−2.5	34.3	4.6
Five non-EC countries[c]	...	2.3	3.7	2.9	−6.6	−5.7	43.9	6.3

Source: IMF, *World Economic Outlook*, October 1993, table 5, p. 400; reproduced by permission of the International Monetary Fund.
[a]Debt data refer to end of year. They relate to general government but may not be consistent with the definition agreed at Maastricht.
[b]Retail price index excluding mortgage interest.
[c]Average weighted by 1992 GDP shares.
[d]The debt-to-GDP ratio would be below 60 percent if adjusted in line with the definition agreed at Maastricht.
[e]General government balance includes capitalized interest; long-term interest rate is twelve-month treasury bill rate.
[f]Unweighted averages. The Treaty does not indicate precisely how these indicators should be weighted across the reference countries.

ferent, as Table 3.1 indicates. The ratio of debt to GDP was close to, or over, 100 percent for Belgium, Ireland, and Italy, and such countries as Greece and Portugal have avoided explosions in their already large debt ratios only by resorting to the inflation tax. Once accumulated, public-sector debts of this magnitude can be safely managed only if the government in question retains ownership of its central bank.

But why might the rules of thumb suggested by Maastricht of, say, keeping debt ratios below 60 percent—or current public deficits below 3 percent—before joining a common currency also be insufficient? For a substantially indebted national government, control over its own central bank confers two major advantages for debt management: (1) in the short run, major rollovers of existing debt are less risky if the central bank acts as the "government's banker," that is, if it can provide liquidity to the market should something go awry, and (2) in the long run, the perceived risk of outright default becomes negligible. Thus, the "real-interest" cost of government-debt finance is reduced. Together, (1) and (2) serve to reduce the risk of a "run" on a highly indebted national government.

The risk of future inflation and exchange-rate devaluation should be distinguished from the risk of outright default and debt repudiation. Joining a common currency might or might not reduce inflation risk, but it surely would increase default risk at the national level. When the government owns its own central bank, the government can always avoid outright default on the face value of its obligations by "printing money," that is, by using the inflation tax, to pay interest and principal. Because owning the central bank greatly reduces the risk of outright default, the government can then preempt the national capital market to issue treasury securities at lower interest rates than can high-quality private borrowers whose debt is also denominated in the national currency.

Apart from the inflation tax, there might remain some residual incentive for a surprise default—or capital levy—on the national debt if the government perceives that traditional methods of tax finance are becoming too expensive and too distortionary (Alesina et al., 1992). Although certainly true in principle, such a default has, to my knowledge, seldom been engineered by any government merely because its use of the printing press was not constrained by a commitment to some external (metallic) monetary standard. One can make a case for instances of outright debt repudiation with regard to the old Soviet Union, but these instances are so unusual that I treat this form of default risk as negligible.

Consequently, government bonds at every term to maturity are considered to be the "safest" financial instruments denominated in the national currency. In the United States, the highest-grade corporate bonds usually pay an interest rate a percentage point or so higher than long-term U.S. Treasury bonds—with "B-grade" corporate bonds paying about 2 percentage points higher and unrated "junk" bonds possibly paying 5 points higher or more. After allowing for tax differences, interest on the debt of American state and local governments is also substantially higher than that on federal debt. The rationale for higher interest rates on private-sector or local-government debt is that companies are subject to commercial risk, that is, the threat of bankruptcy, which the federal government is not, and holders of private securities (or those of local governments) face the same inflation risk as do holders of claims on the federal government. Fiscally weak governments might have to go one step further and use capital controls to make sure this preemption is complete. National savers could then be forced to buy the national government's bonds at lower interest rates than those that would otherwise prevail in world markets. In effect, capital controls are a backdoor method of taxing national savers.

The traditional low-cost financing of the national debt need not hold if the government loses control over its central bank. In the late 1980s, for example, the prospects of moving to a common currency in Europe seemed brighter than in 1993. Had that move occurred, the government of Italy would have lost to the ECB control over the Bank of Italy, that is, over the bank's authority to issue money. What, then, would have been the implications for the cost of servicing the government's debt?

Three Italian economists, Alesina, Prati, and Tabellini (1990) detected an inversion in this traditional relation between interest rates on private and government debt in Italy. After exchange controls were removed in 1987, they found that the average yield on Italian treasury bills was 1 to 3 percentage points higher (after adjusting for tax differences) than on "private" bank certificates of deposit of the same maturity. On medium-term maturities, two-year government bonds yielded interest a percentage point or so higher than did eighteen- to twenty-four-month bank certificates of deposit. These economists also showed that three heavily indebted European countries—Belgium, Italy, and the Netherlands—displayed this interest-rate inversion in their domestic capital markets, whereas other potential common-currency countries with lower debt ratios did not. With Italy falling out of the ERM and its currency depreciating by over 30 percent against the currencies of Germany and other "core" countries in late 1992 and into 1993, one would expect this inversion to disappear as the possibility becomes more remote that Italy, and other European countries, will join together in a common-currency arrangement.

The Italian evidence discriminates between traditional inflation risk on lira-denominated debt and the risk of an outright public-sector restructuring or default. If investors believe that a move to a common European currency (the ECU) will preclude government use of the inflation tax to solve its debt problems, and if the government debt problem is severe enough, the risk premia incorporated in interest rates on Italian government debt may indeed exceed those on high-grade private debt. In the extreme, moving to a common currency in Europe could provoke a run on the Italian government, much of the debt of which is already short-term and turns over every month. Exit from the common-currency agreement would be virtually impossible were a fiscal collapse to occur in one country. Thus, the usual way of settling an untenable national-debt overhang by devaluation and inflation would be blocked.

Under a common-currency arrangement, therefore, a country experiencing a fiscal breakdown would have great leverage on the other member governments. To prevent possible Community-wide bank failures and financial dislocation arising out of one government's threatened default on its ECU debts, the solvent members of the European Community (EC) might be forced to bail it out—whether by asking the ECB to buy the troubled government's bonds or by direct government-to-government lending. Knowing this *ex ante*, politicians in the errant country might become even less willing to take resolute fiscal action. Moral hazard would thus be uncomfortably high. Indeed, the EC has already been significantly weakened by agreeing to large intergovernmental transfers to "distressed" areas and to equalization grants for poorer governments.

So, what might we conclude about the fiscal impediments to a successful common currency in Europe? As long as the main taxing authority and main fiscal problems—the large debt overhangs—remain at the national level, giving up national control over national central banks will be too costly. Government debts of this magnitude can only be accumulated in the first place because each national government owns its own central bank. Thus, suddenly to take away the central bank while leaving the debt residue would make debt management next to impossible.

Is there any way out of this fiscal dilemma? If the national debts and much of the national taxing authority were to be transferred to the emerging European central government, which would also be responsible for issuing the common currency, the fiscal regime would then be consistent with the monetary regime. Indeed, this is just the form of the American monetary union, in which almost all general-obligation government debt is concentrated at the federal level along with the money-issuing authority of the Federal Reserve System. To maintain creditworthiness, the American states have all passed some form of constitutional restraint on deficit financing, and their outstanding general-obligation debts are very small by European standards. Transferring the huge debts of the European national governments to the European central government seems far beyond the realm of current political feasibility.

4 A Common Monetary Standard without a Common Currency

Instead of leaping to a common currency, it would be best to leave in place national central banks and independently circulating national monies separated by narrow exchange-rate margins. A fiscal breakdown in any one country would not then imperil the whole monetary mechanism. Although traumatic for the errant country, exit from the ERM would be relatively easy. The electoral sanctions incurred from losing fiscal control, from inflating, and from falling out of the monetary agreement would fall mainly on the government of the country in question. Because that country's leverage for extracting concessions from the other members would be minimal, it would, *ex ante*, have considerable incentive to keep its fiscal house in order. I would argue that the pressure on each member government to maintain fiscal restraint can be maximized by keeping intergovernmental transfers to a minimum within whatever form of fiscal federalism evolves in Europe. Some influential authors (Eichengreen, 1992) maintain, however, that such transfers are necessary to aid poor areas or to offset region-specific economic downturns.

Within the core group of noninflationary European countries, fixed par values and narrow bands for exchange rates could continue to operate indefinitely. Under such a common monetary standard (as distinct from a common currency), there would be a strong case for (1) defining a common price-level objective for internationally tradable goods within the core group as a whole, rather than just with regard to Germany, and (2) having the core central banks coordinate their monetary policies—mainly domestic-credit expansion—to achieve this objective.

Under (1), zero inflation in a common producer-price index would be the natural target for a common monetary policy in the six core countries, a target that would be consistent with the mutual commitment to fixed nominal exchange rates. Under this arrangement, German producer prices would be given no more weight than Germany's relative GNP would warrant, so the Bundesbank would be bound to a price-level rule at least partly external to Germany. This would, however, be an advantage to the German monetary authorities. The Bundesbank could more easily face down German trade unions if it had to maintain an externally sanctioned price-level objective that it could not easily modify.

Under (2), the monies of the core countries would continue to circulate separately within narrow exchange margins. International currency substitution, however, would make each purely national rate of monetary expansion difficult to control or predict, although the collective money supply of the core group could be a helpful intermediate monetary indicator for targeting the common producer-price level. Under this arrangement, the six central banks would act in concert to determine their respective expansions of domestic credit with a more or less common strategy for adjusting short-term interest rates (McKinnon, 1988; McKinnon and Ohno, 1989).

Because national central banks would continue to collect monetary seigniorage at the national level, they would remain the natural lenders of last resort to national banks in distress and the guarantors of the payments mechanism at the national level—while cooperating to supervise international clearing. Under guidelines similar to the international Basle Accord on capital requirements for reducing regulatory competition, they, or other designated national agencies, would retain supervisory responsibility for regulating banks against undue risk taking.

These proposed reforms to secure better exchange-rate and price-level stability in Europe would have many complications not covered here. Yet, the changes are evolutionary and relatively modest compared to the "leap in the dark" of the Maastricht Treaty's push for a common currency. A common monetary standard that keeps national central banks and national currencies in place is preferable to a common currency.

References

Alesina, Alberto, Mark de Broeck, Alessandro Prati, and Guido Tabellini, "Default Risk," *Economic Policy: A European Forum*, 15 (October 1992), pp. 429–463.

Alesina, Alberto, Alessandro Prati, and Guido Tabellini, "Public Confidence and Debt Management: A Model and a Case Study of Italy," in Rudiger Dornbusch and Mario Draghi, eds., *Public Debt Management: Theory and History,* Cambridge and New York, Cambridge University Press, 1990, pp. 94–123.

Eichengreen, Barry, "The Political Economy of Fiscal Policy After EMU," Center for International and Development Economics Research, University of California, Berkeley, December 1992, processed.

International Monetary Fund (IMF), *World Economic Outlook*, Washington, D.C., International Monetary Fund, October 1993.

Johnson, Harry G., "The Case for Flexible Exchange Rates, 1969," in Harry G. Johnson, *Further Essays in Monetary Economics*, Winchester, Allen and Unwin, 1972, pp. 198–222.

McKinnon, Ronald I., "Optimum Currency Areas," *American Economic Review*, 53 (September 1963), pp. 717–724.

———, "Monetary and Exchange Rate Policies for International Financial Stability: A Proposal," *Journal of Economic Perspectives*, 2 (Winter 1988), pp. 83–103.

McKinnon, Ronald I., and Kenichi Ohno, "Purchasing Power Parity as a Monetary Standard," in Omar F. Hamouda, Robin Rowley, and Bernard M. Wolf, eds., *The Future of the International Monetary System: Change, Coordination or Instability?* Aldershot, Edward Elgar, 1989, pp. 42–67.

Meade, James E., *The Balance of Payments*, London, Oxford University Press, 1951.

Mundell, Robert A., "A Theory of Optimum Currency Areas," *American Economic Review*, 51 (September 1961), pp. 657–664.

Tinbergen, Jan, *On the Theory of Economic Policy*, Amsterdam, North-Holland, 1952.

MICHAEL MUSSA

1 Introduction

On the subject of "One Money for How Many?" I can be brief. The key point that I wish to make is covered very well in Charles Goodhart's stimulating chapter on "The Political Economy of Monetary Union" (Chapter 12). When we look at the factors that actually determine the domains of different monies, we find that they are *not* the economic considerations suggested by the theory of optimum currency areas, as first discussed by Mundell, Kenen, and McKinnon thirty years ago. They are, rather, political. In particular, virtually all of the world's nations assert and express their sovereign authority by maintaining a distinct national money and protecting its use within their respective jurisdictions. Money is like a flag; each country has to have its own.

This dominant political element in the determination of national monetary standards clearly must have an important influence on the way we think about key issues in international monetary economics—from the effort to construct a European Economic and Monetary Union (EMU) to the monetary implications of the destruction of a Soviet Union or a Yugoslavia. As Goodhart has developed his analysis of these issues very well, I shall till somewhat different fields. The question I should like to examine is what type of international monetary system will bring together the domains in which different (national) monetary standards operate. Can we go back to a system such as Bretton Woods in which exchange rates among major currencies were quite tightly linked? Should we want to go back?

These are more than idle questions. It has been only twenty years since the Bretton Woods system finally collapsed following the effort of reconstruction in the Smithsonian Agreement. For most of the preceding century, some form of a fixed-rate system, linked to gold, had prevailed over much of the world. In the century before that, silver, perhaps even more than gold, had formed the basis for the world monetary system, and the relative price of the two metals generally fluctuated within a narrow range. With this historical experience, it seems reasonable to ask if we might someday soon return to an international monetary system in which most of the world's (national) monies are quite tightly linked through a global system of fixed exchange rates.

There is good reason to believe that this will not happen. A fundamental technological, psychological, and political change has occurred during the course of the past fifty years or so that makes a return to a system of fixed exchange rates far less likely than in earlier eras. This change is the advent

The views stated here are the author's and do not necessarily represent those of the International Monetary Fund.

and acceptance of inconvertible paper money as the basis of essentially all national monetary systems.

Paper money has a long history, of course, going back at least a thousand years in China, and passing into modern times through such exciting episodes as the French *assignats* and the German hyperinflation. Until quite recently, however, a pure paper-money standard—not linked to any commodity such as gold or silver—was an aberration associated with wartime finance or other extreme circumstances. Almost always, the expectation was that, once the emergency giving rise to the adoption of a pure paper standard had passed, a more normal monetary system, usually based on gold or silver, would be restored. This was the experience, for example, of Britain after the Napoleonic Wars, of much of Europe after World War I, and of the United States after the Civil War.

In this important respect, national governments, even the most powerful national governments, were not able to exercise full sovereignty in monetary affairs. Until recent times, the popular will compelled governments to pay homage to metallic monarchs. Indeed, it was not until August 15, 1971, that Richard Nixon finally displaced the last illusory vestige of the practical idea of a commodity-based monetary standard. In my view, there is now little chance that key national governments—having once established their sovereign authority over relatively stable paper-money standards—will restore the barbaric relic to the high altar of the Temple of Mammon.

2 Metallic Standards

In three important ways, national monetary systems based on gold or silver had natural advantages in structuring and supporting an international monetary system with tightly controlled exchange rates.

First, the popular sentiment that supported a gold- or silver-based national monetary standard translated automatically into support for a fixed-rate regime vis-à-vis other countries using the same metal as the basis of their national monetary systems. For a long period prior to 1870, the fact that some important countries maintained bimetallic standards also helped to keep fluctuations of the relative price of gold and silver within a relatively narrow range and thereby to limit exchange-rate fluctuations between gold-based and silver-based national monies. With the widespread shift to gold after 1870, and the resumption of the gold standard by the United States in 1879, most countries (excluding those that, like China and Mexico, remained on silver) found themselves in an international system of fixed exchange rates, without any deliberate decision having been made to set up and maintain such a system. Popular support for the gold standard at the national level automatically implied support for the gold-based international monetary system.

Second, widespread acceptance of a common commodity standard in different countries eliminated much of the problem of national jealousies that sometimes arise in asymmetric monetary systems where one country sees itself as subservient to the monetary standard of another country. In the 1960s, President de Gaulle complained about the "exorbitant privilege" enjoyed by the United States because the U.S. dollar (and not really gold) served as the basis of the international monetary system—and this was at a time when the United States was, as one eminent scholar put it, a "giant among nations." More recently, it is clear that part of the impetus to create a European money and a European Central Bank comes from the desire of some countries to move away from an asymmetric system in which the Bundesbank effectively determines monetary policy for other countries the currencies of which are tightly linked to the deutsche mark. The effort is to maintain the Bundesbank's disciplined adherence to the objective of price stability but to "Europeanize" decisions about monetary policy.

There were political complaints about the gold standard, too, perhaps most notably during William Jennings Bryan's presidential campaign of 1896. Bryan's objective, however, was not to introduce a new paper-money standard, but to return to the bimetallic standard (with a silver-to-gold exchange rate of sixteen to one) that had legally prevailed in the United States until 1873—a change that would have been quite inflationary in 1896. For the purpose of the present discussion, it is interesting to speculate whether Bryan might have been more successful politically had he been able to rant not against a golden crucifixion but against the deflationary torments inflicted by the paper pound of perfidious Albion.

Third, under the old metallic standards, each nation individually was responsible only for its own adherence to its preferred monetary standard. This was a political virtue because it did not require different nations to agree either about the nature of the international monetary system or about mechanisms to assure the efficient operation of that system. It was an economic defect because it provided no means for the system as a whole to deal with global shortages or excesses in the supply of gold, the base money of the system. This defect came to the fore in the aftermath of World War I, when the extent of the feasible reversal of wartime inflation proved insufficient to restore a firm foundation for sterling at the prewar parity. This difficulty clearly contributed to the collapse of the gold standard in the early 1930s, as the world slid into deflation and depression.

After World War II, the Bretton Woods system was structured to deal with the perceived defects of the gold standard. It provided for an institution, the International Monetary Fund (IMF), to oversee the operation of the international monetary system—including the adjustment of exchange rates among national currencies—and allowed for adjustments in the official price of gold as a means of assuring an adequate monetary base for the system as a whole.

In actuality, adjustments of the gold price proved politically unpalatable, and the only adjustment occurred in the aftermath of the international monetary crisis of 1971. The effort to reconstruct the system under the Smithsonian Agreement proved short-lived, and, in early 1973, the world moved to a system of floating rates among the leading national currencies.

3 Paper Money

Although gold continued to play a limited and diminishing role until 1971 in official monetary transactions between national governments, monetary gold played no part in ordinary commerce. People generally became accustomed to paper money as the visible national monetary standard. In contrast with earlier experience, these paper-money standards performed quite well. During the 1950s and 1960s, inflation was low in the major industrial countries (at least by subsequent standards) and growth was strong (by both prior and subsequent standards); there was no return to the deflationary experiences of the early 1930s. Some might argue that the final official delinking from gold was responsible for the inflationary excesses of the 1970s, but this is surely not a common perception among the great mass of people, who no longer think about gold as a monetary standard. In any event, the return to significantly lower inflation rates for most industrial countries during the 1980s appears to have established the principle that a well-managed paper standard can deliver reasonable monetary stability while avoiding the evils of both deflation and excessively rapid inflation. As emphasized earlier, there is now no widespread popular sentiment to return to a metallic monetary standard.

It is noteworthy that the Maastricht Treaty does not provide for a return to gold or any other form of commodity standard as the basis of the European Monetary System (EMS). Instead, it provides for the development of a European Central Bank that will be constitutionally dedicated to managing a pure paper-money standard so as to pursue the key objective of price stability. Similarly, elsewhere in the world, one finds considerable emphasis on institutionalizing the objective of price stability as the key goal of monetary policy. There is relatively little discussion of, and little apparent political support for, the reinstitution of the gold standard at either the national or global level.

If the international monetary system is not to have a metallic base enjoying deep and widespread popular support as the "natural" monetary standard for national currencies, how will a system of tightly linked national currencies be made to operate? There are two essential requirements: (1) there must be a high degree of macroeconomic convergence—especially, similar and low inflation rates—among the countries participating in the system, and (2) there must be an acceptable and durable mechanism for determining the monetary policy of the system as a whole.

Under the Bretton Woods system, inflation rates were generally quite low, and most nations seemed reasonably comfortable with the monetary policy conducted by the U.S. Federal Reserve—at least until the late 1960s. Occasional parity adjustments and a relatively low degree of international capital mobility (in comparison with recent times) helped to sustain the system. Since the collapse of the Bretton Woods system, those European currencies that have remained tightly linked to the deutsche mark have been able to remain linked because their national inflation rates have been kept generally in line with those of Germany and because their national monetary policies have been subordinated to a substantial extent to the monetary policy determined by the Bundesbank. The European Monetary System envisioned by the Maastricht Treaty also contains these two essential elements—the requirement for adequate macroeconomic convergence, and the provision for the creation of a European Central Bank to determine monetary policy.

More generally, the major industrial countries seem now to be moving back to similar and relatively low inflation rates. This is a hopeful sign that the wide swings in exchange rates associated with the process of inflation and disinflation during the 1970s and 1980s may be less prevalent in the future. There is little evidence, however, that the essential requirement for a return to a fixed-rate system is likely soon to be met—that is, movement toward the adoption of a common monetary policy by the largest industrial countries. Indeed, despite the fact that monetary policy in the three largest industrial countries appears to be pursuing similar objectives for low inflation in the longer term, there have been particularly wide swings in short-term interest-rate differentials in recent years, as the Federal Reserve, the Bank of Japan, and the Bundesbank have responded to differing cyclical conditions.

Specifically, the short-term interest-rate differential between the U.S. federal funds rate and the German interbank rate was almost 4 percentage points *positive* in early 1989, as the Federal Reserve tightened policy to curb inflationary pressures in the late 1980s. In the summer of 1992, this differential had shifted to more than 6 percentage points *negative* as the Bundesbank confronted postunification inflationary pressures and the Federal Reserve dealt with a particularly sluggish recovery in the aftermath of recession. Recent shifts in the differentials between Japanese short-term interest rates and either U.S. or German short-term rates have been smaller than the unprecedented 10 percentage-point swing in the U.S.-German differential, but the movements have been quite large as Japanese monetary policy has responded, first, to the challenge of the asset-price bubble and, then, to the consequences of its collapse.

Significant movements in exchange rates have of course been associated with these recent cyclical divergences and with the monetary-policy responses to these divergences. Perhaps, if a global system of fixed exchange rates had somehow been preserved, the divergences of performance and policy that contributed to these recent exchange-rate movements among the dollar, yen, and deutsche mark would have been more subdued. I see no reasonable likelihood, however, that these three large countries could have adhered to a commonly accepted monetary policy consistent with the maintenance of mutually fixed exchange rates in the face of recent economic divergences. Surely, the Bundesbank would not have passively agreed to a monetary policy dictated by the Federal Reserve when Germany faced the critical task of containing the inflationary consequences of unification. Similarly, the Federal Reserve would surely have had great difficulty justifying to its political constituency the continued pursuit of a very tight policy in the face of persistent economic sluggishness, on the grounds that it needed to follow the monetary discipline imposed by the Bundesbank. And Japanese monetary policy could not, in my opinion, have passively accepted the monetary dictates of either the Federal Reserve or the Bundesbank in recent economic circumstances. In fact, within Europe, where mutual trade flows form relatively large shares of GDP and where there are strong political commitments to maintain exchange-rate parities, a number of these commitments could not survive the economic strains of recent cyclical divergences.

This should not be regarded as an unsatisfactory situation. Wide swings of nominal and real exchange rates among major currencies, such as the enormous upswing and subsequent downswing of the U.S. dollar between 1980 and 1987, are a serious problem. However, if the monetary policies of the largest countries remain well focused on the objectives of reasonable price and output stability, thereby avoiding the economic strains of substantial inflation followed by disinflation, extremely wide swings of exchange rates should be infrequent if not entirely avoidable. Some inconvenience may be caused by short-term randomness in exchange-rate movements under a floating rate, but this does not appear to be a major obstacle to international commerce. In fact, some flexibility of exchange rates in the face of cyclical divergences among the largest national economies can have beneficial effects, including that of allowing national monetary policies greater flexibility in responding to cyclical disturbances.

The Canadian experience of floating against the U.S. dollar and the Swiss experience of floating against other European currencies suggest that, for highly open economies in which trade constitutes a large fraction of national product, the exchange rate cannot be treated with policy indifference. Recognizing, however, that policy must sometimes adjust to influence the exchange rate or to respond to exchange-rate movements, a number of highly open economies have apparently found that a floating rate functions acceptably well. Other countries, notably those that have participated in the Exchange Rate Mechanism of the EMS, have reached the opposite conclusion and have either pegged unilaterally to a dominant currency (or basket of currencies) or have participated in regional arrangements for pegged exchange rates. So long as there are the political will and popular support to sustain the policy discipline necessary to maintain a pegged exchange rate, such a system also may function acceptably well. Indeed, for Europe, there is reason to hope that conditions similar to those giving rise to recent exchange-market tensions will not soon or often be repeated. Moreover, if it is successful, the move to EMU, including a common currency managed by a European Central Bank, will resolve the politically difficult question of how to determine monetary policy for the European currency area.

4 Conclusion

At the global level, there appears to be neither the political will nor the popular support to commit the economic policies of the largest countries to the maintenance of a global system of fixed exchange rates at the expense of other critical objectives of national economic policy. Neither, apparently, is there much enthusiasm for allowing one national central bank to call the tune for world monetary policy or for creating a world central bank that would play this essential role.

Old systems based on metallic monies, most notably the gold standard, provided natural solutions to these problems. The popular will demanded and supported the adherence of national monetary policies to common metallic standards, and ultimate authority for the management of world monetary policy was not placed in the hands of any one person or group of persons but, rather, was wielded by the more impartial vagaries of the world's supply of precious metals.

For good or ill, these old systems are unlikely to return. At the national level, old fears of the inevitable and excessive inflationary instability of paper money have receded, and reasonably well-managed paper-money standards have demonstrated a capacity to deliver acceptable macroeconomic stability and to sustain widespread political support. With such monetary standards functioning at the national level, there is no longer a natural and obvious candidate for "world money," and there is no longer a strong political basis for subordinating the monetary policies of the world's largest nations to the will of a greater sovereign.

II

EXCHANGE RATES
AND THE ADJUSTMENT PROCESS

4

Exchange Rates, Prices, and External Adjustment in the United States and Japan

PETER HOOPER AND JAIME MARQUEZ

1 Introduction

The experience of the past twenty years with generally floating exchange rates has provided an excellent opportunity to observe and analyze movements in and interactions among exchange rates, prices, and external adjustment. Economists have responded by producing a substantial and wide-ranging literature on the theoretical and empirical linkages between exchange rates and external balances. A significant portion of that literature, concerning the reaction of trade volumes, trade prices, and external balances to changes in exchange rates, will be the focus of our discussion here. Our objectives are to provide an analytical review of the literature and, drawing upon the most commonly used analytical approach, to assess the influence of exchange-rate movements on external adjustment in the United States and Japan, the two countries whose external imbalances have dominated all others over the past decade.

We can draw and build upon several excellent surveys of research on exchange rates, prices, and external balances. Goldstein and Khan (1985) review work on income and price elasticities for much of the floating-rate period. Their survey is augmented by the contributions of Bryant, Holtham, and Hooper (1988) and Marquez (1993). Much of the work in this area since Goldstein and Khan has focused on the relation between exchange rates and trade prices, that is, exchange-rate pass-through. Evidence of incomplete pass-through, or the existence of pricing-to-market behavior by firms engaged in international trade, has implied a weakening of the traditional link between exchange rates and trade volumes. Knetter (1992) surveys a significant portion of this recent literature.

The views expressed in this paper are the authors' and should not be interpreted as reflecting those of the Board of Governors of the Federal Reserve System or other members of its staff. We thank Giuseppe Bertola, William Branson, Neil Ericsson, Jon Faust, Joe Gagnon, Michael Knetter, Catherine Mann, Richard Marston, and Ellen Meade for their helpful comments and suggestions. Mahim Chellappa provided excellent research assistance.

In assessing the recent experience of the United States and Japan, we shall be updating and extending efforts to account for developments in the U.S. external balance by Bryant (1988), Helkie and Hooper (1988), Hooper and Mann (1989a), Cline (1989, 1991), Lawrence (1990), and Krugman (1991) and in the Japanese external balance by Yoshitomi (1991).

The relations between exchange rates and trade prices and volumes are viewed as key parameters in what has become the mainstream macroeconomic model for analyzing external adjustment, the expectations-augmented Mundell-Fleming model.[1] Exchange rates are a primary endogenous channel through which the external balance is influenced by changes in economic policies and shifts in intertemporal preferences among private agents. Movements in exchange rates act by altering relative prices and the allocations of expenditure and production across domestic and foreign goods. Our intent is to assess just how significant the exchange-rate channel has been, after correcting for other influences, especially during the period of floating exchange rates.[2] Typically, empirical estimates of these exchange-rate parameters are derived in a partial-equilibrium framework that takes as given such endogenous variables as expenditures, outputs, and domestic prices. Our survey focuses primarily on this partial-equilibrium framework.

Our review of the literature begins in Sections 2 and 3 with a presentation of the standard theoretical approach to the modeling of trade volumes and prices in a partial-equilibrium framework of demand and supply for imperfect substitutes. We stress recent innovations to theory that are largely on the supply side, pertaining in particular to exchange-rate pass-through. We do not address the intertemporal approach to the external balance, which is covered by Assaf Razin in Chapter 5 of this volume, although the partial-equilibrium parameters we consider could easily be imbedded in a general-equilibrium intertemporal model. In Section 4, we survey empirical estimates of the price elasticities of demand for real exports and imports and estimates of the effects of exchange-rate changes on import and export prices. Our survey is limited to studies employing conventional trade-model specifications that yield readily identifiable price elasticities and/or pass-through coefficients; we do not include, for example, recent studies that have estimated reduced-form equations

---

[1] See Krugman (1991) for a verbal description of this model and Frenkel and Razin (1987b) for a more formal presentation. Frankel (1988) provides a helpful review of the way most of the major global macroeconometric models relate to this simplified two-country theoretical approach.

[2] Strictly speaking, we assess the extent to which movements in exchange rates, whatever the cause, influence the external balance through their effects on the prices of imports and exports. In principle, the exchange rate can also influence the external balance through the effects of a change in the terms of trade on real income and expenditures—the Harberger-Laursen-Metzler effect. Obstfeld (1982), Svensson and Razin (1983), and others have noted that the sign of this effect is ambiguous, because it depends on the persistence of the exchange-rate shock. More recently, Mendoza (1992) has found some empirical evidence to suggest that the effect may be significant for countries that are open to large and sustained exchange-rate shocks.

for the trade balance.[3] Although much of the literature in this area has focused on empirical estimates for the United States, we also devote some attention to studies presenting estimates for Japan. Section 5 contains our analysis of the extent to which movements in exchange rates have contributed to external adjustment since the early 1980s. We review the data for the United States and Japan, estimate trade equations using both standard and nonstandard specifications, and use simulation analysis to illustrate the partial-equilibrium influences of exchange-rate changes. Section 6 presents our conclusions and suggestions for further research.

2 Modeling Demand

To link exchange rates with external balances and trade prices, we begin with the conventional partial-equilibrium demand-side approach to modeling real trade flows.[4] We then extend the conventional theoretical analysis to incorporate recent work on the supply side dealing with the issue of exchange-rate pass-through.

The Conventional Model of the Real Trade Balance

At the most basic level of analysis, the partial-equilibrium model works with two countries, each producing a single tradable good that is an imperfect substitute for the good produced in the other country.[5] Consumers in each country consume both goods and allocate their current nominal expenditures

---

[3] Several such studies, including Rose and Yellen (1989) and Rose (1990, 1991), have investigated the sensitivity of trade to exchange rates in single-equation models of the trade balance. Their results have challenged the prevailing view that exchange-rate changes have potent effects on external balances. Specifically, for the United States and several other industrial countries, Rose and Yellen find little empirical support for a causal long-run relationship running from the real exchange rate to the real trade balance. Meade (1991) has found, however, that many of their study's results are reversed when alternative data sources, different estimation periods, and/or small changes in empirical specification are incorporated.

[4] Good background expositions of this approach and of its relation to the more general two-country model can be found in Kenen (1985), Krugman (1991), and Caves, Frankel, and Jones (1993).

[5] The alternative assumption of perfect substitutes, which implies the law of one price, has been rejected by the data. Wide swings in the relative-price indexes for manufactured goods over the past two decades have indicated that the law of one price fails at the macroeconomic level. Moreover, various studies, including Isard (1977), Kravis and Lipsey (1978), and Giovannini (1988), have shown that, outside the markets for basic raw commodities, which account for a relatively small portion of total trade, the law of one price fails to hold for a wide range of narrowly defined classes of goods. See Goldstein and Khan (1985) for a discussion of the imperfect-substitutes and perfect-substitutes models.

(Y and Y^*) between the quantities of the two goods produced (Q and Q^*), given the prices of those goods (P and P^*), so as to maximize their utilities.[6] Prices of the two goods are assumed to be sticky and, for the time being, are not affected by changes in external demands. The home country's demand for the foreign good measured in terms of home currency at constant prices ($[P^*/S{\cdot}P]DQ^*$) is a function of home expenditure and the prices of the two goods expressed in units of home currency:

$$(P^*/SP)DQ^* = f(Y, P^*/S, P) , \qquad (1)$$

where S is the nominal spot exchange rate in units of foreign currency per unit of home currency, and $f_1 > 0, f_2 < 0$, and $f_3 > 0$, with f_i denoting the partial derivative of f with respect to the ith argument. Assuming that (1) is homogeneous in prices and nominal expenditure yields

$$(P^*/SP)DQ^* = f(y, P^*/S{\cdot}P) , \qquad (2)$$

where $y = Y/P$. Similarly, the foreign country's demand for home goods (D^*Q) is a function of foreign real expenditure and the relative prices of the two goods expressed in units of foreign currency:

$$D^*Q = f^*(y^*, S{\cdot}P/P^*) , \qquad (3)$$

where $f_1^* > 0$, and $f_2^* < 0$. The home country's external balance can be written in real terms as the difference between the quantity of exports and the quantity of imports:[7]

$$D^*Q - P^*/S{\cdot}P)DQ^* = nx(y, y^*, S{\cdot}P/P^*) , \qquad (4)$$

where $nx_1 < 0$, $nx_2 > 0$, and $nx_3 < 0$; the trade balance in nominal terms is

$$P{\cdot}D^*Q - (P^*/S)DQ^* = nxv(y, y^*, S{\cdot}P/P^*, P, P^*/S) . \qquad (5)$$

At this highly simplified level, the ratio $S{\cdot}P/P^*$ can be viewed, alternatively, as the relative price of exports, the inverse of the relative price of imports, the

---

[6] Although theory dictates that wealth or current expenditure is the appropriate scale variable for the import-demand equation, most of the empirical studies we survey employ current GDP. A theoretical case can be made for using output instead of expenditure as the scale variable, inasmuch as a good deal of world trade takes place in intermediate goods and raw materials. In any event, Hooper and Mann (1989a) find that it makes essentially no difference empirically whether one uses domestic expenditure or GDP to model aggregate U.S. import demand.

[7] Quantities are measured in units of home currency valued at constant prices for some base year; prices are indexed to the same base year.

terms of trade, or the real exchange rate. Appendix A outlines how these different measures of relative prices or real exchange rates are related to one another under more realistic assumptions; in Section 5, we consider how much the various measures differ empirically. With sticky prices, a movement in the nominal exchange rate S, induced, for example, by a shift in one country's economic policies, will affect relative prices and the external balance.[8]

Introduction of Nontraded Goods

The model becomes more complex when we allow for nontraded as well as traded goods. We continue to assume that the traded goods produced in both countries are differentiated, but, in this case, we relabel the price terms P and P^*, which in equations (1) through (5) referred to the prices of traded goods only, as P_T and P_T^*, and use P and P^* to denote indexes of the prices of tradables and nontradables:

$$P = \tau P_T + (1 - \tau)P_N , \tag{6}$$

$$P^* = \tau^* P_T^* + (1 - \tau^*)P_N^* , \tag{7}$$

where τ and τ^* are the shares of tradable goods in expenditures at home and abroad.

The home country's import demand is now written as

$$(P_T^*/S \cdot P_T)DQ^* = Q_m = f(y, P_T^*/SP) , \tag{8}$$

where Q_m is the quantity of goods imported. Similarly, the demand for the home country's exports is written as

$$D^*Q = Q_x = f^*(y^*, S \cdot P_T/P^*) . \tag{9}$$

In this case, the real trade balance is written as a function of two expenditure terms and two relative-price terms:

$$Q_x - (P_T^*/S \cdot P_T)Q_m = nx(y, y^*, S \cdot P_T/P^*, P_T^*/S \cdot P) . \tag{10}$$

The nominal trade balance is written as

$$P_T Q_x - (P_T^*/S)Q_m = nxv(y, y^*, S \cdot P_T/P^*, P_T^*/S \cdot P,$$
$$P_T, P_T^*/S) . \tag{11}$$

---

[8] In the presence of fully flexible prices, of course, shifts in nominal exchange rates would not influence relative prices.

Assuming for the moment that the prices of tradable goods are fixed in the currency of the exporting country and not immediately influenced by movements in exchange rates, the effect of a change in the exchange rate on the nominal trade balance depends on three factors. The first is the price responsiveness of real imports, which is defined in elasticity form as

$$\eta_p^{dm} = \partial\log(Q_m)/\partial\log(P_T^*/S{\cdot}P) \tag{12}$$

and is expected to be negative. The second is the price responsiveness of real exports, which in elasticity form equals

$$\eta_p^{dx} = \partial\log(Q_x)/\partial\log(S{\cdot}P_T/P^*) < 0 \ . \tag{13}$$

The third is the valuation effect induced by the change in the exchange rate. Specifically, as equation (11) indicates, changes in the price of imports (P_T^*/S) and therefore the value of imports ($[P_T^*/S]Q_m$) rise in proportion to a depreciation of the home currency (a decline in S).

The Marshall-Lerner Condition

The Marshall-Lerner condition holds that a depreciation of a country's currency will increase its nominal trade balance if the sum of the price elasticities of demand, with signs reversed ($-[\eta_p^{dm} + \eta_p^{dx}]$), exceeds 1. That is, the real trade balance must rise enough to offset the direct effect of the depreciation on the value of imports. This condition assumes that the trade balance is initially zero. If the trade balance is in deficit and the price elasticity of imports (with signs reversed) is less than 1, the elasticities will have to sum to more than 1 for a depreciation to raise the nominal trade balance. For example, if imports are twice as large as exports and the price elasticity of imports is zero, the price elasticity of exports (and therefore the sum of the elasticities, in absolute value) would have to be 2 in order for real exports to rise enough to offset the increase in the value of imports associated with the depreciation. Similarly, if the trade balance is in surplus, the condition can be met with elasticities summing to less than 1.

The Marshall-Lerner condition also assumes that the elasticities of supply of traded goods are infinite and that their prices are fixed in terms of the exporting country's currency. If the prices of traded goods respond to the exchange-rate change, the trade balance could improve even if the price elasticities of demand sum to less than 1 (in absolute value). That is, if the import price (P_T^*/S) rises by less than the full amount of the depreciation, a smaller improvement in the real trade balance is needed to offset the rise in the value of imports.

Dynamics, the J-Curve, and Other Issues

Up to this point, we have used an essentially static framework and have abstracted from dynamics in modeling the adjustment of demand to changes in prices. In empirical models, exchange-rate changes typically affect import prices before trade quantities begin to respond, producing the familiar J-curve in the response of the trade balance to a depreciation (see Meade [1988], Moffet [1989], and Marquez [1991] for more detailed discussions). The trade balance follows a J-curve (relative to its baseline path) because the price and value of imports rise first, causing the trade balance to fall initially. Thereafter, the trade balance rises gradually as real net exports respond positively over time to the changes in relative prices. The Marshall-Lerner condition is based on long-run elasticities, after all adjustment lags have been worked through—lags in the response of trade prices to exchange-rate changes, and lags in the response of real trade flows. The latter can reflect such factors as recognition-response lags, contract lags, and order-delivery lags.

We should also note that empirical trade models increasingly have included in their structural trade-volume equations variables representing cyclical changes in demand (or nonprice rationing) and secular changes in supply (relative capital stocks or a time trend). Nonprice rationing refers in this context to the use of such rationing techniques as changing order backlogs, delivery times, promotional effort, and so forth, that firms may use before altering their prices in the face of a shift in demand (Gregory, 1971). Secular supply variables are discussed further below. Although the inclusion of such variables has been found to have a significant effect on estimated income elasticities, the variables generally have negligible effects on estimated relative-price elasticities (Hooper, 1989; Blecker, 1992; Marquez and Ericsson, 1993).

3 Modeling Supply and Price Determination

The importance of supply and the endogeneity of import prices with respect to import demand has been recognized at least since the work of Orcutt (1950). Nevertheless, as noted by Marquez (1993), most of the empirical studies in this area have continued to assume that prices are determined independently of external demand. This independence is based in some cases on the assumption that export suppliers are perfectly competitive with constant returns to scale, an assumption that yields a perfectly elastic export supply curve. In other cases, the importance of noncompetitive markets is recognized, but price-markup equations are used to determine prices quasi-independently of external demand.

Markup Equations

The markup-equation approach draws on price models developed by Eckstein and Fromm (1968) and Dixit and Stiglitz (1977) and has been applied to trade-price determination by Clark (1974), Helkie and Hooper (1988), Hooper and Mann (1989b), and others. Typically, import prices expressed in terms of the exporting country's currency are set at a markup over foreign costs (C^*):

$$P_T^* = \lambda(C^*) . \tag{14}$$

The markup factor (λ) is treated as a function of excess demand or capacity utilization by the exporter (CU^*), and, assuming some degree of pricing-to-market behavior by the exporter (described in more detail below), the markup in the import market is then represented by

$$\lambda = g(CU^*, S{\cdot}P_T) . \tag{15}$$

Substituting (15) into (14) yields

$$P_T^* = g(C^*, CU^*, S{\cdot}P_T) . \tag{16}$$

Some studies (Helkie and Hooper [1988], for example) have argued that, because of differences between the volatility of exchange rates and of domestic prices or production costs, proportional changes in these variables may not have identical effects on import prices. A more general form of (16) is therefore

$$P_T^* = g(C^*, CU^*, S, P_T, \ldots) , \tag{17}$$

where $g_1 > 0$, $g_2 > 0$, $g_3 > 0$, and $g_4 > 0$.

Exchange-Rate Pass-Through

The markup approach to import-price modeling has been augmented by a substantial and growing literature focusing on exchange-rate pass-through in import-price determination. Early on, this literature focused on the case of perfect competition with less than perfectly elastic supply. More recently, it has concentrated on various models of imperfect competition, including static models of profit maximization by firms with monopoly power and dynamic models of pricing-to-market behavior.

Before surveying this work, we shall define terms more precisely. Pass-through is generally defined as the *ceteris paribus* responsiveness of a country's import prices to changes in its exchange rate. For the moment, we follow the presentation in earlier sections and specify the import price (P_m) as

$$P_m = P_T^*/S \,, \tag{18}$$

so that the rate of exchange-rate pass-through (φ) is defined as

$$\varphi = \partial\log(P_m)/\partial\log(S) < 0 \,. \tag{19}$$

If, for example, a 10 percent depreciation of the dollar (decline in S) raises U.S. import prices by 6 percent, 60 percent of the depreciation is said to have been passed through, that is, $\varphi = -0.6$. Full (100 percent) pass-through would imply that $\varphi = -1$.

Equation (18) shows that the depreciation must be absorbed into lower foreign prices (P_{T*}) to the extent that it is not fully passed through to higher import prices. This effect can be shown more rigorously by taking the logarithm of (18), differentiating the result, dividing through by $\partial\log(S)$, and rearranging terms to obtain

$$\partial\log(P_T^*)/\partial\log(S) = \partial\log(P_m)/\partial\log(S) + 1 = \varphi + 1 \,. \tag{20}$$

Continuing with our earlier example, if pass-through is 60 percent ($\varphi = -0.6$), a 10 percent depreciation implies that the foreign price declines by 4 percent ($\varphi + 1$ [$= 0.4$] times 10 percent).

Static Models

A variety of theoretical models have been used to explain the lack of complete pass-through. Early work on the subject appeared in the wake of currency realignments under the Bretton Woods system and the 1970s depreciation of the dollar during the transition to floating exchange rates. Branson (1972), using an equilibrium demand and supply model in the spirit of Kindleberger (1963) and Haberler (1949), showed that pass-through is less than complete if the price elasticity of the supply of exports is less than infinite, as would be the case for large countries. Specifically, he showed that, under perfect competition and with constant elasticities of demand and supply, the pass-through coefficient is defined as

$$\varphi = -1/(1 - \epsilon/\delta) \,, \tag{21}$$

where ϵ is the price elasticity of demand for imports (assumed to be negative) and δ is the price elasticity of supply (assumed to be positive). It can be seen from equation (21) that pass-through is complete ($\varphi = -1$) when supply is infinitely elastic. Moreover, the smaller the elasticity of supply and the greater the elasticity of demand, the smaller the degree of pass-through coefficient (that is, φ approaches zero). As a depreciation of the importing country's currency raises the import price, import demand shifts down along an upward-sloping foreign-export supply curve, causing the foreign export price to fall. The steeper the export supply curve and the flatter the demand curve, the greater the decline in the foreign price (P_{T*}) and the less the pass-through of the depreciation to import prices.

Interest in the issue of pass-through was sparked again by the U.S. experience from 1985 to 1987, when the dollar depreciated sharply but import prices rose only moderately. Recent work on the subject has focused on various models of imperfect competition. Most studies have assumed static profit maximization by firms with some degree of monopoly power stemming from, for example, product differentiation or oligopolistic market structure.

Profit maximization by the representative foreign exporting firm is written as

$$\text{Max}_{Q_m}[Q_{mS} \cdot P_m - C^*(W^*, S \cdot P_r, Q_m)] \, , \tag{22}$$

where the firm's profits (in its own currency) are equal to the quantity of goods sold times the price the firm sets in the import market (translated into its own currency) minus its costs of production. We assume that costs depend on the wage rate (W^*), the domestic-currency price of raw-material inputs ($P_r^* = S \cdot P_r$), where P_r is the international (dollar) price of raw materials, and (given nonconstant returns to scale) the quantity produced (Q_m).

The first-order condition obtained from (22) is

$$S \cdot P_m(Q_m; y, P)(1 - 1/\eta) - \partial C/\partial Q_m = 0 \, , \tag{23}$$

where $P_m(Q_m; y, P)$ is the inverted import-demand function (solved for price) and $\eta = -(\partial Q_m/\partial P_m)(P_m/Q_m)$ is the associated price elasticity of demand with its sign reversed. Let $Q_m^0 = Q(S, W^*, P_r)$ be the optimal or profit-maximizing level of production associated with (23); substituting Q_m^0 into the inverted import-demand equation yields a reduced-form equation for the import price:

$$P_m = P_m(W^*, P_r, S, y, P) \, . \tag{24}$$

To derive the coefficient for the pass-through of the exchange rates to the import price (φ), we follow Branson and Marston (1989), Feenstra (1989), and Knetter (1992) by totally differentiating (23) and rearranging terms to obtain

$$\varphi = d\log(P_m)/d\log(S)$$

$$= -[(\eta - 1) - \eta\mu/P_m)]/[(\eta - 1) - \eta_q - \theta\eta/S(\partial P_m/\partial Q_m)] \, , \tag{25}$$

where η is the price elasticity of demand (with sign reversed), as defined earlier, and

η_q = $d\log(\eta)/d\log(Q_m)$ is the derivative of the elasticity of demand with respect to quantity (the curvature of the demand schedule);

θ = $(\partial^2 C/\partial Q_m^2)$ is the derivative of marginal cost with respect to output (the degree of returns to scale);

μ = $(\partial^2 C/\partial Q_m \partial P_{r*})P_r[(\partial P_r/\partial S)(S/P_r) + 1]$ is the product of the derivative of marginal cost with respect to raw-material prices $(\partial_2 C/\partial Q_m \partial P_r)$ and the derivative with respect to S of the price of raw materials expressed in the exporter's currency $(P_r[(\partial P_r/\partial S)(S/P_r) + 1])$;[9]

$\partial P_m/\partial Q_m$ is the slope of the demand curve and is negative.

Pass-through will be complete (100 percent) if the elasticity of demand is constant ($\eta_q = 0$), if marginal costs (or returns to scale) are constant ($\theta = 0$), and if raw-material prices in the exporting country are unaffected by exchange rates ($\mu = 0$). In this case, (25) simplifies to

$$\varphi = -(\eta - 1)/(\eta - 1) = -1 . \tag{26}$$

It can also be seen from (25) that pass-through will be less than complete ($-1 < \varphi < 0$) under any of several conditions. One condition is decreasing returns to scale ($\theta > 0$). The intuitive explanation for this result is that a depreciation (decline in S) reduces import demand, which in turn reduces the exporter's unit costs, causing the markup price to rise less than proportionately to the exchange rate. A second condition is the sensitivity of the exporter's production costs to a decline in S resulting from the negative effect of a depreciation on raw-material prices expressed in the exporter's currency ($\mu > 0$).[10] A third involves the response of the price elasticity of demand to changes in quantities sold. If the price elasticity of demand increases in response to lower sales, profit-maximizing producers will raise their prices less than if the elasticity were constant. Pass-through can conceivably be greater than 100 percent if returns to scale are increasing or if the price elasticity of demand declines in response to lower sales.

The monopolistic approach to pass-through has been adopted by a number of economists, using variations on the basic model. Dornbusch (1987), Krugman (1987), Murphy (1989), and Ohno (1989) assume constant marginal costs and nonconstant elasticity of demand. Mann (1986a, 1986b), Giovan-

[9]The latter derivative is obtained by differentiating $P_r^* = S \cdot P_r$ with respect to S.

[10]This condition will hold unless either marginal costs are unresponsive to raw-material prices or the exporter's raw-material prices (P_{r*}) are unresponsive to exchange-rate changes. It can be seen from the second term in the definition of μ that P_r would be unaffected by S only if the elasticity of P_r with respect to S is -1 (that is, if international prices of raw materials in dollars respond inversely in proportion to changes in S).

nini (1988), Branson and Marston (1989), Feenstra (1989), Marston (1990), Gagnon and Knetter (1992), and Knetter (1992) allow for increasing marginal costs. Branson and Marston (1989), Hooper and Mann (1989b), Ohno (1989), and Marston (1990) take into account the role of raw-material prices in reducing pass-through; the other studies do not.

Giovannini, Knetter, Marston, and Ohno consider the case of a firm that sells in more than one market. This generalization allows for more explicit analysis of pricing-to-market behavior or price discrimination across markets (a primary focus of Marston's analysis), but it does not alter the basic insights about pass-through derived from equation (25). Strictly speaking, pricing to market is a special case of incomplete pass-through; it requires some degree of market segmentation so that firms can set prices differently in different markets. In this case, the exporting firm determines not just one price (P_f^*) but multiple prices, each dependent on the demand conditions in a specific market.

Some researchers have modeled pricing-to-market behavior by appealing to alternative market structures that highlight strategic pricing behavior of firms. Dornbusch (1987), Krugman (1987), Fisher (1989), and Knetter (1992) consider oligopolistic markets, where a firm's maximizing decision is directly affected by the prices of its competitors, and where the degree of pass-through depends on the degree of market concentration.[11] One drawback to the oligopoly approach is that it is usually based on the assumption of homogeneous products, whereas most international trade takes place in differentiated products.

Dynamic Models and Hysteresis

The studies of pricing behavior we have surveyed thus far consider primarily longer-term, static explanations for incomplete pass-through and pricing to market, invoking assumptions about market structure. Giovannini (1988) and Feenstra (1989) introduce a dynamic element by assuming that exporting firms maximize expected future profits and must deal with exchange-rate uncertainty. Giovannini finds that, with prices set in advance, pass-through depends on the currency denomination of contracts and the distribution of exchange-rate movements. Under his assumptions, transitory movements in exchange rates are passed through less than permanent movements. In Feenstra's empirical implementation of a similar model, expectations are formed on the basis of current and lagged values of exchange rates. Ohno (1989)

---

[11] In addition to considering alternative market structures, Fisher addresses the role of exchange-rate expectations and the way alternative hypotheses about expectations can interact with alternative assumptions about market structure to influence the rate of pass-through.

introduces dynamic adjustment into the price equation by positing contract lags; exchange-rate changes are passed through gradually over time as existing contracts expire.

Several other studies have focused more comprehensively on short-term, dynamic explanations for pricing-to-market behavior. Krugman (1987) notes that pricing to market can occur in the face of temporary swings in exchange rates when there are significant costs of adjustment. Krugman and Baldwin (1987) and Baldwin (1988) use a monopolistic-competition framework, and Dixit (1989) uses a competitive-market framework to argue that significant fixed costs to market entry can lead to substantial differences in pass-through behavior for large versus small changes in exchange rates. A small appreciation of the home currency, for example, may result in moderate (or no) pass-through, which will then be reversed when the appreciation is reversed. By contrast, an appreciation large enough to overcome the fixed costs of entry will draw additional foreign firms into the home market, increasing competition, pushing down prices, and resulting in proportionately greater pass-through. Furthermore, the change in market structure following the large appreciation will alter the pass-through coefficient for small exchange-rate changes; with profit margins reduced by the entry of new firms, small exchange-rate changes will be passed through more than previously. When the large appreciation is reversed by a large depreciation, the desire not to write off the sunk costs of entry will keep firms from leaving the market and will result in less pass-through than during the large appreciation. This pass-through asymmetry produces hysteresis in import prices; the reversal of a large appreciation leaves import prices permanently lower than they would have been if the swing in exchange rates had not taken place.

In a related study, Froot and Klemperer (1989) postulate an oligopolistic model in which the future demands faced by firms depend on their current market shares (through brand loyalty, and so forth). This intertemporal dependence implies that the degree of pass-through will depend on whether an exchange-rate change is expected to be transitory or permanent. Firms are willing to absorb transitory exchange-rate changes into (or out of) their current profits (that is, they price to market) in order to maintain their current market shares and thus their future sales. Competitive pressures, however, force more complete (and immediate) pass-through of a permanent exchange-rate change. The different effects of transitory and permanent changes in exchange rates when market share matters are therefore analogous to the different effects of small and large changes in the presence of entry costs, and they may likewise lead to hysteresis in import prices.

These dynamic considerations, including both expectations and contracts, have influenced the specification of trade-price equations and pass-through coefficients. They are typically reflected by the use of distributed lags. Froot and Klemperer, however, treat expectations in a more forward-looking manner; they use both forward exchange rates and survey data to represent exchange-rate expectations.

Exchange Rates and Supply in the Long Run

Other research has considered the possibility that firms will shift not only sales and distribution networks in response to large exchange-rate changes, but also the location of their production facilities. When nominal wages are sticky, when labor is relatively immobile across countries, and when capital and labor are complements in production, movements in exchange rates may alter relative labor costs across countries by enough to induce shifts in the location of productive capital. Hooper (1989) finds some evidence to support this hypothesis, indicating the possibility that exchange rates have much longer-lagged partial-equilibrium effects on external balances than are suggested by normal lags on partial-equilibrium price elasticities.[12] In particular, he found that the long-term downward trend in the stock of U.S. manufacturing capital relative to that in other OECD countries was interrupted (and partly reversed) during the late 1970s, after a significant depreciation of the dollar raised average manufacturing unit labor costs of other G-10 countries above those in the United States. The downward trend in the ratio of capital stocks resumed with the appreciation of the dollar during the first half of the 1980s, which moved U.S. unit labor costs back above the average foreign level. Hooper predicted that, in the wake of the dollar's sharp decline through 1987, relatively attractive labor costs in the United States would, *ceteris paribus*, reverse again the downtrend in the capital-stock ratio. This prediction was not realized, however, until cyclical recovery in the United States coincided with economic downturns abroad during 1992.

Although the possibility of a longer-term link between exchange rates and trade flows, through investment- and supply-side developments, may warrant further investigation, several complicating factors must be considered. First, the decisions of firms about the location of production facilities are not based on relative labor costs alone. A domestically generated investment boom in Japan and the stimulus to investment in Europe afforded by Europe 1992 caused the U.S.-to-foreign capital-stock ratio to continue on a strong downward trend during the late 1980s despite a substantial decline in U.S. unit labor costs relative to those abroad. Second, even after the sharp depreciation of the dollar through 1987, U.S. unit labor costs remained far above those in most developing countries, and the U.S. capital stock seemed likely to continue to decline relative to capital stocks in those areas. Third, a currency

---

[12] Several other studies, including Caves (1989) and Froot and Stein (1991), have investigated the effect of exchange-rate changes on direct investment, but these studies have focused on the financial flows associated with direct investment rather than the location of actual plant and equipment.

depreciation would have a significant positive effect on the external balance through this longer-term channel only if it were accompanied (or induced) by a shift in policies or private preferences leading to an increase in domestic saving relative to domestic investment.

Movements in the capital-stock ratio may have implications for views about the longer-term trend in the equilibrium real exchange rate for the dollar. As Krugman (1989a) has noted, the "Houthakker-Magee result," which says that the income elasticity of U.S. imports is substantially greater than that of U.S. exports, implies a secular downward trend in the dollar's equilibrium real exchange rate; if incomes in the United States and elsewhere expand at comparable rates over the long term, the U.S. trade deficit will widen continuously unless the dollar depreciates. Hooper (1976, 1989) and Helkie and Hooper (1988) have argued that the estimated gap in income elasticities reflects, at least in part, secular trends in missing supply factors that are correlated with trends in income variables. Rapid growth in imports relative to income over the past two decades has not necessarily reflected a high income elasticity of U.S. demand for the types of goods being imported. Much of that growth has instead reflected the emergence of new suppliers abroad. In principle, increases in supply abroad should be reflected in declines in U.S. import prices. However, as Feenstra (1991) has noted, existing aggregate price indexes do not adequately capture the introduction of new products (or of existing products by new supplying countries), and they may well be biased upward as a result.

Helkie and Hooper, in their various studies, have attempted to correct for the possible bias in relative prices and have estimated income elasticities by including relative private capital stocks as proxies for the missing supply factors in import- and export-demand equations. They find that inclusion of the capital-stock variable significantly reduces (and in some cases actually eliminates) the difference in income elasticities between U.S. imports and exports, without having much effect on estimated price elasticities.[13] This finding has important implications for the trade effects of shocks to income, but the implications for a possible secular downtrend in the dollar are moot if the longer-term trend in the capital-stock variable persists.

4 Survey of Empirical Studies

Estimates of Price Elasticities

Over the postwar period, a large number of empirical studies, using a wide variety of theoretical models and estimation techniques, have estimated price

[13] Specifically, they find that foreign fixed private capital stocks generally have grown faster than the U.S. capital stock, a result consistent with an increase in the relative supply of foreign goods and a decline in their relative price (if measured correctly). Adding the capital-stock vari-

elasticities in trade. This section attempts to distill the results of a significant portion of these studies into "consensus" estimates and to note how the estimates are affected by alternative estimation techniques. Although our survey is wide-ranging, we have limited our selection in several ways to keep it manageable. First, we focus on estimates that are based on some variant of the conventional theoretical (imperfect-substitutes) model described in the preceding sections. Second, we consider only studies that assume constant elasticities (that is, use a log-linear functional form). Third, we limit our review to studies that report elasticities for aggregate trade flows, whether or not they were estimated directly from those flows. Several studies that are excluded by these criteria are also mentioned briefly. Previous surveys of price elasticities, some of them broader than this, are provided by Stern, Francis, and Schumacher (1976), Goldstein and Khan (1985), Kohli (1991), and Marquez (1993).[14]

Our selection criteria allow for considerable variation in the theoretical and empirical approaches to the estimation of price elasticities. We pay particular attention to differences across studies in whether or not price homogeneity is imposed, in the sample period, in the periodicity of the data (annual versus quarterly), in the estimation technique (single-equation techniques with prices treated exogenously versus one of several simultaneous-equation techniques with prices treated endogenously), in the degree of commodity disaggregation (whether, for example, oil is included or excluded), and in the treatment of adjustment lags (Almon lags, Shiller lags, lagged dependent variables, or no lags).[15] Some of the differences for which we have not attempted to account are differences across studies in the data used for prices, income, and so on, differences with respect to the aggregation or disaggregation of trade flows by region and in the method of aggregation used, and differences arising from the inclusion of additional determinants of demand (rationing variables other than price, and so on).[16]

Table 4.1 lists thirty-seven studies and their estimates of the long-run price elasticities for key industrial countries, Canada, Germany, Japan, the United Kingdom, and the United States.[17] Most of the studies report estimates for the

---

able to the trade equations results in lower estimates of the income elasticity of U.S. imports and somewhat higher estimates of the income elasticity of U.S. exports.

[14] In particular, a large number of unpublished studies have eluded our net.

[15] If $y_t = \Sigma_i \beta_i X_{t-i}$, using Almon lags amounts to assuming that the βs lie on a polynomial curve. In the case of a second-degree Almon lag, for example, the lag coefficients, β_i, are defined by the quadratic equation $\beta_i = \alpha_0 + i\alpha_1 + i^2 \alpha_2$. Shiller lags assume that the polynomial is not known precisely; in the previous example, $\beta_i = \alpha_0 + i\alpha_1 + i^2 \alpha_2 +$ random disturbance.

[16] Some of these measurement issues are discussed in the next section and in Appendix A. Other related measurement issues are considered at length in Hooper and Richardson (1991).

[17] The long-run elasticities measure the full effects of a change in relative prices after all lags have been worked through.

TABLE 4.1

Chronology of Estimated Price Elasticities: Selected Studies for Industrial Countries

Study/Source/Commodity	Estimator/ Price Behavior	Dynamic Structure/ Homogeneity	Price Data/ Frequency; Sample	Country	Price Elasticities	
					Exports	Imports
Chang (1946, table 4) Total	OLS Exog.	Static Yes	Multilateral A; 1924–38	U.S. U.K. Japan Germany		−0.97 −0.28 −0.47 −0.37
Krause (1962, table 2) Nonoil	OLS Exog.	Static Yes	Cross-sec. A; 1947–58	U.S.		−1.98
Kreinin (1967, table 3) Total	OLS Exog.	DL Yes	Multilateral A; 1954–64	U.S.		−1.11
Heien (1968, pp. 705–709) Total	OLS Exog.	DL Yes	Multilateral A; 1951–65	U.S. Germany Canada		−0.62 −1.82 −0.73
Houthakker and Magee (1969, table 1) Total	OLS Exog.	Static Yes	Multilateral A; 1951–66	U.S. U.K. Japan Germany Canada	−1.51 −0.44 −0.80 +1.70 −0.59	−0.54 +0.22 −0.72 −0.24 −1.46
Marston (1971, table 4) Total	OLS Exog.	Koyck Yes	Multilateral Q; 1955–67	U.K.		+0.27

(continued)

TABLE 4.1 (*Continued*)

Study/Source/Commodity	Estimator/Price Behavior	Dynamic Structure/Homogeneity	Price Data/Frequency; Sample	Price Elasticities		
				Country	Exports	Imports
Magee (1972, p. 9) Nonoil	OLS Exog.	Static Yes	Bilateral A; 1951–69	U.S.	−3.75	−1.26
Taplin (1973, table 2) Total	OLS Exog.	Static Yes	Multilateral A; 1953–70	U.S. U.K. Japan Germany Canada		−1.05 −0.22 −0.81 −0.47 −1.59
Clark (1974, pp. 220–228)* Nonoil	OLS Exog.	PDL Yes	Multilateral Q; 1963–73	U.S.	−0.59	−3.72
Miller and Fratianni (1974, table 1) Total	OLS Exog.	Koyck Yes	Multilateral Q; 1956–72	U.S.	−1.30	−0.73
Ahluwalia and Hernández-Catá (1975, table 1, p. 208) Nonoil	ILS Endo.	DL No	Multilateral Q; 1960–73	U.S.		−1.6
Khan and Ross (1975, table 1) Total	OLS Exog.	Static Yes	Multilateral S; 1960–72	U.S. U.K. Japan Germany Canada		−1.00 +0.40 +0.15 −0.53 −2.13

Study	Method	Dynamics	Data	Country		
Hooper (1976, table 2) Nonoil	OLS Exog.	DL Yes	Multilateral Q; 1956–75	U.S.	−0.83	−0.54
Murray and Ginman (1976, table 2) Total	OLS Exog.	Static No	Multilateral Q; 1961–68	U.S.		−1.05
Khan and Ross (1977, table 2) Total	OLS Exog.	Koyck Yes	Multilateral Q; 1960–72	U.S. Japan Canada		−2.16 −3.37 −0.99
Yadav (1977, table 2) Total	OLS Exog.	Koyck Yes	Multilateral Q; 1956–73	Canada		−1.37
Deppler and Ripley (1978, tables 11–18)* Nonoil	OLS Exog.	DL Yes	Multilateral S; 1964–76	U.S. U.K. Japan Germany Canada	−1.05 −0.47 −1.66 −0.60 0	−1.45 −0.30 −0.66 −0.67 −0.75
Goldstein and Khan (1978, table 5)	FIML Endog.	Static Yes	Multilateral Q; 1955–70	U.S. Japan Germany	−2.32 +2.47 −0.83	
Hooper (1978, table 3) Nonoil	OLS Exog.	Static Yes	Multilateral Q; 1955–77	U.S.		−1.04
Lawrence (1978, table 6) Nonoil	OLS Exog.	DL Yes	Multilateral S; 1962–77	U.S.	−1.85	−1.52

(continued)

TABLE 4.1 (*Continued*)

Study/Source/Commodity	Estimator/ Price Behavior	Dynamic Structure/ Homogeneity	Price Data/ Frequency; Sample	Price Elasticities		
				Country	Exports	Imports
Stern, Baum, and Green (1979, tables 2, 4) Total	OLS Exog.	DL No	Multilateral Q; 1953–76	U.S.	−0.20	−2.18
Wilson and Takacs (1979, tables 1, 3–6) Nonoil	OLS Exog.	Shiller No	Multilateral Q; 1957–71	U.S. U.K. Japan Germany Canada	−3.31 −0.37 −11.68 −1.87 −0.24	−4.78 +0.03 −1.25 −0.12 −2.75
Goldstein, Khan, and Officer (1980, table 3) Total	OLS Exog.	Static Yes	Multilateral A; 1950–73	U.S. Germany Canada		−0.68 −0.30 −0.82
Geraci and Prewo (1982, table 1) Total	OLS Exog.	Koyck Yes	Bilateral Q; 1958–74	U.S. U.K. Japan Germany		−1.23 −0.79 −0.72 −0.60
Haynes and Stone (1983, table 1) Total	OLS Exog.	Static No	Multilateral Q; 1955–79	U.S.	−0.77	−0.60
Ueda (1983, table 1) Total	IV Endo.	Koyck No	Multilateral S; 1966–80	Japan	−1.75	−1.40

Study				Country		
Warner and Kreinin (1983, tables 2, 5) Nonoil	OLS Exog.	PDL(M) Static(X)	Multilateral Q; 1970–80 No	U.S.	−0.55	−2.53
				U.K.	−0.86	−1.42
				Japan	−0.30	−0.72
				Germany	−4.98	−0.27
				Canada	−1.37	−1.00
Helkie and Hooper (1988, tables 2–4)* Nonoil	OLS Exog.	PDL Yes	Multilateral Q; 1969–84	U.S.	−0.85	−1.15
Cline (1989, table 4, A.3) Total	OLS Exog.	DL Yes	Multilateral Q; 1973–87	U.S.	−1.09	−1.36
				U.K.	−0.67	−1.04
				Japan	−0.90	−0.69
				Germany	−0.66	−0.48
				Canada	−1.01	−2.35
Deyak, Sawyer, and Sprinkle (1989, table 1) Total	OLS Exog.	Koyck Yes	Multilateral Q; 1958–83	U.S.		−0.29
Krugman (1989, tables 2–3) Nonoil	OLS Exog.	DL Yes	Multilateral A; 1971–86	U.S.	−1.42	−0.93
				U.K.	−0.54	+0.99
				Japan	−0.88	−0.42
				Germany	−0.55	−0.09
				Canada	+0.80	−1.45
Moffet (1989, tables 5-6) Total	OLS Exog.	PDL No	Multilateral Q; 1967–87	U.S.	−0.82	−0.69

(*continued*)

TABLE 4.1 (*Continued*)

Study/Source/Commodity	Estimator/ Price Behavior	Dynamic Structure/ Homogeneity	Price Data/ Frequency; Sample	Price Elasticities Country	Exports	Imports
Noland (1989, table 1) Total	Grid/OLS Exog.	GDL Yes	Multilateral Q; 1970–85	Japan	−0.41	−0.67
Lawrence (1990, tables 8, 10) Nonoil	OLS Exog.	PDL Yes	Multilateral S; 1976–90	U.S.	−1.04	−1.47
Marquez (1990, table 2) Total	OLS Exog.	RL Yes	Multilateral Q; 1973–85	U.S. U.K. Japan Germany Canada	−0.99 −0.44 −0.93 −0.66 −0.83	−0.92 −0.47 −0.93 −0.60 −1.02
Clarida (1991, p. 17) Nonoil	NLS Exog.	ECM/DL Yes	Multilateral Q; 1968–90	U.S.		−0.93
Blecker (1992, tables A1, A5) Nonoil	OLS Exog.	PDL Yes	Multilateral Q; 1975–89	U.S.	−0.72	−0.97

Notes:

*

Commodity   Authors' aggregation of individual elasticity estimates using trade shares.
Total: Measure of trade volume includes oil trade.
Nonoil: Measure of trade volume excludes oil trade.

Homogeneity   Yes: Estimating equation imposes homogeneity of degree zero in prices.

Estimation method   FIML: Full information maximum likelihood.
IV: Instrumental variables.
ILS: Indirect least squares.
NLS: Nonlinear least squares.
NLP: Nonlinear programming.
OLS: Ordinary least squares.

Dynamic structure   DL: Distributed lags.
ECM: Error-correction model.
GDL: Gamma distributed lags.
Koyck: Lagged dependent variable.
PDL: Polynomial distributed lags.
RL: Rational lags.
Shiller: Shiller lags.
Static: No allowance for delay.

Price data   Multilateral: Price data do not differentiate among trading partners.
Bilateral: Price data refer to specific trading partners.

Data frequencies   A: Annual; Q: Quarterly; S: Semiannual.

Exchange-rate system   Fixed: Estimation sample period predominantly pre-1973.
Float: Estimation sample period predominantly post-1973.
Both: Estimation sample period centered approximately on 1973.

United States; several report results for all five countries. The table also lists key attributes of these studies pertaining to the (1) presence or absence of homogeneity constraints, (2) estimation method, (3) dynamic structure, (4) data frequency and sample period, (5) countries covered, (6) estimates for exports, imports, or both, (7) the prevailing exchange-rate system, and (8) the degree of commodity disaggregation.[18] Definitions are presented at the end of the table. With respect to the designation of the exchange-rate system, many of the studies are based largely on data that predate the floating-rate period. These studies were included to see if there is significant evidence of a shift in price-elasticity estimates following the move to more flexible exchange rates. Krugman (1989b), for example, has hypothesized that the increased variability of exchange rates during the floating-rate period has induced a "delinking" of trade from exchange rates that presumably would show up in reduced price elasticities.

Table 4.2 presents the summary statistics for the German, Japanese, and U.S. price elasticities across the studies, including the range of estimates and the means and standard deviations across the studies reporting the relevant estimates. The estimates vary widely across countries. The mean estimates suggest that the Marshall-Lerner condition is easily met for all three countries. The mean elasticity estimate for Japanese exports is substantially higher than the other elasticity estimates reported. This estimate is strongly influenced by the inclusion of an outlier from the study by Wilson and Takacs (1979). Excluding their estimate from the summary statistics yields a mean price elasticity for Japanese exports of −0.96, which is more in line with an average of estimates from studies by Geraci and Prewo (1982), Warner and Kreinin (1983), Cline (1989), Hickok (1989), and Marquez (1990).[19]

The substantial dispersion of elasticity estimates is troublesome but undoubtedly reflects differences across studies with regard to the characteristics listed in Table 4.1 (as well as other differences that we have not tried to identify). In a crude attempt to quantify the relative influence of these charac-

---

[18] The elasticity estimates reported in Table 4.1 are own-price elasticities. This distinction is important for studies that estimate bilateral trade equations in a regionally disaggregated framework. Several of those studies (Magee, 1972; Geraci and Prewo, 1982; Cline, 1989; and Marquez, 1990) include cross-price elasticities (third-country competitive effects) in addition to own-price elasticities. In most cases (Marquez [1990], for example), the cross-price elasticities for total trade by region are not significant. Cline reports sizable cross-price effects; in a large majority of cases, however, those elasticities were not freely estimated but were imposed by constraints used in estimation. Our own estimates, reported in the next section, are designed to capture third-country competitive effects to some degree by using multilateral rather than bilateral trade shares in aggregating foreign prices and exchange rates across countries.

[19] One recent study (Cline, 1989) reports an aggregate own-price elasticity for Japanese exports of about −0.9. With the inclusion of cross-price elasticities, Cline's estimate for Japanese exports rises to −1.3. As noted above, however, the cross-price elasticities reported by Cline are heavily constrained. Finally, Hickok's (1989) estimated price elasticity for Japanese exports is −1.1.

TABLE 4.2
Summary Statistics on Estimates of Price Elasticities

Variable	Mean	Standard Deviation	Minimum	Maximum	Number of Studies
United States					
Exports	−1.31	0.92	−3.75	−0.20	19
Imports	−1.35	0.93	−4.78	−0.29	32
Japan					
Exports	−1.68	3.70	−11.70	2.47	10
Imports	−0.97	0.78	−3.40	−0.26	13
Germany					
Exports	−1.06	1.87	−5.00	1.70	8
Imports	−0.50	0.44	−1.82	−0.09	13

Source: Data in Table 4.1.

teristics on the dispersion of elasticity estimates, we estimate the following "fixed-effect" equation:

$$\epsilon_i = \phi_0 + \phi_1 PREFLOAT + \phi_2 SIMULT + \phi_3 NONHOMOG + \phi_4 ANNUAL + \phi_5 NO\text{-}LAGS + \phi_6 SHILLER + \phi_7 COMMODITY + u_i , \tag{27}$$

where:

ϵ_i	=	the long-run elasticity estimate reported by the ith study;
PREFLOAT	=	a dummy variable equal to 1 if the sample period corresponds to the period of fixed exchange rates, or to 0 if otherwise;
SIMULT	=	a dummy variable equal to 1 if the model is estimated with simultaneous-equation techniques, or to 0 if otherwise;
NONHOMOG	=	a dummy variable equal to 1 if price homogeneity is not imposed, or to 0 if otherwise;
ANNUAL	=	a dummy variable equal to 1 for annual data, or to 0 if otherwise;
NO-LAGS	=	a dummy variable equal to 1 if lagged responses are absent, or to 0 if otherwise;
SHILLER	=	a dummy variable equal to 1 if Shiller lags are used, or to 0 if otherwise;
COMMODITY	=	a dummy variable equal to 1 if oil is included in the measure of trade volume, or to 0 if otherwise;
u_i	=	a random variable having $N(0,\sigma_2)$.

The parameter ϕ_0 in equation (27) is the mean of the elasticity estimates for the prototypical study in our survey, which uses data for the period of floating exchange rates, is estimated by ordinary least squares, assumes price homogeneity, uses semiannual or quarterly data, allows for lagged responses (but does not use a Shiller lag), and excludes oil from the measure of trade volume. The other parameters in the equation measure the extent to which the various characteristics change the mean elasticity. For example, a finding that $\hat{\phi}_1$ is significantly different from zero means that the elasticity estimates shifted between the fixed- and floating-rate periods.[20]

To estimate the parameters of (27), we use weighted least squares in which the weights are the estimated standard errors.[21] The results, shown in Table 4.3, indicate that the estimated price elasticity of the prototypical study is close to -1 for both U.S. exports and U.S. imports. The results also suggest that the methodological characteristics of the various studies can explain a good deal of the variation in elasticity estimates. Estimates for studies focusing on data for the period before floating rates yield significantly higher elasticity estimates (in absolute terms) for U.S. imports, a finding that tends to support Krugman's "delinking" hypothesis. Export elasticities are somewhat higher in the earlier studies as well, but this difference is not statistically significant. Studies that do not assume homogeneity in prices have an (insignificant) tendency to produce lower estimates of the price elasticity of exports and a (significant) tendency to produce higher estimates of the price elasticities for imports. The use of annual data yields larger elasticities for exports but not for imports.[22] The choice of estimating technique (ordinary least squares versus simultaneous) does not significantly affect the elasticity estimates.[23] The inclusion of oil in the measure of trade volume dampens significantly the value of the estimated price elasticity for imports. Finally, the absence of lags yields smaller elasticities for imports, and the use of Shiller lags appears to yield substantially larger elasticity estimates for both imports and exports.[24] On the export side, the small number of studies that have not

---

[20] We stress that this equation is no more than a vehicle to aid in accounting for the effects of alternative research designs. We also recognize that effects attributed to a particular characteristic could reflect the influence of other attributes (such as differences in data and disaggregation) that are not captured by the set of characteristics we have selected.

[21] A few studies do not report estimates of the standard errors. If such a study indicates that the elasticities are statistically significant, however, we impute a t-statistic of 2 to derive an estimate of the standard errors. If the study does not indicate how significant the price elasticities are, we impute a t-statistic of 1.

[22] In the absence of homogeneity, the price elasticity was based on the estimated coefficient for the foreign price, whether or not it was combined with an exchange-rate term.

[23] Only two studies report results based on simultaneous-estimation techniques, Ahluwalia and Hernández-Catá (1975) for import elasticities and Goldstein and Khan (1978) for export elasticities. Both studies report elasticities that were slightly above average. Several other studies reporting ordinary-least-squares results note that, in preliminary testing, simultaneous-equation estimation yielded very nearly the same results as OLS estimation (for example, Geraci and Prewo, 1982; Helkie and Hooper, 1988; and Ericsson and Marquez, 1993).

[24] Despite the fact that only Wilson and Takacs (1979) used the Shiller lag, it was singled out because many of the elasticities they reported were outliers. The extremely high elasticity esti-

TABLE 4.3
Fixed-Effects Model for Long-Run U.S. Price Elasticities

	Exports	Number of Studies	Imports	Number of Studies
Intercept	−0.93		−1.23	
	(−2.9)		(−4.4)	
Prefloat	−0.30	10	−0.96	21
	(−0.7)		(−3.0)	
No homogeneity	0.86	5	−0.74	8
	(1.2)		(−2.4)	
Annual data	−1.40	4	0.04	9
	(−1.7)		(0.1)	
No lags	−0.84	5	0.70	10
	(−1.1)		(2.2)	
Shiller lags	−2.92	1	−1.86	1
	(−3.7)		(−4.2)	
Simultaneity	1.15	1	0.58	1
	(1.5)		(0.7)	
Commodity	—		0.70	18
			(2.9)	
$\bar{R}^2$	0.81		0.88	
Significance	0.00		0.00	
Sample mean	−1.31		−1.35	

Source: Data in Table 4.1.
Note: *t*-statistics are in parentheses.

used lags find *larger* elasticities on average, but this effect is not statistically significant.

Empirical Analysis of Exchange-Rate Pass-Through

The picture that emerges from a variety of empirical analyses is that U.S. exporters, on average, tend to pass through most (80 to 100 percent) of an exchange-rate change into their export prices, whereas Japanese and European exporters pass through considerably less (50 to 70 percent). The lower pass-

---

mates they found, however, may well have been due to characteristics of their study other than the use of Shiller lags.

through for Japan and Europe is consistent with the range of estimates for pass-through into aggregate U.S. import prices (again, 50 to 70 percent). Hooper and Mann (1989b), Moffet (1989), and Lawrence (1990), each use a variant of the markup model (equation [17] above) and find results consistent with these ranges for aggregate U.S. export and/or import prices.

Other empirical studies have been more micro-oriented, focusing on pass-through at the industry level. Gagnon and Knetter (1992) for autos, and Ohno (1989) and Knetter (1993) for a wide variety of industries, find very little or no evidence of pricing-to-market behavior by U.S. exporters. Branson and Marston (1989), Feenstra (1989), Ohno (1989), Marston (1990), and Gagnon and Knetter (1992) all find significant evidence of pricing to market by Japanese exporters in a variety of industries. In most cases, the analysis focuses on the behavior of Japanese export prices to all regions relative to domestic Japanese prices or costs. Hooper and Mann (1989b) and Knetter (1993) employ some regional disaggregation and find no evidence that Japanese exporters behave differently with respect to alternative foreign markets. Knetter (1993) finds that, on average, German and U.K. exporters behave similarly to Japanese exporters. However, Gagnon and Knetter find that evidence of pricing to market for autos is much weaker for German exporters than for Japanese exporters.

Empirical tests of the importance of raw-material prices in reducing pass-through have been limited largely to the behavior of Japanese export prices. In tests for a number of individual Japanese export industries, Ohno (1989) and Marston (1990) find no significant empirical evidence that the influence of exchange rates on raw-material prices affects pass-through. In tests at a more aggregative level, however, Hooper and Mann (1989b) find evidence that such effects are significant for overall Japanese manufactured exports.

With respect to the presence or absence of hysteresis, Baldwin (1988) finds some evidence of a shift in the behavior of U.S. import prices in the wake of the large swing in the dollar during the 1980s. However, Hooper and Mann (1989b), Ohno (1989), and Melick (1990) have all failed to find significant evidence of such shifts.

Cointegration

A method that is gaining attention in the literature is the estimation of price elasticities in the context of cointegrated systems. Clarida (1991) estimates a model for U.S. imports of consumer goods in a framework that allows for the cointegration of U.S. imports and their determinants—that is, the tendency for them to move together in the long run. Clarida finds that the cointegrating relation between imports, income, and relative prices yields income and price elasticities that are very similar to those found by Helkie and Hooper (1988) and Cline (1989), who did not use cointegration analysis.[25] Melick (1990) does much the same for the pass-through relationship and finds cointegrating relationships for U.S. import prices that are consistent with the pass-through coefficients reported by Hooper and Mann (1989b).

5 Exchange Rates and External Adjustment Since 1980

The U.S. Experience

Figure 4.1 shows movements for the past two decades in alternative measures of the dollar's foreign-exchange value against an average of the currencies of major U.S. trading partners. The currencies included are those of the G-7 countries, plus Korea, Mexico, and Taiwan.[26] The indexes are weighted by each country's relative share in world trade and are expressed in units of foreign currency per dollar. The method of constructing these indexes and the underlying data and weights are discussed in Appendixes A and B. Changes since 1980 are of particular interest to the analysis presented later in this section.

In nominal terms, the dollar appreciated by over 60 percent on this basis between 1980 and early 1985. That appreciation was fully reversed by late 1987, and the dollar has fluctuated in a much narrower range, around its 1980 level, since 1987. Figure 4.1 also shows several different measures of the dollar's real exchange rate—the ratios of U.S. to foreign consumer price indexes (CPIs), GDP deflators, producer price indexes (PPIs), and unit labor costs in manufacturing, all in dollars—as well as the relative price of exports, the inverse of the relative price of imports, and the terms of trade. The relative price of exports is the ratio of the price of U.S. exports (excluding agricultural goods and computers) to a weighted average of foreign GDP deflators in dollars; the relative price of imports is described below. The relative price of exports follows essentially the same path as the dollar's nominal exchange rate, indicating that changes in nominal exchange rates were largely passed through to U.S. export prices denominated in foreign currencies; in other words, dollar export prices did not move much in response to exchange-rate changes. The ratio of CPIs also follows much the same pattern as the nominal rate. By contrast, the terms of trade, the relative price of imports, and relative PPIs have not returned to their 1980 levels, although, on the basis of relative GDP deflators and unit labor costs, the dollar's real exchange rate has fallen significantly below its 1980 level.

[25] We also applied Johansen's (1988) cointegration tests to data on per capita nonoil imports, per capita GDP, and relative prices. Using quarterly data for 1949:2 through 1993:1, we found a unique cointegration vector among these variables.

[26] In 1992, these nine countries accounted for two-thirds of combined U.S. exports and nonoil imports.

Figure 4.1 Dollar Exchange Rates: Weighted Averages of Nine Currencies (*foreign currency to dollars*)

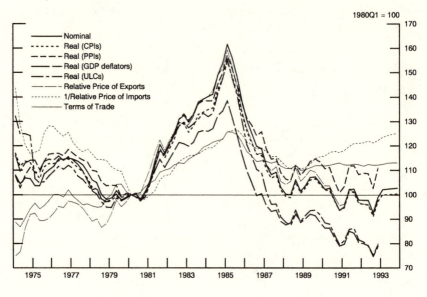

Relative Price of Imports

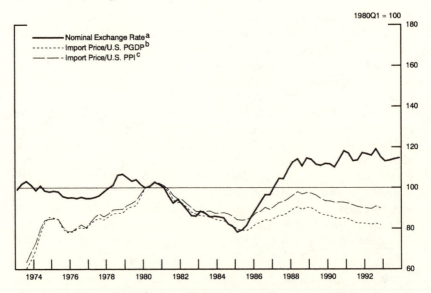

[a]Using bilateral U.S. import weights, dollars to foreign currency; excludes Mexico.
[b]Prices of nonoil imports excluding computers divided by U.S. GDP deflator.
[c]Prices of nonoil imports excluding computers divided by U.S. PPI manufacturing.

Figure 4.2 Price Competitiveness and U.S. Exports

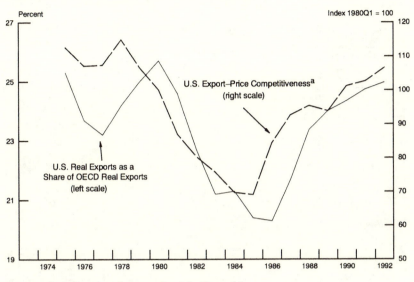

Alternative Measures of U.S. External Balance

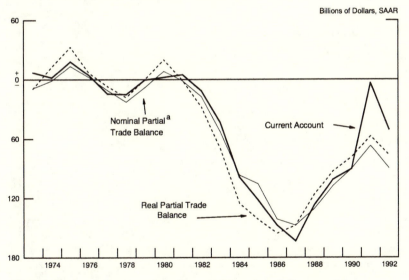

Figure 4.3 Yen Exchange Rates: Weighted Averages of Nine Currencies (*foreign currency to yen*)

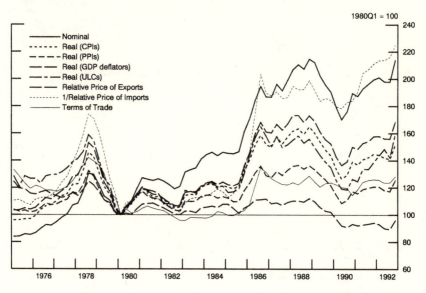

Relative Price of Imports

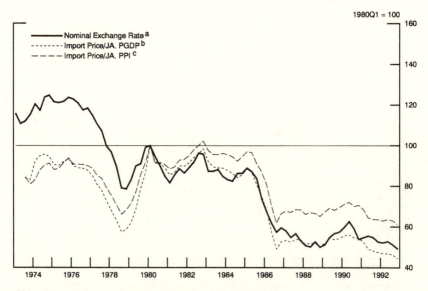

[a]Using bilateral Japanese import weights, yen to foreign currency.
[b]Prices of nonoil imports divided by Japanese GDP deflator.
[c]Prices of nonoil imports divided by Japanese PPI manufacturing.

Figure 4.4 Price Competitiveness and Japanese Exports

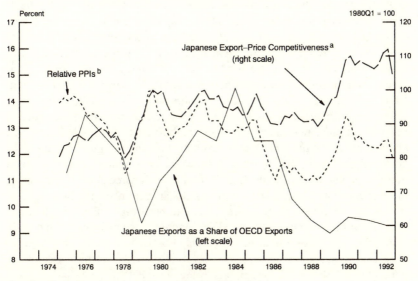

aInverse of relative price of exports as defined in Figure 4.3.
bForeign manufacturing PPIs in yen over Japanese PPI.

Alternative Measures of Japanese External Balancea

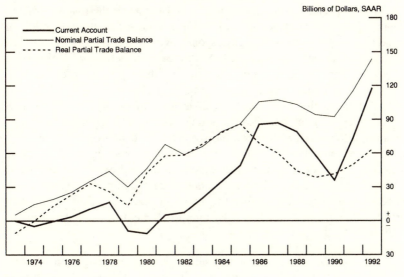

aExports minus nonoil imports.

We suspect that a good deal of the net decline since 1980 in the relative GDP deflator and the unit-labor-cost measure reflects differences in the treatment of computer prices across countries. Rapidly declining computer prices in the United States caused the GDP deflator to rise more slowly than its counterparts abroad, where different measures of computer prices are employed. The same difference caused U.S. manufacturing output (hence, manufacturing productivity) to rise relatively more rapidly, which means that unit labor costs in U.S. manufacturing rose more slowly than those abroad.

The bottom panel of Figure 4.1 shows a different measure of the dollar's nominal exchange rate and two measures of the relative price of U.S. imports: (1) the ratio of the price of imports (excluding oil and computers) to the U.S. GDP deflator (the inverse of which is shown in the top panel) and (2) the ratio of the same import price to the U.S. PPI for manufactured goods. In this case, the exchange rate is expressed in terms of dollars per unit of foreign currency. It uses the same foreign currencies as before but weights them by shares in U.S. imports. On this basis, the dollar appreciated much less in the early 1980s than on a world-trade-share-weighted basis, and it has more than reversed its appreciation since the mid-1980s. Unlike the relative price of exports, the relative price of imports using the GDP deflator has deviated significantly from the nominal exchange rate in recent years. Although it moved about in line with the nominal exchange rate when the dollar appreciated, it rose much less when the dollar depreciated, indicating that the depreciation was not being fully passed through. In the late 1980s, moreover, when the nominal exchange rate moved above its 1980 level, the relative price of imports remained well below its 1980 level, suggesting the possibility of some asymmetry in pass-through response over the period as a whole. The relative price of imports using the U.S. PPI for manufactured goods has risen somewhat more in recent years. Nevertheless, the gap between that relative price and the nominal exchange rate remains sizable.

The effect of the swing in the relative price of exports on U.S. export performance over the past decade is illustrated vividly in the top panel of Figure 4.2. The dashed line is a measure of U.S. export-price competitiveness, the reciprocal of the relative price of exports shown in Figure 4.1. The solid line is the share of U.S. real exports in the real exports of all OECD countries. Movements in the U.S. market share followed movements in the price ratio quite closely, with a lag of about one year. The export share dropped sharply during the first half of the 1980s but had returned to about its 1980 peak by the end of the decade.[27]

[27] We also analyzed the increase in the U.S. share of OECD exports between 1986 and 1991 to determine the extent to which that increase reflected relatively rapid growth in the markets to which the United States exports (as opposed to an increase in U.S. competitiveness). We found that the growth of imports of OECD countries weighted by each country's share in U.S. exports was essentially the same as the growth of total OECD imports. This result indicates that the increase in U.S. market share was attributable primarily to an increase in U.S. competitiveness.

The bottom panel of Figure 4.2 shows movements in various measures of the U.S. external balance, including the current account, the nominal partial trade balance, and the real partial trade balance. The partial trade balances are defined as net exports of goods excluding oil imports, agricultural exports, and imports and exports of computers; the real balance is measured in billions of 1987 dollars. Most of the swings in the current account, from surplus in 1980 to unprecedented deficit in the mid-1980s, then to near zero in 1991 and back into deficit more recently, can be accounted for by swings in the real partial trade balance. The correlation between the two series was remarkably close over this period, with two notable exceptions. One exception occurred in 1987, when the nominal deficit persisted longer than the real deficit because the initial effect of the depreciation of the dollar was to raise the price of imports and therefore to push up nominal imports while depressing real imports. The other notable exception occurred in 1991, when one-time cash grants associated with foreign financing of the Persian Gulf War boosted the U.S. current account by $43 billion.

In the econometric analysis that follows, we focus on the U.S. partial trade balance, partly because it explains most of the movement in the overall current account and partly because the excluded trade categories do not conform to the assumption of imperfect substitutability used in the conventional trade model. Both oil and agricultural commodities can reasonably be viewed as goods that are perfect substitutes across countries. Computers, as Lawrence (1990) and Meade (1991) have shown, present a different problem for empirical analysis of U.S. trade because their prices, measured hedonically, have behaved quite differently from those of other goods.[28] A problem also arises with respect to international comparability because most other industrial countries have not yet applied hedonic techniques to the measurement of computer prices.

The Japanese Experience

Various measures of the yen's weighted average exchange rate are shown in the top panel of Figure 4.3. Movements in these indexes have diverged even more widely since the early 1980s than have those for the dollar. The yen has appreciated substantially less in real terms than in nominal terms, reflecting Japan's relatively low rates of CPI and manufacturing PPI inflation. On a PPI-adjusted basis, the yen appreciated in real terms by about 30 percent on balance between early 1980 and mid-1992. Despite the significant appreciation of the yen in both nominal and real terms, however, Japanese export prices actually declined by 10 percent relative to foreign GDP deflators expressed in

---

[28] Measured in real terms, both imports and exports of computers have grown extremely rapidly over the past decade, but their net effect on the U.S. trade *balance* has been quite small.

yen. The relative price of exports rose by as much as 10 percent during the late 1980s, because of the sharp appreciation of the yen during that period, but that increase was more than reversed after 1989. The reasons for this striking divergence between exchange rates and relative prices relate partly to the strong effects of exchange rates on Japanese import prices and production costs and partly to the pass-through behavior of Japanese exporters. We shall return to this later.

Unlike the relative price of exports, the relative price of Japanese imports has moved very closely in line with the nominal exchange rate since 1980, as indicated in both the top and bottom panels of Figure 4.3.[29] This close correlation suggests that movements in the yen are passed through substantially into Japanese import prices.

The relation between Japan's export-price competitiveness and its export share, shown in the top panel of Figure 4.4, is not as tight as for the United States. As indicated in the bottom panel, Japan's real partial trade balance has accounted for much, but not all, of the variation in the current account since 1980.

Estimated Trade Equations

We now turn to the estimation of a version of the conventional model of trade volumes and prices for the United States and Japan. The volume (structural-demand) equations that we estimate for imports and exports are essentially the same as equations (8) and (9), which we have modified to incorporate distributed lags:

$$Q_m = f(y, p_t, p_{t-1}, \ldots, p_{t-n}) , \tag{8a}$$

$$Q_x = f^*(y^*, p_t^*, p_{t-1}^*, \ldots, p_{t-m}^*) , \tag{9a}$$

where $p_t = P_{mt}/P_t$, $p_{t*} = P_x/(P/S)$.

The price (supply) equations are based on the reduced-form import-price equation (24):

$$P_{mt} = g[(W^*/S)_t, \ldots, (W^*/S)_{t-n}, (P_r^*/S)_t, \ldots, (P_r^*/S)_{t-n},$$
$$y, P_t, \ldots, P_{t-n}] . \tag{24a}$$

The export-price equation is treated symmetrically:

$$P_{xt} = g^*[W_t, \ldots, W_{t-p}, P_{rt}, \ldots, P_{r,t-m}, y^*, (P^*/S)_t, \ldots,$$
$$(P^*/S)_{t-k}] , \tag{23a}$$

[29] As in Figure 4.1, the exchange-rate index in the bottom panel differs from that in the top

where P is the GDP deflator or manufacturing PPI; P_m is the nonoil import-price index denominated in the importer's currency; P_x is the export-price index denominated in the exporter's currency; P_r is the world commodity-price index denominated in the exporting country's currency; Q_m is nonoil import volume; Q_x is export volume; S is the weighted average exchange rate (foreign currency/home currency); W is the unit-labor-cost index in manufacturing; and y is real GDP. Foreign variables, denoted by an asterisk (*), and the exchange rate are weighted averages across the ten countries included in our sample (not including the home country).[30] The data employed, some of which were discussed in the preceding subsections, are described in detail in Appendix B.[31] The two components of cost, W and P_r, did not always perform well in unrestricted estimation, possibly because of significant collinearity among the various price and cost variables. In the results below for the United States, we report estimates for a single regression coefficient on the weighted sum of the two unit costs, $\log C = 0.75 \log W + 0.25 \log P_r$.

The equations were estimated in double-log functional form, so that the coefficients are elasticities. We used Fair's two-stage least-squares method for simultaneous estimation, treating prices as endogenous variables in the demand equation, and used the Cochrane-Orcutt correction for serially correlated residuals. Lags in the response to price and cost changes were represented either by a combination of unrestricted lags and a lagged dependent variable or by Almon distributed lags. These two methods yielded very similar results for long-run relative-price and pass-through elasticities, and we have reported the results for Almon lags. The lags on relative prices in the quantity equations are eight quarters long, and those on the explanatory variables in the price equations are four quarters long. Other lag lengths were tested but generally yielded similar long-run elasticities. The sample period starts somewhere between 1972 and 1976 and ends in mid-1992; it uses quarterly data.[32]

U.S. Estimation Results

The results for the U.S. quantity and price equations are presented in Table 4.4, which reports the long-run elasticity estimates. All of the estimated elasticities have the expected signs and are statistically significant. The long-run

---

panel because it is inverted and is based on Japanese import weights instead of multilateral trade weights. The weights are given in Appendix A.

[30] $P*/S$, for example, is the foreign price measured in the currency of the country for which the import (or export) price is being determined.

[31] Recall that the U.S. equations exclude computers from import and export prices and quantities.

[32] The sample period varied from equation to equation depending upon the availability of data for the relevant variables.

TABLE 4.4
Long-Run Coefficient Estimates for U.S. Trade

	Trade Volumes	
	Exports	Imports
Income	1.00	2.50
	(14.1)	(7.5)
Relative prices	−1.01	−1.03
	(−8.4)	(−3.7)
ρ	0.75	0.81
$\bar{R}^2$	0.99	0.99
Jarque-Bera	0.38	0.61
Serial independence	0.03	0.89
ARCH	0.48	0.76
Sample	1972:2–1992:2	1976:3–1992:2

	Trade Prices	
	Exports	Imports
U.S. costs	0.77	
	(5.9)	
Foreign prices ($)	0.16	
	(2.7)	
U.S. domestic prices		0.51
		(3.2)
Foreign costs ($)		0.55
		(7.8)
$\bar{R}^2$	0.45	0.71
Jarque-Bera	0.97	0.96
Serial independence	0.33	0.03
ARCH	2.70	0.48
Sample	1975:1–1992:3	1975:1–1992:2

Note: *t*-statistics are in parentheses; relative prices enter the volume equations with a second-order Almon lag over eight quarters.

price elasticities in the volume equations are both about −1, very close to the mean estimates we found in our survey of the literature.[33] The income elasticities in the volume equations replicate the Houthakker-Magee asymmetry; the import elasticity is well in excess of the export elasticity.[34]

---

[33] Relative prices enter into the volume equations with a second-order Almon polynomial over eight quarters.

[34] In general here and in Table 4.5 for Japan, the results do not reject the usual assumptions

The results for the price equations indicate that U.S. export prices are quite sensitive to U.S. costs (with an elasticity of 0.77) but not very sensitive to foreign prices expressed in dollars (with an elasticity of 0.16).[35] The coefficient on the foreign price term implies that a 1 percent appreciation of the dollar lowers dollar-denominated export prices by 0.16 percent and raises the foreign-currency value of those prices (the prices paid by foreign importers) by 0.84 percent; the pass-through coefficient for foreign import prices (φ) is thus approximately −0.84.[36] The results for U.S. import prices indicate that a 1 percent increase in foreign costs raises these prices by 0.55 percent, whereas a 1 percent appreciation of the dollar lowers them by 0.55 percent (a pass-through of −0.55).[37] Thus, in contrast to the case of export prices, equal increases in foreign costs and the value of the dollar have similar effects on U.S. import prices. These estimates are fully consistent with those of other studies surveyed in the preceding section.[38]

Japanese Estimation Results

Results for the Japanese equations are shown in Table 4.5. The estimated price elasticities for Japanese exports and imports (−0.8 and −0.7, respectively) are significantly less than those for the United States. These estimates are roughly consistent with results of the most recent five studies reporting estimates for Japan; the averages of the estimates shown in Table 4.1 are −0.7 for both exports and imports.

---

made in estimating trade-volume and price equations. The residuals satisfy the assumptions of normality, serial independence, and homoskedasticity. The exceptions are departures from normality in the U.S. price equations, from serial independence in the Japanese export-volume equation, and from homoskedasticity in the Japanese export-price equation.

[35] These variables enter the export-price equation with a second-order Almon polynomial over four quarters. The results reported for the price equations do not include coefficients for real income in the importing country, as they were found to be uniformly statistically insignificant, and the income variables were dropped from the price equations.

[36] Recall from equation (20) that the pass-through coefficient for import prices (in this case, "foreign" import prices) is equal to the elasticity of the export price with respect to the exchange rate minus 1. The estimated coefficient on the foreign price term expressed in dollars is only an approximation of the elasticity of U.S. export prices with respect to the exchange rate; that coefficient also reflects the effects of independent movements in foreign prices expressed in foreign currency. The approximation is fairly close, however, because exchange-rate changes account for most of the variance in the foreign prices expressed in dollars; the correlation between the foreign price term and the exchange rate over the sample period is 0.68. Pass-through could be somewhat less than 84 percent because we have not factored in the possible effects of exchange-rate changes on the prices of raw materials in the United States.

[37] As in the case of export prices, these variables enter into the export-price equation with a second-order Almon polynomial over four quarters.

[38] However, the results for the export-price equation are less robust than we might have hoped, inasmuch as the residuals do not conform to the underlying assumptions of normality and homoskedasticity.

TABLE 4.5
Long-Run Coefficient Estimates for Japan Trade

	Trade Volumes	
	Exports	Imports
Income	1.06	1.03
	(12.4)	(7.8)
Relative prices	−0.80	−0.73
	(−1.5)	(−6.3)
ρ		0.56
$\bar{R}^2$	0.99	0.98
Jarque-Bera	0.79	0.34
Serial independence	0.99	0.06
ARCH	0.10	0.91
Sample	1976:2–1992:2	1976:4–1992:2

	Trade Prices	
	Exports	Imports
Domestic labor costs	0.61	
	(2.2)	
Commodity prices (¥)	0.34	0.33
	(5.0)	(4.1)
Foreign prices (¥)	0.15	
	(1.7)	
Foreign labor costs (¥)		0.78
		(6.1)
ρ	−0.83	0.85
$\bar{R}^2$	0.98	0.98
Jarque-Bera	0.24	0.60
Serial independence	0.73	0.87
ARCH	2.54	0.88
Sample	1975:3–1992:2	1974:2–1992:2

Note: *t*-statistics are in parentheses.

When the Japanese PPI was included in the Japanese import-price equation as a competitive-price term, it dominated the equation, and the coefficient on foreign costs became insignificant. Given the composition of Japanese imports, many of which do not have domestic substitutes, this result seems implausible, and it may well reflect either multicollinearity or some degree of reverse causation. For this reason, we estimated the import-price equation without including Japanese competitive prices. We also left the components of unit costs unconstrained in the Japanese price equations. The coefficients on unit labor costs and raw-material prices in the export-price equation (0.6 and 0.3, respectively) are consistent with the relative shares of labor and raw materials as inputs into Japanese manufacturing. As in the U.S. case, income variables were uniformly insignificant in the Japanese price equations, and they were dropped.

The results shown in Table 4.5 are consistent with full pass-through of exchange-rate changes to import prices. In fact, the sum of the coefficients on the exchange rate (which appears in both the unit-labor-cost and commodity-price terms) exceeds 1. This result may be attributable in part to some (small) degree of responsiveness of world commodity prices to fluctuations in the effective yen exchange rate.[39]

Exchange-rate pass-through appears to be relatively high for Japanese export prices as well. It appears that 85 percent of exchange-rate changes are passed through into foreign-currency export prices—substantially more than other studies have found. In the Japanese case, however, the exchange rate clearly has a significant effect on export prices through changes in the prices of imported raw materials. Because world commodity prices in dollars are not significantly affected by movements in the yen-dollar exchange rate, prices of raw materials expressed in yen tend to move very nearly proportionately to the exchange rate.[40] Accordingly, the coefficient on the commodity-price term suggests that this effect could reduce exchange-rate "pass-through" by another 30 percentage points or so, to roughly 55 percent. (When the commodity-price term is dropped from the equation, the coefficient on foreign prices rises to 0.43, a result consistent with pass-through of 57 percent.) In brief, these results suggest that the incomplete pass-through of exchange-rate changes to Japanese export prices could reflect the effects of exchange-rate changes on Japanese production costs as much or more than they reflect strategic pricing behavior by Japanese exporters.[41]

This inference is at odds with the findings of Marston (1990) and Ohno (1989), who attach relatively little importance to the channel through which exchange rates influence export prices by affecting prices of raw materials. A possible explanation for this discrepancy may lie somewhere in the empirical differences between industry-level and aggregative analyses. Marston focuses on higher-stage-of-processing industries, such as machinery and transportation equipment, in which raw materials have only a very small direct input. Ohno considers a broader set of industries and finds that raw-material prices

---

[39] To the extent that appreciation of the yen, which reduces the yen-denominated prices of raw materials, stimulates the Japanese demand for those commodities, their world price will rise, offsetting some of the decline associated with the appreciation. This effect is probably small in light of Japan's relatively small share in world absorption of commodities.

[40] The correlation between the dollar commodity-price index and the dollar-yen exchange rate over the sample period is -0.21.

[41] In our review of the literature in preceding sections, we noted several studies that raised this issue.

have very little direct effect in industries such as machinery and transport equipment, but significant effects in lower-stage industries, such as primary metals and chemicals. Our aggregative analysis, which produces results consistent with input-output coefficients for the overall Japanese manufacturing sector, may well be giving more weight to direct effects at lower levels of processing than do studies involving industry-level analysis.[42] Even if this aggregative result holds up, moreover, it does not negate the findings of Marston and Ohno that there is significant pricing to market by Japanese firms. The prices of exports were found to be significantly more sensitive to changes in exchange rates than were domestic Japanese prices for the same categories of goods (which are, of course, subject to the same changes in costs). Similarly, Gagnon and Knetter (1992) find that the prices of identical Japanese exports to different foreign markets are strongly related to exchange-rate movements between those markets.

Whatever the principal reason for incomplete pass-through in the case of Japanese exports, its mere existence weakens the link between exchange-rate changes and changes in Japan's real trade balance. With 60 percent pass-through and an export-price elasticity of -0.8, a 10 percent across-the-board appreciation of the yen results in a less than 5 percent decline in Japan's real exports. Of course, nominal exports (measured in yen) fall noticeably more because of the decline in the yen price of exports associated with the incomplete pass-through of the appreciation.

Model Simulations

To evaluate the performance of the estimated partial-trade-balance equations, we use dynamic simulations to generate predictions for trade volumes and prices. Figure 4.5 compares actual and predicted values for the U.S. partial trade balance in current prices (top panel) and constant prices (bottom panel). Inspection of the results suggests a close fit until 1984. During the mid-1980s, the model predicted a faster turnaround in the trade deficit than actually occurred (in both nominal and real terms), resulting in significant overprediction of the trade balance for several years. This episode, and the failure of the trade deficit to respond quickly to the sharp decline in the dollar, generated considerable interest in the "persistence" of the deficit. With the significant narrowing of the deficit in the later 1980s, however, the model has been much more on track.[43]

---

[42] This explanation is not fully satisfying, however, because, in principle, the effects of raw-material prices at early stages of processing should be reflected in the prices of inputs into higher stages.

[43] Bryant, Holtham, and Hooper (1988) found that a variety of different conventional models of the U.S. current account performed quite well over the period from 1980 to 1986 and that the *ex ante* predictions of many of those models were fairly accurate for the remainder of the 1980s as

Figure 4.6 shows the results of simulations with the same equations used for Table 4.4 and Figure 4.5, but estimated through 1985:2 instead of 1992:2 (that is, based on data ending just before the turning point in the U.S. external balance). The elasticity estimates obtained for this truncated sample period are very similar to those for the full sample, and, as indicated in Figure 4.6, the model's postsample predictions for the 1980s are almost as accurate as the in-sample predictions shown in Figure 4.5.

A similar analysis for Japan is presented in Figure 4.7. The Japanese equations track the overall swing in Japan's external balance reasonably well from 1978 through 1992, but they tend to underpredict the Japanese surplus for the mid-1980s and to overpredict the surplus for recent years.

In both the U.S. and Japanese cases, the presence of sizable and persistent prediction errors for periods of up to several years suggests that there is ample room for further refinement of the conventional model. Problems in measuring prices and quality and the influence of factors affecting demand other than income and relative prices are candidates for further investigation.

Figure 4.8 shows the J-curves produced by our equations for the two countries' partial trade balances. These results were obtained by shocking the relevant country's weighted average exchange rate to produce an immediate and sustained 10 percent depreciation of the domestic currency relative to its baseline path. The simulation was run over the period from 1985 to 1989. Both countries show the conventional J-curve response, with the trade balance falling initially as import prices rise and rising thereafter as real net exports respond positively, but with a lag to the depreciation of the domestic currency. The initial decline is quite small in the U.S. case, however, reflecting the relatively low (55 percent) pass-through of the depreciation to import prices. The initial decline is much more prolonged in the Japanese case, reflecting the very high import pass-through coefficient (in excess of 100 percent) for Japan. The Japanese trade balance does not respond positively to the depreciation until about seven quarters after the shock is imposed. After five years, the 10 percent depreciation of the yen has raised the trade balance by little more than $10 billion. In the U.S. case, by contrast, the depreciation of the dollar raises the trade balance by nearly $35 billion. The longer-term effect is larger in the U.S. case than in the Japanese case, partly because the value of U.S. trade was greater than that of Japanese trade over the simulation period and partly because the sum of the estimated price elasticities for imports and exports is larger for the United States than for Japan.

---

well. Marquez and Ericsson (1993) did an intensive evaluation of the predictive accuracy of alternative trade models for 1985 through 1987 and concluded that the conventional model performed poorly relative to its own measure of uncertainty and the performance of time-series models during that period. Based on analyses of the model's performance over a longer (and more recent) period, Lawrence (1990), Cline (1991), and Krugman (1991) concluded that the conventional model has held up reasonably well.

Figure 4.5 U.S. Partial Balance of Trade

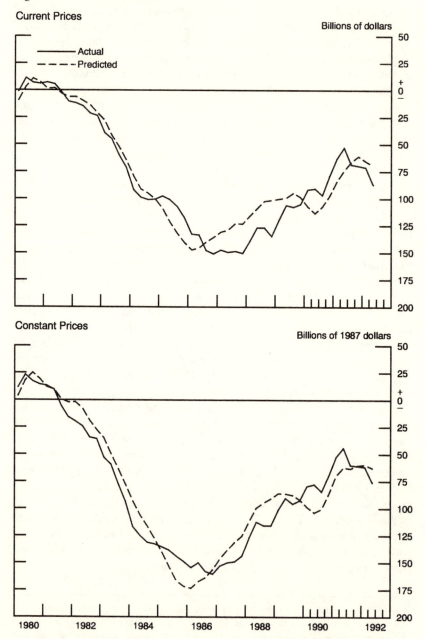

Note: Exports exclude agricultural goods and computers; imports exclude oil and computers.

Figure 4.6 *Ex Post* Forecast of U.S. Partial Balance of Trade

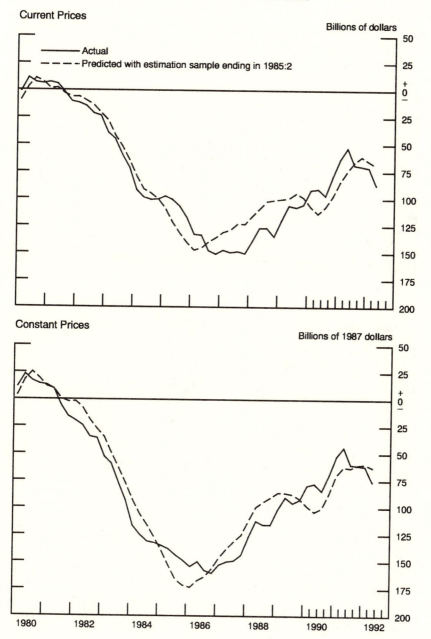

Figure 4.7 Japanese Nonoil Balance of Trade

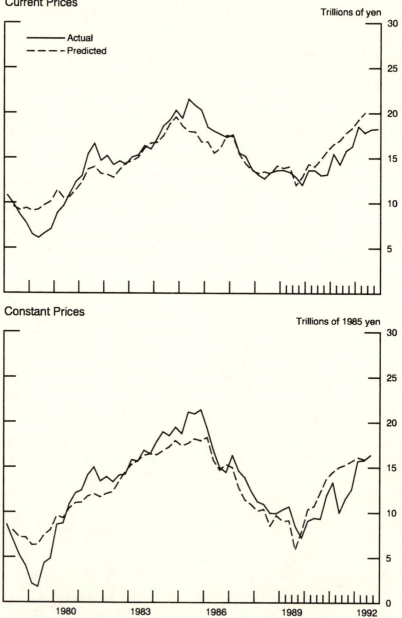

Current Prices

Trillions of yen

Actual
Predicted

Constant Prices

Trillions of 1985 yen

1980   1983   1986   1989   1992

Figure 4.8 Partial Trade-Balance Response to a 10 Percent Depreciation

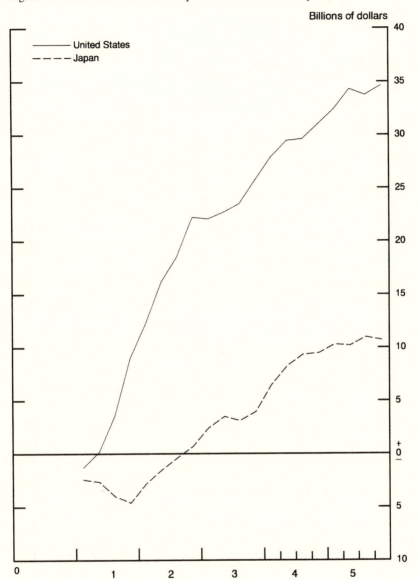

Figure 4.9 Counterfactual Simulations for U.S. Partial Balance of Trade

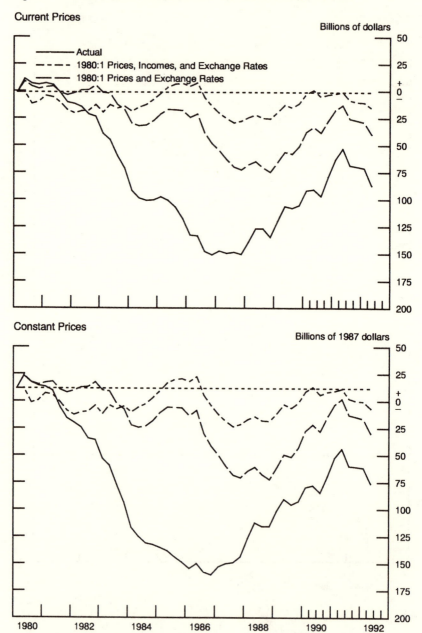

Current Prices

Billions of dollars

——— Actual
– – – – 1980:1 Prices, Incomes, and Exchange Rates
— — — 1980:1 Prices and Exchange Rates

Constant Prices

Billions of 1987 dollars

1980   1982   1984   1986   1988   1990   1992

Note: Dotted line represents 1980:1 value.

Figure 4.10 Counterfactual Simulations for Japanese Nonoil Balance of Trade

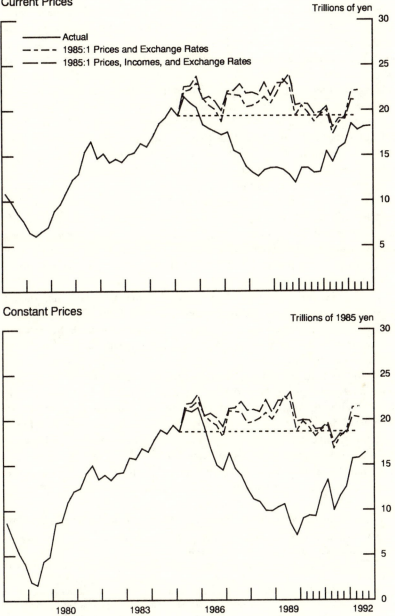

Note: Dotted line equals 1985:1 value.

Figure 4.9 presents two more counterfactual simulations designed to provide a partial-equilibrium accounting of the contributions of changes in relative prices and incomes to movements in the U.S. partial trade balance since 1980. The dashed horizontal line in both top and bottom panels shows the model's prediction of the path of the trade balance if all prices and exchange rates had remained unchanged after 1980:1. The distance between the actual balance and the dashed line can be viewed as the "contribution" of changes in relative (and absolute) prices to the widening of the U.S. trade deficit after 1980.[44] Movements in prices and exchange rates accounted for most of the widening of the real partial trade balance between 1980 and 1986. By 1988–89, after the dollar had reversed its earlier appreciation, the relative-price effect accounted for less than half of the net widening of the deficit from its 1980 level. In 1991, however, it again accounted for most of the gap.

The other factor affecting the external balance was, of course, the path of relative income. The figure shows the model's prediction of the path of the partial trade balance if, in addition to all prices remaining unchanged, U.S. and foreign real incomes had remained at their 1980 levels. The gap between that path and the dashed line can be viewed as the contribution of relative (and absolute) income growth.[45] The income effect reached a maximum around 1988 following the relatively rapid growth of U.S. income to that point.[46] Beyond 1988, however, when U.S. growth slowed noticeably and growth abroad remained strong, the income effect receded sharply. Beginning in mid-1991, the income effect began to widen again as the U.S. economy started to recover from recession and other major industrial countries were, on average, sliding into recession.

A striking feature of Figure 4.9 is the persistence of a significant relative-price effect throughout the period even though the dollar had returned to its 1980 level by the end of 1987. Much of this effect on the real trade balance after 1988 can be attributed to the behavior of imports. As we saw in Figure 4.1, the relative price of U.S. imports has remained significantly below its 1980 level, by contrast with movements in nominal and real exchange rates. This result suggests a somewhat different explanation for the Lawrence-Krugman paradox than the interpretations offered by Lawrence (1990) and Cline (1991).[47]

Figure 4.10 shows a similar set of simulations for Japan. In this case, we

[44] Movements in both relative and absolute prices influence the nominal trade balance, but only relative prices directly affect the real trade balance.

[45] The gap between the horizontal line and the scenario holding all prices and incomes unchanged can be viewed as the "model error."

[46] The income effect was, of course, magnified by the gap between the income elasticities for U.S. imports and exports. As Hooper (1990, 1991) has argued, these "income" effects could well reflect other factors. Nevertheless, it is noteworthy that they are dominated by the relative-price effects for most of the period shown in Figure 4.9.

[47] See also Krugman (1991) and Hooper's comments on Lawrence (1990) and Cline (1991) for

held variables unchanged from their levels at the beginning of 1985, which coincided with a local low point in the yen's real exchange rate. The figure indicates that most of the narrowing of Japan's partial trade balance over the late 1980s can be attributed to the sharp real appreciation of the yen. Relative changes in incomes also contributed to the narrowing of the deficit, but their effect was generally much smaller than the relative-price effect for most of the period.[48] The price effect narrowed substantially toward the end of the period, even though the yen was still significantly above its 1985:1 level in real terms and the relative price of Japanese imports was well below its 1985:1 level. This result can be attributed to the net decline in the relative price of Japanese exports (see Figure 4.3) and to the fact that the estimated price elasticity of exports exceeds that of imports for Japan.

Further work in this area should test the sensitivity of these results to alternative measures of the relative prices of Japanese exports and imports.

6 Conclusions

We can draw a number of conclusions from our investigations. First, the conventional partial-equilibrium model of the trade balance has performed generally fairly well in predicting the paths of the U.S. and Japanese external balances over the past decade. For the United States, the model was somewhat off track for several years during the mid-1980s but has tracked well more recently.

Second, in a partial-equilibrium setting, exchange-rate changes have a significant and substantial influence on movements of external balances. This view is supported by a substantial empirical literature focusing on the estimation of price elasticities in trade, by casual inspection of the data, and by our own econometric estimates of trade elasticities, which are roughly in line with the mean of the estimates obtained by others. The only notable evidence to the contrary, based on single-equation models of the trade balance, does not significantly challenge the conventional result.

Third, estimates of price elasticities reported in studies using data primarily for the floating-rate period (since 1973) are generally smaller than those in studies based primarily on data for the earlier Bretton Woods period. This

---

a discussion of this issue. The Lawrence-Krugman paradox asks why, by 1989–90, the U.S. external deficit had not returned to its 1980 level after the dollar had done so. Lawrence explains the paradox in terms of the Houthakker-Magee result; Cline explains it in terms of errors in the measurement of the real exchange rate (that, on some measures, the dollar's real exchange rate did not return all the way to its 1980 level).

[48] The relatively small role for incomes stems from the similarity of income elasticities for exports (1.1) and imports (1.2) combined with the similarity in the growth rates of Japan's income and of Japan's trade partners' incomes taken together.

observation lends some support to the view that increases in exchange-rate volatility have reduced the sensitivity of trade flows to movements in exchange rates.

Fourth, Japanese real trade flows appear to be considerably less responsive to exchange-rate changes than U.S. real trade flows, and this difference can be traced only in part to evidence that Japanese and U.S. exporters differ in the extent to which they pass through exchange-rate changes to the foreign-currency prices of their exports. The robustness of this result and reasons for it should be explored further. Can the counterpart of relatively high U.S. price elasticities (or relatively low Japanese elasticities) be found in the trade of other countries?

Fifth, further work must be done on the best way to measure (and capture in trade-demand equations) the effects of changes in relative prices or price competitiveness. The various available measures of real and relative exchange rates show widely different movements over relatively brief periods of time.

Sixth, our work draws attention to two especially notable, even paradoxical, developments: the net decline in the relative price of Japanese exports over the past ten years in the face of a sharp appreciation of the yen, and the comparative stability of the relative price of U.S. imports (excluding oil and computers) over roughly the same period in the face of a significant depreciation of the dollar. These two developments are no doubt interrelated to some degree, and the second, in particular, is consistent with, but does not necessarily confirm, the presence of hysteresis.

Seventh, the substantial literature on exchange-rate pass-through that has sprouted during the past decade has contributed some interesting new theoretical insights but has probably not greatly affected the validity of conventional empirical estimates of the effects of exchange rates on import and export prices.

Finally, Japanese exporters tend to pass through a significantly smaller percentage of any given exchange-rate change than do U.S. exporters. Much of this difference may be attributable, however, to the greater sensitivity of Japanese production costs to exchange-rate changes; Japanese export prices fall when the yen appreciates, partly because the prices of petroleum and other raw materials fall in Japan.

Appendix A: Real Exchange Rates, Relative Prices, and the Terms of Trade

As noted in the text, a variety of alternative measures of relative prices and real exchange rates have been used to model trade flows and external balances. These measures are far from uniform, however, and can show widely varying movements over time. The purpose of this appendix is to provide a brief analysis of the conceptual relationships among relative prices, real exchange rates, and the terms of trade and to document how widely these series have differed empirically over the past two decades for both the United States and Japan. Marston (1987) presents a more comprehensive analysis of the theoretical relationships among alternative measures of real exchange rates. Marquez (1992) provides a detailed empirical analysis of several different measures of real exchange rates and their performance in U.S. trade equations.

To begin with the conceptual relationships among the measures, equations (6) to (8) in Section 2 define the *relative price of imports*, inverted as

$$P/P_m = S \cdot [\tau \, P_T + (1 - \tau)P_N]/P_T^* , \qquad (A1)$$

where P_T and P_T^* are the prices of traded goods, P and P^* are indexes of the prices of tradables and nontradables, and τ and τ^* are the shares of tradable goods in expenditures at home and abroad. Here and hereafter, we work with a two-country world, comprising the home country and a foreign country (or rest of the world). From equations (9) to (11), the relative price of exports is defined as

$$S \cdot P_x/P^* = S \cdot P_T/ \, [\tau^* P_T^* + (1 - \tau^*)P_N^*] . \qquad (A2)$$

The terms of trade are defined as

$$P_x/P_m = S \cdot P_T/P_T . \qquad (A3)$$

The real exchange rate is generally defined in terms of the relative levels of broad national price indexes or labor-cost indicators. One such measure is the ratio of output prices in the two countries:

$$S \cdot P/P^* = S \cdot [\tau P_T + (1 - \tau)P_N]/[\tau^* P_T^* + (1 - \tau^*)P_N^*] . \qquad (A4)$$

Another measure of the real exchange rate is the ratio of consumer prices (P_c) in the two countries:

$$S \cdot P_c/P_c^* = S \cdot [\theta P_T + \omega P_N + (1 - \theta - \omega)P_T/S]/[\theta^* P_T^*$$
$$+ \, \omega^* P_N^* + (1 - \theta^* - \omega^*)S \cdot P_T] , \qquad (A5)$$

where θ, ω, and $1 - \theta - \omega$ are the shares of home tradables, home nontradables, and imports in home consumption (the foreign price index is defined similarly). Yet another frequently used measure of the real exchange rate is the ratio of unit labor costs (ULC):

$$S \cdot ULC/ULC^* . \qquad (A6)$$

Relative unit labor costs are generally defined in terms of unit labor costs in the manufacturing or tradables sectors.

An inspection of equations (A1) through (A5) suggests that divergences among the relative prices of exports and imports, the terms of trade, and the real exchange rate will tend to be larger the greater the shares of nontradables in national outputs, the greater the differences between prices of tradables and nontradables within countries, and the greater the differences between prices of nontradables across countries. The real exchange rate measured in terms of consumer prices will deviate from that measured in terms of output prices the greater the difference in prices of tradable goods across countries.

As Marston (1987) notes, the real exchange rate based on output (GDP) deflators is largely influenced by two factors: relative unit labor costs in tradables and the ratios of unit labor costs in tradables and nontradables in each country.

Appendix B: Data Construction and Sources

To compute weighted averages of foreign variables, including effective exchange rates, we used the formula

$$X = \prod_i X_i^{wi} \tag{B1}$$

where X_i is a variable specific to country i, X is aggregated across all i, and wi is the weight given to country i in aggregation. The weights used in aggregation are presented in Table 4.B1; these include bilateral import and export weights and world trade weights.

Our data sources are listed below. Table 4.B2 indicates the source used for each individual variable:[49]

International
  1. Bank for International Settlements
  2. International Monetary Fund, *International Financial Statistics*
Canada
  3. Canadian Statistics, *Canadian Economic Observer*
France
  4. Institute National de Statistiques et Etudes Economiques, *Indices Agrégatifs des Prix de Vente Industriel*
Germany
  5. Deutsche Bundesbank, *Monthly Report of the Deutsche Bundesbank*

---

[49] The exchange-rate indexes and foreign prices in the relative price of exports are weighted by each country's share in world exports. We prefer these weights to bilateral export weights because they allow some scope for third-country competitive effects. For example, although Germany accounts for a relatively small share of total U.S. exports, German exports compete with U.S. exports in other markets, and Germany's relatively large share in world trade reflects to some degree that third-country competition.

Italy

    6. Istituto Nazionale di Statistica, *ISTAT*

Japan

    7. Bank of Japan, *Economic Statistics Monthly of the BOJ*

Mexico

    8. Bank of Mexico, *Indicadores Económicos*

    9. Bank of Mexico, *Avance de Información Económica*

Taiwan

    10. Central Bank of China, *Financial Statistics Monthly*

    11. Central Bank of China, *National Income in Taiwan Area of the Republic of China*

United States

    12. Federal Reserve Board, *Federal Reserve Bulletin*

    13. U.S. Bureau of Labor, Statistics Tapes

TABLE 4.B1

Relative Trade Shares, 1987–89 (percent)

To/From	Share of World Exports	Exports			Imports		
		United States	Japan	Germany	United States	Japan	Germany
Canada	7.1	34	4.3	2.0	24	8.7	1.7
France	10.2	5	2.6	31.3	4	3.3	27.0
Germany	16.3	7	7.7	—	8	7.2	—
Italy	8.2	3	1.2	19.8	4	2.5	23.5
Japan	13.3	16	—	3.4	27	—	11.5
Korea	5.4	6	9.7	1.3	8	8.4	2.5
Mexico	2.3	13	1.2	1.3	9	0.8	0.5
Taiwan	5.5	7	9.7	1.3	11	8.3	2.6
United Kingdom	9.2	9	5.6	19.0	5	3.8	14.3
United States	22.5	—	58.0	20.6	—	57.0	16.4
	(billions of dollars, annual rates)						
Total ten countries (% of world)	1,575.7 (59.4)	191.5 (61.4)	158.7 (61.8)	139.3 (43.6)	313.8 (68.4)	88.2 (48.3)	110.5 (44.3)
Total world	2,650.7	312	257	319.6	459.1	182.7	249.5

Source: Calculated from IMF, *Direction of Trade Statistics.*

TABLE 4.B2

Data Sources by Variable and Country

	Country and Source Number									
	CA	FR	GE	IT	JA	KO	MX	TA	UK	US
Exchange rate	12	12	12	12	12	12	12	12	12	12
Export price			1		1					12
Export value			1		1					12
Import price			1		1					12
Import value			1		1					12
GDP	1	1	1	1	1	2	9	11	1	1
GDP deflator	1	1	1	1	1	2	9	11	1	1
PPI, manufacturing	3	4	5	6	7	2	8	10	1	13
ULC, manufacturing	2	2	2	2	2	13	8	13	2	2
WPI, raw materials					1					
World commodity price	2									

Note: Countries are Canada, France, Germany, Italy, Japan, Korea, Mexico, Taiwan, the United Kingdom, and the United States. Numbers correspond to the list of references in Appendix B.

References

Ahluwalia, Isher, and Ernesto Hernández-Catá, "An Econometric Model of U.S. Merchandise Imports Under Fixed and Fluctuating Exchange Rates, 1959–73," *International Monetary Fund Staff Papers*, 22 (November 1975), pp. 791–824.

Baldwin, Richard E., "Hysteresis in Import Prices: The Beachhead Effect," *American Economic Review*, 78 (September 1988), pp. 773–785.

Bergsten, C. Fred, ed., *International Adjustment and Financing: The Lessons from 1985–1991*, Washington, D.C., Institute for International Economics, 1991.

Blecker, Robert A., *Beyond the Twin Deficits*, New York, M. E. Sharpe, 1992.

Branson, William H., "The Trade Effects of the 1971 Currency Realignments," *Brookings Papers on Economic Activity*, No. 1 (1972), pp. 15–65.

Branson, William H., and Richard C. Marston, "Price and Output Adjustment in Japanese Manufacturing," National Bureau of Economic Research Working Paper No. 2878, Cambridge, Mass., National Bureau of Economic Research, 1989.

Bryant, Ralph C., "The U.S. External Deficit: 'An Update,'" Brookings Discussion Paper in International Economics No. 63, Washington, D.C., Brookings Institution, January 1988.

Bryant, Ralph C., Gerald Holtham, and Peter Hooper, *External Deficits and the Dollar: The Pit and the Pendulum*, Washington, D.C., Brookings Institution, 1988.

Caves, Richard E., "Exchange-Rate Movements and Foreign Direct Investment in the United States," in David R. Audretch and Michael P. Claudon, eds., *The Internationalization of U.S. Markets*, New York, New York University Press, 1989, pp. 199–229.

Caves, Richard E., Jeffrey A. Frankel, and Ronald W. Jones, *World Trade Payments: An Introduction*, 5th ed., Glenview, Ill., Scott, Foresman, 1993.

Chang, Tse Chun, "International Comparison of Demand for Imports," *Review of Economic Studies*, 13 (No. 34, 1946), pp. 53–67.

Clarida, Richard H., "Co-integration, Aggregate Consumption, and the Demand for Imports," Columbia University, 1991, processed.

Clark, Peter B., "The Effects of Recent Exchange Rate Changes on the U.S. Trade Balance, in Peter B. Clark, Dennis E. Logue, and Richard J. Sweeney, eds., *The Effects of Exchange Rate Adjustments*, Washington, D.C., U.S. Treasury, 1974.

Cline, William R., *United States External Adjustment and the World Economy*, Washington D.C., Institute for International Economics, 1989.

———, "U.S. External Adjustment: Progress, Prognosis, and Interpretation," in Bergsten, *International Adjustment and Financing*, 1991, pp. 15–55.

Deppler, Michael, and Duncan Ripley, "The World Trade Model: Merchandise Trade," *International Monetary Fund Staff Papers*, 25 (March 1978), pp. 147–206.

Deyak, Timothy, W. Charles Sawyer, and Richard Sprinkle, "An Empirical Examination of the Structural Stability of Disaggregated U.S. Import Demand," *Review of Economics and Statistics*, 71 (May 1989), pp. 337–341.

Dixit, Avinash, "Entry and Exit Decisions Under Uncertainty," *Journal of Political Economy*, 97 (June 1989), pp. 620–638.

Dixit, Avinash, and Joseph Stiglitz, "Monopolistic Competition and Optimum Product Diversity," *American Economic Review*, 67 (June 1977), pp. 297–308.

Dornbusch, Rudiger, "Exchange Rates and Prices," *American Economic Review*, 77 (March 1987), pp. 93–106.

Eckstein, Otto, and Gary Fromm, "The Price Equation," *American Economic Review*, 68 (December 1968), pp. 1159–1183.

Ericsson, Neil R., and Jaime Marquez, "Encompassing the Forecasts of U.S. Trade-Balance Models," *Review of Economics and Statistics*, 75 (February 1993), pp. 19–31.

Feenstra, Robert C., "Symmetric Pass-Through of Tariffs and Exchange Rates Under Imperfect Competition: An Empirical Test," *Journal of International Economics*, 27 (August 1989), pp. 25–45.

———, "New Goods and Index Numbers: U.S. Import Prices," National Bureau of Economic Research Working Paper No. 3610, Cambridge, Mass., National Bureau of Economic Research, February 1991.

Fisher, Eric, "A Model of Exchange Rate Pass-Through," *Journal of International Economics*, 26 (February 1989), pp. 119–137.

Frankel, Jeffrey A., "Ambiguous Policy Multipliers in Theory and in Empirical Models," in Ralph C. Bryant, Dale W. Henderson, Gerald Holtham, Peter Hooper, and Steven A. Symansky, eds., *Empirical Macroeconomics for Interdependent Economies*, Washington, D.C., Brookings Institution, 1988, pp. 17–26.

Frenkel, Jacob A., and Assaf Razin, *Fiscal Policies and the World Economy*, Cambridge, Mass., MIT Press, 1987a.

————, "The Mundell-Fleming Model a Quarter Century Later," *International Monetary Fund Staff Papers*, 34 (December 1987b), pp. 567–620.

Froot, Kenneth A., and Paul Klemperer, "Exchange Rate Pass-Through When Market Share Matters," *American Economic Review*, 79 (September 1989), pp. 637–653.

Froot, Kenneth A., and Jeremy C. Stein, "Exchange Rates and Foreign Direct Investment: An Imperfect Capital Markets Approach," *Quarterly Journal of Economics*, 106 (November 1991), pp. 1191–1217.

Gagnon, Joseph E., and Michael M. Knetter, "Markup Adjustment and Exchange Rate Fluctuation: Evidence from Panel Data on Automobile Exports," National Bureau of Economic Research Working Paper No. 4123, Cambridge, Mass., National Bureau of Economic Research, July 1992.

Geraci, Vincent, and Wilfred Prewo, "An Empirical Demand and Supply Model of Multilateral Trade," *Review of Economics and Statistics*, 64 (May 1982), pp. 432–441.

Giovannini, Alberto, "Exchange Rates and Traded Goods Prices," *Journal of International Economics*, 24 (February 1988), pp. 45–68.

Goldstein, Morris, and Mohsin Khan, "The Supply and Demand for Exports: A Simultaneous Approach," *Review of Economics and Statistics*, 60 (May 1978), pp. 275–286.

————, "Income and Price Effects in Foreign Trade," in Ronald W. Jones and Peter B. Kenen, eds., *Handbook of International Economics*, Vol. 2, Amsterdam and New York, North-Holland, Elsevier, 1985, pp. 1041–1105.

Goldstein, Morris, Mohsin Khan, and Lawrence Officer, "Prices of Tradeable and Nontradeable Goods in the Demand for Total Imports," *Review of Economics and Statistics*, 62 (May 1980), pp. 190–199.

Gregory, Robert G., "United States Imports and Internal Pressure of Demand: 1948–1968," *American Economic Review*, 61 (March 1971), pp. 28–47.

Haberler, Gottfried, "The Market for Foreign Exchange and the Stability of the Balance of Payments: A Theoretical Analysis," *Kyklos*, 3 (1949), pp. 193–218.

Haynes, Stephen, and Joe Stone, "Secular and Cyclical Responses of U.S. Trade to Income: An Evaluation of Traditional Models," *Review of Economics and Statistics*, 65 (February 1983), pp. 87–95.

Heien, Dale, "Structural Stability and the Estimation of International Import Price Elasticities," *Kyklos*, 21 (1968), pp. 695–711.

Helkie, William, and Peter Hooper, "An Empirical Analysis of the External Deficit, 1980–86," in Ralph C. Bryant, Gerald Holtham, and Peter Hooper, eds., *External Deficits and the Dollar: The Pit and the Pendulum*, Washington, D.C., Brookings Institution, 1988, pp. 10–56.

Hickok, Susan A., "Japanese Trade Balance Adjustment to Yen Appreciation," *Federal Reserve Bank of New York Quarterly Review* (Autumn 1989), pp. 33–47.

Hooper, Peter, "Forecasting U.S. Export and Import Prices and Volumes in a Changing World Economy," International Finance Discussion Paper No. 99, Washington, D.C., Board of Governors of the Federal Reserve System, December 1976.

————, "The Stability of Income and Price Elasticities in U.S. Trade, 1975- 1977," International Finance Discussion Paper No. 119, Washington, D.C., Board of Governors of the Federal Reserve System, June 1978.

————, "The Dollar, External Imbalance, and the U.S. Economy," *Journal of Economic and Monetary Affairs*, 2 (Winter 1988), pp. 30–54.

————, "Exchange Rates and U.S. External Adjustment in the Short Run and the Long Run," International Finance Discussion Paper No. 346, Washington, D.C., Board of Governors of the Federal Reserve System, March 1989.

————, "Comment" on Lawrence, "U.S. Current Account Adjustment: An Appraisal," *Brookings Papers on Economic Activity*, No. 2 (1990), pp. 383–387.

————, "Comment" on Cline, "U.S. External Adjustment: Progress, Prognosis, and Interpretation," in Bergsten, *International Adjustment and Financing*, 1991, pp. 103–112.

Hooper, Peter, and Catherine L. Mann, *The Emergence and Persistence of the U.S. External Imbalance, 1980–97*, Princeton Studies in International Finance No. 65, Princeton, N.J., Princeton University, International Finance Section, October 1989a.

————, "Exchange Rate Pass-Through in the 1980s: The Case of U.S. Imports of Manufactures," *Brookings Papers on Economic Activity*, No. 1 (1989b), pp. 297–329.

Hooper, Peter, and J. David Richardson, *International Economic Transactions: Issues in Measurement and Empirical Research*, Chicago, University of Chicago Press, 1991.

Houthakker, Hendrik, and Stephen Magee, "Income and Price Elasticities in World Trade," *Review of Economics and Statistics*, 51 (May 1969), pp. 111–125.

Isard, Peter, "How Far Can We Push the Law of One Price?" *American Economic Review*, 67 (December 1977), pp. 942–948.

Johansen, Soren, "Statistical Analysis of Cointegration Vectors," *Journal of Economic Dynamics and Control*, 12 (June-September 1988), pp. 231–254.

Kasa, Kenneth, "Adjustment Costs and Pricing to Market," *Journal of International Economics*, 32 (February 1992), pp. 1–30.

Kenen, Peter B., "Macroeconomic Theory and Policy: How the Closed Economy Was Opened," in Ronald W. Jones and Peter B. Kenen, eds., *Handbook of International Economics*, Vol. 2, Amsterdam and New York, North-Holland, Elsevier, 1985, pp. 625–677.

Khan, Mohsin, and Knud Ross, "Cyclical and Secular Income Elasticities of the Demand for Imports," *Review of Economics and Statistics*, 57 (August 1975), pp. 357–361.

————, "The Functional Form of the Aggregate Import Demand Equation," *Journal of International Economics*, 7 (May 1977), pp. 149–160.

Kindleberger, Charles P., *International Economics*, Homewood, Ill., Irwin, 1963.

Knetter, Michael M., "Exchange Rates and Corporate Pricing Strategies," National Bureau of Economic Research Working Paper No. 4151, Cambridge, Mass., National Bureau of Economic Research, 1992.

————, "International Comparisons of Pricing-to-Market Behavior," *American Economic Review*, 83 (June 1993), pp. 473–486.

Kohli, Ulrich, *Technology, Duality, and Foreign Trade*, Ann Arbor, University of Michigan Press, 1991.

Krause, Lawrence, "United States Imports, 1947–1958," *Econometrica*, 30 (April 1962), pp. 221–238.

Kravis, Irving B., and Robert E. Lipsey, "Price Behavior in Light of Balance of Payments Theories," *Journal of International Economics*, 8 (May 1978), pp. 193–246.

Kreinin, Mordechai, "Price Elasticities in International Trade," *Review of Economics and Statistics*, 49 (November 1967), pp. 510–516.

Krugman, Paul R., "Pricing to Market When the Exchange Rate Changes," in Sven W. Arndt and J. David Richardson, eds., *Real-Financial Linkages Among Open Economies*, Cambridge, Mass., MIT Press, 1987, pp. 49–70.

———, "Differences in Income Elasticities and Trends in Real Exchange Rates," *European Economic Review*, 33 (May 1989a), pp. 1031–1054.

———, *Exchange-Rate Instability*, Cambridge, Mass., MIT Press, 1989b.

———, "Has the Adjustment Process Worked?" in Bergsten, *International Adjustment and Financing*, 1991, pp. 277–322.

Krugman, Paul R., and Richard E. Baldwin, "The Persistence of the U.S. Trade Deficit," *Brookings Papers on Economic Activity*, No. 1 (1987), pp. 1–43.

Lawrence, Robert, "U.S. Current Account Adjustment: An Appraisal," *Brookings Papers on Economic Activity*, No. 2 (1990), pp. 343–392.

Magee, Stephen, "Tariffs and U.S. Trade," Working Paper No. 14, Graduate School of Business, University of Chicago, 1972.

Mann, Catherine L., "The Effects of Aggregate Demand and Exchange Rate Shocks on the Profit Margins of Internationally Traded Goods," paper presented at the Conference on Monetary Uncertainty, Financial Futures, and Economic Activity at the International Futures and Commodity Institute, Geneva, November 1986a.

———, "Prices, Profit Margins, and Exchange Rates," *Federal Reserve Bulletin* (June 1986b), pp. 366–379.

Marquez, Jaime, "Bilateral Trade Elasticities," *Review of Economics and Statistics*, 72 (February 1990), pp. 70–77.

———, "The Dynamics of Uncertainty or the Uncertainty of Dynamics: Stochastic J-Curves," *Review of Economics and Statistics*, 73 (February 1991), pp. 125–133.

———, "Real Exchange Rates: Measurement and Implications for Predicting U.S. External Imbalances," International Finance Discussion Paper No. 427, Washington, D.C., Board of Governors of the Federal Reserve System, March 1992.

———, "The Autonomy of Trade Elasticities for Trade Among Canada, Japan, and the United States," *Japan and the World Economy*, 5 (September 1993), pp. 179–195.

Marquez, Jaime, and Neil R. Ericsson, "Evaluating Trade-Account Forecasts," in Ralph C. Bryant, Peter Hooper, and Catherine L. Mann, eds., *Evaluating Policy Regimes: New Research in Empirical Macroeconomics*, Washington D.C., Brookings Institution, 1993, pp. 671–732.

Marquez, Jaime, and Caryl McNeilly, "Income and Price Elasticities for Exports of Developing Countries," *Review of Economics and Statistics*, 70 (May 1988), pp. 306–314.

Marston, Richard C., "Income Effects and Delivery Lags in British Import Demand: 1955–67," *Journal of International Economics*, 1 (November 1971), pp. 375–399.

———, "Real Exchange Rates and Productivity Growth in the United States and Japan," in Sven W. Arndt and J. David Richardson, eds., *Real-Financial Linkages Among Open Economies*, Cambridge, Mass., MIT Press, 1987, pp. 71–96.

———, "Pricing to Market in Japanese Manufacturing," *Journal of International Economics*, 29 (November 1990), pp. 217–236.

Meade, Ellen E., "Exchange Rates, Adjustment, and the J-Curve," *Federal Reserve Bulletin*, 74 (October 1988), pp. 633–644.

————, "Computers and the Trade Deficit: The Case of Falling Prices," in Peter Hooper and J. David Richardson, eds., *International Economic Transactions: Issues in Measurement and Empirical Research*, Chicago, University of Chicago Press, 1991, pp. 61–88.

————, "A Fresh Look at the Responsiveness of Trade Flows to Exchange Rates," paper presented at the Western Economic Association, San Francisco, July 1992.

Melick, William R., "Estimating Pass-Through: Structure and Stability," International Finance Discussion Paper No. 387, Washington, D.C., Board of Governors of the Federal Reserve System, September 1990.

Mendoza, Enrique G., "The Terms of Trade and Economic Fluctuations," International Monetary Fund Working Paper No. 92/98, Washington, D.C., International Monetary Fund, November 1992.

Miller, Joseph, and Michele Fratianni, "The Lagged Adjustment of U.S. Trade to Prices and Income," *Journal of Economics and Business*, 26 (Spring 1974), pp. 191–198.

Moffet, Michael, "The J-Curve Revisited: An Empirical Examination for the United States," *Journal of International Money and Finance*, 8 (September 1989), pp. 425–444.

Murphy, Robert G., "Import Pricing and the Trade Balance in a Popular Model of Exchange Rate Determination," *Journal of International Money and Finance*, 8 (September 1989), pp. 345–357.

Murray, Tracy, and Peter Ginman, "An Empirical Examination of the Traditional Aggregate Import Demand Model," *Review of Economics and Statistics*, 58 (February 1976), pp. 75–80.

Noland, Marcus, "Japanese Trade Elasticities and the J-Curve," *Review of Economics and Statistics*, 71 (February 1989), pp. 175–179.

Obstfeld, Maurice, "Aggregate Spending and the Terms of Trade: Is There a Laursen-Meltzer Effect?" *Quarterly Journal of Economics*, 97 (May 1982), pp. 251–270.

Ohno, Kenichi, "Export Pricing Behavior of Manufacturing: A U.S.-Japan Comparison," *International Monetary Fund Staff Papers*, 36 (September 1989), pp. 550–579.

Orcutt, Guy, "Measurement of Price Elasticities in International Trade," *Review of Economics and Statistics*, 32 (May 1950), pp. 117–132.

Rose, Andrew K., "Exchange Rates and the Trade Balance," *Economics Letters*, 34 (November 1990), pp. 271–275.

————, "The Role of Exchange Rates in a Popular Model of International Trade: Does the Marshall-Lerner Condition Hold?" *Journal of International Economics*, 30 (May 1991), pp. 301–316.

Rose, Andrew K., and Janet L. Yellen, "Is There a J-Curve?" *Journal of Monetary Economics*, 24 (July 1989), pp. 53–68.

Stern, Robert, Christopher Baum, and Mark Green, "Evidence on Structural Change in the Demand for Aggregate U.S. Imports and Exports," *Journal of Political Economy*, 87 (February 1979), pp. 179–192.

Stern, Robert, Jonathan Francis, and Bruce Schumacher, *Price Elasticities in International Trade: An Annotated Bibliography*, London, Macmillan, 1976.

Svensson, Lars E. O., and Assaf Razin, "The Terms of Trade and the Current Account: The Harberger-Laursen-Metzler Effect," *Journal of Political Economy*, 91 (February 1983), pp. 91–125.

Taplin, Grant B., "A Model of World Trade," in Robert J. Ball, ed., *The International*

Linkage of National Economic Models, Amsterdam, North-Holland, 1973, pp. 177–223.

Ueda, Kazuo, "Trade Balance Adjustment with Imported Intermediate Goods: The Japanese Case," *Review of Economics and Statistics*, 65 (November 1983), pp. 618–625.

Warner, Dennis, and Mordechai Kreinin, "Determinants of International Trade Flows," *Review of Economics and Statistics*, 65 (February 1983), pp. 96–104.

Wilson, John, and Wendy Takacs, "Differential Responses to Price and Exchange Rate Influences in the Foreign Trade of Selected Industrial Countries," *Review of Economics and Statistics*, 61 (May 1979), pp. 267–279.

Yadav, Gopal, "Variable Elasticities and Non-Price Rationing in the Import Demand Function of Canada, 1956:1–1973:4," *Canadian Journal of Economics*, 10 (November 1977), pp. 702–712.

Yoshitomi, Masaru, "Surprises and Lessons from Japanese External Adjustment in 1985–91," in Bergsten, *International Adjustment and Financing*, 1991, pp. 123–152.

5

The Dynamic-Optimizing Approach to the Current Account: Theory and Evidence

ASSAF RAZIN

THE PAST decade has witnessed the development of a large theoretical literature on the dynamic-optimizing (or intertemporal) approach to the current account. The models developed have typically emphasized the effects on the current-account balance of real factors such as productivity, the terms of trade, and government spending and taxes, which operate through intertemporal substitution (IS) in consumption, production, and investment.[1] But how important is the role of intertemporal substitution? Might this micro-based theory indeed be wrong? We can answer this question by deriving the empirical implications of the theory and by proving or disproving the importance of the role played by intertemporal substitution. Although the following discussion does not engage in formal statistical testing, the numbers it presents and analyzes shed some light on the validity of the intertemporal theory's key testable hypotheses.

The traditional Mundell-Fleming approach to the macroeconomic modeling of an open economy treats the trade balance as a sideshow, important only for its effect on current output. This is perhaps because it pays little attention to capital and debt accumulation. At center stage are the exchange rate, output, and employment. Under a flexible exchange rate, a current transitory fiscal expansion, which does not alter expectations about the future value of the exchange rate, induces a rightward shift of the IS schedule, raising the level of

I thank Giuseppe Bertola for useful comments.

[1] The intertemporal approach extends Fisher's (1930) analysis to the entire spectrum of macroeconomic decisionmaking, including saving, investment, and labor-supply decisions. Examples of such extensions in the modeling of consumption (saving) decisions are Modigliani and Brumberg (1954), Friedman (1957), and Hall (1978). Examples in the context of investment theory are Lucas (1967), Uzawa (1969), Tobin (1969), Lucas and Prescott (1971), Abel (1979), Hayashi (1982), and Abel and Blanchard (1983). Elements of the intertemporal approach have been used for some time in the modeling of open economies, with special emphasis given to international borrowing and the behavior of the current account. Examples include Bruno (1976), Buiter (1981, 1987), Eaton and Gersovitz (1981), Sachs (1981, 1984), Obstfeld (1982), Dornbusch (1983), Razin (1984), Penati (1987), and Svensson and Razin (1983), who reexamine the much earlier analyses by Harberger (1950) and Laursen and Metzler (1950) on the effects changes in the terms of trade have on saving.

output (under the Keynesian assumption of price rigidity) and raising the domestic interest rate. To maintain interest parity, the rise in the interest rate must result in the appreciation of the domestic currency. The current account must deteriorate, because output has risen and the domestic currency has appreciated. Under a fixed exchange rate, interest arbitrage ensures equality between the domestic and foreign interest rates. Consequently, a fiscal expansion that induces a rightward shift of the IS schedule gains full potency in raising the level of output, because there is no currency appreciation to offset it. The current account must deteriorate in this case, too. Yet the links between the fiscal deficit and the trade deficit, on the one hand, and between the trade deficit and the exchange rate, on the other, are empirically weak (Kotlikoff, 1992, chap. 3).

In contrast with this standard static model, the modern intertemporal optimizing approach provides a framework suitable for positive and normative analyses of current-account dynamics. The predictive content of the model is enhanced by taking explicit account of the intertemporal budget constraint and of optimization by individual households and firms.

The key factors governing the nature of the macroeconomic equilibrium differ drastically across the two models. In the static income-expenditure model, the nature of the macroeconomic equilibrium reflects the relative magnitudes of parameters measuring the effects of changes in income on spending and the demand for money. In the intertemporal model, by contrast, the nature of the equilibrium reflects parameters measuring the effects of intertemporal substitution and the debt-income position. What might we learn about certain recent episodes by following the intertemporal approach rather than the less rigorous Mundell-Fleming approach? Income-expenditure models of the Mundell-Fleming sort suggest a simple relation between the government budget and economic activity: a cut in the government deficit depresses consumption and output. In many countries, however, large cuts in government spending carried out as part of stabilization programs have led to expansions rather than contractions in economic activity and have resulted in improvements in the current-account balance (Giavazzi and Pagano, 1990; Bertola and Drazen, 1993). In Denmark in the early 1980s and in Ireland in the late 1980s, the government deficit was large relative to GDP, and public debt was growing rapidly. Giavazzi and Pagano (1990) show, however, that the consumption-to-GDP ratio rose and the current account improved in the aftermath of stabilization programs that made large budget cuts. These results are inconsistent with the predictions of income-expenditure models but are quite consistent with the predictions of intertemporal models.

A basic assumption that characterizes all intertemporal models is capital mobility. If there is no such mobility, a country cannot engage in intertemporal substitution, and there can be no intertemporal approach. It is suggestive to think in terms of a dichotomy between perfect and imperfect capital mobility. Perfect capital mobility seems to prevail, more or less, between developed countries, whereas imperfect capital mobility seems to prevail between developed and less-developed countries. To the extent that this observation is true, we should expect the intertemporal model to perform better in explaining current-account fluctuations among developed countries (that is, those belonging to the OECD) than among less-developed countries.

Section 1 of this paper builds an empirically implementable model of the current account. Section 2 uses that model to derive the essential time-series properties of the real exchange rate. The positive implications of the intertemporal approach are then checked against panel and international cross-section data in Section 3. The normative implications of the intertemporal approach are examined in Section 4, which highlights the effects of taxes, incentives, and capital controls and the implications of the model for the convergence of growth rates. Section 5 concludes the discussion.

1 Current-Account Theory

The intertemporal approach, like the old absorption approach, begins with the national-income identity. Unlike earlier approaches, however, it models investment and consumption (saving) in ways that focus on intertemporal optimization and the differing effects of various shocks. It distinguishes in particular among four types of shocks: those that are transitory in duration, those that are persistent, those that are country specific, and those that are common across countries. Each type of shock has distinct effects on the dynamics of a country's saving-investment balance. Thus, its current-account balance is driven by different shocks in distinctly different ways.

The benchmark model I use to illustrate the intertemporal approach assumes the existence of riskless assets traded freely, a single representative agent, and perfect competition in the goods market. Nevertheless, the main findings about the different effects of the various shocks carry over to intertemporal models with risky assets, heterogeneous populations, and imperfect competition. The conclusions depend importantly, however, on the implicit assumption, maintained throughout, that only noncontingent borrowing is possible, because that assumption rules out diversification against country-specific shocks (Obstfeld's Chapter 6 in this volume examines the theory and evidence on diversification).

By the national-income identity, the current-account balance is given by

$$CA_t = Y_t - Z_t - C_t + (R - 1)F_{t-1} \, ,$$

where CA_t, Y_t, Z_t, C_t, R_t, and F_{t-1} stand for the current-account surplus, output, investment, consumption, interest factor, and lagged foreign assets, respectively. I look first at the modeling of investment and then at the modeling of consumption (saving).

Investment

Consider a small open economy, producing a single aggregate tradable good (see Leiderman and Razin, 1991; Mendoza, 1991; and Glick and Rogoff, 1992). The production function for that good, Y, is Cobb-Douglas:

$$Y_t = AK_t^\alpha, \tag{1}$$

where A, α, and K denote the productivity level, the distributive share of capital, and the capital stock, respectively. I assume that productivity shocks follow a first-order autoregressive stochastic process:

$$A_t = \rho A_{t-1} + \epsilon_t, \ 0 \le \rho \le 1, \tag{2}$$

where ρ and ϵ denote the persistence parameter and a zero-mean i.i.d. term, respectively.

Firms maximize the expected value of the discounted sum of profits subject to the available production technology and to a cost-of-adjustment investment technology. According to the latter, gross investment (Z) is specified as

$$Z_t = I_t \left(1 + \frac{g}{2} \frac{I_t}{K_t} \right), \tag{3}$$

where $I_t = K_{t+1} - K_t$ and g denote net capital formation (assuming zero depreciation) and the cost-of-adjustment coefficient, respectively. Thus, in the presence of costs of adjustment, gross investment typically exceeds net capital formation, because of the costs of the reorganization and retraining associated with the installation of new capital equipment.

The optimal-investment rule implies that the cost of investing an additional unit of capital in the current period must be equal to the expected present value of the next period's marginal productivity of capital *plus* the next period's induced fall in the adjustment cost of investment resulting from the enlarged stock of capital (that is, the derivative of [3] with respect to K) *plus* the residual value in the next period of the capital remaining for the entire future:

$$E_t R^{-1} \left[\alpha A_{t+1} K_{t+1}^{\alpha-1} + \frac{g}{2} \left(\frac{I_{t+1}}{K_{t+1}} \right)^2 + q_{t+1} \right] = q_t, \tag{4}$$

where E_t is the expectation operator based on period t information, $q_t = 1 + g(I_t/K_t)$ is the firm's market value per unit of capital (the Tobin q measure), and R is the interest factor ($1 +$ the world's real rate of interest).

At a steady state, $I_t = 0$, and the investment rule reduces to an equality between the rate of interest and the marginal productivity of capital:

$$R - 1 = \alpha \bar{A}(\bar{K})^{\alpha-1} , \tag{5}$$

where $\bar{A}$ and $\bar{K}$ are the steady-state levels of productivity and the stock of capital, respectively.

Linearizing (4) around the steady state yields

$$K_{t-1} + a_0 k_t + a_1 E_t k_{t+1} = -b E_t A_{t+1}, \; b > 0 , \tag{6}$$

where $k = K - \bar{K}$ denotes the deviation of the capital stock from its steady-state level. The solution for k_t (Sargent, 1987, pp. 197–204) is given by

$$k_t = \lambda_1 k_{t-1} + \lambda_1 b \sum_{i=0}^{\infty} \left(\frac{1}{\lambda_2}\right)^i E_t A_{t+1+i} , \tag{7}$$

where $\lambda_1 < 1$ and $\lambda_2 > 1$ are the roots of the quadratic equation $1 + a_0 \lambda + a_1 \lambda^2 = 0$. Lagging (7) by one period and subtracting it from the period t equation yields the corresponding solution for the desired investment flow:

$$Z_t \cong I_t = \lambda_1 I_{t-1} + \lambda_1 b \sum_{i=1}^{\infty} \left(\frac{1}{\lambda^2}\right)^{i-1} [E_t A_{t+i} - E_{t-1} A_{t+i-1}] . \tag{8}$$

The first term on the right-hand side of (8) captures the effects on period t investment of lagged productivity shocks, and the second term captures the revisions of expectations about future productivity shocks (revisions based on the change in information from period $t - 1$ to period t). Because such shocks are persistent, realizations convey new information about future shocks.

If the shocks are *country specific* and *permanent*, ρ in equation (2) is equal to 1, and we have a random walk. Substituting (2) with $\rho = 1$ into (8) yields

$$I_t = \lambda_1 I_{t-1} + \left(b \frac{\lambda_1 \lambda_2}{\lambda_2 - 1}\right) \Delta A_t . \tag{9}$$

Subtracting I_{t-1} from both sides yields

$$\Delta Z_t \cong \Delta I_t = (\lambda_1 - 1)\Delta I_{t-1} + \left(b \frac{\lambda_1 \lambda_2}{\lambda_2 - 1}\right) \Delta A_t . \tag{10}$$

Thus, current investment is positively correlated with a permanent country-specific productivity shock.

If, instead, $\rho = 0$ in (2), the country-specific shocks are only *transitory*. Substituting the modified stochastic process into the right-hand side of (8) and recomputing the change in investment yields

$$\Delta Z_t \cong \Delta I_t = (\lambda_1 - 1)\Delta I_{t-1} . \tag{11}$$

Hence, a transitory productivity shock has no impact whatsoever on current investment.

Consider now what happens if productivity shocks are *common* to all countries. The shock will raise the world rate of interest, $R - 1$, whether or not the shock is persistent. If it is persistent, it will tend to raise current investment by raising future productivity, but the rise in the cost of capital will outweigh the expected rise in future productivity, thereby weakening the effect on current investment. If it is not persistent, it will affect current investment only marginally through its impact on world saving and thereby on the world rate of interest.

Consumption

I now turn to the modeling of consumption (saving). Consider the key elements of consumption behavior, based on the familiar permanent-income hypothesis (which holds only when the representative consumer has full access to world capital markets). The representative agent chooses a consumption path so as to maximize its lifetime utility. Using a simple functional form,

$$E_t \sum_{i=1}^{\infty} \delta^i u(C_{t+i}) , \qquad u(C) = hC - \frac{1}{2} C^2 , \tag{12}$$

subject to the constraint

$$C_t + F_t = Y_t + RF_{t-1} , \tag{13}$$

where δ and F denote the subjective discount factor and the stock of foreign assets, respectively. Net output, Y, accounts for the resources used up in investment (that is, Z_t has been subtracted from Y_t). Assuming, for simplicity, that $\delta R = 1$, the solution to the consumer's optimization problem is given by

$$C_t = \beta W_t, \qquad \beta = \frac{R - 1}{R} , \tag{14}$$

where W_t denotes wealth, so that $W(R - 1)/R$ represents the corresponding permanent income flow). Wealth consists of the expected discounted flow of domestic income *plus* income from the initial stock of foreign assets:

$$W_t = E_t \sum_{i=0}^{\infty} \left(\frac{1}{R}\right)^i Y_{t+i} + RF_{t-1} . \tag{15}$$

The general-equilibrium aspect of our framework is reflected by the fact that the representative agent's wealth depends on the economy-wide output stream, which is in turn determined by investment behavior. Accordingly, the realized sequence of current and future productivity shocks (and the induced investment path) are the driving forces behind consumption spending. Specifically, the linear approximation of the production function around the steady state yields

$$Y_t = d_0 + d_k K_t + d_A A_t . \tag{16}$$

Substituting (16), together with (2) and (7), into the wealth term in (14) and (15) yields the closed-form solution for current consumption spending as a function of the observable (current and past) productivity levels and of foreign asset holdings.

Consider specifically the effects on consumption of *persistent* country-specific productivity shocks, representing persistence by the extreme case $\rho = 1$. Writing (16) in first-difference form and substituting (2) and (9) into the resulting expression yields

$$\Delta Y_t = (\lambda_1 - 1)d_K \Delta I_{t-1} + \left(\frac{\lambda_1 \lambda_2}{\lambda_2 - 1} bd_K + d_A\right) \Delta A_t . \tag{17}$$

Writing (17) in first-difference form and substituting (2), (9), and (15) yields

$$\Delta C_t = \left\{\frac{\lambda_1 \lambda_2}{\lambda_2 - 1} bd_k \left(1 + \frac{\lambda_1}{R} \frac{(R-1)}{(R-\lambda_1)}\right) + d_A\right\} \Delta A_t$$
$$+ (R - 1)\Delta F_{t-1} . \tag{18}$$

Observe that the coefficient of ΔA_t in (18) is larger than the corresponding coefficient in (17). The economic intuition is straightforward. The effect of a productivity change (ΔA_t) on current consumption is subject to two reinforcing influences: first, if investment is held constant in response to the shock, current income and current consumption should rise by equal amounts; this effect is captured by the term $\lambda_1 \lambda_2 bd_K/(\lambda_2 - 1) + d_A$ in (17) and (18); second, the productivity shock (ΔA_t), however, raises the entire expected future investment path and thus leads to a larger future capital stock and larger future income. Consequently, permanent income (and, along with it, current consumption) should rise by more than current income. This effect is captured by the term $\{\lambda_1(R - 1)/[R(R - \lambda_1)]\}[\lambda_1\lambda_2 bd_K/(\lambda_2 - 1)]$ in (18).

Consider, instead, a *transitory* productivity shock ($\rho = 0$). It follows from (11) that investment is not affected at all, and the change in wealth must therefore equal the transitory increment to current income with no change in future expected income. Consequently,

$$\Delta C_t = (R - 1) \left(\Delta F_{t-1} + \frac{d_A}{R} \Delta A_t \right) . \tag{19}$$

Comparing (18) and (19), it is evident that transitory shocks have relatively weak effects on current consumption. This is in line with standard consumption theory.

It is noteworthy that disturbances other than productivity shocks, such as changes in government spending, can be incorporated by making only slight modification in the framework. Recall that, even under Ricardian assumptions, government spending can have real effects in an intertemporal framework. Under Ricardian equivalence, an increase in government spending that is fully anticipated reduces a household's wealth and consumption and thus affects the current account. Its effects are weaker in the absence of Ricardian equivalence or when the increase is not fully anticipated (Frenkel and Razin [1987], and Backus, Kehoe, and Kydland [1992], which looks at the effects of temporary and permanent changes in government spending.)

External Balance

Recall the basic equation that defines the current-account balance:

$$\Delta CA_t = \Delta Y_t - \Delta Z_t - \Delta C_t + (R - 1)CA_{t-1} . \tag{20}$$

The effects on the current account of persistent country-specific shocks (with $\rho = 1$) are obtained by substituting (10), (17), and (18) into (20):

$$\Delta CA_t = \left\{ - \frac{\lambda_1\lambda_2}{\lambda_2 - 1} bd_K \frac{\lambda_1}{R} \frac{(R - 1)}{(R - \lambda_1)} - \frac{\lambda_1\lambda_2}{\lambda_2 - 1} b \right\} \Delta A_t$$
$$+ (R - 1)CA_{t-1} - (R - 1)\Delta F_{t-1} - 7(\lambda_1 - 1)\Delta I_{t-1} . \tag{21}$$

The coefficient of ΔA_t in (21) is negative. Consequently, a permanent country-specific productivity-enhancing shock must, for two reasons, worsen the current account. First, it causes investment spending to rise. Second, it causes current consumption spending to rise by more than the current rise in output.

This means that the current account has to be negatively correlated with persistent country-specific productivity shocks.

When shocks of this sort are *not* persistent ($\rho = 0$), however, consumption responds only weakly, and investment does not respond at all. Specifically,

$$\Delta CA_t = \frac{d_A}{R}\Delta A_t + (R - 1)CA_{t-1} - (R - 1)\Delta F_{t-1} - (\lambda_1 - 1)\Delta I_{t-1} \,. \quad (22)$$

The positive coefficient of the productivity term implies that a positive transitory productivity shock tends to move the external balance into surplus. This means that the current account has to be positively correlated with nonpersistent country-specific shocks.

A *global* shock that affects all countries should have a significantly different impact on the external balance than would a country-specific shock. A persistent productivity-enhancing shock common to all countries will raise the world rate of interest. The rise in the interest rate should dampen the increases in current consumption and investment spending that would be produced by a comparable country-specific shock. Thus, the response of the current account to a persistent global shock must be smaller than the response to a country-specific shock. In a world of identical countries, in fact, the ultimate change in the world rate of interest produced by a global productivity-enhancing shock must rule out any observable change in any country's current-account balance, because all countries cannot experience simultaneous improvements in their current accounts. A global nonpersistent positive shock generates excess world saving and thereby exerts a downward pressure on the world rate of interest, which, in turn, will stimulate current spending. Consequently, the response of the current account to a transitory global shock must be weaker than the response to a transitory country-specific shock. The compositional point holds here as well, for, if all countries are identical, the ultimate change in the world interest rate in response to a global shock must be just large enough to prevent any change in any country's current account.

Correlations between Saving and Investment

The typical impulse response of saving (that is, the difference between output and consumption) to a positive, but not fully persistent, productivity shock is presented in Figure 5.1. There is a positive impact effect and a downward monotonic adjustment back to the initial equilibrium, reflecting the fact that consumption is smoothed relative to output. The impulse response of investment shown in the figure indicates a large positive impact effect, followed by a sharp drop and a monotonic convergence to the initial equilibrium, reflecting the intertemporal substitution in investment induced by the shock.

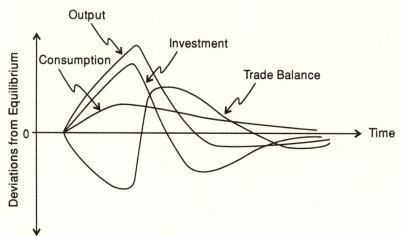

Figure 5.1 Saving-Investment Balance: Impulse Response to Productivity Shock

These patterns explain why the covariance between saving and investment is typically *positive* under the assumption of perfect capital mobility (Obstfeld, 1986). Recall that the covariance includes a quadratic term, the product of saving and investment. Therefore, observations involving large deviations from the initial equilibrium, such as the positive impact effects, take on large weights in the covariance formula, and the covariance becomes positive when the time spent at each point on the impulse function is the same. By implication, a positive covariance between saving and investment should not necessarily be interpreted as an indication of capital immobility, as was argued by Feldstein and Horioka (1980). In fact, the narrow differentials between interest rates on offshore and onshore assets denominated in the same currency indicate that capital mobility is more nearly perfect than zero among the developed countries. Furthermore, the observed positive covariance does not pose a challenge to the intertemporal approach, because it is in fact predicted by that approach.

2 Real-Exchange-Rate Theory

Up to this point, I have assumed that all goods are traded in world markets. In this section, I introduce goods that are not traded; their relative prices are determined exclusively in the domestic economy. In this case, macroeconomic shocks have domestic effects additional to those discussed in the previous section because they affect the relative prices of nontraded goods (that is, the inverse of the real exchange rate).

The intertemporal approach provides important insights into the time-series properties of the real exchange rate, the relative price of tradables in terms of nontradables. Following recent intertemporal models of the trade balance and the real exchange rate (Razin, 1984; Mendoza, 1992; Rebelo, 1992a; and Rogoff, 1992), I assume in this section a stylized two-sector model of a small open economy. Preferences over consumption of tradables, C^T, and nontradables, C^N, are represented by a Cobb-Douglas intratemporal utility function:

$$V(C^T, C^N) = (C^T)^{1-\gamma}(C^N)^\gamma , \tag{23}$$

with the associated first-order condition

$$P = \frac{(1 - \gamma)C^N}{\gamma C^T} , \tag{24}$$

where P denotes the relative price of tradables in terms of nontradables and is thus the real exchange rate.

The representative agent is infinitely lived and seeks to maximize

$$U = \sum_{t=0}^{\infty} \beta^t \left[\frac{1}{1 - \sigma} V_t^{1-\sigma} - 1 \right] . \tag{25}$$

Sectoral outputs are represented by Cobb-Douglas production functions:

$$Y^T = A^T(K^T)^{1-\alpha}(L^T)^\alpha , \tag{26}$$

$$Y^N = A^N(K^N)^{1-\nu}(L^N)^\nu . \tag{27}$$

Intersectoral Factor Mobility

The classic model of the real exchange rate, which was developed by Balassa (1964) and Samuelson (1964), assumes that capital and labor can move freely between sectors. The model thus represents an economy in long-run equilibrium. Given the common wage and rental rates in the two sectors, the standard profit-maximization conditions imply

$$dp = \left(\frac{\nu}{\alpha} \right) da^T - da^N , \tag{28}$$

where a lower-case letter denotes the logarithm of a variable indicated by the corresponding upper-case letter. This equation asserts that the path of the logarithm of the real exchange rate is completely determined by the productivity shocks da^T and da^N, regardless of the aggregate-demand conditions. Under a fixed exchange rate with purchasing-power parity holding for tradable goods, the domestic inflation rate is driven exclusively by shocks to the outputs of tradables and nontradables, as indicated by (27). Therefore, intersectoral factor mobility implies that the real exchange rate is highly sensitive to shocks to the output of the traded good, and, to the extent that these shocks are transitory, the real exchange rate will display a relatively low degree of persistence.

Sector-Specific Factors

The polar opposite to the case considered in (1) is that in which factors are intersectorally immobile. That case can be viewed as describing an economy in short-run equilibrium and thus explaining month-to-month fluctuations of the real exchange rate. As has been emphasized by Rogoff (1992), the equilibrium real exchange rate responds in the short run mainly to aggregate demand shocks in a way that is akin to the behavior of consumption, which smooths out transitory shocks to income.

The intertemporal smoothing of expected marginal utility implies that

$$(x_t)^{1-\gamma}(V_t)^{-\sigma} = \beta R E_t(x_{t+1})^{1-\gamma}(V_{t+1})^{-\sigma}, \qquad x = \frac{C^N}{C^T} . \qquad (29)$$

Setting aside shocks to the supply of nontradable goods (so that C^N is constant) and of consumption tilting (so that $\delta R = 1$), we can substitute (24) into (29) to get

$$P_t^{[1-\gamma(1-\sigma)]} = E_t P_{t+1}^{[1-\gamma(1-\sigma)]} . \qquad (30)$$

Approximating the exponential term P^x for any parameter x by the linear term $(1 + xp)$, where p denotes the logarithm of P, we can rewrite (30) as

$$p_t = E_t p_{t+1} .$$

Thus, the logarithm of the real exchange rate will follow a random walk, regardless of the underlying shocks to the traded-goods sector. Intersectoral factor mobility implies, therefore, that the time series of the real exchange rate will display a relatively high degree of persistence.

3 Positive Implications of the Dynamic-Optimizing Approach

Having set out the theory to highlight the relevant issues, I shall proceed in this section to look at the evidence. I shall be concerned with two types of empirical work, that concerned with the nature of shocks and that concerned with the testable implications of the dynamic-optimizing (intertemporal) approach.

Evidence on Persistence and the Commonality of Shocks

Drawing on Razin and Rose (1992), I provide some evidence on the time-series nature of the shocks that operate on output consumption and investment.[2] The data set comprises 138 countries and spans the period from 1950 to 1988. It is taken from the Penn World Tables, documented in Summers and Heston (1991).

PERSISTENCE

To address the issue of persistence, Razin and Rose (1992) computed simple Dickey-Fuller tests for (the logarithms of) each of our variables. At conventional levels of statistical significance, the data typically do not reject the hypothesis that a single unit root exists in the univariate representations of output, consumption, and investment. Razin and Rose ran separate tests for consumption, output, and investment and for each of the 138 countries; of these, eighteen tests (4.5 percent) rejected the null hypothesis of a unit root at the 5 percent significance level, and five tests (1.3 percent) rejected the null hypothesis at the 1 percent significance level. These results are quite close to what would be expected under the null hypothesis, implying that the data are consistent with the existence of unit roots in the autoregressive representations of the variables.

It is well known that such tests have low power against stationary alternatives and that there are serious problems in interpreting the test results as demonstrating a high degree of persistence. Thus, I view the findings as being consistent with a high degree of persistence in shocks but by no means as definitive.

THE COMMONALITY OF SHOCKS

The models developed earlier in this paper indicate that the dynamics of the saving-investment balance should depend critically on whether shocks are country specific or common across countries. Razin and Rose (1992) therefore tested for the nature of the shocks using standard factor-analytic techniques. The factor analysis was performed across countries on the detrended measures of output, consumption, and investment. The results are given in Table 5.1. Because the national-accounts data in the Penn World Tables are

---

[2] For similar work, focused on segregating global and country-specific shocks, see Glick and Rogoff (1992).

TABLE 5.1

Cross-Country Factor Analysis of Shocks (proportions of total variance explained)

	Output		Consumption		Investment	
	TS	*DS*	*TS*	*DS*	*TS*	*DS*
	Countries with at Least 20 Annual Observations					
1 Factor	43	20	37	16	35	19
4 Factors	85	49	80	45	78	53
	Countries with at Least 35 Annual Observations					
1 Factor	41	18	38	15	35	15
4 Factors	79	41	74	37	68	39

sometimes unavailable for the entire 1950–88 period, Table 5.1 provides results for two sets of countries: those with at least 20 annual observations and those with at least 35 observations; results for the different sets of countries are quite comparable.

Factor-analysis results depend critically on the method of detrending. When the variables are detrended by using the standard linear trend (TS) method, four factors (those corresponding to the largest four eigenvalues) typically account for around three-quarters of the variation in all three series; the first factor alone accounts for over one-third of the total variation. This finding may indicate that only a small number of important shocks have been common across countries. The fractions fall by approximately one-half, however, when the first-differencing (DS) method of detrending is employed (a method that implicitly adopts a random-walk model of trend).

To summarize, the evidence indicates that many business-cycle shocks are both persistent and common to many countries.

Volatility, Persistence, and Correlations

Intertemporal models predict that the degree of capital-market integration and the nature of shocks are key determinants of the volatility of consumption (saving), investment, and the current account. In this subsection, I provide time-series evidence on current-account dynamics so as to shed some light on the empirical importance of the effects identified by the theoretical models discussed in Sections 1 through 3.

Volatility measures for the current account (as a percentage of GDP) and for the logarithms of per capita GDP are exhibited in Figure 5.2 for a sample of fifty-eight countries. The data pertain to the period from 1967 to 1990; as

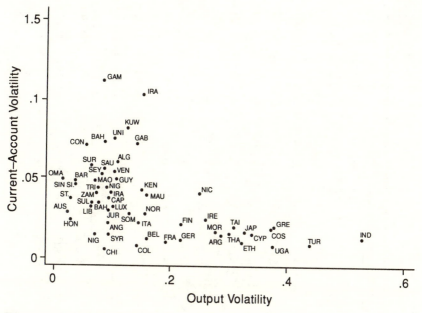

Figure 5.2 Current-Account and Output Volatility (*detrending: first difference*)

before, they come from the Penn World Tables (Mark 5). To measure volatility, I use the standard deviation of the (first-difference) detrended variable. Each country is identified by the first two or three letters of its name.

There is a cluster of mainly developed countries and fastest-growing less-developed countries that show relatively low current-account and output volatility; this group includes countries such as Japan and Indonesia. The group with high current-account volatility and low output volatility includes countries such as Venezuela and Iran, which are major oil producers.

Two major conclusions can be gleaned from Figure 5.2. The less-developed countries show more current-account and output volatility than do the developed countries, and the ratio of current-account volatility to output volatility (measured by the slope of a ray from the origin that fits the cluster of observations) is not markedly different for less-developed and developed countries.

Table 5.2 provides a set of statistics describing the time-series properties of the trade balance, output, the terms of trade, the real effective exchange rate, and the interest rate for each of the seven largest developed countries and for a sample of less-developed countries. It reports measures of volatility and persistence and the correlations between pairs of variables (Mendoza, 1992). Observe that relative price changes (such as changes in the terms of trade, the real exchange rate, and the rate of interest) cause income effects for the country akin to shifts in output, in addition to the direct substitution effects. Thus, for example, because a deterioration in the terms of trade means that, with the

TABLE 5.2
Statistical Properties of Key Variables in Selected Countries

Seven Largest Developed Countries: Standard Deviation and Persistence[a]

	GDP		Terms of Trade		Trade Balance		Real Effective Exchange Rate		Real Rate of Interest	
	σ	ρ	σ	ρ	σ	ρ	σ	ρ	σ	ρ
United States	2.17	0.446	7.11	0.776	9.00	0.509	12.68	0.814	2.46	0.694
United Kingdom	1.98	0.524	4.56	0.460	7.98	0.685	10.83	0.799	3.57	0.676
France	1.49	0.654	5.38	0.683	4.59	0.183	6.11	0.695	2.24	0.449
Germany	1.92	0.439	7.69	0.766	6.19	0.640	6.58	0.751	1.73	0.241
Italy	2.17	0.537	7.83	0.764	10.20	0.496	5.62	0.720	2.84	0.268
Canada	2.01	0.540	3.64	0.577	5.37	0.532	7.76	0.682	2.08	0.565
Japan	3.58	0.812	14.77	0.820	13.48	0.546	9.66	0.670	3.21	-0.166

Seven Largest Developed Countries: Correlations[a]

	$\rho_{tb,tot}$	$\rho_{tot,e}$	$\rho_{tot,r}$	$\rho_{tb,e}$	$\rho_{tb,r}$	$\rho_{e,r}$	$\rho_{tb,y}$	$\rho_{tot,y}$
United States	-0.378	0.393	-0.039	-0.481	0.078	0.712	-0.277	0.197
United Kingdom	0.634	0.499	0.539	0.690	0.816	0.681	-0.538	-0.230
France	0.351	-0.463	-0.530	-0.372	-0.356	-0.183	-0.019	0.287
Germany	0.590	0.458	-0.351	0.299	-0.083	-0.324	-0.299	0.239

Italy	0.572	0.426	−0.231	−0.034	0.021	0.050	−0.210	0.112
Canada	−0.026	−0.312	0.286	0.012	0.430	0.067	−0.709	−0.034
Japan	0.600	0.287	−0.264	0.075	0.122	−0.358	0.054	0.559

Less-Developed Countries: σ, δ, Correlations[a]

	Terms of Trade		Trade Balance		Real Rate of Interest		Correlations		
	σ	ρ	σ	ρ	σ	ρ	$\rho_{tb,tot}$	$\rho_{tot,r}$	$\rho_{tb,r}$
Argentina	10.64	0.295	26.84	0.347	57.44	−0.020	0.179	0.271	0.321
Brazil	14.17	0.614	27.33	0.679	37.14	0.053	0.031	−0.110	0.004
Chile	13.62	0.518	18.86	0.435	8.27	0.127	0.277	−0.540	−0.084
Mexico	14.20	0.741	30.84	0.718	11.50	−0.219	0.368	0.290	0.142
Peru	10.77	0.337	26.57	0.572	13.56	0.385	0.304	−0.016	0.337
Venezuela	35.07	0.786	28.04	0.386	7.72	0.231	0.291	0.341	0.544
Israel	5.94	0.667	11.77	0.490	367.08	−0.574	0.313	0.112	−0.344
Egypt	9.78	0.413	17.35	0.665	3.35	0.092	−0.157	−0.133	0.378
Taiwan	10.44	0.699	13.82	0.575	7.08	−0.023	0.556	−0.063	−0.054
India	10.05	0.667	18.29	0.723	2.55	−0.131	0.439	−0.183	0.114
Indonesia	29.17	0.817	12.35	0.268	3.08	−0.367	0.337	0.181	0.137

(continued)

TABLE 5.2 (Continued)

Less-Developed Countries: σ, δ, Correlations[a]

	Terms of Trade		Trade Balance		Real Rate of Interest		Correlations		
	σ	ρ	σ	ρ	σ	ρ	$\rho_{tb,tot}$	$\rho_{tot,r}$	$\rho_{tb,r}$
Korea	10.56	0.778	16.19	0.574	9.03	0.527	0.243	0.332	0.188
Philippines	13.68	0.815	13.93	0.377	7.69	-0.037	0.444	0.103	-0.002
Thailand	9.76	0.586	13.16	0.551	4.05	0.388	-0.339	-0.491	-0.206
Algeria	35.59	0.761	23.83	0.343	2.70	0.052	0.181	-0.288	-0.450
Cameroon	22.70	0.812	17.25	0.467	2.94	0.322	0.421	0.334	-0.016
Zaire	19.14	0.647	18.97	0.723	16.80	-0.241	0.390	0.276	0.069
Kenya	9.94	0.450	16.05	0.374	4.42	0.416	0.204	-0.064	0.226
Morocco	10.46	0.582	15.86	0.659	3.21	0.207	0.259	0.135	0.192
Nigeria	39.95	0.785	31.33	0.527	9.10	0.181	-0.217	0.022	-0.025
Tunisia	24.09	0.852	12.50	0.452	2.29	0.304	-0.138	-0.620	0.047

Sources: IMF, *International Financial Statistics* and data base for *World Economic Outlook*.

Note: Data for the terms of trade and the trade balance are for the period from 1960 to 1989, and for GDP for the period from 1965 to 1989, expressed in per capita terms and detrended using the Hodrick-Prescott filter with the smoothing parameter set at 100. GDP is gross domestic product at constant domestic prices from National Income Accounts; the terms of trade are the ratio of U.S. dollar unit value of exports to U.S. dollar unit value of imports; the real effective exchange rate is the ratio of unit value of exports to GDP; the trade balance is exports minus imports of merchandise from the Balance of Payments expressed at constant import prices (the detrended trade balance corresponds to detrended exports minus detrended imports).

[a] σ is the percentage standard deviation; ρ is the first-order serial autocorrelation; $\rho_{tb,tot}$ is the correlation of the trade balance with the terms of trade; $\rho_{tot,e}$ is the correlation of the terms of trade with the real effective exchange rate; $\rho_{tot,r}$ is the correlation of the terms of trade with the real rate of interest; $\rho_{tb,e}$ is the correlation of the trade balance with the real effective exchange rate; $\rho_{tb,r}$ is the correlation of the trade balance with the real rate of interest; and $\rho_{e,r}$ is the correlation between the real effective exchange rate and the real rate of interest.

same quantity of exports, the country is able to import reduced amounts of goods and services from abroad, real income falls. The distinction between temporary and permanent changes is as relevant here as for the case of output shocks. The temporary versus permanent distinction is also relevant for the intertemporal substitution effect (Razin and Svensson, 1983).

The main regularities shown in Table 5.2 can be summarized as follows.

(1) There is a significant degree of persistence in output, the terms of trade, and the real exchange rate, a finding similar to our earlier conclusion based on the Penn World Tables.

(2) The trade balance is in most cases more volatile than the terms of trade or output.

(3) The trade balance and the terms of trade are positively correlated for most of the countries, in line with the Harberger-Laursen-Metzler effect. Recall that this proposition predicted that a deterioration of the terms of trade would reduce saving. According to the intertemporal approach, a temporary deterioration of the terms of trade will induce substitution from current to future consumption (that is, will increase saving), but a permanent deterioration will not.

(4) Looking across countries, one cannot detect the link predicted by the theory between the persistence of output or terms-of-trade shocks and the correlation between the trade balance on the one hand and the terms of trade or output on the other. A more structural, econometric approach is needed to test the validity of this implication of the intertemporal approach. It should be noted, however, that Mendoza reproduced the expected relationship by a different method. He constructed two benchmark economies to characterize a "typical" developed country and a "typical" less-developed country. Conditioning them with empirically based parameters pertaining to terms-of-trade shocks, he was able to simulate the Harberger-Laursen-Metzler effect whereby the persistence parameter of the terms-of-trade shocks is positively associated with the correlation between the trade balance and the terms of trade.

(5) The real rate of interest and terms of trade are more volatile for less-developed than for developed countries, and the volatility of the trade balance is also significantly larger for less-developed than for developed countries.

(6) The correlation between the rate of interest and the trade balance is positive for most countries. This is consistent with the presence of intertemporal substitution; the current-account balance will improve if a rise in the interest rate reduces current spending on consumption and investment and augments future spending.

(7) The real exchange rate is only weakly correlated with the trade balance. In contrast to the Mundell-Fleming model, however, the intertemporal model does not make a clear prediction concerning this correlation.

(8) The real exchange rate shows a high degree of persistence and a rela-

tively low correlation with the terms-of-trade shocks. This may support the validity of the consumption-smoothing model of the real exchange rate discussed in the second part of Section 2.

(9) Finally, the trade balance is in most cases negatively correlated with output. Recall that a permanent country-specific shock worsens the trade balance for two reasons. First, it raises investment; second, it causes current consumption to rise by more than the current rise in output.

Sachs (1981) investigated nonstructural regressions describing the behavior of the current account for both developed and less-developed countries. He emphasized that most of the explanatory power of his regressions was the result of an investment surge that led to current-account deficits; saving rates changed little. Further developments in theory and methodology have facilitated structural testing.

Structural Testing

A full-blown optimizing model is difficult to estimate because it is often impossible to reduce it to a small number of tractable equations. There have been, however, a few attempts at empirical implementation.

The intertemporal model predicts that shocks that are persistent and common to all countries (that is, formed by a GNP-weighted average of the individual productivity measures) have no effect on the trade balance. To test this proposition, Glick and Rogoff (1992) computed the Solow residuals for each country and broke them down into country-specific and global shocks and into transitory and persistent shocks. They found that the various shocks enter current-account regressions with the predicted signs. The hypothesis stood up to the annual data of eight developed countries for the period from 1960 to 1990. In particular, Glick and Rogoff found that the coefficient of the productivity variable in their trade-balance equation was, as predicted, larger than the corresponding coefficient in their investment equation. But they did not rigorously incorporate the cross-equation restriction implied by the theory, and the fit of their regression equations was weak in several cases.

Leiderman and Razin (1991) estimated an intertemporal model for Israel using monthly data for the 1980s. They found strong evidence in favor of consumption smoothing (indicated by an offsetting response of private saving to changes in government saving and an absence of liquidity constraints), as well as a strong response of investment to country-specific productivity shocks.

Mendoza (1991, 1992) provides recursive simulations based on a calibrated model with empirically based parameters that lend support to the emphasis that the intertemporal approach attaches to the persistence of shocks and to consumption smoothing.

Finally, Razin and Rose (1992) provide indirect tests of the intertemporal approach. The approach predicts that capital-market integration will lower consumption volatility while raising investment volatility to the extent that productivity shocks are idiosyncratic and nonpersistent. Razin and Rose use a unique panel data set (ranging from the 1950s to the late 1980s and covering developed as well as less-developed countries); it includes indicators of barriers to trade in goods and (financial) capital. The results of their study are inconclusive, for they did not find a strong link between business-cycle volatility and openness. Countries with greater capital mobility (that is, fewer barriers to trade in financial assets), for instance, do not appear to have systematically smoother consumption streams or more volatile investment behavior.

4 Normative Implications of the Intertemporal Approach

Taxes and the Saving-Investment Balance

Taxation on capital income may have large disincentive effects on saving and investment. It is therefore especially relevant to the discussion of the intertemporal approach to the current account.

With the complete integration of capital markets, arbitrage will equalize after-tax rates of return across countries, so that

$$r(1 - t_D) = r^*(1 - t_N^* - t_F) , \tag{32}$$

$$r(1 - t_N - t_F^*) = r^*(1 - t_D^*) , \tag{33}$$

where an asterisk denotes "rest of the world" and the subscripts D, N, and F denote taxes levied on the domestic-source income of residents, taxes levied on nonresidents, and taxes levied on the foreign-source income of residents, respectively. A credit for the tax paid abroad, which is deducted from the tax liability in the home country, is captured by having $t_F = t_N^*$.

In a world with international capital mobility, the equality between saving and investment need not hold for each individual country. This separation implies that different tax principles may have fundamentally different implications for the allocation of saving and investment across countries. The two polar principles of international taxation are the source and the resident principles. According to the source principle, the foreign-source incomes of residents are not taxed, and residents and nonresidents are taxed at a uniform rate on income from domestic sources. According to the residence principle, residents are taxed uniformly on their worldwide income, regardless of its source. For example, the residence principle sets $t_N = t_N^* = 0$, $t_F = t_D$, and $t_F^* = t_D^*$, so that (32) will be $r(1 - t_D) = r^*(1 - t_D^*)$ and (33) will be the same but with asterisks on the t_Ds (that is, t_D^*), whereas the source principle sets $t_F = t_F^* = 0$.

Thus, the residence principle, taken in conjunction with the arbitrage conditions, implies that the marginal productivity of capital (the pre-tax rate of return on capital) will be equalized across countries. At the same time, however, the intertemporal marginal rate of substitution in consumption (which is equated to the post-tax rate of return on capital) will differ with cross-country differences in tax rates. The source principle, taken together with the arbitrage conditions, implies that the intertemporal marginal rate of substitution in consumption will be equalized across residences. At the same time, however, the marginal productivity of capital in each country will depend on its country-specific tax rate (Frenkel, Razin, and Sadka, 1991).

Because the residence principle is the predominant principle in the developed countries, we should expect that the cross-country correlation between saving rates and country-specific tax rates on income from capital will be larger than the corresponding correlation between investment rates and country-specific tax rates.

To understand why the intertemporal approach predicts that the tax on income from capital will be directly related to the saving rate, recall from saving theory how the marginal rate of intertemporal substitution and the after-tax return on capital are brought into equality for every consumer. Writing the utility function in isoelastic form and allowing for the taxation of income from capital yields

$$1 + g_{ct} = [\beta(1 + \bar{r}_t)]^{(1/\sigma)} , \tag{34}$$

where $\bar{r}_t = r(1 - t_k)$ and g_c, β, σ, r, and t_k denote the growth rate of consumption, the subjective discount factor, the reciprocal of the intertemporal elasticity of substitution in consumption, the pre-tax rate of return on capital, and the tax rate on income from capital, respectively. This equation suggests that the negative effect on consumption growth (that is, the positive effect on saving) of the tax on income from capital is directly related to the intertemporal elasticity of substitution in consumption.

Mendoza, Razin, and Tesar (1992) have used OECD data to compute the revenue-based flat-rate equivalents of the taxes on income from capital for the seven major developed countries. This tax-rate equivalent is defined by computing the product of the overall individual tax rate and the sum of the operating surplus of private unincorporated enterprises and household property and entrepreneurial income, adding taxes on the incomes, profits, and capital gains of corporations, and dividing this number by the total operating surplus (as defined by the OECD). Because all sources of individual income are taxed at the same rate, the overall individual tax rate is computed as the sum of taxes on the incomes, profits, and capital gains of individuals, divided by the sum of wages and salaries, the operating surplus of unincorporated enterprises, and the property and entrepreneurial incomes of households. Table 5.3 presents the means and time-series correlations of saving, investment, and the

TABLE 5.3
Saving, Investment, and Capital-Income Tax Rates

Country	Saving/GDP Ratio		Investment/GDP Ratio		Capital-Income Tax Rate
	Mean	Correlation (tk)[a]	Mean	Correlation (tk)[a]	Mean
United States	0.17	0.32	0.18	0.11	0.43
United Kingdom	0.18	−0.23	0.18	−0.37	0.56
Germany	0.25	−0.85	0.22	−0.69	0.25
Italy	0.21	−0.43	0.21	−0.93	0.26
France	0.23	−0.95	0.22	−0.81	0.24
Japan	0.33	−0.45	0.31	−0.58	0.33
Canada	0.24	−0.12	0.22	0.11	0.40

Source: Mendoza, Razin, and Tesar, 1992.

Note: Country data are for the period from 1965 to 1988, except for Italy (1980 to 1988) and France (1970 to 1988).

[a] Contemporaneous correlation with the capital-income tax rate.

computed tax rate for each of the countries. As expected, the saving and investment rates are in most cases negatively correlated with the computed tax rate. Looking across countries, the mean tax rate is negatively associated with the saving and investment rates, except for Japan (which exhibits the highest saving and investment rates despite its relatively high tax rate). The correlations between the saving rate and the tax rate are larger than those between the investment rate and the tax rate, which is consistent with the prediction of the theory for open economies, in which saving and investment are separated by international capital mobility. The tax instruments that drive saving are the individual and corporate income-tax rates, and the corporate tax rate does not affect investment when true depreciation and full interest deductibility are allowed and firms rely on external financing. Hence, taxes on the income from capital can be expected to affect saving more strongly than investment does when there is perfect capital mobility. In a closed economy, by contrast, the close link between saving and investment implies that the all-inclusive tax on income from capital drives both saving and investment.

Capital Movements and Growth

In the literature on open-economy macroeconomics, capital controls are frequently advocated as a stabilization policy instrument under floating exchange rates. With unrestricted capital flows, an expansionary fiscal policy will tend to produce an appreciation of the domestic currency by inducing capital inflows; with restrictions on capital flows, the same fiscal policy will tend to produce a depreciation of the domestic currency because the foreign-exchange market will be dominated by the imbalances in goods flows rather than imbalances in assets flows. Once capital controls are put in place, however, it often proves difficult to remove them, and persistent capital controls have important implications for long-run growth.

Intertemporal optimization tends to be a growth-equalizing force. Recall that free trade equalizes the marginal rates of substitution and transformation between all traded commodities; it does so by imposing a common set of relative prices on consumers and producers in all countries. With intertemporal optimization, moreover, this effect of free trade implies the equalization across countries of the marginal product of capital with the intertemporal marginal rates of substitution in consumption.

With free capital mobility, the law of diminishing returns implies that capital will move from capital-rich to capital-poor countries (that is, from those where the marginal product of capital is low to those where it is high). Over time, such international capital flows will equalize the marginal products of capital across countries. The short-run effect of the capital movements is to shorten the transition path of the capital-importing country and to lengthen that of the capital-exporting country. It is nevertheless essential to distinguish between the dynamics of GNP and GDP; the convergence of GDPs need not imply the convergence of GNPs and thus need not imply the convergence of consumption levels. In the long run, the growth rates of all growing variables will come to be constant (so that ratios among these variables will become time invariant), and total-income growth rates will be uniform across countries (proposition 1 in Razin and Yuen [1992]). This is because the stock of capital flowing from one country to another must be growing at the same rate as the total income of the sending as well as the receiving country in order for growth to be balanced. Two important empirical implications follow this simple reasoning: (1) long-term rates of growth of population and per capita incomes should be negatively correlated across countries, and (2) growth rates of total income should exhibit less variation than growth rates of per capita income. Razin and Yuen (1992) provide some evidence that supports these hypotheses, using data from the *World Development Report* for 120 developed and less-developed countries from 1965 through 1987.

Another important implication of this reasoning is that growth rates of per capita income may not converge and that the diversity among them is affected by the principles governing the taxation of income from capital. Following Rebelo (1992a), assume that the representative household makes its saving decision so as to maximize lifetime utility:

$$U = \Sigma[\beta(1 + g_N)^n]^t u(c_t), \qquad u(c_t) = \frac{c_t^{1-\sigma}}{1-\sigma}, \qquad (35)$$

where g_N denotes the rate of population growth. These preferences are consistent with steady-state growth. They imply that the representative household expands consumption at a constant rate whenever the rate of interest is constant:

$$\frac{(1 - g_N)^t u_c(c_t)}{(1 - g_N)^{t+1} u_c(c_{t+1})} = \beta(1 + r). \qquad (36)$$

In a steady state, where the growth rate of consumption must equal the growth rate of income per capita (g_y) the previous condition yields

$$1 + g_y = [\beta(1 + g_N)^{n-1}(1 + r)]^{1/\sigma}. \qquad (37)$$

This result suggests that if two countries have identical preferences, their rates of consumption growth cannot differ unless they have different population growth rates or different after-tax rates of return on capital. Equalizing the after-tax rate of return on capital across countries, as the "source principle" would do, is growth-equalizing. The "residence principle" would have the opposite effect, because it prevents the equalization of the after-tax rate of return on capital. Capital controls can also perpetuate cross-country differences in rates of return on capital. Thus, the result obtained above suggests that capital controls may account for the observed cross-country diversity in rates of growth of per capita income (Razin and Yuen, 1992).

In the absence of taxes, growth rates of consumption tend to be equalized under capital mobility. Recognizing that this sort of convergence is unrealistic, Rebelo (1992a, 1992b) modifies (37) above by replacing the constant elasticity of intertemporal substitution with a wealth-dependent elasticity. A lower rate of consumption growth is then associated with lower wealth (and GNP) across countries, even after GDP growth reaches a steady state. In reality, of course, levels of GNP and GDP (and their growth rates) are very similar across countries, and there are ways of rationalizing this fact in terms of market imperfections; see, for example, Barro, Mankiw, and Sala-i-Martin (1992), where the accumulation of physical capital but not human capital can be financed by international borrowing.

5 Conclusion

In recent years, we have seen large, unsynchronized changes in national fiscal policies, and these have resulted in substantial budgetary imbalances, volatile real rates of interest and real exchange rates, and large current-account imbalances. The intertemporal approach provides a framework for analyzing these fiscal (and productivity) shocks and offers a coherent theory that can potentially account for the observed diversity of current-account balances. This chapter has illustrated the use of this approach in analyzing current-account dynamics and has reviewed the evidence supporting it.

The intertemporal approach begins with the national-income identity and with detailed descriptions of the intratemporal and intertemporal budget constraints faced by the decisionmaking units. It models investment and consumption (saving) in ways that emphasize intertemporal optimization and the differing effects of various shocks and shows the importance of distinguishing among four types of shocks. These can be transitory or persistent in duration, country-specific or common across countries. Because different shocks have different effects on the saving-investment balance, they have different effects on the trend and volatility of the current-account balance.

Are there easier ways to explain current-account behavior? Can one take shortcuts that are simpler to implement than the rigorous modern approach? A popular method of applied analysis is to regress the current-account balance on such "price" variables as the real exchange rate and interest rates and on such "income" variables as output, government spending, tax-burden indicators, government debt, and money creation. The typical regression uses mostly current variables, except that lagged output is added to function jointly with current output as a proxy for permanent income. Most applied work, however, still emphasizes income and price elasticities of demand for exports and imports, a practice that can be rationalized only by invoking a one-period partial-equilibrium model.

Traditional studies test debt neutrality by asking whether regression coefficients on taxes and debt are significantly different from zero. Similarly, they test whether the exchange rate is effective in improving the trade deficit by the sign and statistical significance of the coefficient of the real exchange rate, allowing possibly for simultaneous-equations bias by the use of instrumental variables. This sort of reduced-form analysis, however, omits all of the variables suggested by the intertemporal model. It also fails to distinguish between the different types of shocks or between types of taxation (that is, taxes on capital income, labor income, or consumption). Accordingly, reduced-form regression analyses of the trade balance are not likely to provide relevant information on the validity of debt neutrality, the sensitivity of the current account to exogenous or policy-induced changes in the exchange rate or the rate of interest, or on a host of other policy-related issues. That is because they ignore an important possibility. If current taxes are a good predictor of future government spending, a tax coefficient significantly different from zero will be consistent with the neutrality proposition and contrary to the traditional interpretation. Furthermore, a large positive current-output coefficient may indicate the presence of persistent productivity shocks, which play no role in the traditional approach.

The empirical implementation of the intertemporal approach has not been widespread, because intertemporal models are inherently intractable and demand much data. Nevertheless, there have been recent attempts to test some of the key hypotheses of this approach, and, as indicated in this chapter, the results are quite encouraging.

A drawback of other existing approaches is their inability to account for changes in the fiscal or monetary regime. An increase in the stock of government bonds, for example, may signal a future increase in taxes, because an increase will be needed to service the new debt. But the increase in debt may also signal a future fall in government spending or forthcoming monetary accommodation and inflation. Current econometric methods cannot distinguish between different types of regime change, with different implications for the debt-neutrality question and other important hypotheses. Innovations in the theory of endogenous policy should prove useful for this purpose.

References

Abel, Andrew B., *Investment and the Value of Time*, New York, Garland, 1979.

Abel, Andrew B., and Olivier Blanchard, "The Present Value of Profits and Cyclical Movements in Investment," *Econometrica*, 51 (May 1983), pp. 675–692.

Backus, David K., Patrick J. Kehoe, and Finn E. Kydland, "International Real Business Cycles," *Journal of Political Economy*, 100 (August 1992), pp. 745–775.

Balassa, Bela, "The Purchasing Power Parity Doctrine: A Reappraisal," *Journal of Political Economy*, 72 (December 1964), pp. 584–596.

Barro, Robert J., N. Gregory Mankiw, and Xavier Sala-i-Martin, "Capital Mobility in Neoclassical Models of Growth," National Bureau of Economic Research Working Paper No. 4206, Cambridge, Mass., National Bureau of Economic Research, 1992.

Bertola, Guiseppe, and Allan Drazen, "Trigger Points and Budget Cuts: Explaining the Effects of Fiscal Austerity," *American Economic Review*, 83 (March 1993), pp. 11–26.

Bruno, Michael, "The Two-Sector Open Economy and the Real Exchange Rate," *American Economic Review*, 66 (September 1976), pp. 566–577.

Buiter, Willem H., "Time Preference and International Lending and Borrowing in an Overlapping-Generations Model," *Journal of Political Economy*, 89 (August 1981), pp. 769–797.

———, "Fiscal Policy in Open Interdependent Economies," in Assaf Razin and Efraim Sadka, eds., *Economic Policy in Theory and Practice*, Basingstoke, Houndsmills, Macmillan, 1987, pp. 101–144.

Dornbusch, Rudiger, "Real Interest Rates, Home Goods, and Optimal External Borrowing," *Journal of Political Economy*, 91 (February 1983), pp. 141–153.

————, "Intergenerational and International Trade," *Journal of International Economics*, 18 (February 1985), pp. 123–139.

Eaton, Jonathan, and Mark Gersovitz, *Poor-Country Borrowing in Private Financial Markets and the Repudiation Issue*, Princeton Studies in International Finance No. 47, Princeton, N.J., Princeton University, International Finance Section, June 1981.

Feldstein, Martin, and Charles Horioka, "Domestic Saving and International Capital Flows," *Economic Journal* (London), 90 (June 1980), pp. 314–329.

Fisher, Irving, *Theory of Interest*, New York, Macmillan, 1930.

Frenkel, Jacob A., and Assaf Razin, *Fiscal Policies and the World Economy*, Cambridge, Mass., MIT Press, 1987.

Frenkel, Jacob A., Assaf Razin, and Efraim Sadka, *International Taxation in an Integrated World*, Cambridge, Mass., MIT Press, 1991.

Friedman, Milton, *A Theory of the Consumption Function*, Princeton, N.J., Princeton University Press, 1957.

Giavazzi, Francesco, and Marco Pagano, "Can Severe Fiscal Contraction Be Expansionary? Tales of Two Small European Countries," *NBER Macroeconomics Annual* (1990), pp. 75–110.

Glick, Reuven, and Kenneth S. Rogoff, "Global versus Country-Specific Productivity Shocks and the Current Account," Working Paper No. 4140, Cambridge, Mass., National Bureau of Economic Research, August 1992 [also issued as International Finance Discussion Paper No. 443, Washington, D.C., Board of Governors of the Federal Reserve System, April 1993].

Hall, Robert E., "Stochastic Implications of the Life Cycle-Permanent Income Hypothesis: Theory and Evidence," *Journal of Political Economy*, 86 (December 1978), pp. 971–987.

Harberger, Arnold C., "Currency Depreciation, Income and the Balance of Trade," *Journal of Political Economy*, 58 (February 1950), pp. 47–60.

Hayashi, Fumio, "Tobin's Marginal q and Average q: A Neoclassical Interpretation," *Econometrica*, 50 (January 1982), pp. 213–224.

Kotlikoff, Laurence J., *Generational Accounting: Knowing Who Pays, and When, for What We Spend*, New York, Free Press, 1992.

Laursen, Svend, and Lloyd A. Metzler, "Flexible Exchange Rates and the Theory of Employment," *Review of Economics and Statistics*, 32 (November 1950), pp. 281–299.

Leiderman, Leonardo, and Assaf Razin, "Determinants of External Imbalances: The Role of Taxes, Government Spending, and Productivity," *Journal of the Japanese and International Economies*, 5 (December 1991), pp. 421–450.

Lucas, Robert E., Jr., "Optimal Investment Policy and the Flexible Accelerator," *International Economic Review*, 8 (February 1967), pp. 78–85.

Lucas, Robert E., Jr., and Edward C. Prescott, "Investment Under Uncertainty," *Econometrica*, 39 (September 1971), pp. 659–681.

Mendoza, Enrique G., "Real Business Cycles in a Small Open Economy," *American Economic Review*, 81 (September 1991), pp. 797–818.

————, "The Terms of Trade and Economic Fluctuations," International Monetary Fund Working Paper No. 92/98, Washington, D.C., International Monetary Fund, December 1992.

Mendoza, Enrique G., Assaf Razin, and Linda L. Tesar, "International Cross Sectional Analysis of Taxation," Washington, D.C., International Monetary Fund, 1992, processed.

Modigliani, Franco, and Richard Brumberg, "Utility Analysis and the Consumption Function: An Interpretation of Cross Section Data," in Kenneth K. Kurihara, ed., *Post-Keynesian Economics*, New Brunswick, N.J., Rutgers University Press, 1954, pp. 383–436.

Obstfeld, Maurice, "Aggregate Spending and the Terms of Trade: Is There a Laursen-Metzler Effect?," *Quarterly Journal of Economics*, 97 (May 1982), pp. 251–270.

———, "Capital Mobility in the World Economy: Theory and Measurement," *Carnegie-Rochester Conference Series on Public Policy*, 24 (Spring 1986), pp. 55–103.

Penati, Alessandro, "Government Spending and the Real Exchange Rate," *Journal of International Economics*, 22 (May 1987), pp. 237–256.

Razin, Assaf, "Capital Movements, Intersectoral Resource Shifts and the Trade Balance," *European Economic Review*, 26 (1984), pp. 135–152.

Razin, Assaf, and Andrew K. Rose, "Business Cycle Volatility and Openness: An Exploratory Analysis," paper presented at the Sapir Conference on International Capital Mobility, Tel Aviv, December 1992.

Razin, Assaf, and Lars E. O. Svensson, "Trade Taxes and the Current Account," *Economic Letters*, 13 (1983), pp. 55–58.

Razin, Assaf, and Chi-Wa Yuen, "Convergence in Growth Rates: The Role of Capital Mobility and International Taxation," National Bureau of Economic Research Working Paper No. 4214, Cambridge, Mass., National Bureau of Economic Research, November 1992.

Rebelo, Sergio T., "Growth in Open Economies," CEPR Discussion Paper No. 667, London, Centre for Economic Policy Research, June 1992a.

———, "Inflation in Fixed Exchange Rate Regimes: The Recent Portuguese Experience," Seminar Paper No. 517, Stockholm, Institute for International Economic Studies, April 1992b.

Rogoff, Kenneth S., "Traded Goods Consumption Smoothing and the Random Walk Behavior of the Real Exchange Rate," National Bureau of Economic Research Working Paper No. 4119, Cambridge, Mass., National Bureau of Economic Research, October 1992.

Sachs, Jeffrey D., "The Current Account and Macroeconomic Adjustment in the 1970s," *Brookings Papers on Economic Activity*, No. 1 (1981), pp. 201–268.

———, *Theoretical Issues in International Borrowing*, Princeton Studies in International Finance No. 54, Princeton, N.J., Princeton University, International Finance Section, July 1984.

Samuelson, Paul A., "Theoretical Notes on Trade Problems," *Review of Economics and Statistics*, 46 (May 1964), pp. 145–154.

Sargent, Thomas J., *Macroeconomic Theory*, 2d ed., Boston, Academic Press, 1987.

Summers, Robert, and Alan Heston, "The Penn World Tables (Mark 5): An Expanded Set of International Comparisons, 1950–1988," *Quarterly Journal of Economics*, 106 (May 1991), pp. 327–368.

Svensson, Lars E. O., and Assaf Razin, "The Terms of Trade and the Current Account:

The Harberger-Laursen-Metzler Effect," *Journal of Political Economy*, 91 (February 1983), pp. 91–125.

Tobin, James, "A General Equilibrium Approach to Monetary Theory," *Journal of Money, Credit, and Banking*, 1 (February 1969), pp. 15–29.

Uzawa, Hirofumi, "Time Preference and the Penrose Effect in a Two-Class Model of Economic Growth," *Journal of Political Economy*, 77 (July/August 1969), pp. 628–652.

III

THE INTEGRATION AND FUNCTIONING OF CAPITAL MARKETS

6

International Capital Mobility in the 1990s

MAURICE OBSTFELD

OVER THE past two decades, global trade in financial assets has been spurred by advances in communication and transaction technologies, by the creation of new financial products, and by a widespread trend toward deregulation of domestic and international capital-market activities. In almost all respects, the consequences of these developments remain controversial.[1]

In theory, the potential benefits of international capital mobility are clear. Individuals gain the opportunity to smooth consumption by borrowing or diversifying abroad, and world savings are directed to the world's most productive investment opportunities. The size of these gains and the extent to which they are being attained in practice remain uncertain and furnish an active research area in which answers are urgently needed. High on the policy agenda in a number of countries is a choice between further integration into world or regional capital markets and the retention of traditional macroeconomic policy options.

This chapter surveys the performance of international capital markets and the literature on measuring international capital mobility. Section 1 reviews the main functions and implications of capital mobility. Section 2 examines recent evidence on the world capital market's ability to arbitrage the prices of similar assets. The market's record in allowing countries to diversify risks is taken up in Section 3. Section 4 focuses on interpreting divergences between national saving and domestic investment rates. Section 5 offers conclusions.

I am grateful to Matthew Jones and Luisa Lambertini for valiant research assistance on this paper and to Polly Allen, Tamim Bayoumi, Giuseppe Bertola, Barry Eichengreen, Jeffrey Frankel, Kaku Furuya, Morris Goldstein, James Nason, Franco Passacantando, and David Romer for helpful suggestions. Discussion at the April 1993 fiftieth anniversary conference for Princeton Essays in International Finance helped sharpen the paper's arguments. Any remaining errors are mine. I acknowledge with thanks financial support from the Centre for Economic Policy Research MIRAGE project; the National Science Foundation; the Ford Foundation (through a grant to the Center for International and Development Economics Research at the University of California, Berkeley); and the University of California, Berkeley, Hewlett Faculty Grant program. David Backus, Tamim Bayoumi, Robert Dekle, Morris Goldstein, Kellett Hannah, Fumio Hayashi, James Poterba, and Data Resources, Inc., generously provided data and advice.

[1] Goldstein et al. (1993) provide an excellent overview of the expanding range of international financial markets.

1 Free International Capital Mobility: Definition and Implications

Capital is freely mobile within a multicountry region when its residents face no official obstacles to the negotiation and execution of financial trade anywhere and with anyone within the region and face transactions costs that are no greater for parties residing in different countries than for parties residing in the same country. The definition implies that national authorities do not interpose themselves between transaction partners from different countries, other than through the provision of a nationality-blind legal framework for contract enforcement.

Actual conditions may differ from this ideal of free international capital mobility. Governments can impose taxes on cross-border financial flows and payments, including certain types of reserve requirements, as well as quantitative limits and outright prohibitions. The mere possibility of such measures can discourage international capital movement, as can official "moral" suasion in which threats of formal regulation may be implicit. The prospect of partial or full government expropriation of foreign-owned assets lowers the financial openness of some economies. Differences in language and business practice can raise the cost of an international financial deal relative to that of a similar bargain between residents of the same country.

In measuring the strength of such barriers to international capital movement, an essential comparative benchmark is the ideal case of *perfect* international capital mobility, in which capital is free to move internationally and transactions costs are literally zero. This section therefore reviews the main implications of perfect capital mobility, implications that will be compared with recent experience in the sections to follow. A main theme of the discussion is that such comparisons are seldom straightforward: many commonly used barometers of capital mobility are based on strong, often questionable, auxiliary assumptions about the world.

The Law of One Price

Perhaps the most basic implication of perfect capital mobility is that an asset's price must be the same wherever it is sold. With sufficiently detailed data, it would be possible to test this implication directly on a wide array of assets. In practice, however, most tests of the law of one price examine the prices in different localities of a narrow set of closely comparable assets, namely, claims on specified future currency payments.

The dollar price of \$1 to be delivered in country A one period from today is $1/(1 + i_\$^A)$, where $i_\$^A$ is the one-period nominal dollar interest rate in country A.

In country B on the same date, the nominal dollar interest rate is $i_\$^B$. Under perfect capital mobility, the price of a future dollar is the same no matter where the claim to the dollar is located. Thus, the equality $i_\$^A = i_\$^B$ holds true (as does the corresponding equality for any other currency).

Empirical studies have pursued this implication of perfect capital mobility by comparing nominal currency interest rates in different financial centers, for example, the interest rates on large dollar certificates of deposit sold in New York and those on London Eurodollar deposits of the same maturity. Strictly speaking, such assets do not guarantee the same payment in all states of nature—for example, the unregulated offshore Eurodollar market may be more prone to a generalized financial crisis than is the onshore U.S. money market. Nonetheless, the relation between nominal interest rates on the same currency in different financial centers is probably the least ambiguous of the commonly used indicators of international capital mobility.

In contrast, little can be learned about international capital mobility from cross-country comparisons of nominal or real uncovered returns on *different* currencies. Such tests are uninformative about capital mobility because they necessarily appeal to auxiliary maintained assumptions that may or may not be valid independently of the degree to which capital is mobile.

To illustrate, let $i_\$^{US}$ be the one-period dollar interest rate in New York, $i_\$^E$ the corresponding rate in the London Eurodollar market, i_{DM}^G the nominal deutsche mark interest rate in Frankfurt, i_{DM}^E the Euro-deutsche mark interest rate, and $x_{\$/DM}$ the subsequent one-period percentage change in the dollar price of deutsche marks.

Consider how information about capital mobility is embedded in the *ex post* difference in dollar returns between dollar deposits in New York and deutsche mark deposits in Frankfurt, $i_\$^{US} - i_{DM}^G - x_{\$/DM}$. Let $E(\cdot)$ denote a conditional expectation. If one decomposes the preceding dollar return differential into

$$(i_\$^{US} - i_\$^E) + (i_\$^E - i_{DM}^E - Ex_{\$/DM}) + (Ex_{\$/DM} - x_{\$/DM}) + (i_{DM}^E - i_{DM}^G) ,$$

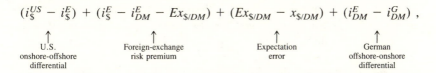

| ↑ | ↑ | ↑ | ↑ |
| U.S. onshore-offshore differential | Foreign-exchange risk premium | Expectation error | German offshore-onshore differential |

it becomes apparent that *all* direct information about international capital mobility is contained in the two onshore-offshore differences. Perfect capital mobility has the clear implication that both of the onshore-offshore interest-rate differentials above must be zero; but the implications of perfect capital mobility for foreign-exchange risk premia and exchange-rate forecast errors are much less obvious.

The risk premium links expected returns on assets (such as different-denomination Eurocurrency deposits) that are identical in location and in all other respects except for currency of denomination. As stressed in my 1986 paper, however, hypotheses about the relative returns on two London deposits can yield no direct information on capital mobility among financial centers.

It is similarly difficult to think of a significant direct link between capital mobility and the exchange-rate forecast errors of market participants. Conceivably, the degree of capital mobility affects the information-revelation process in foreign-exchange markets, with some impact on the distribution of forecast errors, but no definite hypotheses concerning such effects have been advanced, let alone tested.

Thus, only with the aid of specific and probably irrelevant maintained hypotheses about the risk premium and expectations can one glean information about capital mobility from *ex post* uncovered return differentials such as $i_\$^{LS}$ $- i_{DM}^G - x_{\$/DM}$. Tests based on international differences in *real* interest rates —domestic nominal rates less expected domestic inflation—would require even more maintained auxiliary hypotheses than those based on uncovered nominal returns (see Obstfeld [1986] for a detailed discussion). A more direct approach, yielding results vastly easier to interpret, is to analyze the one observable and relatively unambiguous indicator of capital mobility, the onshore-offshore interest differential.[2] Results based on this indicator are reported in Section 2.

Consumption Insurance

Capital mobility allows countries to trade differential consumption risks; the effect is to provide mutual insurance against purely idiosyncratic national consumption fluctuations. In practice, consumption insurance is provided by trade in a wide array of contingent and noncontingent securities: a cross-border exchange of common stock, for example, will alter the statistical distribution of both trading partners' future consumptions. The insurance function of international capital markets is best illustrated, however, by assuming that countries can trade a set of Arrow-Debreu securities, one of which entitles its owner to a specified payment on a particular date if, and only if, a well-defined event, or "state of nature," occurs.

Figure 6.1 illustrates the effect of trade in such securities for a world in which there are two countries peopled by representative agents, A and B, two states of nature, 1 and 2, and in which consumption of a homogeneous non-

---

[2] Tests of *covered* interest parity between different countries, such as those reported by Giavazzi and Pagano (1985) and Frankel (1993), can be formulated so that they are equivalent to comparisons of onshore and offshore interest rates in the same currency. To return to the example, let $f_{\$/DM}$ be the one-period forward premium for deutsche marks in terms of dollars quoted in the London market. Eurocurrency arbitrage ensures that $i_\$^E = i_{DM}^E + f_{\$/DM}$, so the covered differential $i_{DM}^G + f_{\$/DM} - i_\$^E$ between the Frankfurt deutsche mark market and the Eurodollar market is identical to the onshore-offshore deutsche mark differential $i_{DM}^G - i_{DM}^E$.

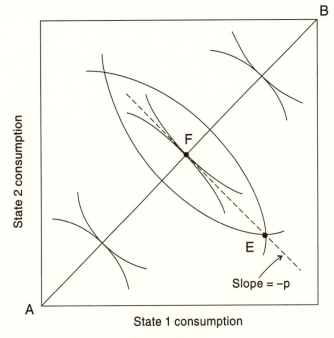

Figure 6.1 Trade across States of Nature

produced output is the only argument in utility functions. At the endowment point E, country A is relatively well-endowed with state 1 consumption and country B with state 2 consumption; that is, state 1 is relatively more favorable to the fortunes of country A; state 2, more favorable to those of country B. Otherwise, the two countries are, for simplicity, portrayed as being identical. If the free exchange of Arrow-Debreu securities is allowed, country A exports and country B imports securities that pay off in state 1; to balance this trade, country A imports and country B exports securities that pay off in state 2. At the resulting free-trade allocation, point F, both countries have raised their utilities by reducing the variability of consumption across states of nature.

Note that this outcome is predicted by the classical principle of comparative advantage, whereby a country exports the good the domestic autarky price of which is relatively low.[3] The relative price of the two available Arrow-Debreu securities can be identified with the price of state 1 consumption in terms of state 2 consumption. As usual, the free-trade price, shown as p in Figure 6.1, lies between the countries' autarky prices; and, in a trading equilibrium, the countries have equated their marginal rates of substitution across states to p, and thus to each other.

[3] Svensson (1988) places this result in a generalized setting.

The key statistical implication of an efficient allocation of consumption risks is that *countries' marginal utilities of consumption are proportional and, thus, perfectly correlated across states of nature.* Note that this proportionality holds true if and only if national marginal rates of substitution across any two states of nature coincide.[4]

The preceding empirical prediction stems from two distinct assumptions: that there is free and costless international asset trade, and that the available set of securities available to trade is *complete*, so that all consumption risks are insurable. In theory, either of these two assumptions can fail independently of the other; in practice, it is clear that the existence of informational asymmetries and limits to enforcement restricts the extent to which individuals can contract to share risks. Even under perfect capital mobility, there thus may be no close *ex post* association between national consumption levels. Other things being equal, however, increasing international capital mobility should entail an increasing tendency for positively correlated consumption comovements among countries. Evidence related to this prediction is discussed in Section 3.

The International Allocation of Investment

If the set of state-contingent assets people trade is sufficiently rich, perfect capital mobility leads to an efficient international allocation of investment: at the margin, a decision to invest a unit of output in country B rather than in country A should not affect the expected value of the flow of future world output.

The clause concerning the richness of the available asset menu is crucial, because the expected value of world output is the sum of output realizations in different states of nature weighted by state-contingent output prices. If the required set of state-contingent assets does not exist, people generally will not have common marginal rates of consumption substitution across all states of nature, and there is no automatic presumption that investment will be efficiently allocated throughout the world.[5]

---

[4] To formalize the one-period example in Figure 6.1, let $c^A(s_j)$ be the consumption of a representative individual from country A in state j ($j = 1, 2, \ldots, N$) and let $U^A[c^A(s_1), c^A(s_2), \ldots, c^A(s_N)]$ be country A's utility from its contingent consumption plans. Then, with similar notation for country B, marginal utilities are proportional if, for some constant $\lambda > 0$ and for every state j, $U_j^A = \lambda U_j^B$, where U_j is a partial derivative with respect to state-j consumption. But this condition implies the international equalization of marginal rates of substitution between any states j and l, that is, $U_j^A/U_l^A = U_j^B/U_l^B$. To show the converse, define $\lambda = U_N^A/U_N^B$.

[5] Under restrictive theoretical conditions, an efficient complete-markets allocation can be reached even when a complete set of state-contingent assets is not traded. For different examples, see Rubinstein (1974) and Cole and Obstfeld (1991).

In a world of uncertainty and incomplete markets, it therefore can be difficult to judge how close global investment patterns are to those that free capital mobility would imply. Researchers hoping to assess capital mobility from this perspective have been forced to rely on very rough measures of constrained investment efficiency.

A number of studies attempt to compare, directly or indirectly through an examination of capital-output ratios, the marginal contribution of installed capital to national outputs. In the presence of capital installation costs, however, this marginal product of capital need not be the same everywhere at every moment. What should be observed under capital mobility is a tendency for time-averaged marginal products of capital in various countries to converge. Correspondingly, world investment should flow disproportionately toward countries where capital is relatively more productive.

A controversial way of evaluating the efficiency of the global allocation of investment is proposed by Feldstein and Horioka (1980) and Feldstein (1983). They argue that the productivity of capital in a country is not systematically linked to the determinants of its saving rate and infer that national saving and domestic investment rates should not be systematically associated either if capital is internationally mobile. Other things being equal, a rise in a country's saving rate should cause a current-account surplus that directs the freed investable resources toward their most efficient worldwide uses, and an increase in the productivity of a nation's capital should cause a current-account deficit that draws in savings from abroad. Feldstein and Horioka's conclusion that this picture does not match the postwar facts has spawned a large literature, which is reviewed in Section 4 below.

2 Evidence on the Law of One Price

Section 1 argued that the least ambiguous evidence on international capital mobility comes from a comparison of nominal interest rates on onshore and offshore loans of the same currency. Under perfect capital mobility, the interest rate on a three-month French franc deposit in Paris, for example, should equal that on a three-month French franc deposit in London.

Numerous studies have compared onshore-offshore interest differentials or the related covered interest differentials; partial surveys are in Obstfeld (1986) and Frankel (1993). Frankel (table 2.4) reports statistics on the size and variability of covered interest differentials for a range of industrialized and developing countries over the period from September 1982 to April 1988. His conclusion is that by that period, departures from perfect capital mobility, indicated by short-term covered interest differentials, were small for a number of countries (Popper, 1993, reaches the same conclusion regarding long-term differentials). Included in Frankel's group of financially open economies are

Austria, Belgium, Canada, Germany, Hong Kong, Japan, the Netherlands, Singapore, Sweden, Switzerland, and the United Kingdom. For other economies in Frankel's sample, most glaringly, Greece, Mexico, and Portugal, substantial barriers to capital movement apparently remained during the period from 1982 to 1988. This latter group also includes France, Ireland, and Italy, European Community (EC) members (now members of the European Union, or EU) that adopted timetables for capital-account liberalization as part of the single-market program set out in the EC's Single European Act of 1987.

Table 6.1 summarizes a set of more detailed and up-to-date data for four industrialized countries, France (panel A), Italy (panel B), Germany (panel C), and Japan (panel D). For each currency, the onshore interest rate is the three-month domestic interbank rate, and the offshore rate is the three-month rate in the London Euromarket. Rates are expressed as basis points per year. Daily Reuters data covering January 1982 through April 1993 (as reported by Data Resources, Inc.) are used. Because these data did not appear to be completely accurate, suspicious observations were checked against the daily reports in the *Financial Times* of London and corrected when necessary.

Many empirical studies ignore the existence of information on both the ask and bid rates of interest at which banks stand ready to supply and accept funds.[6] Ask and bid prices are important data in comparing rates of return internationally, however, because the rates at which interbank transactions actually take place are bracketed by the ask-bid spread. In addition, use of the distinct ask and bid rates allows the researcher to test a wider range of hypotheses about financial market links.

Under free capital mobility, bank borrowers have the option of using whichever market is cheapest, and bank lenders can place funds wherever they get the highest net return. Thus, borrowing rates should be the same in all centers where borrowing is occurring, lending rates should be the same in all centers where lending is occurring, and the ask-bid spread should thus be the same in all centers where both activities are occurring at the ask and bid rates.

The first two columns of numbers in Table 6.1 compute period daily averages of differences between onshore and offshore bid (denoted by an underbar) and ask (denoted by an overbar) rates of interest on loans of domestic currency. As above, the subscripts on the nominal interest rate i refer to currency of denomination, and the superscripts refer to location, either the home country (F for France, I for Italy, G for Germany, J for Japan) or the offshore Eurocurrency market (symbolized by the letter E). The last two columns of Table 6.1 report average onshore and offshore ask-bid spreads, which must be

---

[6] The price of current money in terms of future money at which a bank is willing to supply current funds is 1 plus the ask rate; it always exceeds 1 plus the bid rate, which is the price of current money in terms of future money that a bank stands ready to pay for a loan of current funds.

TABLE 6.1
Domestic Interbank versus Eurocurrency Three-Month Interest Rates: Daily Data, January 1, 1982, to April 30, 1993 (basis points at an annual rate)

A. France

Period	$\underline{i}^F_{Fr} - \underline{i}^E_{Fr}$	$\bar{i}^F_{Fr} - \bar{i}^E_{Fr}$	$\underline{i}^F_{Fr} - \bar{i}^E_{Fr}$	$\underline{i}^E_{Fr} - \bar{i}^F_{Fr}$	Onshore Ask-Bid	Offshore Ask-Bid
Jan. 1, 1982–	−227	−254	−267	214	13	40
Jan. 31, 1987	(336)	(375)	(375)	(336)	(3)	(49)
Feb. 1, 1987–	−11	−10	−23	−2	13	13
June 30, 1990	(16)	(20)	(19)	(17)	(4)	(10)
July 1, 1990–	8	1	−11	−20	12	19
May 31, 1992	(7)	(11)	(7)	(10)	(8)	(5)
June 1, 1992–	−1	−3	−35	−32	32	34
Apr. 30, 1993	(34)	(40)	(45)	(36)	(20)	(38)

B. Italy

Period	$\underline{i}^I_{Li} - \underline{i}^E_{Li}$	$\bar{i}^I_{Li} - \bar{i}^E_{Li}$	$\underline{i}^I_{Li} - \bar{i}^E_{Li}$	$\underline{i}^E_{Li} - \bar{i}^I_{Li}$	Onshore Ask-Bid	Offshore Ask-Bid
Jan. 1, 1982–	−50	−89	−124	15	34	74
Jan. 31, 1987	(262)	(311)	(308)	(265)	(10)	(57)
Feb. 1, 1987–	29	48	−14	−91	62	43
June 30, 1990	(48)	(47)	(49)	(47)	(20)	(7)
July 1, 1990–	56	63	9	−111	55	47
May 31, 1992	(29)	(36)	(29)	(37)	(24)	(6)
June 1, 1992–	36	28	−8	−73	36	45
Apr. 30, 1993	(49)	(50)	(43)	(62)	(42)	(33)

C. Germany

Period	$\underline{i}^G_{DM} - \underline{i}^E_{DM}$	$\bar{i}^G_{DM} - \bar{i}^E_{DM}$	$\underline{i}^G_{DM} - \bar{i}^E_{DM}$	$\underline{i}^E_{DM} - \bar{i}^G_{DM}$	Onshore Ask-Bid	Offshore Ask-Bid
Jan. 1, 1982–	17	16	5	−28	11	13
Jan. 31, 1987	(17)	(17)	(18)	(16)	(4)	(3)
Feb. 1, 1987–	5	3	−8	−15	10	13
June 30, 1990	(10)	(10)	(11)	(10)	(2)	(3)
July 1, 1990–	−5	−5	−18	−8	13	13
May 31, 1992	(9)	(8)	(9)	(8)	(2)	(1)

(*continued*)

TABLE 6.1   (Continued)

	C. Germany					
	$\underline{i}^G_{DM} - \underline{i}^E_{DM}$	$\bar{i}^G_{DM} - \bar{i}^E_{DM}$	$\underline{i}^G_{DM} - \bar{i}^E_{DM}$	$\underline{i}^E_{DM} - \bar{i}^G_{DM}$	Onshore Ask-Bid	Offshore Ask-Bid
June 1, 1992–	7	5	−6	−18	11	13
Apr. 30, 1993	(13)	(12)	(12)	(13)	(2)	(2)

	D. Japan					
	$\underline{i}^J_{¥} - \underline{i}^E_{¥}$	$\bar{i}^J_{¥} - \bar{i}^E_{¥}$	$\underline{i}^J_{¥} - \bar{i}^E_{¥}$	$\underline{i}^E_{¥} - \bar{i}^J_{¥}$	Onshore Ask-Bid	Offshore Ask-Bid
Jan. 1, 1982–	−7	n.a.	−20	n.a.	n.a.	13
Jan. 31, 1987	(28)		(28)			(4)
Feb. 1, 1987–	−60	n.a.	−68	n.a.	n.a.	8
June 30, 1990	(33)		(33)			(3)
July 1, 1990–	9	n.a.	2	n.a.	n.a.	7
May 31, 1992	(37)		(37)			(3)
June 1, 1992–	17	n.a.	10	n.a.	n.a.	7
Apr. 30, 1993	(19)		(19)			(2)

Note: Numbers in parentheses are standard deviations. Subscripts denote asset currency of denomination, franc (*Fr*), lira (*Li*), deutsche mark (*DM*), yen (¥); superscripts denote asset location, London Eurocurrency market (*E*), France (*F*), Italy (*I*), Germany (*G*), and Japan (*J*). Underbars denote bid interest rates (the rates banks pay on deposits); overbars denote ask interest rates (the rates at which banks lend funds); n.a. = not available. Data are daily except for weekends and holidays.

the same if ask and bid rates are the same onshore and off. The use of period averages is not ideal, because large positive and negative daily observations could cancel when the average is taken. The standard deviations given in parentheses below the average return differences offer a rough idea of the extent to which such cancellation has occurred. Figures 6.2 to 6.6, which graph the daily data on onshore-offshore bid differences expressed in percentage points per year, also contain some of this information.[7]

In principle, two financial centers linked by free capital mobility could have different ask rates, if banks are not lending at the ask rate in one center, or bid rates, if no deposits are being taken at the bid rate in one center. This situation seems unlikely to prevail for any length of time, however, and so should not be too problematic for analyzing the period averages reported in the table. In reality, of course, interbank transactions often do not occur at ask or bid rates. As a stronger test, Table 6.1 also reports the returns to a hypothetical arbi-

[7] In comparing these figures, be aware that their left-hand scales differ.

trageur who borrows in one center at the ask rate and lends in the other center at the bid rate. The third column is the return to borrowing offshore and lending onshore; the fourth column is the return to borrowing onshore and lending offshore. Because such arbitrage opportunities would always be exploited, hypothetical arbitrage profits are an unambiguous indicator of capital-market segmentation and must always be absent under free capital mobility. Obviously, the indicators in Table 6.1 are not independent of each other. For example, offshore-to-onshore arbitrage at ask and bid rates is profitable only if the onshore bid exceeds the offshore bid and the offshore ask-bid spread is sufficiently small.

The first period analyzed in the table extends through the entry into force of the Single European Act in January 1987. For France (panel A) there is evidence of significant barriers to capital mobility during this period. Average ask and bid rates of interest on French franc loans are much higher offshore than onshore, and the average profitability of hypothetical onshore-to-offshore arbitrage operations is substantially positive. The interpretation of these results is that France maintained controls on capital outflows that kept domestic interest rates below Eurocurrency rates, particularly around realignments (Giavazzi and Pagano, 1985). The especially high divergences occurring around realignments are apparent in Figure 6.2. Note also that the ask-bid spread is lower onshore than offshore, consistent with the relative thinness of the Eurofranc market in the first half of the 1980s.

The last three periods shown in Table 6.1 begin roughly around the last French realignment within the European Monetary System's Exchange Rate Mechanism (ERM) (February 1, 1987), the deadline for abolition of French capital controls under the Single European Act (July 1, 1990), and the month of the initial Danish referendum (June 1, 1992), which unexpectedly rejected the Maastricht Treaty on European monetary and political union. This last event set off a period of turbulence in exchange markets that culminated in the "flotation" of ERM currencies on August 2, 1993.

In all three of these periods, the average onshore-offshore difference is on the order of 10 basis points in magnitude for both bids and asks. Hypothetical arbitrage profits are negative on average, and average ask-bid spreads are much closer in the two markets. Clearly, the integration of onshore and offshore money markets is much higher than before 1987.

The final period, that of the ERM crisis, is clearly more turbulent than the previous two: the standard errors of returns are much higher, as are ask-bid spreads. As Figure 6.3 (an enlargement of the data from January 1992 to April 1993) shows, some large gaps between onshore and offshore bid rates emerged during September 1992, when the franc first came under concerted attack by speculators. Similar data have been identified as evidence of lingering government interference in capital markets by some commentators ("A Funny Thing Happened," *The Economist*, October 10, 1992, p. 97).

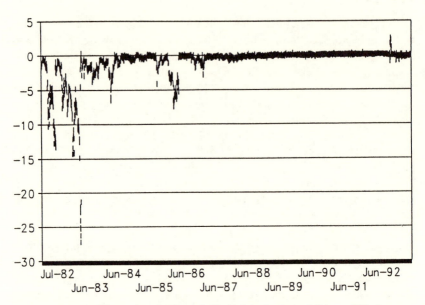

Figure 6.2 French Franc Interest-Rate Differential: Onshore-Offshore Bid, January 1982 to April 1993 (*percentage points at an annual rate*)

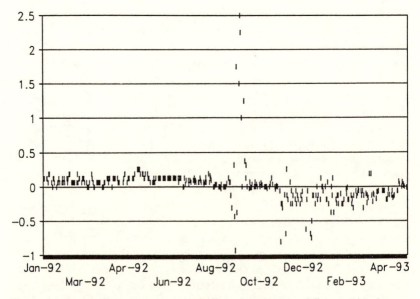

Figure 6.3 French Franc Interest-Rate Differential: Onshore-Offshore Bid, January 1992 to April 1993 (*percentage points at an annual rate*)

Note in Figure 6.3 that the onset of ERM turbulence is the dividing point between a period in which onshore bid rates usually exceed offshore rates by a small amount, and a period in which the reverse is true. This pattern would be consistent with a shift from a regime in which the market attaches a small but positive probability to future capital controls, to a regime in which mild official discouragements to capital outflow are actually in place. Between September 1992 and April 1993 there are, however, only four instances of pure profits from onshore-to-offshore arbitrage, all in 1992: on September 22 and 23, on November 24, and on December 1.

The case of Italy (panel B of Table 6.1) also shows evidence of restricted capital mobility before February 1987. Average offshore bid and ask rates both exceed onshore counterparts, and there exists a small mean (15 basis-point) profit from undertaking a hypothetical onshore-to-offshore arbitrage.[8] As Giavazzi and Pagano (1985) observed using a shorter data sample, domestic Italian interest rates diverge less from the corresponding offshore rates than do French domestic rates during this initial period. Nonetheless, the data are consistent with the view that Italy, like France, restricted capital outflows and thus held domestic interest rates artificially low. As in the case of France, the ask-bid spread before February 1987 is higher offshore.

The next subperiod, February 1, 1987, to June 30, 1990, shows some convergence to offshore conditions: average onshore rates now rise a bit above average offshore rates, average arbitrage opportunities disappear, and the absolute difference between mean offshore and onshore spreads narrows.

After July 1, 1990, average onshore rates actually rise further above offshore rates, and apparent opportunities for profitable offshore-to-onshore (that is, inward) arbitrage open up (see Figure 6.4). Italy adopted a narrow ERM band for the lira in January 1990 and then removed its remaining capital-account restrictions in May. Subsequently, Italy's desire to avoid realignment clashed increasingly with the lira's ongoing real appreciation and with the growth in domestic public debt. The onshore interest premium may have reflected market fears that capital controls might be reimposed in the future to shore up Italy's increasingly strict interpretation of its ERM commitments. Consistent with this view is the behavior of the average onshore premium after June 1, 1992, a period that includes Italy's abandonment of the ERM for a float on September 17, 1992: the average onshore premium drops and average arbitrage profits disappear as one key motive for reimposing capital controls evaporates. After September 1, 1992, one (probably spurious) instance of a pure profit from outward arbitrage occurs on January 4, the first business day of 1993.

Panel C of Table 6.1 shows that, before February 1987, Germany's onshore interest rates were on average slightly above offshore rates, consistent with

---

[8] The large standard error on this small mean value implies episodically large notional profit opportunities.

official measures discouraging capital inflow (see also Figure 6.5). There is even a slight average profit from hypothetical inward arbitrage during this period. Ask-bid spreads, however, are essentially the same in the onshore and offshore markets throughout the full sample period.

In all three subperiods after February 1987, onshore and offshore rates are very close on average and mean arbitrage profits are negative. Some large daily onshore premia emerge during the fall 1992 ERM crisis, however: over the period from September 1992 to April 1993, offshore-to-onshore arbitrage appears profitable on 51 out of 242 business days! This pattern may reflect continuing government intervention in the capital markets. Goldstein et al. (1993, p. 56) mention the "gentlemen's agreement" whereby the Bundesbank may impose high marginal reserve requirements on loans in excess of a certain limit to German banks from their London branches.

For Japan (panel D of Table 6.1), a less complete set of data were available from Reuters. The available data show a very small average difference between onshore and offshore bid rates over the first sample subperiod, consistent with Japan's substantial liberalization of capital movements in December 1980.[9]

Surprisingly, the subperiod beginning with February 1987 shows a 60 basis-point average excess of offshore over onshore bid rates; Figure 6.6 makes clear that this differential is much too long-lived to ascribe to the time-of-day difference in the Japanese onshore and offshore data. Ueda (1993, p. 19) suggests that, before November 1988, the Bank of Japan used heavy administrative guidance to separate the interbank loan market from both the onshore certificate of deposit market and the Euroyen market; during the subperiod in question, the Bank of Japan wished to hold interbank rates below onshore and offshore open-market rates.[10] Thus, the onshore-offshore gaps in Figure 6.6 indicate a segmentation within the *domestic* financial market that, as a side effect, insulated part of that market from global forces.

Over the last two subperiods, the mean onshore bid exceeds the mean offshore bid by relatively small amounts. The ask-bid spread in the Euroyen market is so slim that even the small onshore bid premium implies positive average arbitrage profits from borrowing offshore and investing onshore. These divergences grow stronger in the period starting with June 1992. In light of the data's imperfections, it is unwise to put much weight on these numbers as indicators of capital-market restriction. Faced with a punctured "bubble" economy and a rising yen in these years, however, Japanese officials did have incentives to discourage capital inflows through informal means.

What conclusions follow from these and similar data for other industrial countries? For the four countries in Table 6.1, as well as for others, such as

[9] Marston (1993a) examines differences in Japanese and U.S. short-term interest rates and reviews related literature.

[10] In November 1988, the bank took measures liberalizing the interbank market.

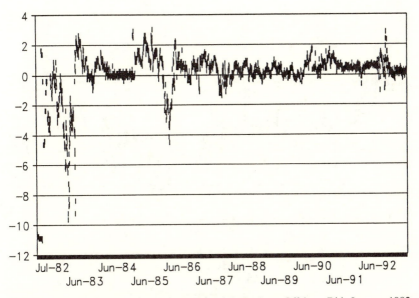

Figure 6.4 Italian Lira Interest-Rate Differential: Onshore-Offshore Bid, January 1982 to April 1993 (*percentage points at an annual rate*)

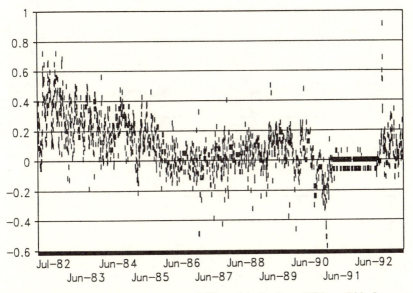

Figure 6.5 German Mark Interest-Rate Differential: Onshore-Offshore Bid, January 1982 to April 1993 (*percentage points at an annual rate*)

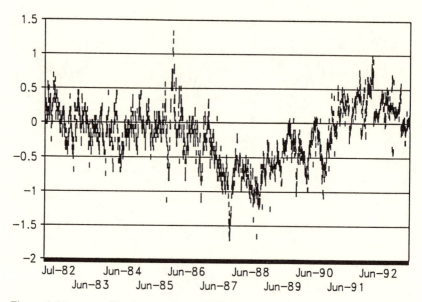

Figure 6.6 Japanese Yen Interest-Rate Differential: Onshore-Offshore Bid, January 1982 to April 1993 (*percentage points at an annual rate*)

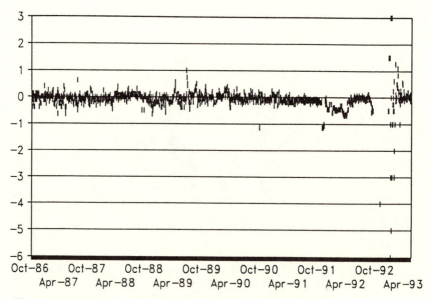

Figure 6.7 Irish Punt Interest-Rate Differential: Onshore-Offshore Bid, October 1986 to April 1993 (*percentage points at an annual rate*)

the United States and United Kingdom, that have liberalized international financial transactions, there are extremely close links between onshore and offshore money markets, links that increased in strength over the 1980s. The data also show, however, that actual or prospective government interventions remain a significant factor in times of turbulence. Industrial-country governments still have instruments that can drive at least temporary wedges between onshore and offshore interest rates. European countries that have not completely opened their capital accounts, such as Greece, Ireland, Portugal, and Spain, openly retain such instruments; all four used them during the ERM currency crisis that began in 1992 (Committee of Governors, 1993; Goldstein et al., 1993). Even these countries tend to have strong links to world capital markets. For example, Ireland's onshore and offshore interest rates were close on the whole from the late 1980s through 1992 (see Figure 6.7).

Matters are different in the developing world, where much higher explicit or implicit barriers to capital flows remain common. Discussions of financial liberalization and international interest-rate linkages for developing regions can be found in Glick and Hutchison (1990), Calvo, Leiderman, and Reinhart (1993), and Mathieson and Rojas-Suarez (1993).

3 The Diversification of Global Consumption Risks

Researchers have taken several approaches to studying the world capital market's success in helping countries trade consumption risks to achieve a mutually preferable allocation of consumption across states of nature. Some look directly at national or regional correlations in consumption. Others look at the extent of trade in explicitly state-contingent assets. As will become apparent in the discussion, the implications of such data for capital mobility are ambiguous unless specific and strong side assumptions are made about the functioning of domestic and international capital markets. Much recent research is aimed at testing these assumptions, and, as difficult as the task is, it is justified by the need to understand better the current and potential risk-allocation role of world capital markets.

International Consumption Correlations

A simple maximization problem illustrates how global consumption allocations would behave in the ideal case of perfect international trade in a *complete* set of state-contingent assets. Because the resulting allocation is Pareto-optimal, its properties can be read off from the first-order conditions that a world planner would derive in maximizing a social-welfare function linear in national utilities.

An analytically convenient starting point is the assumption of a representative national agent for each country. This assumption, which will be discussed further below, amounts to supposing that risks have already been shared optimally *within* each country, leaving only the remaining gains from trade *between* countries as the analytical focus. Country j's representative agent maximizes (from time $t = 0$) the expected utility function

$$U_0^j = E_0 \left[\sum_{t=0}^{\infty} \delta^t u^j(c_t^j, x_t^j) \right] ,$$

where $\delta \in (0,1)$ is a discount factor, c_t^j (as before) is consumption of an internationally tradable good, and x_t^j is consumption of a nontradable good (possibly leisure).[11]

Given N countries and fixed country welfare weights $\omega^j, j = 1, 2, \ldots, N$, the planner maximizes the social-welfare function

$$W_0 = \sum_{j=1}^{N} \omega^j U_0^j$$

by distributing the tradable consumption available on each date, and in each state, among the N countries. If c_t^w is world tradable consumption on date t, a necessary condition for distributing it efficiently among countries is

$$\omega^j u_1^j(c_t^j, x_t^j) = \omega^l u_1^l(c_t^l, x_t^l) \text{ (for all countries } j \text{ and } l) , \quad (1)$$

where $u_1(c, x)$ is a partial derivative with respect to c. Equation (1) implies that, for tradable goods, marginal rates of substitution across states of nature are equalized internationally in an efficient allocation. Because nontradables cannot be shifted among countries, however, the corresponding condition on marginal utilities from the nontradables need not hold.

To derive more specific predictions from (1), suppose that no nontradables x^j are consumed and that utility functions have the specific form

$$u^j(c^j, x^j) = (1 - R_j)^{-1}(c^j)^{1-R_j} .$$

Then, if $\hat{c}_t \equiv \log c_t - \log c_{t-1}$, (1) implies

$$\hat{c}_t^j = (R_l/R_j)\hat{c}_t^l ; \quad (2)$$

---

[11] This formulation already imposes strong restrictions on national utility functions (for example, time and state separability), and more will be imposed later. Without some assumptions on preferences, however, no observable implications of international risk sharing could be derived.

that is, with isoelastic preferences, logarithmic growth rates of consumption are perfectly correlated *ex post* in all countries. If countries have different (fixed) rates of time preference, equation (2) will contain a constant term, but the perfect-correlation prediction will still hold true.

If capital is internationally mobile but asset markets are incomplete, conditions weaker than perfect correlation will characterize the relation between countries' *ex post* intertemporal marginal rates of substitution. As noted above, informational asymmetries generate moral hazards; these or other problems can make certain risks uninsurable. In the extreme case in which only a riskless consumption-indexed bond is traded among countries, expected, but not *ex post*, intertemporal marginal rates of substitution will coincide internationally. This case is the one analyzed in stochastic versions of the life-cycle/permanent-income hypothesis. If only nominally risk-free bonds are traded, expected intertemporal marginal rates of substitution for money (rather than consumption) will be equalized (Obstfeld, 1989; Kollman, 1992). More generally, *ex post* cross-country differences in intertemporal marginal rates of substitution will be uncorrelated with any random variables on which international contracts can be written. Under incomplete markets asset trade allows the sharing of some, but not all, risks.

To compare reality against the predictions of the specific complete-markets model just set out, Table 6.2 examines the correlations of national annual real private consumption growth rates, measured in per capita terms, with rest-of-world per capita private consumption growth over two eras in the development of world capital markets, 1951 to 1972 and 1973 to 1988.[12] The consumption data come from the Penn World Tables assembled by Summers and Heston (1991); the "world" shown in Table 6.2 consists of countries with continuous 1950–88 data rated of quality C− or above by Summers and Heston.

All the correlation coefficients, denoted $\rho(\hat{c}, \hat{c}^W)$, where c^W is rest-of-world real per capita consumption, are below the value of 1 that would obtain with a common world isoelastic utility function were capital perfectly mobile and markets complete. Several regularities in the results are, however, apparent.

For the post-1973 period—a period during which the volume of international financial transactions has increased enormously relative to world output—consumption growth in industrial countries is, on average, somewhat more highly correlated with rest-of-world consumption growth than is consumption growth in developing countries. Within the group of industrial countries, however, there are sharp differences.

For a narrow majority of EU members, domestic and world consumption

---

[12] The current model implies that each country's consumption growth is perfectly correlated with world consumption growth if all countries have the same value of R_j. Looking at correlations with world consumption growth, rather than at the customary pairwise consumption-growth correlations, economizes on the number of estimates reported. This procedure also has some potential statistical advantages (see Obstfeld, 1994a).

TABLE 6.2

Consumption and Output Correlations: International Data, 1951–72 and 1973–88

Country	Correlation 1951–72			Correlation 1973–88		
	$\rho(\hat{c},\hat{c}^W)$	$\rho(\hat{y},\hat{y}^W)$	$\rho(\hat{c},\hat{y})$	$\rho(\hat{c},\hat{c}^W)$	$\rho(\hat{y},\hat{y}^W)$	$\rho(\hat{c},\hat{y})$
Industrial Countries						
EU members						
Belgium	0.50	0.47	0.66	0.49	0.58	0.81
Denmark	0.09	−0.04	0.75	0.60	0.39	0.80
France	0.26	0.41	0.64	0.50	0.56	0.71
Germany	−0.11	0.31	0.78	0.72	0.87	0.68
Greece	−0.10	0.03	0.69	0.13	0.41	0.56
Ireland	0.58	0.58	0.77	0.48	0.57	0.76
Italy	−0.02	0.35	0.62	0.27	0.61	0.90
Luxembourg	0.14	−0.18	0.20	0.21	0.73	0.19
Netherlands	0.49	0.27	0.77	0.56	0.59	0.75
Portugal	−0.10	0.18	0.55	0.06	0.44	0.89
Spain	−0.33	0.01	0.90	0.32	0.39	0.93
United Kingdom	0.29	0.49	0.60	0.59	0.66	0.81
Others						
Australia	0.39	0.06	0.88	−0.00	0.72	0.66
Austria	0.33	0.27	0.59	0.29	0.55	0.71
Canada	0.43	0.42	0.71	0.10	0.30	0.90
Finland	0.20	0.34	0.82	0.19	0.06	0.46
Iceland	0.17	−0.18	0.91	0.05	0.27	0.85
Japan	0.06	0.43	0.57	0.62	0.71	0.86
New Zealand	0.38	−0.07	0.81	−0.03	0.16	0.77
Norway	0.36	0.01	0.56	0.05	0.37	0.43
Sweden	0.27	0.07	0.74	0.18	0.04	0.36
Switzerland	0.32	0.50	0.56	0.64	0.53	0.79
United States	0.26	0.19	0.59	0.31	0.67	0.81
Developing Countries						
Argentina	0.00	0.02	0.96	−0.04	0.25	0.92
Bolivia	−0.07	0.34	0.59	0.29	0.08	0.74
Chile	−0.32	0.02	0.69	0.44	0.62	0.85
Colombia	0.28	0.11	0.89	0.29	0.51	0.79
Costa Rica	0.15	−0.09	0.89	0.63	0.65	0.95
Cyprus	0.20	−0.04	0.62	0.64	0.64	0.92
Dominican Rep.	0.03	0.10	0.92	0.11	0.26	0.88
Ecuador	−0.01	0.19	0.63	−0.17	0.05	0.67
El Salvador	0.38	0.21	0.89	0.56	0.44	0.95
Guatemala	−0.28	−0.40	0.81	0.39	0.48	0.95
Honduras	0.16	0.20	0.58	0.54	0.68	0.91
India	−0.13	−0.09	0.59	−0.13	−0.16	0.93

(*continued*)

TABLE 6.2 (*Continued*)

Country	Correlation 1951–72			Correlation 1973–88		
	$\rho(\hat{c},\hat{c}^W)$	$\rho(\hat{y},\hat{y}^W)$	$\rho(\hat{c},\hat{y})$	$\rho(\hat{c},\hat{c}^W)$	$\rho(\hat{y},\hat{y}^W)$	$\rho(\hat{c},\hat{y})$
Kenya	−0.04	0.24	0.93	−0.08	0.20	0.82
Mexico	−0.01	0.22	0.92	−0.27	0.02	0.98
Morocco	−0.18	−0.05	0.94	0.22	−0.04	0.62
Pakistan	0.03	0.33	0.59	−0.20	0.06	0.44
Paraguay	0.13	−0.21	0.78	−0.32	0.01	0.93
Peru	0.11	0.35	0.60	−0.26	−0.18	0.94
Philippines	0.03	−0.15	0.77	−0.06	−0.12	0.80
South Africa	0.39	0.20	0.85	−0.49	−0.10	0.88
Thailand	−0.27	−0.23	0.94	0.51	0.61	0.84
Trinidad & Tobago	−0.20	−0.09	0.69	−0.30	−0.33	0.95
Turkey	−0.13	0.21	0.96	0.06	−0.18	0.86
Uruguay	0.17	0.42	0.95	0.09	0.28	0.90

Note: The numbers $\rho(\hat{c},\hat{c}^W)$, or $\rho(\hat{y},\hat{y}^W)$, are simple correlation coefficients between the annual change in the natural logarithm of the country's real per capita consumption (or output) and the annual change in the natural logarithm of the rest of the world's real per capita consumption (or output), with the "world" defined as the sample listed in the table. National per capita consumptions and outputs were calculated using variables 1, 3, and 6 listed in appendix A.1 of Summers and Heston, 1991. The numbers $\rho(\hat{c},\hat{y})$ are correlations between the logarithms of each country's consumption per capita and output per capita changes.

growth are relatively strongly correlated; Greece, Portugal, and Spain, which still maintain capital controls, as well as Italy, which did so through early 1990, are in the minority, as, surprisingly, is Luxembourg. For virtually all EU countries, and most dramatically for Germany, the correlation coefficient rises between the first and second subperiods. Multiple regressions show that this last result persists even after one controls for possible parallel responses to the two OPEC oil-price shocks (see Obstfeld [1994a] for further discussion).

For industrial countries outside the EU, the consumption correlations tend to be lower in the recent period except for Switzerland and Japan. Moreover, apart from those two countries, there is a tendency for the correlations to decrease, not increase over time. To explain the contrast with the EU countries would require a country-by-country analysis. One general factor, however, may be the exchange-rate regime: these countries opted for greater exchange-rate flexibility than the EU countries in the early 1970s partly because they desired to decouple domestic from world consumption growth. The Japanese example shows, however, that floating exchange rates, and even capital controls (which persisted in Japan through 1980), need not rule out a strong coherence between domestic and world consumption growth.

One way to highlight the change in German and Japanese consumption behavior after 1973 is through a simple regression. Let y^j denote country j's real per capita GDP, inv^j its real per capita investment, and g^j its real per capita government spending. Absent international asset markets, domestic per capita consumption c^j would be limited to $y^j - inv^j - g^j$. The regression

$$\hat{c}_t^j = \alpha_0 + \alpha_1 \hat{c}_t^W + \alpha_2 \Delta\log(y_t^j - inv_t^j - g_t^j) + \epsilon_t^j$$

gives an indication of whether consumption growth is more strongly associated with global or with domestic factors.[13] The Summers-Heston data lead to the following results:

	Germany		Japan	
1951–72	$\alpha_1 = -0.18$	$\alpha_2 = 0.76$	$\alpha_1 = -0.15$	$\alpha_2 = 0.76$
	(0.33)	(0.13)	(0.37)	(0.13)
1973–88	$\alpha_1 = 1.07$	$\alpha_2 = 0.02$	$\alpha_1 = 1.18$	$\alpha_2 = 0.35$
	(0.32)	(0.20)	(0.42)	(0.26)

The regressions show a stunning reversal for both countries. In the earlier period, national consumption growth is insignificantly correlated with world consumption growth but moves nearly one-for-one with the growth of GDP net of investment and government spending. From 1973 on, the opposite is true.

A fundamental identification problem is suggested by the columns in Table 6.2 labeled $\rho(\hat{y}, \hat{y}^W)$, which report correlations between national per capita output growth rates and rest-of-world per capita output growth. For most of the industrial countries, these correlations rise between the two subperiods shown. Thus, although any increase over time in the correlation between national and world consumption growth could be due to increased risk sharing through the international capital market, it could also be explained by other mechanisms, such as a naive Keynesian consumption function in which consumption merely tracks current output or by one of the richer behavioral models discussed by Carroll and Summers (1991). The Table 6.2 correlations $\rho(\hat{c}, \hat{y})$ between domestic output and consumption growth are high in most cases, although often they are well below unity.

Again, only country-by-country analysis can resolve this question. For example, tests reported in Obstfeld (1994a) suggest that the high post-1973 correlation of Japanese with world consumption growth may reflect only the high correlation coefficient between world consumption and Japanese output (0.72), coupled with the high correlation of Japanese consumption and output. In contrast, German output growth also has a very high correlation coefficient with world consumption growth (0.84), yet adds no significant explanatory

---

[13] See Obstfeld (1994a) for more discussion of this equation and its estimation.

power to a regression of German on world consumption growth. These regressions are somewhat analogous to those Campbell and Mankiw (1991) examine in modeling departures from the permanent-income theory.

Among the developing countries in Table 6.2, a few have reasonably high post-1973 correlation coefficients with world consumption growth—notably, Chile, Cyprus, Thailand, and a few Central American countries. But this is not the norm. Note that the developing countries with high post-1973 values of $\rho(\hat{c}, \hat{c}^W)$ also have high values of $\rho(\hat{y}, \hat{y}^W)$.

Before drawing strong conclusions from Table 6.2 about feasible gains from risk sharing, recall that (2) was based on some restrictive auxiliary assumptions, for example, the assumption that nontradables are not consumed. If some consumption goods are nontradable, there is no necessity for national consumptions to be perfectly correlated: risks relating to the consumption of nontraded goods may be impossible to share (Stockman and Dellas, 1989). At best, consumption of tradables will obey (2) if the utility function $u^j(c^j, x^j)$ is separable (but still isoelastic in c^j). In more complicated models, even this simple property can fail despite complete markets.[14]

By investigating the stochastic consequences of a labor-leisure trade-off and/or nontradables, several studies have tried to reconcile consumption correlations such as those shown for the industrial countries in Table 6.1 with complete markets and perfect capital mobility.

Backus, Kehoe, and Kydland (1992) and Stockman and Tesar (1990) observe that the pairwise correlation coefficients between (Hodrick-Prescott [1980]–filtered) industrial-country consumption levels tend to be lower than the corresponding output correlations. This property of the data is quite evident in Table 6.2: after 1973, $\rho(\hat{c}, \hat{c}^W)$ exceeds $\rho(\hat{y}, \hat{y}^W)$ only for Denmark, Finland, Sweden, and Switzerland among twenty-three industrial countries. Backus, Kehoe, and Kydland fail to replicate this pattern using a plausibly calibrated two-country intertemporal production model with uncertainty.

Stockman and Tesar introduce nontradable consumption into a similar equilibrium business-cycle model and find that the addition of preference shocks allows a closer approximation to the empirical correlation coefficients for national consumptions and outputs. Devereux, Gregory, and Smith (1992) show that a specific utility nonseparability between consumption and labor supply allows an equilibrium business-cycle model to replicate the U.S.-Canadian consumption-correlation coefficient. They do not, however, subject their model to the tougher test of fitting other moments of the data. Van Wincoop (1992c, table 1) adjusts annual 1970–88 consumption data from the United Nations System of National Accounts for both nontradability and durability. He finds

---

[14] Stulz (1981) addresses these questions in a general setting. Note that if there is heterogeneity in national preferences over tradables, results based on total tradables consumption will be misleading. Under full risk sharing, national marginal utilities for individual tradable commodities move in proportion.

that for most industrial countries, the correlation between the growth of adjusted domestic per capita consumption and adjusted world per capita consumption is much higher than in Table 6.2 above (albeit still imperfect). His calculations do not, however, control for the possibility that correlations are also higher among the growth rates of similarly adjusted per capita domestic outputs.

Lewis (1993) carries out a panel study of the growth of nondurable, tradable consumption, using data from forty-eight countries sampled at five-year intervals from 1970 to 1985. Remarkably, she finds that, although domestic output growth is a strong and significant determinant of *total* consumption growth in her panel, its effect on nondurable, tradable consumption growth is statistically insignificant; furthermore, domestic output growth explains less than a hundredth of the dependent variable's variance (as opposed to about two-thirds of the variance of total consumption growth). Although imprecisely estimated, the coefficient of output growth in Lewis's equation for nondurable, tradable consumption remains sizable. In light of possible measurement errors, and her panel methodology's merging of countries with different degrees of financial openness, a judicious conclusion is that durability and nontradability go part, but probably not all, of the way in explaining why total consumption growth is highly correlated with domestic output growth. Lewis does not look at the influence on consumption of idiosyncratic factors other than income growth, so her results do not explain why, as in van Wincoop's (1992c) study, international consumption correlations remain imperfect even after attention is restricted to nondurable tradables.

The message of this body of work seems to be that, after allowing for nontradables and durables, equilibrium complete-markets models that assume perfect capital mobility still cannot provide a satisfactory explanation of international consumption correlations unless unexplained preference shifts are assumed as in Stockman and Tesar (1990). Taste shocks are not inherently implausible, but, until they are modeled more fully, there is no way of telling if the heavy explanatory burden they bear in the Stockman-Tesar model is reasonable.[15]

An alternative approach starts by acknowledging that the assumption of complete asset markets is glaringly at odds with the facts. Events such as job loss generally are not completely insurable because of the potential for moral hazard. More generally, labor incomes cannot be privately insured against all contingencies. Some shocks simply cannot be foreseen with sufficient clarity to be provided for in contracts. Thus, even with free and costless international trade in the same range of assets traded domestically, there is no reason to

---

[15] Canova and Ravn (1993), Lewis (1993), and Obstfeld (1994a) all allow for preference shocks in their formal tests of consumption risk-sharing models. In tests on quarterly data for nine OECD countries, Canova and Ravn find little evidence against moment restrictions implied by a model based on equation (2) above. They do, however, reject long-run implications of the model.

expect high correlations even between the tradable-goods consumptions of different countries.

Empirical studies of U.S. microeconomic data, such as Cochrane (1991), Mace (1991), and Mankiw and Zeldes (1991), confirm that, even within modern industrial economies, there are unexploited opportunities for risk sharing.[16] In line with this conclusion, van Wincoop (1992b) finds that the correlations among (Hodrick-Prescott-filtered) per capita consumption levels in Japanese prefectures are well explained by a simulation model in which domestic Japanese financial markets are incomplete and subject to limited participation.[17] Work by Baxter and Crucini (1993a) and Kollmann (1993) suggests that general-equilibrium real-business-cycle models in which countries trade only consumption-indexed bonds can mimic the actual stochastic behavior of consumptions and outputs far better than can otherwise similar models that assume complete asset markets.

These considerations have three implications for the class of models discussed so far in this section. First, the representative national consumer is a hypothetical construct that, although perhaps useful for illustrating the incremental gains from international compared with national risk sharing, gives a misleading picture of how national consumption levels actually are determined. Second, imperfect correlations among industrial-country consumptions are likely to be in large measure the result of generalized asset-market incompleteness rather than of international capital-market segmentation. Third, studies of international consumption correlatedness that counterfactually assume complete markets probably cannot throw much light on the international mobility of capital. A more fruitful approach is to consider models admitting alternative financial-market structures (for example, Cole, 1988) and, ultimately, models in which market incompleteness arises endogenously (for example, Gertler and Rogoff, 1990; Lucas, 1992).

Comparing Regional and International Risk Sharing

If asset markets are incomplete, is there any way that consumption correlations or related measures can throw light on the extent of international capital mobility? Atkeson and Bayoumi (1993) propose an imaginative approach to this problem: they use the measured extent of *regional* risk sharing within the United States as a benchmark against which the efficiency of *international* risk sharing among a group of industrial countries can be judged. In principle,

---

[16] Indeed, Altonji, Hayashi, and Kotlikoff (1992) find such unexploited opportunities even within extended U.S. families. Deaton (1992, p. 37), who surveys the related microeconomic literature, reminds us that moral-hazard problems arise even within families.

[17] Van Wincoop (1992a) shows that such a model also can rationalize cross-country consumption correlations.

this methodology can help determine the extent to which low international consumption correlations are due to international asset-trade barriers as opposed to incomplete markets.

The findings, although generally pointing to higher regional than international financial integration, are somewhat ambiguous. Regional financial transfers within the United States appear to be much larger in absolute value than resource transfers into or out of the main industrial countries, suggesting more extensive asset trade within the United States. In contrast, U.S. regional growth in real retail sales (a consumption proxy) is no less correlated with regional ouput growth than is OECD national consumption growth with national output growth.

Atkeson and Bayoumi also find that in U.S. data, shifts in state capital income are virtually uncorrelated with state capital product but are highly correlated with U.S. capital income. In Europe, national capital incomes, although uncorrelated with national capital products, seem much less correlated than in the United States with total European capital income. Atkeson and Bayoumi interpret this result as indicating better capital-income diversification within the United States than within Europe.

Table 6.3 provides another regional-to-international comparison using yearly data assembled by Robert Dekle on per capita consumption and income (which is interpreted here as an output proxy) in forty-five of the forty-seven Japanese prefectures from 1975 to 1988.[18] The column labeled $\rho(\hat{c}, \hat{c}^j)$ shows the correlation of prefectural per capita private consumption growth with mean per capita consumption growth in the other 44 prefectures; these numbers are similar on the whole to those reported for countries in Table 6.2. Slightly less than half the time, the consumption correlations are below the corresponding income correlations, labeled $\rho(\hat{y}, \hat{y}^j)$. The column labeled $\rho(\hat{c}, \hat{y})$ shows the correlation between per capita consumption and income growth by prefecture. In about two-thirds of the cases, these numbers are rather high, as are most of the corresponding numbers for national economies in Table 6.2; but, in other cases, the correlations are relatively low and are sometimes even negative. Although there is thus some limited evidence that risk sharing within Japan may be more efficient than is risk sharing among industrial countries, this is not evident in the intranational consumption correlations.

In contrast to these results for Japan, Crucini (1992) finds in annual data for 1971 to 1990 that consumption growth rates among Canadian provinces are generally more highly correlated than are provincial output growth rates or different countries' consumption growth rates.

A problem in comparing regional risk sharing within nations with risk sharing among nations when asset markets are incomplete is that a predominance

---

[18] See Dekle (1993) for a description of these data and an econometric analysis of their implications for interregional capital mobility.

TABLE 6.3
Consumption and Output Correlations by Prefecture:
Japanese Data, 1975–88

Prefecture	$\rho(\hat{c}, \hat{c}^J)$	$\rho(\hat{y}, \hat{y}^J)$	$\rho(\hat{c}, \hat{y})$
Aichi	0.349	−0.004	−0.265
Akita	0.219	0.433	0.367
Aomori	−0.096	0.196	0.905
Chiba	0.547	0.267	0.693
Fukui	0.012	−0.106	0.849
Fukuoka	0.319	0.123	0.569
Fukushima	0.065	0.386	0.898
Ehime	0.277	0.215	0.577
Gifu	0.258	0.423	−0.313
Gunma	0.644	0.668	0.444
Hiroshima	0.661	0.075	0.736
Hokkaido	0.595	0.165	0.339
Hyogo	0.480	−0.000	0.742
Ibaraki	0.077	0.205	0.630
Ishikawa	0.723	0.380	0.764
Kagawa	0.610	0.494	0.555
Kagoshima	0.046	0.218	0.982
Kanagawa	0.240	−0.015	0.872
Kochi	0.070	0.122	0.115
Kumamoto	0.059	0.221	0.907
Kyoto	0.682	0.149	0.778
Mie	0.039	0.211	−0.618
Miyagi	0.750	0.555	0.420
Miyazaki	0.010	0.528	0.824
Nagano	0.252	0.358	−0.474
Nagasaki	−0.218	0.254	0.704

(*continued*)

TABLE 6.3   *(Continued)*

Prefecture	$\rho(\hat{c},\hat{c}^J)$	$\rho(\hat{y},\hat{y}^J)$	$\rho(\hat{c},\hat{y})$
Nara	0.181	0.766	−0.211
Oita	−0.020	0.096	0.537
Okayama	0.245	0.103	−0.568
Okinawa	−0.249	0.036	0.949
Osaka	0.719	0.053	0.776
Saga	0.505	0.534	0.913
Saitama	0.404	0.337	0.696
Shiga	0.625	0.602	−0.142
Shimane	0.170	0.551	0.717
Shizuoka	0.297	0.415	0.081
Tochigi	0.100	0.115	−0.589
Tokushima	0.313	0.613	0.705
Tokyo	0.238	0.055	0.978
Tottori	0.413	0.858	0.491
Toyama	0.098	0.232	−0.713
Wakayama	0.136	0.105	0.455
Yamagata	0.496	0.303	0.748
Yamaguchi	0.777	0.331	−0.201
Yamanashi	0.658	0.513	0.567

Note: The numbers $\rho(\hat{c},\hat{c}^J)$, or $\rho(\hat{y},\hat{y}^J)$, are simple correlation coefficients between the annual change in the natural logarithm of the prefec-
ture's real per capita consumption (or output) and the annual change in the
natural logarithm of the other forty-four prefectures' average real per capita
consumption (or output). The numbers $\rho(\hat{c},\hat{y})$ are correlations between the
logarithms of prefecture consumption per capita and output per capita
changes. Data were supplied by Robert Dekle.

of uninsurable country-specific shocks can create a spurious impression of
greater risk sharing within than between countries. Another drawback of the
method is that more goods are nontradable across *national* borders than across
regional borders, so that, other things being equal, one would naturally expect
interregional consumption correlations to be higher than international ones.
Finally, government-mediated transfers and spending play a vital role in pool-

ing risks within national borders. It is conceivable that any finding of higher interregional compared with international consumption correlation is entirely an artifact of redistributive domestic fiscal policies. Despite these and other ambiguities, however, refinements of the general approach described above offer the promise of a better understanding of how international and intranational financial linkages differ.

The Extent of International Portfolio Diversification

Further evidence on the world capital market's promotion of risk sharing among countries comes from a direct examination of international portfolio positions. The consensus of studies such as French and Poterba (1990, 1991), Golub (1991), and Tesar and Werner (1992) is that there is a substantial "home bias" in the portfolios of industrial-country investors. French and Poterba and Tesar and Werner argue that conventional models of portfolio choice can explain these patterns only if domestic investors have a much more optimistic view of the expected return on domestic assets than do foreign investors. Alternatively, imperfect capital mobility simply could make extensive international diversification prohibitively costly or infeasible. But, in view of the efficiency of international interest-rate arbitrage among industrial countries (Section 2), no one believes that transactions costs or official impediments to foreign investment are universally high enough fully to explain the home bias in equity portfolios. Thus, there is an *international diversification puzzle*.[19]

One widely cited estimate reports that, in December 1989, U.S. investors held 94 percent of their stock-market wealth in home equities; Japanese investors, 98 percent; and U.K. investors, 82 percent (French and Poterba, 1991). These figures apparently do not control for holdings by "home"-based corporations of assets located abroad, for example, Nissan's Sunderland, U.K., auto plant. Investors may diversify, moreover, through holdings of assets other than equities, such as direct investments and bonds. French and Poterba (1991) report, for example, that 79 percent of German corporate equity was domestically owned at the end of 1989, which suggests a substantial home bias in German investors' portfolios. Germany's December 1991 gross external assets, however, amounted to 72.9 percent of its GDP and its gross external liabilities to 51.4 percent of its GDP—numbers that could be indicative of more extensive foreign diversification.[20] Such diversification might help ex-

---

[19] Dumas (1994) surveys models of international portfolio choice from the perspective of the international diversification puzzle and other asset-market puzzles. Current trends such as the rapid recent growth of international stock-market mutual funds suggest that the diversification puzzle may well disappear before the middle of the twenty-first century.

[20] Data on total German external assets and liabilities come from Deutsche Bundesbank (1993, p. 45). I have supplemented these numbers with a 1991 GDP estimate of $1.58 trillion.

plain the robust correlation of German with world consumption growth noted above.

The German case may be atypical; U.S. and Japanese investors, for example, probably have not used foreign diversification opportunities as extensively.[21] Several explanations for this puzzle have been proposed. Stockman and Dellas (1989) argue that the presence of nontraded goods and services may impart a significant home-asset bias to investors' portfolio decisions. The empirical explanatory ability of home-asset bias due to nontradables remains to be established, however.[22] Another explanation hinges on the argument that the appropriate criterion for evaluating a country's gains from international risk pooling is not the impact of global portfolio diversification on the statistical distribution of national equity investment income, but, rather, the scope for raising mean consumption and lowering its variance. And, if this scope is limited, international diversification may be discouraged by even minimal investment barriers such as small transactions costs.

Cole and Obstfeld (1991) use a model calibrated to U.S. and Japanese data to illustrate that, at the aggregate or national level, the efficiency gains from risk sharing among industrial countries may be as small as 0.2 percent of GNP per year.[23] Golub (1991) takes issue with this result, arguing on the basis of 1970–87 data that, despite small *aggregate* gains, Japanese and U.S. recipients of exclusively corporate income cannot pool risks with human or noncorporate capital and, as a result, would gain substantially from freer asset trade. Thus, strong individual incentives for cross-border diversification might remain. Van Wincoop's (1992a) calibration model similarly implies that owners of capital can face significantly stronger incentives to diversify than aggregate consumption figures suggest. A useful extension of this line of work would attempt to distinguish empirically between the labor incomes of stockholders and nonstockholders.

Brainard and Tobin (1992) and Baxter and Jermann (1993) argue that because human capital is largely nontradable, its owners have a strong incentive to go short in domestic equities and long in foreign equities when the returns to domestic human and physical capital are highly positively correlated.

[21] For the United States, external assets were 34.5 percent of GDP at the end of 1991, and external liabilities were 40.9 percent. The corresponding Japanese figures are 59.2 percent (external assets) and 47.9 percent (external liabilities). Position data come from Deutsche Bundesbank (1993, p. 45). My GDP estimates are $5.68 trillion for the United States and $3.39 trillion for Japan. These figures show considerable growth over the comparable 1987 figures reported by Brainard and Tobin (1992, p. 536). Their numbers show that, for the United Kingdom, assets and liabilities already exceeded GNP in 1987.

[22] Alternative theoretical models of home-asset bias are proposed by Eldor, Pines, and Schwartz (1988), by Tesar (1993), and by Feeney and Jones (1994).

[23] See also Mendoza (1991a) and Obstfeld (1992), who present alternative estimates of small industrial-country gains from asset trade.

Whether this deepens the home-bias puzzle in practice requires further research on the international and domestic correlations among returns to human and physical capital. Golub (1991), for example, shows that human and physical capital returns (measured by labor income and corporate profits, respectively) appear *negatively* correlated for Japan, and that the optimal portfolio of a Japanese worker can be skewed toward home equities. This inference depends, however, on Golub's assumption that the national-income-account proxies he uses to measure returns to human capital and to equities adequately capture the true statistical relation between those variables.

Even the magnitudes of the aggregate national gains from risk sharing among industrial countries are in dispute. Van Wincoop (1992c), who examines a larger sample of countries, assumes a lower rate of time preference, and allows for some nondiversifiable consumption risk, finds national gains from risk sharing much larger than those found by Cole and Obstfeld (1991). Obstfeld (1994c) shows that financial integration can bring very large welfare gains if diversification has effects on investment and output growth rates.[24] Before the puzzle of low diversification is resolved, more work on understanding both the magnitude and distribution of the gains from international risk sharing is needed.

The importance of transactions costs also is unclear. Cole and Obstfeld argue that small transactions barriers—for example, the extra paperwork needed to obtain a tax credit for asset income withheld by a foreign government or a security registration requirement—could substantially discourage international diversification. Backus, Kehoe, and Kydland (1992) confirm this as a theoretical possibility. They show that introducing small costs of international transactions into their empirically calibrated model leads to an equilibrium very close to the autarky allocation. This result, however, is based on a representative-agent model that may seriously understate individual, as opposed to aggregate, gains from trade. Tesar and Werner (1992) find that the turnover rate for foreign equity investments is higher than that in domestic equity markets and offer this difference as evidence that transactions costs are not important in promoting international equity-market segmentation. Transactions costs other than turnover costs could, however, be important impediments to cross-border investments.

To summarize, the available data on international portfolio positions suggest that many industrial countries are not diversified nearly to the extent that standard models of global portfolio choice would predict. The reasons could range from transactions costs to internationally asymmetric information (Gehrig, 1993) to differential tax treatment of domestic and foreign investors (Gor-

---

[24] The model in Obstfeld (1994c) is based on constant expected returns to investment. An alternative model of the way in which diversification affects growth, based on learning-by-doing effects, is proposed by Feeney (1993).

don and Varian, 1989) to irrational expectations concerning the relative returns on domestic and foreign investments.[25] Future progress in unraveling the apparent puzzle may come from a more disaggregated analysis of the investing behavior of different income groups. Even at the aggregate level, more detailed information on national balance sheets would give a better perspective from which to evaluate the risk and return characteristics of national portfolios.

Such analyses might throw light on the related outstanding puzzle of reconciling convincingly the possibly small aggregate gains from pooling national consumption risks with the apparently large unexploited gains to expected wealth maximizers from international equity diversification. The literatures on stock-market volatility and the equity-premium puzzle show how hard it is to rationalize the behavior of equity returns on the basis of simple optimal-consumption models with representative national consumers (see, respectively, Grossman and Shiller, 1981, and Mehra and Prescott, 1985). Asset prices that appear excessively volatile from the perspective of such models could easily give rise to the divergent estimates of international diversification gains. Partly explaining both the discrepancy in efficiency-gain estimates and the asset-pricing puzzles is imperfect domestic risk sharing, as suggested by Mankiw's and Zeldes's (1991) observation that U.S. stockholders have more variable consumption than have nonstockholders. Even this finding, however, does not enable Mankiw and Zeldes fully to resolve the equity-premium puzzle for the United States. It remains to be seen if general-equilibrium models assuming realistically imperfect asset markets or some form of asset-market segmentation can rationalize both equity-price behavior and the coexistence of small aggregate gains from international risk pooling with large private gains to equity holders.[26] Such models would, in turn, provide useful vehicles for understanding why limited international equity diversification has persisted.

Gains from Risk Sharing by Developing Countries

Even if it is true that industrial countries would reap only modest gains from further international pooling of risks, there is little doubt that developing countries could benefit enormously.

Lucas (1987) proposed the thought experiment of eliminating the variability of U.S. consumption around its trend path. For the United States and for most other industrial countries, the aggregate or social benefit this hypothetical event would confer is small, far less than 1 percent of GNP per year in most cases. These small numbers are upper bounds on the aggregate gains to

---

[25] Morris Goldstein has suggested that there is also a noticeable *regional* bias in international investment, a phenomenon consistent with the notion that informational barriers to international investment are important.

[26] Van Wincoop (1992a) is a partial step in this direction.

industrial countries from international risk sharing (absent dynamic investment effects or uncertainty over trend growth rates themselves).

The Lucas aggregate cost of consumption variability is, however, substantial for most developing countries. For a representative sample, Table 6.4 shows the welfare gain per year from eliminating consumption variability, expressed as a percent of annual consumption. The calculations use the Summers-Heston (1991) data on per capita consumption and assume that the natural logarithm of real per capita consumption follows a random walk with trend. Consumers have generalized isoelastic utility functions with annual

TABLE 6.4

Gains from the Elimination of Consumption Variability in Selected Developing Countries

Country	Annual Percent Consumption Gain
Argentina	1.94
Bangladesh	3.04
Barbados	2.69
Botswana	4.56
Brazil	1.80
Chile	2.75
India	0.93
Kenya	4.27
Malaysia	1.17
Mexico	0.54
Morocco	1.54
Tanzania	4.53
Thailand	1.07
Turkey	1.52
Venezuela	2.22
Zimbabwe	5.31

Note: The calculations assume that the logarithm of per capita consumption follows a random walk with trend and that individuals have generalized isoelastic utility functions with annual time-discount factor 0.95, relative risk-aversion parameter 1, and intertemporal-substitution elasticity 0.25. Data are taken from Summers and Heston, 1991. For details on the calculation, see Obstfeld, 1994b.

time-discount factors of 0.95 (Lucas's number), relative risk-aversion coefficients of 1, and intertemporal-substitution elasticities of 0.25.[27]

The numbers in Table 6.4 are based on a greater reduction in consumption variability than would be feasible in reality. But they suggest that for many developing countries, mechanisms to reduce consumption risk, such as increased access to world financial markets or Shiller's (1993) proposed market in perpetual claims to national GDPs, could yield a dramatic payoff.

4 The Allocation of Global Investment

A well-functioning world capital market should direct investment toward its most productive global uses. Economic efficiency requires that the expected value of investment in any location be the same. The most direct approach to evaluating efficiency would compare capital's rate of return in different countries, but it is difficult to find internationally comparable measures of the *ex ante* return to capital.[28] This section therefore focuses on two indirect approaches. One indirect approach argues that capital should flow from countries where it is relatively abundant to countries where it is relatively scarce. A second indirect approach is based on an examination of countries' saving and investment patterns.

Does Capital Flow to Capital-Poor Countries?

In the simplest one-sector growth models, capital mobility ensures that countries sharing a common technology will converge to identical capital-output ratios. Figure 6.8 shows that, for the two years 1973 and 1987, this equality was not even approximately true among the six OECD countries for which Maddison (1991) has constructed comparable capital-stock data. Moreover, there is little discernible tendency for capital-output ratios to converge between 1973 and 1987. A cross-sectional regression of the change in the log capital-output ratio K/Y on the initial log capital-output ratio yields a small and insignificant slope coefficient:

$$\log(K/Y)_{1987} - \log(K/Y)_{1973} = 0.16 - 0.07 \log(K/Y)_{1973} \; ; R^2 = 0.01 \; .$$
$$(0.13) \quad (0.47)$$

---

[27] For details on the formulas used, see Obstfeld (1994b). The assumptions on time preference, risk aversion, and intertemporal substitutability are conservative; more realistic assumptions would raise the costs in Table 6.4.

[28] Strictly speaking, one would wish to examine the after-tax marginal rates of return that capital investments in different countries offer to various domestic and foreign investors. Even the states within a national federation may tax capital at different effective rates.

Figure 6.8 Industrial-Country Capital-Output Ratios, 1973 and 1987

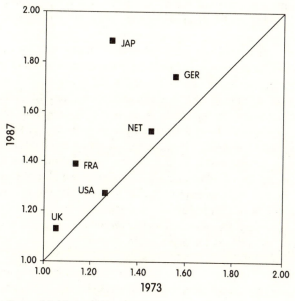

Source: Maddison, 1991.

Are such persistent international differences in capital-output ratios *prima facie* evidence of capital market failure? Suppose aggregate output in a country is produced through the (possibly country-specific) Cobb-Douglas production function of capital K and N other productive factors L_j,

$$Y = (\theta_K K)^\alpha \prod_{j=1}^{N} (\theta_j L_j)^{\alpha_j} . \tag{3}$$

The marginal product of capital in this economy is $MPK = \alpha/(K/Y)$. If two countries' outputs are given by Cobb-Douglas production functions of form (3), then even when those production functions differ in factor productivities (the θs) and in the array of noncapital inputs, the countries' MPK ratio will equal the inverse of their relative capital-output ratio provided only that they share a common value of α, capital's share in GDP.

This simple result has strong implications. Figure 6.8 suggests, for example, that, as of 1987, K/Y was about 1.9 for Japan but under 1.3 for the United States. With a common $\alpha = 1/3$, the value suggested by Mankiw, Romer, and Weil (1992), the marginal product of capital would have been 17.4 percent in Japan, much below its predicted value of more than 25.3 percent in the United

States. Under free capital mobility, investment should have been higher in the United States than in Japan; in reality the reverse was true. If one applies this type of argument to compare returns to capital in developed and developing countries (as do Lucas [1990] and King and Rebelo [1993]), the discrepancies are even greater.

One major pitfall in the preceding reasoning is the assumption of an aggregate production function of form (3). If there are multiple production activities with different capital requirements, aggregate capital-output ratios can differ widely between economies that pay the same factor rewards. Furthermore, factors could be more substitutable in some activities (at least in the long run) than the Cobb-Douglas form assumes. For example, capital substitutes for land in some Japanese production activities that are carried out in the United States with more land and less capital. The evidence that α is a universal constant is weak. Expected changes in relative prices will influence expected rates of return. Finally, uncertainty is being ignored. If the productivity coefficients θ are stochastic and imperfectly correlated across countries, we would not expect to observe the same K/Y ratio everywhere: more capital should be placed in countries where the payoff to investment is most highly correlated with the marginal utility of world consumption.[29]

Examination of countries' aggregate capital-output ratios cannot, in itself, be informative about opportunities for efficiency-enhancing international investment flows. A more convincing, albeit painstaking, method is to evaluate sectoral rates of return directly, as in Minhas's (1963) famous monograph. This work, like Harberger's (1980) later summary of more aggregative studies, suggests that *ex post* international differences in the return to capital have been relatively moderate in the recent past. Unfortunately, little up-to-date research along these lines is readily available.

The Feldstein-Horioka Approach

As Section 1 described, Feldstein and Horioka (1980) and Feldstein (1983) proposed as a barometer of capital mobility the size of the association between economies' saving rates and their investment rates. They reasoned that, in a world of capital mobility, each country's savings are free to flow to their most productive uses anywhere in the world; thus, there is no reason for an increase in national saving necessarily to augment the source country's domestic capital stock. These papers use regressions of domestic investment rates on national saving rates to measure the fraction of an exogenous increase in national savings that will remain at home, the "savings retention coefficient," as Feldstein and Bacchetta (1991) call it. The saving-investment puzzle is to explain

---

[29] Bardhan (1993) explores several deterministic models in which big international wage discrepancies coexist with small international differences in returns to capital.

why this coefficient appears to be high, even in recent data, despite the high international capital mobility suggested by the evidence on interest-rate links reviewed in Section 2.

Informed policy decisions may depend on whether the saving-investment puzzle really is explained by low capital mobility, or by other factors that simultaneously drive both saving and investment. For example, under perfect capital mobility, an increase in the government budget deficit of a small economy need not crowd out domestic investment, even if consumers do not behave according to the Ricardian equivalence proposition; instead, foreign savings are available in perfectly elastic supply to finance additional national borrowing. Feldstein and his collaborators have, by contrast, interpreted their saving-investment regressions as implying that any fall in national saving will, over the long run, cause a commensurate fall in domestic investment, as in a closed economy.

The Feldstein-Horioka approach raises two distinct questions. First, is a close association between saving and investment in fact evidence of low international capital mobility, as argued in the initial papers by Feldstein and Horioka? Second, do regressions of investment on saving actually measure the investment effect of an exogenous change in the saving rate, for example, one caused by fiscal policy? These two questions are inseparably linked: before the investment effect of a change in national saving can be predicted, the precise mechanism underlying the estimated saving-investment association must be understood. Because of space limitations, however, this chapter will focus on the first question, the relevance of the statistical saving-investment relationship for assessing international capital mobility.[30]

CROSS-SECTIONAL VERSUS TIME-SERIES ESTIMATION

It is helpful to distinguish between two possible econometric approaches to estimating saving-investment relationships. Feldstein and Horioka (1980) implemented a *cross-sectional* estimation strategy. In this approach, each observation consists of a country j's average investment and saving rates over a given time period; the estimated regression equation based on a cross-sectional sample of N countries is

$$(I/Y)_j = \alpha^{CS} + \beta^{CS}(S/Y)_j + u_j , \qquad (4)$$

where $(I/Y)_j$ is country j's average nominal investment rate out of nominal GNP or GDP over the chosen time period, $(S/Y)_j$ is its average saving rate over the same period, and u_j is a random disturbance.

A second estimation strategy is based on *time-series* data. In this approach, each observation consists of a given country's investment and saving rates

[30] Obstfeld (1991) analyzes econometric pitfalls of using saving-investment regressions to predict the effects of exogenous shifts in saving.

over some time period t. The estimated regression equation based on a time-series sample for a single country is

$$(I/Y)_t = \alpha^{TS} + \beta^{TS}(S/Y)_t + u_t \qquad (5)$$

(or the corresponding equation in first differences).[31]

In a world of completely immobile capital, the error terms in (4) and (5) represent measurement error, and both estimation strategies yield estimated slope coefficients near 1. More generally, however, the two estimation strategies could yield quite different slope coefficients, even when all countries are integrated into world capital markets to a similar degree, because β^{CS} in (4) and β^{TS} in (5) measure very different things.

Suppose, for example, that in the sample of N countries, mean saving rates have a high positive cross-sectional association with mean investment rates, but that for each country, deviations of saving rates from the time-series mean are uncorrelated with deviations of investment rates from the time-series mean. Suppose also that the cross-sectional observations are country averages over T periods. Then the ordinary-least-squares (OLS) estimate β^{CS} will be high if T and N are sufficiently large, but β^{TS} will be near zero for each country. If, instead, mean saving rates and investment rates have a zero cross-sectional correlation, but for each country, deviations from its mean saving and investment rates tend to be close, β^{CS} will be near zero for sufficiently large T and N, but the estimates β^{TS} will be high.

The cross-sectional estimation strategy attempts to capture the relation between *long-run* saving and investment rates. For this strategy to succeed, each country's saving and investment rates must be averaged over a sufficient interval to eliminate the influence of short-run fluctuations around long-run means. The time-series estimation strategy is meant to uncover the *short-run* relation between national saving and domestic investment. Both long-run and short-run relationships are pertinent to an assessment of capital mobility. Explanations of the time-series relation between saving and investment will not, however, throw much light on the cross-sectional relationship unless the time period chosen for cross-sectional estimates is so brief that transitory shocks to saving and investment swamp underlying long-run patterns. Conversely, explanations of true long-run patterns may have little power to explain short-run comovements.

RESULTS OF CROSS-SECTIONAL ESTIMATION

Feldstein and Horioka (1980) estimated equation (4) for a sample of sixteen OECD countries, averaging annual data for subperiods from 1960 to 1974.[32]

---

[31] Feldstein (1983) reports panel estimates that combine the cross-sectional and time-series strategies by assuming that β^{CS} and β^{TS} are equal.

[32] Their country sample was Australia, Austria, Belgium, Canada, Denmark, Finland, Ger-

Data on gross saving and investment rates[33] averaged over the entire 1960–74 period led to a representative OLS result:

$$(I/Y)_j = 0.035 + 0.887(S/Y)_j + u_j \; ; R^2 = 0.91 \; .$$
$$(0.018) \quad (0.074)$$

Feldstein and Bacchetta (1991) provide an update; a typical estimate of β^{CS} based on a sample of twenty-three OECD countries over the more recent period from 1974 to 1986 is 0.868 (with a standard error of 0.145), a result quite close to the original findings.[34] This regression presents a much starker puzzle about the international capital market than those based on 1960–74 data because it is generally believed that the world capital market, although relatively shallow and segmented prior to the early 1970s, has become less regulated and has expanded vigorously since then (Marston [1993b] gives evidence for the 1960s). Notwithstanding this evolution, the Feldstein-Bacchetta findings still imply that a 1 percent increase in the national saving rate remains cross-sectionally associated with a nearly equal increase in the domestic investment rate.

A further update is provided in Table 6.5, which presents the result of estimating (4) for twenty-two OECD countries for subperiods from 1974 to 1990.[35] Saving and investment rates are gross nominal flows divided by nominal GDP or GNP.

The point estimates for β^{CS} in Table 6.5 are lower than those that Feldstein and Horioka (1980) report and somewhat lower, on the whole, than those that Feldstein and Bacchetta (1991) report. The R^2 statistics are also below the ones in Feldstein and Horioka (1980). Figure 6.9 shows a scatter plot for the 1981–90 data, together with the fitted regression line.

The results are suggestive of a decade-to-decade downward trend in β^{CS}: the estimated coefficient for the 1974–80 period, 0.867, has dropped to 0.636 by 1981–90. Such a trend, even if established, would be difficult to interpret unambiguously. For example, the 1986–90 estimate of β^{CS} is higher than that for the 1981–85 period, yet would not be taken as evidence of a decreasing degree of international capital mobility. Another reason for caution is that the coefficient differences in Table 6.5 are not statistically significant.

The basic finding is that the positive cross-sectional association between OECD saving and investment rates is economically and statistically signifi-

---

many, Greece, Ireland, Italy, Japan, the Netherlands, New Zealand, Sweden, the United Kingdom, and the United States.

[33] Gross, rather than net, rates are more appropriate for this regression. A regression in net rates imposes the assumption that all replacement investment is financed by domestic savings.

[34] The countries are the sixteen listed by Feldstein and Horioka (1980) plus France, Iceland, Norway, Portugal, Spain, Switzerland, and Turkey.

[35] The countries are the Feldstein-Bacchetta sample minus Turkey, which can be classified as a developing country. Luxembourg traditionally is omitted from this sample; it is such an extreme outlier that its addition reduces the cross-sectional regression coefficient to insignificance.

TABLE 6.5
Cross-Sectional Regressions
of Investment Rates on Saving Rates:
Period Average Data, 1974–90

Period	$\hat{\beta}^{CS}$	R^2
1974–90	0.715 (0.131)	0.60
1974–80	0.867 (0.170)	0.56
1981–90	0.636 (0.108)	0.64
1981–85	0.567 (0.147)	0.43
1986–90	0.636 (0.094)	0.69

Note: Estimates of equation (4) in text. Standard errors appear in parentheses below estimates of slope coefficient β^{CS}. The sample of twenty-two countries consists of Australia, Austria, Belgium, Canada, Denmark, Finland, France, Germany, Greece, Iceland, Ireland, Italy, Japan, the Netherlands, New Zealand, Norway, Portugal, Spain, Sweden, Switzerland, the United Kingdom, and the United States.

cant, although far from perfect and possibly declining over time. Although the cross-sectional results are less striking than those for the 1960–74 period, they may present more of a puzzle given the current level of industrial-country residents' participation in international capital markets (Goldstein et al. [1993] document this activity).

Results for a wider sample including developing countries are not reported, because there is less of a saving-investment puzzle as far as those countries are concerned. Most of those countries even now control capital flows and in some periods have faced binding external credit constraints. Notwithstanding these tangible impediments to capital flow, the cross-sectional association of saving and investment rates is often found to be lower for the developing countries than for the OECD countries over the period from 1960 to the early 1980s, when the debt crisis began (Fieleke, 1982; Dooley, Frankel, and Mathieson, 1987; and Summers, 1988).

RESULTS OF TIME-SERIES ESTIMATION

Table 6.6 examines the time-series properties of annual saving and investment rates from 1974 to 1990 for the twenty-two countries that made up the cross-

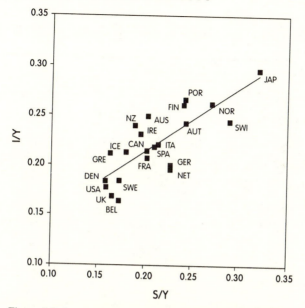

Figure 6.9 Average Saving and Investment Rates for Twenty-Two Industrial Countries, 1981–90 (*fraction of GNP/GDP*)

sectional sample, plus Luxembourg. "Levels" estimates of β^{TS} come from OLS estimation of equation (5), with a time trend included in the regression. "Differences" estimates come from the regression

$$\Delta(I/Y)_t = \alpha^{TS} + \beta^{TS}\Delta(S/Y)_t + u_t .$$

Table 6.7 reports the corresponding simple correlation coefficients between linearly detrended and differenced saving and investment rates.

There is a wide dispersion of outcomes, a reflection not only of different degrees of financial openness, but also of different country sizes and the different shocks that have buffeted these diverse economies. For most countries, the saving and investment time series are positively related, and the relationship is typically strong. Australia, New Zealand, and Portugal all show positive time-series saving-investment associations despite having run sizable current-account deficits over parts of the sample period. (Portugal's 1982 deficit was 13.5 percent of GDP.) Norway, which also ran a deficit, shows a strongly negative relationship. These findings underscore the point that annual time-series correlations contain little information about the relation between saving and investment over long periods.[36]

Even under perfect capital mobility, positive regression coefficients such as

[36] Observe that the choice between levels and differences can matter, at least in this finite sample (for example, for the United Kingdom).

TABLE 6.6
Time-Series Regressions of Investment Rates on Saving Rates:
Annual Data, 1974–90

Country	$\hat{\beta}^{TS}$ (levels)	$\hat{\beta}^{TS}$ (differences)
Australia	0.792	0.857
Austria	0.825	0.732
Belgium	0.637	0.749
Canada	1.097	0.963
Denmark	0.727	0.657
Finland	1.803	1.172
France	0.909	1.101
Germany	0.327	0.561
Greece	0.845	0.892
Iceland	−0.450	−0.654
Ireland	−0.037	0.208
Italy	0.214	1.154
Japan	1.161	1.100
Luxembourg	−0.135	0.042
Netherlands	0.381	0.457
New Zealand	1.154	0.787
Norway	−0.614	−0.515
Portugal	0.736	0.718
Spain	1.104	0.246
Sweden	0.717	0.574
Switzerland	1.221	1.547
United Kingdom	0.113	1.002
United States	0.848	1.090

Note: Estimates of levels are based on the OLS regression $(I/Y)_t = \alpha^{TS} + \beta^{TS}(S/Y)_t + \gamma^{TS}t + u_t$; *estimates of differences are based on the OLS regression* $\Delta(I/Y)_t = \alpha^{TS} + \beta^{TS}\Delta(S/Y)_t + u_t$.

TABLE 6.7
Time-Series Correlation Coefficients between Saving
and Investment Rates: Annual Data, 1974–90

Country	$\hat{\rho}^{TS}$ (levels)	$\hat{\rho}^{TS}$ (differences)
Australia	0.834	0.742
Austria	0.746	0.575
Belgium	0.848	0.773
Canada	0.745	0.823
Denmark	0.783	0.662
Finland	0.846	0.682
France	0.851	0.710
Germany	0.401	0.610
Greece	0.836	0.750
Iceland	−0.333	−0.333
Ireland	−0.031	0.157
Italy	0.150	0.560
Japan	0.837	0.795
Luxembourg	−0.247	0.071
Netherlands	0.505	0.518
New Zealand	0.517	0.562
Norway	−0.659	−0.474
Portugal	0.591	0.584
Spain	0.711	0.193
Sweden	0.785	0.514
Switzerland	0.784	0.736
United Kingdom	0.092	0.668
United States	0.773	0.895

Note: Estimates of levels are simple correlation coefficients between $(I/Y)_t$ and $(S/Y)_t$, where both variables are linearly detrended. Estimates of differences are correlation coefficients between $\Delta(I/Y)_t$ and $\Delta(S/Y)_t$.

those reported in Table 6.7 are not hard to explain. If labor is internationally immobile, for example, positive shocks to investment productivity can cause both investment and saving to rise (Obstfeld 1986; Finn 1990; Tesar, 1991; Ghosh, 1994). If the usual outcome of such a shock is a current-account deficit, and, if productivity shocks are the dominant form of disturbance, then it would not be surprising to find an estimate of β^{TS} above 1, a result found for several countries in Table 6.6 but difficult to explain if capital is internationally immobile. A positive time-series correlation between saving and investment is reinforced if global as well as local shocks to investment and saving are important (as found by Glick and Rogoff [1993]).[37]

Unlike the time-series results, which can be rationalized in several plausible ways, the cross-sectional finding that countries with higher long-term saving rates also have higher long-term investment rates is more difficult to explain in a world of capital mobility. The balance of this section therefore focuses on alternative interpretations of the cross-sectional saving-investment pattern as it persisted through the 1980s.

Explanations for the Cross-Sectional Saving-Investment Relationship

Many researchers have taken the high estimates of β^{CS} in (4) as evidence that national savings for the most part are still retained at home and are not channeled toward their most efficient global uses by the world capital market. Others have tried to approach the saving-investment puzzle by identifying economic forces that underlie both saving and investment and cause long-term averages of these two variables to move together. A wide variety of contributory mechanisms has been proposed.

DEMOGRAPHIC FACTORS

Characteristics of a nation's labor force can simultaneously affect national saving and the profitability of domestic investment. Labor-force growth provides one example: higher growth can raise national saving by increasing the ratio of young savers to old dissavers. At the same time, higher growth raises the investment needed to keep the labor force equipped with capital (Black 1982; Obstfeld 1986). Higher productivity growth concentrated among prime-age workers would likewise raise trend saving as well as trend investment.

Summers (1988) and Feldstein and Bacchetta (1991) dismiss the hypothesis that growth, either in the labor force or in factor productivity, is the primary factor generating the cross-sectional saving-investment relationship. They

---

[37] Stockman and Tesar (1990), Mendoza (1991a, 1991b), Cardia (1992), and Baxter and Crucini (1993a, 1993b) explore simulation models in which free international asset trade is consistent with high time-series correlations between saving and investment.

show that the addition of growth variables to the cross-sectional regression does not reduce the apparent influence of saving on investment. Notwithstanding these regressions, it remains quite plausible that labor-force developments are a part of the story, more important in some countries than in others. Tesar (1991) presents evidence along these lines, showing that the fraction of the population between ages 15 and 64 is positively related to both saving and investment rates. In a more recent contribution, Taylor (1993) uses the Summers-Heston data to estimate versions of the Feldstein-Horioka regression that control for measures of domestic relative prices, the age structure of the population, and the interaction of the age structure with the growth of domestic output. He finds that, in a number of country samples, the cross-sectional saving-investment association disappears. The role of growth clearly deserves further detailed study.

Other potential links between household intertemporal allocation decisions and investment remain to be investigated. For example, are there systematic links among fertility rates, saving, expenditures on schooling, and the profitability of domestic investment?

REAL INTEREST RATES

Even if capital is perfectly mobile and uncovered interest parity holds true, national real interest rates need not be equal. Frankel (1986, 1993) claims that this point resolves the Feldstein-Horioka puzzle. The apparent puzzle arises, he argues, because increases in national saving depress the local real interest rate, spurring investment and inducing a statistical correlation between saving and investment rates.

Although this mechanism may help us understand *time-series* correlations between saving and investment rates, its bearing on the longer-run cross-sectional patterns is less obvious. Under perfect capital mobility and uncovered interest parity, the real-interest differential between two countries equals the expected percentage change in their currencies' real exchange rate. If real-interest effects are to explain the cross-sectional regression results, countries with high saving and investment rates must have low real interest rates and so their currencies must be *continually* appreciating in real terms against foreign currencies.

Cardia (1992) describes a simulation model that is based on Frankel's suggested mechanism but that nonetheless may have some explanatory power for the cross-sectional Feldstein-Horioka pattern. In her model, adjustment to shocks can be drawn out over decades because of capital-installation costs and an overlapping-generations population structure. Although Cardia does not report cross-sectional simulations, the long-lived effects of the disturbances she considers probably would contribute to a strong cross-sectional association between long saving- and investment-rate averages.

As Balassa's (1964) work implies, models with different sectoral productivity growth rates can exhibit permanently trending real exchange rates. This suggests another potential mechanism causing high-saving, high-investment countries also to be countries with low real interest rates.

Imagine a small open economy producing traded and nontraded goods using capital, which is internationally mobile, and labor, which is not. Assume that initially all countries are identical, with growing labor forces. Consider the effect of a permanent increase in traded-goods productivity growth in one economy.

The currency of this economy will begin to appreciate in real terms, its real interest rate will fall, and its investment rate will rise. Saving, which depends on the real interest rate, also may change. If the average domestic intertemporal-substitution elasticity is below 1, as several empirical studies suggest, the fall in the real interest rate can cause saving to rise. Saving and investment may therefore show a positive cross-sectional correlation, seemingly driven by cross-country real-interest-rate differences but really driven by differences in traded-goods productivity growth.[38]

No one has yet established a robust cross-sectional relationship among saving, investment, the real interest rate, and the real exchange rate's expected path. Mechanisms such as the one described thus remain speculative.

HYSTERESIS OF FACTOR SUPPLIES

Results presented above (Figure 6.8) show that OECD countries are characterized by wide and persistent differences in capital-output ratios. This pattern suggests another possible explanation for the saving-investment puzzle.

European countries entered the postwar era burdened by external payments controls and limited access to foreign resources. For some time, therefore, countries had to finance most of their capital accumulation through domestic savings. High-saving countries accumulated large capital stocks and specialized in capital-intensive industries, and low-saving countries produced a more labor-intensive product mix.

The substantial liberalization of capital movements starting in the 1970s need not have disturbed this production pattern greatly. In the presence of labor-force growth, however, high-capital countries required high investment rates to maintain their established industries, whereas low-capital countries could get by with lower investment rates. Because the high-capital countries were also those with high saving rates, a high cross-sectional correspondence

---

[38] In general, when an economy has several sectors of differing capital intensity, some of which produce nontraded goods, there is no longer a presumption that the economy's consumption side and its production side (including investment) can be analyzed separately, even under capital mobility. This point is made through various examples by Murphy (1986), Engel and Kletzer (1989), and Wong (1990).

between saving and investment rates was the result. On this view, the historical accident of capital immobility during the first part of the postwar period had an effect on the distribution of national investment rates that persisted even after capital mobility returned.

If the preceding interpretation is valid, countries with higher saving and investment rates should have higher shares of capital income in GDP. Mankiw, Romer, and Weil (1992) argue, however, that this is not the case and that, in fact, there is little international variation in capital's GDP share.[39] Their argument, based on limited data from the 1960s and 1970s, contradicts Kaldor's (1961, p. 178) fifth "stylized fact" of economic growth of "a high correlation between the share of profits in income and the share of investment in output." More research on this point would be useful.

CORPORATE FINANCING FRICTIONS

The need for firms facing imperfect domestic capital markets to finance investment out of corporate savings has been suggested as another explanation of the Feldstein-Horioka puzzle. But is a tight link between corporate saving and investment enough to produce a tight link between national saving and investment? A dollar rise in corporate saving may raise domestic investment if firms are borrowing-constrained, but it will raise national saving only if shareholders fail to pierce the corporate veil and adjust their own total saving downward by a dollar. The largest corporations, moreover, probably do not face binding finance constraints. The general hypothesis is that strict *domestic* segmentation of financial markets might generate a country-by-country saving-investment association. Empirical documentation for this mechanism has not yet been produced.

A related hypothesis concerns the possibility that domestic and foreign residents value domestic equities differently, as might (but need not) be the case in the absence of efficient consumption risk sharing among countries (Dooley, Frankel, and Mathieson [1987] examine a polar case in which claims to domestic physical capital are nontradable). In this situation, domestic saving and investment could be positively correlated, even for a small country, despite perfect international arbitrage in bonds. A strong positive correlation is not a necessity, however, because there remains the possibility in principle of substantial bond-intermediated foreign financing of investment. Equity-market segmentation along national lines underlies the international diversification puzzle; but can the phenomenon help explain the cross-sectional saving-investment relationship? Different plausible models yield different answers. One obvious empirical strategy would be to look for a negative cross-sectional

[39] This pattern would be consistent with a world in which national outputs are produced according to equation (3), with α the same in all countries, and capital is internationally immobile.

correlation between the cost of capital and the saving rate in industrial countries.[40]

GOVERNMENT POLICIES

Systematic current-account targeting by governments would, if successful, tend to produce a strong cross-sectional association of saving and investment even with high capital mobility (Fieleke, 1982; Summers, 1988). Fiscal and monetary policy, as well as capital controls, have all been used to limit the sizes of current-account imbalances. There is some evidence that government policies in a number of countries have aimed to curtail external imbalances (Artis and Bayoumi, 1989), but it is difficult to judge how well these policies succeeded. It is also possible that government policies aimed at domestic stabilization or international reserve management have effects similar to current-account targeting.

THE ECONOMY'S INTERTEMPORAL BUDGET CONSTRAINT

An open economy faces an intertemporal budget constraint relating the difference between its saving and investment, the current account, to the change in its net external assets. Under some economic conditions this constraint alone implies that saving and investment ratios averaged over sufficiently long periods must be close despite capital mobility (Obstfeld, 1986; Vikøren, 1991; Sinn, 1992).

To appreciate this point, let A_t denote a given country's nominal net foreign assets at the end of period t and recall the current-account identity's implication that $A_t - A_{t-1} = S_t - I_t$.[41] Suppose that the data are average saving and investment rates over T periods. Let $a_t = A_t/Y_t$ be the ratio of external assets to income and $g_t = (Y_t - Y_{t-1})/Y_t$, the growth rate of nominal income. Then the current-account identity implies that the difference between the averaged saving and investment rates is[42]

---

[40] There is some limited evidence of such a relationship in the past; see McCauley and Zimmer (1989). However, it is hard to disentangle the effect of saving from the effect of tax provisions that simultaneously affect saving and the cost of capital. Obviously, such tax effects could be another influence on the cross-sectional pattern of saving and investment rates.

[41] This relation will not hold exactly in the data because saving as measured by national income and product accounts does not include capital gains or losses on foreign assets (Obstfeld, 1986).

[42] The income growth rates below are nominal rather than real rates because the national-income and product-account concept of saving does not correct income for the inflationary erosion of the real values of nominal assets.

$$\frac{1}{T} \sum_{t=1}^{T} \frac{S_t - I_t}{Y_t} = \frac{1}{T} \sum_{t=1}^{T} \frac{A_t - A_{t-1}}{Y_t}$$

$$= \frac{1}{T} \left[a_T + \left(1 - \frac{Y_{T-1}}{Y_T} \right) a_{T-1} + \ldots - \left(\frac{Y_0}{Y_1} \right) a_0 \right]$$

$$= \frac{1}{T} (a_T - a_0 + g_T a_{T-1} + \ldots + g_2 a_1 + g_1 a_0) . \tag{6}$$

In principle, the foregoing identity alone places no constraints on the average difference between saving and investment rates. Suppose, however, that there is a steady-state ratio of net foreign assets to income from which the economy does not greatly diverge between the start and end of the sample period. Then, if nominal income growth is moderate, equation (6) implies that the averaged difference between saving and investment rates may well be small.

Mature economies may have attained a stationary distribution of the foreign-assets-to-GNP ratio; the intertemporal trade gains that arise between mature economies will generally be transitory and their distribution symmetrical.[43] This conjecture may help explain why, even in the late 1980s, a fairly high cross-sectional saving-investment relation persisted for the industrial countries. The conjecture also explains why, before the debt crisis of the 1980s, developing countries displayed lower cross-sectional saving-investment correlations than did the industrial countries. Developing countries with significant unexploited investment opportunities have external debts well below their steady-state levels. This perspective suggests that, ultimately, the cross-sectional saving-investment correlation within a group of countries with open capital markets depends on the extent of each one's long-term intertemporal trade gains with other countries. Attempts to assess these gains (as in Glick and Rogoff [1993] and Ghosh [1994]) are critical for understanding how puzzling the saving-investment puzzle really is.

Comparisons with the Gold Standard and with Regional Data

An indirect way to judge whether the Feldstein-Horioka puzzle reflects true capital immobility or some subset of the alternative factors listed above is to examine the strength of the cross-sectional saving-investment association in

---

[43] An exception is Norway, which borrowed abroad so heavily during the 1970s to develop its oil production that, by 1978, its foreign-debt-to-GDP ratio stood near 60 percent (Vikøren, 1991). Norway repaid this debt quickly. By 1985, the country's net foreign debt stood at around 12 percent of GDP, its 1970 level. The U.S. current-account deficit, driven by government deficits and demographic shifts, is another exception.

settings of presumed high capital mobility. Data from the gold-standard period and regional data have both been used for this purpose.

THE SAVING-INVESTMENT RELATION UNDER THE GOLD STANDARD

Table 6.8 reports results for three data samples. The first consists of Australia, Canada, Denmark, France, Germany, Italy, Norway, Sweden, the United Kingdom, and the United States with data averaged over the period from 1880 to 1913. The second sample adds Japan, using data averaged over 1885 to 1899 and 1900 to 1913. The third sample, based on 1926–38 data, subtracts France but adds Finland, which gained independence from Russia in 1917. I first discuss the pre-1914 results, which fall under the classical gold standard (Jones and Obstfeld [1994] give details on data construction).

For 1880 to 1913, the estimated regression coefficient β^{CS} is almost significant (with a one-tailed test) and not very different from the estimates in Table 6.5 based on data from the 1980s (the R^2 is, however, much lower in Table 6.8). For 1885 to 1899, the estimate β^{CS} is about the same but is significant.

TABLE 6.8
Cross-Sectional Regressions
of Investment Rates on Saving Rates
during the Gold Standard and Interwar
Period: Period Average Data

Period	$\hat{\beta}^{CS}$	R^2
1880–1913	0.576 (0.335)	0.27
1885–99	0.568 (0.228)	0.41
1900–13	0.774 (0.436)	0.26
1926–38	0.959 (0.082)	0.94

Note: Estimates of equation (4) in text. Standard errors appear in parentheses below estimates of slope coefficient β^{CS}. The 1880–1913 sample consists of Australia, Canada, Denmark, France, Germany, Italy, Norway, Sweden, the United Kingdom, and the United States. The samples for 1885 to 1899 and 1900 to 1913 add Japan. The sample for 1926 to 1938 subtracts France and adds Finland.

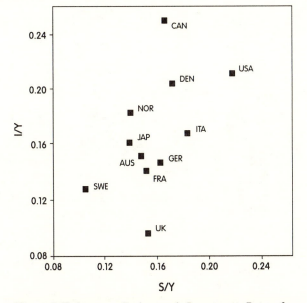

Figure 6.10 Average Saving and Investment Rates for Eleven Countries under the Gold Standard, 1900–13 (*fraction of GNP/GDP*)

For 1900 to 1913 (with data pictured in Figure 6.10), the coefficient rises to 0.77 but loses significance.[44]

To the extent that the classical gold standard was a period of high international financial integration, the pre-1914 findings in Table 6.8 and Figure 6.10 suggest that the recent long-run behavior of saving and investment rates is not inconsistent with substantial capital mobility.

True, the dispersion of saving and investment rates during the gold standard is greater than among industrial countries over the 1980s; and among the largest economies we now see nothing like the surpluses the United Kingdom persistently ran. Three factors should be considered, however, in assessing capital mobility under the classical gold standard and comparing it with current conditions. First, as Nurkse (1954) emphasized, international capital movements were abetted by complementary large-scale labor movements from Europe into regions of recent (white) settlement. Pre-1914 levels of international migration have not been approached in the recent postwar era.[45]

[44] Bayoumi (1990) finds no cross-sectional saving-investment association for a smaller eight-country sample over any subperiod of 1880 to 1913. Eichengreen (1990) amends Bayoumi's data and adds the United States. The results in Table 6.8 are very similar to Eichengreen's, despite my use of an expanded set of countries and of different data for some of them.

[45] See Razin and Sadka (1993) for a recent discussion of international labor mobility.

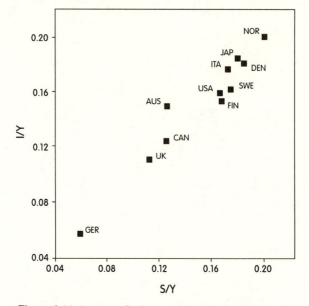

Figure 6.11 Average Saving and Investment Rates for Eleven Countries in the Interwar Period, 1926–38 (*fraction of GNP/GDP*)

Second, the inclusion of Australia and Canada means that developing- and industrial-country data are being pooled, a procedure that would loosen the saving-investment association in modern data. Finally, Britain's close cultural and political ties with some borrowers certainly facilitated its large-scale foreign lending. As is evident from Figure 6.10, Canada and the United Kingdom are behind the poor fit of the regression for 1900 to 1913.

Table 6.8 also reports a regression for the interwar period following the (short-lived) reinstatement of the international gold standard, 1926 to 1938; the data are displayed in Figure 6.11. The results stand in the sharpest possible contrast to those for the classical gold standard and show a stronger saving-investment association even than the Feldstein-Horioka 1960–74 results. Eichengreen (1990) discusses possible reasons for this contrast, which are complex but seem related to a genuine post–World War I decline in capital mobility. One factor behind this decline was the rise of the political Left. This development made international investors less secure in their property rights than they were before 1914. It also focused the attention of policymakers on domestic economic problems at the expense of laissez-faire principles of international economic relations.

Governments practiced less pervasive management of their economies during the classical gold-standard era than they did later. Do the results discussed here therefore show that the hypothesis of current-account targeting is not needed to explain the current cross-sectional saving-investment relation? Not at all. Even under the gold standard, some governments may have curtailed current-account imbalances as a side effect of actions taken to maintain gold convertibility, or in pursuit of foreign-policy aims.

REGIONAL SAVING-INVESTMENT LINKS

The use of regional saving and investment data is a potentially fruitful way to throw light on the saving-investment puzzle.[46] Bayoumi and Rose (1993) construct saving and investment data for eleven British regions for 1971 to 1985; they find no significant positive cross-sectional relation between saving and investment rates. Bayoumi and Sterne (1993) find a similar result for Canadian provinces. Sinn (1992), who looks at both 1953 and 1957 data for the forty-eight U.S. states and Alaska, finds a negative cross-sectional relation between saving and investment rates. Data for 1975 to 1988 on average saving and investment rates for the forty-five Japanese prefectures listed in Table 6.3 are graphed in Figure 6.12. Again, no positive relationship is apparent.

The data used in these calculations are not always ideal. For example, Bayoumi and Rose have data for only part of regional expenditure and investment. In addition, data limitations force Bayoumi and his coauthors to define saving as regional GDP less a regional consumption measure, not as GNP less that measure. Thus, these measures of saving fail to include in income not only net interest and dividend payments from outside the region, but also net transfers from the domestic central government and others. The much greater dispersion of saving as compared to investment rates in Figure 6.12 raises suspicions that measurement errors are a problem in the Japanese "saving" data shown there, despite their definition as prefecture GNP less consumption.

There are, moreover, differences between regions and countries that might weaken the saving-investment link. The comparative ease with which labor can migrate between regions could alter the response of regional saving and investment to disturbances (this is especially possible in Japan, where commuting between prefectures is significant). Furthermore, regions within countries tend to be more specialized in their production activities than are countries themselves. Thus, some of the shocks that can make national saving and domestic investment move together may not induce similar comovements in regional saving and investment.

The strength of factors such as these is unknown at present. Until more work is done and better data assembled, the regional saving-investment re-

---

[46] Murphy (1984) applied an analogous idea to the 143 largest industrial corporations from the 1981 Fortune 500. He found a significant cross-sectional relation between corporate saving and investment. It would be interesting to know if this relationship has held up in view of financial-market developments since the early 1980s.

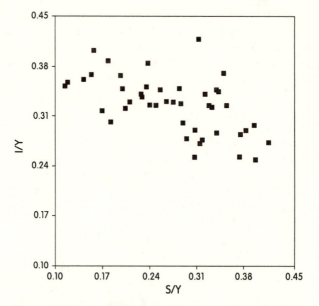

Figure 6.12 Average Saving and Investment Rates for Forty-Five Japanese Prefectures, 1975–88 (*fraction of prefecture income*)

gressions provide the most persuasive evidence that national boundaries or macroeconomic policies contributed to limiting industrial-country current-account imbalances through the 1980s.

Because regional current accounts are not objects of government policy, the regional results leave current-account targeting as one of the prime suspects generating the positive cross-sectional saving-investment relationship that has persisted in international data. The results are also consistent with the view that capital is still not as mobile between as within countries.

5 Conclusion

The main conundrum in thinking about international capital mobility is to reconcile measures of mobility that superficially contradict each other. How can one square the generally smooth international interest-rate arbitrage documented in Section 2 with the low international consumption correlations and home portfolio bias discussed in Section 3 or the still-sizable cross-sectional coherence between saving and investment documented in Section 4? In this chapter, I have reviewed a number of economic models and data limitations that potentially can contribute to a reconciliation. Despite years of research, however, economists still have not reached the semblance of a consensus on which factors are most relevant. Much work remains to be done; one can hope that the rapid evolution of world capital markets, if not braked by renewed regulation, will furnish more clues as well as data.

After this lengthy and arduous trek through the literature, I owe the reader more, however, than just a plea for more of the same. So, here are my tentative conclusions.

How mobile is capital in the world economy? As far as industrial countries are concerned, capital mobility appears substantial when judged by past experience, such as that of the gold-standard era. Although the experience of the developing countries is diverse and the market access of many of them is currently in flux, it is clear that much of the developing world still stands outside the nexus of industrial-country financial markets.

Capital mobility appears noticeably lower between industrial economies than within them, although intereconomy capital mobility certainly has increased over time. The threat of government intervention in cross-border capital movements has not disappeared. Indeed, in the wake of the August 1993 ERM collapse, European Commission president Jacques Delors signaled support for concerted EC measures to limit capital mobility ("Return of Capital Controls Raised by Delors," *Financial Times*, September 16, 1993). Financial flows apparently are less extensive between than within countries. International portfolio diversification appears inexplicably limited for some major countries. And long-run saving and investment rates remain positively associated in international cross sections to an extent greater than is true in the (usually imperfect) regional data that are available. This last phenomenon could reflect central-government policies that have the effect of limiting national current-account imbalances.

It is doubtful that capital will ever be fully as mobile between nations as it can be within them. The mere existence of national governments sovereign within their borders means that no investor can think about domestic and foreign assets in quite the same way. What is at issue, then, is the extent to which actual conditions approximate free capital mobility. Among industrial countries, the approximation has become better and better in recent years, but scope for greater financial integration clearly remains.

References

Altonji, Joseph G., Fumio Hayashi, and Laurence J. Kotlikoff, "Is the Extended Family Altruistically Linked? Direct Tests Using Micro Data," *American Economic Review*, 82 (December 1992), pp. 1177–1198.

Artis, Michael J., and Tamim A. Bayoumi, "Saving, Investment, Financial Integration, and the Balance of Payments," International Monetary Fund Working Paper No. 89/102, Washington, D.C., International Monetary Fund, December 1989.

Atkeson, Andrew, and Tamim A. Bayoumi, "Do Private Capital Markets Insure Regional Risk? Evidence from the United States and Europe," *Open Economies Review*, 4 (1993), pp. 303–324.

Backus, David K., Patrick J. Kehoe, and Finn E. Kydland, "International Real Business Cycles," *Journal of Political Economy*, 100 (August 1992), pp. 745–775.

Balassa, Bela, "The Purchasing-Power Parity Doctrine: A Reappraisal," *Journal of Political Economy*, 72 (December 1964), pp. 584–596.

Bardhan, Pranab, "Disparity in Wages But Not in Returns to Capital between Rich and Poor Countries," Working Paper C93–017, Center for International and Development Economics Research, University of California, Berkeley, July 1993.

Baxter, Marianne, and Mario J. Crucini, "Business Cycles and the Asset Structure of Foreign Trade," University of Rochester and Ohio State University, June 1993a, processed.

———, "Explaining Saving/Investment Correlations," *American Economic Review*, 83 (June 1993b), pp. 416–436.

Baxter, Marianne, and Urban J. Jermann, "The International Diversification Puzzle is Worse Than You Think," Working Paper No. 350, Rochester, N.Y., Rochester Center for Economic Research, May 1993.

Bayoumi, Tamim A., "Saving-Investment Correlations," *International Monetary Fund Staff Papers*, 37 (June 1990), pp. 360–387.

Bayoumi, Tamim A., and Andrew K. Rose, "Domestic Savings and Intra-National Capital Flows," *European Economic Review*, 37 (August 1993), pp. 1197–1202.

Bayoumi, Tamim A., and Gabriel Sterne, "Regional Trading Blocs, Mobile Capital, and Exchange Rate Coordination," London, Bank of England, January 1993, processed.

Black, Stanley W., "Discussion," in *Saving and Government Policy*, Conference Series No. 25, Boston, Federal Reserve Bank of Boston, 1982, pp. 158–161.

Brainard, William C., and James Tobin, "On the Internationalization of Portfolios," *Oxford Economic Papers*, 44 (April 1992), pp. 533–565.

Calvo, Guillermo A., Leonardo Leiderman, and Carmen M. Reinhart, "Capital Inflows and Real Exchange Rate Appreciation in Latin America: The Role of External Factors," *International Monetary Fund Staff Papers*, 40 (March 1993), pp. 108–151.

Campbell, John Y., and N. Gregory Mankiw, "The Response of Consumption to Income: A Cross-Country Investigation," *European Economic Review*, 35 (May 1991), pp. 723–767.

Canova, Fabio, and Morten Overgaard Ravn, "International Consumption Risk Sharing," San Domenico di Fiesole, European University Institute, March 1993, processed.

Cardia, Emanuela, "Crowding Out in Open Economies: Results from a Simulation Study," *Canadian Journal of Economics*, 25 (August 1992), pp. 708–728.

Carroll, Christopher D., and Lawrence H. Summers, "Consumption Growth Parallels Income Growth: Some New Evidence," in B. Douglas Bernheim and John B. Shoven, eds., *National Saving and Economic Performance*, Chicago, University of Chicago Press, 1991, pp. 305–343.

Cochrane, John H., "A Simple Test of Consumption Insurance," *Journal of Political Economy*, 99 (October 1991), pp. 957–976.

Cole, Harold L., "Financial Structure and International Trade," *International Economic Review*, 29 (May 1988), pp. 237–259.

Cole, Harold L., and Maurice Obstfeld, "Commodity Trade and International Risk Sharing: How Much do Financial Markets Matter?" *Journal of Monetary Economics*, 28 (August 1991), pp. 3–24.

Committee of Governors of the Central Banks of the Member States of the European Economic Community, *Annual Report 1992*, Basle, April 1993.

Crucini, Mario J., "International Risk Sharing: A Simple Comparative Test," Ohio State University, August 1992, processed.

Deaton, Angus, *Understanding Consumption*, Oxford, Clarendon, 1992.

Dekle, Robert, "Saving-Investment Correlations and Capital Mobility: On the Evidence from Japanese Regional Data," Boston University, October 1993, processed.

Deutsche Bundesbank, "The Trend in Germany's External Assets and Investment Income," *Monthly Report of the Deutsche Bundesbank*, 45 (January 1993), pp. 43–66.

Devereux, Michael B., Allan W. Gregory, and Gregor W. Smith, "Realistic Cross-Country Consumption Correlations in a Two-Country, Equilibrium, Business-Cycle Model," *Journal of International Money and Finance*, 11 (February 1992), pp. 3–16.

Dooley, Michael P., Jeffrey A. Frankel, and Donald J. Mathieson, "International Capital Mobility: What Do Saving-Investment Correlations Tell Us?" *International Monetary Fund Staff Papers*, 34 (September 1987), pp. 503–530.

Dumas, Bernard, "Partial-Equilibrium vs. General-Equilibrium Models of International Capital Market Equilibrium," in Frederick van der Ploeg, ed., *Handbook of International Macroeconomics*, Oxford, Blackwell, forthcoming 1994.

Eichengreen, Barry, "Trends and Cycles in Foreign Lending," in Horst Siebert, ed., *Capital Flows in the World Economy*, Tübingen, Mohr, 1990, pp. 3–28.

Eldor, Rafael, David Pines, and Abba Schwartz, "Home Asset Preference and Productivity Shocks," *Journal of International Economics*, 25 (August 1988), pp. 165–176.

Engel, Charles, and Kenneth Kletzer, "Saving and Investment in an Open Economy with Non-Traded Goods," *International Economic Review*, 30 (November 1989), pp. 735–752.

Feeney, JoAnne, "International Financial Markets and Learning-by-Doing in a Small Economy," University of Colorado, Boulder, July 1993, processed.

Feeney, JoAnne, and Ronald W. Jones, "Risk Aversion and International Markets: Does Asset Trade Smooth Real Income?" *Review of International Economics*, 2 (February 1994), pp. 13–26.

Feldstein, Martin, "Domestic Saving and International Capital Movements in the Long Run and the Short Run," *European Economic Review*, 21 (March/April 1983), pp. 129–51.

Feldstein, Martin, and Philippe Bacchetta, "National Saving and International Investment," in B. Douglas Bernheim and John B. Shoven, eds., *National Saving and Economic Performance*, Chicago, University of Chicago Press, 1991, pp. 201–220.

Feldstein, Martin, and Charles Horioka, "Domestic Saving and International Capital Flows," *Economic Journal* (London), 90 (June 1980), pp. 314–329.

Fieleke, Norman S., "National Saving and International Investment," in *Saving and*

Government Policy, Conference Series No. 25, Boston, Federal Reserve Bank of Boston, 1982, pp. 138–157.,

Finn, Mary G., "On Savings and Investment Dynamics in a Small Open Economy," *Journal of International Economics*, 29 (August 1990), pp. 1–21.

Frankel, Jeffrey A., "International Capital Mobility and Crowding-Out in the U.S. Economy: Imperfect Integration of Financial Markets or of Goods Markets?" in Rik W. Hafer, ed., *How Open is the U.S. Economy?* Lexington, Mass., and Toronto, Heath, 1986, pp. 33–67.

———, "Quantifying International Capital Mobility in the 1980s," in Jeffrey A. Frankel, *On Exchange Rates*, Cambridge, Mass., MIT Press, 1993, pp. 41–69.

French, Kenneth R., and James M. Poterba, "Japanese and U.S. Cross-Border Common Stock Investments," *Journal of the Japanese and International Economies*, 4 (December 1990), pp. 476–493.

———, "Investor Diversification and International Equity Markets," *American Economic Review*, 81 (May 1991), pp. 222–226.

Gehrig, Thomas, "An Information Based Explanation of the Domestic Bias in International Equity Investment," *Scandinavian Journal of Economics*, 95 (March 1993), pp. 97–109.

Gertler, Mark, and Kenneth S. Rogoff, "North-South Lending and Endogenous Domestic Capital-Market Inefficiencies," *Journal of Monetary Economics*, 26 (October 1990), pp. 245–266.

Ghosh, Atish R., "Capital Mobility amongst the Major Industrial Countries: Too Little or Too Much?" *Economic Journal*, 104 (forthcoming 1994).

Giavazzi, Francesco, and Marco Pagano, "Capital Controls and the European Monetary System," in Francesco Giavazzi and Marco Pagano, *Capital Controls and Foreign Exchange Legislation*, Milan, Euromobiliare, June 1985, pp. 19–38.

Glick, Reuven, and Michael Hutchison, "Financial Liberalization in the Pacific Basin: Implications for Real Interest Rate Linkages," *Journal of the Japanese and International Economies*, 4 (March 1990), pp. 36–48.

Glick, Reuven, and Kenneth S. Rogoff, "Global versus Country-Specific Productivity Shocks and the Current Account," International Finance Discussion Paper No. 443, Washington, D.C., Board of Governors of the Federal Reserve System, April 1993.

Goldstein, Morris, David Folkerts-Landau, Peter M. Garber, Liliana Rojas-Suarez, and Michael G. Spencer, *International Capital Markets*, Part I. *Exchange Rate Management and International Capital Flows*, Washington D.C., International Monetary Fund, April 1993.

Golub, Stephen S., "International Diversification of Social and Private Risk: The U.S. and Japan," Swarthmore College, November 1991, processed.

Gordon, Roger H., and Hal R. Varian, "Taxation of Asset Income in the Presence of a World Securities Market," *Journal of International Economics*, 26 (May 1989), pp. 205–226.

Grossman, Sanford J., and Robert J. Shiller, "The Determinants of the Variability of Stock Market Prices," *American Economic Review*, 71 (May 1981), pp. 222–227.

Harberger, Arnold C., "Vignettes on the World Capital Market," *American Economic Review*, 70 (May 1980), pp. 331–337.

Hodrick, Robert J., and Edward C. Prescott, "Post-War U.S. Business Cycles: An Empirical Investigation," Carnegie-Mellon University, November 1980, processed.

Jones, Matthew T., and Maurice Obstfeld, "Saving and Investment under the Gold Standard," University of California, Berkeley, 1994, processed.

Kaldor, Nicholas, "Capital Accumulation and Economic Growth," in Friedrich A. Lutz and Douglas C. Hague, eds., *The Theory of Capital*, New York, St. Martin's, 1961, pp. 177–222.

King, Robert G., and Sergio T. Rebelo, "Transitional Dynamics and Economic Growth in the Neoclassical Model," *American Economic Review*, 83 (September 1993), pp. 908–931.

Kollmann, Robert, "Consumptions, Real Exchange Rates and the Structure of International Asset Markets," Université de Montréal, March 1992, processed.

———, "Fiscal Policy, Technology Shocks and the US Trade Balance Deficit," Université de Montréal, April 1993, processed.

Lewis, Karen K., "What Can Explain the Apparent Lack of International Consumption Risk Sharing?" University of Pennsylvania, July 1993, processed.

Lucas, Robert E., Jr., *Models of Business Cycles*, Oxford, Blackwell, 1987.

———, "Why Doesn't Capital Flow from Rich to Poor Countries?" *American Economic Review*, 80 (May 1990), pp. 92–96.

———, "On Efficiency and Distribution," *Economic Journal* (London), 102 (March 1992), pp. 233–247.

McCauley, Robert N., and Steven A. Zimmer, "Explaining International Differences in the Cost of Capital," *Federal Reserve Bank of New York Quarterly Review*, 14 (Summer 1989), pp. 7–28.

Mace, Barbara J., "Full Insurance in the Presence of Aggregate Uncertainty," *Journal of Political Economy*, 99 (October 1991), pp. 928–956.

Maddison, Angus, *Dynamic Forces in Capitalist Development*, Oxford, Oxford University Press, 1991.

Mankiw, N. Gregory, David Romer, and David N. Weil, "A Contribution to the Empirics of Economic Growth," *Quarterly Journal of Economics*, 107 (May 1992), pp. 407–437

Mankiw, N. Gregory, and Stephen P. Zeldes, "The Consumption of Stockholders and Nonstockholders," *Journal of Financial Economics*, 29 (1991), pp. 97–112

Marston, Richard C., "Determinants of Short-Term Real Interest Differentials between Japan and the United States," *Bank of Japan Monetary and Economic Studies*, 11 (July 1993a), pp. 33–61.

———, "Interest Differentials under Bretton Woods and the Post-Bretton Woods Float: The Effects of Capital Controls and Exchange Risk," in Michael D. Bordo and Barry Eichengreen, eds., *A Retrospective on the Bretton Woods System*, Chicago, University of Chicago Press, 1993b, pp. 515–538.

Mathieson, Donald J., and Liliana Rojas-Suarez, *Liberalization of the Capital Account: Experiences and Issues*, Occasional Paper No. 103, Washington, D.C., International Monetary Fund, March 1993.

Mehra, Rajnish, and Edward C. Prescott, "The Equity Premium: A Puzzle," *Journal of Monetary Economics*, 15 (March 1985), pp. 145–161.

Mendoza, Enrique G., "Capital Controls and the Gains from Trade in a Business Cycle

Model of a Small Open Economy," *International Monetary Fund Staff Papers*, 38 (September 1991a), pp. 480–505

———, "Real Business Cycles in a Small Open Economy," *American Economic Review*, 81 (September 1991b), pp. 797–818.

Minhas, Bagicha Singh, *An International Comparison of Factor Costs and Factor Use*, Amsterdam, North-Holland, 1963

Murphy, Robert G., "Capital Mobility and the Relationship between Saving and Investment Rates in OECD Countries," *Journal of International Money and Finance*, 3 (December 1984), pp. 327–342.

———, "Productivity Shocks, Non-Traded Goods and Optimal Capital Accumulation," *European Economic Review*, 30 (1986), pp. 1081–1095.

Nurkse, Ragnar, "International Investment Today in the Light of Nineteenth-Century Experience," *Economic Journal* (London), 64 (December 1954), pp. 134–150

Obstfeld, Maurice, "Capital Mobility in the World Economy: Theory and Measurement," *Carnegie-Rochester Conference Series on Public Policy*, 24 (Spring 1986), pp. 55–103

———, "How Integrated Are World Capital Markets? Some New Tests," in Guillermo A. Calvo, Ronald Findlay, Pentti Kouri, and Jorge Braga de Macedo, eds., *Debt, Stabilization and Development: Essays in Memory of Carlos Díaz-Alejandro*, Oxford, Blackwell, 1989, pp. 134–155.

———, "Comment," in B. Douglas Bernheim and John B. Shoven, eds., *National Saving and Economic Performance*, Chicago, University of Chicago Press, 1991, pp. 261–270

———, "International Risk Sharing and Capital Mobility: Another Look," *Journal of International Money and Finance*, 11 (February 1992), pp. 115–121.

———, "Are Industrial-Country Consumption Risks Globally Diversified?" in Leonardo Leiderman and Assaf Razin, eds., *Capital Mobility: The Impact on Consumption, Investment, and Growth*, Cambridge, Cambridge University Press, 1994a.

———, "Evaluating Risky Consumption Paths: The Role of Intertemporal Substitutability," *European Economic Review*, 38 (forthcoming 1994b).

———, "Risk-Taking, Global Diversification, and Growth," *American Economic Review*, 84 (forthcoming 1994c).

Popper, Helen, "Long-Term Covered Interest Parity: Evidence from Currency Swaps," *Journal of International Money and Finance*, 12 (August 1993), pp. 439–448.

Razin, Assaf, and Efraim Sadka, "The Interactions between International Migration and International Trade," Research Memorandum 316, Vienna, Institute for Advanced Studies, February 1993.

Rubinstein, Mark, "An Aggregation Theorem for Securities Markets," *Journal of Financial Economics*, 1 (September 1974), pp. 225–244.

Shiller, Robert J., "Aggregate Income Risks and Hedging Mechanisms," Cowles Foundation Discussion Paper No. 1048, Yale University, June 1993.

Sinn, Stefan, "Saving-Investment Correlations and Capital Mobility: On the Evidence from Annual Data," *Economic Journal* (London), 102 (September 1992), pp. 1162–1170.

Stockman, Alan C., and Harris Dellas, "International Portfolio Nondiversification and Exchange Rate Variability," *Journal of International Economics*, 26 (May 1989), pp. 271–289.

Stockman, Alan C., and Linda L. Tesar, "Tastes and Technology in a Two-Country Model of the Business Cycle: Explaining International Comovements," National Bureau of Economic Research Working Paper No. 3355, Cambridge, Mass., National Bureau of Economic Research, December 1990.

Stulz, René, "A Model of International Asset Pricing," *Journal of Financial Economics*, 9 (1981), pp. 383–406.

Summers, Lawrence H., "Tax Policy and International Competitiveness," in Jacob A. Frenkel, ed., *International Aspects of Fiscal Policies*, Chicago, University of Chicago Press, 1988, pp. 349–375

Summers, Robert, and Alan Heston, "The Penn World Tables (Mark 5): An Expanded Set of International Comparisons, 1950–1988," *Quarterly Journal of Economics*, 106 (May 1991), pp. 327–368.

Svensson, Lars E. O., "Trade in Risky Assets," *American Economic Review*, 78 (June 1988), pp. 375–394.

Taylor, Alan M., "Domestic Saving and International Capital Flows Reconsidered," Northwestern University, November 1993, processed.

Tesar, Linda L., "Savings, Investment, and International Capital Flows," *Journal of International Economics*, 31 (August 1991), pp. 55–78.

———, "International Risk-Sharing and Nontraded Goods," *Journal of International Economics*, 35 (August 1993), pp. 69–89.

Tesar, Linda L., and Ingrid M. Werner, "Home Bias and the Globalization of Securities Markets," National Bureau of Economic Research Working Paper No. 4218, Cambridge, Mass., National Bureau of Economic Research, November 1992.

Ueda, Kazuo, "A Comparative Perspective on Japanese Monetary Policy: Short-Run Monetary Control and the Transmission Mechanism," in Kenneth J. Singleton, ed., *Japanese Monetary Policy*, Chicago, University of Chicago Press, 1993, pp. 7–29.

van Wincoop, Eric, "International Risksharing," Milan, Innocenzo Gasparini Institute for Economic Research, 1992a, processed.

———, "Regional Risksharing," Milan, Innocenzo Gasparini Institute for Economic Research, 1992b, processed.

———, "Welfare Gains from International Risksharing," Milan, Innocenzo Gasparini Institute for Economic Research, 1992c, processed.

Vikøren, Birger, "The Saving-Investment Correlation in the Short Run and in the Long Run," Oslo, Norges Bank, 1991, processed.

Wong, David Y., "What Do Saving-Investment Relationships Tell Us about Capital Mobility?" *Journal of International Money and Finance*, 9 (March 1990), pp. 60–74.

7

A Retrospective on the Debt Crisis

MICHAEL P. DOOLEY

1 Introduction

In 1992 and 1993, private capital inflows to Mexico equaled about 7 percent of Mexico's gross domestic product (GDP). These private capital inflows were larger than in any year before 1982, when Mexico's suspension of debt-service payments marked the beginning of the debt crisis that dominated the economic circumstances of many developing countries for a decade. The resurgence of private capital inflows to developing countries has been widely distributed but has been particularly evident in developing countries that did not experience debt-servicing difficulties and in countries that have participated in Brady Plan rescheduling agreements (Calvo, Leiderman, and Reinhart, 1993).

This remarkable turnaround makes it particularly important to take a retrospective look at what has been called a "lost decade" of economic stagnation for the debtor countries.[1] Only a few years ago, experts agreed that the developing countries would not return to private international credit markets for at least a generation. Do we now understand enough about the 1982 crisis to predict that a renewed accumulation of external debt will not lead to a repeat of 1982 and to the considerable costs that followed for the debtor countries? Unless the memories of investors and debtor-country governments are very short, they must believe this new round of international lending will have a different outcome.

It is very likely that economic developments external to the debtor countries, in particular recent declines in interest rates in industrial countries, explain an important share of recent capital inflows (Bulow, Rogoff, and Bevilaqua, 1992; Dooley and Stone, 1993). It therefore follows that highly indebted developing countries will remain vulnerable to external shocks, particularly to a combination of recession and high real interest rates in the industrial countries. The analysis of the 1982 crisis developed in this chapter

I would like to thank Polly Allen and Kenneth Rogoff for their helpful comments.

[1] See Dooley and Corden (1989), Cohen (1991, 1992), Cooper (1992), and Arora (1993) for comprehensive reviews of the debt crisis.

suggests, however, that the recent buildup in external debt is unlikely to generate economic costs for debtor countries comparable to those that followed 1982, even if bad luck or bad policies lead to another round of debt-servicing difficulties. By contrast, those debtor countries that have not restructured and reduced their existing debt to commercial banks are vulnerable to a return to economic stagnation.

The basic theme of this discussion is that the enormous costs borne by the debtor countries after 1982 were the result of prolonged self-interested bargaining between the commercial banks and their own governments, not between the banks and the debtor countries. The new buildup of debt will not generate similar bargaining because recent lending has not involved the commercial banks of the industrial countries.

The origins of the bargaining game between international commercial banks and industrial-country governments are found in relationships among creditors established long before the summer of 1982. For this reason, I begin with a brief review of the buildup of the external debt of developing countries in the 1970s.

2 Accumulation of External Debt, 1970–82

Historical Review

The striking aspect of the debt buildup before 1982 is the dominant role of commercial banks in providing medium- and long-term credits to residents of developing countries. Following widespread defaults on international bonds issued by developing countries in the 1930s, new lending to developing countries before 1974 was generally restricted to government-to-government loans or loans from international organizations such as the World Bank and the International Monetary Fund (IMF). One of the keys to the interpretation of the debt crisis offered in this chapter is that the emergence of banks as financial intermediaries in the 1970s can best be understood as a process in which the banks replaced the governments of industrial countries as lenders to developing countries but did so with the approval, encouragement, and implicit support of the governments of the industrial countries.

The economics behind the debt buildup are straightforward. The dramatic rise in the price of oil in 1974 and again in 1979 generated huge current-account surpluses for oil-exporting countries. As shown in Table 7.1, the counterparts of current-account surpluses for the oil exporters were deficits for both the industrial and the developing countries. The oil exporters' current-account surpluses reflected their desire to smooth consumption. This implied that a large share of their revenues had to be "recycled" to oil-importing countries in the form of capital flows from oil exporters to oil importers.

TABLE 7.1
Current-Account Balances (billions of U.S. dollars)

	All Industrial Countries	Fuel Exporters	Non-Fuel Exporters
1970	6	2	−9
1971	9	1	−11
1972	6	2	−5
1973	11	6	−4
1974	−27	65	−22
1975	7	33	−31
1976	−15	31	−18
1977	−20	20	−13
1978	11	−5	−21
1979	−27	53	−32
1980	−64	94	−52
1981	−23	32	−68
1982	−27	−20	−59

Source: IMF, *World Economic Outlook.*

The economics behind the pattern of financial intermediation between surplus and deficit countries is much less obvious. Although private capital markets were the obvious vehicle for capital inflows to industrial countries, the traditional pattern would have been for governments and international organizations to act as intermediaries for lending to developing countries. Governments, however, particularly the U.S. government, were reluctant to take on this responsibility either directly through an expansion of government-to-government loans or indirectly through international organizations.

Oil exporters were also an unlikely source of direct credit for the developing countries. In fact, oil-exporting countries realized that they were not the most popular investors at that time and wanted financial assets that were as liquid and immune from political reprisals as possible. Direct loans to residents of developing countries did not fit this description.

Bank deposits were an ideal instrument from the point of view of the oil exporters, and commercial banks saw the recycling of oil money as a profitable new business. Banks operated in many offshore banking centers, and deposits were typically passed on to several banks in different countries before being loaned to a nonbank. There was thus no correspondence between the location of a deposit and the location of the ultimate loan to a nonbank. Moreover, it was generally recognized that banks were special institutions that had proven to be "too big to fail." Governments had consistently stepped in to save large banks in order to prevent a general financial panic.

On the other side, borrowers in both industrial and developing countries preferred bank credits to more traditional private and official financial intermediaries because banks were willing to charge only a small margin over their cost of funds when setting lending rates. The wisdom of banks in entering into this business and lending at very narrow spreads to compensate for credit risk has been widely questioned in recent years. My interpretation of this phase of the crisis is that banks were rational; they realized a bad outcome was possible but also realized that the losses generated by bad outcomes could be shifted to their own governments.

In summary, the buildup of external debt in the 1970s is generally attributed to a series of external events that seemed to provide economic reasons for lending to the developing countries. Relative price increases for oil and other commodities provided a demand for credit, and the surplus of the Organization of Petroleum Exporting Countries (OPEC) provided a supply of internationally mobile savings. Low *ex post* real interest rates on loans denominated in major currencies may have contributed to the willingness of the developing countries to incur debt, although those low interest rates should have encouraged other borrowers equally.

Policy during the Buildup of Debt

The hypothesis that banks relied on their own governments' implicit guarantees of their loans to developing countries helps to make sense of the implausibly naive statements by bankers about the inability of countries to fail. The one thing that could stop the banks from taking on this profitable but risky loan portfolio was the attitude of regulators toward country risk. The banks knew that their exposure to individual countries was much larger than would normally be permitted under domestic concentration ratios. Thus, the banks had every incentive to reassure the regulators that there was no risk involved in the quite clearly risky positions the banks were taking.

An alternative interpretation is that banks really were naive but turned to their governments for a bailout after the crisis occurred and used the earlier official support for the recycling of oil money as a convenient *ex post* rationalization for help from their governments. The banks were quick to point out after 1982 that "the public and government applauded them for successfully 'recycling' the soaring revenue of oil-producing countries in the 1970s" (Lawrence Rout, "A New Solution for the World's Debt Crunch," *Wall Street Journal*, March 3, 1983).

The conjecture that creditor governments were expected *ex ante* to guaran-

tee bank claims on the developing countries is important to my interpretation
of the buildup in debt but is less important to my interpretation of the subsequent bargaining between banks and their governments, which can be explained in terms of an *ex post* claim to support. In either case, the banks saw a
good chance of collecting from their own governments what they could not
collect from their developing-country debtors following 1982. The policy decision that led to protracted negotiations between the banks and creditor governments was the refusal of conservative governments in the United States
and other industrial countries to provide the expected backup. The longer this
game went on, the higher was the loss to the debtor countries.

There is ample evidence for the existence of an implicit backup by creditor
governments before the debt crisis became apparent in 1982. Officials of the
Federal Reserve System, for example, were concerned about the size of the
banks' exposure. As early as 1974, Arthur Burns (1978), then chairman of
the Federal Reserve Board, warned that banks were taking excessive risks in
international lending. Governor Henry Wallich (1981, 1987) repeatedly
pointed out before 1982 that the banks' exposure to sovereign risk threatened
their capital and argued that additional lending should be constrained by the
regulatory authorities.

Economists also pointed out the potential problem arising from the excessive concentration of country risk on the banks' balance sheets. John Kereken
(1977, p. 506) warned that, "at the end of 1976, Citibank had LDC loans
amounting to about 6 percent of its total assets. And we know it had capital,
as conventionally measured, amounting to 5 percent of its assets. That suggests, at least to me, that there may be some slight danger, particularly if
Citibank is not all that untypical. The Federal Reserve, which along with
other central banks can make good loans out of bad, may in certain circumstances, be tempted to do just that." Marina Whitman (1978, p. 151) argued
that the official sector should play a larger role in intermediating oil surpluses
through the IMF. "Should the pessimists turn out to be right," she wrote, "and
widespread defaults loom, the American banks would look for bailout, not to
an IMF facility totaling less than $10 billion, but to the incomparably greater
resources of our own Federal Reserve System."

By contrast, the U.S. Treasury consistently argued that the banks were the
preferred financial intermediaries for loans to developing countries. As De
Vries (1985) shows in her history of the IMF, Treasury secretary William
Simon was the main opponent of an expanded role for official lending through
the IMF. Moreover, as Weintraub (1983) notes, the U.S. Treasury had encouraged U.S. banks to pursue international lending long before the first oil shock.

Finally, the fact that regulatory agencies allowed banks to "bet the bank" on
loans to individual countries suggests that the official community believed that
the public benefits of smoothly and efficiently recycling oil money would
exceed the potential costs of bailing out the banks. Wellons (1987) documents

the cautious approach taken by U.S. regulators in defining limits on lending to individual developing countries and argues that U.S. bank regulators responded to strong political pressure against interfering with recycling to developing countries by declining to enforce such lending limits.

In summary, the governments of the industrial countries had conflicting policy objectives. Oil money had to be recycled, but the governments did not want to do it themselves. Moreover, the majority of industrial countries were not enthusiastic about expanding the roles of international organizations as financial intermediaries. A widely held view was that market forces would lead to the most efficient allocation of financial resources across countries.

Was it rational for the governments of the industrial countries to permit their banks to intermediate loans to developing countries? It could be argued that the governments had little choice. The financial intermediation was thought to be important for maintaining aggregate demand in the oil-consuming world. If this premise is accepted, *some* government or private institution had to accept the country risk associated with international lending. The governments of the industrial countries seem to have believed that official lenders were not very good at identifying the most efficient allocation of funds. The banks took the same view, pointing out that they were experts at the analysis of country risk and that the discipline of the marketplace was preferred to bureaucratic decisions by the IMF and other multilateral institutions (Friedman, 1977). In the following pages, I argue that, once committed, the creditor governments made a major policy error in refusing to provide the expected backstop. This policy choice transformed an unremarkable financial crisis into a decade-long economic crisis for the debtor countries.

Analytical Literature during the Buildup

The buildup of the external debt of the developing countries generated a substantial academic literature both before and after the crisis of 1982. The majority of papers before the crisis dealt with the ability of the debtor countries to repay their loans. Until very late in the day, the consensus was that servicing the loans was not likely to be a problem (Solomon, 1977).

In retrospect, an important element missing from the evaluation of debtor countries during the years when debt was growing rapidly is that the private sector of the debtor countries was typically accumulating gross claims on the rest of the world at an impressive rate.[2] There are several reasons why what later came to be known as capital flight was entirely missed at the time. Pri-

---

[2] See Dooley (1986) for estimates of the stock of flight capital for debtor countries and comparisons between balance-of-payments data and debt-reporting-system estimates of external debt. In 1983, I and others prepared a paper for the Board of Governors of the Federal Reserve System that provided comprehensive statistical estimates of capital flight (see Dooley et al., 1986).

vate capital outflows from the debtor countries were largely unrecorded and did not show up in balance-of-payment statistics of the debtor or creditor countries. Perhaps more surprising, medium- and long-term borrowing was also not always reported in the balance-of-payments statistics of the debtor countries, even when it carried official guarantees.

The lack of attention to gross capital flows may be explained by the fact that there is no particular reason to be concerned about the scale of financial intermediation as long as all goes well. It is only after an accident that the consequences for different groups of debtors and creditors have to be sorted out. Cooper (1992) makes the interesting point that the fact that a substantial part of the stock of external debt was "matched" by capital flight is one reason why creditor governments were unwilling to support proposals that would have provided the bailout the banks had anticipated. More generally, the cost of the debt crisis to debtor countries arose largely because the participants had perverse incentives to jockey for position in the workout process.

There were interesting attempts to explain why banks had "overlent" to developing countries. Kletzer (1984) argued that the fact that banks were poorly informed about the loans other banks had made or would make to developing countries could account for what appeared *ex post* to be excessive lending. Guttentag and Herring (1986) argued that banks and most of the rest of us seem to suffer from "disaster myopia," in the sense that decisionmakers systematically ignore really bad outcomes. Devlin (1989) argued that banks are complex organizations that tend to do what other banks are doing to maintain market share. He also mentions the possibility that banks have to keep growing so that they remain too large to fail.

My explanation is that the banks acted rationally. If all went well, they would have enjoyed substantial profits; if things went badly, they planned to shift the loans to their governments on terms that were not well defined but that were unlikely to call into question the wisdom of making the loans. In the event of trouble, creditor governments were expected to "nationalize" the banks' claims on the developing countries and then collect what they could. This argument is appealing because it avoids the need to invent naive or poorly informed bankers (specimens I have seldom encountered in negotiations over restructuring packages). More important, it provides a better basis for understanding the negotiations that followed the 1982 crisis.

3 A Banking Crisis

Historical Review

The system of financial intermediation through commercial banks that had developed to accommodate international transactions among residents of industrial countries was easily modified to channel funds to, and from, developing countries. Moreover, syndicated credits commonly used in Euromarkets were uncritically adopted for lending to developing countries. Unfortunately, just as generals prepare to fight the previous war, financial markets design contracts to accommodate the previous shock. The floating-rate loan contracts used for the bulk of commercial-bank lending to the developing countries were ready for an increase in the rate of inflation, the dominant shock in the 1970s. The shock in 1982, however, was recession and a fall in the rate of inflation in the industrial countries that was accompanied by a spectacular and durable rise in real interest rates, a rise in the real value of the dollar, and a fall in the relative prices of oil and other commodities.

In my view, the probability of such a shock to the system was very low *ex ante*. No one predicted in the late 1970s that a conservative Republican president would generate fiscal deficits that far exceeded any outside those produced by major wars, and that the Federal Reserve would launch a major disinflation initiative at the same time.

The resulting rise in the real interest rate on dollar-denominated loans to the developing countries fell entirely on the debtors. The floating-interest-rate credits that generated this result were widely used in Euromarket lending and were a natural reaction to the inflationary shock in the industrial countries in the 1970s. Commercial banks had learned the hard way that fixed-interest assets placed them at risk in the event of unexpected increases in inflation rates. Thus, the dominant form of debt contract for all international lending was medium term in maturity but with an interest rate that was adjusted twice yearly and was tied to the six-month London interbank offer rate (LIBOR) for the currency of denomination. The popularity of these floating-rate loans was based on the fact that both the banks and debtors would be protected from surprises in the inflation rate.

The banks hedged currency risk by matching deposits to loans and hedged interest-rate risk by using floating-rate loans. The latter, however, shifted the surprise in real interest rates entirely and almost immediately to the debtor countries and for this reason contributed to credit risk. The spread over LIBOR on loans determined profit margins and presumably reflected expected losses from credit risk. As is natural for banks, their attitude toward credit risk was influenced less by the quality of the borrower than the quality of the collateral. In this case, the collateral was, first, a debtor-government guarantee of loans to the residents of the developing countries and, ultimately, the political commitment of a creditor-country government to the debtor government. When the credits were put at risk by the new economic conditions, the banks called the collateral, pointing out that they had been asked to recycle the oil money and that the solvency of the banking system was very important to the governments of the industrial countries.

Policy Response and Damage Control

The initial reaction to the banks' refusal to roll over credits was as expected. First, developing-country private debt was rapidly transformed into developing-country government debt even in countries like Chile where there was no formal guarantee and the government had said that it would not step in to bail out private debtors. Second, there were immediate calls on the governments of the creditor countries to provide the debtor governments with the means to meet their obligations to the banks. Third, bank regulators in all the industrial countries reassured the markets that they would not close banks the capital of which was threatened by losses on developing-country loans.

But the surprise was that the creditor governments refused to provide the banks with an opportunity to sell their doubtful credits to their governments on any terms, favorable or not. Proposals for a comprehensive debt facility were met with considerable hostility in several important creditor countries. The strategy, instead, was to "coordinate" continued bank lending until IMF programs could put the debtor countries back on their feet. Thus, the initial official credit was typically a short-term bridge loan that was supposed to be liquidated after a few months by an IMF credit.[3] Some important officials apparently saw this as a unique opportunity to force debtor countries to embrace the reforms that they believed had been postponed unduly by the developing countries' easy access to credit before 1982. This call for "conditionality" found wide acceptance at international organizations and among academic economists who had favored greater official involvement with recycling.

Analytical Literature

The academic literature immediately following the debt crisis pursued a number of interesting lines of thought. The classic theoretical treatment of sovereign debt by Eaton and Gersovitz (1981) developed the idea that the key difference between a sovereign debtor and other debtors is that the creditor cannot seize collateral in the event of default. Put differently, a bank cannot force liquidation of the debtor and thus make the best of a bad loan judgment. For this reason, the creditor has to rely on the ability to impose punishments on the debtor. Eaton and Gersovitz considered punishment in the form of trade sanctions, and the related loss of gains from trade in the form of exclusion from future lending and the associated loss of the debtor's ability to smooth consumption. This basic framework helps explain why a sovereign-debt problem can take an extended time to resolve. Because there is no outside arbiter

---

[3] See Sachs (1989) for a description of the immediate official response to the crisis.

to divide the collateral and "protect the debtor" from residual claims, default will be followed by prolonged renegotiation for partial payment. The basic insight provided by this theory is that sovereign default normally results in a continuous renegotiation of payments based on the changing power of the two sides in an ongoing game.

This emphasis on a game between a debtor and a representative creditor, however, was adopted with too much enthusiasm by subsequent researchers. I have argued that loss of reputation or fear of trade disruption was not the basis for the enormous private loans extended to developing countries through 1982. More important from our point of view is that the events following the debt crisis cannot be adequately modeled as a game involving only debtors (developing-country governments) and creditors (commercial banks). By leaving out the interested and relatively wealthy third parties (industrial-country governments), this framework fails to capture the basic nature of the problems generated by the crisis. An important exception is the paper by Bulow and Rogoff (1989b), which shows that the governments of creditor countries may have good reasons to make side payments to banks and debtor countries in order to resolve conflicts over repayment. In the context of the argument presented in this chapter, this insight might be seen as a reason why the banks expected the creditor governments to make good on their implicit guarantees.

The refusal of creditor governments to "bail out the banks" was consistent with another important strand of academic inquiry, which developed the idea that the debtors faced a temporary "liquidity" problem but were "solvent" in the long run. This judgment was based on calculations that suggested that the debt was small relative to the payments capacity of the debtor country. Influential studies by Cline (1983) and Feldstein (1986) argued that a normal recovery by the industrial countries from the recession would provide export markets to developing countries and thus allow them to service their debt. This analysis fit the policy of concerted lending and conditional official lending to get the debtor countries over a brief liquidity crisis.

A number of researchers, including Sachs (1984) and Krugman (1985), sought to explain why banks refused to lend to illiquid but basically solvent countries. The basic idea in these papers is that the value of individual loans depends on the continued participation of other lenders. An individual bank would prefer to wait for other banks to make new loans so that it could receive full payment without increasing its exposure. This interesting line of research followed the earlier convention of modeling a game between the debtor and a group of commercial banks. It argued that the banks would find it difficult to organize themselves to make loans that were in their mutual interest. It recognized that there might be an expected loss to be distributed among the banks but pointed out that even a small expected loss could paralyze new lending unless an outside force were to organize concerted lending. The free-rider problem provided an elegant justification for concerted lending and appeared to explain the inability of private markets to keep on lending to the developing countries. The same line of analysis is also consistent with the idea that an official debt facility (Kenen, 1983, 1990; Corden, 1989) or a private investor (Dooley, 1989) would have an economic incentive to buy up all the existing debt and internalize the coordination problem. If debtor countries were solvent, this could be done at no expected cost.

Early proposals for a debt facility implicitly addressed the issue I turn to next, the coordination problem among official creditors, private creditors, and potential investors in the debtor country. In retrospect, it is unfortunate that these proposals did not have more influence on the analytical work that followed. The conflict among the creditors is at least as important as the conflict between debtors and creditors for understanding the ensuing economic crisis of the debtor countries.

A debt facility would have resolved the conflict between the banks and official creditors. The proposals for such a facility called for the official creditors to buy the debt from the banks, perhaps at a discount, and hold it until the debtor countries benefited from the expected turnaround in the world economy.[4] In one important sense, these proposals focused on the key problem associated with the debt. The commercial banks expected to be bought out and viewed the refusal to do so, particularly by the U.S. government, as an *ex post* change in the rules of the game. The struggle that followed between the official and private foreign creditors left the debtors without a basis for entering into credible contracts with new creditors.

4 Conflict among Creditors and Economic Stagnation in the Debtor Countries

Historical Review

The years following the debt crisis are marked by a prolonged struggle among broad groups of creditors and the related dismal economic performance of the debtor countries. The rough outline of how the creditors fared is shown in Table 7.2. At the end of 1982, debtor countries owed $278 billion to commercial banks and $115 billion to official creditors. Over the next seven years, the *real* value of commercial-bank debt fell to $241 billion, whereas the *real* value of official debt rose to $236 billion (both in 1982 dollars).

How did this happen? Clearly, the commercial banks did not forgive any of the debt, and (before 1989) only small amounts were exchanged for nondebt claims on the debtor governments. The answer, first, is that most debtor countries made all their interest payments to commercial banks. Given an average

---

[4] See Dornbusch (1989, chap. 5) for a comprehensive review of proposals for a debt facility.

TABLE 7.2

Real Debt of Developing Countries with Debt-Servicing
Difficulties (billions of 1982 U.S. dollars)

	To Commercial Banks	To Official Creditors
1982	278	115
1983	290	129
1984	286	143
1985	276	162
1986	278	187
1987	283	224
1988	254	232
1989	241	236
1990	222	251
1991	213	251
1992	200	252

Source: IMF, *World Economic Outlook.*

inflation rate of about 4 percent in industrial countries, this means that a debt of $100 in 1982 on which all interest payments were made would still have a nominal value of $100 in 1989. But the real value of debt would have fallen to about $79. This is roughly what happened after 1983. From where did the interest payments come? They must have come partly from new credits provided by the official lenders and partly from earnings through net exports. This process insured that the historically unusual bulge in private lending in the 1970s was being slowly returned to its historical norm as official credits once again dominated lending to the developing countries.

The second important aspect of this phase of the crisis is the dismal economic performance of the debtor countries. Table 7.3 shows growth rates for per capita GDP for developing countries with and without debt-servicing difficulties. Slow growth in the industrial countries surely accounts for some of the slowdown of growth in the developing countries, but, as discussed in detail below, it seems likely that the overhang of external debt also played a role in this weak economic performance.

The third important institutional development was the emergence of a secondary market for external debt. As shown in Figure 7.1, starting in 1985, a well-organized secondary market allowed banks to buy and sell their participation in syndicated credits. This market is important because it gives a sensitive barometer of the expected value of future payments on this type of debt.

TABLE 7.3
Per Capita GDP Growth in Developing Countries, 1972–91

	All Developing Countries	Countries with Recent Debt-Servicing Difficulties	Countries without Debt-Servicing Difficulties
1972–81[a]	2.3	1.7	3.5
1982	−0.2	−2.0	3.3
1983	−0.1	−3.9	5.1
1984	1.8	0.4	5.8
1985	1.7	1.1	4.8
1986	1.7	1.3	4.2
1987	1.4	0.3	5.3
1988	2.1	−0.2	5.6
1989	0.9	−0.5	2.6
1990	0.4	−2.5	3.5
1991	1.9	0.8	3.4

Source: IMF, *World Economic Outlook.*
[a]Average of compound annual rates of change; excludes China.

In 1985 and 1986, prices settled at about $0.60 per dollar of face value. If a credit was supposed to pay LIBOR, plus a typical spread of about 1 percent, the secondary-market yield was roughly (LIBOR + 0.01)/0.60. Falling prices through 1989 indicated that an increasing risk premium was demanded by investors to induce them to hold the existing stock of bank debt.

Policy of Muddling Through

Regardless of the merits of the case, a comprehensive debt facility was politically unacceptable in most creditor countries. The preferred alternative was "concerted rescheduling," in which all creditors did their "share" in providing credit to debtor countries. The banks cleverly called their contribution "new money," which, in reality, was neither new nor money. An only slightly cynical view of this process is that the banks organized the official creditors rather than the reverse.

This strategy was formalized in the Baker Plan announced in 1985. The essence of the plan was that industrial-country governments would provide (a little) new lending to the debtor countries, both directly and through the inter-

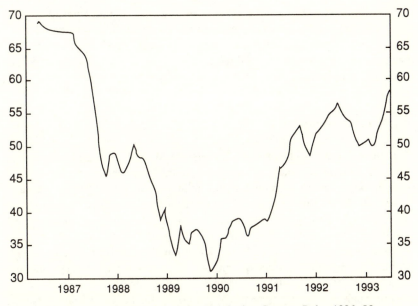

Figure 7.1 Secondary-Market Prices for Developing-Country Debt, 1986–93

national institutions they both financed and controlled, and would thereby "catalyze" (a large volume of) new credits from the banks. The Baker Plan added "catalyze" to the list of terrible international finance jargon but did not result in new lending by the banks. As shown above, the key in interpreting how private and official creditors were working out their relative positions during this phase of the crisis is to look at their balance sheets rather than to listen to their words.

The banks were the clear winners of this phase of the game, because the expected bailout was forthcoming, although at a very slow rate, as official debt gradually displaced bank debt. I believe that the banks understood the nature of the game very well but, of course, were not anxious to discuss the matter in these terms.[5] The official sector was less well informed. In retrospect, it seems to me that, for a long time, the strategy that was intended to force the banks to continue to lend while the debtor countries embarked on reform programs worked in the narrow interests of the banks.

It was, and is, easy to miss the essential nature of this game between the banks and their governments. The argument did not usually explicitly focus on which creditor would receive interest payments but on the mirror-image question of which creditor would make a new loan. Given payments from the debtors' resources, making a new loan is the same thing as giving a payment

---

[5] Calvo (1989) and Cohen (1992) give an interesting calculation of the *ex post* returns realized by the banks over the entire period.

to the other creditor. Neither the banks nor the creditor governments, however, saw any advantage to presenting their position with excessive clarity.
Banks were winning the game as it was being played, and governments that
had asserted they would not "bail out the banks" were not anxious to concede
that they were doing slowly what they would not do quickly.

Analytical Literature

This phase of the debt crisis can be interpreted as a protracted negotiation
between heavily indebted developing countries and their creditors—and,
more important in my view, among the creditors—to rationalize contracts and
implicit understandings that could not be carried out as written or understood
by the various participants. As discussed above, the analytical literature immediately following the crisis emphasized the conflict between a debtor and a
representative creditor. This framework continued to dominate the subsequent
literature, which turned to the question of the effects of debt on the economic
performance of debtors and the effects of debt forgiveness. As outlined above,
an important aspect of this phase of the crisis was the miserable economic
performance of the debtor countries. The key to the academic literature that
addressed this issue was to model the relation between existing debt and economic performance.

One approach was to model debt-service payments as a tax on future output
(Krugman, 1988; Sachs, 1988; Froot, 1989; Helpman, 1989, 1990; Dooley
and Helpman, 1992). Like any expected tax on current investment, debt service can be expected to discourage investment and encourage current consumption in debtor countries. The link between the contractual value of debt
and its market value can be summarized in a "debt Laffer curve" that relates
the stock of debt to its market value. The market value of debt will increase as
the stock of debt rises as long as tax receipts rise. But, as the tax rate rises, the
disincentives from a higher tax rate eventually generate a decline in investment and income that dominates the increase in tax rates.

These models emphasize the behavior of the debtor in evaluating the effects
of a debt overhang and debt reduction. Forgiveness of debt is in the interest of
creditors as a group if the country is on the wrong side of the debt Laffer
curve, that is, only if the market value of debt rises as debt is forgiven. Empirical estimates of the relation between the stock of debt and its market value
suggest that very few debtor countries have been in such a position (Claessens, 1990).

An alternative approach developed by Dooley (1986) focuses on the behavior of various groups of existing and potential creditors. This approach emphasizes the expected sharing of a given pool of debt-service payments among
creditors. It seems clear in retrospect that there are at least four important

classes of creditors of debtor-country governments. These include banks, official creditors, domestic creditors, and potential investors in real capital in the debtor country.

Potential investors in a debtor country are the most important and least obvious of the government's creditors. Investors are creditors because they implicitly enter into a tax contract with the government that sets out how revenues are to be shared with the government. In that sense, potential investors are offered contracts by governments that are similar to those held by the internal and external creditors. In an environment where there is uncertainty concerning the government's ability to satisfy its obligations, all creditors and potential creditors will position themselves to maximize their payments at the expense of other creditors. A new investor has the option of moving to a country that does not have a debt overhang.

The interdependence among creditors suggests that there is a strong relation between the market return available on existing debt and the rate of return on additions to the capital stock located in the debtor country. Because rates of return on existing debt had risen by 1986 to four to ten times the risk-free interest rate, this argument implies that existing creditors expected to be subject to a very high marginal tax rate. If new investors expected to be subject to that same marginal tax rate, few new investment projects could plausibly promise such a high rate of return. The critical issue is the expected seniority of various creditors. The assumption that all existing and potential creditors face the same expected marginal tax rate seems the most appropriate. Dooley and Svensson (1994) show that it is difficult for a debtor government credibly to establish seniority that will protect a new investor from existing creditors.

The interdependence of old and new creditors has important implications for the behavior of individual creditor groups. For example, for the commercial banks as a group, the unilateral debt reduction that made sense in the context of the debt Laffer curve discussed above would generate capital gains for official creditors, domestic creditors, and taxpayers in the debtor countries. More important, if transfers to the debtor by official creditors were related to the level of misery in the debtor country, banks would have even less reason to be concerned about the negative incentives for investment generated by a debt overhang. It is possible in this situation that, even if a country were on the "wrong" side of a debt Laffer curve (so that debt forgiveness by banks would increase expected payments by debtors), the gain for the banks would be more than offset by lower expected transfers from official creditors because of better economic conditions in the debtor country.

In summary, an emphasis on the interdependence of the creditors is based on the view that the banks did not see much payoff in trying to influence the behavior of the debtor-country governments. They were, however, accustomed to influencing their own governments, and, in crude terms, that is where the money was.

The economic consequences of what came to be known as a debt overhang have been evaluated in a number of empirical models (Borensztein, 1990; Cohen, 1992). There remains a wide range of opinion about the importance of the overhang for the economic performance of debtor countries and, therefore, about the benefits from reducing debt through various techniques. It seems very likely that, among the players in this game, the debtor countries had the most to lose from the inability of the banks and the official creditors to resolve their conflict.

5 Confrontation among Creditors

Historical Review

The rescheduling of Mexico's debt in 1986 was the beginning of a new and more confrontational relation between the official and bank creditors. Periodic reschedulings were necessary because most external debt had been combined into a multiyear rescheduling agreement that had to be renegotiated every few years. Naturally, all the creditors saw these negotiations as opportunities to reduce their exposure on terms better than they could get on the secondary market. The real problem, however, was not coordination among the banks. In my view, the banks did not believe they could gain much at the expense of other banks. The real payoff was in convincing official creditors to increase lending.

The 1986 negotiations were different in that they started with an explicit statement by the Mexican government that expressed the interest payment to be made to the banks as a percentage of GDP. This opening bid by the debtor forced official creditors to take a stand on whether the Mexican offer was reasonable in light of the debtor's economic condition. In addition, it was clear that any financing gap between the debtor's offer and the banks' counter-offer would have to be filled by official credits. If the official creditors did not provide the residual financing, no agreement was possible and interest arrears would emerge. The banks felt abused in this negotiation in that the creditor governments reportedly assigned "new-money" quotas to the banks.

Shortly after this episode, U.S. banks created substantial loan-loss provisions against their developing-country debt, and market prices for all sovereign debt fell dramatically. The initial Mexican offer put all creditors on notice that the debtor countries were unwilling or unable to continue to tap domestic credit markets in order to make external debt payments. The resulting fall in market prices was the natural consequence of the fall in the de facto senior status relative to other creditors that bank debt had enjoyed since 1982 (see Dooley and Stone [1993] for an empirical analysis of this conjecture).

Policy Options

The showdown in the Mexican deal in 1986 clarified the conflicting interests of the creditors. It clearly demonstrated that the official and bank creditors were competing for the same limited pool of payments from the debtor countries. The insistence on the part of official creditors that banks provide new money was equivalent to their insistence that their own lending not be used to amortize bank claims.

At the same time, the fall in market prices for the debt made the proposition that the debtors were solvent increasingly difficult to sell. The substantial discounts on secondary markets seemed to offer the official creditors better terms for reducing bank claims than they were getting through concerted lending packages. After all, interest payment to another creditor is a buyback at a price of unity. Moreover, the process of slowly financing interest payments to banks with new official credit was proving very tough on the debtor countries.

The Brady Plan was an amazingly muddled attempt to deal with the conflict. The original Brady Plan proposal was thought by its proponents to offer a great deal of debt reduction at little cost to the official creditors providing the resources. Those with a more analytical frame of mind, including the banks, recognized that the resources available to support the plan would generate significant debt reduction only if the banks were given no choice but to sell at existing market prices—which had, at the time the plan was first announced, reached a low of about $0.30 on the dollar.[6] The U.S. Treasury, however, never had any intention of making the plan mandatory. The Treasury view was that each agreement would be purely voluntary. This was practical, in a way, because it was not clear how the U.S. government could force the banks to accept an agreement that was contrary to the interests of their shareholders.[7]

The result, in addition to a good deal of confusion, was a protracted series of negotiations that usually began with the debtor expecting and asking for a large amount of debt reduction and ended with an agreement involving debt reduction at prices that reflected the market's view of the value of debt remaining after the debt reduction. For this reason, the amount of debt reduction in the Brady deals was quite limited, especially when new official debt was added to the calculation of net debt reduction.[8] As late as the spring of 1990,

---

[6] Krugman (1989) and Dooley and Symansky (1989) discuss why the ancillary aspects of the Brady rescheduling agreements did not allow official resources to retire more debt than is suggested by a simple buyback at prices expected to prevail after the buyback.

[7] The Federal Reserve was particularly hostile to forced write-downs of debt and rightly questioned the practical difficulties in defining and administering an equitable administrative restructuring (Volcker and Gyohten, 1992).

[8] See Claessens, Diwan, and Fernandez-Arias, 1992, for a careful evaluation of the Brady Plan agreements.

economists agreed that the scale of debt reduction possible under voluntary agreements could not make a material difference in the fortunes of the debtor countries (Dornbusch, 1989; Krueger, 1989; U.S. Congress, 1990).

Analytical Literature

The main topic in the theoretical literature relevant to this phase was the analysis of debt reduction and restructuring. An important issue was the extent to which a secondary-market discount on sovereign debt offered an opportunity for official creditors to purchase the debt cheaply, forgive a portion of the contractual value, and enjoy the capital gains on the remaining debt when the debtor economies revived.

A very simple analysis made it clear that any voluntary transaction would generate a rise in the price at which the debt could be purchased, because the expected value of the existing debt would rise (Bulow and Rogoff, 1988, 1989a; Dooley, 1988a, 1988b). This placed the official creditors in direct and open conflict with the commercial banks. If, for example, the industrial-country governments were to offer to buy all private debt and forgive all of it, an individual bank would hold out and expect to receive full payment following the deal. The obvious solution would be to threaten to default on any debt not sold at a price set by the buyer, but the industrial-country governments refused to force the banks into that position.

In practical terms, this meant that the market value of claims surrendered by the banks in a Brady restructuring had to be comparable to the expected market value of the new claims or cash acquired. If this condition was not met, the banks had the option of refusing to grant the waivers necessary for a restructuring and of waiting for a better offer. The banks were "held together" by the requirement that 60 to 100 percent of the participants holding existing credits had to vote to approve the waivers required for a restructuring agreement. The creditor governments that financed the deals also had the option to set conditions and wait for a better agreement. It follows that the division of the surplus provided by the creditor governments between the banks and the debtors reflected the relative bargaining power or the impatience of the banks and their governments.

In an extreme case in which the creditor governments have no bargaining power, it is clear that, once the market is aware of the resources available for the buyback, the market price will be set equal to a rational forecast of the value of debt after the buyback. Some simple arithmetic will help develop the point (Dooley, 1988a, 1988b). Suppose the expected present value of payments from the debtor is $100. Initial debt consists of dollar-dominated loans —$100 "bank debt" held by foreign banks and $100 "official debt" held by creditor governments. Suppose also that all creditors expect to share all future payments strictly in proportion to the contractual value of their claims. This is sometimes called an "equal-sharing clause," and it is found in all syndicated credit agreements. The market price of both types of debt would be $0.50, the expected present value of payments divided by the contractual value of total debt. If official creditors lend $10 to the debtor government for a buyback, it is clear that the debt remaining after the restructuring will be $210 − $10/$p$, where p is the price at the time of the transaction. If market participants are rational, they will set p at the level expected to prevail following the restructuring. Setting the buyback price equal to the expected market price, $p = \$100/(\$210 − \$10/p) = \$0.524$. It follows that the rise in the market price generates a capital gain for the banks, a net loss for the official creditors, and no direct gain for the debtor.[9] In addition, the scale of debt reduction possible is constrained by the resources available to compensate creditors.

In most restructuring agreements, a menu of options has been offered to the banks. The basic points made above, however, are not altered by an expansion of the instruments involved. Most agreements, for example, include a variety of new bonds, often convertible into equity, that carry guarantees of interest and/or principal. As long as the assumption of equal sharing is maintained, however, a new instrument can be decomposed into country risk that has the same market value as other unsecured claims on the country and a risk-free component the value of which is equal to the collateral behind the guarantee. Arbitrage conditions insure that, if the same $10 were used to collateralize the principal and interest of a new instrument, an exchange of old for new debt would generate the same equilibrium as shown above.

A related issue is whether or not voluntary debt reduction is an efficient use of resources. The fact that banks realize capital gains as debt prices rise suggests that most of the benefits might go to existing creditors rather than to the debtors. In the above example, it is difficult to see what difference a small amount of debt reduction could make for the debtor. A market price of $0.52 rather than $0.50 is unlikely to generate a measurable change in the investment in the debtor country (Bulow and Rogoff, 1988; Dooley, 1988a). The debtor might be better off to keep its resources and invest in reserves or domestic activities.

A buyback makes more sense in the context of a three-party game when one of the existing creditors is financing the buyout of another creditor. In the simple example above, the official creditor makes a new loan that immediately falls to a discount on the secondary market. This loss can be interpreted as a side payment by one creditor to another. The circumstances under which this is a rational policy choice are presented in Bulow and Rogoff (1989b). Their framework shows that a range of outcomes is possible depending on the pref-

---

[9] Dooley, Haas, and Symansky (1993) provide an accounting framework for evaluating the effects of debt restructuring on various classes of creditors.

erences and market power of the lenders. For example, it shows that, if lenders are competitors and thus have no market power, side payments from creditor governments will go entirely to the debtor. This framework also helps clarify the extent to which the market value of the debt depends on expected side payments from the creditor governments and expected payments from the debtor.

It is certainly possible that the Brady restructuring agreements were able to exploit the power of creditor governments to force the banks to make concessions to consummate the deals. In fact, empirical evaluations of the agreements suggest that the debtor countries and the banks shared about equally the surplus generated by side payments from creditor governments (Van Wijnbergen, 1991; Bulow, Rogoff, and Bevilaqua, 1992; Claessens, Diwan, and Fernandez-Arias, 1992). Nevertheless, as shown in Dooley (1993), it is difficult to rule out the possibility that all the direct benefits of the Brady deals to date went to the banks. Moreover, it is generally agreed that the direct benefits of the Brady restructurings have been too small to account for much of the increase in the secondary-market prices since 1990.

6 Another Debt Buildup, 1990–93

Historical Review

Why, then, have the financial positions of debtor countries improved since 1990? As mentioned in the introduction, private capital inflows into Brady Plan countries have been very strong, prices for external debt have risen, and stock and real-estate markets have seen large increases in prices. Is the debt crisis dead, as suggested by several observers recently, or is it only sleeping?

As documented by Bacha (1991), the increase in debt prices has been greater for Brady Plan countries than for other debtor countries.[10] There are good reasons to guess that the crisis is over for some countries. A clear change in economic policies has been an important aspect of the turnaround in some countries. In Mexico, Argentina, and Chile, for example, impressive reform programs have included substantial increases in the primary budget surpluses and the amortization of internal and external debt. In addition, privatization of important financial and nonfinancial enterprises and a significant opening up to foreign competition promise to provide a lasting improvement in the return on investment. Although the relative contributions of debt reduction and economic adjustment are difficult to disentangle for these countries, it makes little difference for the purpose of assessing the permanence of the turnaround as long as policy reforms are maintained.

---

[10] Bacha includes Chile even though Chile's debt-reduction program relied on debt-equity swaps rather than on a formal restructuring.

Even in the cases above, however, reversible good luck also appears to have played a role. The rise in international interest rates that caused the problem in the first place was gradually reversed after the first quarter of 1989, and real interest rates have continued to fall to very low levels. This will change as the industrial countries recover from the current recession and real interest rates begin to regain historically normal levels.

The recovery in debt prices since 1989 has been highly correlated with the fall in real and nominal interest rates in the industrial countries. This comovement is consistent with the possibility that expected payments by debtor governments are independent of market interest rates, so that the market value of the debt rises as expected payments are discounted at lower interest rates (Cohen and Portes, 1990; Dooley and Stone, 1993). But we do not have a good statistical model of debt prices that would discriminate among reasonable alternative hypotheses.

It is certainly possible that the important forces behind the recent return of many debtors to the markets could be quickly reversed. The argument developed here, however, suggests that the consequences of such a reversal might be less serious than in 1982 for the subset of debtor countries that have restructured their external bank debt. In particular, a fall in the expected value of the new debt would not generate the drawn-out conflict among creditors that characterized the previous experience. By the same logic, however, countries that still have a large stock of floating-rate bank debt, and arrears on that debt, could be very vulnerable to a new period of economic stagnation. It should be remembered that only a handful of countries have taken advantage of the improved climate since 1990 to reduce or transform a significant part of their debt.

Recent capital inflows to Brady Plan countries may well generate capital losses for investors, but it is unlikely that the debtor countries will suffer from a debt overhang. Under the Brady Plan, foreign investors have acquired domestic-currency claims on the developing countries. This might suggest that a relatively painless (from the debtors' point of view) currency depreciation would reduce the value of debt if expectations were to change. A qualification of this argument is that, in many cases, debtor governments have staked the credibility of their anti-inflation programs on maintaining a fixed nominal exchange rate. Moreover, the debtor governments have accumulated large reserve positions that would presumably be used to defend the exchange rate.

To reduce the chances that private debts will become socialized this time, some debtor governments have placed limits on their commercial banks' foreign borrowing or have imposed high reserve requirements against foreign deposits in order to limit the governments' implicit guarantees of such deposits. If the incentives for capital inflows are not reduced, however, foreign borrowing by domestic nonbanks will surely replace borrowing by banks.

Moreover, should foreign creditors call in loans, domestic banks might not be able to let firms with large domestic bank loans default to foreign lenders without calling into question their own claims on these firms. It thus appears at least possible that private domestic-currency debt could once again be quickly transformed into government liabilities effectively denominated in dollars because of the fixed exchange rate.

The important contrast to 1982 is that commercial banks in the industrial countries are not the lenders this time. Instead, investors, including residents of the debtor countries, have acquired claims on developing countries through a variety of nonbank financial intermediaries. These intermediaries include high-yield bond funds and emerging market-equity funds located in both the industrial and developing countries, and they are not likely to receive much sympathy from their creditor governments if losses on their holdings should occur. A tentative conclusion is that there will be winners and losers in this new round of debt accumulation in the developing countries but that recent inflows will not set the stage for a repeat of the 1982 crisis.

By contrast, debtor countries that still have large stocks of floating-rate bank debt outstanding are vulnerable to a continuation and intensification of the economic consequences of a decade-long failure to resolve the debt over-hang from the 1970s. In fact, attention should now focus on the majority of countries that have not taken advantage of the recent decline in interest rates or the availability of official credit to finance debt reduction. For these countries, voluntary, and therefore expensive (from the point of view of the creditor governments), debt-reduction deals remain the best solution to the debt problem.

The relative effectiveness of official lending for debt reduction and official lending to support economic-adjustment programs remains an open empirical question. In the face of considerable uncertainty about what went right for Brady Plan countries to date, it seems clear that the best strategy is to continue to support "voluntary" debt-reduction programs even if all the direct benefits go to the banks. I do not believe we have learned enough about the costs and benefits to advise debtors to hold out for better terms that might someday be available in the unlikely event that creditor governments decide to impose settlements on their commercial banks.

References

Arora, Vivek B., "Sovereign Debt: Survey of Some Theoretical and Policy Issues," International Monetary Fund Working Paper No. 93/56, Washington, D.C., International Monetary Fund, July 1993.

Bacha, Edmar L., "The Brady Plan and Beyond: New Debt Management Options for Latin America," Discussion Paper No. 257, Department of Economics, Pontifícia Universidade Católica, Rio de Janeiro, May 1991.

Borensztein, Eduardo, "Debt Overhang, Credit Rationing and Investment," *Journal of Development Economics*, 32 (April 1990), pp. 315–335.

Bulow, Jeremy, and Kenneth S. Rogoff, "The Buyback Boondoggle," *Brookings Papers on Economic Activity*, No. 2 (1988), pp. 675–698.

————, "A Constant Recontracting Model of Sovereign Debt," *Journal of Political Economy*, 97 (February 1989a), pp. 166–177.

————, "Multilateral Negotiations for Rescheduling Developing Country Debt," in Frenkel, Dooley, and Wickham, *Analytical Issues in Debt*, 1989b, pp. 194–207.

————, "Sovereign Buybacks: No Cure for Overhang," *Quarterly Journal of Economics*, 96 (June 1991), pp. 1219–1235.

Bulow, Jeremy, Kenneth S. Rogoff, and Alfonso S. Bevilaqua, "Official Creditor Seniority and Burden-Sharing in the Former Soviet Bloc," *Brookings Papers on Economic Activity*, No. 1 (1992), pp. 195–234.

Burns, Arthur F., *Reflections of an Economic Policy Maker: Speeches and Congressional Statements, 1969–1978*, Washington, D.C., American Enterprise Institute for Public Policy Research, 1978.

Calvo, Guillermo A., "A Delicate Equilibrium: Debt Relief and Default Penalties in an International Context," in Frenkel, Dooley, and Wickham, *Analytical Issues in Debt*, 1989, pp. 172–193.

Calvo, Guillermo A., Leonardo Leiderman, and Carmen M. Reinhart, "Capital Inflows and Real Exchange Rate Appreciation in Latin America: The Role of External Factors," *International Monetary Fund Staff Papers*, 40 (March 1993), pp. 108–151.

Claessens, Constantijn, "The Debt Laffer Curve: Some Estimates," *World Development*, 18 (December 1990), pp. 1671–1677.

Claessens, Constantijn, Ishac Diwan, and Eduardo Fernandez-Arias, "Recent Experience with Commercial Debt Reduction," Working Paper No. 995, Washington, D.C., World Bank, October 1992.

Cline, William R., *International Debt and the Stability of the World Economy*, Institute of International Economics, Washington, D.C., 1983.

Cohen, Daniel, *Private Lending to Sovereign States*, Cambridge, Mass., MIT Press, 1991.

————, "The Debt Crisis: A Postmortem," *NBER Macroeconomics Annual* (1992), pp. 64–114.

Cohen, Daniel, and Richard Portes, "The Price of LDC Debt," CEPR Discussion Paper No. 459, London, Centre for Economic Policy Research, June 1990.

Cooper, Richard N., *Economic Stabilization and Debt in Developing Countries*, Cambridge, Mass., MIT Press, 1992.

Corden, W. Max, "An International Debt Facility," in Frenkel, Dooley, and Wickham, *Analytical Issues in Debt*, 1989, pp. 151–171.

Devlin, Robert, Debt and Crisis in Latin America: *The Supply Side of the Story*, Princeton, N.J., Princeton University Press, 1989.

De Vries, Margaret Garritsen, "The International Monetary Fund, 1972–1978: Cooperation on Trial," Washington, D.C., International Monetary Fund, 1985.

Dooley, Michael P., "Country Specific Risk Premiums, Capital Flight and Net Investment Income Payments in Selected Developing Countries," Washington, D.C., International Monetary Fund, 1986.

————, "Market Valuation of External Debt," *Finance and Development*, 24 (March 1987), pp. 6–9.

————, "Buy-Backs and the Market Valuation of External Debt," *International Monetary Fund Staff Papers*, 35 (June 1988a), pp. 215–229.

————, "Self-Financed Buy-Backs and Asset Exchanges," *International Monetary Fund Staff Papers*, 35 (December 1988b), pp. 714–722.

————, "Debt Relief and Leveraged Buy-Outs," *International Economic Review*, 30 (February 1989), pp. 71–75.

————, "Is the Debt Crisis History?" University of California, Santa Cruz, March 1993, processed.

Dooley, Michael P., and W. Max Corden, "Issues in the Debt Strategy: An Overview," in Frenkel, Dooley, and Wickham, *Analytical Issues in Debt*, 1989, pp. 10–37.

Dooley, Michael P., Richard D. Haas, and Steven A. Symansky, "A Note on Burden Sharing Among Creditors," *International Monetary Fund Staff Papers*, 40 (March 1993), pp. 226–232.

Dooley, Michael P., William Helkie, John Underwood, and Ralph W. Tryon, "An Analysis of External Debt Positions of Eight Developing Countries through 1990," *Journal of Development Economics*, 21 (May 1986), pp. 283–318.

Dooley, Michael P., and Elhanan Helpman, "Tax Credits for Debt Reduction," *Journal of International Economics*, 32 (February 1992), pp. 165–177.

Dooley, Michael P., and Mark Stone, "Endogenous Creditor Seniority and External Debt Values," *International Monetary Fund Staff Papers*, 40 (June 1993), pp. 395–413.

Dooley, Michael P., and Lars E. O. Svensson, "Policy Inconsistency and External Debt Service," *Journal of International Money and Finance* (forthcoming 1994).

Dooley, Michael P., and Steven A. Symansky, "Comparing Menu Items: Methodological Considerations and Policy Issues," in Frenkel, Dooley, and Wickham, *Analytical Issues in Debt*, 1989, pp. 398–411.

Dornbusch, Rudiger, *The Road to Economic Recovery: Report of the Twentieth Century Fund Task Force on International Debt*, New York, Priority Press, 1989.

Eaton, Jonathan, and Mark Gersovitz, "Debt with Potential Repudiation: Theoretical and Empirical Analysis" *Review of Economic Studies*, 48 (April 1981), pp. 289–309.

Feldstein, Martin, "International Debt Service and Economic Growth—Some Simple Analytics," National Bureau of Economic Research Working Paper No. 2046, Cambridge, Mass., National Bureau of Economic Research, 1986.

Frenkel, Jacob A., Michael P. Dooley, and Peter Wickham, eds., *Analytical Issues in Debt*, Washington, D.C., International Monetary Fund, 1989.

Friedman, Irving, *The Emerging Role of Private Banks*, New York, Citicorp, 1977.

Froot, Kenneth A., "Buybacks, Exit Bonds, and the Optimality of Debt and Liquidity Relief," *International Economic Review*, 30 (February 1989), pp. 49–70.

Guttentag, Jack M., and Richard J. Herring, *Disaster Myopia in International Banking*, Essays in International Finance No. 164, Princeton, N.J., Princeton University, International Finance Section, September 1986.

Helpman, Elhanan, "Voluntary Debt Reduction: Incentives and Welfare," *International Monetary Fund Staff Papers*, 36 (September 1989), pp. 580–611.

————, "The Simple Analytics of Debt Equity Swaps," *American Economic Review*, 79 (June 1990), pp. 440–451.

International Monetary Fund (IMF), *World Economic Outlook*, Washington, D.C., International Monetary Fund, various issues.

Kenen, Peter, "A Bailout for Banks," *New York Times*, March 6, 1983.

————, "Organizing Debt Relief: The Need for a New Institution," *Journal of Economic Perspectives*, 4 (Winter 1990), pp. 7–18.

Kereken, John H., Discussion, *Brookings Papers on Economic Activity*, No. 2 (1977), pp. 505–508.

Kletzer, Kenneth, "Asymmetries of Information and LDC Borrowing with Sovereign Risk," *Economic Journal* (London), 94 (June 1984), pp. 287–307.

Krueger, Anne O., "Resolving the Debt Crisis and Restoring Developing Countries' Creditworthiness," *Carnegie-Rochester Conference Series on Public Policy*, 30 (Spring 1989), pp. 75–113.

Krugman, Paul R., "International Debt Strategies in an Uncertain World," in Gordon W. Smith and John T. Cuddington, eds., *International Debt and the Developing Countries*, Washington, D.C., World Bank, 1985.

————, "Financing vs. Forgiving a Debt Overhang: Some Analytical Notes," *Journal of Development Economics*, 29 (December 1988), pp. 253–268.

————, "Market Based Debt-Reduction Schemes," in Frenkel, Dooley, and Wickham, *Analytical Issues in Debt*, 1989, pp. 258–278.

Sachs, Jeffrey D., *Theoretical Issues in International Borrowing*, Princeton Studies in International Finance No. 54, Princeton, N.J., Princeton University, International Finance Section, July 1984.

————, "The Debt Overhang of Developing Countries," in Jorge Braga de Macedo and Ronald Findlay, eds., *Debt, Growth, and Stabilization: Essays in Memory of Carlos Dias Alejandro*, Oxford, Blackwell, 1988.

————, *New Approaches to the Latin American Debt Crisis*, Essays in International Finance No. 174, Princeton, N.J., Princeton University, International Finance Section, July 1989.

Solomon, Robert, "A Perspective on the Debt of Developing Countries," *Brookings Papers on Economic Activity*, No. 2 (1977), pp. 479–510.

U.S. Congress, Senate Committee on Finance, Subcommittee on International Debt, *Hearings on the Implementation of the Brady Plan*, 101st Congress, 2d Session, 1990.

Van Wijnbergen, Sweder, "Mexico's External Debt Restructuring in 1989/90: An Economic Analysis," *Economic Policy*, 12 (April 1991), pp. 13–56.

Volcker, Paul A., and Toyoo Gyohten, *Changing Fortunes: The World's Money and the Decline of American Supremacy*, New York, Time Books, 1992.

Wallich, Henry C., "LDC Debt . . . to Worry or Not to Worry," *Challenge*, 24 (September/October 1981), pp. 28–34.

————, *Central Banks as Regulators and Lenders of Last Resort in an International Context: A View from the United States*, New York, St. Martin's, 1987.

Weintraub, Robert E., "International Lending by U.S. Banks: Practices, Problems, and Policies," George Mason University, August 1983, processed.

Wellons, Phillip A., *Passing the Buck: Banks, Governments, and Third World Debt*, Boston, Harvard Business School Press, 1987.

Whitman, Marina von Neumann, "Bridging the Gap," *Foreign Policy*, 30 (Spring 1978), pp. 148–156.

IV

STABILIZATION AND LIBERALIZATION

8

Trade Liberalization in Disinflation

DANI RODRIK

1 Introduction

Respectable economists are quick to disavow claims to knowing much about the appropriate sequencing of economic reforms. Economic theory gives very little guidance, it is often said, about the dynamics of the transition away from highly distorted, inflationary situations. One enduring piece of conventional wisdom, however, is the desirability of achieving macroeconomic stabilization *before* the removal of microeconomic distortions. A concise and representative statement to this effect is made by Corbo and Fischer:

> In countries with acute macroeconomic problems, structural reforms designed to increase efficiency and restore growth, whose own efficiency depends on a predictable macroeconomic situation, should be initiated only when sufficient progress has been made in reducing the macroeconomic imbalances. . . . The importance of this sequence—first reforms oriented mainly towards reducing severe macroeconomic imbalances and then reforms aimed at improving the allocation of resources and the restoration of growth—has become increasingly clear with experience. At the same time, the approach has strong analytical underpinnings: macroeconomic instability in the form of high and variable inflation and of balance-of-payments crises reduces the benefits of structural reforms aimed at improving the allocation of resources through changes in incentives—benefits that generally are transmitted through changes in relative prices. (Corbo, Fischer, and Webb, 1992, p. 7)

This advice was completely disregarded in some of the most important reforms during the last decade—in Bolivia and Mexico in 1985, Poland in 1990, and Argentina in 1991, for example. In these countries and quite a few others, radical trade-liberalization measures were put in place, or existing programs speeded up, *in conjunction with* macroeconomic stabilization packages. So far at least, it is not evident that the policymakers in these countries were mistaken in ignoring conventional wisdom.[1]

I am grateful to Giuseppe Bertola, Max Corden, Rudiger Dornbusch, Michael Gavin, and, especially, Susan Collins for very helpful comments on the conference version of this paper, and to Leilynne Lau for excellent research assistance.

[1] The conventional wisdom is in part based on reforms in Argentina, Chile, and Uruguay

There are essentially three arguments why it makes sense to postpone trade liberalization until disinflation takes root. First, as mentioned by Corbo and Fischer, the relative-price variability that typically characterizes high-inflation environments is not conducive to the realization of the efficiency benefits generally expected from the removal of price distortions. Second, trade liberalization requires a reduction in trade taxes, which may conflict with the need to shore up government revenues during stabilization. Third, the liberalization will typically require a compensating devaluation to protect the trade balance and domestic employment, whereas the success of stabilization may hinge on a fixed, or at least stable, exchange rate. For useful discussions that expand these arguments, see Mussa (1987) and Sachs (1987).

Closer examination suggests that the first two of these arguments are not particularly damaging to the liberalization-cum-stabilization strategy. The low likelihood of efficiency gains materializing in a high-inflation environment may weaken the case for liberalization, but it does not reverse it. If policymakers find it politically expedient to package the trade reforms alongside the stabilization measures, as they apparently have done, the fact that the benefits will take some time to show up is no argument for delaying the liberalization. With respect to fiscal impact, a serious trade liberalization is as likely to increase revenues as it is to reduce them: the elimination of tariff exemptions and of quantitative restrictions, and the ensuing import boom, may more than outweigh the reduction in (statutory) tariffs. The practical importance of removing exemptions can be grasped by considering that actual import-tax revenues stood at no more than 2 percent of import value in Argentina prior to the recent reforms, despite an average statutory tariff rate of above 30 percent.[2] A recent study by Greenaway and Milner (1991) finds no evident relation between trade reform and the amount of revenue collected from trade taxes.

The most serious objection by far to trade liberalization is therefore that having to do with exchange-rate management. The problem arises from the constraint that the exchange rate can be used in only one of two ways, *either* as an instrument to achieve a real target (the trade balance or employment) *or* as a nominal anchor for the domestic price level (Corden, 1991). Under the first strategy, exchange-rate policy is responsive to developments in the economy, and policy *follows* wage and price setting; under the second, the exchange rate is precommitted, and government policy *leads* the private sector.

In practice, there may be ways to alleviate the conflict. For example, a

---

during the late 1970s. The experience in these countries with liberalization accompanied by simultaneous stabilization is now routinely judged to have been a failure (*World Development*, Special Issue, August 1985).

[2] These figures are from GATT (1992a). See also Pritchett and Sethi (1992) on the difference between statutory tariff rates and trade-tax collections. It should be noted that the presence of exemptions does not necessarily reduce the efficiency costs of protection: their discretionary and arbitrary implementation generates a great deal of uncertainty and rent-seeking.

maxi-devaluation at the outset of the stabilization (as in Bolivia in 1985 and Poland in 1990) can provide some extra margin of competitiveness to help with the tough times to come. Once inflation is under control, moreover, a downward crawl in the nominal exchange rate can be instituted with less fear of inflation. These are palliatives, which do not entirely solve the problem. Unless the currency is inconvertible and domestic price setters have already internalized the more depreciated parallel exchange rate, a maxi-devaluation will necessarily raise the price level and be inflationary under conditions of imperfect credibility and staggered contracts.[3] Giving up the nominal anchor is always a risky option in countries with long inflationary experience. The Bolivian case, discussed below, is a good example.

In most of the successful stabilizations of the past decade, and certainly in all of those involving triple-digit or higher levels of inflation, fixing the exchange rate has played an important role in coordinating expectations around a low-inflation equilibrium and in achieving a quick break in the inflationary cycle. The exchange rate, often along with other nominal variables, has been used as a nominal anchor. Although the importance of fixing the exchange rate to conquer inflation can be debated,[4] the more relevant point is that policymakers *have* chosen this strategy and that this choice has left the exchange rate unavailable for maintaining external competitiveness.

This choice would not be of great consequence if nominal wages were fully flexible. In the absence of such flexibility, however, a trade liberalization has to be coupled with a devaluation to offset its negative impact on the trade balance and on employment. If the devaluation cannot be undertaken for fear of complicating the stabilization, trade liberalization will simply result in overvaluation. Indeed, this overvaluation will be particularly costly to the economy, for it will *aggravate* the real appreciation that will take place even in the best of circumstances, because domestic and world inflation will necessarily converge only gradually.

This risk is not a hypothetical one. Overvaluation of the currency is one of the most important reasons for the failure and abandonment of liberalization. Krueger (1978, p. 230), in her review of the evidence for the well-known National Bureau of Economic Research project on trade liberalization, found that twelve out of thirteen failures occurred because the real exchange rate became too overvalued "to permit sustained liberalization." The more recent

[3] A devaluation aimed at unifying the official and black-market rates can also be inflationary. The larger-than-expected jump in the Polish price level in early 1990 has often been attributed to a maxi-devaluation judged by many to have been excessive.

[4] Anne Krueger (1978, pp. 231–237), for one, has argued that a sliding-peg strategy for the exchange rate need not be incompatible with the goal of reducing inflation. She cites South Korea and Brazil in 1964 as two success stories of simultaneous trade-regime liberalization and inflation control in the context of a sliding peg. For a more recent skeptical view, see Kenen (1992). Edwards (1992) presents a broad discussion on the pros and cons of using the exchange rate as a nominal anchor.

nineteen-country World Bank study organized by Michaely, Papageorgiou, and Choksi (1991, p. 196) reaches the even stronger conclusion that a real-exchange-rate depreciation "appears to be almost a necessary condition for at least partial survival of a liberalization policy." These authors find that none of the liberalizations that took place during a real appreciation was fully sustained (see their table 13.4).

The present discussion revisits this policy dilemma by focusing on recent liberalizations in Latin America. The first half of the chapter briefly reviews the evidence from the last fifteen years. It asks if trade reform has created economies that are more open and if it has complicated macroeconomic stabilization and engendered doubts regarding its sustainability when undertaken in the midst of macroeconomic instability. The answer in both instances is yes.

The second half of the chapter suggests that the theoretical case for the existence of a policy dilemma in exchange-rate management may be weaker than we usually suppose. It shows, in particular, that, in the context of a standard model, a credible nominal anchor—a necessary condition for the success of an exchange-rate-based stabilization—leads to the disappearance of the nominal-wage rigidity that lies at the root of the dilemma. There is, in theory at least, a way out.

The argument that underlies the last point is the following. Trade liberalization has to be accompanied by devaluation when nominal wages are rigid, but nominal wages are most likely to be rigid (that is, predetermined with respect to the nominal exchange rate and monetary policy more generally) when policymakers cannot or do not commit credibly. Therefore, a commitment to a pegged exchange rate can, if credible, actually solve rather than intensify the potential conflict between trade liberalization and exchange-rate stability.[5] "If credible," however, carries a big "if." I shall discuss credibility issues briefly in the penultimate section of the chapter.

2 Recent Trade Reforms and Their Consequences

A synopsis of recent Latin American trade reforms is presented in Table 8.1. To underscore the point made above regarding the unorthodox sequencing commonly selected, the table shows the inflation rate prevailing at the time the reforms were initiated. I shall focus on five countries: Chile, Bolivia, Mexico, Argentina, and Brazil. The first two have the longest-running significant trade-liberalization programs on the continent; the last three are important because of their size (de Melo and Dhar [1992] give a recent overview of trade reforms in the region; Rodrik [1992a, 1992b] reviews the reforms in Eastern Europe and elsewhere).

[5] I am shamelessly borrowing language here from Peter Kenen, who suggested that I include a verbal explanation of the model at this point of the paper.

TABLE 8.1

Trade Liberalization in Selected Latin American Countries

Country and Start of Program	Inflation Rate at Start	Maximum Tariff		Number of Brackets		Average Tariff	
		Initial	Current	Initial	Current	Initial	Current
Argentina 1987	132	115	20	n.a.	4	43	9
Bolivia 1985	11,805	150	10	n.a.	1	12	10
Brazil 1988	683	105	60	29	7	51	17[a]
Chile 1973	350	220	11	57	1	94	11
Mexico 1985	58	100	20	10	5	24	10[b]
Peru 1990	7,482	110	25	53	3	66	15 & 25[c]
Venezuela 1989	84	135	20[d]	41	6	35	9.5

Sources: Economic Commission for Latin America and the Caribbean (on the basis of country figures); U.S. Department of Commerce; IMF, *International Financial Statistics.*

Note: Nontariff barriers include:

Argentina: In 1987–88, the value of industrial output subject to restrictions was reduced from 62 to 18 percent. In 1989–90, the remaining licensing restrictions were eliminated. Liberalization began in 1987 and accelerated in 1989.

Bolivia: All prohibitions and license requirements on imports were abolished, except for controls on sugar and wheat and on goods affecting health and endangering safety.

Brazil: In 1990, the list of prohibited imports was abolished, but importation of forty-seven computer-related products was forbidden until October 1992, and local-content rules for intermediate and capital goods were maintained. Tariffs began to be restructured in 1988–89.

Chile: Quantitative import restrictions were eliminated in the 1970s, except for those on second-hand automotive vehicles. The uniform tariff of 10 percent was raised to 20 percent in 1983, and to 35 percent in 1984, in response to a balance-of-payments crisis. It was then reduced in successive stages to 15 percent in 1988 and to 11 percent in 1991.

Mexico: Coverage of import licenses was reduced from 92.2 percent of production in June 1985 to 17.9 percent in December 1990, and government import prices were eliminated. Prior licenses were maintained for some agricultural and food products, petroleum and its byproducts, and some products used in industrial-development programs.

Peru: Licenses, controls, import permits, quotas, and prohibitions were eliminated in March 1991. The program began in August 1990, when the maximum tariff of 50 percent was established. It went further in March 1991, when the maximum tariff was reduced to 25 percent for consumer goods and 15 percent for the rest.

Venezuela: The number of headings subject to restriction was reduced from 2,204 in 1988 to 200 currently. The tariff-reduction program, initially to be completed in 1993, was accelerated in March 1992.

[a] Fourteen in July 1993.

[b] Varies.

[c] Two-tiered system.

[c] Except car imports, which are at 25.

Chile

Chile's trade reform, beginning in 1973, constitutes the longest-running experiment with openness in Latin America, and it has had an important demonstration effect on other countries in the region. Between 1973 and 1979, quantitative restrictions were entirely eliminated and tariffs were reduced in stages down to a uniform rate of 10 percent. Following the debt and financial crisis of 1982, which hit Chile particularly hard, tariffs were raised, first to 20 percent (in 1983) and then to 35 percent (in 1984), the highest rate allowed under Chile's GATT binding. By 1988, the uniform tariff was down to 15 percent, and it was further reduced to 11 percent in 1991. Aside from the uniformity of tariffs and their comparatively low level, the Chilean trade regime is distinguished by an institutional framework that renders the exercise of discretionary protectionism (over time and across goods) very difficult (GATT, 1991).

Figure 8.1 shows why Chile is now the envy of Latin America. Chile's trade has more than doubled in dollar terms since the lows of 1983 and 1984. Moreover, the expansion of trade has been a balanced one, with imports *and* exports growing at commensurate rates. The path of the real exchange rate (also shown in Figure 8.1) yields the reason.[6] From 1982 to 1985, the Chilean government was able to engineer a real depreciation of about 50 percent through successive devaluations. In the following three years (1986 to 1989), the real rate was maintained as roughly constant. Thus, a highly supportive exchange-rate policy provided an ideal environment for the liberalization.

This textbook performance was enabled in turn by the absence of a protracted inflation problem in Chile. The fiscal imbalances that developed during the 1982–83 crisis, brought about by the socialization of the insolvent financial sector, were quickly reversed. There was consequently no need to use the exchange rate as a nominal anchor, and so exchange-rate policy could be targeted on the competitiveness of the tradables sector. It is only since 1990, with the trade boom (as well as a boom in private investment) safely under way, that the government has allowed the exchange rate to lag behind domestic prices (Figure 8.1).

Bolivia

Bolivia's trade liberalization is more recent than Chile's, but it is equally impressive. A major trade liberalization was implemented in August 1985

---

[6] The real exchange rate in this and the following figures is calculated as the ratio of the nominal exchange rate (national currency per U.S. dollar) multiplied by the U.S. wholesale price index (WPI) to the relevant country's domestic WPI (where available; consumer price index [CPI] otherwise). All data come from the IMF, *International Financial Statistics*, unless otherwise specified.

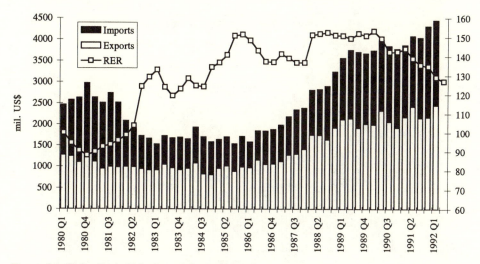

Figure 8.1 Chile: Trade Volume and the Real Exchange Rate

alongside the stabilization program that ended the hyperinflation. The unification of the exchange rate as part of the stabilization eliminated a huge implicit
export tax. In addition, practically all quantitative restrictions were lifted and
the maximum tariff was lowered to 20 percent. In 1991, a further reduction in
tariffs took place, with a 10 percent rate applying to all imports except capital
goods, which were subject to a tariff of 5 percent.

Bolivia is often portrayed as a case in which the economy has responded
very sluggishly to structural reforms. A casual look at the dollar value of
Bolivia's trade (Figure 8.2) would seem to support this view: there has been
only a modest increase in exports and in the overall trade volume since the
liberalization-cum-stabilization of August 1985. This modest increase, however, has taken place during a period when Bolivia's export prices tumbled by
50 percent, mainly because world tin prices collapsed (Figure 8.2). Moreover,
nontraditional exports have been growing at double-digit rates since 1987 (de
Melo and Dhar, 1992, p. 22).

Exchange-rate policy in Bolivia illustrates well the conflict between the
real-target and nominal-anchor strategies.[7] The textbook prescription to a
country experiencing a large, apparently permanent, terms-of-trade deterioration would be a devaluation. Yet Bolivian authorities have been loath to
undertake a maxi-devaluation for fear that it might reignite inflationary expectations. Exchange-rate policy has consequently not been used to counter the
effects of either the drop in export prices or the 1991 liberalization.

---

[7] The Bolivian exchange rate is determined in a currency auction and so is nominally free to
fluctuate. In practice, however, the institutional framework of the auction allows the government
considerable discretion in setting the rate (Dominguez and Rodrik, 1990).

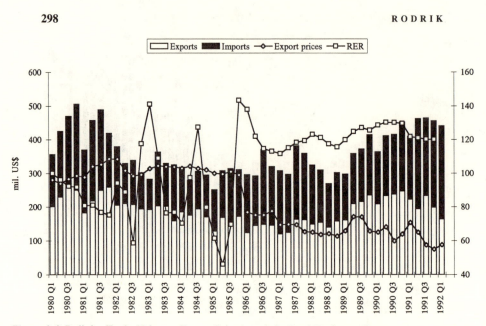

Figure 8.2 Bolivia: Trade Volume, Export Prices, and the Real Exchange Rate

Mexico

Mexican trade liberalization began in 1985 but was accelerated in late 1987 as part of the Economic Solidarity Pact negotiated between the government, labor, and employers. Since then, quantitative restrictions on imports have been substantially eliminated, and the maximum tariff has been progressively reduced from 100 to 20 percent, with the average tariff coming down to 11 percent by 1991. In 1986, Mexico joined the GATT, and the Mexican government looks at the successful completion of the North American Free Trade Agreement (NAFTA) as an important final step in the institutionalization of its reforms.

Since the Economic Solidarity Pact, the Mexican peso has been targeted firmly on the domestic price level despite the substantial trade liberalization that has taken place. Thanks to a serious fiscal adjustment, the strategy has worked in reducing inflation to below 20 percent. Figure 8.3 illustrates the consequences for trade and the real exchange rate. Since the end of 1987, the real value of the peso has appreciated steadily, imports have more than tripled, and the trade surplus has turned into an awesome deficit. Taking the total value of trade as the appropriate indicator of success, we can say that the trade reform has achieved a remarkable opening up of the economy. Microeconometric studies have already documented the positive consequences of this opening up for domestic price-cost margins and, less solidly, for productive efficiency (Grether, 1992; Tybout and Westbrook, 1992). Trade liberalization has, thus, clearly "worked" in the sense of resource allocation. Without the confidence engendered by the presence of NAFTA on the horizon, however,

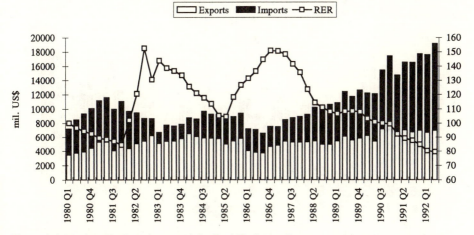

Figure 8.3 Mexico: Trade Volume and the Real Exchange Rate

the accompanying real appreciation would have made this liberalization a prime candidate for reversal. Even with NAFTA, it remains to be seen whether domestic costs will fall sufficiently to validate a real value of the peso that is now higher than on the eve of the 1982 crisis. In all likelihood, Mexican policymakers will face the tough task of generating a real depreciation without upsetting existing agreements with labor and without destabilizing the price level.[8]

Argentina

Argentina has gone through several cycles of liberalization and protection. The liberalization that started in 1976 was undone with the onset of the debt crisis in 1982, at which point quantitative restrictions and licensing requirements were reimposed. By 1986, half of Argentine production was protected by import quotas, import-licensing requirements were ubiquitous, and tariffs that were already high were augmented by surcharges and additional import taxes. Special exemptions and rebates, however, prevented the collection of most of the import taxes (GATT, 1992a, Vol. 1, p. 7). These restrictions were substantially eliminated beginning in 1987. By mid-1992, import licensing had been entirely abolished, the maximum tariff was brought down to 22 percent, and quantitative restrictions were virtually eliminated (except for the automotive sector). The current trade regime essentially consists of a three-tier tariff schedule, with rates set at 5 percent, 13 percent, and 22 percent.[9]

[8] Dornbusch (1993) examines the sustainability of Mexico's exchange-rate stance.
[9] The GATT Trade Policy Review Mechanism (TPRM) report on Argentina mentions that

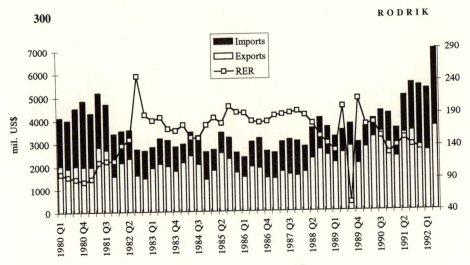

Figure 8.4 Argentina: Trade Volume and the Real Exchange Rate

Figure 8.4 shows a moderate increase in Argentine exports subsequent to the onset of liberalization in 1987. More striking, however, is the import boom that has taken place since the Cavallo stabilization in 1991. Imports from the United States have increased at an astounding annual rate of 65 percent during the two years following the stabilization, whereas exports have stagnated. The immediate culprit is the exchange rate once again. The Convertibility Law of April 1991 has fixed the value of the Argentine currency (renamed "peso" after January 1992) against the dollar. Despite the dramatic reduction in inflation, now at single-digit levels annually, a creeping real appreciation has been the inevitable result. Amid industrialists' complaints regarding loss of competitiveness, the government has already experimented with a simulated devaluation by instituting a scheme combining export subsidies with import surcharges.

Brazil

In Brazil, a complex, discretionary, and highly protective trade regime was in place until the late 1980s. Trade reform was begun in 1988 and was greatly accelerated in early 1990 in conjunction with the first Collor stabilization plan, when virtually all nontariff barriers were lifted (GATT, 1992b). Brazil's infamous restrictions on computer and software imports were completely liberalized by October 1992. Export licensing and taxes had been largely elimi-

---

there have been fourteen tariff reforms since 1987, not all of which have been in a downward direction. In July 1991, for example, the duty on electronics and automotive items was raised to 35 percent (to be lowered again to 22 percent on January 1, 1992).

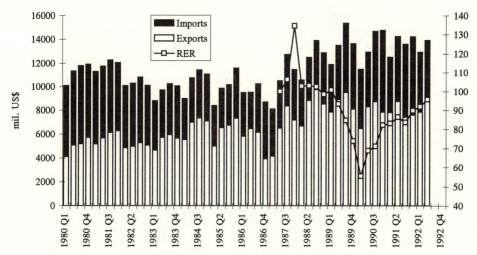

Figure 8.5 Brazil: Trade Volume and the Real Exchange Rate

nated. And the average tariff was down from 51 percent in 1987 to 21 percent in January 1992, with further reductions scheduled. Brazil has offered to bind its tariffs at 35 percent in the context of the Uruguay Round (the same level as the Chilean binding), but only for industrial goods.

Unlike the other countries discussed above, Brazil is continuing to struggle with extremely high inflation (of more than 20 percent a month). Exchange-rate policy has gone through different phases, targeting the price level at some points and competitiveness at others—shifts that have caused widely fluctuating cycles in the real exchange rate (Figure 8.5). Brazil's trade volume has expanded noticeably since the liberalization (also Figure 8.5) but, like the rest of the economy, remains unstable.

To summarize the evidence, trade liberalization has clearly been successful in the sense of increasing overall trade. The strongest gains, however, have been recorded for countries in which macroeconomic instability has been substantially reduced. Moreover, whether exports have taken off as rapidly as imports has depended heavily on the exchange-rate stance. In Mexico (since 1988) and Argentina (since 1991), the use of the exchange rate as a nominal anchor has led to significant real appreciations, import booms, and potentially unsustainable trade deficits.

3 Trade Policy and Disinflation with Endogenous Nominal-Wage Rigidity

Policymakers in Latin America have not been entirely oblivious to the risk of denying themselves the use of the exchange rate as a tool for enhancing competitiveness. From their perspective, however, the dilemma has looked less compelling. This is because the now prevailing view among policymakers is that chronic inflation is deep down the result of insufficient discipline exerted by a weak, accommodating government on wage and price setters in the private sector. Bruno (1991, p. 4) writes that "although the origin of high chronic inflation, like hyperinflation, lies in the existence of a large public-sector deficit, the quasi stability of the dynamic process comes from an inherent inertia strongly linked with a high degree of indexation or accommodation of the key nominal magnitudes (wages, the exchange rate, and the monetary aggregates) to the lagged movements of the price level." If this view is correct, it follows that a credible commitment not to accommodate, exemplified by an exchange-rate commitment, should not only take care of inflation, but also remove the nominal rigidities that require the use of devaluation for purposes of competitiveness. In other words, the exchange-rate dilemma may be illusory when nominal rigidities and the inflationary bias both have the same root: a weak government facing cartelized labor and business groups.

Opening up, then, should also help disinflation, because it creates competition and imposes market discipline on cartelized groups. This lumping-together of the sources of microeconomic and macroeconomic distortions is quite common. The official Argentine view is that "unlike previous experiments in adjustment and stabilization, the current strategy aims to increase the overall efficiency of the economy through the liberalization of all the available variables, so that the *reduction of costs* as a result of the ongoing structural transformations will eliminate the recurrent fiscal deficits as well as the handicaps borne by the production sector in terms of international competition" (GATT, 1992a, Vol. 2, p. 15, emphasis added). The Brazilians state that "openness, transparency and deregulation . . . are the main features of an economic program aimed at eliminating inflation, increasing investments and ultimately resuming sustained economic development in Brazil" (GATT, 1992b, p. 1).

From this perspective, one can perhaps understand why the prospect of overvaluation due to liberalization is not viewed as an independent source of risk when compared to the prospect that the nominal anchor itself may not hold. In view of the primacy of the concern with inflation, the former would certainly appear to be of less consequence.

I shall briefly sketch out a model to clarify the links between nominal-wage rigidity and the credibility of an exchange-rate commitment. The basic model is a familiar one from the literature on time inconsistency. The only new wrinkle is the differentiation between the import-competing and export-oriented sectors of the economy and the incorporation of a tariff. The model's basic structure is given by the following four equations:

$$W = -\gamma\pi^2 - (l - l^*)^2 , \qquad (1)$$

$$U = U(w - \pi, 1) , \qquad (2)$$

$$\pi = \alpha(e + t) + (1 - \alpha)e = e + \alpha t , \qquad (3)$$

$$l = l^* + \phi(e - w) + \phi\lambda t . \qquad (4)$$

The first equation shows the objective function of the government. It is a conventional quadratic-loss function defined over prices (π) and employment (l), with γ denoting the relative weight placed on inflation and l^* denoting the government's employment target. Equation (2) is the general formulation of labor's objective function and shows that workers care about their real-wage levels as well as their level of employment. Equation (3) is the definition of the CPI, with e denoting the nominal exchange rate and import-competing products receiving a weight α and exportables, a weight $1 - \alpha$. Note the role of import protection, captured by the parameter t. Foreign prices of importables and exportables are taken to be exogenous, so their logarithmic levels are fixed at zero with no loss of generality.

Economy-wide labor demand is given by equation (4). To see how this equation is derived, note, first, that (inverse) product real wages are $e - w$ and $e + t - w$ in the two sectors. Let each sector have a common elasticity of labor demand with respect to the product wage (ϕ) and let the share of employment in the import-competing sector be γ. The result is the labor-demand function expressed in equation (4), with prices normalized so that l^* is the full-employment level. I ignore the effect on aggregate labor demand of any changes in allocative efficiency brought about by trade liberalization.

I compare two situations in this model, one in which the government sets the exchange rate after the nominal wage is selected (*discretion*) and another in which the government makes a credible exchange-rate commitment prior to wage setting (*commitment*). Because our interest lies in the way that trade policy affects equilibrium outcomes under these two scenarios, I take t to be predetermined relative to e and w in both cases.

Discretion

Under discretion, the government maximizes its objective function (1) with respect to e, taking w as given. Substituting (3) and (4) into (1) and solving for the first-order condition yields

$$e = \frac{\phi^2}{\gamma + \phi^2} w - \frac{\alpha\gamma + \lambda\phi^2}{\gamma + \phi^2} t . \qquad (5)$$

Increases in wages are accommodated by a compensating depreciation of the currency so as to reduce the impact on employment. The accommodation is

less than full, however, as long as the government attaches a cost to the inflationary consequences (that is, as long as $\gamma > 0$). A tariff reduction, in turn, is
also met with a depreciation, again to dampen the effect on employment.

A useful simplification at this point is to assume that the import-competing
sector's share in aggregate employment matches its share in the CPI, so that $\lambda = \alpha$. This reduces (5) to

$$e = \mu w - \lambda t , \qquad (6)$$

with

$$0 < \mu \equiv \frac{\phi^2}{\gamma + \phi^2} < 1 .$$

Equation (6) generates the conventional prescription for exchange-rate management in the presence of nominal-wage rigidity—that is, match trade liberalization with a compensating devaluation.

Workers, in turn, set w by taking the decision rule expressed in (6) into
account and maximizing (2). In view of (6), real wages and employment are
given by

$$W - \pi = (1 - \mu)w , \qquad (7)$$

$$l = l^* - \phi(1 - \mu)w . \qquad (8)$$

Because t does not enter into either expression, we can immediately conclude
that, in the discretionary equilibrium, the nominal wage is rigid with respect
to the tariff. Wage setters disregard trade liberalization. The reason is that they
know the exchange rate will be set so as to insulate them from its effects.
Furthermore, this is true regardless of the specific functional form taken by
$U(w - \pi,l)$.[10]

What we have shown is that, when the government cannot credibly commit
to a fixed exchange rate, the nominal wage will indeed be rigid in the sense
that it will be unresponsive to changes in commercial policy (*even though* no
money illusion or long-term contracting has been assumed), and it will thus be
optimal for the government to devalue the currency whenever it liberalizes
trade.

Commitment

Suppose now that the government can credibly commit (through a convertibility law as in Argentina, for example) to a fixed exchange rate. Without loss
of generality, let $e = 0$. How is the nominal wage set in this case?

---

[10] This conclusion, however, is sensitive to the equality between λ and α. When these two

Because there is no feedback from the exchange rate, the levels of the real wage and of employment are now given by

$$w - \pi = w - \lambda t , \tag{9}$$

$$l = l^* - \phi(w - \lambda t) . \tag{10}$$

By inspection, we can see that, in this case, real wages and employment are both affected by t (the first negatively, and the second positively), holding w constant. Further, because $w - \lambda t$ enters (9) and (10) in exactly the same way, we know that the optimal response of nominal wages to changes in trade policy will be given by

$$\left. \frac{dw}{dt} \right|_{\text{commitment}} = \lambda .$$

A reduction in tariffs will be matched by a proportionate reduction in nominal wages, with the proportion equaling the share of the import-competing sector in the economy. Once again, this result is independent of the functional form taken by $U(.)$. Thus, under a credibly fixed exchange rate, the flexibility of nominal wages is regained.

To get closed-form solutions for variables of interest and to carry out a more explicit comparison of outcomes under the two scenarios, we need to assume a specific functional form for workers' utility function. If this function is given by

$$U = \beta \log(w - \pi) + \log l , \tag{11}$$

with β capturing the relative weight placed on real wages, we can obtain the solutions shown in Table 8.2.

Several points about these results are notable.[11] First, the real variables (employment and real wages) are invariant to the exchange-rate regime. This is the usual policy-ineffectiveness result. Second, there is an inflationary bias under discretion, because the government is encouraged to push employment above the level regarded as desirable by wage setters. This is also the standard result.[12] Third, nominal wages are unresponsive to a change in trade policy under discretion but responsive to it under commitment. This is the point

---

parameters are not equal to each other, the wage-setting rule will depend on the level of t. However, $\lambda = \alpha$ would seem to be an appropriate benchmark.

[11] Note that we can think of all price variables in the model as being expressed in rates of change, so that we can talk about inflation rather than changes in the price level.

[12] An inflationary bias under discretion also exists when the government is motivated by seigniorage revenues (and not by the short-run Phillips curve as in this model). Bruno (1991) discusses this.

TABLE 8.2
Solutions for Variables of Interest

Variable	Under Discretion	Under Commitment
Nominal wages	$\dfrac{\beta}{\phi(1 + \beta)(1 - \mu)}\, l^*$	$\dfrac{\beta}{\phi(1 + \beta)}\, l^* + \lambda t$
Employment	$\dfrac{1}{1 + \beta}\, l^*$	$\dfrac{1}{1 + \beta}\, l^*$
Real wages	$\dfrac{\beta}{\phi(1 + \beta)}\, l^*$	$\dfrac{\beta}{\phi(1 + \beta)}\, l^*$
Inflation	$\dfrac{\mu\beta}{\phi(1 + \beta)(1 - \mu)}\, l^*$	λt
Nominal exchange rate	$\dfrac{\mu\beta}{\phi(1 + \beta)(1 - \mu)}\, l^* - \lambda t$	0

made above, and it shows that stickiness of the nominal wage is endogenous to the policy regime. Fourth, the aggregate price level is a function of the tariff under commitment, but it is independent of the tariff under discretion. This implies that trade liberalization can serve as a credible disinflation strategy only when a credible exchange-rate commitment exists. In the absence of such a commitment, the beneficial impact on prices of trade liberalization is undone by the depreciation necessitated by nominal-wage rigidity.

To summarize, what this framework has shown is that the circumstances under which a successful exchange-rate-based stabilization will work— that is, conditions of credibility, which will in turn depend partly on fiscal fundamentals—are the same as those under which nominal-wage rigidity will disappear endogenously. Consequently, provided the nominal anchor is credible, the trade-off between using the exchange rate for disinflation and using it for competitiveness disappears also. In addition, trade liberalization can buy added disinflation at no cost to employment or the trade balance.

How do we interpret the evidence discussed earlier in light of the present model? In particular, can we put a more optimistic gloss on the real-exchange-rate appreciation experienced by the liberalizing and stabilizing countries? The answer is "not necessarily." The real exchange rate is the inverse of the real-wage rate in the present model and should therefore remain unaffected by the switch to an exchange-rate commitment. Strictly speaking, the observed real appreciation is inconsistent with the implication that nominal-wage rigidity will disappear in a successful stabilization.

Two more optimistic possibilities need to be discussed, however. First, in the real world, the exchange-rate commitment may lack full credibility at the outset and may gain credibility as time passes. Real appreciation is a feature shared by all exchange-rate-based stabilizations, whether trade liberalization accompanies the stabilization or not (see, for example, Kiguel and Liviatan, 1988; Végh, 1992). Consequently, the disappearance of nominal-wage rigidity can be expected to take some time, too.

In this interpretation, the observed real appreciation is a *temporary* one that will eventually reverse itself as the change in policy regime takes root. This view resuscitates the trade-off between the nominal-anchor and the real-target strategies but confines it to the short term. Any country with a sufficient cushion of foreign reserves would be able to survive the trade-off. The experience of the 1980s is perhaps too recent to provide any clues as to whether this process is in motion or not, and earlier cases of exchange-rate-based stabilizations are unclear tests because of complicating features: the Argentine *tablita* stabilization from 1979 to 1981 was undone by lack of fiscal discipline, and the Chilean stabilization from 1976 to 1981, by backward indexation of wages.

A second possibility is that the observed real appreciations simply reflect the appreciation of the long-run, sustainable equilibrium exchange rate. In our model, the switch in policy regimes is associated with a transformation of the economy from a fixed-wage to a flexible-wage regime. Should not this change have beneficial real consequences for the economy? Indeed, in a more fully fleshed-out model, it is possible that the added flexibility of the economy would show up in a higher level of the equilibrium real wage and a lower (more appreciated) real exchange rate. The simplest way to see this is to consider what would happen to labor demand as nominal wages become more flexible. It is not unreasonable to suppose that increased labor-market flexibility would be rewarded in practice by an outward shift in the labor-demand schedule, that is, by an increase in l^* in equation (4). It is clear from the solutions (Table 8.2) that the upshot would be an increase in employment and in real wages and, consequently, an appreciation of the real exchange rate.

An important clue with regard to the relevance of this second scenario is provided by the behavior of private investment. Where the real-exchange-rate appreciation is a sustainable, equilibrium phenomenon, we would expect it to go alongside a revival in private investment. The latter would indicate increased confidence on the part of the private sector and would form the natural real-world counterpart to an increase in l^* in the model above.[13]

The experiences of Chile, Argentina, and Mexico in the second half of the 1980s present three rather different pictures with regard to private investment. In Chile, the comparatively mild real appreciation since 1988 has been accompanied by a doubling of private investment: from 1989 to 1991, private

---

[13] The counterargument is that nothing favorable can be ascribed to an investment boom that takes place in the context of a real appreciation of the currency: a (temporary) overvaluation acts as an investment subsidy because imported capital goods are (temporarily) cheap (see Dornbusch, 1985). An investment boom that takes place under these conditions, however, has at least the potential of validating the contemporaneous level of the real exchange rate, provided it is not narrowly focused on nontradables, because it expands the production capacity of the economy.

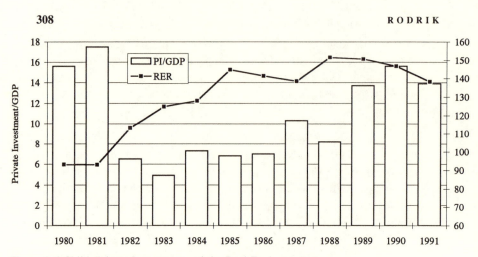

Figure 8.6 Chile: Private Investment and the Real Exchange Rate

investment averaged 14.4 percent of gross domestic product (GDP), compared to 7.3 percent from 1982 to 1988 (Figure 8.6).[14] As Figure 8.6 makes
clear, the appreciation still leaves the Chilean peso highly depreciated relative
to the heights reached prior to 1982, although the private-investment share has
practically caught up with its peak during the earlier period. These facts
would lead one to remain relatively sanguine about the appreciation of the
Chilean peso. Of course, Chile is one country that did not experience triple-
digit inflation and a protracted stabilization crisis during the 1980s, so it may
not be a very good case on which to try out the scenario above.

Argentina's experience from 1987 to 1991 has been opposite that of Chile.
The trend real appreciation of the Argentine currency has taken place alongside a continued squeeze in private investment, to the point at which *gross*
private investment stood at barely over 4 percent of GDP in 1990 (Figure 8.7).
In light of the inability of successive stabilization packages to conquer inflation during this period, the result is not surprising. Since the Cavallo stabilization of 1991, private investment has apparently shot up, so future statistics
could conceivably tell a different story.

The Mexican case stands between the Chilean and Argentine extremes.
Unlike in Argentina, the real appreciation followed a successful stabilization
in 1988, and private investment has risen by a couple of percentage points of
GDP since then (Figure 8.8). The magnitude of the real appreciation, however, has been much larger, and the investment boom much smaller, than in
Chile. As pointed out above, it remains to be seen whether NAFTA and overall confidence in the health and stability of the Mexican economy can sustain a
real exchange rate that has appreciated by 35 percent since 1987.

[14] The source for all private-investment data in Figures 8.6 through 8.8 is Pfefferman and
Madarassy (1992).

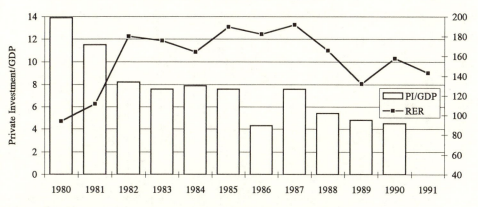

Figure 8.7 Argentina: Private Investment and the Real Exchange Rate

To sum up, it may be viewed as encouraging that in all cases where disinflation has worked (Chile and Mexico, and Argentina after 1991), private investment has increased. This may be seen as making the real appreciations less threatening to the sustainability of the trade reforms. Nonetheless, Chile is the only one among the three countries considered here where there is no *prima facie* case that the observed real appreciation poses a future risk. The model considered above was designed to illustrate a best-case scenario under which the conflicting demands made on exchange-rate management by stabilization, on the one hand, and trade liberalization, on the other, can prove to be illusory. The evidence for this scenario is mixed, and it is unlikely to be fully sorted out for some time.

4 Early Trade Liberalization and the Credibility of the Nominal Anchor

Even if trade liberalization is fully compatible with a *credible* disinflation, the reality that any disinflation strategy is likely to face imperfect credibility at the outset raises additional problems. Early liberalization may be costly both because it exacerbates the transitional costs, as discussed in Section 1, and because it may affect adversely the credibility of the disinflation itself. I focus here on the latter possibility. By simply assuming an exchange-rate commitment, the model discussed above sidestepped the crucial question of how early trade liberalization affects the credibility of the anchor. Does it endanger credibility by complicating the transition, or does it enhance credibility by raising the stakes?

Liberalization clearly aggravates the costs (both economic and political) of the transitory real appreciation experienced by disinflating countries. In addition, it forces policymakers to confront an additional powerful group—the

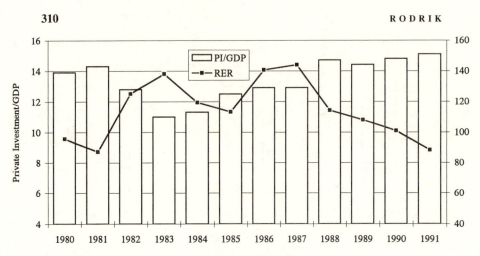

Figure 8.8 Mexico: Private Investment and the Real Exchange Rate

import-competing interests—in addition to those adversely affected by the fiscal retrenchment. Finally, by linking in the public's mind the fortunes of stabilization and liberalization, it creates the danger that any reversal of the liberalization will contaminate the disinflation process. These are powerful arguments suggesting that early liberalization may be costly to the credibility of disinflation.

These arguments, however, have to be set against the potential signaling value of tackling stabilization and liberalization simultaneously. To a jaded public that has seen too many disinflation plans fail for lack of political backbone, an ambitious package that attacks all the sacred cows at once may well communicate the presence of a "tough" government that means business (or a naive one that will disappear before long). The fact that linkage raises the costs of failure has a beneficial flip side as well: it makes reversal less likely in the face of temporary setbacks.

Arguments can thus be made on either side. As is usual with anything of practical consequence, economics provides only so much guidance; responsible policymakers have to judge the politics of the situation for themselves. It should be stressed again, however, that the exchange-rate conflict need not render stabilization-cum-liberalization inherently incredible, because the conflict may well disappear under a successful nominal peg.

5 Concluding Remarks

It is clear that, in all the reforms considered here (except Chile's), policymakers were concerned first and foremost with controlling inflation. Opening up to foreign trade was a secondary priority and was largely undertaken for its anti-inflationary (rather than resource-allocation) benefits. Policymakers have been more sanguine than academics about avoiding the risk of overvaluation, and there is at least a theoretical possibility that they may yet prove to be right. As we have seen, the use of the exchange rate as a nominal anchor is not necessarily in conflict with the requirements of trade liberalization. If the nominal anchor works, nominal-wage rigidity will eventually disappear; if it ultimately proves unsustainable, competitiveness will have taken a serious blow, but so will have the fight against inflation.

This discussion has been an attempt to put the best possible face on the preference of policymakers for early liberalization. In view of the preference for price stability, it is not clear that packaging trade reform with stabilization has seriously compounded the downside risks. And if the stabilization works, the economy will reap the obvious upside gains from having integrated into the world economy. As discussed above, however, the strategy is not without serious problems, and its success remains to be demonstrated.

References

Bruno, Michael, *High Inflation and the Nominal Anchors of an Open Economy*, Essays in International Finance No. 183, Princeton, N.J., Princeton University, International Finance Section, June 1991.

Corbo, Vittorio, and Stanley Fischer, "Adjustment Programs and Bank Support: Rationale and Main Results," in Vittorio Corbo, Stanley Fischer, and Steven B. Webb, eds., *Adjustment Lending Revisited: Policies to Restore Growth*, Washington, D.C., World Bank, 1992.

Corden, W. Max, "Exchange Rate Policy in Developing Countries," in Jaime de Melo and André Sapir, eds., *Trade Theory and Economic Reform—North, South, and East: Essays in Honor of Bela Balassa*, Cambridge, Mass., Blackwell, 1991.

de Melo, Jaime, and Sumana Dhar, "Lessons of Trade Liberalization in Latin America for Economies in Transition," World Bank Working Paper No. 1040, Washington, D.C., World Bank, November 1992.

Dominguez, Kathryn M., and Dani Rodrik, "Exchange Rate Management and Growth in the Aftermath of Stabilization: The Bolivian Case," Harvard University, May 1990, processed.

Dornbusch, Rudiger, "External Debt, Budget Deficits, and Disequilibrium Exchange Rates," in Gordon W. Smith and John T. Cuddington, eds., *International Debt and the Developing Countries*, Washington, D.C., World Bank, 1985, pp. 213–235.

————, "Mexico: How To Recover Stability and Growth," Massachusetts Institute of Technology, February 1993, processed.

Edwards, Sebastian, "Exchange Rates as Nominal Anchors," National Bureau of Economic Research Working Paper No. 4246, Cambridge, Mass., National Bureau of Economic Research, December 1992.

General Agreement on Tariffs and Trade (GATT), *Trade Policy Review: Chile*, Geneva, Switzerland, 1991.

————, *Trade Policy Review: Argentina*, Vols. 1 and 2, Geneva, Switzerland, 1992a.

————, *Trade Policy Review: Brazil*, Geneva, Switzerland, 1992b.

Greenaway, David, and Chris Milner, "Fiscal Dependence on Trade Taxes and Trade Policy Reform," *Journal of Development Studies*, 27, 1991, pp. 96–132.

Grether, J.-M., "Trade Liberalization, Market Structure and Performance in Mexican Manufacturing, 1984–89," Washington, D.C., World Bank, 1992, processed.

Kenen, Peter B., "Financial Opening and the Exchange Rate Regime," in Helmut Reisen and Bernhard Fischer, eds., *Financial Opening: Policy Issues and Experiences in Developing Countries*, Development Centre Documents, Paris, Organisation for Economic Co-operation and Development, 1993, pp. 237–262.

Kiguel, Miguel A., and Nissan Liviatan, "Inflationary Rigidities and Orthodox Stabilization Policies: Lessons from Latin America," *World Bank Economic Review*, 2 (September 1988), pp. 273–298.

Krueger, Anne O., *Liberalization Attempts and Consequences*, Cambridge, Mass., Ballinger, for the National Bureau of Economic Research, 1978.

Mussa, Michael L., "Macroeconomic Policy and Trade Liberalization: Some Guidelines," *World Bank Research Observer*, 2 (January 1987), pp. 61–77.

Papageorgiou, Demetris, Michael Michaely, and Armeane M. Choksi, eds., *Liberalizing Foreign Trade: Lessons of Experience in the Developing World*, Oxford and Cambridge, Mass., Blackwell, 1991.

Pfefferman, Guy P., and Andrea Madarassy, *Trends in Private Investment in Developing Countries*, Discussion Paper No. 13, Washington, D.C., International Finance Corporation, 1992.

Pritchett, Lant, and Geetha Sethi, "Tariff Rates, Tariff Revenue and Tariff Reform: Some New Facts," Washington, D.C., World Bank, 1992, processed.

Rodrik, Dani, "Foreign Trade in Eastern Europe's Transition: Early Results," National Bureau of Economic Research Working Paper No. 4064, Cambridge, Mass., National Bureau of Economic Research, May 1992a.

————, "The Rush to Free Trade in the Developing World: Why So Late? Why Now? Will It Last?" National Bureau of Economic Research Working Paper No. 3947, Cambridge, Mass., National Bureau of Economic Research, June 1992b.

Sachs, Jeffrey D., "Trade and Exchange-Rate Policies in Growth-Oriented Adjustment Programs," in Vittorio Corbo, Morris Goldstein, and Mohsin Khan, eds., *Growth-Oriented Adjustment Programs*, Washington, D.C., International Monetary Fund and World Bank, 1987, pp. 291–325.

Tybout, James R., and M. Daniel Westbrook, "Trade Liberalization and the Dimensions of Efficiency Change in Mexican Manufacturing Industries," Georgetown University, July 1992, processed.

Végh, Carlos A., "Stopping High Inflation," *International Monetary Fund Staff Papers*, 39 (September 1992), pp. 626–695.

9

Inflation and Growth in an Integrated Approach

MICHAEL BRUNO

1 Introduction

The events of the last decade or two provide cumulative empirical evidence that macroeconomic factors in general, and the macroeconomic policy response to external shocks in particular, play a dominant role in the protracted growth crises of countries and in the renewal and long-term sustainability of growth. Ongoing studies based on cross-country regressions bear this out, as do the individual case-history projects carried out by the World Bank (Corden et al., 1993).[1] Indeed, part of the *World Development Report 1991* was devoted to the role of macroeconomic stability in comparative development experience.

The fact that seemingly transitory disturbances may have long-term effects on productivity and growth is also consistent with two distinct theoretical developments of the last decade. One is the methodological econometric attack on the conventional distinction between cycle and trend,[2] which has developed an alternative econometric approach that allows stochastic disturbances to affect long-term trends. The other, largely disconnected from the new econometrics and hitherto primarily theoretical, is the work on endogenous growth theory.[3] In this latter framework, the existence of increasing

I am grateful to David Coe for helpful discussions during a 1992 stay as a visiting scholar at the Research Department of the International Monetary Fund. I also thank colleagues at the Economics Department at Hebrew University and participants of the Centre for Economic Policy Research 1993 Summer Symposium in Macroeconomics for discussion at seminars. For very valuable comments on earlier drafts, I am thankful to Roland Benabou, Giuseppe Bertola, Rudiger Dornbusch, Stanley Fischer, and Andrés Solimano. Finally, I wish to thank Margret Eisenstaedt for preparing the figures and Benny Daniel for help with data and computations. This paper is part of a study that formed the basis for a set of three Kuznets Memorial Lectures on "Short-Term Adjustment and Long-Run Growth," delivered at Yale University in April 1993.

[1] Cross-sectional studies were recently carried out under the project "Do National Policies Affect Long-Run Growth?" (and presented in a conference bearing that title) by Easterly et al. (1992), Easterly and Rebelo (1993), Fischer (1993), and Saint-Paul (1993).

[2] In a series of papers by Nelson and Plosser (1982); for a recent survey, see Stock and Watson (1988).

[3] This renewed interest in the role of learning and increasing returns in growth begins with the work of Romer (1986) and Lucas (1988). See also Grossman and Helpman (1991) and a more recent paper by Galor and Tsiddon (1992).

returns or externalities can, in principle, make long-term growth depend at least partly on transitory disturbances and the policy response to them.

Despite the growing empirical evidence, however, the mainstream dichotomy between short-term and long-term analytical frameworks persists. A most elementary, and almost trite, statement is that the long term is a succession of short terms. Yet, in our basic macroeconomic models, in our teaching, and, to a considerable extent also in the design of macroeconomic policies, we tend to separate into analytical compartments the frameworks within which we discuss short-term adjustment and long-term growth (and structural reform). Nowhere is this better exemplified than in the basic macroeconomic textbooks and teaching, where we devote most of the space and time to the time-honored "short-term" framework in which the capital stock and productivity are kept constant and aggregate demand management carries most of the action.[4] In the remaining, usually end-of-course residual lectures, we confine the discussion to standard smooth long-term-growth models, in which the supply of capital and labor plays the dominant role, but from which inflation, the short-term macroeconomic disturbances, and the policy reactions are abstracted.[5] In the large cross-sectional regressions mentioned above, macroeconomic variables such as inflation and its variability are typically introduced as extraneous arguments within a framework of steady-state long-term growth, rather than as simultaneously determined components of a more complete macroeconomic model.

Similarly, we tend to distinguish policies that deal with adjustment (centered on inflation and the balance of payments) from policies that address structural reform (mainly targeted on productivity and growth), as if that division of instruments can be clearly made. Take, for example, fiscal policy in the form of a permanent fiscal adjustment. Is it a short-term macroeconomic instrument or is it a long-term policy to affect growth through crowding-in of investment or through direct expenditure allocation (on infrastructure investment and human-capital development)? Maybe the effects of exchange-rate and monetary policies are of a more purely short-term adjustment nature? But was not the U.S. fiscal and monetary stance in the Vietnam War aftermath the main element that triggered the collapse of Bretton Woods, that at least partly induced the oil shocks and thus had a lasting effect on world inflation and

---

[4] The price shocks of the 1970s have encouraged the incorporation of independent shifts in the aggregate supply schedule into the standard macroeconomic model, but this has been confined mainly to the short-term effect of terms-of-trade or real-wage shocks.

[5] Empirically based country models have to integrate short-term fluctuations with medium- or long-term effects, but these are usually *ad hoc* and have not found their way into the standard macroeconomic model. A possible reason for the persistence of this bias is the fact that most textbooks are written for the U.S. market, an economy in which a relatively high frequency of the more conventional business cycles still plays a major role. Most of Europe has been considerably less cyclical in the conventional sense and most middle- and low-income countries even less so.

growth patterns? Or consider the more recent events following German unification. Although it is too early to assess the long-term consequences for
growth in Germany and the rest of Europe, it is clear that the particular mix of
(no) fiscal and (harsh) monetary response to the unification shock in Germany
had far-reaching repercussions on the sustainability of the Exchange Rate
Mechanism (ERM) and on the protracted recession in Europe (with repercussions for the medium term).

As an illustration, consider the representation of postwar growth and inflation for the countries of the Organisation for Economic Co-operation and
Development (OECD) and for the subgroup of European Community (EC)
countries. Figure 9.1 presents data for the inflation of the consumer price
index (CPI) and growth of the gross domestic product (GDP). Because annual
fluctuations make it difficult to follow the developments over the medium and
long term, the figures show the five-year moving averages of these rates.[6]
Five years is a sufficiently long period to overcome very short-term cyclical
effects or "political cycles" (even though the conventional "business cycle" is
variable and often somewhat longer).

The end of each quinquennium is marked on these curves to show also the
actual average trajectory of nonoverlapping average rates of change; the five-
year end posts, starting from the quinquennium ending in 1970, all stand for a
particular worldwide development. The second half of the 1960s is important
in terms of high growth and the approach to full-capacity utilization; 1970
signals the beginning of the breakdown of Bretton Woods, building up to the
first oil shock; 1975 signals the depth of the recession; 1980 signals the second
oil shock and the beginning of the monetary squeeze with the steep rise in real
interest rates (which is also very significant for the debt-crisis shock in the
middle-income countries discussed in Section 5); 1985 signals a drop in oil
prices and real interest rates, the beginning of the last large recovery, and a
series of attempts at stabilization and reform among some middle-income
countries; 1990 signals the full breakdown of the Soviet block and German
unification.[7]

The most marked feature of these curves, which will also be shown to apply
to individual industrial countries, is the apparent twenty-year cycle, or "loop,"
that marks the period between 1970, or thereabouts, and 1990 (1988 for the
OECD as a whole); by the end of this period, inflation returns to its earlier
levels, although growth fails to do so, at least on average (which is also true

[6] The starting observation marked 1955 is the average for the *preceding* period, 1950 to 1955,
and the same applies for each of the subsequent years marked on the curves. The estimate for
1993 (included in the average for 1988 to 1993), which is the last observation marked in these
figures, was taken from the IMF's *World Economic Outlook, Interim Assessment*, January 1993.

[7] The exact timing of events and responses has differed among countries, but there is an
advantage in considering a common external framework of time that enables international comparisons in an interdependent world.

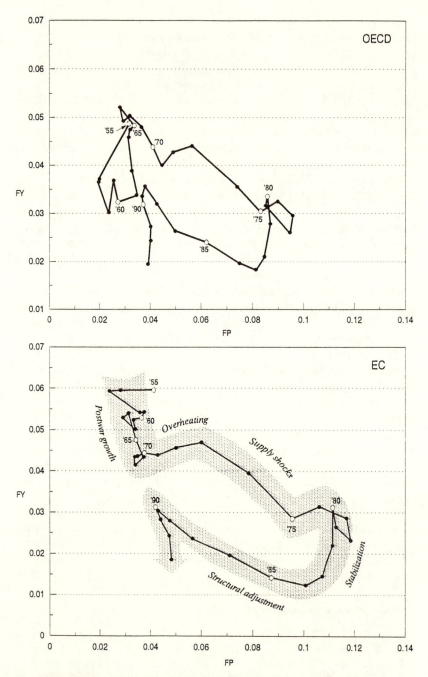

Figure 9.1 Phases of Growth and Inflation in the OECD and EC, 1950–93 (*percentages, five-year moving averages*)

for most individual countries).[8] Superimposed on the curve for the EC is a stylized representation of major phases in this apparent loop. I shall return to this in Section 3.

The approach taken in this chapter thus derives from the fact that country (and intercountry) growth, inflation, and stabilization have become increasingly linked during the last two decades. The premise is that long-term growth is not only in theory the outcome of a succession of short-term equilibria, but that it has for that reason been predominantly path dependent in recent decades for both industrial and semi-industrial countries. Once that line is taken, we can begin to resolve the seeming empirical paradox of the coexistence of very high persistence of the standard growth-determining characteristics of countries across recent decades with the very low persistence (that is, extreme instability) of productivity and output growth.[9] Part of the reason for this apparent paradox is that a series of external shocks that have affected all countries have met with differential macroeconomic responses, not only between countries, but also within the same countries over time. These, in turn, have had long-lasting effects on growth, sometimes extending over two decades. It is apparent, however, that the time profiles of inflation and GDP growth across both the advanced and many of the middle-income countries during this period are very similar when the moving averages of both variables are viewed simultaneously. An integrated view is also important for discussing questions of cause and effect; for example, are inflation and growth determined simultaneously, is the relationship always negative, does one cause the other, and do some of the relationships vary for countries at different rates of inflation (a question to be discussed in Section 5)? An integrated view is also important for the joint evaluation of adjustment and structural-reform policies, for issues of sequencing, and the like.

To argue the point, one needs a simple unifying device to combine the short and long terms. Part of this chapter attempts to construct and apply just such a simple (to some extent, simple-minded) framework, within which medium- and long-term output and price behavior over time are considered. This can be done by starting with a rudimentary short-term aggregate supply (AS) and aggregate demand (AD) framework and extending it into the medium and long term. I develop this framework in Section 2 and apply it in Section 3 to reinterpret the growth slowdown of the 1970s and the partial recovery of

[8] For the OECD as a whole, the period from 1961 to 1989 looks like a closed longer thirty-year loop, but, as we shall see, this is only the result of averaging over a larger group of countries, in which lumping Japan, the United States, and the European Economic Community (EEC) together gets this result.

[9] Easterly et al. (1992) find that, in a comparison of about one hundred countries across the three recent decades, the time-correlation coefficient of basic growth characteristics or "regressors" such as the level of education, share of urban population, trade share, and government consumption levels, is close to unity, whereas the cross-decade correlation of growth of GDP per worker is only of the order of 0.1 to 0.3.

the 1980s in the industrial countries. This spells out a common "cycle" of approximately the above duration over which macroeconomic adjustment to common shocks interacted with structural characteristics of countries (in particular, those of labor markets) to account for both the similarities as well as differences in inflation and growth profiles.

Of particular concern in the present context are the medium-term dynamics of investment and their link to short-term macroeconomic developments. Section 4 analyzes the empirical determinants of capital formation for panel data of sixteen industrial countries, centering on the role of profits and real interest rates in the investment squeeze and subsequent recovery phase in the industrial countries. A possible separate role in investment determination for short-term growth and inflation behavior is also discussed. Among competing or complementary theoretical rationales for these links is the recent option-pricing theory of irreversible investment, to which some reference will also be made.

Section 5 applies corresponding tools to the analysis of an analogous, usually much more extreme, inflation and growth loop in some groups of high- as well as moderate-inflation middle-income countries. The structural and political economic factors that affect the probability of rescheduling debt (Berg and Sachs, 1988), as well as the political constraints on the ability to use restraining fiscal and monetary policies, explain quite well why several countries, particularly in Latin America, entered deep crises of high inflation and low growth in response to external shocks.[10] Also discussed is the aftermath of successful sharp stabilizations from high inflation and the medium-term dynamics of recovery of growth. Private and public investment and savings behavior, as well as the political economy of exchange-rate policy, play an important role in this process. The chapter ends with a brief reference to some analogies of the framework used here with the sequencing of growth crises, adjustments, and structural reforms in Central and Eastern Europe.

2 Inflation and Output Growth: Analytical Framework and Illustrations

My point of departure is a conventional AS and AD framework, which is drawn in Figure 9.2 in terms of the logarithm of GDP (y) on the vertical axis and the logarithm of the price level (p) on the horizontal axis. The distance traveled between two points of intersection of shifting AS and AD curves will then measure, respectively, the growth rate (g) and the inflation rate (π).

I assume an open economy producing a single final good that competes

[10] A control group of East Asian countries, most of which responded well to the same shocks, was included in this analysis but, for lack of space, is not included in this chapter.

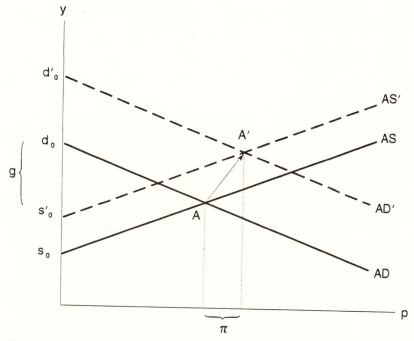

Figure 9.2 Aggregate Supply and Demand Framework

with foreign goods and uses an importable intermediate import. Consider a gross-output function of the final good $Q = Q[Y(K, L), N;A(t)]$, in which Y is GDP, K is the capital stock, L is the labor input, N represents material inputs, and $A(t)$ is time shift or total factor productivity (TFP); W is the nominal-wage rate, P is the price level, t is time, P_n^* is the world price of input (oil), P^* is the world price of final good, E is the nominal exchange rate, and Y^* is the foreign GDP level. Lower-case letters denote logarithms of their equivalent capital letters.

Assuming constant returns to scale and proportionality of marginal products of L and N to respective real-factor prices, one may obtain, by log-linearizing, the GDP supply schedule (y^s):

$$y^s = k + \lambda t - b_1(w - p) - b_2 (e + p_n^* - p) . \qquad (1)$$

The major, subsequently to be endogenized, shift factor is k; λ may stand for a variety of predetermined "residual" shift factors (to be discussed below).

Next, assume a simplified aggregate demand schedule (y^*):

$$y^d = a_0 + a_1 (m - p) + a_2 (e + p^* - p) + a_3 y^* , \qquad (2)$$

where a_0 represents the effect of fiscal policy. The second term, monetary policy, and the other terms come from export demand.[11]

The supply and demand schedules can be abbreviated as

$$y^s = s_0 + sp \,, \tag{3}$$

$$y^d = d_0 - dp \,, \text{ where} \tag{4}$$

$$s_0 = k + \lambda t - b_1 w - b_2 e - b_2 p_n^* = \text{supply shifts} \,; \; s = b_1 + b_2 \,,$$

$$d_0 = a_0 + a_1 m + a_2 p^* + a_2 e + a_3 y^* = \text{demand shifts} \,; \; d = a_1 + a_2 \,,$$

and s and d are the slopes of the short-term AS and AD curves, respectively.

The way the curves have been defined assumes short-term wage (and exchange-rate) stickiness. I shall subsequently modify this assumption for medium-term changes over time. Solving (3) and (4) for $y = y^s = y^d$ yields

$$y = (s_0 d + d_0 s)/(s + d) \,, \tag{5}$$

$$p = (d_0 - s_0)/(s + d) \,. \tag{6}$$

For given slopes s and d, y rises with positive Δd_0 and Δs_0 shifts, whereas p rises only with $\Delta d_0 > \Delta s_0$.

The slope of the joint expansion path of y and p will then be

$$\frac{\Delta y}{\Delta p} = \frac{s + (\Delta s_0/\Delta d_0)\, d}{1 - \Delta s_0/\Delta d_0} \,, \tag{7}$$

which is the slope of the line AA′ in Figure 9.2. The growth-to-inflation ratio ($\Delta y/\Delta p$) increases with $\Delta s_0/\Delta d_0$, s, or d (but *be warned*: the axes are reversed from the conventional P-Y diagram). The slope of the expansion curve in a P-Y diagram will thus fall more the larger are the positive demand shocks (Δd_0) and negative supply shocks ($-\Delta s_0$).

Figure 9.3 illustrates the above analysis for the joint profile of GDP and CPI[12] log-level development for the six large industrial countries during the period from 1950 to 1990, which can be viewed as the time profile of intersections of the short-term aggregate supply and aggregate demand curves for each country. The mid-year 1970 was chosen as the joint reference point (log = 0). The other points on the curves mark common five-year signposts that

[11] Under a clean float or a closed economy, the exchange-rate term will not appear.

[12] I use CPI rather than GDP prices throughout because these are generally more consistently measured across different types of countries. Using GDP prices would be more consistent with the quantity measure of GDP but would also lend itself to the problem of bias in measurement of GDP, because this would automatically bias quantity and price measures in opposite directions.

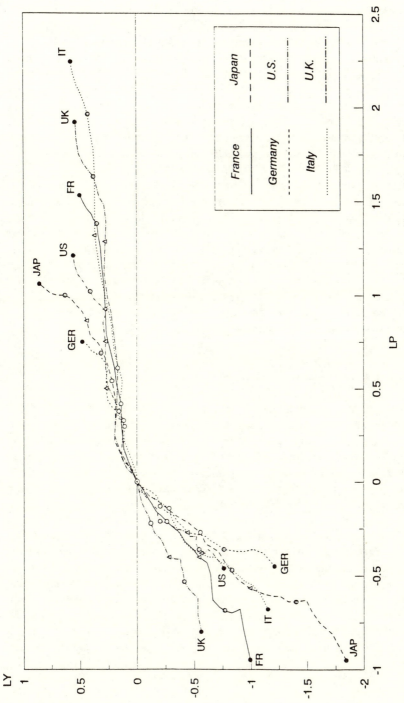

Figure 9.3 Output and Price Expansion in the G-6 Countries, 1950–90 (*natural logs of GDP and CPI, 1970 = 0*)

enable some impression of the distance traveled in terms of output and prices across the different countries over time. The figure underscores the marked difference between the two halves of the forty-year period. In the pre-1970 period, there was fast growth and relative price stability, with the ratio $\Delta s_0/\Delta d_0$ almost equal to unity, and thus the slope $\Delta y/\Delta p$ was relatively high. Beginning in the early 1970s, there was low growth and higher inflation, with the negative supply shocks leading to a drop in the above two ratios. The figure marks Japan as the highest cumulative growth country over both halves of the forty-year period, and Germany as the least inflationary (Italy was the most inflationary from 1970 to 1990; France and Japan were the most inflationary from 1950 to 1970). A comparison of the four European countries after 1970 suggests a positive long-term average trade-off between cumulative price inflation and cumulative output growth. Germany was the most stable, but it had lower growth. The reverse was true for Italy, which had, on average, the most expansionary macroeconomic policy. (If we exclude the United Kingdom, the trade-off was reversed before 1970.) A very weak, slightly positive association between inflation and growth appears to be evident during the 1970–90 period when the sample of OECD countries is enlarged to include the smaller members, and it is in marked contrast to the highly negative relation between inflation and growth among the group of Latin American countries (discussed in Section 5).

Representing Changes over Time

Consider now the output and price relations of equations (1) through (6) in time-difference form, using deltas (Δ) to represent average time changes (for example, three- to five-year moving averages, as discussed below). In Figure 9.4, we use the horizontal axis of the first quadrant for logarithmic changes in the price level (Δp) to represent the average inflation rate (π) and the vertical axis for logarithmic changes in the GDP level (Δy) to represent the average growth rate (g). The vertical axis will also be used to measure the growth rate of the capital stock (to be denoted Δk or k).

The time changes in output supply (g^s) and demand (g^d) will be shown as curves (ΔAS and ΔAD in Figure 9.4). The respective convex and concave shapes of these curves beyond a certain threshold inflation rate come from assuming that, with rising inflation, there is partial indexation (accommodation) of wages, money, and the exchange rate, the degree of which rises with the rate of inflation, reaching a limit with 100 percent indexation (or accommodation), at which point the curves become horizontal. This can be shown by writing the first difference of the supply and demand schedules, respectively, as

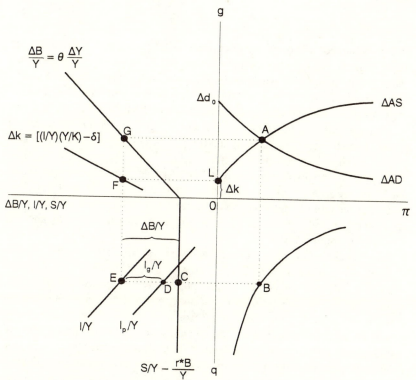

Figure 9.4 Determinants of Growth and Inflation

$$g^s = \Delta k + \lambda + b_1(\pi - \omega) + b_2(\pi - \epsilon - \pi^*)$$
$$- b_2(\pi_n^* - \pi^*) , \tag{8}$$

$$g^d = \Delta a_0 - a_1 (\pi - \mu) - a_2(\pi - \epsilon - \pi^*) + a_3 g^* . \tag{9}$$

The rate of change of nominal wages is given by ϵ, the rate of monetary expansion by μ, and the rate of nominal devaluation by ϵ; π_n^* is the rate of change of world prices of raw materials, π^* is the rate of change of final goods, and g^* is the growth rate of world output.

In equation (8), the first two elements represent capital accumulation and TFP, respectively; the first brackets give the rate of drop of real wages; the second brackets give the rate of real appreciation; and the last brackets represent the effect of a change in the terms of trade. In (9), real depreciation and the rate of change of world output (g^*) represent the effect of exports on the demand growth side, and Δa_0 represents expansionary fiscal policy.

For the change of nominal wages,

$$\omega = \alpha\pi + (1 - \alpha)\pi^e + \nu \qquad (10)$$

may be assumed, where π^e is the expectation of inflation as reflected in the wage contract, which also incorporates a partial cost-of-living adjustment, and ν stands for all other wage-shifting factors (such as the distance of unemployment from the natural rate). Accelerating inflation will tend to motivate an increase in α, which will enhance the inertia of the inflationary process and will make it concave in terms of the g_s curve, until, in the limit—with 100 percent formal indexation ($\alpha = 1$) and full purchasing-power parity ($\pi - \epsilon - \pi^* = 0$)—the curve will become horizontal.[13]

To argue for analogous curvature of the g_d curve, we need to assume that the respective rates of devaluation and monetary expansion also partly accommodate to the rate of inflation. The degree of accommodation is an increasing function of the rate of inflation (π) up to full purchasing-power parity and full monetary accommodation.

The intersection of the two curves represents, at best, a temporary equilibrium of inflation and growth and cannot represent a long-term steady state, because steady-state inflation will take place only when all nominal magnitudes, the wage, exchange rate, and money, grow at the same rate. In that case, however, both curves become horizontal, and only the growth rate will be determined by the underlying production model.[14] To obtain the steady-state inflation rate, we need a mechanism to determine money growth, as, for example, seigniorage finance of the budget deficit determines the inflation rate. Before turning to possible applications of this framework for joint inflation and growth response to shocks and macroeconomic policy, I shall, for subsequent reference, supplement the short-term determination of inflation and growth with the medium-term link through the effect on profitability and investment.

The intercept of the dynamic supply schedule (Δs_0) incorporates the rate of change of the capital stock (Δk),[15] which is related to the investment ratio through the identity

[13] The gradual nature of the slope hinges on the assumption that there is sluggishness in the adjustment of wages, that is, long-term contracts extending beyond the length of the period over which averages are calculated, or sluggishness in the adjustment of inflationary expectations. In the case of perfect foresight, the respective real-wage brackets disappear at once. As to the catchall shift factor ν in equation (10), the part that comes from actual unemployment could be solved out by assuming an Okun-type relation between the growth rate and the unemployment rate, leaving the factors underlying the natural rate of unemployment affecting ν positively. The way the equation is set up, the shift factor ν must also include the productivity part of real-wage growth as well as indirect taxes on wages (because producers equate the marginal product to wage costs).

[14] Some mechanism, such as savings-investment adjustment, is required to get to equilibrium from between the demand and the supply sides.

[15] As shown above, the intercept also includes the effect of "total productivity" (λ), as well as time shifts in the other components of the supply schedule, in particular input (oil) price changes.

$$\Delta k = (I/Y)(Y/K) - \delta \, , \tag{11}$$

where δ is the depreciation rate, and Y/K (the slope of the Δk line in the top left quadrant of Figure 9.4) measures the average productivity of capital (or degree of utilization).

The line drawn in the bottom left quadrant of Figure 9.4 relates the rate of inflation (through its variance) by way of a general q factor to the private investment rate (I_p/Y). The position of the q schedule will depend on a number of other factors, including the rate of growth and the real rate of interest (r^*). These will be mentioned in the empirical discussion below. For the moment, I write

$$I_p = f[q(\underset{-}{\pi}, \underset{+}{g}, \underset{-}{\pi_n^*}, \underset{-}{r^*} \ldots)] \, . \tag{12}$$

Total investment (I) is composed of private investment (I_p) and public investment (I_g), where the latter is determined by government:

$$I_p/Y + I_g/Y = I/Y \, . \tag{13}$$

This is shown in the bottom left quadrant of Figure 9.4 along with the net-savings (here, vertical) line that is measured net of interest payments on the foreign debt (r^*B/Y).

The increment to debt (ΔB) can be assumed to depend on growth, with a coefficient θ that will be negatively related to the level of the existing debt ratio, to the foreign interest rate (r^*), and to a country risk factor (σ) and is shown as the line $\Delta B/Y$ in the top left quadrant.

Thus, we have

$$\frac{\Delta B}{Y} = \frac{I}{Y} - \left(\frac{S}{Y} - \frac{r^*B}{Y} \right) = \theta(\underset{-}{B/Y}, \underset{-}{r^*}, \underset{-}{\sigma}) \, g \, . \tag{14}$$

This completes the very rudimentary framework that links the short- and long-term components.[16] It will mainly be used as a descriptive device. Now consider a few illustrations, following from the main shocks (oil prices and real interest rates) that have affected industrial and/or middle-income countries during the 1970–90 period.

It could also be affected, however, by other supply constraints, such as credit ceilings and interest rates on working capital. In Figure 9.4, I abstract from the other shift factors or assume g^s is measured net of them.

[16] There are some implicit additional interdependencies within this framework, such as those between the savings ratio (S/Y) and the intercept of the aggregate demand curve (Δd_0), as well as other elements that will be mentioned in the discussion.

Terms-of-Trade Shocks

An import-price shock will lead to a temporary downward shift of the AS curve because it directly affects output supply. This shift will persist over time when the higher *rate* of change of the relative price (including devaluation of the exchange rate) persists. Similarly, as shown in the various quadrants of Figure 9.4, the price shock reduces q, and thereby I_p/Y, and thus leads to a lower growth rate of the capital stock (Δk). A concomitant drop in foreign demand will also show in a downward shift of the AD curve. The effect of a terms-of-trade shock will thus be a drop in the growth rate and a rise in the inflation rate, the size of which can be mitigated at the expense of an even larger output drop by contractionary macroeconomic (fiscal and monetary) policy. In this case, the AD curve shifts further down and to the left, at least temporarily.

The output effects, by contrast, can be mitigated at the cost of higher inflation by an upward shift of Δd_0 and the AD curve, with temporary equilibrium shifting up along the AS curve. Pure AD movements, that is, cyclical Phillips-curve shifts, at given AS, will show as northeast and southwest fluctuations of inflation and growth unless the cycle is averaged out over a longer time span. If a five-year moving average is used, as in Figure 9.1, the mean fluctuations of the AD curve will average out for most of the period, and the set of equilibria will be dominated by the negative supply shocks during the 1970s and the positive supply shifts in the 1980s. Thus, the observations in Figure 9.1 (see the stylized representation on the curve for the EC) approximately trace "average" downward-sloping demand curves for the "supply-shocks" and "structural-adjustment" phases and likewise trace "average" upward sloping supply curves for the "overheating" and "stabilization" phases.[17]

Positive and Negative Debt Shocks

Consider an increase in the θ coefficient in equation (14), as a result of a fall in the world interest rate and/or the alleviation of ceilings on the availability of funds, as after the first oil shock. This enables an increase in I/Y (through government investment) and/or a drop in the savings rate. The former will show in an increase in k and a possible shift up of the AS curve; the latter will show in an upward shift of the AD curve. In both cases, an increase in the growth rate is possible, or, at least, the ability to prevent a drop that would otherwise be mandated by the oil shock (for an oil-importing country). The

[17] Obviously, these are only broad descriptions. The movement from 1975 to 1980, for example, represents a mini-loop caused by both AS and AD shifts.

outcome for inflation depends on the relative strength and persistence of the supply and demand shifts. The propensity to incur a crisis later on depends, of course, on whether the larger foreign borrowing has been channeled into productive investment or into higher consumption levels (that is, the dominance of a permanent upward shift of the AS curve or a temporary upward shift of the AD curve).

The debt crisis shows in this framework as a reverse phenomenon. It takes the form of a supply shock, namely, a downward shift of the AS curve, because of short-term increases in interest rates and the availability of working capital and/or in raw-material imports. A step devaluation or the acceleration of an exchange-rate crawl will likewise shift the AS curve down, at least temporarily, whereas the expansionary effect on the AD curve will be mitigated by the required cut in domestic absorption. The depressing influence on public as well as private investment (an inward shift of the q line) will in turn feed through the k line into a reduction in the rate of growth of the capital stock. The extent of the squeeze on investment depends, of course, on the compensating increase in the domestic savings rate, which in turn must show in a leftward shift of the AD curve (the experience of different countries is discussed in Section 5). Again, there is a trade-off between growth and inflation, because higher savings rates imply a greater squeeze on consumption (private and public), which shows up, in the short term, in lower economic activity and higher unemployment, with the benefit of a smaller acceleration in inflation. The inflationary outbursts that were common in the 1980s reflect the inability to reconcile conflicting demands on budgetary and political commitments as well as money financing of gaping fiscal deficits as inflation ran into three digits. Distortionary effects of very high inflation, for which empirical evidence exists, will show in a drop in the "residual," or TFP, factor, which again will be reflected in a further downward shift of the AS curve.

A useful summary measure of the response of different countries to the various crises is the ratio of the average growth rate to the inflation rate. In terms of the geometry of the two figures, this is represented by the slope of the expansion curve in Figure 9.2 or the slope of the ray from the origin to the equilibrium point in the first quadrant of Figure 9.4.

Interactions of Adjustment and Structural Reform

Inflation stabilization (a shift back along the horizontal inflation axis) is conventionally regarded as macroeconomic adjustment in which the dominant tools are monetary and fiscal, effecting a leftward shift of the dynamic AD curve. A given shift in the AD curve, however, can involve a larger drop in growth and/or a lesser drop in the inflation rate depending on the slope of the AS curve. This is where incomes policy (heterodox stabilization, removal of indexation mechanisms, and so on) comes in. In the absence of credibility or explicit social compacts, movements upward or downward along a given AS curve will not be symmetric, because indexation (both *ex post* and *ex ante*) usually applies only for inflation acceleration. Deceleration will thus be along a steeper AS slope unless wage earners are explicitly willing to take a cut in nominal-wage growth as inflation decelerates.

Structural reform, however, usually consists of measures that affect the position of the AS curve (all the factors that may increase the "total productivity" parameter Δ), shifting it gradually upward and to the left. It will thus bring about an increase in the growth rate (a shift along the vertical axis). Some measures, such as fiscal and monetary reform, work through both blades of the scissors. The convenience of a framework in which *both* inflation and growth appear simultaneously comes precisely from the fact that adjustment and structural reform are often intertwined and, as we shall argue from the reform experience of middle-income countries, often inseparable. The closer one looks at Central and East European reform, the more blurred this distinction becomes. I take this up briefly at the end of the chapter.

The following section examines some of the worldwide experience with short-term adjustment and longer-term growth in the last two decades, using elements of the above general framework where convenient. It begins with the industrial countries, if only to prove that, even in the most developed part of the world, the simultaneous examination of past price and output developments yields some useful insights.

3 Supply Shocks and the Industrial Countries Revisited

Much has been written about the general slowdown of growth and productivity in the industrial countries since the 1970s. Two somewhat complementary views have been prevalent. One starts from the events of the early 1970s, particularly the first large oil-price shock, and ascribes the poorer performance directly to the oil (and commodity) stagflationary price shock and to the effect on resource allocation and growth of the macroeconomic response to the shock. This was the main line taken in my work with Jeffrey Sachs (1985). The other, and in a sense complementary, view centers primarily on an analysis of the U.S. economy. It uses a multifactor productivity approach along the lines of Denison (1979) and Kendrick (1983), in which the productivity "residual" that is obtained after accounting for quantities of labor and capital is systematically chiseled away by accounting for changing quality of factors, diminished research and development effort, environmental factors, increasing returns to scale, and so forth. Most, although not all, of the slowdown can be accounted for in this way.[18]

---

[18] For selected discussions, see Maddison (1987) and the 1988 symposium in the *Journal of Economic Perspectives*. Within that literature, the role ascribed by different authors to the oil

There are weaknesses in both approaches. The multifactor productivity approach is problematic in that its components, almost by definition, make for a gradual deceleration, rather than the seemingly abrupt shift in the growth trend that has actually taken place. In addition, one can ascribe to the side effects of the 1973 crisis some of the underlying changes in quantity or quality of factors, which are taken as exogenous in this type of decomposition. Even so, however, there remains an unexplained residual, which, for the case of the United States, Maddison (1987) estimates to be of the order of 60 percent (!) of the deceleration from the 1950–73 period to the 1973–87 period. This large discrepancy comes mainly from the large margin that is unexplained during the high-growth period. A larger percentage of the slowdown is explained for five other industrial countries.[19]

The other line of explanation that builds on the shock itself and its ramifications, has been less grounded on hard quantitative evidence. The direct impact of the oil input price increase cannot account for the full measure of the drop in productivity,[20] within a conventional neoclassical production framework, even after one takes into account the indirect effect on the cost of machinery. The complementary arguments about reduced resource mobility, general effect of unemployment on productivity, and the like make intuitive sense but are hard to quantify. The main argument in Bruno and Sachs (1985) about persistent unemployment hinges on the real-wage gap. This seemed to work reasonably well in explaining high unemployment, especially in Europe, until the early 1980s, but not after that, and recourse had to be made to hysteresis effects and insider-outsider models of the labor market of the kind brought forward by Blanchard and Summers (1986) and Lindbeck and Snower (1986).

The 1970–90 Loop: A Descriptive Account

Consider once more the growth and inflation trajectories of individual industrial countries (Figure 9.5). The analytical framework suggests that the slope of the output-and-price-expansion curve (the ratio of the growth rate to the inflation rate) is a summary measure of economic performance. I call this the

---

shock itself varies. Jorgenson (1984) and his associates, for example, examine in great detail the sectoral breakdown and ascribe quite a large role to the oil-price increase through both the direct use of oil and the effect of the increase on machinery inputs.

[19] The percentage explained is 57 to 58 percent for France and Germany, 81 percent for Japan, 89 percent for the Netherlands, and 99 percent for the United Kingdom.

[20] My own work on the subject took into account other raw materials the price of which increased in the early 1970s. This part of the explanation, however, is problematic because the relative price of raw materials is mainly cyclical and there was no apparent reversion to trend when raw-material prices bounced back. So this explanation, just as the assumption of a role for a sharp short-term recession, can only work if one assumes asymmetry of response, threshold effects on investments, and/or hysteresis effects.

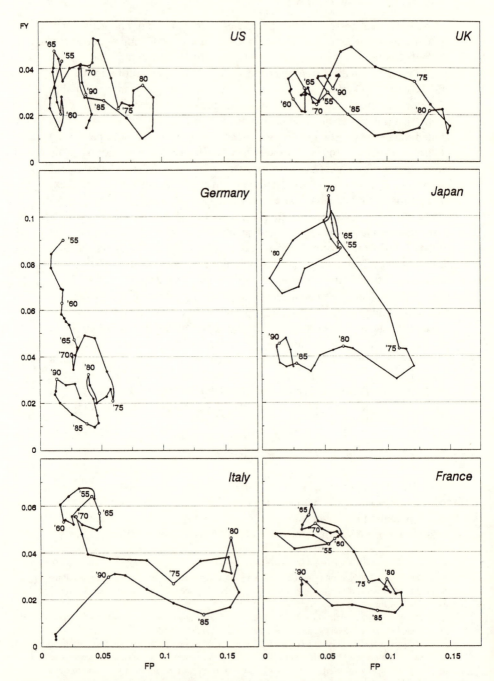

Figure 9.5 GDP Growth and CPI Inflation in the G-6 Countries, 1955–93 (*five-year moving averages, annual rates*)

G/I, or GRIN, ratio. The slope of the ray to the origin from each point in the panels of Figure 9.5 shows that ratio for a five-year moving average. The slope is plotted on a time scale in Figure 9.6 for the six large industrial countries.[21] Several observations emerge from these figures.

FROM POSTWAR GROWTH TO OVERHEATING

In almost all countries, the golden age until the end of the 1960s was marked, with few interruptions, by high growth, low inflation, and high rates of growth-inflation trade-offs (coefficients of at least 1). For most countries, the years from 1950 to 1970 were marked by relatively small fluctuations of growth and inflation, in line with a standard "cycles-around-deterministic-trend" model, but the synchronization of business cycles was far from perfect. The amplitude of the growth fluctuations in the United States was relatively large, and the German drop in growth rate came from the inevitable adjustment following the very high growth after the war. Almost without exception, the second half of the 1960s marked the beginning of a worsening trade-off ratio.[22] This was the period of boom in which unemployment rates throughout the industrial world fell to historically low levels and economies were reaching capacity levels. The worsening trade-off until 1970 was more marked in the United States than in Europe, where it was relatively mild. The United States both experienced and exported the inflationary fiscal and monetary pressures of the Vietnam War (which eventually led to the breakdown of Bretton Woods), whereas, in Europe, the countervailing beneficial effects of the common market and the internal migration of labor were still at work.

One way or another, 1970 or thereabouts marks an almost synchronized end of the golden age of postwar growth. It also marks the collapse of the Bretton Woods system. The demise of Bretton Woods was preceded by the GATT rounds of tariff reductions, the large expansion of world trade and multinational investment in the 1960s, and the expansion of the European financial markets, all of which had contributed to a growing interdependence of the OECD economies and increasing synchronization of cycles of expansion and deflation (Bayoumi and Eichengreen [1992] discuss the relevance of pre- and post-1970 exchange-rate regimes to these developments). The actual breakdown began with the suspension of dollar convertibility to gold in August 1969 following a worsening of the U.S. trade balance. This was followed by a gradual suspension of dollar parities and by the floating of major currencies by 1972–73.

---

[21] The underlying data for a set of sixteen OECD countries during five-year intervals from 1950 to 1993 are given in Table 9.A3 of the Appendix.

[22] Italy seems to have been an exception among the European countries, and so was Japan, presumably because both countries still had untapped resources, mainly surplus labor power in agriculture.

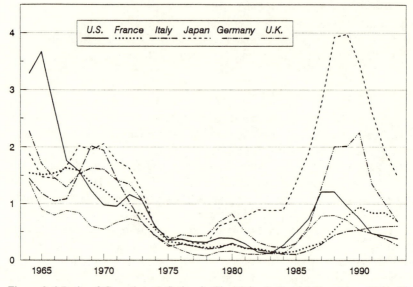

Figure 9.6 Ratio of Growth to Inflation in Six Major Industrial Countries, 1964–90 (*based on GDP and CPI, five-year moving averages*)

In a recent study, Glyn, Hughes, Lipietz, and Singh (1990) stress, even more than do Bruno and Sachs (1985), that the roots of the 1970s crisis lay in the external developments and increasing internal tensions of the late 1960s. The 1950s and 1960s in Europe had been marked by considerable internal labor migration away from agriculture, and by international migration from poorer regions of Europe (together accounting for 80 percent of EEC employment growth from 1955 to 1970 [Bernabe, 1982]). By the end of the 1960s, all of this came to an end, and, with approaching full employment, labor started exercising stronger market power. This marks the beginning of the "overheating" phase, at least in Europe (Figure 9.1). The student and labor unrest in 1968 and the real-wage explosion (Crouch and Pizzorno, 1978; Soskice, 1978; Sachs, 1983) transformed the system into one of *real-* (rather than *nominal-*) wage rigidity even before the first oil shock set in. An increasing measure of formal wage-indexation schemes took place in a number of European economies. Our measure of the GRIN ratio (Figure 9.6), as well as the behavior of business-sector profits (Figure 9.7), show the worsening performance for the second half of the 1960s. As in some middle-income countries, unresolved conflict over shares of labor and capital in government budgets for social services and redistribution, or in income distribution more generally, was bound to lead to accelerated inflation at a time when overheating and external shocks caused reduced growth. This had, indeed, already begun in the late 1960s.

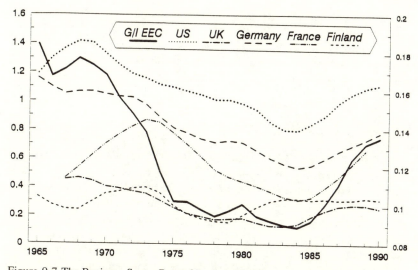

Figure 9.7 The Business-Sector Rate of Profit in Five Selected Countries and the Average Ratio of Growth to Inflation in the EEC, 1960–90 (*five-year moving averages*)

THE SUPPLY-SHOCKS PHASE

In the aftermath of the first supply shock, there was a temporary growth recovery from 1975 to 1980. This resulted from an aggregate demand expansion, which in most countries showed in a simultaneous acceleration in growth and in inflation (with the exception of Germany, where inflation fell first, followed by a crash after the second oil shock, and Japan, where performance worsened until 1977 and then turned around). A further drop in growth, at the time of the second oil shock, was experienced by all the European countries, more briefly by the United States, and only mildly by Japan (see labor-market interpretation below). The drop in output growth following the oil shocks came from the direct shift of the supply curves, exacerbated by real-wage rigidity and the need for internal demand contraction to counteract pressures on prices and current accounts, as well as by the reinforcing effects of export contraction (all leading to inward shifts of the AD curves).

Note the already familiar difference in trade-off between the first and second oil shocks, which varies across countries depending on the immediate macroeconomic policy response to the shock. Only Japan's GRIN ratio (Figure 9.6) shows a *rise* from 1980 to 1985, reflecting the much improved policy response to the second oil shock relative to its own performance following the first. The main reason for this was real-wage flexibility, that is, a sharp drop in the consumption real wage while the product wage stayed constant relative to trend (Bruno and Sachs, 1985, chap. 13). At the same time, most of the other industrial countries show a marked worsening of response in the aftermath of the second oil shock.[23] Germany's poor macroeconomic response to the second oil shock is particularly conspicuous compared to Japan's and probably accounts for its relatively worse growth performance (and, thus, GRIN ratio) in the subsequent decade—testimony to short-term path dependence of the growth process, to which I shall return in the context of the link with investment.

THE STRUCTURAL-ADJUSTMENT PHASE

The period from 1985 to 1990 marks, for all countries, a substantial recovery in growth and in the growth-inflation trade-off, a recovery that had already started in most countries in 1983 or 1984. The period is marked by a downward reversion in oil prices and a general rise in profitability levels (Figure 9.7), reflecting, *inter alia*, moderating changes taking place in the labor market after a long period of very high unemployment rates that peaked in and around that time. The systematic improvement in both growth and inflation (and the trade-off measure) continued, for most countries, until the end of the 1980s (Japan, the United Kingdom, and the United States reversed course from 1988 to 1990).

Labor Relations, Corporatism, and the Differential Macroeconomic Response to Shocks

To what extent can structural factors, in addition to macroeconomic policies, account for the differential response of countries to the same shocks? In the earlier study with Sachs, a welfare "misery index," which *subtracts* the growth rate from the inflation rate (following the work of Tarantelli [1983]), relates the change across countries for the pre- and post-oil-shock periods (1965–73 and 1973–79) to the degree of corporatism of these countries (based on the work of political scientists, Soskice [1978] and Crouch [1985]).[24] The present framework suggests a measure of economic performance in the form of the *ratio* of growth to inflation, the rationale of which follows directly from the slope of the y on p expansion curve.

The GRIN ratio is inversely related to the misery index, but it is defined in terms of ratios rather than sums, a difference that can be significant, especially at low rates of inflation (see below). As discussed in Section 2, the GRIN ratio

[23] Some Scandinavian countries, such as Finland, however, pursued a successful medium-term adjustment strategy and showed a better aggregate performance from 1980 to 1985 (see the profit rate for Finland in Figure 9.7 and the data for Finland and Sweden in Table 9.A3).

[24] A corporatism rank order and index was based on a composite measure involving the degree of union-movement centralization, shop-floor autonomy, employer coordination, and the existence of workers' councils. The index runs from 0 to 4; see Bruno and Sachs (1985, table 11.3).

should be positively related to the slope of the AS curve (which in turn is negatively related to the degree of indexation in the economy), as well as to the ratio of shifts of the AS and AD curves along the growth axis.

Table 9.1 gives, for sixteen OECD countries, the GRIN ratios in the two subperiods 1965–73 and 1973–80 (columns 1 and 2) as well as the *drop* in these ratios between the two subperiods (column 4). A regression of the GRIN reductions (column 4) on the corporatism index (column 5) for fifteen countries (excluding Japan) gives a coefficient of 0.084 (standard error of 0.021) and a relatively high $R^2 = 0.54$ (the adjusted R^2 is 0.51).

In this context, one should also mention an interesting study by Calmfors and Driffill (1988) that compares the various measures of macroeconomic performance. Focusing in particular on the role of the degree of unionization of economies in the increase in unemployment between 1963–73 and 1974–85, the authors show that the relationship should, in theory, be hump shaped, a hypothesis for which they provide some empirical evidence. Both the most centralized and the most decentralized economies in terms of union membership seem to have had more real-wage restraint and smaller increases in unemployment than the group of countries that are intermediate, such as Australia, Belgium, Germany, and the Netherlands.[25] The three-way classification of countries by Calmfors and Driffill by centralized (C), intermediate (I), and decentralized (D) unionization appears in column 6 of Table 9.1, and the unemployment rate for the year 1985 appears in column 7.

Neither corporatism nor the degree of wage responsiveness (another measure applied with positive results in the study by Bruno and Sachs [1985]) yields any explanation of the change in GRIN, or the misery index, for the period of recovery after 1980. There is, however, some evidence that differential changes in inflation rates across countries are related to the size of the unemployment rate, which in turn is related to contractionary macroeconomic policies. A least-squares regression of the change in the average inflation rate between 1975–80 and 1985–90 (column 8 of Table 9.1) and the 1985 unemployment rate gives a significant coefficient of 0.39 (standard error of 0.15) and R^2 of 0.33 (adjusted 0.29), suggesting that conventional Phillips-curve moderation of wage behavior must eventually have played a significant role in the disinflation. I have not found any relation between the change in growth rate and the unemployment rate, but there is other evidence from a study by Saint-Paul (1991) that cross-country TFP growth is positively related to the rate of unemployment after 1974.

What these findings suggest is that, although differential institutional and structural factors may have attenuated the worsening of macroeconomic performance in terms of unemployment and the reduction in GRIN ratios in re-

---

[25] For a recent survey of the extensive literature on European unemployment and its determinants, see Bean (1992).

TABLE 9.1
Measures of Structure and Economic Performance in Sixteen OECD Countries, 1965–90

	Growth/Inflation Ratios			Drop from (1) to (2) (4)	Corporatism Index (5)	Degree of Trade Union Centralization (6)	Unemployment Rate in 1985 (7)	Inflation-Rate Change from 1975–80 to 1985–90 (8)
	1965–73 (1)	1973–80 (2)	1985–90 (3)					
Norway	0.73	0.54	0.16	0.19	4	C	2.6	−2.0
Denmark	0.54	0.16	0.39	0.38	3	C	7.3	−6.0
Sweden	0.68	0.19	0.34	0.49	4	C	2.8	−4.0
Netherlands	0.84	0.33	3.62	0.51	4	I	10.6	−5.2
Switzerland	0.65	0.08	1.10	0.57	2	D	0.9	0.2
Germany	1.07	0.47	2.25	0.60	4	I	7.2	−2.6
Finland	0.85	0.23	0.70	0.62	1.5	C	5.0	−5.4
United Kingdom	0.70	0.08	0.54	0.62	0	D	11.2	−7.7
Austria	1.12	0.43	1.42	0.69	4	C	3.6	−3.0
France	0.98	0.22	0.95	0.76	0	D	10.2	−6.9
Canada	1.21	0.42	0.67	0.79	0	D	10.4	−4.0
United States	1.03	0.23	0.74	0.80	0	D	7.1	−4.6
Belgium	1.15	0.31	1.51	0.84	0.5	I	11.3	−4.1
Italy	1.15	0.23	0.54	0.92	0.5	D	9.6	−9.9
Australia	1.17	0.24	0.35	0.93	0	I	8.2	−2.4
Japan	1.56	0.36	3.45	1.20	1.5	D	2.6	−5.1

Sources: Cols. (1)–(4): GDP and CPI data, IMF, *International Financial Statistics.* Col.(5): Based on Crouch, 1978; see Bruno and Sachs, 1985, table 11.3. Col. (6): Calmfors and Driffill, 1988, table 2. Col. (7): OECD data. Col. (8): CPI data, IMF, *International Financial Statistics.*

sponse to the oil shocks, higher unemployment eventually helped countries partly to correct such disparities through wage moderation.[26] The self-correcting mechanism is at least partly at work, but at a considerable time lag. The other medium-term channel of inflation, profits, and investment will be taken up in the next section.

One way of observing the process of divergence and convergence of country performance over the so-called twenty-year cycle is to look at the cross-country ranking of the five-year average GRIN ratio over five-year intervals. Appendix Tables 9.A1 through 9.A3 show that, although the country ranking within the 1970–90 period changed substantially, the changes are much less when we compare the end-point 1965–70 and 1985–90 ratios. In only three countries out of sixteen was there a dramatic change in the ranking. Italy moved from position 2 to 12; Australia, from position 3 to 14; and the Netherlands, in a dramatic positive shift, from position 10 to 1 (the 1985–90 ratios also appear in column 3 of Table 9.1).[27] The United Kingdom and United States each moved up four to five places, and all other nine countries moved no more than one or two places. The shifting of rankings is considerably larger when time intervals *within* the 1965–90 period are considered. Because there was convergence in inflation rates across countries toward the end of the period and relatively similar low inflation at the beginning, the above ranking of GRIN ratios could imply a process of convergence to the pre-1970 ranking of growth rates. The growth ladder, although not the actual numbers, may be more stable in the much longer term in which the fundamental growth factors play their dominant role, and it would pay to test that hypothesis, which I have not done. Twenty years, however, is a very long period, corresponding almost to the lifetime of a generation, and it would make little sense to ignore the prolonged systematic departures from the "very" long-term-growth trend even if that hypothesis were to hold.

To see the qualitative similarities and quantitative differences among groups of countries, I take up in Section 5 a parallel discussion of the inflation-and-growth framework applied to groups of middle-income countries of both high and moderate inflation. First, however, I turn to the macroeconomic investment-growth nexus.

4 Inflation, Profitability, and Investment

A major link between the short and the long term that needs to be considered in the present context is the one that connects fluctuations in growth and

---

[26] There is also an empirical negative link, although not a very significant one, between the above measure of corporatism and the rate of unemployment.

[27] The figure for the Netherlands is a bit misleading; only in the quinquennium 1985 does the Netherlands surpass Japan. Minor perturbations in the period of measurement would take

inflation to the profitability of capital and to the investment process. Figure 9.7 indicated a synchronization between the long cycle of inflation and growth and the behavior of the average profit rate for a number of industrial countries. Similarly, the rate of capital formation has also, at a lag, demonstrated a long cycle of recession and recovery during the 1970–90 period. The business-sector gross capital stock in Europe grew at rates of 5 to 6 percent a year throughout the 1960–72 period, and then gradually dropped to rates of 3 percent in the early 1980s.

A strong positive link between profitability and the rate of investment (and a somewhat weaker negative link with respect to the real interest rate) can be established from the data for individual countries and also from the pooling of country data over time (to which we turn below).[28] There also appears to be a link, which an accelerator model of investment would suggest, between the rate of investment and the lagged growth rate. Another significant empirical link to the short-term macroeconomic developments is the apparent negative effect of inflation on capital accumulation (emphasized by a recent cross-sectional study by Fischer [1993]). It is not clear *a priori* to what extent the growth rate has acted on capital formation independently from the profit rate, because their respective movements over time, in response to the supply shocks, have been closely synchronized. There is some evidence, to which Benabou (1988, 1992) has given a theoretical basis, for a line of causality running from inflation to reduced markups. Consider, first, the components and the role of profits.

The average nominal or real rate of profit on capital can be written as the product of the GDP-to-capital ratio (nominal or real), which is average capital productivity, or "capacity utilization," and the profit share. In the following identity, this is written in relative nominal-value terms as

$$R = (P_yY/P_kK) \; [(P_yY - WL)/P_yY] \;, \tag{15}$$

where WL is the nominal wage bill, Y is real GDP, K is the real capital stock, and the Ps are the corresponding price indexes.[29] A fall in R may come as a result of a fall in capacity utilization or in the share of profits or in both.

Looking at the components of the OECD data used below but not analyzed further here reveals that the decomposition of the movement of the profit rate

---

the Netherlands out of first place but would still keep it in the top three to five countries. The relatively high GRIN numbers obtained for some countries suggest a problem with the comparative use of a level *ratio* measure when inflation drops to very low rates.

[28] An earlier study of the link between capital-stock growth and the profit rate for the period up to 1982 is reported in Marglin and Schor (1990).

[29] Here, R is nominal profits over nominal capital, and the first bracket on the right is the capacity ratio in value terms. Both can be turned into real expressions by moving the price ratio P_y/P_k from the right- to the left-hand side.

differs by type of country, even though capacity utilization, the share, and R are all correlated (a rough U-shape) along the twenty-year period. In Canada, the United Kingdom, and the United States, which have been more short-term cyclical (mainly because of aggregate demand shifts), most of the action has come from changes in capacity utilization. In France, Germany, and Sweden, most of the movement has been in changes in the profit share in response to changing real-wage behavior. For some countries (for example, Finland), both factors have been at play. The real-wage profit nexus is a reflection of the aggregate supply response to the oil shocks that has simultaneously also appeared in an increase in inflation and a drop in the growth rate.[30]

I use the *nominal* rate of profit here because it seems to fit the data and the empirical relation between investment and profits better. The reason may be the effect of liquidity (resulting from credit constraints) that larger relative nominal profits give, in addition to the "neoclassical" effect of the real-profit rate on the expected marginal productivity of capital. The importance of financing constraints in explaining investment behavior for a broad class of firms, even in a most advanced financial system, is well brought out in the U.S. context in an extensive recent study by Fazzari, Hubbard, and Petersen (1988).[31]

I have run a panel regression in which the cross-section of data for sixteen countries is pooled and runs jointly over the 1961–91 period (approximately 460 observations, taken from the OECD Analytical Data Base). This yields the following two regressions, which also incorporate country and time dummies (not shown):

$$\dot{k} = \underset{(0.027)}{0.722} \dot{k}_{-1} + \underset{0.015}{0.137}\, R_{-1} - \underset{(0.009)}{0.021}\, r_{-1}, \tag{16}$$

$$(R^2 = 0.95)$$

$$\dot{k} = \underset{(0.025)}{0.745}\, \dot{k}_{-1} + \underset{(0.013)}{0.105}\, R_{-1} - \underset{(0.008)}{0.037}\, r_{-1} + \underset{(0.010)}{0.087}\, g_{-1} - \underset{(0.009)}{0.030}\, \pi_{-1}. \tag{17}$$

$$(R^2 = 0.96)$$

In both equations, the coefficients for R and r are highly significant. In the second equation, the lagged business-sector growth rate (g) and the rate of

---

[30] This longer-term effect of real-wage gaps on investment was analyzed in Malinvaud (1982) and Bruno and Sachs (1985).

[31] Their empirical work relates the traditional study of financial effects on investment to recent literature on capital-market imperfections by studying investment behavior in groups of firms of different sizes and different financial characteristics. It is thus possible to rationalize the finding that real factors affect investment in some firms (as in neoclassical models of the Jorgenson type, which would also be consistent with the Modigliani-Miller neutrality theorem), but that they do not in others. Nevertheless, it puts into doubt the use of a "representative firm" model in investment theory. I am indebted to Ariel Pakes for the above reference.

inflation in terms of GDP prices (π) were included, and these only slightly change the coefficient of R and r. This could suggest that both of these factors may play an independent role in affecting capital formation. The long-term elasticity of capital-stock growth (k) with respect to the lagged rate of profit (R_{-1}) is 0.41 or 0.49, depending on whether we apply the second or the first set of coefficients, while the elasticity with respect to the growth rate (in equation [17]) is 0.34 and with respect to the inflation rate is 0.12.[32]

How does the inflation rate affect the rate of investment? One possible avenue may be suggested by recent theoretical developments in investment theory, based on option value pricing (Dixit, 1989, 1992; Pindyck, 1991) linking investment with macroeconomic uncertainty, which raises the volatility of the marginal productivity of capital and pushes up the threshold of the value of irreversible investment below which investment will not take place. A recent empirical study by Pindyck and Solimano (1993) based on that theory finds that, in addition to the conventional lagged link from the growth rate to the investment rate, the inflation rate (which is highly correlated with its variability) is the "only robust explanator of the marginal profitability of capital."

A panel regression was run by the two authors, in which the dependent variable is the investment-to-GDP ratio, I/Y (rather than k; the two can be related through multiplication of k by the capital-to-output ratio). This is carried out for six industrial countries (France, Germany, Japan, the Netherlands, the United Kingdom, and the United States) over the 1962–89 period, and the variables on the right-hand side of the regression are the lagged dependent variable I/Y (with a coefficient of 0.89), the lagged GDP growth rate (with a highly significant coefficient of about 0.1), and the contemporaneous inflation rate (with a highly significant coefficient of 0.088). Incorporating the standard deviation of inflation (which is highly correlated with inflation) adds nothing, but adding the standard deviation of the real exchange rate gives a slight additional negative effect that increases in impact and significance when the inflation rate is left out of the regression.

To compare the above estimates with those given in Table 9.2, the short-term coefficients have to be turned into implied long-term ones (by dividing the coefficient by $0.11 = 1 - 0.89$) and to be multiplied by an estimate of the capital-to-GDP ratio (about 2.5). This would imply the marginal effect of the

[32] When only the growth rate is incorporated in the regression, the coefficients are almost the same as in equation (17) except for the coefficient of r_{-1}, which gets close to its value in (16). When only the inflation rate is incorporated, its coefficient rises to 0.043, that of R_{-1} rises to be the same as in (16), and r_{-1} is as in (17), suggesting the direction collinearity may be taking between the two pairs of variables. In an earlier draft of this chapter, a regression was included in which there appeared to be an additional direct negative effect of inflation on the profit rate, but it was not considered robust. Ideally, one would want to estimate a model in which the growth rate and inflation rate, as well as the profit rate, are determined endogenously within a larger framework in which both the supply shocks and the macroeconomic policy variables appear explicitly.

TABLE 9.2

Regression Coefficients of Profit and Investment Equations in Sixteen OECD Countries, 1960–91

	Coefficient of R on:		Long-Term Effect on π on R	Coefficient of Δk on:			Long-Term Effect of R on Δk
	R_{-1}	π		Δk_{-1}	R_{-1}	r_{-1}	
Australia	0.62 (0.12)	−0.23 (0.06)	−0.61	0.49 (0.10)	0.15 (0.05)	0.02 (0.02)	0.29
Austria	0.87 (0.09)	−0.05 (0.07)	—	0.66 (0.09)	0.47 (0.11)	0.08 (0.06)	1.36
Belgium	0.87 (0.09)	−0.15 (0.04)	−1.15	0.81 (0.05)	0.17 (0.02)	0.02 (0.01)	0.89
Canada	0.88 (0.09)	−0.02 (0.07)	—	0.53 (0.12)	0.12 (0.04)	−0.11 (0.02)	0.25
Denmark	0.68 (0.12)	−0.13 (0.05)	−0.41	0.74 (0.08)	0.10 (0.09)	−0.06 (0.03)	0.39
Finland	0.38 (0.16)	−0.09 (0.04)	−0.15	0.85 (0.08)	0.38 (0.08)	−0.03 (0.02)	2.55
France	0.88 (0.06)	−0.17 (0.02)	−1.42	1.02 (0.08)	0.08 (0.04)	0.08 (0.03)	. . .
Germany	0.80 (0.06)	−0.19 (0.06)	−0.95	0.53 (0.07)	0.34 (0.06)	−0.06 (0.04)	0.47
Italy	0.64 (0.14)	−0.06 (0.03)	−0.17	0.92 (0.09)	0.17 (0.08)	0.01 (0.02)	2.23
Japan	1.01 (0.05)	−0.24 (0.05)	—	0.35 (0.12)	0.39 (0.07)	0.02 (0.02)	0.60
Netherlands	0.74 (0.18)	−0.14 (0.08)	−0.54	0.77 (0.07)	0.24 (0.05)	−0.08 (0.03)	1.06
Norway	0.59 (0.19)	−0.04 (0.04)	—	0.59 (0.24)	0.46 (0.21)	−0.03 (0.03)	0.76
Sweden	0.56 (0.14)	−0.17 (0.06)	−0.39	0.81 (0.09)	0.19 (0.05)	0.00 (0.02)	0.99
Switzerland	0.93 (0.03)	−0.08 (0.04)	−1.14	0.80 (0.14)	0.06 (0.07)	0.01 (0.04)	. . .
United Kingdom	0.56 (0.11)	−0.09 (0.02)	−0.20	0.69 (0.11)	0.33 (0.10)	−0.03 (0.02)	1.05
United States	0.78 (0.07)	−0.19 (0.04)	−0.86	0.69 (0.12)	0.11 (0.05)	−0.03 (0.03)	0.37

GDP growth rate on capital growth to be 0.37 (similar to the result obtained from equation [17]) and that of inflation to be -0.32, which is stronger than that in (17). A major difference between the two regressions is, of course, the absence of the R and r variables from the Pindyck-Solimano regressions, which are based on a different underlying model.

Through whichever channel inflation affects capital accumulation (this must at the moment remain an open question that calls for more research), these groups of results suggest the existence of a strong path dependence of growth on the shocks and the macroeconomic responses to them, as well as a substantial time span over which these short- and medium-term developments can affect the long-term-growth outcome. They also lend added importance to the policy link between short-term adjustment, structural features of economies, and long-term growth, a link that assumes even greater importance when I discuss, in the next section, the inflation and growth crisis among middle-income countries.

5 Shocks and the Crisis and Recovery Cycle in Middle-Income Countries

I now shift the view to some of the semi-industrial countries, beginning with Latin America. Figures 9.8 and 9.9 (log Y on log P) apply the previous output-and-price-expansion-curve framework to a group of thirteen Latin American economies, from which some of the main elements of inflation and growth can be read. The examples are grouped into the post-1970 high- and moderate-inflation countries, respectively. As with the OECD countries, the 1950s and 1960s were for these countries a golden age of generally high growth, albeit with moderate inflation.[33] The differences between countries were considerable, however, and all of them show much greater variance of behavior over time than do the OECD countries. This variability is mainly a manifestation of terms-of-trade shifts that have always played an important role in countries for which primary exports are an important source of production and revenue. My main concern here, however, is with the 1970s and 1980s (the intermediate thick dots on the curves in Figure 9.9 mark the year 1980). Note that Chile (and to some extent Argentina) is an exception in that Chile had already undergone a sharp growth and inflation crisis in the early 1970s, triggered by very large terms-of-trade shifts. It entered its second major crisis in 1981. For most other countries, which benefited from the large-scale borrowing that became feasible in the aftermath of the first oil shock, the 1970s marked a period of high growth and high investment financed by exten-

---

[33] The figures start in 1960. Tables 9.A1 and 9.A2 in the Appendix give average growth and inflation data that for some of the countries go back to the 1950s.

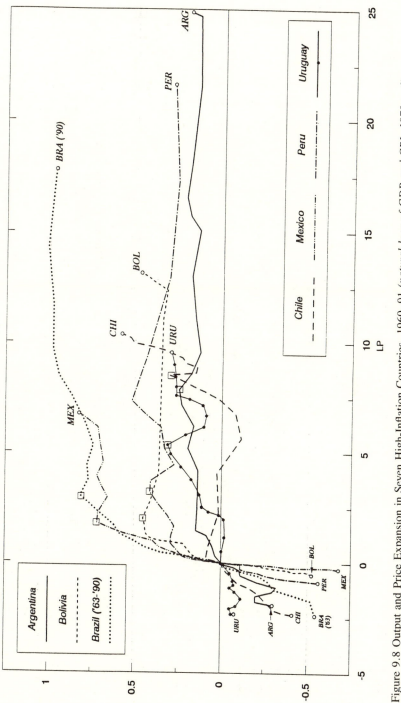

Figure 9.8 Output and Price Expansion in Seven High-Inflation Countries, 1960–91 (*natural logs of GDP and CPI, 1970 = 0*)

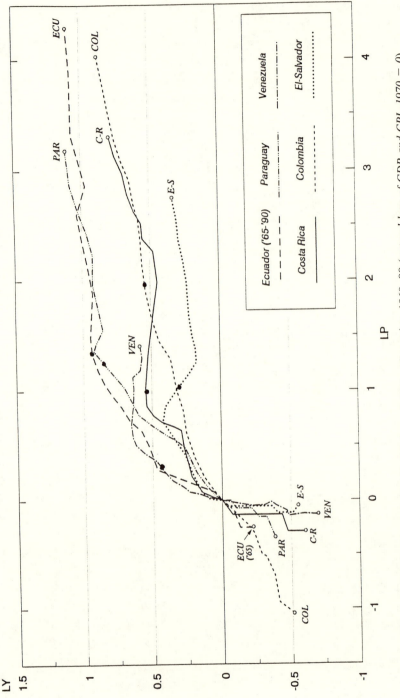

Figure 9.9 Output and Price Expansion in Six Moderate-Inflation Countries, 1960–90 (*natural logs of GDP and CPI, 1970 = 0*)

sive and cheap capital inflow, until the increase in real interest rates and the debt crisis arrived with a vengeance in 1981–82. Figure 9.10 depicts investment and savings for four large borrowers before and after the 1981 crises (more on this below).

The group shown in Figure 9.8 includes, in addition to Uruguay, the six countries showing the highest inflation from 1960 to 1991. Of these, only Brazil stayed in very high inflation by 1993, but only Chile and Mexico (and, to a lesser extent, Bolivia and Argentina) were in what might be termed renewed growth. The six countries displayed in Figure 9.9 had more minor crises and cumulative inflation that was markedly different from that of the first group.

One overriding difference with respect to the OECD countries marks the inflation and growth of this group of countries (as well as of Israel, which will be discussed below) during the 1970–91 period as a whole.[34] Not only are entirely different orders of magnitude of inflation encountered (the horizontal axis of Figure 9.8 multiplies that of Figure 9.3 by a factor of 10!), but the cross-country correlation between growth and inflation is clearly negative here, with only Brazil being the most marked outlier.[35] As Table 9.3 shows, the Spearman rank-correlation coefficient between cumulative growth and cumulative inflation for the twelve countries (excluding Brazil) over the 1970–90 period is −0.48 (it is even more negative for the preceding decade from 1960 to 1970), whereas the figure for the OECD countries is +0.31. This latter figure, however, may be misleading.[36]

The depth of the joint growth and inflation crisis in these countries, as well as in some other middle-income countries (such as Israel), is not related specifically to the size of the terms-of-trade shocks, because these did not markedly differ across countries. It relates, rather, to the differential domestic macroeconomic response to the shocks, notably large fiscal budget deficits and monetary accommodation. The easy access to large-scale foreign borrowing in most cases only postponed the crisis and accentuated it later on. Should we look at output and inflation as jointly determined in this case, in terms of our initial framework, as we did with the case of the OECD countries? I have

[34] In terms of the scale of Figure 9.8, Israel's *LP* figure for 1991 (1970 = 0) is 9.96, like Chile's, and its *LY* value (1970 = 0) is 0.89, between Brazil's and Mexico's.

[35] Over the 1970–90 period as a whole, Brazil had the third-highest (after Ecuador and Paraguay) cumulative GDP growth and also the third-highest cumulative price increase (after Argentina and Peru). The simultaneous high growth no longer applied in the latter part of the period, when, after the mid-1980s, Brazil joined the rest of the low-growth countries. Note, however, that Brazil's relative performance in terms of the GRIN ratio had already in the mid-1970s begun to worsen, first absolutely, then also in comparison to some of the other Latin American countries (Figure 9.11).

[36] An ordinary-least-squares (OLS) regression of the output expansion over the price expansion gives a significantly negative coefficient, with an $R^2 = 0.46$ for the twelve countries but only 0.23 when Brazil is included. An OLS regression for the sixteen OECD countries gives a positive but insignificant coefficient and an R^2 of close to zero.

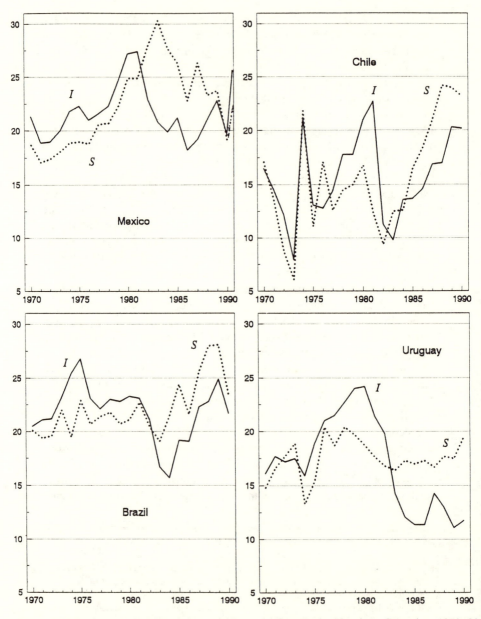

Figure 9.10 Investment (*I*) and Savings (*S*) Rates in Four Latin American Countries, 1970–90 (*percent of GDP*)

TABLE 9.3

Rank Correlation (ρ) of Inflation and Growth by Subperiod and Country Group, 1950–90

	1960–70			1970–90		
	GDP Annual Growth (%)	CPI Inflation %	ρ	GDP Annual Growth (%)	CPI Inflation %	ρ
Latin American (10–13)[a]	4	9	−0.75	3	46	−0.48[b]
OECD[c] (16)	5	4	0.14	3	7	0.31

[a]For 1960 to 1970, the ten countries are Argentina, Bolivia, Colombia, Costa Rica, El Salvador, Mexico, Paraguay, Peru, Uruguay, and Venezuela. For 1970 to 1990, Ecuador and Chile are also included.

[b]When Brazil is included, the rank correlation falls to −0.31

[c]The sample includes the G-6 and ten smaller economies (Australia, Austria, Belgium, Canada, Denmark, Finland, the Netherlands, Norway, Sweden, and Switzerland). For the OECD, the first period extends over the entire twenty years from 1950 to 1970.

already argued in Section 3 that for very high rates of inflation, moving intersections within the underlying AS and AD framework cannot capture the dynamics of inflation. The cumulative experience with episodes of extreme inflation shows that beyond a certain inflation threshold, the economy may lose its nominal anchor and a "neoclassical dichotomy" between the real and the nominal system sets in, so that the nominal system "lifts off," so to speak, into a life of its own. It will distort the real economy and reduce its TFP, but the conventional short-term Phillips-curve trade-offs no longer exist (in terms of Figure 9.4, this implies a position on the horizontal portion of the AS and AD curves). The nominal components of pricing may still be applied as the basis for analysis of the dynamics of inflationary spirals, and the real demand-side fiscal-seigniorage-based model can be applied to determine the "equilibrium" steady-state rates of inflation, if equilibrium exists.[37] The growth rate and the rest of the real system can be determined within an AS and AD framework along with *relative* prices, leaving the *rate of change* of nominal magnitudes—prices, wages, exchange rates, and monetary aggregates—to be determined by one of the above dynamic mechanisms.

High Inflation and Low Growth: Joint Determination and Two-Way Causality

What are the interactions between the growth rate and the inflation rate in such a system, and is there any clear causal link between the two? The answer to

---

[37] Bruno (1991, 1993a) discusses the neoclassical dichotomy of Patinkin (1989) in the context

this question is not independent of the intensity of inflation and the nature of the crisis, and there may be causal mechanisms working in both directions. I shall start with the more generally acceptable causality running from inflation to growth. The conventional argument invokes the distortions caused by the variability of price levels and of relative prices (especially for *unanticipated* inflation); these will affect the TFP residual for given inputs of productive factors. In addition, there is the argument that was applied in Section 4, running from inflation or inflation uncertainty through the rate of profit to depressed capital accumulation. To this can be added the pressure to cut government budgets where it hurts least in the short term, namely, investment in infrastructure. There will also be the distortive effects of high inflation on the structure of production, in particular the inflation of financial-service activities at the level of both the economy and the firm.[38]

In an open economy, the frequent coexistence of high inflation with considerable balance-of-payments problems often forces governments to reduce the growth rate in order to economize on imports of raw materials and capital goods. Such contraction is often also coupled with price-shocking policies (such as subsidy cuts and devaluations) that lead, under monetary accommodation, indexation, or both, to jumps in the inflation rate. This would be one additional explanation why high inflation and low growth tend to occur simultaneously.[39]

Are there causal links working in a clear reverse direction from low growth to high inflation? At least two related channels link the inflation rate with unexpected drops in the growth rate. In an economy running a high growth rate with relative price stability, as did many of the semi-industrial economies in the 1960s, a given preexisting government budget deficit that for political reasons cannot be reduced may turn highly inflationary once there is an exogenous shock to the growth rate. This is because the growth in demand for real government bonds and real money holdings will drop along with the growth rate. Thus, a hitherto noninflationary budget deficit may become inflationary as a result of an exogenous shock to growth. There is no doubt that this factor plays an important role in explaining the jump of the Israeli inflation rate, in response to the large drop in the growth rate, after 1973 (Melnick and Sokoler, 1984).

---

of the high-inflation dynamics of Israel and the extreme-inflation cases of Latin America. Bruno and Fischer (1990) analyze the seigniorage model. In terms of Figure 9.4, the dichotomy implies that AS = AD becomes a horizontal line and that inflation is separately determined.

[38] On this and related arguments, see Fischer and Modigliani (1978). Although these growth costs apply to sustained inflationary processes, there are also the separate, more dramatic disruptions of the economic system during brief, but extreme, hyperinflation episodes. I am indebted to Nissan Liviatan for suggesting these distinctions.

[39] Israel's experience in the 1970s and several Latin American episodes would be cases in point.

More generally, the argument has been made, particularly in the context of several Latin American economies at the turn of the 1970s, that expectations of continuing growth from the golden age of the 1960s and expectations of better living standards on the part of underprivileged social classes forced democratic governments into "populist" policies that increased budget deficits.[40] In some of the cases, these could initially be financed through the easier access to foreign borrowing, for which the inflationary price had to be paid later; in others, the finance was inflationary from the start. Finally, the events of 1968 in the industrial countries (the student unrest and workers' strikes) were not confined to the industrial world but affected countries elsewhere. As Figure 9.11 and Table 9.A3 in the Appendix show, the worsening GRIN ratio had already occurred at the turn of the 1970s, even for countries such as Bolivia and Mexico, and Argentina and Brazil, for which the extreme inflation and growth collapse occurred only much later.

What all of these elements have in common is the fact that an exogenous real shock reduces GDP (or at least its growth rate) and imposes a real burden on society. Inflation, low, moderate, or high, is a measure and a manifestation of the irreconcilability of conflicting claims on a diminishing pie. In a corporatist democratic society, institutional arrangements exist by which such claims can be settled by consensus, at a lower inflation (or additional growth-reduction and unemployment) cost. In an authoritarian regime, the burden sharing can sometimes be settled by decree, but, even under an authoritarian regime, coalitions and pressure groups may be formed, and compromises must often be made to avoid unnecessary social conflict.[41]

Interactions of Shocks, Macroeconomic Response, and Structural Features

What, then, are the structural explanations that can account for the differences in country inflation and growth response at the time of crisis? A study by Berg and Sachs (1988) has asked a related question with respect to the prediction of different countries' *ex ante* probability of incurring debt rescheduling. The same type of argument can also be applied to the predicted position on the inflation and growth-performance scale. The Berg-Sachs study develops a cross-country statistical model of debt rescheduling and secondary-market

[40] For more detailed discussions of individual country histories in this context, see the volumes edited by Sachs (1989) and Dornbusch and Edwards (1991). Alesina and Rodrik (1992) and Persson and Tabellini (1992) present two broad cross-sectional studies that link political factors and distributional conflict with economic growth.

[41] Both Mexico at the turn of the 1970s, and even Chile under dictatorship in the mid-1970s, bear witness to this reality (for example, the 100 percent wage indexation introduced in Chile in 1974).

evaluation of developing-country debt that links these variables to several important structural characteristics of developing countries—the trade regime (the degree of inward or outward orientation that is inferred from a World Bank comparative study), the degree of income inequality (which is measured by the ratio of the top and bottom quintiles and is shown to increase significantly the probability of debt rescheduling),[42] and the share of agriculture in GNP (a high degree of urbanization increases the probability of political instability and thus motivates more "populist" policies).

Applying a probit model based on these characteristics, Berg and Sachs (1988) estimate the debt-rescheduling probability for a set of thirty-five countries (of which twenty-four have comparatively full measurable trade indicators) mainly in Latin America and Asia. The eight Latin American economies included in the smaller sample are listed in Table 9.4 for 1970 to 1990. Column 1 ranks countries by the average inflation rate in terms of logarithmic differences (the most stable country is given the rank of 1); column 2 does the same for the average GDP growth rates; and column 3 ranks in terms of the GRIN ratio (logarithm of difference in GDP over the difference in CPI). Column 4 gives the calculated ranking by the Berg-Sachs measure, which runs from 0.46 for Colombia, the lowest in the group, to 1 for Peru.

I first underscore the Berg-Sachs finding that the calculated probability to reschedule is a good predictor of the actual debt burden and the secondary-market price measure.[43] In terms of the topic of concern here, note that the economic performance measures, the average GRIN ratio as well as the inflation rate (and, to a somewhat lesser extent, the growth rate) are rank-correlated with the calculated probability to reschedule, which is a composite structural index that in some sense is a counterpart of the measure of corporatism for an industrial country. Only one country is removed by more than two positions for at least one of the two rankings: Uruguay, for which the macroeconomic performance was considerably worse than would be predicted by any of the structural or actual debt measures.

Brazil, as mentioned earlier, fits well in terms of inflation but not in terms of growth (and thus in terms of GRIN, for the period as a whole). Although Brazil was relatively more outward oriented among the Latin American economies and suffered less from balance-of-payments crises, it had the most unequal income distribution within the group (Table 9.4, column 7). This basic fact prevented successive democratic governments, at the end of a long period

---

[42] It is interesting to note that this reverses the causality of the well-known Kuznets correlation between income inequality and economic growth.

[43] Colombia is the only country in the above group that had no debt rescheduling but was on the borderline in terms of the market price of its debt. It was an outlier in terms of low share of urban population, low degree of populism, and appropriately low government budget deficits during the period in question. This position shows in the moderate behavior of the growth-to-inflation measure over time (see Figure 9.11).

TABLE 9.4
Economic Performance and Structural Factors in Eight Latin American Borrowers, 1970–90

	Ranking by:				Debt and Income Distribution			
	GDP Growth (1)	Inflation (2)	G/I (3)	Berg-Sachs Index (4)	Debt/ Exports (5)	Public Debt/Exports (6)	Debt Discount (7)	Income Distribution (8)
Colombia	2	2	1	1	121	108	19	21.3
Venezuela	5	1	2	3	129	71	33	18.0
Mexico	3	3	3	5	239	100	47	15.1
Brazil	1	7	4	7	268	85	45	33.3
Chile	4	4	5	4	273	93	33	11.4
Uruguay	6	5	6	2	100	45	32	10.8
Peru	7	7	7	8	160	142	89	32.1
Argentina	8	8	8	6	269	109	53	11.4

Sources: Cols. (1)–(2): Calculated on the basis of IMF, *International Financial Statistics* data. Cols. (4)–(8): Berg and Sachs, 1988, tables 1, 2, 7, 8.
Notes: Col. (4): Ranking by 'probability to reschedule debt' estimated from profit model by Berg and Sachs, 1988, based on trade regime, urbanization, and income distribution. Cols. (5)–(6): Debt-to-export ratio (percentage) for 1981, total (5) and public only (6). Col. (7): Bid price for $100 claim of debt to financial institutions and secondary market, July 1987. Col. (8): Ratio of highest to lowest quintile.

of military government, from adopting the required austerity measures or from adopting stringent monetary policies with regard to the business sector. Brazil proves the point that you may continue with high growth and high inflation for a while, but not without limit. Its GRIN ratio for 1980 to 1990 would have placed it much closer to its true position in the ranking by the debt-rescheduling predictor. Indeed, by 1993, Brazil remained the only economy in the region with annual inflation of more than two digits.[44]

The Dynamics of Recovery from Extreme Inflation

Figure 9.11 shows the development of the GRIN ratio for several countries over the last fifteen years in comparison to the OECD curve. Israel is included, because the depth of its high-inflation and low-growth crisis in the 1970s and early 1980s assumed Latin American dimensions.[45] Among the countries that have successfully come out of the deep crisis, Chile is particularly remarkable. After initial success at stabilization and reform during the 1970s debt crisis, its relative position worsened again and, to most observers, looked no better than Argentina's and Uruguay's in terms of a failed reform process. The speed with which Chile came out of the crisis after a successful 1982–83 stabilization effort is shown by the rapidly rising GRIN curve in Figure 9.11 and can be ascribed to the series of structural reforms Chile had undertaken in the earlier years.

Figure 9.12 shows the cycle of crisis and recovery for four successful stabilizers from extreme inflation. It is interesting to note the qualitative similarity of the twenty-year loop with that of a typical OECD country.[46] There are two notable differences, however. One is the obviously larger amplitude on the inflation axis for Bolivia (10 and 20 times) and the temporary shift into the negative growth region for three or four other countries. The other is the *anti-clockwise* movement of the trajectory during recovery. The fact that growth is systematically higher after a sharp stabilization is consistent with the finding *that very high rates of inflation are definitely harmful to growth*. Stabilization, by itself, improves resource allocation and total factor productivity, even before sustainable resumption of investment and long-term growth.[47]

[44] It is probably no accident that Peru, the worst off of the economies in terms of the composite predictor, finally stabilized—before Brazil—only after giving up democracy.

[45] The same cannot be said of the elements that make up the Berg-Sachs structural predictor, in which Israel ranks among the lowest (0.012 probability of rescheduling), together with several East Asian economies, as a result of a more egalitarian income distribution and a more outward trade orientation than that of the average Latin American economy.

[46] The five-year averaging adopted here makes Mexico's cycle look incomplete because its stabilization took place only in 1988 and the last observation on the curve is the average for 1986 through 1991. The actual numbers for 1991–92, however, place it closer to the end of the loop.

[47] In the case of Israel, for example, average annual TFP growth rose from −0.5 percent for 1981–84 to 2.6 percent for 1986–90.

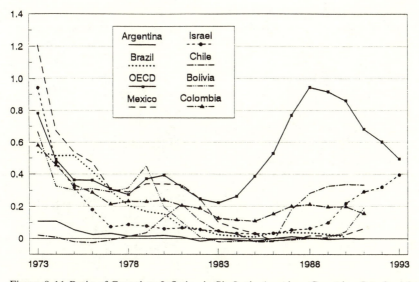

Figure 9.11 Ratio of Growth to Inflation in Six Latin American Countries, Israel, and the OECD, 1973–91

In all four countries, the initial stabilization included a sharp cut in the fiscal deficit and a sharp devaluation coupled with a credit squeeze. In two of the countries, Mexico and Israel, stabilization was *heterodox*; that is, direct intervention in the dynamics of inflation in the form of a wage and exchange-rate freeze, coupled in the case of Israel with temporary price controls, supplemented the fiscal cut.[48] *Structural reforms*, which in most cases accompanied the initial adjustment (in Israel, these came gradually during the post-stabilization period), consisted of trade liberalization, financial deregulation, privatization, and the introduction of greater flexibility in the labor market.

Figure 9.10 shows the diverse behavior of investment after stabilization for two of the countries. Chile, which was the earliest reformer (mid-1970s) showed a strong effect, mainly a composition switch; private investment rose from 5.3 percent for 1971–75 to 11.2 percent for 1976–81, whereas public investment was cut in half, from 10.6 to 5.8 percent. Subsequently, Chile's 1982–83 crisis was one of the worst, with a 10 percent drop in investment to GDP (11 percent for private investment), but with a sharp rebound in investment later on. As can be seen from Figure 9.10, Chile's medium-term adjustment also involved a large increase in the savings rate.

In Mexico, investment to GDP fell by 8 percent between 1978–81 and 1982–89, but most of the decrease (5 percent) was in public investment, with only a moderate temporary fall in private investment. This contrasts with a

---

[48] For a detailed analysis as well as cross-country comparisons, see Bruno (1993a).

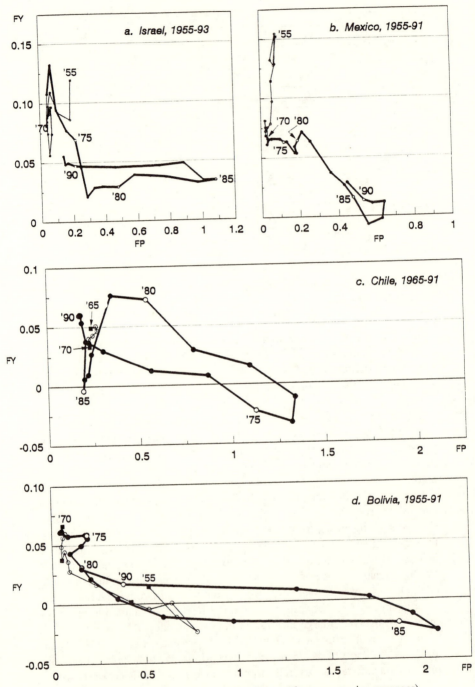

Figure 9.12 Inflation and Growth, Successful Stabilizers (*five-year moving averages*)

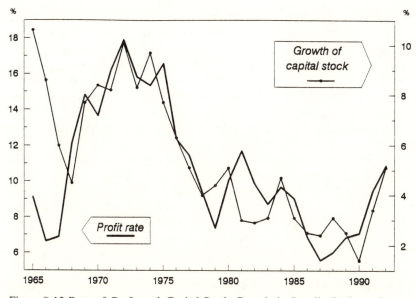

Figure 9.13 Rate of Profit and Capital-Stock Growth in Israel's Business Sector, 1965–92

sharp drop in investment in Israel, from a high of above 30 percent of GDP in the early 1970s to below 20 percent after stabilization; a rebound occurred only more recently, five to six years after the successful 1985 stabilization. The numbers for the growth rate of the capital stock in Israel's business sector appear in Figure 9.13. The marked difference between Israel and Mexico can be explained in terms of the different behavior of two key real-factor prices, real wages and real interest rates. In both of these, a substantial overshooting in the case of Israel caused a sharp two-year recession two years after stabilization (see Bruno [1993a, chap. 6] for a more detailed comparison).

High real interest rates have characterized virtually all sharp stabilizations and are one of the reasons holding up investment renewal, along with uncertainty about the sustainability of stabilization. The case of real-wage overshooting is confined to the existence of a rigid labor market, like Israel's, where a reputation game had to be played between the government (mainly the Bank of Israel), the employers, and the labor unions to establish the credibility of a stable exchange-rate anchor. The cost was the need to go through a period of unemployment before real wages started falling, and a precondition was the existence of a sufficient exchange-reserve cushion to carry the government over a period of real appreciation and loss of competitiveness. In Israel, this post-stabilization adjustment to more flexible exchange-rate and interest-rate policy, as well as to greater wage moderation, took three to four years, during which profits continued to be squeezed.

Figure 9.13 shows the close relation in the Israeli case between profitability (in turn affected by unit labor costs) and investment. A least-squares regression of capital-stock growth on the contemporaneous rate of profit in the business sector over the 1968–92 period (25 observations) gives a highly significant coefficient of 0.64 (standard error of 0.06) with an adjusted $R^2 = 0.82$ (and a Durbin-Watson coefficient of 1.73), suggesting that the link may be mainly through the financial channel mentioned in the context of the industrial countries. Lack of data prevents a similar analysis of other countries in our sample.

Can a link between inflation, investment, and growth be established in this case, as with the OECD countries? The previously quoted study by Pindyck and Solimano (1993) includes a separate panel regression for the group of six high-inflation economies—Argentina, Bolivia, Brazil, Chile, Mexico, and Israel—for the thirty-year period from 1960 to 1990. Here again, the investment-to-GDP ratio is regressed over its own lag (with a coefficient of 0.76) on the growth rate (0.17), the inflation rate (-0.00016), and the variability of the real exchange rate (-0.0924). All the coefficients are highly significant. Working out the long-term response of growth and inflation, we get coefficients of 0.73 for the growth rate but only -0.00067 for inflation. Thus, roughly speaking, a 500 percent increase in inflation had the same effect on the I/Y ratio in a high-inflation country as a 1 percent increase had for an industrial country (where the implied long-term inflation coefficient was 0.32). Moderate inflations of the 1960s and early 1970s apparently did not affect investment rates among these countries, but the very high inflations later on and, in particular, the hyperinflations of Bolivia and Argentina did have an effect, although the estimates seem surprisingly small. The coefficient for the growth rate, however, was larger than for the industrial countries, and, with much deeper growth collapse, the total investment response (both private and public) to the debt shock was sizable. Investment ratios in some of these countries typically fell by 5 to 7 percentage points between the decades of the 1970s and 1980s. Resumption of investment once stabilization has been achieved is, in theory as well as practice, extremely slow.[49] So, in these countries even more than in the industrial countries, the deep crisis of the 1970s (and, even more, of the 1980s), and the delayed adjustment to the external shocks, has had and must continue to have a very marked effect on long-term growth.

Endnote on Central and Eastern Europe

This chapter is already too long to include a separate detailed discussion of Central and East European reform (see Bruno [1993a, 1993b] for a more

---

[49] See discussion in Dornbusch (1990). An extreme example not shown here is Bolivia, for

detailed discussion). The only point to be mentioned in the present context is that, although the region has brought up a great many new and substantially uncharted problems, some of the issues can be cast into an inflation-and-growth framework of the type used here.

In almost all the cases of protracted inflation and growth collapse of the kind discussed in the Latin American context, the crisis involved several dimensions, a drop to zero (or negative) growth lasting for a considerable length of time and a worsening of *both* the macroeconomic imbalance of the economy and the structural maladjustment dimension of the microeconomy. The former usually involves both internal fiscal imbalances as well as external imbalance; the latter involves distorted production structures and distorted signals of relative prices. With time, the various dimensions of the crisis tend to reinforce one another. A sustained (open or repressed) high inflation, for example, exacerbates the microeconomic distortions in the economy, whereas distorted labor-, commodity-, or financial-market structures may worsen the extent of macroeconomic imbalance in the economy.

How relevant is this to Central and Eastern Europe? Because the systems in the region lacked the basic attributes of market economies, the problem of restructuring was clearly different. Yet, at a level of macroeconomic generalities, there are some analogies. All the Central and East European countries went through a phase of sharp growth slowdown with repressed inflation that burst out into the open once the price system was liberalized. The outcome, in terms of the drop in growth and the rise in inflation in 1989–90, had supply-shock properties. As to the adjustment and structural-reform phase, the difference is considerable and, in analytical terms, would show in the steepness and distancing of the AS curves. The existence of substantial distortions in the financial markets, for example, would make much more costly in terms of the output loss the monetary contraction required to achieve a given reduction in inflation, that is, the g_s curve would be much steeper (in the context of Figure 9.4).

Figure 9.14 gives a stylized representation of the phases of crisis and reform into which most countries in question can be classified. All of the Central and East European countries went through a prolonged growth crisis in the second half of the 1970s and into the 1980s (a shift from A to B). At different times, they have all, or are still, in the process of a price liberalization that takes the form of a price shock and a sharp drop into negative growth (from B to C). Czechoslovakia, Hungary, and Poland (Hungary much more gradually than the others) have gone through price liberalization and stabilization and now find themselves somewhere in the structural-adjustment phase (between

---

which the 1985 stabilization was a success, yet GDP growth per capita by 1991 hardly returned to positive, and investment has remained depressed at barely positive net investment; gross investment in 1990 was of the order of 12 percent, down from close to 30 percent in the first half of the 1990s.

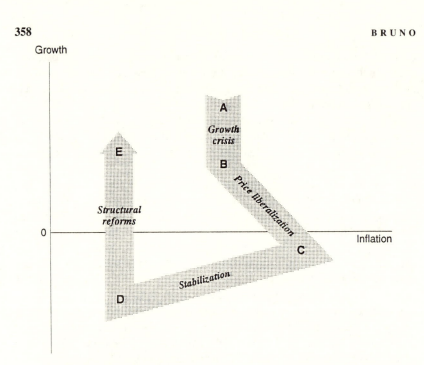

Figure 9.14 Stylized Representation of Crisis, Adjustment, and Reform in Central and Eastern Europe

D and E), with Poland the only country in the region that by 1992 was beginning to show positive growth (with the Czechs soon to follow). Romania and Bulgaria had opened up and were still in the process of stabilization (somewhere between C and D), and most members of the former Soviet Union (with the exception of some of the Baltics) had not quite reached point C, yet were in very high inflation and negative growth.

One of the many interesting questions that both the Latin American experience and the more recent Central and East European episodes raise is that of the sequencing of stabilization and structural reforms. Stabilization, in stylized terms, implies a sharp inward movement along the horizontal inflation axis with smaller or larger output sacrifice; structural reform is depicted as the subsequent vertical movement along the growth axis amid relative price stability. Can stabilization be achieved without some simultaneous structural reforms? Moreover, are there "diagonal" shortcuts between C and E, by which some structural reforms can also be achieved amid very high inflation? I shall not attempt to answer these questions in this chapter but shall end instead by reiterating the point made at the beginning and followed as a premise throughout, that both the positive economics of growth and growth crises in recent decades, as well as the policy and reform options, are, for very dissimilar types of economies, best discussed within a framework that considers growth and inflation simultaneously.

Appendix

TABLE 9.A1

Average Rate of GDP Growth, 1950–90 (annual percentage, based on log differences)

	1950–55	1955–60	1960–65	1965–70	1970–75	1975–80	1980–85	1985–90
OECD countries								
Australia	3.9	4.0	4.8	5.6	3.6	2.8	3.1	2.7
Austria	6.2	5.4	4.0	5.2	3.8	3.3	1.3	3.0
Belgium	3.3	2.6	4.9	4.7	3.4	3.0	0.8	3.1
Canada	5.1	3.9	5.6	4.5	4.9	3.8	2.9	2.9
Denmark	2.0	4.3	5.1	3.6	1.9	2.5	2.6	1.5
Finland	5.1	4.5	4.8	4.7	3.9	3.0	2.8	3.4
France	4.4	4.6	5.6	5.2	2.7	2.8	1.5	2.9
Germany	9.0	6.3	4.7	4.1	2.1	3.3	1.1	3.1
Italy	6.4	5.3	5.7	5.6	2.7	4.6	1.4	3.0
Japan	8.7	8.2	8.9	0.9	4.4	4.5	3.7	4.6
Netherlands	5.2	3.8	4.7	5.2	3.2	2.6	1.0	2.6
Norway	3.9	3.5	4.5	3.7	4.5	4.7	3.3	0.9
Sweden	3.0	3.4	6.1	3.9	2.6	1.3	1.8	2.0
Switzerland	4.8	4.2	5.1	4.1	0.8	1.7	1.4	2.7
United Kingdom	3.0	2.7	3.2	2.5	3.4	2.2	2.0	3.1
United States	4.3	2.1	4.7	4.1	2.3	3.3	2.6	2.9
OECD total	4.9	3.2	4.8	4.4	3.0	3.4	2.4	3.2

(continued)

TABLE 9.A1 (Continued)

	1950–55	1955–60	1960–65	1965–70	1970–75	1975–80	1980–85	1985–90
Latin America								
Argentina	5.9	1.2	1.7	4.2	2.7	2.2	-2.2	0.3
Bolivia	1.4	0.2	3.8	6.6	5.7	3.1	1.9	1.7
Brazil				6.2	9.9	6.4	1.1	2.0
Chile			4.9	3.3	-2.2	7.2	0.4	6.0
Colombia			4.6	5.6	5.5	5.2	2.2	4.5
Costa Rica			5.0	6.8	5.8	5.1	0.3	4.5
Ecuador			-4.3	4.3	11.5	6.4	2.2	1.9
El Salvador			6.6	4.4	5.3	1.1	-1.8	2.2
Mexico	5.2	11.4	6.9	6.7	6.3	6.4	1.6	1.3
Paraguay			3.4	4.1	6.5	10.2	1.7	3.8
Peru			6.9	4.3	5.1	2.0	-0.2	-1.8
Uruguay		0.0	-0.0	0.8	1.4	4.4	-3.7	3.3
Venezuela			6.8	7.1	4.7	4.7	3.3	-1.1
Israel	11.9	8.5	9.7	8.1	6.9	2.9	3.4	4.7

Source: IMF, International Financial Statistics.

TABLE 9.A2

Average Rate of CPI Inflation, 1950–90 (annual percentage, based on log differences)

	1950–55	1955–60	1960–65	1965–70	1970–75	1975–80	1980–85	1985–90
OECD countries								
Australia	8.5	3.1	1.8	3.1	9.7	10.1	8.0	7.6
Austria	7.8	2.1	3.8	3.2	7.0	5.1	4.8	2.1
Belgium	2.1	1.7	2.5	3.4	8.0	6.2	6.8	2.1
Canada	2.5	1.9	1.5	3.8	7.1	8.4	7.2	4.4
Denmark	4.1	1.8	5.2	6.2	8.9	9.9	7.6	3.9
Finland	4.4	6.4	5.2	4.6	11.1	10.2	8.2	4.8
France	5.3	5.8	3.7	4.2	8.5	9.9	9.1	3.0
Germany	1.9	1.8	2.8	2.5	5.9	4.0	3.8	1.4
Italy	4.2	1.8	4.8	2.9	10.7	15.4	13.2	5.5
Japan	6.2	1.5	6.0	5.3	10.8	6.4	2.7	1.3
Netherlands	2.9	3.1	3.2	4.7	8.3	5.9	4.1	0.7
Norway	2.9	3.1	3.2	4.7	8.1	8.1	8.6	6.1
Sweden	5.5	3.6	3.6	4.4	7.7	10.0	8.6	6.0
Switzerland	1.6	1.2	3.2	3.4	7.4	2.3	4.2	2.5
United Kingdom	5.4	2.6	3.5	4.5	12.2	13.4	6.9	5.8
United States	1.9	1.8	1.3	4.1	6.5	8.5	5.3	3.9
OECD total	3.2	2.7	3.4	4.1	8.3	8.6	6.2	3.7

(continued)

TABLE 9.A2 (Continued)

	1950–55	1955–60	1960–65	1965–70	1970–75	1975–80	1980–85	1985–90
Latin America								
Argentina	13.9	35.8	20.8	17.8	49.8	107.4	144.1	192.3
Bolivia	51.8	42.3	5.0	5.7	18.7	15.7	186.3	38.2
Brazil			47.9	24.3	19.1	41.3	91.2	203.8
Chile	34.7	27.0	24.0	23.2	112.6	54.3	19.3	17.7
Colombia			11.0	9.8	16.5	21.8	20.2	22.3
Costa Rica			3.1	2.7	12.8	7.8	29.9	15.7
Ecuador			6.7	5.0	12.6	11.1	24.3	37.7
El Salvador			0.0	1.1	8.2	12.0	13.7	21.1
Mexico	8.7	5.7	2.5	3.3	11.8	19.0	47.5	52.9
Paraguay			5.2	1.5	10.9	13.7	14.6	24.7
Peru	7.0	8.0	8.5	9.3	11.9	40.9	70.4	222.3
Uruguay	0.0	11.2	20.0	26.1	52.5	44.8	37.0	57.7
Venezuela			2.3	0.3	1.6	5.6	10.5	10.5
Israel	19.4	44.4	6.9	3.9	21.6	47.9	108.3	21.3

Source: IMF, *International Financial Statistics.*

TABLE 9.A3
Ratio of Growth to Inflation, 1950–90

	1950–55	1955–60	1960–65	1965–70	1970–75	1975–80	1980–85	1985–90
OECD countries								
Australia	0.459	1.306	2.683	1.817	0.366	0.274	0.386	0.352
Austria	0.798	2.571	1.057	1.605	0.541	0.640	0.269	1.416
Belgium	1.602	1.485	1.954	1.375	0.423	0.484	0.112	1.505
Canada	2.060	2.094	3.641	1.190	0.697	0.454	0.399	0.674
Denmark	0.478	2.388	0.979	0.578	0.217	0.250	0.339	0.394
Finland	1.169	0.707	0.917	1.022	0.354	0.294	0.346	0.699
France	0.825	0.793	1.511	1.241	0.323	0.287	0.164	0.948
Germany	4.689	3.493	1.710	1.612	0.355	0.822	0.297	2.252
Italy	1.532	2.898	1.191	1.945	0.250	0.302	0.104	0.541
Japan	1.404	5.482	1.480	2.061	0.406	0.697	1.373	3.448
Netherlands	1.814	1.220	1.477	1.107	0.383	0.439	0.241	3.618
Norway	1.340	1.136	1.419	0.789	0.559	0.580	0.379	0.156
Sweden	0.548	0.921	1.704	0.885	0.334	0.132	0.210	0.339
Switzerland	2.949	3.512	1.608	1.214	0.109	0.723	0.329	1.101
United Kingdom	0.554	1.035	0.902	0.552	0.280	0.163	0.293	0.544
United States	2.239	1.146	3.667	0.984	0.353	0.387	0.493	0.743
OECD total	1.540	1.185	1.433	1.065	0.365	0.394	0.387	0.859

(continued)

TABLE 9.A3 (*Continued*)

	1950–55	1955–60	1960–65	1965–70	1970–75	1975–80	1980–85	1985–90
Latin America								
Argentina	0.428	0.034	0.083	0.235	0.055	0.020	−0.016	0.001
Bolivia	0.027	0.004	0.764	1.155	0.303	0.199	−0.010	0.044
Brazil				0.254	0.517	0.155	0.012	0.010
Chile			0.205	0.143	−0.020	0.133	−0.020	0.337
Colombia			0.417	0.564	0.335	0.240	0.110	0.200
Costa Rica			1.629	2.530	0.455	0.655	0.011	0.290
Ecuador			−0.637	0.853	0.911	0.575	0.092	0.050
El Salvador				3.809	0.637	0.088	−0.132	0.102
Mexico	1.756	2.006	2.749	2.058	0.539	0.339	0.033	0.025
Paraguay			0.655	2.772	0.599	0.746	0.118	0.155
Peru			0.813	0.461	0.432	0.050	−0.003	−0.008
Uruguay		0.000	−0.002	0.031	0.022	0.098	−0.099	0.058
Venezuela			2.899	21.388	3.013	0.843	0.310	−0.102
Israel	0.616	1.894	1.410	2.055	0.318	0.061	0.031	0.220

Source: Tables 9.A1 and 9.A2.

References

Alesina, Alberto, and Dani Rodrik, "Distribution, Political Conflict and Economic Growth: A Simple Theory with Some Empirical Evidence," in Alex Cukierman, Zvi Hercowitz, and Leonardo Leiderman, eds., *Political Economy, Growth, and Business Cycles*, Cambridge, Mass., MIT Press, 1992.

Bayoumi, Tamim A., and Barry Eichengreen, "Macroeconomic Adjustment Under Bretton Woods and the Post-Bretton-Woods Float: An Impulse-Response Analysis," National Bureau of Economic Research Working Paper No. 4169, Cambridge, Mass., National Bureau of Economic Research, September 1992.

Bean, Charles R., "European Unemployment: A Survey," Discussion Paper No. 71, London, Economic and Social Research Council, London School of Economics, March 1992.

Benabou, Roland, "Search, Price Setting and Inflation," *Review of Economic Studies*, 55 (July 1988), pp. 353–376.

———, "Inflation and Markups," *European Economic Review*, 36 (April 1992), pp. 566–574.

Berg, Andrew, and Jeffrey D. Sachs, "The Debt Crisis: Structural Explanations of Country Performance," *Journal of Development Economics*, 29 (November 1988), pp. 271–306.

Bernabe, Franco, "The Labour Market and Unemployment," in Andrea Boltho, ed., *The European Economy: Growth and Crisis*, New York, Oxford University Press, 1982, pp. 159–188.

Blanchard, Olivier J., and Lawrence H. Summers, "Hysteresis and the European Unemployment Problem," *NBER Macroeconomics Annual* (1986), pp. 15–78.

Bruno, Michael, *High Inflation and the Nominal Anchors of an Open Economy*, Essays in International Finance No. 183, Princeton, N.J., Princeton University, International Finance Section, June 1991.

———, *Crisis, Stabilization and Economic Reform: Therapy by Consensus*, New York, Oxford University Press, 1993a.

———, "Stabilization and the Macroeconomics of Transition—How Different is Eastern Europe?" *Economics of Transition*, 1 (January 1993b), pp. 5–19.

Bruno, Michael, and Stanley Fischer, "Seignorage, Operating Rules and the High Inflation Trap," *Quarterly Journal of Economics*, 105 (May 1990), pp. 353–374.

Bruno, Michael, and Jeffrey D. Sachs, *Economics of Worldwide Stagflation*. Cambridge, Mass., Harvard University Press; Oxford, Blackwell, 1985.

Calmfors, Lars, and John Driffill, "Centralization of Wage Bargaining," *Economic Policy*, 3 (April 1988), pp. 14–61.

Corden, W. Max, Richard N. Cooper, Ian M. D. Little, and Sarath Rajapatirana, *Boom, Crisis and Adjustment: The Macroeconomic Experience of Developing Countries*, Washington, D.C., World Bank, 1993.

Crouch, Colin, "Conditions for Trade Union Wage Restraint" in Leon Lindberg and Charles S. Maier, eds., *The Politics of Inflation and Economic Stagflation: Theoretical Approaches and International Case Studies*, Washington, D.C., Brookings Institution, 1985.

Crouch, Colin, and Alessandro Pizzorno, eds., *The Resurgence of Class Conflict in Western Europe Since 1968*, London, Holmes and Meier, 1978.

Denison, Edward F., *Accounting for Slower Growth: The United States in the 1970s*, Washington, D.C., Brookings Institution, 1979.

Dixit, Avinash, "Entry and Exit Decisions Under Uncertainty," *Journal of Political Economy*, 97 (June 1989), pp. 620–638.

———, "Investment and Hysteresis," *Journal of Economic Perspectives*, 6 (Winter 1992), pp. 107–132.

Dornbusch, Rudiger, "Policies to Move from Stabilization to Growth," in *Proceedings of the World Bank Annual Conference on Development Economics*, Supplement to *World Bank Economic Review*, Washington, D.C., World Bank, 1990, pp. 19–48.

Dornbusch, Rudiger, and Sebastian Edwards, eds., *The Macroeconomics of Populism in Latin America*, Chicago, University of Chicago Press, 1991.

Easterly, William R., Michael Kremer, Lant Pritchett, and Lawrence H. Summers, "Good Policy or Good Luck? Country Growth Performance and Temporary Shocks," Washington, D.C., World Bank, March 1992, processed.

Easterly, William, and Sergio T. Rebelo, "Fiscal Policy and Economic Growth: An Empirical Investigation," Washington D.C., World Bank, December 1993, processed.

Fazzari, Steven M., R. Glenn Hubbard, and Bruce C. Petersen, "Financing Constraints and Corporate Investment," *Brookings Papers on Economic Activity*, No. 1 (1988), pp. 141–206.

Fischer, Stanley, "The Role of Macroeconomic Factors in Growth," Department of Economics, Massachusetts Institute of Technology, January 1993, processed.

Fischer, Stanley, and Franco Modigliani, "Towards an Understanding of the Real Effects and Costs of Inflation," *Weltwirtschaftliches Archiv*, 114 (No. 4, 1978), pp. 810–832.

Galor, Oded, and Daniel Tsiddon, "Transitory Productivity Shocks and Long-Run Output," *International Economic Review*, 33 (November 1992), pp. 921–933.

Glyn, Andrew, A. Hughes, A. Lipietz, and A. Singh, "The Rise and Fall of the Golden Age," in Marglin and Schor, *The Golden Age of Capitalism*, 1990, pp. 153–186.

Grossman, Gene, and Elhanan Helpman, *Innovation and Growth in the Global Economy*, Cambridge, Mass., MIT Press. 1991.

Jorgenson, Dale W., "The Role of Energy in Productivity Growth," in John W. Kendrick, ed., *International Comparisons of Productivity and Causes of the Slowdown*, Cambridge, Mass., Ballinger, 1984, pp. 270–323.

Kendrick, John W., "International Comparisons of Recent Productivity Trends," in Sam H. Schurr, ed., *Energy, Productivity and Economic Growth*, Cambridge, Mass., Oelgeschlager, Gunn, and Hain, 1983, pp. 71–120.

Lindbeck, Assar, and Dennis J. Snower, "Wage Setting, Unemployment and Insider-Outsider Relations," *American Economic Review*, 76 (May 1986), pp. 235–239.

Lucas, Robert E., Jr., "On the Mechanics of Economic Development," *Journal of Monetary Economics*, 22 (June 1988), pp. 3–42.

Maddison, Angus, "Growth and Slowdown in Advanced Capitalist Economies: Techniques of Quantitative Assessment," *Journal of Economic Literature*, 25 (June 1987), pp. 649–698.

Malinvaud, Edmond, "Wages and Unemployment," *Economic Journal* (London), 92 (March 1982), pp. 1–12.

Marglin, Stephen A., and Juliet B. Schor, eds., *The Golden Age of Capitalism: Rein-*

terpreting the Postwar Experience, Oxford, Clarendon; New York, Oxford University Press, 1990.

Melnick, Raphael, and Meir Sokoler, "The Government's Revenue Creation and the Inflationary Effect of a Decline in the Rate of Growth of GNP," *Journal of Monetary Economics*, 13 (March 1984), pp. 225–236.

Nelson, Charles R., and Charles I. Plosser, "Trends and Random Walks in Macroeconomic Time-Series," *Journal of Monetary Economics*, 10 (September 1982), pp. 139–162.

Patinkin, Don, *Money, Interest and Prices*, Cambridge, Mass., MIT Press, 2d rev. ed., 1989.

Persson, Torsten, and Guido Tabellini, "Growth, Distribution and Politics," in Alex Cukierman, Zvi Hercovitz, and Leonardo Leiderman, eds., *Political Economy, Growth and Business Cycles*, Cambridge, Mass., MIT Press, 1992.

Pindyck, Robert S., "Irreversibility, Uncertainty and Investment," *Journal of Economic Literature*, 29 (September 1991), pp. 1110–1152.

Pindyck, Robert S., and Andrés Solimano, "Economic Instability and Aggregate Investment," Massachusetts Institute of Technology, February 1993, processed.

Romer, Paul, "Increasing Returns and Long-Run Growth," *Journal of Political Economy*, 94 (October 1986), pp. 1002–1037.

Sachs, Jeffrey D., "Real Wages and Unemployment in the OECD Countries: A Comparative Study," *Brookings Papers on Economic Activity*, No. 2 (1983), pp. 255–303.

———, ed., *Developing Country Debt and Economic Performance*, Vols. 1–3 [Vol. 3 edited with Susan M. Collins], Chicago, University of Chicago Press, 1989.

Saint-Paul, Gilles, "Productivity Growth and Unemployment in OECD Countries," Working Paper No. 91–09, Paris, Département et Laboratoire d'Economie Théorique et Appliquée, 1991.

———, "Productivity Growth and the Structure of the Business Cycle," CEPR Discussion Paper No. 709, London, Centre for Economic Policy Research, October 1992.

Soskice, David W., "Strike Waves and Wage Explosions, 1968–70: An Economic Interpretation," in Colin Crouch and Alessandro Pizzorno, eds., *The Resurgence of Class Conflict in Western Europe Since 1968*, London, Holmes and Meier, 1978, pp. 221–246.

Stock, James H., and Mark W. Watson, "Variable Trends in Economic Time Series," *Journal of Economic Perspectives*, 2 (Summer 1988), pp. 147–174.

Tarantelli, Ezio, "The Regulation of Inflation in Western Countries and the Degree of Neocorporatism," *Economia Internazionale*, 2 (May 1983), pp. 199–238.

10

Panel: The Outlook for Stabilization and Reform in Central and Eastern Europe

THE POLITICAL and economic transformation of Central and Eastern Europe is the most urgent and complicated task facing the international community. Success will depend primarily on the skills and commitment of those directly involved—the leaders and citizens of the countries themselves—but the West can help. What are the chief obstacles to transformation? How can they be overcome? What can the West contribute? How much difference can it make?

Three economists were asked to answer these questions, paying particular attention to the external dimensions of the process—the roles of exchange-rate arrangements and convertibility, of foreign investment and assistance, and of trade policies, not only those of the countries involved but those of the West as well. The panelists were not asked to focus primarily on Russia, but all of them chose to do so, because Russia faces the most formidable problems and its success or failure can have fateful consequences for the entire world.

Each panelist has given much attention and effort to the problems of transformation and reform. Stanley Fischer has served as vice president and chief economist of the World Bank. John Odling-Smee is director of the European II Department of the International Monetary Fund, which deals with the problems of Central and Eastern Europe. (His duties prevented him from attending the conference, and his paper was presented by his colleague, Thomas Wolf.) John Williamson, senior fellow at the Institute for International Economics, has written extensively on the problems of reform in Central and Eastern Europe, with particular attention to exchange-rate arrangements and convertibility.

Readers of these papers should bear in mind the situation in April 1993, when the papers were presented. The Western governments had just agreed to provide large amounts of financial assistance to Russia, bilaterally and by way of the multinational institutions. The International Monetary Fund was about to establish a Structural Transformation Facility, designed to provide transitional assistance to the countries of Central and Eastern Europe until they are able to implement policies that will give them access to ordinary drawings on the Fund. Within Russia itself, the process of reform appeared to be gathering momentum, although there were widespread concerns, even then, about the amounts of subsidized credit being granted by the Central Bank of Russia. Few people foresaw the crises ahead—the disruptive and demoralizing currency reform, the rapid acceleration of credit creation, the dissolution of Parliament, and the election of December 1993, which led to a discouraging retreat from reform. Although the papers that follow were written before these events, they are no less relevant now. The issues they raise have not been resolved, and some are more urgent than ever.

STANLEY FISCHER

1 The Current Situation

To understand the prospects for economic reform in Russia, one must consider the singularly difficult conditions from which Russia began its reform program in November 1991. Not only were the Soviet economy and its central planning system breaking down but the highly centralized state and government were breaking up into fifteen republics, none of which, except Russia, had any recent experience of political, administrative, or economic self-government. In addition, although a new president had been elected to lead the new Russian state, the Congress was a holdover from the previous regime, with members who knew they would lose power in the next election. Finally, reform began as the result of a massive historical defeat, not, as in Eastern Europe, as a result and component of a national triumph. Two years earlier, Russia had been a feared superpower at the heart of an empire of 420 million people; now, though feared for its nuclear arms, it was reduced to 150 million people, with its empire lost and its economy in tatters.

Russia had one potential advantage over the other reforming countries: Russians had been discussing reform strategy and preparing reform plans over the previous several years. All of the plans, even those of the Soviet government, agreed that it would be necessary to move to a market economy within a space of no more than a few years. The plans tended to put little emphasis on the international dimensions of reform—international trade, currency convertibility, and Western aid. In addition, they tended to differ from the reform strategy followed later, both in the proposed sequencing of reforms and with regard to interrepublican relations.

The differences in sequencing arose with respect to macroeconomic stabilization, demonopolization, price liberalization, and privatization. Russian planners were reluctant to privatize before either breaking up firms or putting antimonopoly regulations into effect. They proposed privatizing before, or as part of, stabilization, on the argument that the sell-off of firms would help mop up the liquidity overhang.

Some of the leading reformers, notably Grigory Yavlinsky, while recognizing that the republics would have far greater economic and political independence under a new economic regime, believed it would be important to set up an orderly system of interrepublican relations before reforms began. Indeed, Yavlinsky and his team, together with the international financial institutions, were working on an interrepublican treaty even after it became clear that the Soviet Union would collapse. The reformers within the Russian government, however, led by Yegor Gaidar, were Russia-firsters, both from conviction and, more important, because they did not want to be delayed by the impossible task of coordinating reform with the twelve non-Baltic republics.

The initial reform program, which began in January 1992, violated most of the rules learned from the experiences of developing countries and from Eastern Europe. The reforms began with partial, but substantial, price and trade liberalizations. In the presence of a liquidity overhang, and with budget control far from assured, this ensured a massive initial increase in price levels.

Oil prices were kept well below world levels, limiting the amount of tax revenue the government could collect from the oil industry and thereby hindering the attainment of macroeconomic stability. The Soviet budget deficit in 1991 was at least 10 percent of GNP, and it was not known how or whether taxes would be collected. The Yeltsin government introduced a value-added tax and left most Soviet taxes in place while reducing some subsidies. It did not control the central bank, although the problems that would create were not yet fully recognized. The government announced its intention of moving ahead with privatization but had made no decisions about how to handle economic relations with the other former Soviet republics, none of which was ready to begin reforms as soon as Russia was.

The most visible result of the Russian program was a tripling of prices within a month, a far greater rise than previous calculations of the money overhang had projected. The ruble devalued massively, although many firms continued to obtain foreign exchange at subsidized rates.

After the initial shocks, and further shocks associated with the resolution of the buildup of arrears in mid-1992, the Russian economy has settled into quasi-stability. For about six months, inflation has been in the range of 20 to 30 percent per month, broadly matching the growth in money and credit. The conflict between the finance ministry and the Central Bank of Russia, which is responsible to the Congress, has become the crux of the Russian policy debate. The data show that output declined quickly to about 70 percent of the 1989 peak and maintained that lower level for nearly six months. The real wage has settled at 50 to 60 percent of the previous peak, and unemployment has risen only slowly.

The Central Bank of Russia has issued credit amounting to 30 to 40 percent of GDP over the past year. The three recipients of this credit are enterprises, the government, and other republics. The government budget deficit is somewhere between 5 and 10 percent of GDP, excluding foreign-exchange subsidies, which amounted to more than 10 percent of GDP in 1992. By allocating the foreign exchange received through foreign-export credits to domestic firms at heavily subsidized rates, the Russian government ensured that this aid would be mostly wasted. This practice will have to be stopped if Western assistance is to be used successfully.

Nominal credit creation in a high-inflation economy may, of course, be accompanied by a decline in the real volume of credit, thus leading to an unstable hyperinflation. In Russia, the real volume of credit is now probably below its mid-1991 level but is greater than it was after the 300 percent price-level adjustment of January 1992. That is why the inflationary process has stabilized.

Although the macroeconomic situation in Russia is chaotic, there has been real progress in privatization. As in Eastern Europe, small-scale privatization has been quite rapid. More important, voucher privatization of medium- and large-scale enterprises is under way and is, indeed, proceeding more rapidly than in some of the successful reforming countries of Eastern Europe. There are now over 200,000 private farms, although they account for only 5 percent of the arable land. Progress in privatizing housing and land has been slow.

Although large amounts of financing have been poured into Russia, the Western aid effort has been ineffective. Details of the financial assistance are surprisingly unclear. It seems that about $12 billion in export credits flowed to Russia last year. In addition, the IMF approved a loan of $1 billion, some of which has been drawn upon. Perhaps as much as $20 billion can be counted as debt relief, although Russia's inability to pay would have ensured that it receive this funding one way or another. In addition, technical assistance is being provided in large, though uncoordinated, amounts.

Two features of the aid effort to date will influence the future prospects for a successful use of aid in support of Russian stabilization and reform. The first is that the details of the $24 billion aid package announced in April 1992 were never fully clarified, an omission that has greatly increased cynicism about aid to the former Soviet Union, both locally and in the West. The second is that, although the IMF was put in overall charge of the Western effort, it has been unable to deliver much aid and has played a disappointingly inactive role in coordinating the many interested aid givers.

2 Russian Reform

The prospects for stabilization in Russia are clouded by the political uncertainties continuing even after the April 25 referendum. The key question is whether Yeltsin will face continuing opposition from the present Congress and the central bank or will be able to call elections and work with a Congress that supports reform. Elections are in any case unlikely to happen before the end of 1993, so that, for six months at least, the present political situation will remain essentially the same.

Although the Russians are making real progress in privatization, an early stabilization remains either a precondition or at least a lubricant for other market-oriented reforms. The priority in stabilization is to reduce the rate of credit creation. But because there is a real problem behind the creation of credit, namely, the political power of the industrial lobby and the widespread fear of unemployment among the general public, alternative means will have to be found to finance those firms that should survive and perhaps to ease the transition for those that will have to shut down. Credit from the central bank to the government and to other republics will also have to be reduced. This means that the government budget deficit will have to be cut, or at least that the part of the budget deficit financed by domestic credit creation will have to be cut.

Both Russians and potential foreign investors complain about high taxes. It is often asserted, for instance, that taxes on oil profits exceed 100 percent. Some Russian complaints relate to tax rates—around 30 percent—that would be considered quite normal in other countries. But there is no doubt that the problems of conflicting jurisdictions and uncertainties about tax collection complicate business in Russia. The cure is easily stated, but the restoration of governmental authority in Russia is not.

The problem of dealing with the other republics has not yet been resolved. There are two main difficulties. First, the republics need to cut loose from the Central Bank of Russia and to introduce their own currencies. This is gradually, although belatedly, being done, with the absolutely essential aid of external technical assistance. Second, Russia is still subsidizing the republics by charging less than world prices for oil. This aid may well be in the interests of Russia, both because it wants the other republics to be dependent upon it, and because Russian industry needs markets in, and inputs from, other republics. It would make more sense, however, for Russia to raise the price of oil to world levels and to compensate the republics with economic assistance, preferably provided through the budget.

The Russian government plans to reduce the rate of credit creation from the 25 to 35 percent per month rate during the first quarter of 1993 to 5 percent per month in the last quarter. This would be a significant achievement. At the same time, Russia needs urgently to move to a more uniform exchange-rate policy and, in particular, to stop providing foreign exchange to privileged importers at a subsidized rate. A reduction of the rate of credit creation to 5 percent per month and unification of the exchange rate for current-account transactions would be significant achievements. If these goals are attained, it would also make sense for Russia to fix the exchange rate for a protracted period—up to a year—in order to reduce inflation further. It would be essential, however, in pursuing a policy of fixed exchange rates, to know when to get off the train, namely, before the currency becomes overvalued. With the real exchange rate now at about one-fifth the level it would be according to the standard Heston-Summers regression, there is room for a real appreciation of about 100 percent, but not much more.

Macroeconomic stabilization in Russia would be accompanied by a tightening of credit conditions and thus the hardening of budget constraints for Russian enterprises. This will be needed if privatization is also to result in the restructuring of industry. There is increasing and encouraging evidence from Poland that the hardening of budget constraints results in improved performance by state-owned enterprises as well.

For both moral and political reasons, industrial restructuring should be accompanied by improvements in the social safety network, including improved training for those who lose their jobs. And it is not only industry that needs restructuring, but also agriculture, where private farms are being created but marketing and distribution systems need to be developed. As already indicated, special attention will have to be given to the oil industry, which is the great potential earner of foreign exchange.

In the prerevolutionary era, Russia was a major agricultural exporter, and there is no good reason why it should not return to that position. World markets in agriculture are notoriously protected, however, and the precedent of EC treatment of East European agriculture does not bode well for Russia. Similarly, Western sensitivity to Russian exports of high-tech items, such as satellite launchers, is creating problems for Russian economic adjustment. Russia would surely benefit if the West would agree to more trade at the expense of somewhat less aid.

As in all the formerly centrally planned economies, the financial system in Russia is underdeveloped. Although many banks have been set up, most merely funnel central-bank credit at highly negative real interest rates to firms authorized to receive it. Valuable experience in operating banks is being gained, nonetheless, and a healthier banking system can develop if inflation is brought down to a reasonable level. At the same time, the central bank will have to create instruments that will enable it to affect interest rates and the supply of credit through open-market operations rather than through the direct provision of credit. The national savings bank that existed in the former Soviet system provides a valuable national network of offices through which a commercial banking system could expand.

As essential as all these reforms are to the creation of a market economy, there is also the need for a coherent system of commercial law and for general adherence to the law. It is well known that lines of authority in Russia are very weak, and that foreign investors do not know with whom to negotiate. As with the tax system, this is part of the enormous weakening of the central government that has accompanied the breakup of the old order. The problem cannot be quickly repaired, although stabilization would help.

3 Western Assistance

Given the starting conditions, Russia's transformation into a market economy is bound to be extremely difficult. Although success or failure depends primarily on the Russians themselves, the attitude and support of the West can make the crucial difference. The success of Russian reform is far too important politically to the West for it to take a laissez-faire attitude. We will all benefit if, after the end of the Cold War, Russia joins the community of democratic nations, just as we have benefited from the extraordinarily successful reintegration of Japan and Germany into the democratic world after World War II.

In April 1993, one year after President Bush and Chancellor Kohl announced a $24 billion aid package for Russia, the Group of Seven (G-7) announced a $28 billion package. Russia needs aid in the first instance to finance its general budgetary expenses and thereby to help reduce inflationary pressure. Although it at one time looked attractive for the West to support the Russian social safety net, many Russians have said they would prefer support for more productive government expenditures. Because budgetary financing is fungible, the West should simply agree with the Russians on whether they want to designate budgetary support for a particular category of spending or for general budgetary financing.

The Russians are also requesting about $4 billion for an enterprise-restructuring fund. To help ensure that the fund will assist restructuring rather than just keep firms alive through artificial means, such a fund should be comanaged by the aid donors. The European Bank for Reconstruction and Development (EBRD) is expected to manage a $200 to $300 million fund for the financing of small enterprises.

Beyond these general forms of aid, the World Bank has prepared a large loan to support the restructuring of the oil industry. Further such loans may be expected, along with loans to the agricultural sector.

As, and if, the Russians make progress toward reducing the rate of credit creation, it will at some point—perhaps toward the end of 1993—become appropriate to move to an exchange-rate peg. The $6 billion stabilization fund that was proposed in 1992, administered through the IMF, remains available for that purpose.

In addition to direct financial assistance, the Russians will need technical assistance, not only at the governmental but also at the enterprise level. There are already some examples of successful technical assistance, not least in the privatization ministry, where the combination of determined Russian political leadership, highly skilled Russian experts, and intentionally inconspicuous Western experts has made genuine progress possible.

The Russians would benefit if Western assistance were to take the form of long-term loans rather than short-term export credits, but that appears un-likely. Given the desirability of restarting the aid process very soon, it would also be useful if the first tranches of assistance were bilateral rather than from the international financial institutions. That, too, appears unlikely.

There has for some time been an Alphonse and Gaston problem in the aid process: the West will give aid if the Russians stabilize, and the Russians will stabilize if they receive aid. The laudable initiative of the International Mone-tary Fund in creating a new facility that will make it possible to start the aid process before a full standby agreement is reached should help break the im-passe. The conditionality for such aid will be that the Russians take steps toward reducing credit expansion and inflation. Further aid from the interna-tional financial institutions will depend on the usual conditions.

4 Prospects

The Russian government is now likely to attempt gradually to reduce the inflation rate and to restore a semblance of macroeconomic stability. This attempt will likely be supported by a large initial dose of financial assistance from the West. Although the inflation rate will be reduced in the early stages of such a program, the more detailed restructuring of the economy will take much longer and will be hampered by the lack of Russian administrative and technical expertise. It is therefore possible that the new G-7 aid initiative will bog down after a promising start. To reduce the possibility of failure, the West will have both to improve its own aid process and to provide assistance to the Russians for implementing their reforms.

It would certainly help for the G-7 to put an aid coordinator in charge of the overall aid program in Moscow. This coordinator would be charged with (1) ensuring that the aid program is moving ahead on all fronts and that the multilateral and bilateral agencies are doing what they are supposed to do, (2) identifying gaps and problems in the aid effort, (3) coordinating with the Russian government and helping it organize to receive and deal with aid, and (4) reporting back to the G-7 and calling it in when needed.

If the aid effort bogs down and the Russians are unable to meet the normal conditions of the international financial institutions, the best course for the West would be to put aid on a low-level maintenance basis, consisting mainly of export credits. This would show continuing Western support but would not put the international financial institutions at risk by asking them to make bad loans.

The arguments for a special aid program for Russia suggest also that a similar, but much smaller, effort should be made to assist Ukraine when it shows its willingness to begin reforms. Other republics of the former Soviet

Union will continue to rely on assistance from the international financial institutions.

It must be recognized that it will take several years at least for the decline in Russian output to cease and the upturn to begin. In Poland, which began with far more favorable conditions, the turnaround took three years. Russia will be doing well if growth resumes by 1995. The difficulties the society is now facing, and will continue to face, make it quite likely that there will be several changes of government during the reform process. That is another reason why the West needs now to show strong and concrete support for democratic reformers; the Russian people and future governments should know that the West stands ready to support democratic economic reform.

JOHN ODLING-SMEE AND HENRI LORIE

I focus explicitly in my remarks on the process of economic reform in Russia, although much of what I say is also relevant to the other states of the former Soviet Union. Following comments on the ways in which Russia differs from other countries undergoing major reforms, I shall discuss some key features of Russia's reform process, especially with regard to enterprises, and shall comment briefly on the role of external financial assistance.

1 Is Russia Different?

It is now more than a year since Russia took decisive steps to reform its economic system in the direction of a market economy. By 1991, years of failed partial reforms, instead of improving the situation, had brought about a full macroeconomic and balance-of-payments crisis.

The economic difficulties confronted by Russia at the end of 1991 seemed to combine most of the economic ills suffered by Argentina, Mexico, and Brazil in the early 1980s with many of the problems posed by the economic reconstruction of Europe and Japan following World War II. Russia was faced with stagnant economic growth, in part brought about by too much government intervention and protection, with domestic and external disequilibria reflecting large fiscal imbalances, with price distortions and accompanying resource misallocation, and with substantial rent-seeking stimulated by the lack of economic freedom and transparency. In addition, much of Russia's capital stock had become obsolete and its trade patterns disrupted. The country faced a massive military conversion problem; its infrastructure was run

The views expressed here are the authors' and do not necessarily correspond to those of the International Monetary Fund.

down; and it was confronted by considerable ecological devastation. As in Argentina in the 1980s and Japan in the 1940s, Russia faced the urgent need to downsize (and privatize) very large monopolistic state enterprises with a view to instilling competition and innovation to recreate growth.

Russia differed from these countries in one critical respect, however. Prior to 1992, 95 percent of the Russian economy (roughly the output share of its state-enterprise sector) operated entirely outside market mechanisms. In Mexico, by contrast, a thriving private-market economy had continued to account for more than 85 percent of gross domestic product (GDP), even at the peak of the expansion of its state-enterprise sector.

Russia's problems of structure and stabilization, as well as its lack of market mechanisms and infrastructure, are shared in varying degrees by the transition countries of Eastern Europe. Their experience in moving toward a market economy—a process initiated some two years earlier than in Russia—is for this reason the most relevant point of reference both for Russia and for the Western economists and international institutions providing policy advice. Poland is a particular case in point, although the initial conditions in Russia were in many ways more similar to those of the less celebrated example of Bulgaria.

Despite many setbacks and frequent minor revisions in financial and macroeconomic targets, Poland, Czechoslovakia, Hungary, and even Bulgaria, have made significant progress toward macroeconomic stabilization; they have improved their balance-of-payments positions and have created conditions attracting both new home-grown private entrepreneurs as well as foreign investors. After cumulative output declines of about 20 to 30 percent, there were clear indications by the end of 1992 that output growth had turned positive in several of the countries. These developments point to hopeful directions for Russia.

The East European experience provides ample support for the view that the transition to a market economy must pass through a period of temporarily lower output. Replacing one system of economic coordination (the plan) with another (the decentralized behavior of profit- and utility-maximizing economic agents) inevitably implies a short-term decline in overall production, even if supporting policies and institutions are in place. The more ambitious the reform program, the deeper (although shorter) this output dip is likely to be. Thus, a fall in output is not necessarily a signal that the reform process is not working, and a small fall in output is not necessarily better than a large one if the latter is indeed the byproduct of an ambitious and successful reform.

Several factors point in the direction of a more arduous and longer transition for Russia: (1) the dissolution of the Soviet Union, and with it, the breakdown in the trade, payments, and monetary systems that made the former Soviet republics even more dependent on one another than were the members of the former Council for Mutual Economic Assistance (CMEA), (2) the greater geographical, historical, and psychological remoteness of Russia from experiences with a market economy, (3) the sheer size of the country, which had compounded coordination and distribution problems even under central planning, (4) Russia's diversity ethnically and with regard to regional distribution of resources, which carries the risk that powerful regional interests could preempt the effective functioning of the central government, (5) the weak political and social cohesion undermining support for firm reform and stabilization policies, and a breakdown in the ability to enforce law and order, which discourages law-abiding entrepreneurs, (6) large macroeconomic disequilibria (larger in Russia than in most East European countries), and (7) the relatively small amount of financial assistance that will likely be made available relative to the large absolute size of financial need.

But, although the transition may be longer and more arduous in Russia, and there may be a need for realism about what can be accomplished in the short run, it does not follow that the broad policy approach for economic reform in Russia should be any different from that adopted in Eastern Europe. In particular, to create conditions in which market mechanisms will eventually grow, it is at least as important in Russia as in Eastern Europe to make rapid progress in both macroeconomic stabilization and structural reform.

There are also factors that appear to be particularly favorable to the reform process in Russia, specifically the fact that the dissolution of the CMEA—and of the Soviet Union itself—has resulted in a concentration of Russia's exports in energy and raw materials, and therefore to an improvement in Russia's terms of trade. This same abundance of energy and raw materials gives Russia a long-term economic potential that should make it particularly attractive for foreign direct investment.

It is useful to consider China's reform experience, which has differed significantly from that of the European transition countries. The introduction of market mechanisms in China was largely incremental, but it is difficult to attribute the remarkable progress achieved in China (particularly with regard to economic growth) solely to this more gradual approach. China has many other special circumstances that appear to have played important roles. Its labor-intensive agriculture has been well suited to rapid productivity gains once market-oriented institutions were allowed to predominate in the agricultural sector. It withdrew early from the politically motivated and stifling CMEA trade arrangements. It was able to initiate economic reforms prior to any emergence of a macroeconomic crisis and to dissociate economic reforms from more intractable political reforms. And it has benefited greatly from the proximity of highly dynamic economies (in particular, Hong Kong and Taiwan) with plenty of excess capital to invest, and from a large Chinese diaspora. None of these circumstances apply to Russia.

2 Reforming Russia's Economy

Price Liberalization

What clearly differentiates economic reforms in Russia from reforms in countries such as Argentina and Mexico is the sheer dimension of systemic changes implied by the transition from a centrally planned to a market-oriented economy. Despite weaknesses, and an often large gap between *de jure* and *de facto* changes, it is fair to say that much has been accomplished since 1991, and Russian reforms have begun to yield fruit. Witness, for instance, the successful privatization of retail trade and apartments and the creation of new owner-operated private businesses and farms.

Rather than review all the systemic changes, I wish today just to emphasize and assess the one stemming directly from the main objective of the transition, which is to replace plan directives with a system of decentralized economic relations springing from the pursuit of individual utility and profit maximization. This essential change is trade and price liberalization, and it is no coincidence that the freeing of most prices was the first momentous decision taken by the Russian authorities at the start of 1992.

Although the process of price liberalization has not yet been completed, decisive progress has been made. Even so, some people continue to argue that demonopolization and the establishment of a market infrastructure should have preceded price and trade liberalization. It is true that price behavior early in 1992 was less than competitive and that the break-up of very large enterprises into smaller units ought to be given greater priority under a strengthened antimonopoly program. Instead of adjusting to the new economic environment, enterprises attempted to maintain both profits and wages by continuing with cost-plus-margin pricing and, because little of the production could be sold at such prices, by financing their cash-flow problem through recourse to arrears and subsequently to bank credit.

It must be recognized, however, that neither competition nor markets can be created entirely in a vacuum; they are partly the result of the dynamic process brought about by price and trade liberalization. The changes in relative prices following liberalization stimulate competition as producers respond to the new situation and new entrants identify activities in which temporary monopoly profits can be made. Furthermore, although monopolistic behavior can explain higher than competitive prices, it cannot explain high inflation. A monopolist whose only interest is to earn high profits will not be able to increase profits by raising prices continuously if money and credit growth are held down to a level consistent with zero inflation.

In addition to breaking up large enterprises, an antimonopoly program should emphasize the removal of barriers to entry for new enterprises and should free competition with unfettered imports. Direct controls on prices or profit margins, although playing a role in the regulation of natural monopolies, should be eschewed with regard to Russia's temporary monopolies because of the risk that they will be applied inappropriately and will damage incentives and the development of managerial initiative.

Stabilization and Hard Budget Constraints

Inflation and balance-of-payments difficulties are almost invariably the results of credit policies that are inconsistent with an economy's productive capacities. To correct these problems, one must tighten credit policies, and usually also fiscal policy, which is closely related. Only then will structural reform measures aimed at restoring sustainable growth succeed. This is clearly the lesson from the experience of Latin America and even of China, as well as from the example of the drastic stabilization effort of Japan under the Dodge Plan, an exercise that laid the foundation for decades of price stability and growth.

It cannot be overemphasized that credibility is critical to the early success of such a financial stabilization program. In Russia, the attempt in early 1992 to stabilize the economy through a tightening of financial policies seems not to have been sufficiently credible. How else can one explain the behavior of enterprises that failed to adjust to the new economic environment and opted instead to run up a significant stock of interenterprise debt? The managers of these enterprises expected that the government would eventually bail them out, and the Russian authorities' response, which involved a considerable loosening of both monetary and fiscal policies, fulfilled their expectations. This response separates Russia's experience from that of Poland, Czechoslovakia, and even Bulgaria, and it brought Russia to the edge of hyperinflation by the end of 1992.

Russia's failure to stabilize in 1992 illustrates that the successful imposition of hard budget constraints on enterprises is a necessary condition for effective financial stabilization. The evidence clearly demonstrates that the much higher than projected credit expansion and fiscal deficit for 1992 resulted largely from decisions and measures taken to alleviate the impact of new relative prices and demand conditions on the cash flow and financial position of enterprises. A hardening of budget constraints on enterprises is also a necessary condition for economic restructuring. Without it, any systemic reforms will inevitably fail to provide an effective set of incentives.

Enterprise Reform

Because hardening of budget constraints encourages enterprises to adjust their behavior in response to financial difficulties rather than to extend their indebtedness, the core of the reform program must be the reform of the enterprises themselves. Most transitional East European countries have approached this issue with varying degrees of benign neglect pending privatization. Government subsidies have been sharply curtailed, and the task of assessing creditworthiness has generally been left to the banks, which display increasing signs of more prudential lending behavior. This approach seems to have had some success in forcing enterprises to improve management and to find new markets. The plight of loss-making large-scale enterprises with few prospects for privatization, however, remains largely unanswered. The governments of both Poland and Hungary have been assuming greater responsibilities in this regard, particularly with respect to financial restructuring of banks and enterprises.

In Russia, the scale of the transformation required is huge, and it may not be possible to follow such a clean policy of zero subsidies, government noninterference, and benign neglect of nonadjusting and nonprivatizing enterprises. Temporary government assistance may be necessary, for example, in downsizing very large enterprises located in single-enterprise towns. Nevertheless, for reforms to take place, any assistance must be very tightly controlled to ensure compatibility with both inflation objectives and the creation of incentives.

More specifically, there should be four guiding principles in granting subsidies to enterprises: (1) The aggregate amount of the subsidies must be consistent with the overall fiscal and macroeconomic program and must be explicitly budgeted *ex ante*. Total subsidies in 1992 were close to 30 percent of GDP, including interest-rate and import subsidies. (2) The subsidies must be transparent and as nondistortionary as possible (which calls for lump-sum rather than price subsidies). (3) They must be strictly temporary, with targets for their phased elimination clearly stated at the outset. (4) The mechanism for the allocation of subsidies must be based on conditionality, which should be part of, and consistent with, quantified financial and restructuring plans for the enterprises concerned and should include incentives for privatization and the breaking up of monopolies. Assessment and monitoring of the implementation of these plans should probably be undertaken by a special government entity in close collaboration with both the finance ministry and privatization agency.

The provision and allocation of credit to enterprises through the finance ministry and the central bank is now very large—over 20 percent of GDP for 1992. This allocation has not been based on economic grounds, and the aim ought to be to move as quickly as possible to a market-based and decentralized process of financial intermediation. Only under such a system will safeguards be sufficient to ensure that financial savings are being allocated to the most productive uses. This should also encourage the mobilization of such savings. In Russia, this necessitates eliminating as quickly as possible the policy of so-called "directed credit," in particular by the central bank. I fully realize that the present state of the commercial banking system is far from meeting the above standards (notwithstanding growing signs of more profit-maximizing behavior), in part because the *de facto* insolvency position of many banks deprives them of the right incentives, and the practice of lending to large shareholders of the banks remains largely unregulated. But the answer lies largely in financial-sector reform rather than in more government involvement. Admittedly, this will take time.

An important question is what to do with the state enterprises temporarily or indefinitely remaining in the public sector that are now in need of, but unable to finance, restructuring because the existing financial system cannot or will not provide credits for such purposes. The answer may involve some assistance from the government, perhaps in the establishment of a special restructuring fund or development bank. Such an entity could be funded by government or from capital markets and could also serve as a conduit for external assistance.

A question often raised in this context is whether government ought to target specific priority sectors for a development effort toward which assistance, including foreign financing, will be channeled on a preferential basis. My reaction is, first, to point out that, under price, trade, foreign-exchange, and financial liberalization, one would expect such sectors to emerge naturally, without government encouragement, as the most promising for investment, and second, to ask why, in case of market imperfection, one should necessarily assume that government is better equipped to "pick winners," at either the enterprise or the sectoral level. In this context, I should point to the fact that, given its still recent emphasis on central planning, the Russian civil service cannot be expected to undertake the same kind of market-based assessments as are made by the governments in Japan and some other industrial countries. In addition, the allocation of government assistance remains exposed to political pressures and corruption. Finally, recent experience in Poland suggests that there are successful enterprises in every sector, and so a policy of discriminating among sectors would not necessarily maximize the success of the economy as a whole.

Sectors frequently mentioned for targeting are oil and agricultural. Oil is the single most important source of foreign exchange, and agriculture has great potential as a source for future growth. These sectors may be fairly safe bets, but let me stress that they faced difficulties in attracting investments in 1992, not so much because of financial-market failure, which could in principle justify intervention, but because of continued distortions. Liberalization, in particular price liberalization, has not been allowed to proceed as quickly in these sectors as in others, and institutional factors, particularly in the area of property rights, have not been sufficiently clarified. Potential investors have understandably been put off, and removal of these barriers should be the first priority. Of course, when there are clear positive externalities, the government *ought* to take the initiative and mobilize the necessary financing. This is more likely to be the case for the modernization of the administrative and physical infrastructure than for sectors in tradable goods.

3 External Financial Assistance

Let me conclude by addressing the question of external financial assistance for Russia. Here again, the historical experience of other countries is relevant. I earlier compared Russia's economic problems to those of several Latin American countries and those of post–World War II Europe and Japan. In both instances, governments in the international community that were able to help did assist, in the form of both debt relief and new financing flows. Under the Marshall Plan for Europe, new financing was on a very large scale.

On the face of it, Russia's short-term needs for financial assistance appear to be comparable in scale to those faced by Europe and Japan at the end of World War II. There are three reasons for this:

(1) Russia will have to smooth the consumption stream of its population. An excessive short-term decline in standards of living, in line with the unavoidable short-term fall in output (which cumulatively could well be anywhere between 30 and 50 percent before recovery), would not only be unnecessarily painful from a human point of view, but would also increase the risk of social unrest and provide arguments for a gradual approach that, from a broader perspective, would likely be suboptimal even if achievable. Foreign financing that directly or indirectly enables the government to provide an adequate social safety net would seem to be an excellent investment, especially if linked to measures encouraging labor mobility.

(2) Much of the administrative, service (particularly health), and productive infrastructure (including transportation and communication) is in great need of repair, modernization, and new investment. Without these, productivity gains from the restructuring of enterprises, the development of the private sector, and the attraction of foreign capital will be delayed. It is certain, however, that such outlays, which are the responsibility of the government, will, under even the most optimistic scenario, be severely constrained by the availability of domestic savings for the national budget. Foreign-financed investment projects will need to be fully assessed for their social rates of return and carefully ranked within a fully articulated public-investment program.

(3) It is difficult to imagine a major transformation in the enterprise sector without a substantial influx of foreign investment and expertise. In the long run, this will have to take the form largely of foreign direct investment, in ways that take account of sensitivities about foreign control and exploitation. In the short run, however, there is a role for official financial flows to govern-

ment agencies responsible for providing finance for reforming and restructuring enterprises, such as a restructuring fund or development bank. Western managerial expertise could be associated with such assistance.

I do not wish to enter here into the debate about the appropriate scale of financial assistance. On the one hand, the Marshall Plan analogy points to a large sum, and financial assistance from the western to eastern part of Germany has exceeded $100 billion a year (nearly all of it falling into one of the three categories just set out). On the other hand, there must be a willingness and an ability on the Russian side to pursue economic policies to ensure that the external financial assistance has the desired effects. This requires policies aimed at achieving macroeconomic stability, so that people have the confidence to invest in Russia rather than to take capital out of the country as fast as it comes in. It also requires rapid progress on a wide range of systemic reforms, including the creation of the legal and institutional framework for a market economy, the further removal of direct controls such as export quotas, and the elimination of state trading in the form of so-called centralized exports and imports. Finally, it requires administrative arrangements enabling the proper monitoring and receipt of assistance. The slow pace of the progress made in some of these areas accounts for the delay in disbursements of assistance from international financial institutions such as the IMF, EBRD, and World Bank.

JOHN WILLIAMSON

Because the presentations by Fischer and Odling-Smee and Lorie focused on only one of the twenty-seven independent countries in Central and Eastern Europe, it falls on me to redress the balance. It seems natural to divide the twenty-seven countries in the region into five groups:

(1) The first group consists of those countries that, in terms of Michael Bruno's useful schematic diagram (Figure 9.14), have already passed point D. In this category, I place Poland, the Czech Republic, and Hungary, as well as Estonia and Slovenia. These countries have succeeded in stabilizing their economies; their transformation is well along; and they are just about ready to start growing again. A year ago, it was expected that one of these countries would already register positive growth in 1992. That proved to be correct, although the country in question turned out to be Poland rather than Hungary.

The key query about these countries is whether they are going to launch into a sustained period of catch-up growth comparable to that enjoyed by Western Europe after 1950 or currently in progress in East Asia. There are two obvious economic dangers. One is that some of them may encounter secondary recessions, as Hungary did last year when it began to enforce bankruptcy legislation. One wonders whether they might not be wise to move to a more gradual imposition of the hard budget constraint than Hungary did, allowing a few prominent bankruptcies of particularly badly managed enterprises to serve as a warning before proceeding to general enforcement. Better still might be to move away from aping Western bankruptcy legislation and to implement instead the proposals of Aghion, Hart, and Moore (1992), which involve two basic ideas: first, to solicit bids for a bankrupt company from all and sundry, expressed in either cash or equity, or a combination of the two; second, to allow a vote on which of those offers to accept, after converting the senior claims on the bankrupt company into equity, subject to a right of the junior creditors to buy out senior creditors at the face value of their previous claims if they wish to retain a stake in the firm.

The other danger, which I fear is altogether more serious, is that the open-trade system will erode to the point where the process of catch-up growth is no longer possible. The Uruguay Round remains in trouble. The Clinton administration seems consumed by the desire to win privileges for U.S. exporters rather than inspired by a vision of the strategic benefits of open trade. And the EC is imposing additional restrictions on Central European exports of "sensitive" items, that is, those in which they have a comparative advantage. These are not hopeful omens.

(2) The second group of countries consists of those that seem to have passed through the process of price liberalization without succumbing to hyperinflation and to be now in the process of stabilization (between points C and D in Bruno's figure). Countries in this category include Albania, Bulgaria, Latvia, Lithuania, Romania, and Slovakia, with some of them (such as Bulgaria and Latvia) close to point D. This is a more dangerous phase than Bruno's figure might suggest, for there is no assurance that a country will arrive successfully at point D. On the contrary, there is always debate about whether the time for relaxation (that is, point D) has not already arrived. Premature relaxation can simply revive the inflationary crisis, and excessive delay can cause the fall of the government. If these shoals are avoided, however, and if Western markets stay reasonably open, the presumption is that these countries can make the transition successfully whatever happens eastward of them.

(3) Russia falls into a category of its own, still in the liberalization phase of the Bruno diagram (between points B and C), but big enough to succeed whatever happens to its neighbors. I return to discuss its problems shortly.

(4) In category four, I place the remaining former Soviet republics (that is, all but the Baltic states and Russia). Many of these are at a still earlier stage on the road to liberalization than Russia is and/or are suffering even higher inflation. All of them remain highly dependent on events in Russia despite having achieved political independence, and that will remain true for some time even if they move to separate currencies and even though it is forecast that, in the longer term, their trade will be dramatically reoriented toward countries outside the former CMEA. Further disruptions in their trade among themselves and with Russia are all too likely to occur as Russia establishes monetary

control or liberalizes the price of energy. This can be expected to push point C in Bruno's diagram even farther to the southeast. These problems of inter-republic relations are certainly important, but, in the absence of a satisfactory outcome in Russia, even their satisfactory resolution cannot be expected to allow for rapid recovery in the other republics.

(5) In the last category, I place all the former Yugoslav republics except Slovenia. It will be a happy day when the security issues that currently dominate attention recede far enough to justify worrying about their economic future.

Returning to Russia, my argument implies that, although Russia contains slightly less than 40 percent of the region's total population, its transition to a market economy is critical to the success of transition for more than 70 percent of the region's people. Hence, I cannot resist adding a few comments to those offered by the two preceding panelists.

I certainly agree with the view that Russia has already made a quite extraordinary change in ridding itself of central planning, even if the Klondike capitalism that has emerged in its stead leaves a great deal to be desired as a system of social organization. I also endorse the extreme concern already voiced by Fischer and Odling-Smee and Lorie regarding the current state of near hyperinflation. But we should recognize that universal concern with this problem is not enough, for agreement on the diagnosis does not imply a similar accord on prescription. I recently heard a deputy governor of the Central Bank of Russia declare that we need not be concerned about the big new credits that his bank had found necessary to extend to industry, because inflation in Russia was caused, not by monetary expansion, but by the irresponsibility of the media, which forecast price rises and in that way provoked them. One has to retain doubts about the wisdom of making available large sums of aid to those who see the solution to inflation lying in media, rather than monetary, control.

If Boris Yeltsin remains in power and committed to reform, and, if the reformers establish a stabilization program that is worth backing, the West should certainly be prepared to put in the serious money that will maximize the program's chance of success. One idea that I hope the reformers will consider is to begin with a general cancellation of interenterprise debt, so as to clear the ground for a rapid enforcement of relatively hard budget constraints (something that is not feasible as long as enterprises can plead plausibly that their difficulties arise from bad debts inherited from the prereform era). Obviously, it would be important to do this in a way that minimizes expectations that the exercise will be repeated in the future.

If Yeltsin's position is no more than marginal, however, or if he proves unwilling to commit himself wholeheartedly to a determined stabilization program, I am not sure we would do either him or his country a service by giving large-scale aid that could serve to reduce the pressure to make timely reforms.

By all means show goodwill with modest sums targeted on specific policy initiatives—especially if the aid requires no additional Russian expenditure (so that the cause of stabilization will be furthered). And, as with Central Europe, a fair chance to compete in Western markets without protectionist restrictions will enhance the prospects for Russian reform. Furthermore, in the absence of a decisive stabilization program, it might make more sense not to send the big money directly to Russia but, rather, to give it to the other republics to enable them to pay the world price for their energy imports from Russia if and when Russia liberalizes energy prices. By means such as these, we can try to nudge Russia toward adopting those policies that will make a successful transition possible even without the decisive commitment to stabilization that most of us would like to see.

Reference

Aghion, Philippe, Oliver Hart, and John Moore, "The Economics of Bankruptcy Reform," *Journal of Law, Economics, and Organization*, 8 (October 1992), pp. 523–546.

V

COORDINATION AND UNION

11

International Cooperation in the Making of National Macroeconomic Policies: Where Do We Stand?

RALPH C. BRYANT

THIS CHAPTER revisits the question of whether international cooperation can contribute to the design and implementation of national macroeconomic policies. It was originally commissioned as a survey of the benefits and costs of international coordination, but, as it evolved, my goals shifted. The early parts of the chapter now try to clarify concepts. I draw a somewhat different map of international cooperation, in effect redefining the space where we locate the subject and clarifying the terms we use to describe its main manifestations—in particular, the "coordination" of national policies. The chapter also summarizes analytical insights in the existing literatures—I say literatures, plural, because, in the course of drafting this paper, I have dabbled in the international-relations literature as well as reviewing economic research and commentary. The final sections of the chapter analyze the implications of uncertainty for the desirability and feasibility of international cooperation.

The discussion is selective and idiosyncratic. It does not attempt to survey the existing literatures in a balanced fashion. I have felt free to present a personal view, in large part because several useful surveys of the economics literature are already available.[1]

1 International Cooperation: General Terminology

Nation-states are the primary political units in the world today and will remain so for the foreseeable future. Nations have separate currencies, separate central banks, and separate fiscal authorities. "Domestic" politics within each

The views in this paper are those of the author and should not be attributed to the trustees, officers, or other staff members of the Brookings Institution.

[1] Listed roughly in chronological order of preparation, these include Hamada (1985), Cooper (1985), Artis and Ostry (1986), Fischer (1988), Horne and Masson (1988), Group of Thirty (1988), McKibbin (1988), Currie, Holtham, and Hughes Hallett (1989), Frenkel, Goldstein, and Masson (1990), Kenen (1990), Canzoneri and Henderson (1991), Dobson (1991), Solomon (1991), and Ghosh and Masson (1994). My views at earlier dates are summarized in Bryant (1980, chap. 25; 1987a; 1987b, chap. 9; and 1990b).

nation tend to have much greater influence than "international" politics, though the latter are not negligible. Each nation's citizens, and hence national governments, are predominantly concerned with the welfare of "home" citizens.

Despite the preoccupation with own-nation welfare, the effects of home national policies spill over into foreign nations. Some cross-border effects operate through market forces, for example, affecting interest rates and exchange rates and, through them, variables such as outputs and prices. Other spillovers, however, can give rise to externalities (gains or losses not adequately reflected in market prices).

Because each nation's policymakers are not usually rewarded for any favorable effects of their policies abroad or penalized for any bad effects, nations may collectively fail to foster their own interests if spillovers and externalities are ignored in national decisionmaking. Moreover, cross-border spillovers and externalities may have grown larger and more salient over time—hence the broad issue addressed in this chapter: should national governments cooperate in making decisions about their economic policies?

Many words beginning with C pervade discussion of this topic. These include "cooperation," "consultation," "collaboration," "coordination," "collusion," and "coalition." Unfortunately, different authors use the words differently, which leads to some confusion.

I prefer to use "cooperation" as an umbrella term for an entire spectrum of interactions among national governments designed to deal with "arbitrage pressures" and cross-border spillovers among national economies (Bryant, 1987a). "Consultation," "mutual recognition," various forms of "coordination," and "explicit harmonization" are varieties of intergovernmental cooperation, each involving some element of management of the interactions among nations. Consultation alone involves only a small degree of cooperative management. Coordination is more ambitious. Each of these concepts is discussed below.

With this richer terminology, the issue addressed in this paper can be restated: under what circumstances should national governments cooperate in making decisions about their macroeconomic policies, and, if they do cooperate, how ambitious should that cooperation be? In particular, should governments go beyond the exchange of information and consultation and attempt explicitly to coordinate their policy decisions? Alternatively, should they cooperate by agreeing on presumptive rules that constrain the use of national policy instruments?

2 Top-Level Cooperation: International "Regime" Environments

It is helpful to think of international cooperation as a two-level process. During brief, exceptional episodes of negotiations at a "top level," typically characterized by intensive consultations and bargaining, national governments reach understandings or formal agreements defining the processes and institutions through which they will interact with one another. Such intermittent agreements, at the time they are reached, usually seem to the participating governments to be one-time decisions (although valid for the foreseeable future). During the lengthy periods between these top-level negotiations, governments interact with one another through the agreed processes and institutions at a "lower level." At this lower level, each government makes its ongoing decisions in a largely decentralized way, independently choosing settings for the policy instruments under its control. The "regime environments" agreed episodically at the top level can be interpreted as traffic regulations (sometimes loosely called "rules of the game") that govern continuing interactions at the lower level.[2]

The regime environments negotiated at the top level are usually labeled simply as "regimes" in the international-relations literature. Economists analyzing macroeconomic policies use "regime," however, to refer to the week-to-week operating procedures used by an individual national central bank (fiscal authority) to implement its monetary policy (fiscal policy). The dual connotations of "regime" can be confusing, especially if (as in this chapter) both meanings are sometimes required in the same sentence or paragraph. Later in the chapter, where confusion might arise, I use "international regime environment" or "international regime" for the first connotation and "national operating regime" or "domestic policy regime" for the second.[3]

My notion of an international regime environment is associated exclusively with episodic, top-level decisions by national governments. The most widely used definition of a regime in the international-relations literature, which captures well the main elements in my notion, describes a regime as

> sets of implicit or explicit principles, norms, rules and decision-making procedures around which actors' expectations converge in a given area of international relations. Principles are beliefs of fact, causation, and rectitude. Norms are standards of behavior defined in terms of rights and obligations. Rules are specific prescriptions or proscriptions for action. Decision-making procedures are prevailing practices for making and implementing collective choice. (Krasner, 1983, p. 2; see also Keohane, 1984, pp. 57–61)

Some parts of the international-relations literature define "regime" even more

---

[2] The last century and a half of intergovernmental economic relations have conformed moderately well to this characterization. Economic theorists, notably Hamada (1974, 1977), have applied the idea of two levels of cooperation in game-theoretic analyses of interdependence in macroeconomic policies. I used the distinction in Bryant (1987b). The two-level characterization is implicit if not explicit in much of the literature on international relations among nation-states.

[3] In the draft of this essay prepared for the April 1993 conference, I used the label "regimen" for an international regime environment and reserved "regime" for the ongoing operating procedures of domestic policy. Because that effort to clarify was disliked by some readers and criticized by others as a proliferation of terminology, I have retreated to using "regime" for both concepts.

broadly, equating it comprehensively with any patterned regularity in the behavior of national governments interacting with one another. Other international-relations authors prefer a more restricted definition, reserving the concept for explicit multilateral agreements among nation-states that regulate national actions within an issue area (in effect, only the rules, but not the principles and norms, in the preceding quotation).[4]

At least two dimensions are involved in identifying an international regime, as suggested in Figure 11.1. The horizontal spectrum in Figure 11.1 refers to the incidence of agreements and treaties among national governments and the principles, norms, rules, and decisionmaking procedures around which actors' expectations converge. The vertical dimension indicates the numbers and strengths of non-national institutions and the forums, processes, and decision-making procedures that may be associated with them. Such institutions are "international" or "supranational" in the strict sense of those words.

A vertical movement in Figure 11.1 from top to bottom involves a shift from complete decentralization of authority among nation-states (northern border) to international regimes in which there is more—but not complete (even at the southern border)—centralization of authority through international or supranational institutions. A horizontal movement from left to right, for any given degree of decentralization, entails more cooperative activity through the establishment of agreed principles and norms and the acknowledgment of constraints (rules and decisionmaking procedures) that have prescriptive and proscriptive force for the "local" decisions of national governments.

The space in the extreme northwest corner of the diagram, a polar case, may be labeled "national sovereignty with little or no international cooperation." For such an international regime, the exclusive determinant of relations among national governments (which would be noncooperative and probably limited) would be the relative powers of the nation-states. As one moves to the southeast, the regimes still involve essentially decentralized national decisions but begin to have elements of international cooperation. The larger the movement to the southeast, the more salient become transnational norms and non-national institutions.

International regimes near the extreme southeast corner of the diagram are hypothetical in today's world. But such regimes can be imagined and can be used as benchmarks for analyzing other spaces in the diagram. The southeast extreme would entail "mutual governance" facilitated by strong federal, su-

---

[4] Haggard and Simmons (1987) discuss differences among definitions of "regime" in international relations. The concept seems to have been introduced in Ruggie (1975) and used by Keohane and Nye (1977) and Keohane (1980). Two issues of *International Organization* were devoted to the subject in 1982, with much of the material republished in Krasner (1983); see especially the introductory and concluding pieces by Krasner and the chapters by Ruggie, Haas, Keohane, and Strange. For subsequent discussion, see Keohane (1984), Haggard and Simmons (1987), and a special 1992 issue of *International Organization* devoted to multilateralism, which includes contributions by Caporaso (1992), Kahler (1992), and Ruggie (1992).

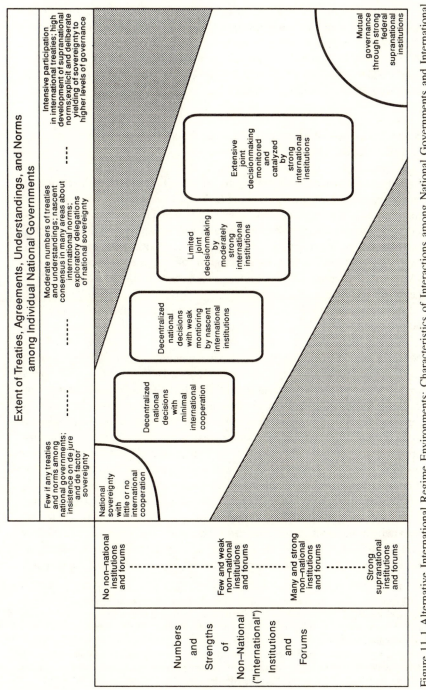

Figure 11.1 Alternative International Regime Environments: Characteristics of Interactions among National Governments and International Institutions

pranational institutions. When dealing with an extensive range of economic
and social concerns, national governments would be restricted to local roles;
close political union would have evolved and transnational norms would be
salient. In such a regime, the locus of political authority would have shifted
substantially away from national governments to the federal, supranational
level (regionally, globally, or both).[5]

3 Lower-Level Cooperation: Mutual Recognition and Coordination

Figure 11.2 extends the taxonomy in Figure 11.1 to another dimension by
considering the interplay between top-level episodic decisions and lower-level
intermittent decisions. The vertical axis in Figure 11.2 represents the degree
of "ongoing cooperation" affecting lower-level decisions, with little or none at
the extreme north and continuous, intensive amounts at the extreme south.
The horizontal axis, representing the northwest-southeast diagonal of Figure
11.1, lists the international regimes established in the periodic, top-level
negotiations.

The taxonomy resulting from the combination of Figures 11.1 and 11.2
helps to define and classify several of the concepts widely used in the literature, such as "mutual recognition" and "international coordination." These
concepts can be associated with particular regions in Figure 11.2.

"National autonomy," in the northwest corner in Figure 11.2, is one polar
case. It is useful as a benchmark in analyzing differing degrees of international
cooperation in either or both dimensions. Going roughly in a southeasterly
direction, I define the regions as "mutual recognition with infrequent consultations," "mutual recognition in the context of an internationally monitored
presumptive-rule regime," "weak-form coordination," and "strong, activist
coordination." The polar case in the southeast corner may be called "federalist
mutual governance with continuous bargaining and joint decisionmaking."

"Mutual recognition" is a term that has become popular in recent years,
primarily in discussions about European integration. It is sometimes defined
narrowly in the context of European Community (EC) trade and regulatory
policies.[6] Broadly defined, as here, mutual recognition presumes decentralized decisions by national governments, entails minimal traffic regulations,

[5] Recent political discussion in Europe has focused some attention on alternative (regional)
models of federalism and alternative visions of how a federal Europe might eventually be organized. Continental concepts of subsidiarity have been contrasted with Anglo-Saxon concepts of
federalism (for example, as manifested within the United States). See, for example, Peters (1992)
and Sbragia (1992).

[6] The term, narrowly interpreted, originates from the 1979 decision of the European Court of
Justice in the now familiar Cassis de Dijon case. Mutual recognition is discussed in several of the
chapters in Sbragia (1992), including those by Guy Peters and Martin Shapiro.

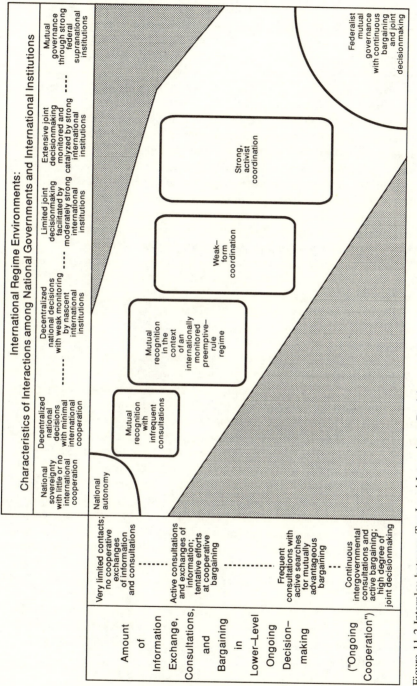

Figure 11.2 Interplay between Top-Level Intermittent Decisions and Lower-Level Ongoing Cooperation

and relies on competition among national policies and regulations—through private decisions and market forces—to guide transactions among nations. Mutual recognition, however, can involve exchanges of information and consultations among governments and even nascent reliance on non-national forums or institutions.

For international regimes embodying more intergovernmental agreements and some international monitoring of the agreements, and especially as intergovernmental consultations become more frequent and intensive, the term "mutual recognition" becomes less appropriate. Governments may operate under internationally agreed and monitored "presumptive rules" that constrain their ongoing policy decisions. In such a situation, the emphasis is not only on (mutually recognized) competition among the decentralized national decisions, but also on some agreed rules that condition the national decisions themselves. The meaning of "rules" in this context is discussed below. As the international monitoring of compliance with such rules becomes more important, one might begin to speak of this situation as "monitored decentralization."

Regions in Figure 11.2 still further to the south and east may be characterized as domains in which "international coordination" occurs. Depending on the degree of cooperation built into the international regime as a result of the intermittent top-level decisions, but depending especially on the frequency and intensity of the ongoing consultations and bargaining, the coordination can vary from weak and hesitant to strong and activist.

Because the horizontal and vertical dimensions in Figures 11.1 and 11.2 are continuums, it would be artificial to draw a precise boundary line between mutual recognition and coordination. One could well argue that the two are partly overlapping. Seen in terms of Figure 11.2, however, most of the domain of coordination lies to the east, and especially to the south, of mutual recognition. Some significant amount of information exchange and consultation must occur even under mutual recognition. More frequent and intensive consultations will typically occur, however, if the cooperation is sufficiently ambitious to achieve coordination. "International coordination," in my view, is best defined as coordination that goes further than mutual recognition in focusing on the cross-border spillovers and arbitrage pressures that erode the differences among national economies and policies. And coordination is more ambitious than mutual recognition in promoting intergovernmental cooperation to deal with these spillovers and pressures. Coordination involves jointly designed, mutual adjustments of national policies—commitments about the time paths of policy instruments, not merely aspirations about the time paths for ultimate-target variables. In clear-cut cases of coordination, bargaining occurs, and governments commit themselves to behave differently—to implement different settings for policy instruments—than they would have behaved without the coordination.

"Strong, activist coordination" differs from "weak-form coordination" mainly in the frequency and strength of consultations and bargaining. Strong, activist coordination is characterized by fairly continuous exchanges of information and consultations and by more frequent and intense bargaining about alternative outcomes.

States of the world near the southeast corner of Figure 11.2 can be imagined, perhaps for middle or late decades of the twenty-first century. International cooperation would intensify still further because, presumably, the economic and political integration of the world would be highly advanced, making it mutually advantageous to create political institutions that would reach centralized decisions for the entire integrated economic domain. In the extreme, for example, monetary policies for the entire integrated area would be explicitly harmonized, with a supranational central bank and probably with a single unified currency. The supranational institutions would have a central fiscal budget, which would become an increasingly important part of total governmental expenditures and revenues for the entire integrated area (supranational + national + within-nation local).[7] In this region of Figure 11.2, one would want to reinterpret "top-level" decisions as those made by federal supranational institutions, whereas "lower-level" decisions would be those decisions that were still made by national governments (now "local" political authorities in the highly integrated area).[8]

The distinctions made in Figures 11.1 and 11.2 help to locate the subject of policy coordination more clearly in a larger context. The figures also clarify other matters. For one thing, debates about policy coordination (and, by extension, different varieties of mutual recognition) have paid much more attention to the vertical dimension in Figure 11.2 than to the horizontal dimension. Protagonists of all positions have tended to take as given (implicitly) the international regime they believe to be in place in the world economic system. In other words, they take for granted some point on the horizontal dimension in Figure 11.2. They then focus on the pros and cons of varying the degree and nature of cooperation along the vertical dimension. Most of the economics literature cited in this paper, for example, is preoccupied with the conduct of lower-level, ongoing decisions. I, too, believe that many of the controversial aspects of policy coordination turn on the most appropriate way to conduct

[7] Important differences between monetary and budgetary policies—not least their macroeconomic stabilization aspects—would arise in such a highly integrated world. "Explicit harmonization" has a relatively clear-cut meaning for monetary policy, but a less clear meaning for the different layers of governmental revenues and expenditures. Fiscal policies (still plural, not singular) for such a world would require analysis of all the political and economic issues that have been discussed within federal nation-states as "fiscal federalism." See, for example, Oates (1972, 1977) and Olson (1969).

[8] Here, and also below in introducing Figure 11.3, I speak of "world" political and economic integration, and the harmonization of national policies into "world" policies. At least for the early decades of the next century, such ideas are likely to have relevance, if at all, for multicountry regions—for example, the European Community—rather than for the world as a whole.

these lower-level decisions. But my taxonomy serves as a reminder that some salient and consequential aspects of intergovernmental cooperation cannot be thoughtfully appraised by restricting attention solely to lower-level, ongoing decisions.

The preceding discussion has not differentiated macroeconomic policies from other types of policies. Although my taxonomy is applicable to a wide range of other policies, I restrict attention hereafter to the policy instruments for which macroeconomic stabilization is a primary objective—the monetary policies of national central banks and the budgetary (expenditure, tax, transfer, and debt) policies of national fiscal authorities.

4 Rules and Discretion in National Macroeconomic Policies

To discuss macroeconomic stabilization policies in either their domestic or international manifestations, one needs to extend the taxonomy in at least one more dimension. Accordingly, I now introduce the spectrum of possibilities for national macroeconomic policies running from simple rules at one extreme to highly activist discretion at the other.

A single nation's monetary or fiscal policymakers can be seen as trying to attain certain ultimate objectives, which can be stated in terms of time paths desired for certain ultimate-target variables. The policymakers have at their disposal certain instruments of policy. These instruments are the variables that policymakers can and do control precisely at each point in time. The problem of instrument choice is to select particular variables as operating instruments. The problem of instrument variation is to choose how to vary the settings of the policy instruments over time. The way that policymakers resolve the issues of instrument choice and intertemporal instrument variation results in an operating regime for policy.

This definition of a (national, in effect, "domestic") operating regime pertains solely to a single nation's lower-level, ongoing decisions for monetary and fiscal policies. It must be differentiated from the concept of an international regime, defined earlier, and in particular from an international regime embodying intergovernmentally agreed constraints on national policies taking the form of "presumptive rules."[9]

Differences in judgment about the conduct of macroeconomic stabilization policies arise from several sources. Differences in views exist about instrument choice per se, and still more about the relative merits of single-stage versus intermediate-target strategies.[10] Most prominently, however, judg-

---

[9] For elaboration of the national, domestic definition of "regime" in the economics literature on macroeconomic policy and the identification of alternative regimes for ongoing decisions about national monetary policies, see Bryant, Hooper, and Mann (1993, chap. 1).

[10] Intermediate-target and single-stage strategies are defined and discussed in, for example,

ments differ about the role of "activism" in varying the policy instruments intertemporally (especially for monetary policy). Controversy about the appropriate degree of activism is often couched in terms of the relative merits of "rules" versus "discretion."

Activist approaches to instrument variation tend to be defended in the policy community but are often criticized in academic circles. Advocates of activist discretion stress the probable need for policymakers to adjust their instruments in the light of new information about the evolution of the economy or changed perceptions of how the economy does or should function. Critics of activist discretion emphasize the benefits of "commitment" to an announced rule. Discretion gives policymakers flexibility with respect to their future actions. Commitment to a rule is like a binding contract that specifies in advance the actions that policymakers will (and will not) take.

The term "rule" has two connotations frequently encountered in macroeconomics. Sometimes, as in the preceding paragraph, "rule" is used as an antonym of "activist discretion." In that usage, a rule for policy is a determinate procedure, often simple and rigid, indicating how policy will be implemented. Such a rule gives little or no scope to policymakers for activist discretion. At other times, "rule" has a looser, more general connotation. It may indicate only a prescribed guide for conduct, which need not be simple and rigid and does not necessarily deny policymakers substantial scope for discretion in the future. In this chapter, I reserve the word "rule" for situations in which the nondiscretionary connotation is dominant. I identify an operating regime as a (nondiscretionary) rule if the regime permits only limited flexibility for policymakers to adjust the settings of their instruments in response to new data, to changes in their perceptions of how the economy works, or to alterations in their ultimate objectives. Analogously, the more flexibility available to policymakers, the greater the degree of discretion—potential activism —permitted by a particular regime.

The debate about nonactivist rules versus activist discretion has a long history. But it took on new intensity in the 1970s and 1980s, when inflation rates rose dramatically and economic theory began to focus more intensively on expectations, issues of "time consistency" and reputation, and the potential benefits of credible commitment to an announced policy rule. An operating regime announced by policymakers may be described as time-consistent if there is no incentive for the policymakers to change the regime even though they are free to do so. If, as was increasingly argued in the 1970s and 1980s, society is afflicted with an inflation bias, policymakers acting in the interests of the society should tie their own hands by commitment to a rule that will, if followed, credibly prevent inflation. The rationale is analogous to Ulysses'

Kareken, Muench, and Wallace (1973), Waud (1973), Friedman (1975, 1990), Bryant (1980, 1983), and McCallum (1985, 1990).

behavior in putting wax in his crew's ears and having them tie him to the mast as their ship sailed by the Sirens' rocks.[11]

The debate about rules and discretion, with its associated themes of time consistency and the alleged benefits of credible commitment to a simple rule, is certain to continue in the 1990s. This debate, moreover, has important implications for the conduct and analysis of international cooperation, although the connections are not always acknowledged.

Figure 11.3 emphasizes the likely interplay between the degree of activist discretion in national operating regimes and the characteristics of international cooperation among national governments (in both their lower-level, ongoing decisions and their episodic agreements about international regime environments). All regions of the space in Figure 11.3 can, in principle, be relevant (in contrast with Figures 11.1 and 11.2). A situation near the northwest corner, national autonomy with simple rules for national policies, is the preferred position for those who dislike both discretionary instrument variation in national operating regimes and efforts to cooperate internationally. A position not far from the southwest corner comes closest to characterizing the actual world economy for most of the twentieth century. Policymakers within each national government have tended to use activist discretion in their own decisions about intertemporal instrument variation but have resisted most pressures to agree on international regimes and to engage in intensive consultations and bargaining with other national governments. The far right-hand side of the space in Figure 11.3 might characterize a highly integrated world economy in the middle or late twenty-first century, with outcomes varying all the way from locations near the northeast corner (if advocates of committed rules were to have their case fully accepted by decisionmakers in federalist supranational agencies) to locations near the southeast corner (if advocates of highly activist discretion were to prevail).

The regions in Figure 11.3 of greatest relevance to this chapter are the two identified most prominently. The larger region in the northwest quadrant (not the corner region itself) is labeled "international cooperation with presumptive-rule national operating regimes" (henceforth, "cooperation with presumptive rules"). Mutual recognition is the characteristic mode of international cooperation in this region, with the degree of cooperation (for example, the intensity of international monitoring and surveillance) rising as one moves from west to east. The other prominent space, occupying the central southern space, is the domain of "explicit international policy coordination." This domain does not extend to the northern border, of course, because "coordination" presumes some degree of discretionary activism in the use of national policy instruments.

---

[11] For the recent literature on rules versus discretion, pertinent references include Kydland and Prescott (1977), Barro and Gordon (1983), Rogoff (1985b, 1987), Barro (1986), Fischer (1990a), Canzoneri (1985), Flood and Isard (1989), and Canzoneri and Henderson (1991).

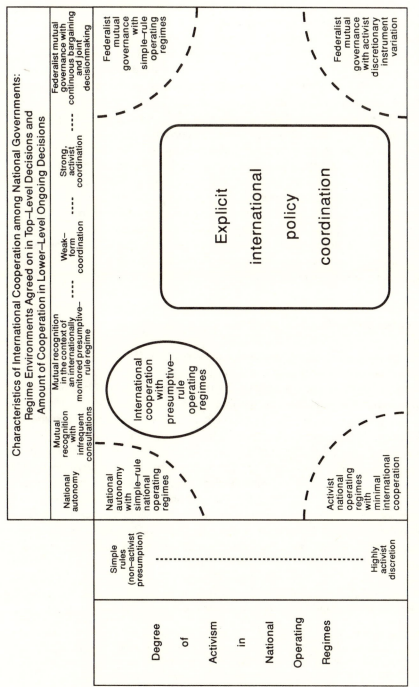

Figure 11.3 Interplay between Characteristics of International Cooperation among National Governments and Degree of Activism in National Operating Regimes

Certain regions in Figure 11.3 can be identified with actual historical experience or with prominent proposals for "reform" of the international regime environment. All of historical experience lies within the western half of the space. Developments since World War II have resulted in some small movements, though all within the southwest quadrant of the diagram. The collapse of Bretton Woods in the early 1970s and the move to more flexible exchange rates resulted in a modest movement to the southwest; international cooperation was somewhat diminished, and the flexibility of exchange rates encouraged marginally more activism in national operating regimes for monetary policies. Efforts to strengthen multilateral surveillance and cooperation, primarily through consultations and economic summit meetings of the Group of Seven (G-7), can be interpreted as a small movement eastward after the mid-1980s. Virtually all proposals for reforming the international regime would marginally enhance international cooperation (an eastward movement), sometimes simultaneously adjusting the degree of activism characteristic of national operating regimes.[12] Proposals for more ambitious explicit coordination of macroeconomic policies involve a move eastward from recent experience, but probably with little movement to the north or south.

5 Three Analytical Perspectives

The preceding cartography sketches a map of the intellectual territory. What analytical perspective is most useful in studying this territory, in particular the categories of mutual recognition and international coordination? Each of three perspectives has something to contribute.

Rule analysis concentrates on international cooperation through presumptive rules or guidelines; its preoccupation is with questions that arise within the mutual-recognition domains in Figures 11.2 and 11.3. *Policy-optimization analysis* concentrates on explicit policy coordination. *Institutionalist analysis* describes a third perspective, which is not so much an alternative to the other two but, rather, a broad perspective that can subsume them. Institutionalist analysis represents in part a reaction by noneconomists to the preoccupations of policy-optimization analysis and emphasizes what I subsequently call "satisficing stabilization" and "maintenance of the international regime environment."

---

[12] For example, McKinnon's (1984, 1988) ideas for encouraging monetary stabilization among the largest industrial countries must be placed fairly far north in the diagram, given his suggestions for rules constraining national monetary policies. Target-zone proposals, such as the Williamson-Miller (1987) blueprint for coordination, lie to the southeast of McKinnon's proposals but clearly to the northeast of where matters stand today; Williamson and Miller suggest several types of constraints on national policies, with rulelike features but with substantial residual scope for discretion.

Policy-optimization analysis is the most familiar and most developed of the three. It dominates the existing literature. Policy optimization grows out of the tradition in economics of studying choices of rational agents; it embeds the logic of rational choice in game-theoretic contexts, in which two or more agents interact with each other. An analogous tradition is labeled "realism" or "neorealism" in international-relations theory.[13] The agents in the analysis are national governments, each of which has well-defined, exogenously given preferences (loss functions) biased toward home-nation welfare.[14] As with the loss functions, the interactions among national economies (the ways in which policies and shocks originating in one country affect other countries) and the alternative strategies available to governments (choice options) are exogenous inputs to the analysis.

Each national government is treated analytically as an individual decision-making agent acting strategically to further its own interest (defined by its loss function). National decisions are seen as plays in "noncooperative games" or, alternatively, "cooperative games." Cooperation and actual coordination characterize outcomes in which the national governments adjust their own policy actions to take into account the preferences and actions of other governments. Both the strengths and weaknesses of this analytical perspective rest on its unitary-actor, rational-choice assumptions.

The policy-optimization perspective has generated valuable insights (to be summarized momentarily). Until recently, I have been content to adopt this perspective when discussing international cooperation. But some critics see shortcomings, and I, too, am now a bit restive—hence, the attention I give in this chapter to the complementary perspectives of rule analysis and institutionalist analysis.

Unlike the explicit coordination that is a main focus of the policy-optimization perspective, rule analysis presupposes uncoordinated decisions by national governments. The national decisions are decentralized, but they are also rule constrained. Rule analysis is based on the presumption that discretionary "activism" in national decisions about monetary and fiscal policies may have undesirable consequences.

---

[13] For archetypal references for this analytical perspective in international economics, see Hamada (1985), Cooper (1985), and Canzoneri and Henderson (1991). Representative references in international relations include Waltz (1979) and Strange (1983). Keohane (1984) represents a modified structuralist, or neorealist, perspective. Krasner (1983) compares this perspective with others in international relations.

[14] The underlying assumption is that citizens of a home nation give little or no weight in their utility functions to the welfare of the citizens of foreign nations. Hence analysts seeking to study international economics and politics simplify by postulating that each nation's government operates with a national loss function. That function is assumed to be predominantly, if not exclusively, a function of home-nation variables. If taken literally, the assumption of a national loss function assumes that each national government behaves as if it is a unitary actor with a capacity unambiguously to rank alternative outcomes and to make rational choices among them.

The term "rules" in the context of the rule-analysis perspective effectively performs double duty. The rules can refer to aspects of the international regime environment that have been accepted as constraints on national decisions (for example, limiting exchange-rate movements or exchange-market intervention). Such rule features of the international regime, if they exist, will have resulted from past top-level international negotiations. But the rules constraining national decisions may be simply domestic, representing the rule aspects of the nation's own independently chosen operating regimes for monetary and fiscal policies (for example, a simplified rule for money targeting or nominal-income targeting followed by the nation's central bank). Although the rule features of the international regime environment will have been agreed in top-level international negotiations, both the international and the domestic aspects of the rules themselves will pertain to the conduct of macroeconomic policies in ongoing, lower-level decisions.

It might seem tempting to refer to international cooperation through presumptive rules as "implicit coordination" or perhaps "rule-based coordination." Advocates of presumptive rules hope that the behavior of national governments, when constrained by the rules, will generate world macroeconomic outcomes more favorable than would otherwise occur. If successful outcomes do occur, there is a sense in which one might want to say that the rules "implicitly" induce behavior similar or preferable to that achievable through explicit coordination.[15] But it is more straightforward and less likely to cause confusion to reserve the word "coordination" for situations characterized by explicit bargaining and explicitly agreed mutual adjustment of ongoing decisions about policy instruments.[16]

The "institutionalist" analytical perspective originates mainly outside economics. One of its distinguishing features is a focus on information exchanges, norms that govern behavior, and the processes through which

[15] Explicit coordination conducted through policy optimization will generate Pareto-optimal outcomes (by construction, given the assumptions of the analysis as typically conducted). Advocates of policy optimization thus argue that simplified rules cannot produce outcomes more favorable than those attainable with explicit coordination. Advocates of presumptive rules counter this argument by emphasizing the benefits of credible commitment to a simple, time-consistent rule and (what they believe to be) the dangers of discretionary activism.

[16] Kenen (1990, p. 67) makes a distinction between "bargaining about specific policy packages" and "a once-for-all bargain about policy rules or guidelines" and refers to the latter as "rule-based policy coordination." My terminology and his are not compatible, in part because I wish to emphasize the distinction between simpler rules and policy activism and so must consider the domestic as well as international features of rule-constrained policies. But the differences between Kenen and me are only semantic. Note, for example, his description of the Bretton Woods system as "too vague to meet my definition of full-fledged coordination" because, although "the exchange-rate obligations were explicit, the corresponding policy commitments were implicit." The presumption in the Articles of Agreement of the International Monetary Fund (IMF) about national operating regimes was that they would be relatively activist and discretionary, not rule based.

persuasion and learning take place. More than rule analysis, and much more than policy-optimization analysis, institutionalist analysis emphasizes general principles of conduct and the institutional infrastructure in which they are embodied. It is also defined by an emphasis on "diffuse reciprocity" (see below) and by a concern with the management of crisis periods and, more generally, with the episodic aspects of international cooperation. Indeed, institutionalist analysis focuses not merely on lower-level, ongoing decisions, but also, perhaps even especially, on the episodic, top-level interactions that determine international regime environments.

6 Explicit International Coordination Analyzed through Policy Optimization

In this section, I look through the lenses of the policy-optimization perspective at the more ambitious forms of international cooperation called "explicit coordination." Most of the resulting insights, which I summarize here selectively and subjectively, have by now become familiar in the literature on international cooperation.

Applications of game theory in economics make more precise the insight, recognized in political and economic theory for centuries, that decentralized, noncooperative decisionmaking can produce outcomes that are decidedly inferior to a set of efficient, Pareto-optimal outcomes attainable through collective action. Numerous studies of market failures, externalities, public goods, and strategic interactions within national economies identify instances in which unconstrained maximization by individual decisionmaking agents, though rational for each agent, can produce suboptimal outcomes for all agents together. The possible suboptimality of decentralized decisions extends naturally to many types of interactions between national governments and to international collective goods. In principle, therefore, when transnational externalities are important and if coordination among governments is feasible, it may be possible to "internalize the externalities" and reach mutually preferable outcomes through cooperative decisionmaking. This fundamental insight is the starting point for most of the literature adopting the policy-optimization perspective.[17]

A closely related insight is the appreciation that neither international cooperation nor explicit coordination is a synonym for altruism or benevolence. On the contrary, cooperation and coordination can result from completely selfish

---

[17] References to the older game-theory and market-failure literatures are given in Bryant (1980, chap. 25); see Canzoneri and Gray (1985), Canzoneri and Henderson (1991), and Ghosh and Masson (1994) for more recent references. The earliest discussions of the basic insight applied to international cooperation include Niehans (1968), Hamada (1974, 1976, 1979), and Cooper (1969).

bargaining. Coordination does not require that national governments have common or even compatible goals, or that some governments must sacrifice their own goals in deference to the goals of others. Cooperation and coordination merely imply the self-interested mutual adjustment of behavior. The potential for large gains from cooperation in all its forms may well be greatest when goals are inconsistent and discord is high.

Explicit coordination of macroeconomic stabilization policies should not be confused with "harmonization." The harmonization of national policies and standards (alternatively stated, the evolution of world policies and standards) is an extraordinarily advanced form of international cooperation. It can be imagined for the hypothetical regions along the extreme eastern border of Figure 11.3. In the limit, as noted earlier, one can even imagine currency unification and a single monetary policy for a region or the world, which would harmonize monetary policies "completely" across nations. Even under federalist mutual governance, however, not all types of policies would be harmonized; national budgetary policies would be one notable exclusion.

The differences between coordination and harmonization are still more fundamental for the domains of explicit policy coordination identified in Figure 11.3. Normally, one would *not* expect coordinated national monetary and fiscal policies to be harmonized. For example, national governments will not necessarily move in similar directions, even when undertaking "optimal" coordination. If asymmetric disturbances hit their economies, the optimal policies will typically require governments to do different things. The further the distance away from the eastern border in Figure 11.3, the less likely that harmonization will be an appropriate benchmark for "full coordination."

Cooperation, and still more, coordination, pose a theoretical problem for game-theoretic analysis of strategic interactions among individual decisionmakers. The most basic results in the theory, often expounded in terms of game situations such as the prisoner's dilemma, explain why noncooperative decisions may be dominant strategies for all agents. "Free riders" inhibit cooperative decisionmaking. The "supply of cooperation" is likely to fall short of what would be mutually beneficial because collective action is a public good. Interdependent groups of agents, with their individual members making decentralized (rational) decisions, may fail to foster their mutual interests (Olson, 1971; Hirsch, 1976). These general points seem to apply with even greater force to a situation in which national governments are the individual decisionmaking agents. How is it, then, that intergovernmental cooperation and coordination do sometimes occur?

Policy-optimization analysis has explored three categories of explanation for the emergence of cooperation. First and most straightforward, side payments may be made to governments that ought to be included in a cooperative agreement but may not have sufficient incentives to participate. Only if such free-rider governments can be bribed through side payments of some sort, thereby raising their own gains from cooperation, will they be willing to help other prospective participants move toward the Pareto-optimal frontier.

The second explanation explored by policy-optimization analysis is to focus on repetition of the strategic interactions and, hence, on the phenomena of reputation and credibility. Most of game theory initially explored games that, analytically, were played only once. In such one-shot games, illustrated by the prisoner's dilemma, the strategy of defection (not to cooperate) typically dominates. Once the one-shot framework is relaxed, however, the range of possible outcomes is greatly increased. Analysis must then focus on strategic time paths rather than single moves. Issues of trustworthiness and credibility can become paramount. Broadly speaking, cooperative outcomes are more often observed in repeated than in one-shot games (Hardin, 1982; Kreps et al., 1982; Kreps and Wilson, 1982; Axelrod, 1984; Taylor, 1987).

Some strategies for such iterated games call for contingent or "conditional" cooperation. A conditional cooperator agrees to cooperate only on the condition that some or all of the other players will also cooperate. The tit-for-tat strategy explored extensively by Axelrod (1984) and others is the most prominent example of a conditional strategy. By definition, conditional cooperators have to monitor the actions of other players to enforce compliance with the cooperative decisionmaking. The study of repeated games therefore involves careful analysis of enforceability. Canzoneri and Henderson (1991, chaps. 4 and 5) explore this set of issues in detail for the case of international cooperation in monetary policies. They show how policymakers in a repeated game can, if they do not discount the future too heavily, make decisions in a decentralized manner without explicit coordination but nonetheless produce outcomes resembling those attainable through explicit coordination.

The third type of explanation for the emergence of cooperation focuses on entrepreneurial leadership and the formation of a cooperating subgroup by some of the participants in a game situation. The traditional free-rider analysis, which predicts a suboptimal supply of collective action, tends not to give adequate emphasis to the potential role of leadership. Imaginative political entrepreneurship can sometimes circumvent the inability of unorganized groups to cooperate by packaging potential benefits so as to induce collective action (Frohlich, Oppenheimer, and Young, 1971; Olson, 1971, appendix). Not all of the n agents in a strategic situation, moreover, need necessarily cooperate. It may be possible for a k subset of the n agents to form a smaller group, members of which agree to cooperate regardless of what the remaining $n - k$ agents choose to do.[18]

Despite the possibility that a subgroup may coalesce around a cooperative

---

[18] Applications of these ideas to intergovernmental cooperation are numerous; see, for example, Canzoneri and Henderson (1991, chap. 3) and Kahler (1992). The theory of "hegemonic stability" emphasizes the leadership of a hegemon in facilitating desirable systemic outcomes; see Kindleberger (1973), Gilpin (1975), and Keohane (1984).

outcome, the forces that threaten cooperation may still be significant. Indeed, it has been another fundamental insight of the policy-optimization perspective to point out that cooperative solutions tend to be more difficult to attain in larger than in smaller groups. The original statement of this conclusion in Olson (1971) rested on three assertions: that the fraction of a collective benefit enjoyed by any individual agent tends to decline as the size of the group increases; that larger groups are less likely to exhibit the small-group strategic interactions that facilitate the supply of collective goods; and that organization costs tend to increase with an increase in group size. Authors such as Hardin (1982) and Michael Taylor (1987) take issue with the last two of these assertions; their arguments are summarized in Kahler (1992). But Taylor (1987, p. 105) himself emphasizes still another reason for believing that larger groups have more difficulty than smaller groups in achieving collective action. He observes that conditional cooperation becomes more difficult as the size of a cooperating group grows. Cooperation and coordination tend to be sustainable only when conditional cooperators play an important role. But conditional cooperators need to monitor the compliance of others, and the costs and difficulties of monitoring compliance tend to increase with the number of participants. International economics and intergovernmental political agreements provide numerous illustrations of this phenomenon.

The literature on policy optimization applied internationally has naturally devoted considerable attention to the size of the potential gains from intergovernmental cooperation and, more narrowly, from the explicit coordination of macroeconomic policies. How much has been learned about this question, either from the exploration of small theoretical models or from examining empirical models?

The first point to stress is that significant gains may result merely from governments' exchanging information and acting strategically rather than acting in an insular or myopic manner. Benefits may be achieved, in other words, without trying to move all the way to the explicit coordination of national policy instruments, but merely by moving from outcomes where international interdependence receives little attention to noncooperative outcomes where national decisions are decentralized, yet governments exchange information about their economies and policies.[19]

Some limited evidence exists to support this favorable view of consultations and information exchanges, and I know of none that generally contradicts it.

[19] Both the international-relations and international-economics literatures have long conjectured that "mere" consultations and information exchanges are extremely important aspects of international cooperation. For examples, see Keohane and Nye (1977), Keohane (1984), Bryant (1987a), and Currie, Holtham, and Hughes Hallett (1989). Policy-optimization analysis notes that information exchanges about the "initial conditions" in which economies are currently located and about the shocks they are thought to be currently experiencing can help to reduce uncertainty and thereby facilitate national decisions even when there is no intention of explicitly coordinating policies.

Hughes Hallett (1986a; Brandsma and Hughes Hallet, 1989), for example, carried out some loss-function calculations showing that the welfare gains for the United States and Europe associated with moving from a baseline situation to a noncooperative solution (that is, to optimized policies with strategic behavior) were substantially larger than the additional gains associated with moving from that noncooperative solution to a fully coordinated solution. Edison and Tryon (1988) and Canzoneri and Minford (1989) likewise report estimates affirming that large gains are attainable when nations act strategically rather than myopically (insularly). Canzoneri and Edison (1990) study gains realizable from information exchanges and surveillance and from agreement about instrument choice. Their principal conclusion is that the gains from information sharing and from agreement on instrument choice tend to be much larger than the incremental gains from going further to full-scale cooperation (explicit coordination).[20]

It is possible to imagine circumstances in which information exchanges among governments could lower welfare. Ghosh and Masson (1994, chap. 8) construct an example using a simple model of official exchange-market intervention in which governments exchange information that is asymmetrically available about certain types of shocks. What makes the Ghosh-Masson illustration produce its counterintuitive result is the temptation of one government to mislead another given that the governments are merely sharing information rather than making policy commitments. This illustration seems contrived, however, and does not provide insight into the welfare consequences of most types of international communications and exchanges of information.[21]

The subject that has commanded the lion's share of attention in the policy-optimization literature is the size of potential gains attainable from choosing a cooperative solution embodying explicit coordination (sometimes referred to as "full coordination"). Analytically, the issue is typically addressed by seeking to measure the potential gains associated with moving from a Nash nonco-

---

[20] The terminology in the Canzoneri and Edison paper is inconsistent with my terminology in this essay. "Coordination" for Canzoneri and Edison is the process of agreeing on the preferred Nash noncooperative solution. Their (full-scale) cooperation is my explicit coordination. Estimates of the gains from optimized strategic interaction of the type cited in this paragraph cannot be regarded as definitive evidence about the potential gains from information exchanges among national governments. Such calculations do not clearly distinguish between gains associated with efficient use of information about cross-border spillovers and foreign governments' loss functions versus gains associated with efficient use of information about a country's own economic structure.

[21] An institutionalist analyst appraising this illustration might regard it as another example of policy-optimization analysis gone astray (see discussion below). The institutionalist would probably emphasize the continuous dealings that governments have with one another in the context of the existing international regime. Because of those dealings, he would argue, any clear-cut effort to deceive in period t is likely to become apparent in period $t + 1$ or $t + 2$; thus the norms and institutional-process aspects of the international regime would discipline information exchanges and discourage such "deception-motivated information exchanges."

operative solution to a solution characterized by Nash bargaining.[22] A sizable number of studies have tackled this question since the initial paper by Oudiz and Sachs (1984). Many investigations have been conducted in the context of smaller theoretical models.[23] A variety of others have used one or more empirical models.[24]

It has become conventional wisdom, based on the existing empirical studies, to say that the incremental gains from coordination for the largest OECD economies are small or at most modest in size. The original Oudiz and Sachs (1984) study suggested incremental gains on the order of 0.5 percent of real GNP, or less. Most of the other studies fail to show substantially larger gains. As shown by Hughes Hallett, Frankel and Rockett, and Nedde (among others), however, estimates of the size of the gains are significantly sensitive to the models used and the definitions of the noncooperative and cooperative solutions. In any case, potential gains on the order of 0.5 percent of real GNP are far from negligible, even though, as emphasized by Currie, Holtham, and Hughes Hallett (1989), the forecast standard errors of target variables tend to be this large.

The most prudent stance on this question has not changed much since my earlier conclusion (Bryant, 1987a) that the evidence is inconclusive and that the sensitivity of the estimated gains to different models and to alternative specifications of the underlying assumptions needs to be studied further. Canzoneri and Henderson (1991) review only the theoretical literature, but they, too, suggest that "the jury is still out" on the size of the potential gains from explicit coordination.

7 Rule Analysis of International Regime Environments

Policy-optimization analysis presumes that national governments should be able, through international consultations and bargaining, to make mutually

[22] In models where intertemporal dynamics are explicit, several alternative types of Nash noncooperative solutions can be defined. Nash cooperative bargaining solutions can also vary depending on the specification of national and joint loss functions. Thus, a precise analysis of the question identified in the text is more complex than it may at first appear. The activities of consultation and information exchange, furthermore, cannot be rigidly compartmentalized from explicit coordination. Thus, it is not straightforward to separate the potential gains associated with "mere" consultation from the potential gains associated with explicit coordination.

[23] These include Carlozzi and Taylor (1985), Currie and Levine (1985), Miller and Salmon (1985), Oudiz and Sachs (1985), Taylor (1985a), Ghosh (1986), Turnovsky and d'Orey (1986), Levine and Currie (1987), Turnovsky, Basar, and d'Orey (1988), van der Ploeg (1988), Ghosh and Ghosh (1991), Masson (1992), and Ghosh and Masson (1994, chap. 4).

[24] These contributions include Hughes Hallett (1986a, 1986b, 1987, 1989), Currie, Levine, and Vidalis (1987), Holtham and Hughes Hallett (1987, 1992), Canzoneri and Minford (1988, 1989), several of the contributions in Currie and Vines (1988), Edison and Tryon (1988), Frankel and Rockett (1988), Brandsma and Hughes Hallett (1989), Hughes Hallett, Holtham, and Hutson (1989), Nedde (1989), Canzoneri and Edison (1990), Ghosh and Ghosh (1991), and Ghosh and Masson (1988, 1991, 1994).

agreed on, discretionary adjustments of the policy instruments in their national operating regimes. But advocates of rules for national operating regimes are uncomfortable with the activist resetting of national instruments associated with explicit international coordination. Not surprisingly, therefore, rule advocates prefer to distance themselves from many aspects of policy optimization.

Rule analysis of international cooperation, in contrast to policy optimization, is preoccupied with the evaluation of alternative international regime environments and their associated national operating regimes. As indicated in Figure 11.3, rule analysis rests on the premise that decisions about national macroeconomic policies will not be explicitly coordinated but will be constrained by presumptive rules. It envisages mutual recognition as the general mode of international cooperation, with each nation's presumptive rules subject, at least to some degree, to multilateral surveillance.

Some advocates of international cooperation with presumptive rules regard such international regimes as unambiguously first best—better than more ambitious forms of cooperation, such as explicit coordination. Other advocates support such international regimes as an attainable second best; they believe that explicit full coordination is not feasible and that presumptive rules may be able to emulate some of the favorable consequences that would be achieved if full coordination were feasible.

Rule analysis must somehow evaluate the likely performance of national economies under alternative international regime environments and rank the international regimes against one another. The analytical task is analogous to that involved in evaluating alternative domestic operating regimes for monetary or fiscal policy in a single economy. Analysts must have at their command one or more structural models of macroeconomic behavior that represent, *endogenously*, not only the key aspects of private behavior but also the main features of the policymakers' behavior. The behavior of the policymakers is represented by "reaction functions," which summarize how the actual instruments of monetary and fiscal policy vary intertemporally in response to evolution of the economy.[25]

---

[25] Reaction-function equations for a structural model are derived, either explicitly or implicitly, from policy loss functions (which could be, but do not have to be, well-defined specifications of preferences for a "unitary actor"). Reaction functions typically take the form

$$\underset{\substack{\text{actual}\\\text{value of}\\\text{policy}\\\text{instrument}}}{X_t} = \underset{\substack{\text{ultimate-target}\\\text{or benchmark}\\\text{value of}\\\text{instrument}}}{X_t^{U*}} = \underset{\substack{\text{responses to}\\\text{disequilibrium}\\\text{deviations of}\\\text{goal variables}}}{f(G_t - G_t^{U*})} + \underset{\substack{\text{nonmodeled}\\\text{residual}\\\text{elements of}\\\text{policy}}}{Z_t}\,,$$

where X is a particular policy instrument and G represents a vector of the policymakers' ultimate-target variables. The reasons why structural models used for rule analysis must include explicit endogenous equations for the behavior of policymakers and the difficult issues of how to specify reaction-function equations are discussed in Bryant (1991) and Bryant, Hooper, and Mann (1993).

Rule analysis in an international context, however, is even more complex. The structural models that are a prerequisite for the analysis must be *multicountry* models, because the overriding purpose is to evaluate the performance of international regimes, taking into account the cross-border as well as domestic effects of macroeconomic policies and nonpolicy shocks. And separate reaction functions are required to represent the behavior of each nation's monetary and fiscal authorities. In effect, every international regime to be studied must be a complex combination of the domestic operating regimes of each country or region represented in the corresponding structural model. Descriptions of alternative international regimes must specify the different underlying types of simple rules in the national operating regimes together with, where applicable, the different types of internationally agreed constraints on the national rules.

One fundamental goal of rule analysis is to assess the performance of alternative international regimes in stabilizing ultimate-target variables in the face of various economic disturbances (nonpolicy shocks and policy actions themselves). A related issue, important for the analysis of some types of rules, is to assess the ability of any one nation's policymakers to identify in a timely and accurate manner the disturbances that are hitting the national economy.

The potential benefits from credible commitments to simple, time-consistent rules is still another major subject for analysis. Analysts need to quantify these benefits for different international regimes and to rank the international regimes against one another on this dimension. Alternatively stated, we need to understand how credibility is earned for various international regimes (and for their national component regimes) and how it can be eroded by various types of discretionary departures from a particular international regime. Not least important, rule analysis should be able to examine the possibly difficult trade-offs between the commitment properties and the stabilizing properties of international regimes.

The stabilizing properties of alternative international regimes have received most of the attention in the limited research carried out thus far. Some of that research has focused on simplified theoretical models for which analytical solutions can be obtained. More complex structural models require simulation analysis. Most studies working with multicountry empirical models have used the techniques of deterministic simulation, examining the consequences of a series of individual shocks. In a few cases, researchers have employed the techniques of stochastic simulation, in which the shocks passed through a structural model are random draws from the model's own residuals, with the shocks occurring to multiple variables and varying in size from period to period. In principle, stochastic simulation provides a more realistic basis for evaluating the robustness of alternative international regimes in stabilizing ultimate-target variables in the presence of multiple shocks.

The most comprehensive effort thus far undertaken to analyze alternative

national operating regimes in an international setting stems from a collaborative project of multicountry modeling groups. The volume resulting from the
project (Bryant, Hooper, and Mann, 1993) contains illustrations of all the
complementary approaches: analyses with simplified theoretical models, deterministic simulations, and stochastic simulations. The strategy of the project
was to get the ten participating model groups to run "horse races" among four
highly simplified intermediate-target regimes for national monetary policies:
money targeting, nominal-income targeting, real-GNP-plus-inflation targeting, and exchange-rate targeting. The policymakers for each country represented separately in a particular model were presumed to implement one of
these national operating regimes, and the world combination of the national
regimes constituted an international regime environment in the sense discussed here. For the purposes of the project, exchange-rate targeting evoked
the main features of the Bretton Woods system; Germany, Japan, and other
countries outside the European Monetary System (EMS) were assumed to
target their nominal bilateral exchange rates against the U.S. dollar, and the
United States was assumed to target its own money supply independently of
exchange rates.[26]

This particular project was stimulated in part by three papers presented at a
December 1988 conference, all of which used stochastic simulations to evaluate alternative monetary-policy regimes. Several additional pieces of exploratory research in a similar vein appeared in recent years.[27] Another group of
research papers was sparked by the Williamson-Miller (1987) extended
target-zone proposal.[28]

Apart from the preceding studies, discussions of presumptive rules in international regimes have not struggled with the issues in a modeling framework.
Instead, commentary has typically focused attention only on exchange rates,
exchange-rate targeting, and exchange-market intervention. Policymakers
themselves appear to have made exchange rates the principal focus of international cooperation (or, at least, the rhetoric of cooperation) in the late 1980s
and early 1990s.

That exclusive focus of attention on exchange rates seems to me misplaced.
To be sure, I share with many economists the sense that exchange rates can be
buffeted by excessive volatility or become temporarily misaligned, thus stray-

---

[26] Countries in the EMS other than Germany were assumed to use their monetary-policy
instrument to target their bilateral exchange rates against the deutsche mark.

[27] The three papers from the 1988 conference are Frenkel, Goldstein, and Masson (1989),
McKibbin and Sachs (1989), and Taylor (1989). The other exploratory research includes Currie
and Levine (1985), Taylor (1988), Frenkel, Goldstein, and Masson (1990), Levine, Currie, and
Gaines (1989), McKibbin and Sachs (1988, 1991), Hughes Hallett (1992, 1993), and Frenkel and
Chinn (1993).

[28] Efforts to study that international regime include Edison, Miller, and Williamson (1987),
Currie and Wren-Lewis (1989a, 1989b, 1990), Hughes Hallett, Holtham, and Hutson (1989), and
Nedde (1989).

ing away from values consistent with fundamental economic determinants. I, too, believe that private exchange-market participants could benefit from having a more solid analytical anchor for their expectations about future exchange rates (Bryant, 1987b; Holtham, 1989; Currie, Holtham, and Hughes Hallett, 1989). But I feel even more strongly that it is a mistake to become preoccupied with the exchange-rate aspects of an international regime. The domestic-monetary and the fiscal aspects of national operating regimes are more important. Without an internally consistent specification of all aspects of an international regime, moreover, there are good reasons to doubt that any effort at exchange-rate management can be successful.

From the perspective of a single nation's policymakers, there is no logically valid dividing line between the external and domestic aspects of operating regimes for monetary policy and no way of compartmentalizing the external and domestic impacts of fiscal actions. Internationally agreed on presumptive rules—traffic regulations—that apply exclusively to exchange rates or external reserves are thus bound to be analytically unsound. There may exist rules that can make an international regime successful, but they will have to encompass the instruments, once thought to be "domestic," of national monetary and fiscal policies.

This basic point about international regimes is recognized in the most prominent academic proposals for presumptive rules, such as those of Williamson and Miller (1987), McKinnon (1984, 1988), and Frankel (1990). It is less clear that policymakers themselves have adequately acknowledged the point in their intergovernmental bargaining about the management of exchange rates.

The limited empirical evidence available, at least as I read it, does not show exchange-rate targeting to be a promising international regime environment. One of the robust generalizations emerging from Bryant, Hooper, and Mann (1993) was the relatively poor performance of exchange-rate targeting relative to the other international regimes studied. For most types of shocks, either real-GNP-plus-inflation targeting or nominal-income targeting outperformed both money targeting and exchange-rate targeting in stabilizing national economies when policymakers were assumed to stress real ultimate targets, such as output or employment, or when they were assumed to stress a combination of such real variables and nominal ultimate targets, such as the inflation rate or the price level. This ranking was evident in a large majority of the theoretical analyses, in nearly three-fourths of the many deterministic simulations run for the ten models, and in more than five-sixths of the stochastic simulations.[29]

By reporting these negative results about exchange-rate targeting, I do not

[29] The better overall performance of real-GNP-plus-inflation targeting and nominal-income targeting was less clear-cut for productivity and other supply shocks and for certain assumptions about the relative importance that policymakers attach to various ultimate-target variables. For example, the theoretical analysis suggested, and the two types of empirical simulation tended to confirm, that money targeting or exchange-rate targeting could be the preferred regime under one

imply that the *Evaluating Policy Regimes* project (Bryant, Hooper, and Mann, 1993) produced a definitive reading. A minority of the participating model groups could not implement exchange-rate targeting in the form requested. The EMS was taken into account in only a rudimentary way, and, most important, the project focused only on simple rules for national *monetary* policies, not on the combined functioning of monetary-policy and fiscal-policy operating regimes. At a minimum, however, these extensive empirical experiments place a greater onus on the proponents of exchange-rate targeting as an international regime to come up with evidence that such an international regime is likely to have welfare-improving effects for individual countries and for the world as a whole. One can also interpret the turbulent EMS experience in September 1992 as raising anew questions about the dynamic stability of exchange-rate targeting.[30]

The preceding paragraphs have focused on the stabilizing properties of alternative international regimes. To repeat, a balanced and complete rule analysis would have to offer satisfactory answers to all the questions raised earlier in this section. In particular, policymakers need sound advice on how to trade off the stabilizing properties and commitment properties of alternative international regimes.

8 Cooperation and Coordination as International Regime Maintenance and Satisficing Stabilization

From the viewpoint of proponents of simple rules, the major difficulty with policy-optimization analysis is its presumption in favor of discretionary activism. I now turn to quite different criticisms of policy optimization that have

---

or (especially) both of two conditions: (1) if productivity or other supply shocks are the most prevalent disturbances to economies, and (2) if policymakers place great weight on stabilization of the inflation rate or the price level and place little or no weight on stabilization of output or employment. The project also found that, if policymakers placed significant weight on dampening the variability of financial variables such as interest rates and exchange rates, the case for preferring real-GNP-plus-inflation targeting and nominal-income targeting became still less strong and could conceivably be overturned. Interest rates and exchange rates tended to be *more* variable under those two regimes, especially under real-GNP-plus-inflation targeting.

[30] Such questions were rarely addressed in the European context during the four to five years preceding September 1992. The empirical assessment of the extended target-zone proposal conducted by Currie and Wren-Lewis (1990), using the global economic model (GEM) of the National Institute of Economic and Social Research, suggested that policy cooperation based on those presumptive rules would have led to substantial welfare gains for the Group of Three (G-3) countries *relative to historical experience* from the mid-1970s to mid-1980s. But even Currie and Wren-Lewis stress that much additional work evaluating the proposal needs to be carried out. Hughes Hallett's (1992) analysis of exchange-rate targeting reinforces this judgment. Eichengreen (1992), Eichengreen and Wyplosz (1993), and Williamson (1993) analyze the EMS experience of September 1992.

led some analysts to adopt an institutionalist perspective. These other critics wish to emphasize aspects of international cooperation that may be labeled "satisficing stabilization" and "maintenance of the international regime environment" ("regime maintenance," for short).

Institutionalist analysts tend to regard policy optimization as tied to unrealistic or misleading assumptions and, therefore, as unlikely to be feasible in practice. One objection asserts that policy optimization fails to focus sufficiently on the management of crisis situations. A second line of criticism attacks the unitary-actor assumption as implausible and thus views the conclusions reached by policy-optimization analysis as lacking operational relevance. A third class of objections turns on issues of uncertainty, claiming that policy-optimization analysis often ignores uncertainty about countries' macroeconomic interactions and thereby fails to focus on the issues of international cooperation that national governments actually face. A final group of critics, especially noneconomists, argue that policy optimization takes too many institutional aspects as being exogenously given, with the result that it overlooks or downplays important dimensions of international cooperation. These last critics see policy optimization as paying little attention to international regimes and other important institutional aspects of cooperation.

Kenen (1990) stresses a distinction between a "policy-optimizing approach" and a "regime-preserving approach" to international policy coordination. In describing the latter (in which "regime" means "international regime environment" in my terminology), Kenen emphasizes its reliance on "mutual persuasion" in contrast to the "adversarial bargaining" of policy optimization. The regime-preserving approach, he writes (p. 69), is concerned with "defend[ing] the international economic system from economic and political shocks, including misbehavior by governments themselves." Institutionalist analysis, as I identify it here, is broader than Kenen's regime-preserving approach, and it draws explicitly on the international-relations literature.[31]

The notion that an international regime may be threatened by occasional crises, involving extreme turbulence in financial and economic transactions or in political interactions, grows naturally out of historical experience. International cooperation has not been so extensive and ingrained that it can be taken for granted by national governments. Actual international regimes, to the limited degree that they have existed, have been a fragile nexus of principles,

[31] My reasons for highlighting institutionalist analysis and regime maintenance are similar to Kenen's reasons for stressing regime preservation. Goldstein and Isard (1992), Masson (1992), and Ghosh and Masson (1993) echo the notion of regime preservation. Kenen cites Cooper (1985) and Kindleberger (1986) as economists writing in the vein of a regime-preserving approach. He places Putnam and Bayne (1984, chap. 1) in this tradition as well, quoting their remark that "public goods must be produced and institutional arrangements defended by common or collective action." Fischer (1990b), in commenting on Kenen (1990), describes the distinction between regime-preserving and policy-optimizing coordination as "suggestive but elusive" and expresses doubt about its usefulness in debates about national policies.

norms, and decisionmaking procedures around which expectations can converge.

Many observers have suggested that international cooperation, when it has been manifest, often arises in response to shared perceptions of a crisis (for example, Pauly, 1992). An extension of this suggestion might claim that the bulk of observed international cooperation is best explained as actual or latent crisis management. A key part of this idea is the presumption that an existing international regime is valued by national governments (and at one remove by their citizens), even if national policymakers cannot readily demonstrate how the regime is beneficial in each and every circumstance. If this framework of international comity is threatened—if it looks as though major disruptions might cause one or more governments to act so as to undermine the international regime—then high priority is given to rallying round in the crisis.

The argument can be carried further. If national governments feel a need to maintain readiness to deal with possible future disruptions, it may even be possible to interpret the ongoing intergovernmental consultations held in normal (noncrisis) periods as preparation for or insurance against latent crises. Without the regular, noncrisis consultations and without the bonding and sense of mutual confidence to which they give rise, the policymakers in national governments might be significantly less able to act effectively if and when actual crises materialize. During his tenure as economic counselor at the IMF, Jacob Frenkel frequently made this point by invoking the analogy of firefighters who can be observed in noncrisis times lounging about the firehouse playing cards. Their apparent nonproductiveness in normal times cannot be appropriately judged unless one also takes into account their behavior when a fire has to be put out promptly.

Consider next the assumption, typical of policy optimization, that each national government can be analytically treated as a unitary actor. We economists use this abstraction in virtually all of our prescriptive theory of economic policy, even when we ignore international aspects. Yet the concept of a single, unified policy authority and the consequent assumption of an integrated approach to macroeconomic policy within each national government are false representations of the political and bureaucratic facts of life. In all nations, the ship of state has many captains, and policy decisions are far from fully integrated. With a multiplicity of domestic agents pulling and pushing against each other, it requires a big stretch of the imagination to see the national government as a unitary actor with a well-defined national loss function.

All theory must do violence to reality. Lack of realism is thus not by itself a damaging criticism of the traditional theoretical approach to economic policy and international cooperation. But the economists' practice of treating each national government as a unitary actor is open to criticism on a more fundamental point: this abstraction has inhibited thoughtful analytical study of the within-nation politics of macroeconomic policy. According to some critics, these domestic politics are so crucial as to render misleading the unitary-actor policy-optimization analysis that ignores them.[32]

Various types of institutionalist analysis pay much more explicit attention to domestic politics. Approaches emphasizing "organizational process" focus on the institutional forms and procedures of the individual agencies composing the national government. Models of "governmental or bureaucratic politics" emphasize the different perceptions, motivations, and powers of those agencies and the results of bargaining among them. More broadly still, other approaches encompass domestic actors outside as well as inside the national government.[33] Putnam and Henning, addressing the deficiencies of the unitary-actor model, introduce the idea of international economic policy coordination as a "two-level game":

> Games at both the domestic and international level are played simultaneously, so that national policies are in some sense the result of both the domestic and international parallelograms of forces. . . . Each national political leader appears at both game boards. Across the international table sit his foreign counterparts. . . . Around the domestic table behind him sit party and parliamentary figures, spokesmen for the great domestic ministries, representatives of key domestic interest groups, and the leader's own political advisers. . . . The special complexity of this two-level game is that moves that are rational for a player at one board . . . may be quite irrational for that same player at the other board. (Putnam and Henning, 1989, pp. 111–112)

Applying these ideas in a study of the 1978 Bonn economic summit, Putnam and Henning (1989, p. 112) assert that "this two-table metaphor captures the dynamics of the 1977–78 negotiations better than any model based on unitary national actors."[34]

Seen from an institutionalist perspective, "satisficing stabilization" may be a more appropriate label for what is sought and sometimes achieved in international cooperation about national macroeconomic policies. Rather than at-

[32] For example, Putnam and Henning (1989, p. 106) remark that "the right question is not whether the unitary-actor assumption is unrealistic, but whether it is misleading. Unfortunately, we believe that it is the latter."

[33] In comments on the conference draft of my paper, Jerry Cohen emphasized the variety of approaches to domestic politics in the political-science and international-relations literatures and criticized my treatment of these approaches as incomplete and inadequate. In Cohen (1990), he discusses the levels-of-analysis issue in political science; one of these levels of analysis (the second image, or unit level) focuses on the roles of heterogeneous domestic politics and institutions.

[34] The two-table-game metaphor is discussed in Putnam (1988); the concept originated in a 1986 Putnam-Henning draft of the essay published in 1989. For earlier illustrations of different institutionalist approaches, see Allison's (1971, esp. chaps. 3–5) study of the Cuban missile crisis, Simon (1959), March and Simon (1958), Steinbruner (1974), Halperin, Clapp, and Kanter (1974), and Katzenstein (1978).

tempting policy optimization through explicit full coordination, governments constituted of many heterogeneous actors may have to settle for a satisficing second best that, though less precise, is also more attainable and less politically contentious.

Institutionalist analysis takes issue not only with the unitary-actor assumptions of policy optimization but also with several of its other simplifying assumptions. The relevant question here also is whether those assumptions are productive or misleading, not whether they are realistic. Many analysts in international relations believe that policy optimization has too narrow a focus and fails to take into account important institutional aspects of international cooperation, a failure that renders its conclusions misleading or at least only partly illuminating.

One point of departure for these critics is that state-centered, unitary-actor theories in both economics and international relations "build very little sociality into their premises" and thus "are of limited value in explaining multilateral cooperation." Such theories underestimate "the extent to which cooperation depends on a prior set of unacknowledged claims about the embeddedness of cooperative habits, shared values, and taken-for-granted rules. Further, its assumption that preferences are exogenously given reduces multilateralism to a question of strategic interaction, making it difficult to comprehend multilateralism propelled by collective beliefs, presumptive habits, and shared values. . . . Shared understandings and communicative rationality are as important as instrumental rationality" (Caporaso, 1992, pp. 630–631).[35]

The flavor of institutionalist views is well captured in another quotation from Caporaso's (1992) survey article on multilateralism. Institutionalism is preoccupied with the relations among preferences, norms, beliefs, and institutions and aspires to "rethink the conventional relationships":

> Conventional rational choice models in neoclassical economics start with exogenous preferences, a given distribution of endowments, and a given technology. . . . In the institutional approach, however, norms, beliefs, and rules occupy a more central position. Individuals come to politics not only with preferences for particular outcomes but also with shared and divisive values and variously developed beliefs about the political process. . . . politics and individual preferences undergo change: not only do individuals "act out" their preferences politically, but . . . the political process is a forum within which their preferences and beliefs change "as in the rest of life, through a combination of education, indoctrination, and experiences."[36]

[35] Caporaso (1992, pp. 630–631). Caporaso's survey of different approaches in the international-relations literature is helpful, and I have based some of my comments on his summaries of the views of others.

[36] Caporaso (1992, pp. 624–625). The quotation within the quotation is from March and Olsen (1984, p. 739). In addition to March and Olsen, Caporaso cites Keohane (1988) and Powell and DiMaggio (1991) as overviews of a growing literature on institutionalism.

Policy optimization and institutionalism tend to have analogously contrasting interpretations of historical experience. Traditional economic theory predicts outcomes, including institutional outcomes, largely on the basis of choice-theoretic efficiency (with given preferences, technology, and endowments). In contrast, the institutionalist perspective emphasizes the contingent, path-dependent nature of institutional change (Caporaso, 1989, 1992).

Diffuse reciprocity, in the context of institutionalist analysis, is the notion that each nation engaging in international cooperation expects to benefit over many periods on many issues, not necessarily to benefit in every period on every issue. The emphasis on diffuse reciprocity is another characteristic that differentiates institutionalism from policy optimization (Krasner, 1983, p. 3; Keohane, 1986). If one thinks in terms of the concepts of Hirschman (1970), there is much more emphasis on "voice" in institutionalist analysis than on "exit," with exit interpreted broadly to mean that a nation will not play the game unless the game will yield good outcomes judged by the benchmark of the national loss function.

How much weight should economists accord to these points? At the very least, the institutionalist criticisms should caution us not to lose sight of the extreme nature of some of the analytical abstractions that we employ. There is great force in the contention that unitary-actor analysis of national government decisions may be misleading. Focusing on the multiplicity of agents and forces within a national government—the juxtaposition of a domestic bargaining table with the international game board—reinforces the conclusion that international cooperation becomes more difficult as the number of inter-acting agents increases (and thus is an order of magnitude more difficult than it is made to appear when national governments are treated as unitary actors). Similarly, the crisis-management line of reasoning merits further careful attention by economists. My conjecture is that the varieties of institutionalist analysis, when developed further, will generate many additional insights. To state the obvious, however, I do not know the relevant literatures sufficiently well to be able to give institutionalist ideas a balanced appraisal, and I have only tentative views about how best to use these ideas to modify conclusions reached in the economics literature.

Perhaps because I am unable to wriggle far enough out of the straitjacket of my economics training, I am reluctant to bet the bulk of my chips on institutionalist analysis. That training reminds me, moreover, that policy-optimization analysis is itself flexible. By thoughtfully amending some of its assumptions or by casting its net more widely, it can be extended to tackle some of the issues emphasized in institutional analysis. We have surely not learned all we can by operating with the as-if assumptions that nations have well-defined loss functions and act to optimize their decisions accordingly. For example, it may be possible creatively to adapt national loss functions to include variables that represent some of the diversity of domestic politics or that capture some aspects of the international regime that nations regard as shared goals. Institutionalist critics should also acknowledge that economists' analyses of repeated games, reputation, and credibility are aimed at the very phenomena that institutionalists wish to discuss under the heading of diffuse reciprocity. Most important, policy-optimization analysis can take into account uncertainty of various types. Indeed, as I discuss below, traditional economic analysis has probably done more to incorporate the consequences of uncertainty into our conclusions than have the institutionalist critics who assert the importance of uncertainty but have not taken many steps to study it analytically.

9 Arguments That Cooperation May Be Counterproductive

Several arguments have been advanced from time to time claiming that efforts to cooperate internationally will have undesirable consequences. I turn here to the most important.

One line of argument asserts that efforts to cooperate are not desirable because they may deflect the attention of national governments from higher-priority (domestic) policy choices or may give the governments incentives to delay policy actions they ought to be taking regardless of international considerations. Some economists even see international negotiations and bargaining as providing a smokescreen, enabling a government to blame foreigners for its own failure to take responsible action.[37]

Most critics adopting this position appear to be primarily worried about international efforts to achieve explicit coordination. Few seem to object to some degree of ongoing consultations and exchanges of information. As far as I know, moreover, such critics do not object to the crisis-management cooperation emphasized by institutionalist analysts (although they might be uncomfortable with a low-threshold definition of "crisis" that made it too easy for governments to invoke the crisis-management rationale).

I have never been able to regard this line of criticism as compelling. Governments are capable of short-sighted behavior. Individual policymakers within a government can be tempted to deflect attention from difficult issues and choices by invoking foreign pressures or external constraints on policies. But obfuscating behavior by politicians can occur over any issue, domestic or international. The possibility of obfuscation is seldom invoked as a rationale for preventing a government from pursuing one or another domestic objective. If international cooperation, including explicit coordination, can offer opportunities for a nation to benefit significantly, *provided the cooperation is*

---

[37] For examples of those doubting the usefulness of international cooperation, especially efforts to achieve explicit coordination, see Stein (1978, 1987), Corden (1983, 1985, 1986), Vaubel (1983, 1985), and Feldstein (1987, 1988a, 1988b). Fischer (1988) is a partial doubter.

pursued wisely and without obfuscation, why should the risk of deflected priorities be used as an argument against the international cooperation? The remedy for the risk of deflected priorities is to straighten out the erring policy-makers rather than to choose to forgo the benefits from cooperation. The situation is analogous to the risks that doctors run when prescribing medications that must be wisely used. The risk that a few patients may swallow an entire bottle of aspirin is not accepted as a valid reason for urging the doctors not to prescribe aspirin at all.

A weightier line of argument asserts that international cooperation, explicit coordination in particular, can be counterproductive if a subgroup of agents cooperates in the absence of relevant third parties. Rogoff (1985a) articulated this criticism clearly in an influential article identifying circumstances in which explicit coordination between two national governments could actually reduce welfare. The mechanism causing this result in Rogoff's theoretical model is the exclusion of the private sector from the coordinating bargain; in effect, one of the key players in the game-theoretic situation is not permitted at the bargaining table, and the outcome that results from the bargaining does not reflect that player's interests. When the two governments in Rogoff's model do not coordinate their policies, each government is constrained because of a knowledge that a monetary expansion will depreciate its currency (the exchange rate in the model is flexible) and thereby cause higher inflation. In effect, the noncooperative solution restrains central-bank temptation. If the two governments are permitted to coordinate their policy actions, however, a joint monetary expansion will not lead to a depreciation of either currency, and the restraint that prevents the central banks from pursuing overly expansionary policies is removed. But the forward-looking agents in the private sector understand that international coordination removes the restraint on temptation and raise their wage demands accordingly. The coordination outcome thus produces higher inflation and reduces welfare relative to noncoordination.[38]

Some adherents of a "public-choice" view of economics take the argument even further. They argue that governments are organizations with interests of their own, which are different from, and potentially inimical to, those of general populations. Consequently, these public-choice economists wish to prevent national governments from "colluding" (their interpretation of international cooperation, especially explicit coordination). Instead, they advocate intergovernmental competition, not coordination, as being more likely to

---

[38] Other papers that explore cooperative solutions to games that decrease rather than increase welfare include Miller and Salmon (1985), Kehoe (1986, 1989), Currie, Levine, and Vidalis (1987), and Levine and Currie (1987). Carraro and Giavazzi (1991) take issue with the Rogoff (1985a) model and provide a counterexample in which, with three agents per economy (government, firms, and trade unions), cooperation is welfare enhancing. Tabellini (1988) is also relevant.

serve the interests of general populations. Seen in the context of Figure 11.3, such critics favor mutual-recognition types of international regime, if any international regime at all. Most are also proponents of simple rules rather than activist discretion.[39]

I take this argument against cooperation and coordination seriously but do not find it persuasive on balance. In practice, as with most issues pertaining to government behavior, a judgment has to be made about the greater danger: that collusion between governments will work against the public interest or, alternatively, that the absence of international cooperation will allow cross-border spillovers and externalities to work to the detriment of the public interest. Public policy, for all its imperfections, is virtually the only vehicle we have to represent the public purpose. If public goods and collective action are necessary, then governments are necessary, and this proposition carries over to the international domain. The premise underlying my personal views is that, on the whole, international cooperation among governments, particularly democratically elected governments, can be plausibly expected to further the collective interests of their citizens.[40]

10 Uncertainty about National Objectives and Intentions

Even analysts who would like national governments to cooperate acknowledge that such efforts may not be feasible. The fundamental obstacles to feasibility are various types of uncertainty. In real-life circumstances, policymakers and analysts in a "home" nation are uncertain about (a) the current positions of the home and foreign economies—the so-called initial conditions and shocks that are currently buffeting those economies; (b) the objectives and intentions of policymakers in other national governments—the loss functions that guide the policymakers' decisions; and (c) the actual functioning of the world economy, including especially the ways in which policy actions themselves influence the home and foreign economies—the analytical model that represents interactions within and among the national economies. All three aspects of uncertainty can have decisive consequences for international cooperation.

Even when analysts look through the lenses of game theory and policy optimization, uncertainty about the policymakers' loss functions can have an important bearing on analytical conclusions. Although the outside analyst is likely to assume correct knowledge of each (unitary-actor) player's loss func-

[39] James Buchanan is a noted expositor of the public-choice view; see, for example, Brennan and Buchanan (1980).

[40] For examples of other papers that share this political premise, see Artis and Ostry (1986), Frenkel, Goldstein, and Masson (1989), Dobson (1991), and Solomon (1991). Bryant (1987b, 1990b) has more discussion of the general political background to international cooperation.

tion, the individual players themselves can be assumed to have only imperfect information about the others' functions. Such uncertainty leads naturally to issues of bluffing, deception, and reputation, and thus to the consideration of reneging on agreements, of monitoring compliance with agreements (enforceability), and of the use of "trigger mechanisms" to facilitate enforceability.

From an institutionalist perspective, uncertainty about the objectives and intentions of national governments may be even more important. When it is acknowledged that each national government is composed of multiple agents interacting with one another—when the "domestic game board" is crowded and confusing—the issues of bluffing, deliberate deception, and willful reneging at the international game board will probably be less relevant. But the ability of national governments to make and effectively "deliver" on international agreements, and therefore also the problem of monitoring compliance, will have still greater salience.

Uncertainty about policymakers' objectives and intentions is thus a major stumbling block for international cooperation, and all the more so for explicit coordination. A considerable part of the policy-optimization literature discusses this nexus of issues by emphasizing reneging, cheating, and the "sustainability" of cooperation. It is more revealing, in my opinion, to emphasize other aspects of uncertainty.

Reneging on an international agreement ("defection") can be voluntary or involuntary (Putnam and Henning, 1989). Voluntary reneging is the deliberate decision of a rational agent to defect from an agreement because he expects to improve his strategic situation by doing so. Bluffing, deception, and apprehension about other agents' compliance may precede the decision. Voluntary reneging is typically studied under the assumption that national governments behave as if they were unitary actors. Involuntary reneging is a notion that stems from an institutionalist perspective on agreements. It occurs when an individual policymaker, being part of a national government that does *not* behave as a unitary actor, is unable to deliver on a previous promise.

Institutionalists tend to believe that game-theoretic economics has exaggerated the importance of voluntary reneging. Putnam and Henning (1989), for example, find the concept unhelpful in studying the 1978 Bonn summit and argue that such behavior is much less common, particularly among Western democratic governments, than policy-optimization theorists would predict. The institutionalist presumption is that conditional cooperators in repeated games, concerned about their reputations and credibility and judging their participation in international cooperation by the standard of diffuse reciprocity, will hesitate to deceive or renege voluntarily for the purpose of capturing short-run advantages.

Much of the game theorists' emphasis on time consistency and trigger mechanisms likewise seems artificial to institutionalist analysts. For example, they doubt that real-life policymakers are so averse to "giving up some sovereignty" to a third-party monitor (such as an international institution) that they will search for a complex trigger mechanism as a substitute for third-party oversight.

My sympathies lie with the institutionalists on these points, largely because the policy-optimization perspective on reneging and compliance pays too little attention to uncertainty. In real life, the multiple agents within national governments and all the private-sector agents in their economies have too little information, of too low a quality, to identify reneging behavior (Bryant, 1987a). Imagine the possibility of a government's voluntarily reneging in period 2 on policies announced in period 1. What can reneging mean? In real life, it cannot plausibly mean that the government "reoptimizes" in period 2 and thus changes its instrument settings away from the preannounced settings that were derived from optimization calculations in period 1. Private-sector agents and other governments should not rationally want the government to stick to a previously announced "open-loop" path for its instruments if new disturbances have occurred in the meantime. Thus, the only logically sound notion of reneging must imply that the government announces in period 1 future paths for its instrument settings—in effect, a complex set of "closed-loop" reaction-function equations—that are explicitly contingent on the occurrence of every conceivable type of future disturbance. Reneging must then be defined as a departure from these complex, reaction-function "rules." Under this definition, however, the information presumed to be available to governments and private-sector agents is enormously greater than what they actually have. The concept of reneging that has received such attention in the game-theory literature thus has limited practical applicability.[41]

Although an institutionalist perspective may downplay the importance of reneging, cheating, and willful deception, it will nonetheless assign great importance to issues of monitoring and ability to deliver. Putnam and Henning, for example, argue that deliverability was a prominent feature of the negotiations for the 1978 Bonn summit, even though concern about cheating and reneging were not.[42]

Uncertainty about the objectives and intentions of national governments, about their ability to deliver on agreements, and about their ability to monitor the compliance of other governments, is a troublesome type of uncertainty that can undermine the feasibility of international cooperation. But it is not as consequential as the type of uncertainty I turn to next.

[41] Note, however, the similarity to the analytical issues that have to be faced in specifying and evaluating the presumptive rules to be studied in the rule analysis of international regimes!

[42] "The Americans worked hard to convince the others, first, that [President Carter] was under severe domestic political constraints on energy issues that limited what he could promise, but, second, that he could deliver on what he was prepared to promise" (Putnam and Henning, 1989, p. 105).

11 Uncertainty about the Functioning of the World Economy

Policymakers and their advisers have only limited knowledge about the functioning of their national economies and even less knowledge about the ways in which national economies interact to generate global economic outcomes. This analytical ignorance—for brevity, "model uncertainty"—is the single greatest impediment to sound policymaking within national governments and to successful international cooperation for macroeconomic policies.

Real-life policymaking is bedeviled by the competing-model problem. To formulate alternative courses of action and to clarify the likely costs and benefits associated with them, a decisionmaker and his or her advisers must employ some sort of analytical model that connects actions to expected outcomes. But several rival models will be available, often embodying significantly different analytical views and having conflicting implications for policy decisions. Basic disagreements exist, for example, about how to characterize the behavior of private economic agents, how to describe the behavior of policy authorities themselves, how to treat expectations of future economic developments, and what to assume about the current and future values of the driving forces not treated endogenously in a model. The decisionmaker will accordingly be uncertain about which of the competing models represents the least inadequate approximation of the "true" model (the actual relationships that will determine the consequences of his or her actions).

When focusing on the competing-model problem, it is helpful to distinguish between model construction, model evaluation, model improvement, and model selection. Model construction is the initial process of building some piece of analytical machinery to shed light on issues of interest. Construction of a model or several alternative models is self-evidently a prerequisite for model evaluation and model improvement. Similarly, there is no competing-model problem facing a policymaker unless several different explicit models have already been constructed. I am concerned here with issues that postdate model construction.

Model evaluation systematically compares a model with the objectives for which it has been constructed and assesses its performance using theoretical and economic criteria thought to be characteristic of a "good" model. Model evaluation can also entail systematic comparisons of the performances (and thus the relative strengths and weaknesses) of competing models.[43] Model improvement attempts to remedy the inadequacies of individual models and to

---

[43] Since the mid-1980s, the Brookings Institution, together with other organizations, has sponsored a series of international collaborative projects among model groups that have constructed empirical multicountry models. The resulting publications include Bryant et al. (1988), Bryant, Holtham, and Hooper (1988), Hooper et al. (1990), Bryant et al. (1989), and Bryant, Hooper, and Mann (1993).

promote convergence among competing models. If the processes of model evaluation and model improvement were to work ideally, inconsistencies across models would be gradually eliminated and a single model would become the encompassing, consensus model (for a particular analytical purpose).

Because the processes of model evaluation and improvement do not work ideally, policymakers are confronted with the thorny issues of model selection, that is, the competing-model problem proper. This problem presupposes that several alternative models have been constructed, all presumptively relevant to the analytical problem facing a policymaker, but that no professional consensus exists about the single best model.

Accumulation of robust empirical knowledge does not occur quickly, at least not in macroeconomics. The techniques of model evaluation do not seem sufficiently robust or the prospects for model improvement sufficiently good to permit policymakers to believe that macroeconomists will soon converge on a single, "true" model for any single economy, let alone for the global economy.

Both classical and Bayesian statistical theory rest on the hope that model evaluation and improvement will eventually lead to an encompassing model. But this hope may be forlorn. The "true" structure to be estimated may change over time (or, if one prefers, the true "deep" parameters that are time invariant cannot be reliably identified and estimated). Statistical theory presumes that a researcher can obtain a lengthy sample of data or draw repeatedly from the invariant true structure. In practical macroeconomics, however, the usable samples are likely to be small, because data from periods far in the past may be relatively uninformative, measured with large errors, or utterly unavailable. The awkward fact is that policymakers will have to wait a very long time for model evaluators and model improvers to reach a degree of convergence sufficient to make the competing-model problem unimportant in practice.

The competing claims of rival models and the other dimensions of model uncertainty would not vex policymakers greatly if policymakers could safely downplay uncertainty. But they cannot do so. In any practical policy situation, uncertainty should be taken explicitly into account when formulating and implementing decisions.

Uncertainty about the consequences of a policymaker's own actions—about the time paths of the policy "multipliers" associated with the policymaker's instruments—is an especially critical type of uncertainty. Policymakers should never ignore uncertainty about policy multipliers. Even if it were feasible to use policy doses of any size, it would be inappropriate to select those instrument settings that would be dictated by focusing on the expected values of multipliers while ignoring their variances and covariances. All available instruments should be fully utilized, moreover, no matter how few the target variables that are the objective of policy and no matter how plentiful the instruments. As a general presumption, the more uncertain the multipliers of an individual policy instrument are, the less aggressively one should use it. More broadly stated, the greater the uncertainty associated with the policy multipliers, the less active policymakers should be in adjusting the settings of the corresponding instruments.[44]

Policymakers in a hypothetical, completely closed national economy would be confounded by numerous types of "domestic" uncertainty, but "international" uncertainties are often even more troublesome. Only limited analytical agreement exists about the ways in which policy actions and nonpolicy disturbances originating in one nation spill across borders to influence economic developments in other nations. Increasing economic interdependence would substantially complicate policymaking, moreover, even if governments had reliable estimates of the cross-border spillovers. Typically, larger cross-border spillovers reduce the effects of a country's policy instruments on its own national variables relative to their effects on variables in other countries and hence reduce the autonomy of economic policy. Externally originating forces constrain the ability of a government to achieve its goals, thereby diminishing the degree of control that a nation's policymakers can exert over its own national target variables. The closer intertwining of economies renders policy decisions in any single nation more difficult (Bryant, 1980).

The difficulties for policy are magnified by great uncertainty about the empirical magnitudes, and sometimes even the directions, of the cross-border spillovers. A nation's policymakers know that policy actions and nonpolicy shocks originating abroad will constrain their own policy choices, and that their actions will alter outcomes and policy choices in other countries, but the forms and magnitudes cannot be well estimated.

These points bear powerfully on conclusions about international cooperation reached through the policy-optimization perspective. But they have the same importance for rule analysis and institutionalist analysis as well. All three perspectives share the presumption (albeit with different nuances) that national governments can sometimes foster their nations' interests by framing their policies cooperatively. But how can governments cooperate when they are so uncertain about the ways in which nations' actions influence each other? More of a consensus about the direction and size of cross-border interactions is a necessary—although far from sufficient—condition for significant progress in facilitating cooperation for national macroeconomic policies.

Is model uncertainty a valid reason for believing that international cooperation, in particular explicit coordination, may not be *desirable* (as opposed to

---

[44] The basic reference for these generalizations is the seminal article by Brainard (1967). Many subsequent researchers have confirmed the importance of this line of inquiry. For applications to international cooperation, see, among others, Ghosh (1986), Ghosh and Ghosh (1991), Masson (1992), and Ghosh and Masson (1994). Bryant (1985) emphasized the importance of uncertainty issues.

being infeasible)? In a widely cited study, Frankel and Rockett (1988) appeared to think so (see also Frankel, 1988). Frankel and Rockett drew on the extensive simulation experiments in the first Brookings comparative-model evaluation to calculate gains and losses from policy coordination for the United States and an aggregate comprising the rest of the OECD region. Because multiplier estimates were available for ten models, the Frankel-Rockett calculations were done for $1,000 (= 10 \times 10 \times 10)$ possible combinations of assumptions; each of the two "governments" was presumed to use each of the ten models, with each model treated in turn as being the "true" model. For any combination of two models, the two governments in the Frankel-Rockett analysis could find a set of adjustments in policy instruments that each believed would raise its own nation's welfare. Frankel and Rockett concluded that such policy adjustments could, in fact, lower welfare as easily as raise it when the consequences of the adjustments were evaluated using a third model as the "true" model.[45] Frankel (1989, p. 52) subsequently summarized the research with remarks such as "coordination in the presence of model uncertainty can leave countries worse off ex post as easily as better off."

It is incontrovertible that policymakers can lower welfare by using an incorrect model. And, because no one can know with any confidence what the true model is, policymakers will inevitably make mistakes. Yet policymakers necessarily rely on some form of analytical model. A model of *some* sort is a logical prerequisite for decisions on what to do with policy instruments. Policymakers cannot set all their instruments at "zero" values, so to speak, and decide to have no policy at all. If policymakers choose to ignore all explicit models, in essence they choose to use an implicit model, which is typically still more flawed and unreliable than the explicit models. Explicit models can at least be analyzed, criticized, and improved. Implicit models can be badly wrong and can stay wrong because they are not subjected to criticism.

How, then, should one interpret the Frankel-Rockett analysis? In my view, the authors overstate the pessimistic inferences drawn from their analysis. Unfortunately, many casual readers of their paper have gone still further astray in misrepresenting the inferences. The Frankel-Rockett analysis has been loosely cited—wrongly I believe—as strong evidence for the view that international coordination is undesirable.

Constructive adjustments to, and reinterpretations of, the Frankel-Rockett analysis emerged from the criticisms of Holtham and Hughes Hallett (1987), first made in 1986 in response to the original Frankel and Rockett paper and eventually published in full in Holtham and Hughes Hallett (1992) together with a response from Frankel, Erwin, and Rockett (1992). Holtham and Hughes Hallett distinguish between "weak-condition" and "strong-condition"

---

[45] The counting of cases was done in several different ways, but Frankel and Rockett typically found that coordination was beneficial to both the United States and the rest of the OECD countries in only 50 to 65 percent of the possible combinations.

bargains in policy coordination. For a weak-condition bargain to be struck, each government must expect to gain according to its own preferred model, but it does not ask whether the models preferred by other governments also predict that it will gain. For a strong-condition bargain to be struck, each government must expect to gain not only according to its own model but also according to the preferred models of other governments. (Holtham and Hughes Hallett also discuss a "superstrong" bargain in which each government would expect to gain according to all available models.) Holtham and Hughes Hallett initially conjectured, and confirmed, using Frankel and Rockett's own calculations, that restricting coordination to instances in which a proposed package of policy changes satisfies a robustness criterion has the effect of significantly raising the frequency of outcomes that improve welfare.[46] For example, if the initial Frankel-Rockett exercise is restricted to strong-condition bargains (each government expects to gain according to its own and the other government's model), only 410 cases out of 1,000 result in actual coordination; within that subset, however, both the United States and the remaining OECD countries gain in slightly more than three-fourths of the cases. More generally, as the robustness requirement is tightened (that is, as both governments must expect to gain according to each of a larger proportion of the ten models), the number of cases of actual coordination shrinks further but the probability of welfare gains rises still higher (Frankel, Erwin, and Rockett, 1992, table 1).

Ghosh and Masson (1994), in a series of important papers culminating in a book, have taken different tacks from Frankel and Rockett and Holtham and Hughes Hallett in studying the implications of model uncertainty for international cooperation. In a theoretical model drawn from Oudiz and Sachs (1985), Ghosh (1986) showed that sufficiently high degrees of uncertainty could eliminate gains from coordination. In a further theoretical exploration that partly reverses Ghosh (1986), however, Ghosh and Masson (1988) and Ghosh and Ghosh (1991) derive conditions under which uncertainty, rather than precluding coordination, may provide an additional incentive to coordinate. Ghosh and Masson (1991) emphasize learning issues and allow decisionmakers to update their priors in a Bayesian fashion over the set of possible models.

Masson (1992) studies uncertainty about portfolio preferences and its interaction with the potential gains from coordination. These various contributions are summarized and extended in the new book.

---

[46] Frankel and Rockett themselves further confirmed the Holtham–Hughes Hallett conclusion in their subsequent review of the original calculations (Frankel, Erwin, and Rockett, 1992). Kenen (1989) offers a double rationale for the Holtham–Hughes Hallett strong bargain: *prudence* requires a policymaker to ask whether his own economy would gain if the model of the other country's policymaker were true, whereas *reputation* requires him to ask whether the other country would gain if his model were true and he were to persuade the other country's policymaker to take advice based on his model.

As in Brainard (1967), Ghosh and Masson stress the distinction between "additive uncertainty" and "multiplier uncertainty." They argue that the former has unimportant implications for the gains from international coordination because it does not change the expected values of the policy spillovers from one nation to another.[47] Multiplier uncertainty, in contrast, does alter those cross-border spillovers and can significantly alter the gains from coordination. Multiplier uncertainty can thus provide incentives to coordinate policies even where such incentives would not otherwise exist. Ghosh and Masson (1994, chap. 4) also differentiate between domestic multiplier uncertainty and multiplier uncertainty associated with cross-border transmission of policy actions. They show that "a sufficiently high degree of uncertainty about domestic multipliers reduces the gains from coordination while increased transmission multiplier uncertainty raises the welfare gains."

Ghosh and Masson (1994, chap. 3) provide a clear exposition of the point that increases in the magnitude of cross-border spillovers can magnify externalities and international collective-goods problems. They illustrate how changes in structural parameters for cross-border spillovers can alter the means and increase the variances of reduced-form transmission multipliers by much more than they affect the means and variances of reduced-form domestic multipliers.

Two more conclusions of Ghosh and Masson warrant emphasis here. Their analysis (1991; 1994, chap. 7) reinforces the point that national economies can become dynamically unstable and suffer welfare losses from efforts at coordination if policymakers assign little weight to the "correct" model and exhibit no learning behavior. Under such circumstances, the performance of the Ghosh-Masson model economies can be more robust under simple presumptive rules than under activist coordination. If policymakers can engage in Bayesian learning, however, the risks of dynamic instability are reduced, and the *ex post* gains from international policy coordination are systematically positive in the Ghosh-Masson simulations. Ghosh and Masson (1994, chap. 7) are appropriately cautious about their learning results, preferring not to make general claims about the desirability of policy coordination in the presence of model uncertainty. "At the very least, however," they write, "all of our results suggest that countries would be no worse off by coordinating their macroeconomic policies so long as policymakers do not stick dogmatically to incorrect models."

The various points about model uncertainty made in this section lead to the conclusion that the *feasibility* of cooperation and coordination, not the desirability, should be the primary focus of attention in policy analysis. There is no question whatever that model uncertainty makes explicit coordination very difficult, if not completely infeasible. Model uncertainty also makes it more

---

[47] In private correspondence with me, Andrew Hughes Hallett has questioned the point that additive uncertainty is unimportant for international policy coordination, drawing on the results reported in Brandsma and Hughes Hallett (1989).

difficult to agree on international cooperation through presumptive rules. An extended target-zone proposal, to take only one prominent illustration, would require an internationally agreed calculation of the exchange-rate zones. Despite the work of Williamson (1991, 1993) and others on fundamental equilibrium exchange rates, difficult analytical questions remain unresolved about how to make such calculations merely in the context of a single multicountry model. The difficulties are made much greater by the competing-model problem. The available evidence, moreover, suggests that the performance of national economies in a target-zone international regime could depend quite sensitively on the choice of the fundamental equilibrium exchange rates.[48]

The posture that Holtham and Hughes Hallett recommend at the end of their comment on Frankel and Rockett's work appeals to me as a balanced overall assessment of the implications of model uncertainty for international cooperation. Holtham and Hughes Hallett (1992, p. 1051) argue that policymakers considering cooperation should "seek to use all available information to take account of uncertainty" but should not try to "suppress or eliminate any remaining differences in view." They should try to identify policies that promise gains on any of the views held by the participating countries. "There is no assurance that such policies exist in any particular case; but that is no reason not to look for them, nor to eschew bargains should such policies be found."

12 Concluding Note

This chapter has concentrated on analytical points about international cooperation rather than commenting on recent historical experience. To conclude, I briefly consider where the actual process seems to be going and make a recommendation for facilitating further progress.[49]

The primary institutional forums for international (as opposed to regional) consultations about macroeconomic policies are the G-7 ministers' meetings and summit meetings, supplemented by contacts and meetings among the G-7 sherpas; periodic meetings of the IMF Interim Committee, backed up by regular meetings of the IMF Executive Board; meetings of ministers at the OECD and of its Economic Policy Committee and Working Parties (especially Working Party Three); and regular meetings of central-bank governors at the Bank for International Settlements (BIS). These forums are ongoing activities. If a

---

[48] For discussion, see Edison, Miller, and Williamson (1987), Currie, Holtham, and Hughes Hallett (1989), Hughes Hallett, Holtham, and Hutson (1989), Currie and Wren-Lewis (1989a, 1989b, 1990), and Hughes Hallett (1989, 1992, 1993).

[49] Several recent publications, notably Dobson (1991) and Solomon (1991), have made practical recommendations for strengthening international cooperation about macroeconomic policies. See also Artis and Ostry (1986). Crockett (1989) reviews the roles of international institutions in supporting and monitoring international economic cooperation.

perceived crisis arises, with implications for macroeconomic policies, some of the same forums may be called into play for discussion and management of the crisis.

These forums serve, and are perceived as serving, important communicative goals. Indeed, they constitute the core of the existing weak international regime for macroeconomic stabilization policies. From my outside perspective, however, I see little evidence that consultations and information exchanges through these forums have intensified during, say, the last ten years. Speaking loosely, the international regime appears to be firmly established but subject to few if any evolutionary adaptations. One has to examine institutions with a specific regional focus, especially institutions of the European Community, for any evidence of an intensification of intergovernmental communication and an evolutionary adaptation of institutions.

The series of G-7 and summit meetings appears, at least on the surface, to have markedly less continuity and institutional infrastructure than consultations conducted through the IMF, the OECD, or the BIS. The G-7 meetings are not backstopped by consistent staff support. The G-7 governments have not wanted to establish a new secretariat to support the G-7 process but have also been unwilling to allow existing international organizations such as the IMF or OECD to become actively enough involved to play that role.

Although an improved analytical understanding of macroeconomic interactions among national economies is a prerequisite for the development of enhanced cooperation through presumptive rules or for more successful efforts at explicit coordination, the governments of the major countries have taken little direct interest in promoting an improvement in such understanding. And they have not put pressure on the international organizations to make this objective a high priority for staff work. Such efforts as have been made have been sponsored by individual central banks, individual groups within international organizations, or research or academic institutions.

Several years ago, in conjunction with a comment on Frankel's proposal for international nominal-income targeting (Frankel, 1990), I sketched a vision of the way in which the institutional evolution of international macroeconomic cooperation might proceed (Bryant, 1990a). But I failed to emphasize enough the importance of establishing a group charged with the task of improving analytical knowledge about international macroeconomic interactions and diffusing that knowledge more widely. I now believe that staff support of this type is a necessary precondition for progress of other sorts. The IMF, perhaps in combination with the OECD and the World Bank, is the most logical institutional locus for this staff support. An inferior alternative would be to establish an explicit secretariat for the G-7 and to locate the analytical staff support in that secretariat.[50]

[50] Both Dobson (1991) and Solomon (1991) argue for more active use of the IMF and its staff rather than the creation of a competing G-7 secretariat. I share that judgment, both about general

This discussion is not the place to present details of an evolutionary vision of the ways in which international cooperation could be improved if national policymakers had the benefit of enhanced analytical support, both within national governments and from a secretariat located within the international organizations. The key elements of such a process, however, are straightforward to describe.

Each national government aspiring to participate actively in the ongoing (lower-level) process of international macroeconomic cooperation would submit periodic projections of a "baseline outlook" to the international secretariat responsible for administrative and analytical support. The frequency of the projection rounds and meetings associated with them might presumptively be two or three times a year. At a minimum, each of the G-7 countries would be involved. The nature of the consultations and cooperation within each country, involving the fiscal authority, the central bank, and other government agencies, would, of course, vary across the participating countries. Delicate, controversial issues of central-bank independence and the allocation of responsibilities for economic policy within governments have so far inhibited a deeper involvement of central banks in G-7 consultations. But more extensive central-bank involvement would improve the quality and relevance of the consultations.

The baseline outlook prepared by each national government would either assume no departures from macroeconomic policies currently in force or, alternatively, could incorporate policy changes already decided or very likely to be made. Each national projection would preferably be derived using one or more analytical frameworks (models) that would try to be internally consistent; each government would be willing to exchange information about its models and projection methods. An individual government would concentrate most on projecting the key macroeconomic variables pertaining to its own economy, but each government would be free to submit projections for other economies. The supporting international secretariat would provide its own baseline projection of the outlook for each major country or region.[51]

The international secretariat would play a key analytical role in the evaluation of the different versions of the baseline outlook. For example, the secretariat would prepare a systematic comparison of the new baselines prepared for the current round, pointing out inconsistencies between the different nations' versions and the secretariat's version. The secretariat would also systematically compare the *ex ante* outlooks submitted in the preceding round with updated information about *ex post* outcomes.

---

staff support for the backstopping and monitoring of G-7 consultations ("surveillance," broadly defined) and in particular for the location of a special support staff charged with strengthening the analytical foundations for international cooperation.

[51] One may think of the IMF World Economic Outlook and the OECD Economic Outlook exercises as nascent prototypes for the baseline outlooks of the international secretariat.

"What-if" simulations, judiciously chosen to shed light on issues of current relevance, would examine the consequences of changing this or that policy instrument or postulating such and such a nonpolicy shock. These what-if scenarios would be prepared, at a minimum, by the international secretariat. Ideally, national governments would also prepare them, especially for changes in their own policy instruments, but even for changes in other governments' policy instruments and for various nonpolicy shocks. Differences in models would, of course, lead to differences in the answers to the what-if questions. No attempt would be made to suppress differences due to model uncertainty. On the contrary, they would be important grist for the mill of the analytical support group, suggesting problems with differing models or properties needing clarification.[52]

Periodic meetings of the national policymakers, and preparatory meetings of their deputies, would typically examine the baseline-outlook projections, some of the most relevant what-if scenarios, and the associated evaluations prepared by the secretariat. The discussions would involve frank exchanges of information about the individual governments' goals. Efforts would be made to classify differences in the baseline projections and what-if scenarios according to whether they were due to differences in identification of initial conditions (current positions of the national economies), to differences in national goals, to differences in preferred models, or to differences in assumptions about expected future nonpolicy shocks.

A rudimentary variant of the preceding vision could be implemented in the near future. It is even possible to interpret the last few years of G-7 discussions as hesitantly groping in this direction. The all-important missing ingredient in actual experience, however, has been the supporting role of an international secretariat charged with catalyzing the process. An improved analytical understanding of macroeconomic interactions among national economies is a prerequisite for making progress on virtually every significant macroeconomic issue, positive or normative, confronting national policymakers. Is it too much to hope that the governments of the largest nations will soon perceive their collective interest in establishing adequate analytical support for international cooperation and then give the supporting group sufficient resources and authority to foster that collective interest?

References

Allison, Graham T., *Essence of Decision: Explaining the Cuban Missile Crisis*, Boston, Little, Brown, 1971.

[52] The analytical support group could also be charged with carrying out what-if simulations examining alternative presumptive rules. Analysis would have to begin with quite simplified specifications of international regimes before eventually examining more complex and realistic alternatives.

Artis, Michael J., and Sylvia Ostry, *International Economic Policy Coordination*, Chatham House Papers No. 30, Royal Institute of International Affairs, London, Routledge & Kegan Paul, 1986.

Axelrod, Robert, *The Evolution of Cooperation*, New York, Basic Books, 1984.

Barro, Robert J., "Reputation in a Model of Monetary Policy with Incomplete Information," *Journal of Monetary Economics*, 17 (January 1986), pp. 3–20.

Barro, Robert J., and David Gordon, "Rules, Discretion and Reputation in a Model of Monetary Policy," *Journal of Monetary Economics*, 12 (July 1983), pp. 101–121.

Brainard, William C., "Uncertainty and the Effectiveness of Policy," *American Economic Review*, 57 (May 1967), pp. 411–425.

Brandsma, Andries S., and Andrew Hughes Hallet, "Macroeconomic Policy Design with Incomplete Information," *Economic Modelling*, 6 (October 1989), pp. 432–446.

Branson, William H., Jacob A. Frenkel, and Morris Goldstein, eds., *International Policy Coordination and Exchange Rate Fluctuations*, Chicago, University of Chicago Press, 1990.

Brennan, Geoffrey L., and James M. Buchanan, *The Power to Tax: Analytical Foundations of a Fiscal Constitution*, Cambridge, Cambridge University Press, 1980.

Bryant, Ralph C., *Money and Monetary Policy in Interdependent Nations*, Washington, D.C., Brookings Institution, 1980.

———, *Controlling Money: The Federal Reserve and Its Critics*, Washington, D.C., Brookings Institution, 1983.

———, "Comment" on Marcus Miller and Mark Salmon, "Policy Coordination and Dynamic Games," in Buiter and Marston, *International Economic Policy Coordination*, 1985, pp. 213–219.

———, "Intergovernmental Coordination of Economic Policies: An Interim Stocktaking," in Paul A. Volcker, Ralph C. Bryant, Leonhard Gleske, Gottfried Haberler, Alexandre Lamfalussy, Shijuro Ogata, Jesús Silva-Herzog, Ross M. Starr, James Tobin, and Robert Triffin, *International Monetary Cooperation: Essays in Honor of Henry C. Wallich*, Essays in International Finance No. 169, Princeton, N.J., Princeton University, International Finance Section, December 1987a, pp. 4–15.

———, *International Financial Intermediation*, Washington, D.C., Brookings Institution, 1987b.

———, "Comment" on Jeffrey Frankel, "Obstacles to Coordination, and a Consideration of Two Proposals to Overcome Them: International Nominal Targeting (INT) and the Hosomi Fund," in Branson, Frenkel, and Goldstein, *International Policy Coordination*, 1990a, pp. 145–153.

———, "The Evolution of the International Monetary System: Where Next?" in Yoshio Suzuki, Junichi Miyake, and Mitsuaki Okabe, eds., *The Evolution of the International Monetary System: How Can Efficiency and Stability Be Attained?* Tokyo, University of Tokyo Press, 1990b.

———, "Model Representations of Japanese Monetary Policy," *Monetary and Economic Studies* (Bank of Japan), 9 (September 1991), pp. 11–61; also available as Brookings Discussion Paper in International Economics No. 84, Washington, D.C., Brookings Institution, January 1991.

Bryant, Ralph C., David A. Currie, Jacob A. Frenkel, Paul R. Masson, and Richard Portes, eds., *Macroeconomic Policies in an Interdependent World*, Washington,

D.C., Brookings Institution, Centre for Economic Policy Research, and International Monetary Fund, 1989.

Bryant, Ralph C., Dale W. Henderson, Gerald Holtham, Peter Hooper, and Steven A. Symansky, eds., *Empirical Macroeconomics for Interdependent Economies*, Washington, D.C., Brookings Institution, 1988.

Bryant, Ralph C., Gerald Holtham, and Peter Hooper, eds., *External Deficits and the Dollar: The Pit and the Pendulum,* Washington, D.C., Brookings Institution, 1988.

Bryant, Ralph C., Peter Hooper, and Catherine L. Mann, eds., *Evaluating Policy Regimes: New Research in Empirical Macroeconomics*, Washington D.C., Brookings Institution, 1993.

Buiter, Willem H., and Richard C. Marston, eds., *International Economic Policy Coordination*, Cambridge and New York, Cambridge University Press, 1985.

Canzoneri, Matthew B., "Monetary Policy Games and the Role of Private Information," *American Economic Review*, 75 (December 1985), pp. 1056–1070.

Canzoneri, Matthew B., and Hali J. Edison, "A New Interpretation of the Coordination Problem and Its Empirical Significance," in Peter Hooper, Karen H. Johnson, Donald L. Kohn, David E. Lindsey, Richard D. Porter, and Ralph W. Tryon, eds., *Financial Sectors in Open Economies: Empirical Analysis and Policy Issues*, Washington, D.C., Board of Governors of the Federal Reserve System, 1990, pp. 399–433.

Canzoneri, Matthew B., and Jo Anna Gray, "Monetary Policy Games and the Consequences of Non-Cooperative Behavior," *International Economic Review*, 26 (October 1985), pp. 547–564.

Canzoneri, Matthew B., and Dale W. Henderson, *Monetary Policy in Interdependent Economies: A Game-Theoretic Approach*, Cambridge, Mass., MIT Press, 1991.

Canzoneri, Matthew B., and Patrick Minford, "When International Policy Coordination Matters: An Empirical Analysis," *Applied Economics*, 20 (September 1988), pp. 1137–1154.

———, "Policy Interdependence: Does Strategic Behavior Pay? An Empirical Investigation Using the Liverpool World Model," in Donald Hodgman and Geoffrey Wood, eds., *Macroeconomic Policy and Economic Interdependence*, New York, St. Martin's; London, Macmillan, 1989, pp. 158–179.

Caporaso, James A., "Introduction: The State in Comparative and International Perspective," in James A. Caporaso, ed., *The Elusive State: International and Comparative Perspectives*, Newbury Park, Calif., Sage, 1989, pp. 7–16.

———, "International Relations Theory and Multilateralism: The Search for Foundations," *International Organization*, 46 (Summer 1992), pp. 599–632.

Carlozzi, Nicholas, and John B. Taylor, "International Capital Mobility and the Coordination of Monetary Rules," in Jagdeep Bhandari, ed., *Exchange Rate Management Under Uncertainty*, Cambridge, Mass., MIT Press, 1985, pp. 186–211.

Carraro, Carlo, and Francesco Giavazzi, "Can International Policy Coordination Really Be Counterproductive?" in Carlo Carraro, Didier Laussel, Mark Salmon, and Antoine Soubeyran, eds., *International Economic Policy Coordination*, Oxford and Cambridge, Mass., Blackwell, 1991, pp. 184–198.

Cohen, Benjamin J., "The Political Economy of International Trade," *International Organization*, 44 (Spring 1990), pp. 261–281.

Cooper, Richard N., "Macroeconomic Policy Adjustment in Interdependent Economies," *Quarterly Journal of Economics*, 83 (February 1969), pp. 1–24.

———, "Economic Interdependence and Coordination of Economic Policies," in Richard N. Cooper, *Economic Policy in an Interdependent World*, Cambridge, Mass., MIT Press, 1986, pp. 289–331; originally published in Ronald W. Jones and Peter B. Kenen, eds., *Handbook of International Economics*, Vol. 2, Amsterdam and New York, North-Holland, Elsevier, 1985, pp. 1195–1234.

Corden, W. Max, "The Logic of the International Monetary Non-System," in Fritz Machlup, Gerhard Fels, and Hubertus Muller-Groeling, eds., *Reflections on a Troubled World Economy: Essays in Honor of Herbert Giersch*, New York, St. Martin's, 1983, pp. 59–74.

———, *Inflation, Exchange Rates, and the World Economy: Lectures on International Monetary Economics*, 3d ed., Oxford, Clarendon, 1985.

———, "Fiscal Policies, Current Accounts and Real Exchange Rates: In Search of a Logic of International Policy Coordination," *Weltwirtschaftliches Archiv*, 122 (No. 3, 1986), pp. 3–18.

Crockett, Andrew, "The Role of International Institutions in Surveillance and Policy Coordination," in Bryant et al., *Macroeconomic Policies in an Interdependent World*, 1989, pp. 343–364.

Currie, David A., Gerald Holtham, and Andrew Hughes Hallett, "The Theory and Practice of International Policy Coordination: Does Coordination Pay?" in Bryant et al., *Macroeconomic Policies in an Interdependent World*, 1989, pp. 14–46.

Currie, David A., and Paul Levine, "Macroeconomic Policy Design in an Interdependent World," in Buiter and Marston, *International Economic Policy Coordination*, 1985, pp. 228–268.

Currie, David A., Paul Levine, and Nic Vidalis, "International Cooperation and Reputation in an Empirical Two-Bloc Model," in Ralph C. Bryant and Richard Portes, eds., *Global Macroeconomics: Policy Conflict and Cooperation*, London, Macmillan, 1987, pp. 73–121.

Currie, David A., and David Vines, *Macroeconomic Interactions between North and South*, Cambridge and New York, Cambridge University Press, 1988.

Currie, David A., and Simon Wren-Lewis, "An Appraisal of Alternative Blueprints for International Policy Coordination," *European Economic Review*, 33 (December 1989a), pp. 1769–1785.

———, "Evaluating Blueprints for the Conduct of International Macropolicy," *American Economic Review*, 79, No. 2, Papers and Proceedings (May 1989b), pp. 264–269.

———, "Evaluating the Extended Target-Zone Proposal for the G3," *Economic Journal* (London), 100 (March 1990), pp. 105–123.

Dobson, Wendy, *Economic Policy Coordination: Requiem or Prologue*? Policy Analyses in International Economics No. 30, Washington, D.C., Institute for International Economics, April 1991.

Edison, Hali J., Marcus H. Miller, and John Williamson, "On Evaluating and Extending the Target Zone Proposal," *Journal of Policy Modelling*, 9 (Spring 1987), pp. 199–224.

Edison, Hali J., and Ralph W. Tryon, "An Empirical Analysis of Policy Coordination in the United States, Japan, and Europe," in Homa Motammen, ed., *Economic Modelling in the OECD Countries*, London and New York, Routledge, 1988, pp. 53–70.

Eichengreen, Barry, *Should the Maastricht Treaty Be Saved?* Princeton Studies in International Finance No. 74, Princeton, N.J., Princeton University, International Finance Section, December 1992.

Eichengreen, Barry, and Charles Wyplosz, "The Unstable EMS," *Brookings Papers on Economic Activity*, No. 1 (1993), pp. 51–124.

Feldstein, Martin, "The End of Policy Coordination," *Wall Street Journal*, November 9, 1987.

———, *International Economic Cooperation*, Chicago, University of Chicago Press, 1988a.

———, "Distinguished Lecture on Economics in Government: Thinking about International Economic Cooperation," *Journal of Economic Perspectives*, 2 (Spring 1988b), pp. 3–13.

Fischer, Stanley, "International Macroeconomic Policy Coordination," in Martin Feldstein, ed., *International Economic Cooperation*, Chicago, University of Chicago Press, 1988, pp. 11–43.

———, "Rules versus Discretion in Monetary Policy," in Benjamin M. Friedman and Frank H. Hahn, eds., *Handbook of Monetary Economics*, Vol. 2, Amsterdam and New York, North-Holland, Elsevier, 1990a, pp. 1155–1184.

———, "Comment" on Peter B. Kenen, "The Coordination of Macroeconomic Policies," in Branson, Frenkel, and Goldstein, *International Policy Coordination*, 1990b, pp. 105–108.

Flood, Robert P., and Peter Isard, "Monetary Policy Strategies." *International Monetary Fund Staff Papers*, 36 (September 1989), pp. 612–632.

Frankel, Jeffrey A., *Obstacles to International Macroeconomic Policy Coordination*, Princeton Studies in International Finance No. 64, Princeton, N.J., Princeton University, International Finance Section, December 1988.

———, "Comment" on David Currie, Gerald Holtham, and Andrew Hughes Hallett, "The Theory and Practice of International Policy Coordination: Does Coordination Pay?" in Bryant et al., *Macroeconomic Policies in an Interdependent World*, 1989, pp. 51–58.

———, "Obstacles to Coordination, and a Consideration of Two Proposals to Overcome Them: International Nominal Targeting (INT) and the Hosomi Fund," in Branson, Frenkel, and Goldstein, *International Policy Coordination*, 1990, pp. 109–145.

Frankel, Jeffrey A., and Menzie Chinn, "The Stabilizing Properties of a Nominal GNP Rule in an Open Economy," Working Paper No. 259, Department of Economics, University of California, Santa Cruz, March 1993.

Frankel, Jeffrey A., Scott Erwin, and Katharine E. Rockett, "Reply [to Holtham and Hughes Hallett]," *American Economic Review*, 82 (September 1992), pp. 1052–1056.

Frankel, Jeffrey A., and Katharine E. Rockett, "International Macroeconomic Policy Coordination When Policymakers Do Not Agree on the True Model," *American Economic Review*, 78 (June 1988), pp. 318–340.

Frenkel, Jacob A., Morris Goldstein, and Paul R. Masson, "Simulating the Effects of Some Simple Coordinated Versus Uncoordinated Policy Rules," in Bryant et al., *Macroeconomic Policies in an Interdependent World*, 1989, pp. 203–239.

———, "The Rationale for, and Effects of, International Economic Policy Coordination," in Branson, Frenkel, and Goldstein, *International Policy Coordination*, 1990, pp. 9–62.

Friedman, Benjamin M., "Targets, Instruments, and Indicators of Monetary Policy," *Journal of Monetary Economics*, 1 (October 1975), pp. 443–473.

———, "Targets and Instruments of Monetary Policy," in Benjamin M. Friedman and Frank H. Hahn, eds., *Handbook of Monetary Economics*, Vol. 2, Amsterdam and New York, North-Holland, Elsevier, 1990, pp. 1185–1230.

Frohlich, Norman, Joe A. Oppenheimer, and Oran Young, *Political Leadership and Collective Goods*, Princeton, N.J., Princeton University Press, 1971.

Ghosh, Atish R., "International Policy Coordination in an Uncertain World," *Economics Letters*, 21 (No. 3, 1986), pp. 271–276.

Ghosh, Atish R., and Swati R. Ghosh, "Does Model Uncertainty Really Preclude International Policy Coordination?," *Journal of International Economics*, 31 (November 1991), pp. 325–340.

Ghosh, Atish R., and Paul R. Masson, "International Policy Coordination in a World with Model Uncertainty," *International Monetary Fund Staff Papers*, 35 (June 1988), pp. 230–258.

———, "Model Uncertainty, Learning, and the Gains from Coordination," *American Economic Review*, 81 (June 1991), pp. 465–479.

———, *Economic Cooperation in an Uncertain World*, Oxford and Cambridge, Mass., Blackwell, 1994.

Gilpin, Robert, *U.S. Power and the Multinational Corporation: The Political Economy of Foreign Direct Investment*, New York, Basic Books, 1975.

Goldstein, Morris, and Peter Isard, "Mechanisms for Promoting Global Monetary Stability," in Morris Goldstein, Peter Isard, Paul R. Masson, and Mark P. Taylor, *Policy Issues in the Evolving International Monetary System*, Occasional Paper No. 96, Washington, D.C., International Monetary Fund, June 1992.

Group of Thirty, *International Macroeconomic Policy Coordination*, New York, Group of Thirty, 1988.

Haggard, Stephan, and Beth A. Simmons, "Theories of International Regimes," *International Organization*, 41 (Summer 1987), pp. 491–517.

Halperin, Morton H., Priscilla Clapp, and Arnold Kanter, *Bureaucratic Politics and Foreign Policy*, Washington, D.C., Brookings Institution, 1974.

Hamada, Koichi, "Alternative Exchange Rate Systems and the Interdependence of Monetary Policies," in Robert Z. Aliber, ed., *National Monetary Policies and the International Financial System*, Chicago, University of Chicago Press, 1974, pp. 13–33.

———, "A Strategic Analysis of Monetary Interdependence," *Journal of Political Economy*, 84 (August 1976), pp. 677–700.

———, "On the Political Economy of Monetary Integration: A Public Economics Approach," in Robert Z. Aliber, ed., *The Political Economy of Monetary Reform*, London, Macmillan, 1977.

———, "Macroeconomic Strategy Coordination under Alternative Exchange Rates," in Rudiger Dornbusch and Jacob A. Frenkel, eds., *International Economic Policy*, Baltimore, Johns Hopkins University Press, 1979, pp. 292–324.

———, *The Political Economy of International Monetary Interdependence*, Cambridge, Mass., MIT Press, 1985.

Hardin, Russell, *Collective Action*, Baltimore, Johns Hopkins University Press, 1982.

Hirsch, Fred, *Social Limits to Growth*, Cambridge, Mass., Harvard University Press, 1976.

Hirschman, Albert O., *Exit, Voice, and Loyalty*, Cambridge, Mass., Harvard University Press, 1970.

Holtham, Gerald, "Foreign Exchange Markets and Target Zones," Brookings Discussion Paper in International Economics No. 73, Washington, D.C., Brookings Institution, June 1989.

Holtham, Gerald, and Andrew Hughes Hallett, "International Policy Cooperation and Model Uncertainty," in Ralph C. Bryant and Richard Portes, eds., *Global Macroeconomics: Policy Conflict and Cooperation*, London, Macmillan, 1987, pp. 128–177.

———, "International Macroeconomic Policy Coordination When Policymakers Do Not Agree on the True Model: Comment," *American Economic Review*, 82 (September 1992), pp. 1043–1051.

Hooper, Peter, Karen H. Johnson, Donald L. Kohn, David E. Lindsey, Richard D. Porter, and Ralph W. Tryon, eds., *Financial Sectors in Open Economies: Empirical Analysis and Policy Issues*, Washington, D.C., Board of Governors of the Federal Reserve System, 1990.

Horne, Jocelyn, and Paul R. Masson, "Scope and Limits of International Economic Cooperation and Policy Coordination," *International Monetary Fund Staff Papers*, 35 (June 1988), pp. 259–296.

Hughes Hallett, Andrew, "Autonomy and the Choice of Policy in Asymmetrically Dependent Economies: An Investigation of the Gains from International Policy Coordination," *Oxford Economic Papers*, 38 (November 1986a), pp. 516–544.

———, "International Policy Design and the Sustainability of Policy Bargains," *Journal of Economic Dynamics and Control*, 10 (December 1986b), pp. 467–494.

———, "The Impact of Interdependence on Economic Policy Design: The Case of the US, EEC and Japan," *Economic Modelling*, 4 (July 1987), pp. 377–396.

———, "What Are the Risks in Co-ordinating Economic Policies Internationally?" in Ronald MacDonald and Mark P. Taylor, eds., *Exchange Rates and Open Economy Macroeconomics*, Oxford and Cambridge, Mass., Blackwell, 1989, pp. 307–341.

———, "Target Zones and International Policy Coordination: The Contrast between the Necessary and Sufficient Conditions for Success," *European Economic Review*, 36 (May 1992), pp. 893–914.

———, "Exchange Rates and Asymmetric Policy Regimes: When Does Exchange Rate Targeting Pay?" *Oxford Economic Papers*, 45 (June 1993), pp. 1–16.

Hughes Hallett, Andrew, Gerald Holtham, and Gary Hutson, "Exchange Rate Targeting as a Surrogate for International Policy Coordination," in Marcus H. Miller, Barry Eichengreen, and Richard Portes, eds., *Blueprints for Exchange Rate Management*, London and New York, Academic Press, 1989, pp. 239–278.

Kahler, Miles, "Multilateralism with Small and Large Numbers," *International Organization*, 46 (Summer 1992), pp. 681–708.

Kareken, John H., Thomas Muench, and Neil Wallace. "Optimal Open Market Strategy: The Use of Information Variables," *American Economic Review*, 63 (March 1973), pp. 156–172.

Katzenstein, Peter J., ed., *Between Power and Plenty: Foreign Economic Policies of Advanced Industrial States*, Madison, University of Wisconsin Press, 1978.

Kehoe, Patrick J., "International Policy Cooperation May Be Undesirable," Federal Reserve Bank of Minneapolis Staff Reports No. 103, Minneapolis, Minn., Federal Reserve Bank of Minneapolis, 1986.

———, "Policy Cooperation Among Benevolent Governments May Be Undesirable," *Review of Economic Studies*, 56 (April 1989), pp. 289–296.

Kenen, Peter B., *Exchange Rates and Policy Coordination*, Manchester, Manchester University Press, 1989.

———, "The Coordination of Macroeconomic Policies," in Branson, Frenkel, and Goldstein, *International Policy Coordination*, 1990, pp. 63–108.

Keohane, Robert O., "The Theory of Hegemonic Stability and Changes in International Regimes," in Ole R. Holsti, Randolph M. Siverson, and Alexander L. George, eds., *Change in the International System*, Boulder, Colo., Westview, 1980, pp. 131–162.

———, *After Hegemony: Cooperation and Discord in the World Political Economy*, Princeton, N.J., Princeton University Press, 1984.

———, "Reciprocity in International Relations," *International Organization*, 40 (Winter 1986), pp. 1–27.

———, "International Institutions: Two Approaches," *International Studies Quarterly*, 32 (December 1988), pp. 379–396.

Keohane, Robert O., and Joseph S. Nye, *Power and Interdependence*, Boston, Little, Brown, 1977.

Kindleberger, Charles P., *The World in Depression, 1929–1939*, Berkeley, University of California Press, 1973.

———, "International Public Goods without International Government," *American Economic Review*, 76 (March 1986), pp. 1–13.

Krasner, Stephen D., ed., *International Regimes*, Ithaca, N.Y., Cornell University Press, 1983.

Kreps, David, Paul Milgrom, John Roberts, and Robert Wilson, "Rational Cooperation in the Finitely Repeated Prisoners Dilemma," *Journal of Economic Theory*, 27 (August 1982), pp. 245–252.

Kreps, David, and Robert Wilson, "Reputation and Imperfect Information," *Journal of Economic Theory*, 27 (August 1982), pp. 253–279.

Kydland, Finn E., and Edward C. Prescott, "Rules Rather Than Discretion: The Inconsistency of Optimal Plans," *Journal of Political Economy*, 85 (June 1977), pp. 473–491.

Levine, Paul, and David A. Currie, "Does International Macroeconomic Policy Coordination Pay and Is It Sustainable? A Two Country Analysis," *Oxford Economic Papers*, 39 (March 1987), pp. 38–74.

Levine, Paul, David A. Currie, and Jessica Gaines, "The Use of Simple Rules for International Policy Agreements," in Barry Eichengreen, Marcus H. Miller, and Richard Portes, eds., *Blueprints for Exchange Rate Management*, London and New York, Academic Press, 1989.

McCallum, Bennett T., "On Consequences and Criticisms of Monetary Targeting," *Journal of Money, Credit, and Banking*, 17, pt. 2 (November 1985), pp. 570–597.

———, "Targets, Indicators, and Instruments of Monetary Policy," in William S. Haraf and Phillip Cagan, *Monetary Policy for a Changing Financial Environment*, Washington, D.C., American Enterprise Institute for Public Policy Research, 1990, pp. 44–70.

McKibbin, Warwick J., "The Economics of International Policy Coordination," *Economic Record*, 64 (December 1988), pp. 241–253.

McKibbin, Warwick J., and Jeffrey D. Sachs, "Coordination of Monetary and Fiscal Policies in the Industrial Economies," in Jacob A. Frenkel, ed., *International Aspects of Fiscal Policies*, Chicago, University of Chicago Press for the National Bureau of Economic Research, 1988, pp. 73–113.

———, "Implications of Policy Rules for the World Economy," in Bryant et al., *Macroeconomic Policies in an Interdependent World*, 1989, pp. 151–194.

———, *Global Linkages: Macroeconomic Interdependence and Cooperation in the World Economy*, Washington, D.C., Brookings Institution, 1991.

McKinnon, Ronald I., *An International Standard for Monetary Stabilization*, Policy Analyses in International Economics No. 8, Washington, D.C., Institute for International Economics, 1984.

———, "Monetary and Exchange Rate Policies for International Financial Stability: A Proposal," *Journal of Economic Perspectives*, 2 (Winter 1988), pp. 83–103.

March, James G., and Johan P. Olsen, "The New Institutionalism: Organizational Factors in Political Life," *American Political Science Review*, 78 (September 1984), pp. 734–749.

March, James G., and Herbert A. Simon, *Organizations*, New York, Wiley, 1958.

Masson, Paul R., "Portfolio Preference Uncertainty and Gains from Policy Coordination," *International Monetary Fund Staff Papers*, 39 (March 1992), pp. 101–120.

Miller, Marcus H., and Mark Salmon, "Policy Coordination and Dynamic Games," in Buiter and Marston, *International Economic Policy Coordination*, 1985, pp. 184–213.

Nedde, Ellen Marie, "Dynamic Gains to Strategic Policy-Making and International Economic Policy Coordination," Ph.D. diss., University of Maryland, 1989.

Niehans, Jurg, "Monetary and Fiscal Policies in Open Economies Under Fixed Exchange Rates: An Optimizing Approach," *Journal of Political Economy*, 76 (July/August 1968), pp. 893–920.

Oates, Wallace E., *Fiscal Federalism*, New York, Harcourt Brace Jovanovich, 1972.

———, ed., *The Political Economy of Fiscal Federalism*, Lexington, Mass., Lexington Books, 1977.

Olson, Mancur, "The Principle of 'Fiscal Equivalence': The Division of Responsibilities Among Different Levels of Government," *American Economic Review*, 59, Papers and Proceedings 1968 (May 1969), pp. 479–487.

———, *The Logic of Collective Action: Public Goods and the Theory of Groups*, 2d ed., Cambridge, Mass., Harvard University Press, 1971 (originally published in 1965).

Oudiz, Gilles, and Jeffrey D. Sachs, "Macroeconomic Policy Coordination Among the Industrial Economies," *Brookings Papers on Economic Activity*, No. 1 (1984), pp. 1–64.

————, "International Policy Coordination Among the Industrial Economies," in Buiter and Marston, *International Economic Policy Coordination*, 1985, pp. 274–319.

Pauly, Louis W., "The Political Foundations of Multilateral Economic Surveillance," *International Journal*, 47 (Spring 1992), pp. 293–327.

Peters, B. Guy, "Bureaucratic Politics and the Institutions of the European Community," in Alberta M. Sbragia, ed., *Euro-Politics: Institutions and Policymaking in the 'New' European Community*, Washington, D.C., Brookings Institution, 1992, pp. 75–122.

Powell, Walter W., and Paul J. DiMaggio, eds., *The New Institutionalism in Organizational Analysis*, Chicago, University of Chicago Press, 1991.

Putnam, Robert D., "Diplomacy and Domestic Politics: The Logic of Two-Level Games," *International Organization*, 42 (Summer 1988), pp. 427–460.

Putnam, Robert D., and Nicholas Bayne, *Hanging Together: The Seven-Power Summits*, Cambridge, Mass., Harvard University Press, 1984.

Putnam, Robert D., and C. Randall Henning, "The Bonn Summit of 1978: A Case Study in Coordination," in Richard N. Cooper, Barry Eichengreen, Gerald Holtham, Robert Putnam, and Randall Henning, *Can Nations Agree? Issues in International Economic Cooperation*, Washington, D.C., Brookings Institution, 1989, pp. 12–140.

Rogoff, Kenneth S., "Can International Monetary Policy Coordination Be Counterproductive?" *Journal of International Economics*, 18 (May 1985a), pp. 199–217.

————, "The Optimal Degree of Commitment to an Intermediate Monetary Target." *Quarterly Journal of Economics*, 100 (November 1985b), pp. 1169–1190.

————, "Reputational Constraints on Monetary Policy," *Carnegie-Rochester Conference Series on Public Policy*, 26 (Spring 1987), pp. 141–181.

Ruggie, John Gerard, "International Responses to Technology: Concepts and Trends," *International Organization*, 29 (Summer 1975), pp. 557–584.

————, "Multilateralism: The Anatomy of an Institution," *International Organization*, 46 (Summer 1992), pp. 561–598.

Sbragia, Alberta M., "Thinking about the European Future: The Uses of Comparison," in Alberta M. Sbragia, ed., *Euro-Politics: Institutions and Policymaking in the 'New' European Community*, Washington, D.C., Brookings Institution, 1992, pp. 257–292.

Simon, Herbert A., "Theories of Decision-Making in Economics and Behavioral Science," *American Economic Review*, 49 (June 1959), pp. 253–283.

Solomon, Robert, "Background Paper" in *Partners in Prosperity: The Report of the Twentieth Century Fund Task Force on the International Coordination of National Economic Policies*, New York, N.Y., Priority Press, 1991.

Stein, Herbert, "International Coordination of Domestic Economic Policies," *AEI Economist*, June 1978.

————, "International Coordination of Economic Policy," *AEI Economist*, August 1987.

Steinbruner, John D., *The Cybernetic Theory of Decision: New Dimensions of Political Analysis*, Princeton, N.J., Princeton University Press, 1974.

Tabellini, Guido, "Domestic Politics and the International Coordination of Fiscal Policies," Working Paper No. 226, London, Centre for Economic Policy Research, January 1988.

Taylor, John B., "International Coordination in the Design of Macroeconomic Policy Rules," *European Economic Review*, 28 (June/July 1985a), pp. 53–81.

———, "The Treatment of Expectations in Large Multicountry Econometric Models," in Ralph C. Bryant, Dale W. Henderson, Gerald Holtham, Peter Hooper, and Steven A. Symansky, eds., *Empirical Macroeconomics for Interdependent Economies*, Washington, D.C., Brookings Institution, 1988, pp. 161–182.

———, "Policy Analysis with a Multicountry Model," in Bryant et al., *Macroeconomic Policies in an Interdependent World*, 1989, pp. 122–141.

Taylor, Michael, *The Possibility of Cooperation*, Cambridge and New York, Cambridge University Press, 1987.

Turnovsky, Stephen, Tamer Basar, and Vasco d'Orey, "Dynamic Strategic Monetary Policies and Coordination in Interdependent Economies," *American Economic Review*, 78 (June 1988), pp. 341–361.

Turnovsky, Stephen, and Vasco d'Orey, "Monetary Policies in Interdependent Economies with Stochastic Disturbances: A Strategic Approach," *Economic Journal* (London), 96 (September 1986), pp. 696–721.

van der Ploeg, Frederick, "International Policy Coordination in Interdependent Monetary Economics," *Journal of International Economics*, 25 (August 1988), pp. 1–23.

Vaubel, Roland, "Coordination or Competition among National Macroeconomic Policies?" in Fritz Machlup, Gerhard Fels, and Hubertus Muller-Groeling, eds., *Reflections on a Troubled World Economy: Essays in Honor of Herbert Giersch*, New York, St. Martin's, 1983, pp. 3–28.

———, "International Collusion or Competition for Macroeconomic Policy Coordination? A Restatement," *Recherches Economiques de Louvain*, 51 (December 1985), pp. 223–240.

Waltz, Kenneth, *Theory of International Relations*, Reading, Mass., Addison-Wesley, 1979.

Waud, Roger N., "Proximate Targets and Monetary Policy." *Economic Journal* (London), 83 (March 1973), pp. 1–20.

Williamson, John, "FEERs and the ERM," *National Institute Economic Review*, 137 (August 1991), pp. 45–50.

———, "Exchange Rate Management," *Economic Journal* (London), 103 (January 1993), pp. 188–197.

Williamson, John, and Marcus H. Miller, *Targets and Indicators: A Blueprint for the International Coordination of Economic Policy*, Policy Analyses in International Economics No. 22, Washington, D.C., Institute for International Economics, 1987.

12

The Political Economy of Monetary Union

CHARLES A. E. GOODHART

1 One Hundred Lums in a Dram

In the last few years, while Western Europe has been preoccupied with its fitful progress toward economic and monetary union, previous monetary unions to the east have been unraveling. Wherever political unity and central control have ended in Central and Eastern Europe, monetary separation has rapidly followed. This was true in Czechoslovakia, where political division was comparatively friendly and peaceful, as well as in Yugoslavia, where it has been hostile. Despite a Czech-Slovak agreement on October 29, 1992, to use a common currency for an unspecified period after formal separation, Slovaks rushed to get rid of Czech banknotes almost as soon as the breakup occurred on January 1, 1993, and the Czech and Slovak central banks began overprinting banknotes in preparation for the new separate currencies (Reuters, January 11, 1993). In Yugoslavia, not only were the Slovenian tolar and Croation dinar established separately from the Yugoslav (Serbian) dinar, but separate new dinars were planned for Muslim-held parts of Bosnia-Herzegovina and the self-proclaimed "Serbian Republic of Bosnia-Herzegovina." Thus, Sarajevo radio announced on August 15, 1992, that the old Yugoslav dinar would be scrapped in favor of a new Bosnian dinar, pegged to the German mark at 350 to 1 (Reuters, August 15, 1992).

It is the former Soviet Union (FSU), however, that has spawned the greatest number of new and projected new currencies. My own favorite is the proposed Armenian currency, which will have banknotes worth between 1 and 500 drams and coins worth 10 lums to 10 drams. A dram will contain 100 lums (Interfax, September 4, 1992). Other republics have moved varying distances

My thanks are due to those participating in discussions of this paper at Columbia, Liverpool, and Princeton Universities; to Michael Artis, Andrew Crockett, Phillipa Gaster, Dieter Guffens, Rosa Lastra, Jacques Melitz, Robert Nobay, Lionel Price, and Christian Schluter for help and suggestions; and to Benjamin Cohen, Alberto Giovannini, and Andrew Hughes Hallett for acting not only as discussants, but also as friendly advisers. They are not, however, to be chided for my opinions and errors.

toward introducing separate currencies; the range and state of play in May 1993 is shown in Table 12.1. Of the countries listed, only Estonia had managed a full transformation to an independent currency. Latvia, Lithuania, and Ukraine were using temporary coupons or currencies intended to supplant the Russian ruble, and Azerbaijan and Kazakhstan were using new currencies side by side with the ruble (Hansson, 1993).

No one suggests that the defections from the ruble area occurred because the region was too large to be an optimum currency area (OCA). Indeed, the preference of Soviet planners for huge centralized plants serving, in some cases, the entire Soviet Union and the other members of the Council for Mutual Economic Assistance (CMEA) made the single-currency area more efficient than not, and it has greatly increased the real economic cost of the region's breakup (Havrylyshyn and Williamson, 1991; Williamson, 1992a). Political, not economic, events have caused the monetary changes in Central and Eastern Europe; economic considerations, although important, have been secondary.

It is probable that those favoring monetary unification within the European Community (EC) are also motivated mainly by political considerations,[1] although the change in the monetary constitution, set out in the Maastricht Treaty, has been discussed largely in economic terms. The Zollverein may be remembered as an example of monetary unification being used as an important stage, even a precondition, for political unification (Holtfrerich, 1988, 1992).

Evidence that politics determine currency questions has generally been sought from recent or prospective examples of changes in existing circumstances. We might consider also the status quo. How many economists seriously argue that the great federal countries, Australia, Brazil, Canada, the former Soviet Union, and the United States, are too large to be optimum currency areas and that they should be disbanded? How many argue that certain small nations using the dollar, such as Liberia and Panama, belong optimally to the U.S. currency area? Does anyone suggest that OCA considerations have determined the use of the dollar in countries with hyperinflation (for example, Argentina and Russia)?

At the opposite end of the size spectrum are Iceland, with a separate currency for about 250,000 people, and Liechtenstein, San Marino, and Monaco, whose economies are so closely joined to their neighbors that having separate currencies would be economically inefficient. Size alone seems not to be the most important criterion.

Many countries peg their currencies to others, of course, often so irrevoca-

---

[1] Fratianni, von Hagen, and Waller (1992, pp. 1–2) concur: "Although there are surely economic benefits to be expected from a monetary union, the main driving force for its [EMU's] resurgence remains the quest for the political integration of Europe. . . . The main objections to monetary union have also been largely political."

TABLE 12.1
The Status of Currencies in the Former Soviet Union in May 1993

State	Currency	Current Position	Comment	Reuters Date(s)
Russia	Ruble	Existing	On verge of hyperinflation; may need currency reform	December 4, 1992
Turkmenistan	Manat	Introduced August 1992	Parallel with ruble	December 15, 1992
Azerbaijan	Manat	Introduced January 1993	Manat and ruble used side by side	December 11, 1992
Latvia	Lat	Phased introduction planned from March 1993, alongside Latvian ruble	Lat and Latvian ruble initially to be used side by side; Latvian ruble devalued 25 percent in October 1992	November 30, 1992
Ukraine	Hrivnya	Coupons (karbovanets) deemed only legal tender, November 1992	Coupon is halfway stage to new currency	November 12, 1992
Lithuania	Litas	Coupons (talonas) termed "zoo tickets" because of animal motif, issued at end September 1992; sole legal tender since October 1992	Coupon is halfway stage to new currency	October 12, 1992
Tatarstan[a]	Ruble	New national coins ordered from Yugoslave supplier	To enable citizens to buy bread	September 14, 1992
Armenia	Dram	Planning stage only	"unprofitable to leave ruble zone at present" (Reuters)	September 2, 1992

Country	Currency	Status	Notes	Date
Tajikistan	Ruble	Order given to Canada's Bank Note Company to print new money; possibly to be called "somon"	At early planning stage	August 10, 1992
Kazakhstan	Tanga	Introduced August 1992 for limited groups, e.g., pensioners	Tanga and ruble used side by side	May 22, 1992 August 5, 1992
Estonia	Kroon	Introduced June 1992	Pegged to deutsche mark; backed by prewar gold	June 21, 1992
Uzbekistan	Ruble	Early planning stage		June 3, 1992
Belarus	Rubel	Interim currency issued June 1992; sole legal tender since November 1992	1 rubel = 10 rubles	May 16, 1992
Moldova	Lei	Already printed in Romania, but not issued		May 9, 1992
Kyrgyzstan	Som	Introduced May 1993 as sole legal tender[b]		
Georgia	Ruble	Plans made for new currency, the lary		

Source: Reuters reports in 1992 and 1993.

Note: I thank Philippa Gaster for enabling me to update this table to May 1993.

[a] Tatarstan may now be moving toward a national currency. Although it has indicated its desire over the last year to become more independent, it is technically still part of Russia (one of twenty autonomous republics) and is required to comply with Russia's monetary policies. Its attempt, as yet modest, to nationalize the currency is significant in terms of probable Russian fragmentation.

[b] See also John Lloyd, "IMF Watches as Kyrgyzstan Fights the Battle of the Som," *Financial Times,* May 21, 1993.

bly that the currencies are accepted as interchangeable (Newlyn and Rowan, 1954; Hanke and Schuler, 1990, 1991; Walters and Hanke, 1992; Hanke, Jonung, and Schuler, 1993). Even so, the smaller pegged countries generally maintain separate banknotes in order to enjoy prestige and seigniorage (when the backing is in the form of earning assets) and, just possibly, security against a day when the "irrevocable" ceases to be unalterable, as, for example, when Luxembourg broke with the Belgian franc or Ireland ended a half-century of equivalency with sterling (Walsh, 1993). No independent country, however, has unilaterally abandoned its own note issues for another's currency. There was some discussion in Israel, during a period of severe inflation, of stopping the inflation by replacing the shekel with the U.S. dollar. Imaginative as the cure was, however, it was quickly dismissed as both too radical and too politically humiliating to be acceptable (Glasner, 1989; see Chown and Wood [1992–93] for a somewhat similar proposal in Russia). There are many instances of currency substitution and dollarization during inflationary processes (Fischer, 1982), but national authorities have generally seen these as threats to their ability to generate seigniorage.

The evidence therefore suggests that the theory of optimum currency areas has relatively little predictive power. Virtually all independent sovereign states have separate currencies, and changes in sovereign status lead rapidly to accompanying adjustments in monetary autonomy. The boundaries of states rarely coincide exactly with optimum currency areas, and changes in boundaries causing changes in currency domains rarely reflect shifts in optimum currency areas.

Why do currency questions have such political resonance? Section 2 examines the symbolic significance of national currencies as emblems of sovereignty, the role of seigniorage, particularly as revenue of last resort, and the economic benefits of monetary autonomy. But can we really believe these issues are so important? Symbols are, after all, just symbols; the use of seigniorage to obtain control over real resources is, and should remain, low in most stable, industrial countries; and, if monetary autonomy is beneficial in, for example, adjusting to asymmetric, local shocks, why has no federal country considered the adoption of a multiplicity of currencies for its constituent states? Will political considerations, in fact, hinder or even preclude the prospective move to Economic and Monetary Union (EMU) in the EC?

Section 3 examines the reasons and incentives to move to EMU and reviews the European Commission's analysis of the economic benefits and costs of EMU within an OCA framework (Commission, 1990). The Commission compares largely unquantifiable gains from greater microeconomic efficiency in the functioning of money as a medium of exchange and unit of account with more tangible losses in the authorities' ability to conduct macroeconomic demand management (see Krugman, Chapter 13). Neither the benefits nor costs appear to be large (Bean, 1992). Moreover, judging by the usual criteria of convergence, frequency of asymmetric shocks, and flexibility of labor markets, it is doubtful that the EC is an OCA at all, at least outside the core area of North-Central Europe (Austria, Denmark, France, Germany, Switzerland, and the Benelux countries); it is equally doubtful that several existing EC states (reunified Germany, Italy, Spain, and the United Kingdom) are OCAs. It can also be argued, however, that, if there is no long-term trade-off between inflation and output, if there is considerable real-wage rigidity throughout Europe (Layard, Nickell, and Jackman, 1991), and if exchange-rate adjustment is not the appropriate response to many (perhaps most) shocks, then abandoning the exchange rate as an instrument of demand management may involve no serious cost (Artis, 1991; Melitz, 1993a).

If it is difficult to make a strong case for EMU along OCA lines, and, if the political concerns seem trivial, what is all the fuss about? To answer this question, Section 4 returns to an earlier line of argument, pioneered by Kenen (1969), that there is an essential interaction between the currency domain and the domain in which certain other policies can effectively operate. Kenen emphasizes the interaction between the monetary and fiscal domains. Most assessments of EMU ask whether some significant fiscal centralization is a necessary adjunct to a currency union, and that issue is reviewed here, but the point stressed by Kenen and often overlooked is that a considerable degree of currency stability may also be necessary if a federal fiscal system is to work satisfactorily. This reverse causation, from currency stability to federal fiscalism, is assessed in the second part of Section 4.

Not only do currency and fiscal domains interact, but the currency domain also interacts with the relative freedom of trade and the free movement of factors of production. The influence the degree of economic openness has on the case for monetary union and on OCA theory has been clear in the literature from the start (Mundell, 1961; McKinnon, 1963). What I emphasize in Section 4 is the reverse causation whereby the nature of the currency and exchange-rate regime may influence political decisions on the future of the single market. Anglo-Saxon commentators often assert that an open single market with common minimum standards is perfectly consistent with flexible exchange rates and autonomous monetary policies; continental European commentators usually take the opposite tack.

The history of the European Monetary System (EMS) shows that it has been possible to move to a single market before achieving a single currency. Although it is uncertain that the benefits of the single market can survive freely floating exchange rates within the EC, the events of 1992 have thrown into doubt the proposed transition to EMU whereby a single currency will eventually supplant ever more tightly fixed, then irrevocably locked, nominal exchange rates. Much of the early discussion of EMU took place either in terms of comparative statics, involving the comparison of the benefits and costs of different but established exchange-rate systems, or under the assumption that the transition would follow the orderly process laid down by the Delors Committee (Committee, 1989) and amended in the Maastricht Treaty (Council, 1992).

Some of these transitional issues are examined in Section 5, which considers three main issues. First, it examines the long-standing dispute between the "monetarists" and the "economists." The monetarists believe that early moves toward monetary union will put pressure on members to converge in other economic respects; the economists hold to the German "coronation" theory and maintain that monetary union can be securely achieved only as the culmination of a general process of convergence. Second, it examines the likely costs and disturbances of moving from Stage 3A, with irrevocably locked exchange rates between national currencies, to Stage 3B, with a single currency (Melitz, 1991a; Gros and Thygesen, 1992). Advocates of EMU have been largely silent, and occasionally cavalier, about these costs and disturbances, which are potentially severe. A variety of proposals for reducing them are discussed. Third, it argues that Stage 3A may last longer than is generally expected, perhaps up to four or five years, and it examines the operational problems that may arise with respect to the functioning of the financial system and the conduct of monetary policy.

2 The Political Imperative

The Symbolism of National Currencies

From the earliest days of minted coins, images on currencies have celebrated sovereign majesty and power. A strong currency is in itself grounds for national satisfaction, and devaluation is seen as a humiliation, a sign of national weakness. When decimalization was introduced in the United Kingdom (from 1967 to 1971), the authorities retained the pound as the main unit, rather than switch to the mathematically more convenient ten-shilling note. This was partly a matter of national prestige, for the pound was the heaviest, most valuable monetary unit among the industrialized nations.

In several EC countries, and especially in Germany, citizens are concerned about losing their national note issues under EMU and having to accept an unfamiliar and perhaps less stable currency, produced and controlled by foreigners. Because currency is the most tangible and commonly used claim to goods and services, the significance attached to its imagery and control is not so surprising. The seigniorage derived from note issue, moreover, can be an important source of revenue for countries, especially in times of war or other crises, when revenue from taxes or bond issues is difficult or impossible to raise. It is, therefore, understandable that emerging countries, such as Slovenia or the Baltic states, should regard as a top priority the establishment of national currencies and the concomitant demonetization of the dinar and ruble (Havrylshyn and Williamson, 1991; Williamson, 1992b; Hansson, 1993). Even the Archbishop of Canterbury, Dr. George Carey, is reported to have "draw[n] the line at the idea of monetary union leading to the head of his Church disappearing from English pound notes. . . . 'I want the Queen's head on the banknotes,'" he is quoted as saying. "'The point about national identity is a very important one. For me, being British is deeply important. I don't want to become French or German'" (Interview, *Financial Times*, February 15, 1993).

Seigniorage

David Glasner (1989, p. 31), in his chapter on "Money and the State," asks why money, of all goods and services, has led governments of all types to try to control its production and supply. His answer is that state monopoly of money "was founded on security considerations . . . [as] an instrument of wartime finance," There is thus "a real, if only historical, connection between control over money and the protection of sovereignty, . . . [a connection that] would also explain the otherwise surprising fact that counterfeiting was a treasonable offence under English law," and that the primary duties of the Secret Service in the United States are protection of the president and prevention of counterfeiting.

Glasner's hypothesis has a number of testable implications. One is that "governments most likely to relinquish control over the creation of money are ones with no defense responsibilities" (p. 36). This fits the early American experience, Glasner argues, and, certainly, it fits current European experience. The political cement of the EC has been the determination of the French and Germans to end their rivalry and the series of European wars. If the nations of Western Europe no longer expect to wage wars among themselves, they no longer need national instruments of wartime finance. Moving to a single EC currency therefore represents both an actual and a symbolic renunciation of any anticipated need to finance the protection of national, as opposed to EC, sovereignty. In Central and Eastern Europe, the reverse is true. Political upheavals have caused concern about the status and nature of independence, and continuing hostilities in the former Yugoslavia and potential rivalries between former Soviet republics (Ukraine and Russia, Armenia and Azerbaijan, Georgia and Abkhazia, for example) have naturally led the new East European states to consider all possible means of reinforcing their recently won independence.

Another testable implication is that the national-defense rationale "implies that governments optimally exploit the monopoly by avoiding inflation in peacetime. If they don't avoid inflation, they risk being left defenseless in wartime" (p. 39). This accords well with the history of the nineteenth century, when nearly all governments and central banks strove to maintain a noninflationary monetary rule in peacetime but readily abandoned it for inflationary note finance in times of war. It fits less well with the largely peaceful years since 1945, during which both inflation and currency devaluation have been frequent. Perhaps a nuclear-age war is considered so remote, or so apocalyptic, that the need to hold monetary finance in reserve for such an occurrence is perceived as much reduced or even pointless. Glasner explains this by the currently fashionable theory of time inconsistency. Thus, "one disincentive to investing in the monopoly over money in peacetime is that the government decision makers have a limited tenure in office and have no transferable property rights in the assets [low inflation expectations] they create while in office" (p. 39). Notwithstanding the popularity of this theory, evidence for the existence of a regular Nordhaus political business cycle is surprisingly weak (Alesina, 1989). History may record that the genesis of the inflationary upsurge in recent decades, especially in the 1970s, was much more specific to the context of the period, combining a continuing belief in a potential trade-off between inflation and output along a declining Phillips curve with specific inflationary oil shocks.

A state must nevertheless be able to undertake certain costly functions to ensure its own survival. Even in peacetime, the maintenance of civil authority requires a variety of expenditures, including disbursements to avert disaffection, disobedience, and insurrection. At times of crisis, when a government is not fully in control and its ability to raise funds from taxation and bond issues is reduced, it may well revert to issuing notes. Such monetary expansion leads to inflation, of course, which erodes still further the government's access to ordinary funding sources and leads inevitably to hyperinflation (Havrylyshyn and Williamson, 1991).

The time-inconsistency model suggests that the use of seigniorage as a means of government finance will be inversely related to the stability of the national government; the weaker the government's authority, the greater its reliance on seigniorage as an instrument of finance (Leijonhufvud, 1992). Thus, asking whether seigniorage is at an optimal level in some absolute sense is misguided, because the question must be conditioned on the strength and ability of the government to tap alternative sources of finance. Italy, for example, might be concerned that the reduction of the national debt required by the Maastricht Treaty, combined with a simultaneous reduction in seigniorage and the loss of monetary autonomy, could lead to so great an increase in tax rates or so significant a reduction in public-sector expenditures that the cohesion of the Italian state could be put at risk (Dornbusch, 1988; Giavazzi, 1989; Grilli, 1989; Gros and Thygesen, 1992).

Monetary Autonomy

The value of seigniorage to a stable country with low inflation is small, and the arrangements made under the Maastricht Treaty for returning seigniorage to the constituent national central banks suggest that the net loss or gain to most EC states will be of secondary importance. The considerations raised above may therefore be regarded as of relatively minor importance for EC countries, although this assessment would surely not hold for most of the states in Central and Eastern Europe.

The main cost perceived for the EC states is the loss of monetary policy as a national instrument for demand management. Monetary policy can be used, at least in the short run, to control interest rates or exchange rates, key prices within any economy. It cannot by itself, however, achieve differing and separate objectives for both of these rates without the deployment of another instrument, for example, exchange controls. The attempt in the Maastricht Treaty to assign exchange-rate decisions to politicians and to assign the operation of monetary policy to an independent European System of Central Banks (ESCB) has therefore generated considerable concern (Begg et al., 1991; Goodhart, 1992b; Kenen, 1993). It can be argued that national governments should not, and in some cases cannot, optimally control nominal interest rates and exchange rates in a discretionary fashion. The ability to engineer short-term increases in output, whether by exploiting agents' misperceptions or temporary rigidities, carries with it the cost that private-sector agents will be led to revise upward their expectations of inflation. Given that the long-term optimal position is to maintain near-zero inflation at an unemployment rate consistent with nonaccelerating inflation, the best long-term monetary policy would be to stick to a noninflationary path, unless the rigidities were extensive and very long lasting or the time-discount rates of private agents were very high. The danger is that governments, particularly when seeking reelection, will have higher rates of time discount than those of the public and will therefore be tempted to undertake expansionary policies that risk reigniting both inflation and inflationary expectations.

Concern over this problem has been central in the drive to achieve independence for central banks. Even when governments deny that they have pursued expansionary policies, they are worried about the perceived lack of credibility attaching to their counterinflationary commitments. One solution would be to transfer to an independent central bank the power to determine the *tactics* of monetary policy, but to restrict the bank's *strategic* objectives to the primary, overriding task of achieving price stability. This has been done in the Reserve Bank of New Zealand Act and suggested to, but rejected by, the current U.K. government; it is the scheme adopted in the Maastricht Treaty for the prospective European Central Bank (ECB).

A second solution was sought by governments participating in the Exchange Rate Mechanism (ERM) of the EMS. They hoped that their commitment to the ERM would reward them with the reputation for maintaining low inflation already enjoyed by the Bundesbank. This commitment was modest before 1983, however, requiring only that realignments be less than sufficient to recoup the prior losses of competitiveness caused by higher inflation rates. With the increasingly successful operation of the ERM, the commitment progressively hardened, until, from 1987 to 1992, there seemed to be a strong preference for avoiding any realignments.[2]

Insofar as the ERM had hardened by the end of the 1980s, and members' strategies were based on holding their ERM parities against the deutsche mark, adherence to the ERM tightly constrained the use of monetary policy and, in particular, the level of interest rates. The discretion of member governments became more and more limited, especially as exchange controls were progressively abandoned. It is arguable that, having accepted ERM membership in this context, governments had already abandoned discretionary monetary policy and that there would be virtually no economic cost in doing so formally and completely by moving to a full monetary union. This issue is examined further in Section 5.

3 Steady-State Economic Benefits and Costs of Monetary Union

The Economic Benefits

The economic gains from monetary union would accrue primarily in the form of increased microeconomic efficiency. As listed by the Commission (1990, pp. 63–84), these are as follows:

(1) REDUCTION IN TRANSACTIONS COSTS

EMU would allow the redeployment to more profitable uses of the resources used in exchange-rate transactions. Transactions savings are calculated to be 4 percent of Community GDP, with smaller countries and trading companies benefiting more than larger ones. Associated improvements in cross-border payments facilities would provide additional savings.

---

[2] This is an oversimplification. The core countries, France, Denmark, and the Benelux group clearly renounced any further realignment against the deutsche mark. The problem for the peripheral countries was that they would have been willing to participate in a general realignment against the deutsche mark but were unwilling to do so individually, as that would have demonstrated weakness and diminished their credibility.

(2) REDUCTION IN THE RISK OF REALIGNMENT AND DEVALUATION

EMU should result in a reduction of the risk premia currently included in the interest rates of most EC countries, relative to German rates. These can be large in countries whose peg to the deutsche mark is threatened. If, in turn, that threat is perceived as greatest when undesirable economic outturns (such as high unemployment) would result from maintaining the peg, these risk premia may be larger in the intermediate ERM stage than in a managed float or with a single currency.

The existence of such risk premia is clear. Compare, for example, French, Danish, or Spanish real interest rates in the winter of 1992–93 with those of Germany. The average long-term level is less certain, however, and the Commission's (1990, pp. 63, 77–83) estimates of the long-term effect on real incomes of reducing the premia seem optimistic: "Preliminary estimates show that even a reduction in the risk premium of 0.5 percentage points could raise income in the community significantly, possibly up to 5–10% in the longer run." The Commission would count as yet another gain from EMU the more buoyant expectations of business leaders following the successful achievement of EMU. The possibility that a differential "default" premium on government (for example, Italian) bonds may replace some part of the prior devaluation-risk premium is not addressed (Baldwin, 1991).

(3) EFFICIENCY GAINS TO TRADE AND CAPITAL MOVEMENTS

Gains should result from both the reductions in exchange-rate uncertainty and the greater price transparency that EMU would bring across EC countries, but these are difficult to quantify. Without good regional trade data and the opportunity to regress trade flows on both distance (gravity-model) variables and exchange-rate volatility, it is hard to tell how far monetary separation and volatility reduce the scale of the market. The studies quoted by the Commission (1990) concerning the effect of exchange-rate variability on trade are inconclusive and suggest that the effect is small (Feldstein, 1992).

(4) STABLE PRICES

Stable prices are clearly beneficial, but it is difficult to say whether they should be ascribed, if achieved, to EMU or to the structural and constitutional foundations of the ESCB, which mandate the bank's independence from political influence and require that its overriding objective be to "maintain price stability" (Treaty, Article 105, 1, and Protocol on the ESCB Statute, Article 2; also, Fratianni and von Hagen, 1990; Currie, 1992). If such structural and constitutional amendments were introduced at the national level, would the

effect not be the same? What, if anything, does EMU add beyond the establishment of an independent central bank? Hughes Hallett and Vines (1993)
estimate the additionality to be minuscule. Indeed, the continuing confusion
over the relation between external exchange-rate policies, to be left in the
hands of the politicians, and monetary policy, to be controlled by the ESCB,
may suggest that the added European dimension could have adverse effects on
price stability (Treaty, Article 109; Commission, 1990; Begg et al., 1991;
Goodhart, 1992b; Kenen, 1992a).

(5) INTERNATIONALLY STRONGER CURRENCY

The Commission (1990, pp. 178–198) argues that a single, unified European
currency would have more authority than the sum of the currencies of middle-
sized European countries (sec. 7.1) and that the change would allow Europe a
stronger voice in negotiations with the United States (secs. 7.2 and 7.3; see
also Alogoskoufis and Portes, 1991). This argument appeals particularly to
those in the EC who are jealous of the dollar's predominant role in international finance and of the asymmetric power of the United States in international conclaves. The Commission makes the curious conjunction of claims
that EMU would enable the EC to match the United States in international
weight and that this could lead to greater harmony and coordination. Risks
that antagonistic trading blocks could develop are noted but dismissed as negligible (Commission, 1990, p. 196). Recent history of the EC's trade negotiations with the United States in the GATT and with Central and Eastern Europe
gives little reason for optimism in this respect. The final two arguments for
EMU, that it may be necessary for the continued success and development of
the single market and that it is a prerequisite for further fiscal federalism, are
taken up below.

The Costs of Monetary Union

The main cost of moving to monetary union has generally been identified as
the loss of an instrument of national demand management, domestic monetary
policy, and of the associated ability to adjust exchange rates. As noted above,
the loss is less if the ability to use monetary policy has already been constrained by membership in the ERM. Indeed, the Commission (1990) reduces
considerably its estimates of this cost because it assumes the existence of the
"EMS and the 1992 Single Market" (see chaps. 6 and 2, esp. sec. 2.1.2,
p. 40, on "Alternatives to EMU").

Leaving to one side the problem of deciding how far national authorities
still retain control over monetary policies in the initial regime, the cost of

losing this instrument will depend, in part, on (1) the extent to which the participating nations and regions are likely to suffer asymmetric shocks, (2) the speed and flexibility of the adjustment process whereby disequilibria can be resolved by wage flexibility and the migration of the factors of production, especially labor, and (3) the extent to which fiscal policy, at either the national or federal level, can, and should, serve as an alternative to the use of monetary policy to foster adjustments. The need for fiscal policies that are more active than in recent years raises the question of how to fund deficits that may be disproportionately large in some regions; this is discussed below.

The founders of OCA theory, Mundell, McKinnon, and Kenen, identified three main criteria to define an optimum currency area. The first, emphasized by McKinnon, is the openness of the economies involved to trade among themselves. This is discussed in Section 4. The second criterion, emphasized by Kenen, concerns the susceptibility of the constituent economies to asymmetric shocks. The third criterion, emphasized by Mundell, pertains to the flexibility of adjustment to such shocks (Melitz [1991b] has a slightly different approach). As De Grauwe and Vanhaverbeke (1993, p. 111) state, "This theory says that when regions or countries are subjected to different disturbances (asymmetric shocks), the adjustment process will require either real exchange rates to adjust, or factors of production to move, or a combination of these two. In the absence of real exchange-rate flexibility and factor mobility, regional or national concentrations of unemployment will be inevitable." This analysis has led to a burgeoning of empirical research comparing the incidence of common and idiosyncratic shocks with the extent of nominal- and real-wage flexibility and of labor and capital mobility between and within the countries in Europe and the regions of the United States (Eichengreen, 1992c).

The Commission (1990, p. 147) argues that asymmetric shocks "are likely to diminish with the disappearance of trade barriers through the completion of internal market[s]," but that they still exist within the EC. They are notably less, however, for the core countries of northern Europe—Austria, France, Denmark, Germany, and the Benelux nations—than for the peripheral Mediterranean and British Isles countries. For the core countries, the ratio of common to idiosyncratic shocks is higher between themselves than between them and the United States (Cohen and Wyplosz, 1989), and it is broadly similar to the ratio between U.S. regions (Bini-Smaghi and Vori, 1992; Bayoumi and Eichengreen, 1993; De Grauwe and Heens, 1993).

Taken by themselves, these results suggest that the structures of the EC core countries have converged sufficiently for monetary union to be feasible. Whether the peripheral countries can reach an adequate level of convergence without severe adjustment difficulties is much more problematic. Yet, as Gros and Thygesen (1992) and Malo de Molina (1992) point out, the advantages of

EMU for the peripheral countries may be greater, in terms of lower transactions costs, lower risk premia, and greater price stability, than for the core countries.

There is also a question whether the dynamic effects of EMU are likely to make regions more similar, because they will become more "converged," or more dissimilar, because they will become more specialized. The Commission believes that economic integration in Europe will make local economics more similar and thus subject to fewer asymmetric shocks (Gros and Thygesen, 1992; Spahn, 1992); some economists, arguing in part from American experience, claim the reverse (Eichengreen, 1992c; Feldstein, 1992; Krugman, 1992). The literature must be read, however, with a significant caveat. Since 1989, Germany has suffered a massive idiosyncratic shock as a result of reunification. Because of Germany's position as the anchor country, this has been particularly damaging to the ERM and a major cause of the setbacks to EMU in 1992 and 1993. How should one view this event when looking to the future—as a unique shock that will never happen again or as a striking example that effectively destroys the validity of earlier work on the ratio of common to asymmetric shocks among the core countries?

There has been an enormous amount of work in recent years on rigidities in nominal and real wages, mostly at the national level, but also at the regional level. Although this research has chiefly tried to explain the persistence of high unemployment levels in Europe (Bruno and Sachs, 1985; Drèze and Bean, 1990; Layard, Nickell, and Jackman, 1991; Bini-Smaghi and Vori, 1992), the findings are significant for EMU. In general, the conclusions are that EC countries, especially the United Kingdom, suffer from considerable real-wage rigidity but little nominal-wage rigidity, whereas the United States shows more nominal-wage stickiness but much less real-wage rigidity.

This finding can be used to argue both for and against EMU. It supports EMU in that the existence of real-wage rigidity makes improved competitiveness through nominal devaluations much harder to achieve and maintain. It opposes EMU in that the sclerotic workings of European labor markets make it unlikely that wage adjustment can play a significant role in alleviating regional disequilibria. De Grauwe and Vanhaverbeke (1993, pp. 123–124) challenge this argument, observing that "the regional variability of output is relatively well correlated with the regional variability of the real exchange rates. . . . that this correlation is stronger and more significant at the regional than at the national level. This suggests that, although the regional variability of real exchange rates is relatively small, it nevertheless plays a significant role in regional adjustment." They point out that "the correlation between the variability of real exchange rates and employment is much weaker" but that the evidence is only suggestive, and that correlation coefficients say nothing "about the direction of the causality. These correlations can also be interpreted to mean that relative price shocks cause variability in output and employment." They stress, in addition that "there is evidence . . . that real exchange-rate changes have also been quite important in the adjustment process of individual EMS countries that have chosen to limit the changes in their nominal exchange rates. Countries like Belgium and the Netherlands, for example, allowed significant real depreciations of their currencies of 20–30 percent to occur during the early part of the eighties" (see also Poloz, 1990).

There are, furthermore, disputes about the effect that EMU, a regime change, would have on the future interregional flexibility of wages. The optimists think that abandoning the option of national monetary management and exchange-rate adjustment would force workers and unions into greater local flexibility. The pessimists perceive that the greater transparency of international differences in nominal wages following the adoption of a single currency would likely lead, through demonstration effects, to less flexibility in labor markets than now exists (see Doyle, 1989; also Horn and Zwiener [1992], who model the effects of differing wage regimes in Europe). The demand in the former East Germany for nominal-wage parity with West Germany within a few years, largely irrespective of productivity differentials, supports this view. Certainly, special factors are involved in Germany, but can we be confident that monetary union in the EC would not lead to similar tendencies?

De Grauwe and Vanhaverbeke (1993, p. 111), perhaps echoing the belief that a single currency would promote a single labor market with insufficient regional flexibility, claim that "the theory of optimum currency areas has also established a presumption that in a monetary union the adjustment mechanism will rely more on factor mobility than on real exchange-rate flexibility." This is certainly true in the United States (Blanchard and Katz, 1992).

The largest question, therefore, about identifying the EC as an optimum currency area arises from the empirical studies revealing that labor migration in Europe is minuscule in comparison to that in the United States, and that any large increase would cause political problems (Doyle, 1989). Eichengreen (1993, p. 131) notes that

in comparison, little systematic attention has been directed toward the analysis of labor mobility. Previous studies cited in Eichengreen (1992b) indicate that observed migration rates are lower in Europe than in the US. Not only are migration rates between European nations relatively low, but so are migration rates within those nations. Americans move between US states about three times as frequently as Frenchmen move between *départements* and Germans move between *länder*. If Europeans move little among regions of European nations within which culture and language are relatively minor barriers to mobility, they can hardly be expected to move between European nations once statutory barriers to migration are removed. On the basis of this evidence, Mundell's second criterion also suggests that the EC is less of an optimum currency area than the United States.

Eichengreen (1993) follows prior work by Pissarides and McMaster (1990) and by Attanasio and Padoa-Schioppa (1991) and models the propensity of labor to migrate between regions in Italy, in the United Kingdom, and in the United States in response to changes in relative regional unemployment and wage levels. He concludes (p. 150) that

> the models estimated here confirm the tendency for inter-regional labor flows to respond to economic conditions. In all three countries, immigration is encouraged by relatively high wages and relatively low unemployment. But the elasticity of migration with respect to wage differentials is very much larger in the United States. Similarly, US labor exhibits a greater tendency to move in response to regional unemployment differentials. This, then, is systematic evidence in support of the presumption of greater labor mobility in the US. As Eichengreen realizes, this latter finding poses an important question, because Italy and the United Kingdom *already are* single-currency areas, yet his evidence suggests that the low level of mobility *within* these countries makes them, *prima facie*, unsuitable to be so. Apart from political stirrings in Lombardy and Scotland, however, nobody has seriously suggested dividing these countries into separate currency areas.

In addition, using a cointegration approach, Eichengreen (1993, p. 155) finds that regional labor markets in Italy and the United Kingdom, and to a lesser extent in the United States, tend to revert quite quickly to a normal relationship with aggregate unemployment (that is, the series are cointegrated), although this "normal" relationship implies that some regions remain worse, and others better, than average.[3] Idiosyncratic shocks, however, do not appear to make regional unemployment deviate indefinitely from the average, as in a random walk. Even if labor-market forces, real-wage adjustment and mobility, are comparatively weak within Italy and the United Kingdom, other factors, "perhaps including relative wage adjustments, inter-regional capital mobility, and government policy," appear capable of providing a spatially unifying effect. The implication is that these factors could work as powerfully in EMU as in Italy or the United Kingdom to offset the inflexibility of labor markets. One such possibility is that capital mobility might substitute for labor mobility, with new firms and new investment being attracted to areas of available, low-wage labor, and that EMU would thereby bring particular benefits in cheaper capital to the smaller peripheral regions (Bayoumi and Rose, 1993).[4]

Much current research on capital mobility has asked whether the financial equity markets in the EC have become more integrated in recent years (Sen-

---

[3] Note that, for the time being, such "normality" has ceased to hold in the United Kingdom.

[4] Thus, Spahn (1992, p. 12) states that "the benefit is, of course, greatest for the smaller, peripheral monies, the escudo, the krona. Portugal and Denmark, by their belonging to the Ecu zone, would thus automatically appear on the map for Japanese institutional investors; and this would lower their costs of raising money and capital to a considerable degree."

tana, Shah, and Wadhwani, 1992; Atkeson and Bayoumi, 1993; Fraser and MacDonald, 1993). The results are inconclusive, but financial-market integration may be a necessary, although insufficient, condition for capital mobility to preserve the cohesion of a monetary union. Indeed, a strong body of academic argument sees unification as likely to exacerbate regional divergences by attracting investment and activity to the already successful regions rather than to the comparatively unsuccessful periphery (Masera, 1992).[5]

Masson and Taylor (1993), who have looked at the issue in the U.S. context, compare the regional deviations of real output per capita within the United States with the national deviations within the EC. Regional disparity in the United States was markedly less than in the EC and fell over time, whereas the dispersion of real output per capita among EC nations remained roughly constant, except for Greece, Portugal, and Spain, where output per capita diverged sharply until the early 1970s and converged somewhat thereafter. Masson and Taylor (1993, p. 31) note that, "there is certainly no presumption from the US data that currency union makes convergence of living standards difficult. However, how much of the convergence was facilitated by fixity of exchange rates—encouraging both capital and labor mobility—and how much was due to fiscal transfers from richer to poorer regions . . . is unclear."

This is one of the problems facing empirical econometric work in this field. The domain of a single currency has generally had the same boundaries as its central political and fiscal system, and areas with independent currencies have likewise had separate political and fiscal centers. It is therefore difficult to distinguish between the roles played by monetary union and by the redistributive role of the federal fiscal center in bringing about convergence. I turn now to this interaction between monetary and fiscal policies.

4 Interactions between the Currency Domain and the Fiscal and Trade Domains

Most modern federal countries (Australia, Brazil, Canada, Germany, the former Soviet Union, the United States, and Yugoslavia) have had strong central political institutions, single currencies, and central control over most of the fiscal flows. Switzerland, with the least centralization, still has several orders of magnitude more central power than that proposed for the EC (Schneider, 1993). It is therefore not surprising that many economists have looked at existing federal states when trying to decide whether EMU can survive without comparable fiscal centralization. This issue goes back to the Werner Report

---

[5] A discussion of whether monetary union is more likely to lead to convergence or divergence in per capita incomes in the constituent regions has been omitted from this section to economize on space.

(Council, 1970), which made more ambitious proposals for an associated EC fiscal function than did the Delors Report (Committee, 1989) or the Maastricht Treaty (Council, 1992; see also Gros and Thygesen, 1992, chap. 1).

Is Federal Fiscalism Needed to Support a Single Currency?

Insofar as the main economic cost of abandoning separate currencies lies in losing control over monetary policy, it would appear that more weight should be placed on alternative mechanisms of demand management, such as fiscal policy. The two main concerns about EMU are that parts of the union might suffer from asymmetric shocks and that unification might lead to a divergence, rather than a convergence, of economic performance (Giersch et al., 1992). Fiscal measures aimed at both stabilization and redistribution could mitigate these concerns.

As Goodhart and Smith (1993) emphasize, these two fiscal functions should be carefully distinguished, although many measures, such as income taxes and unemployment benefits, simultaneously stabilize and redistribute. Stabilization is concerned with dynamic changes in economic conditions. It involves changing fiscal flows (expenditures and revenues) in response to economic changes relative to the normal trend, irrespective of initial levels. Redistribution adjusts expenditures and taxes in response to relative levels of economic activity, irrespective of the direction or extent of previous change. If asymmetric shocks are the primary concern, stabilization policies should be emphasized; if regional divergence is anticipated, redistribution should be stressed.

Virtually all stabilizing and redistributive fiscal functions in the EC are currently undertaken at the national level, with the monetary and fiscal authorities having the same boundary. Why, when the monetary boundary is enlarged to replace national currencies with a single currency, cannot the fiscal functions of stabilization and redistribution be left at the national level and, if necessary, be pursued at that level more vigorously than before?

There are several arguments for shifting these fiscal functions partly to the federal center. Specific to the EC is the conflict between national needs and the restrictions imposed on national autonomy. The Maastricht Treaty (Article 104c, 2, and Protocol on the Excessive Deficit Procedure, Article 1) established reference values to limit both the ratio of national debt to income and the government deficit, with the normally acceptable limit for the planned or actual government deficit set at 3 percent of gross domestic product. In the course of the 1993 recession in Europe, however, every EC member except Luxembourg expected, indeed planned, to exceed the 3 percent limit. This implies that the ability of national governments to undertake countercyclical fiscal stabilization could be seriously constrained by strict adherence to the Treaty (Buiter, 1992).

Insofar as fiscal constraints designed to counter budgetary indiscipline could yield insufficient scope for national stabilization, a case can be argued for transferring the function to the federal level. A more general argument for centralizing fiscal functions at the federal level is that fiscal-policy measures in one area may spill over into neighboring areas. Some overspills, such as those resulting from a high marginal propensity to import, may make a national or regional authority less fiscally active than desirable (see Knoester, Kolodziejak, and Muijzers [1992] with respect to the smaller EC countries). Other overspills, such as the reduced effect of national fiscal policies on national interest rates and exchange rates, and their effect, instead, on the general level of EC interest rates, may encourage national fiscal policymakers to be less disciplined. The Delors Report (Committee, 1989) and the Maastricht Treaty (Article 104c) have given enormous emphasis to this problem and to the necessity of avoiding "excessive" governmental deficits.

Overspills can, of course, be internalized by appropriate coordination, without shifting actual operational control and responsibility to the federal center. The Maastricht Treaty (Article 103) requires that "Member States shall regard their economic policies as a matter of common concern and shall coordinate them within the Council." But, beyond publicity (Article 103, 4), the Council can impose no penalties on a state that refuses to coordinate its fiscal policies for the common European benefit. It is therefore unlikely that there will be much effective coordination of national fiscal policies at the EC level. Moreover, to the extent that national policies are effectively coordinated at the federal level, a key policymaking role is transferred *de facto* to the federal level.

A second argument for centralizing fiscal functions is that their continued exercise at the national or regional level is likely to affect not only current levels of public-sector expenditures and tax rates, but also expected future levels. The achievement of EMU may not only require a high level of factor mobility, at least in theory, but may also induce greater future mobility in response to differing tax rates. It is already increasingly difficult within the EC to impose differential taxes on highly mobile tax bases, such as financial transactions, savings, or corporate profits. If labor should also become highly mobile, it would be difficult to differentiate nationally benefits to, or taxes on, labor. With levels of labor mobility remaining low, however, this constraint is of academic interest only (Eichengreen, 1990; Bean et al., 1992).

A third argument for centralizing these functions is to insure against having to meet locally the full costs of an asymmetric downturn or of a shock producing a more permanently depressed economy. This involves some moral hazard, however, in that policies might become more reckless or natural market adjustments might be more muted. Moral hazard could be much reduced, however, by a specialized stabilization scheme (proposed by Goodhart and Smith [1993]) that would tie stabilization more closely to random asymmetric shocks. Each participating nation would then have an almost equal chance of benefiting, and transfers would be triggered only by a worse than average downturn and would be strictly temporary (see also van der Ploeg, 1991; Van Rompuy, Abraham, and Heremans, 1991; and Italianer and Vanheukelen, 1992). Redistribution, by contrast, is usually a function not of accidents but of a need for predictable long-term transfers, so moral hazard would be much increased by its centralization (as reported for the Canadian Maritimes by Courchene [1992], or for the Mezzogiorno by De Nardis and Micossi [1991] and Micossi and Tullio [1991]). The insurance argument is consequently best applied to well-designed stabilization mechanisms with minimal redistributive content (Persson and Tabellini, 1992a, 1992b).

The fourth, and most powerful, argument for centralization refers to the condition of "social union," when people in a particular area agree that all of them should be treated alike. Assuming that the benefits go to people who are dependent, unemployed, or poor, and that taxes are raised on the usual principles relating to personal expenditure, income, or wealth, there will generally be, often without much public notice, spatial transfers from more prosperous to less prosperous regions (for example, from northern European to Mediterranean regions). Within the EC, however, there is not now, or in sight, an agreement that all area inhabitants should have broadly the same menu of benefits and taxes. Indeed, there is scarcely accord on minimum standards for the provision of public goods. Insofar as redistribution takes place at all, it occurs through the more covert mechanism of structural, or cohesion, funds, which are themselves subject to a variety of operational problems.[6]

Any new steps in the direction of social union will be either voluntary, in response to a stronger feeling of common citizenship and solidarity than is currently apparent, or forced, if the international mobility of people interferes with national attempts at interpersonal redistribution. Neither prospect looks likely in the foreseeable future. Steps taken so far have been to set down conditions for raising the volume of interregional transfers and for making them unconditional. But, because equity normally relates to the reduction of interpersonal, not interregional, income disparities, interregional transfers have two disadvantages (Prud'homme, 1993). They will not automatically narrow interpersonal differences, for poor people in rich regions may end up supporting rich people in poor regions. Similarly, aid to a region may not be used to support its most needy inhabitants. For these reasons, regional policies in several federal and unitary countries have been scaled down to put greater emphasis on "people-oriented" instruments.

Considerations of interpersonal equity obtain, in principle, in the EC as

---

[6] Although a definitive judgment has to await the completion of the Commission's evaluation that is currently under way, the reform of the Structural Funds may need to be carried beyond the stage reached in 1988. If not, the Structural Funds, which are meant as conditional specific-purpose grants, risk remaining a set of disguised block grants, which, because their implementation procedures are rather convoluted, may produce neither an efficient nor a fair outcome.

well, but they need to be set beside the powerful political-economic arguments against a large role for central government in interpersonal redistribution (Forte, 1977; Tresch, 1981). A large central role can be contemplated only when altruism has taken on so strong a European dimension that nationality is dominated by solidarity, and national preferences for redistribution have closely converged. Until then, redistribution in the EC will continue to be limited, disguised, and somewhat inefficient.

Virtually no stabilization is achieved through the current federal budget. The gross flows are very small relative to national budgets; the form of the expenditures, mainly through the Common Agricultural Policy (CAP), and of the taxes, mainly through the value-added tax, are not highly responsive to economic fluctuations; and the EC cannot, by law, run a deficit.

Does this matter for the success of EMU? How extensive are federal, "automatic" stabilizers in existing federal countries? Sala-i-Martin and Sachs (1992) argue that such stabilizing flows offset about 35 to 44 percent of divergences between regional income levels in the United States, and they suggest that attempting to move to EMU without a similar supporting fiscal mechanism in the EC would be difficult. Their findings are criticized by von Hagen (1992), partly on the grounds that their percentages relate to redistribution rather than stabilization. When von Hagen repeated the exercise in first-difference form on state-level data, he found much lower figures, about 10 percent for the tax offset to changes in incomes. Since then, a number of studies have given generally higher figures for the extent of regional stabilization (for example, Pisani-Ferry, Italianer, and Lescure, 1993). These are summarized in Table 12.2.

I conclude from these various studies that both stabilizing and redistributive functions have been actively carried out through existing federal fiscal systems. It would be reckless to dismiss the potential importance of these activities for the cohesion and success of such monetary unions,[7] but it is reasonable to ask if the fiscal authority carrying out such functions needs to be a federal center (Bean, 1992; von Hagen, 1993). As noted earlier, there is no likelihood whatsoever of transferring overt, unconditional redistributive functions to Brussels. That is ruled out by the principle of "subsidiarity," by the fact that regional disparities within EC countries, for example, Italy, Spain, and the United Kingdom, are greater than most disparities between those countries, and, above all, by the lack of political cohesion.

That the scheme proposed by Goodhart and Smith (1993) will be seen as a welcome and useful supplement to existing national systems of automatic

---

[7] A counterargument is that the gold standard operated successfully without any such international fiscal transfers. A recent book by Panić (1992) specifically considers what lessons the gold standard may hold for EMU. The gist of Panić's conclusions was that the success of the gold standard was the result of unrepeatable, serendipitous circumstances and cannot serve as a useful analogy or basis for assessing the probable outcome of EMU. Eichengreen (1992a) concurs.

TABLE 12.2

Estimates of the Degree of Interregional Income Redistribution and Regional Stabilization through Central Public-Finance Channels in Selected Federal and Unitary Countries (percent)

Country	Interregional Redistribution		Regional Stabilization	
Australia	50	Commission, 1977		———
Canada	30	Commission	17	Bayoumi and Masson, 1991
			24	Goodhart and Smith, 1993
France	53	Commission	37	Pisani-Ferry, Italianer, and Lescure, 1993
Germany	35	Commission	33–42	Pisani-Ferry, Italianer, and Lescure, 1993
Switzerland	15[a]	Commission		———
United Kingdom	34	Commission	34	Goodhart and Smith
United States	35–44	Sala-i-Martin and Sachs, 1992	10[b]	von Hagen, 1992
			28	Bayoumi and Masson
	25	Commission	29	Goodhart and Smith
			17	Pisani-Ferry, Italianer, and Lescure

Source: Adapted from Commission, 1993, table 9, p. 37.

[a]Incomplete data.

[b]Tax side only.

stabilization is doubtful. Some oppose on broad political grounds any further transfer of fiscal powers to Brussels. Melitz and Vori (1992) argue against the adoption of any federal insurance scheme, given those already available at the national level. They believe that the likelihood of sizable asymmetric shocks and the benefits of federal insurance are both too small, and that there are large risks both of moral hazard and of a benefit's being triggered by an event that could be held to be a nation's own fault (a strike, a mistaken policy). How would other EC members have reacted, for example, to a call in recent years to transfer funds to East Germany?

A final argument for adopting some federal stabilization insurance scheme is, again, unashamedly political. It is that, once Stage 3 is achieved, politicians and commentators will, rightly or wrongly, blame the severity of cyclical downturns on monetary union. They will argue that, without such a union, monetary policy would have been relaxed. So long as the downturn is symmetric over the entire EC, the answer will be straightforward, but, in an asymmetric, particularly adverse situation, how can a supporter of EMU counter the accusation that monetary union involves a sizable net disadvantage? A significant, timely, and visible fiscal federal transfer to temporarily disadvantaged countries could help to sustain political support for EMU at especially difficult times.

Is a Single Currency Needed to Support Fiscal Federalism?

In many, perhaps most, of the large federal countries, there are regions that are both distant from the industrial heartland of the country and specialized in production, often in certain primary commodities. Examples are Western Australia, the oil-producing states of the United States, and Alberta, Canada; no doubt similar examples can be found in Brazil, the former Soviet Union, and elsewhere. Given the separation and specialization of these divergent states and regimes, there would seem to be *prima facie* grounds, according to OCA theory, for them to have currencies separate from those of the states to which they belong. Does Western Australia, for example, form an OCA with the rest of Australia? Yet these large federal nations never choose to maintain a multiplicity of currencies. Why not?

In Section 3, I stated that microeconomic efficiency gains from currency unions were mostly unquantifiable and, quite probably, relatively minor. If they are not minor, however, and those gains in economic efficiency explain the maintenance of currency unions in huge federal states, why is it so rare, and apparently difficult, to combine several sovereign countries in a currency union? The more political considerations addressed in Section 2, symbolism, seigniorage, and the power to control a key economic instrument, are no longer such compelling reasons.

If there are economic benefits to having more currencies and monetary authorities, from being able to offset asymmetric shocks, for example, why not enjoy these within a larger federation? Yet no stable, autonomous, federal government has voluntarily chosen to allow separate currency areas and regional central banks within its own domain. How can American economists, such as Feldstein (1992), advise European countries against monetary union, while appearing entirely content with their own even wider monetary union?

The answer, as Feldstein puts it, lies in the interrelations between monetary policy, on the one hand, and fiscal and trade policies, on the other.[8] Yet I have just argued that it might be possible to operate EMU with a strictly limited transfer of stabilizing and redistributive functions to the federal budget; the bulk of these functions could remain at the national level. By the same token, Western Australia, the southwestern states of the United States, and the west-

---

[8] Feldstein's other arguments for leaving the U.S. monetary union intact are historical inertia and the "reputation" of the U.S. dollar. I find these less convincing.

ern provinces of Canada could look after their own internal stabilization and redistribution. The adoption and implementation of a carefully focused and cost-effective stabilization scheme in the EC would, of course, alleviate short-term adjustment pressures after the advent of EMU. Nevertheless, it is hard to prove that such a comparatively limited scheme is essential to the success of EMU.

A move to comparatively fixed exchange rates, however, may be necessary for the success of any centralized fiscal domain; that is, the thrust of causation may run opposite to that normally discussed. Certainly, the problems of trying to run the system of levies and subsidies that constitute the CAP were made so complicated by flexible exchange rates that the agreement nearly collapsed. The political process that sustains agreements such as these requires centralized payoffs. This concern played a major role in the establishment of the ERM; as Giavazzi and Giovannini (1989, p. 7) note, "[T]he common market [in cereals under the CAP] could only function if intra-Community exchange rates remained stable."

The response can be made that such arrangements require no more than the adoption of pegged but adjustable exchange rates, not a move all the way to a single currency. Indeed, the subsequent experience of the EC suggests that currency adjustments in member states would not impede the continuation of the CAP, the progress toward a single market, or any further transfer of fiscal responsibilities to Brussels, so long as two conditions are met: first, that the adjustments are infrequent, and, second, that the sizes and occasions of the adjustments are subject to multilateral oversight and agreement, for example, within the Monetary Committee of the EC.

Thus, the move toward a single market in Europe may have been conditional on the continued perceived success of the ERM. If so, a policy dilemma arises. A system of pegged but adjustable exchange rates is well known to be fragile under the "unholy trinity" of free movement of goods and capital, stable exchange rates, and autonomous monetary policies (Cohen, 1993b). What is surprising about disturbances in European exchange markets in 1992 and 1993 is not so much their occurrence, but that the ERM had operated so successfully for so long (from 1987 to 1992) without such disturbances. To revert to more flexible exchange rates would make the system less susceptible to such "speculative" attacks, although not necessarily less prone to medium-term misalignment. But would such flexibility in exchange rates dampen political enthusiasm for a single market and for greater centralization of fiscal and political powers?

The fragility of pegged but adjustable exchange rates in the absence of exchange controls suggests that the continuation of such a regime for an extended period may not be viable. But, even if it were, there are reasons for doubting whether any regime with periodic exchange-rate adjustments is consistent with sizable transfers of fiscal responsibility to a federal center. Such doubts become more pronounced the more flexible the exchange-rate regime is, whether a float, a crawling peg, or, as advocated by *The Economist*, an arrangement with soft bands ("Can Europe Put EMU Together Again?" May 8–14, 1993, pp. 17–18).

The first argument is largely presentational, though not less important for that. It is that the existence of separate national currencies facilitates the calculation of the net fiscal transfer among the member states, indeed, almost requires such calculations when transfers involve conversions between domestic currencies and ECUs. Partly in consequence, the identification of net fiscal winners and losers within the EC is regularly made in terms of the overall position of each country, rather than of diverse groups of individuals within the whole of the EC. This means that, despite the best preventive efforts of the Commission, the identification of "gainers" or "losers" from the majority of EC economic measures is made largely in terms of the effects the measures have on separate countries. Thus, the battles over EC fiscal policies in Brussels are not about how these affect the welfare of the representative European, but how they change the net position of each separate state. Although it is possible to estimate the net benefits to Queensland, Indiana, or Manitoba from a change in the federal budgets of their respective countries, the existence of a single currency tends to shift the focus of debate toward the effect on the representative agent defined by type, for example, age, income, and job, and not by geographical locality.

It is true that U.S. senators support the interests of their own states within the United States, just as heads of member states do in the EC, but they do so to a somewhat lesser extent, I believe, and not so single-mindedly. As Giovannini (1993) stated in his comment on this chapter, it is often difficult to identify exactly who the gainers or losers are from a switch to a single-currency regime. Thus, "the political debate on EMU . . . is not characterized by the confrontation of those [intranational] constituencies that gain or lose from the introduction of a single currency, since these constituencies do not have a clear identity." When the fiscal assessment concentrates on type rather than geographical residence, moreover, the perceived gainers or losers will only occasionally be concentrated in any one locality and, when they are, will often constitute producer groups, such as miners or farmers, whose political clout far outweighs their numerical strength. The rise of the Lombard League as a political power in Italy is an interesting exception to this generalization. Its rallying cry is partly that heavy tax burdens are placed on Northern Italian taxpayers to finance (corrupt) expenditures in Rome and the Mezzogiorno.

Because the continuation of separate currencies encourages the calculation of benefits and costs in national terms, it exerts a centrifugal force, causing national politicians to fight for "our money," the *juste retour*, and so forth. By contrast, calculations that concentrate on a similar treatment of similar types of agents, irrespective of location, exert a centripetal force. Adopting a single currency would be an important step in moving in this latter direction.

I argued earlier that the development of certain centralized, federal powers, for example, fiscal powers, could ease the strain of asymmetric shocks and localized disturbances in a coherent, cohesive federal country. It is far from certain, however, that the analogy can be directly applied to Europe, where there is as yet little fundamental cohesion. Would transferring more powers to the center not just result in more disputes and bickering over the division of political rents between nation-states? See Aghion and Bolton (1990), Buiter and Kletzer (1991), and Persson and Tabellini (1992a) for theoretical analyses of cooperation under heterogeneous preferences.

Whenever fiscal expenditures are financed by taxes, some regions will gain and some lose. If each fiscal decision were considered on its own and each region had a veto, it would become impossible to reach any agreement, because the losers on each issue would veto it. Some political scientists therefore ask how the EC has achieved as much agreement and cohesion as it has. One answer (Martin, 1993, p. 127) is that "international organizations such as the EC facilitate stable linkages among issues that are not inseparably intertwined for functional reasons." As Keohane (1984, p. 91) put it, "Clustering of issues under a regime facilitates side-payments among these issues: more potential *quids* are available for the *quo*. Without international regimes linking clusters of issues to one another, side-payments and linkages would be difficult to arrange in world politics."

Cohen (1993a, p. 200) suggests that the very factors determining "the sustainability of EC monetary cooperation under the Maastricht Treaty" would, no doubt, affect fiscal cooperation. He claims that "studies of currency integration that principally emphasize either economic variables (Masson and Taylor, 1992 [here 1993]) or organizational characteristics (Griffiths, 1992) miss the main point. . . . The primary question is whether there is likely to be either a local hegemon or a fabric of related ties with sufficient influence to neutralize the risk of time inconsistency."

There is no single hegemon in Europe. Moreover, differences in language, culture, history, legal systems, and so forth, often divide countries. The attempt to find unity through diversity is, in addition, not particularly well served by the political process at the European center, whereby decisionmaking remains firmly in the hands of national politicians. Thus, the European federal political system is *indirectly* democratic, rather than *directly* accountable to the European people. Europeans do not vote for the appointee to the presidency of the Commission. The Council has the power, whereas the European Parliament is largely a cipher (Martin, 1993).

Cohen (1993a, p. 200), referring to the Scandinavian monetary union of 1873 to 1931, notes that "given the density of existing ties, creation of a common currency system seemed not only natural but almost inevitable." The concern of a European federalist must be to extend and strengthen ties between European states. Adopting a single currency in the EC would seem to be a potent measure for this purpose, for it could refocus the attention to gainers and losers on the status of the agent involved, rather than his or her country of residence.

As Cohen points out, the process of currency union is mutually interactive. Sharing a single currency could so shift perceptions that it would encourage federalism in other, notably fiscal, spheres. This would, in turn, reinforce a network of other existing ties that could support the single currency. The combination could bring about a markedly different, and preferable, balance to the discussion concerning the level of authority—local, regional, state, or federal—at which fiscal measures should be undertaken.

Some groups fear and oppose EMU as an important step in the path to a federal Europe in which the power and identity of the nation-states would be much reduced. Lady Thatcher is an example. For these opponents, the pros and cons of monetary union are a secondary matter. The hidden agenda is federalism and the locus of political sovereignty. I agree with much of their analysis, although not with their prejudices. Other groups, especially in Germany, believe that monetary union cannot easily survive unless it is accompanied by greater fiscal and political federalism. They fear that the loss of national control over monetary policy would enable local politicians to blame federal European constraints for any future severe or persistent national depression. On this view, more political and economic cohesion and integration must be achieved at the federal level for monetary union to withstand the centrifugal force of nationalism.

There is, thus, a division of opinion between those who believe that monetary union can work only if it is, or already has been, accompanied by a transfer of political and fiscal powers to a federal center, and those who believe that monetary union can precede any such large-scale transfer. This division pits the German coronation theorists (or economists), who support the first view, against the monetarists, who support the second (Gros and Thygesen, 1992; Bini-Smaghi, Padoa-Schioppa, and Papadia, 1993). Most of the monetarists also hope, however, that monetary unification would accelerate the transfer of fiscal powers. This conflict goes back to the time of the Werner Report (Council, 1970). Thus, Giavazzi and Giovannini (1989, p. 25) record that, at the Hague Summit in 1969, "the six EEC countries agreed on the principle of monetary unification, but expressed divergent opinions on how to implement the transition. . . . The French wanted the immediate abolition of fluctuation bands, and the transition to irrevocably fixed exchange rates; the Germans thought that precondition for a monetary union was the convergence of macroeconomic policies and performances, and the transfer of powers in the area of economic policy-making to the EEC Commission. The French thought that a clear commitment to irrevocably fixed rates would be sufficient to force policy convergence; the Germans thought instead that irrevocably fixed rates were incompatible with decentralized policy-making, and put forth a program of step-by-step transition toward supranational decision-making first, and currency unification later."

These differences have led the proponents of EMU and the Maastricht Treaty into some difficult policy dilemmas and areas of argument. The Commission finds itself in a delicate position between those who bitterly oppose the "hidden agenda" of federalism and those who believe that monetary union without federalism is not viable. Should the Commission try to pacify the Danes and U.K. Euroskeptics by claiming that EMU need not imply any further federalism in, for example, defense, political processes, and fiscal affairs? This argument would cause those who hold to the German view to be even more skeptical about the viability of a monetary union pushed ahead of supporting federal measures. The conflict helps to explain why the Commission (1990, p. 32) has embraced the principle of subsidiarity, which asserts that policies should be decided at the lowest effective level of government: "In the Community context, the application of this principle should ensure that a policy function is assigned to the Community level only when it can be performed in a more efficient way at that level than by national or local governments." This is a clever compromise.[9] It enables politicians to address the antifederalists by stating that powers will be transferred to the federal center only when it can be clearly demonstrated that they can be used more efficiently there. It also enables them to respond to the federalists by asking them whether they would really argue for a transfer to a higher level of government of powers that can better be exercised at a lower level.

In addition to providing an intellectual balance between two strongly opposed pressure groups, the principle of subsidiarity shifts the continuing argument from the general to the particular. On what grounds, and by what criteria, can one decide whether a function can be handled "more efficiently" at one level of government rather than another (Adonis and Tyrie, 1990)? There are methods for so doing in the area of fiscal federalism (Oates, 1972; Walsh, 1992; von Hagen, 1993), but how would one decide in the fields of defense, diplomacy, or law and order?

In one sense, the principle of subsidiarity provides an intellectual smokescreen behind which the ongoing decisionmaking process in the EC can result in a series of pragmatic determinations leading either toward or away from greater federalism. For the time being, general questions about the relation between monetary union and the appropriate extent of federalism are being purposefully masked as being both too difficult and too potentially inflammatory to attempt to answer directly.

---

[9] Not perhaps surprisingly in this context, the British government has also been pushing the concept of subsidiarity, but it supports the principle only when it is applied between Brussels and Westminster. The government appears aghast when anyone asks that the same principle be applied between Westminster and the local authorities in Scotland and Wales.

Should there be any significant shift of sovereignty to the federal center, however, involving diplomacy or defense, heavy expenditures would be required and would need to be financed. There would then be a problem with multiple currencies, varying flexibly against each other within the federation. The comparative regional benefits and costs of the central fiscal policy would be disturbed and distorted by the monetary fluctuations. At best, this would lead to great complexities; almost certainly, it would lead to dissatisfaction resulting, perhaps, in dissension and the progressive division of the federal state into its component parts. Even under a pegged, but occasionally adjustable, exchange-rate regime, a realignment would alter either the real fiscal impact on individual member states, if monetary transfers (fiscal expenditures and receipts) were denominated in terms of a federal currency such as the ECU, or the real fiscal outturn for the federal budget, if transfers were denominated in national currencies. And what would happen if the realignment were to occur partway through the fiscal year, with more accruals than disbursements completed?

One of the main questions raised by Kenen (1969) is whether the currency and fiscal domains need to have identical boundaries. It is difficult to answer this question empirically, because there are virtually no instances of single, unified fiscal authorities spanning a multiplicity of currency domains connected by flexible exchange rates. Indeed, one of the few available examples is the early EC, which had extremely limited federal fiscal powers. This is, in itself, suggestive. Note, for example, that, in the FSU, responsibility for fiscal policy has accompanied the shift to separate currency regimes among the independent former republics.

Interactions between Currency Regimes and Trade Policies

The extent to which two regions with initially separate currencies are linked by sizable trade flows has been a main criterion for currency union since the earliest discussions of the subject (for example, McKinnon, 1963; and Melitz, 1993a). I shall take this strand of the literature as given and simply consider the influence of the currency regime on trade policies. Does the existence of a single market depend on the existence of a single currency? The argument largely follows that on the need for a single currency to support a unified federal fiscal system. Giavazzi and Giovannini (1989), for example, give even greater weight to the role of exchange-rate stability in maintaining trading relationships within the common market than to its role in maintaining the viability of the CAP.

Although currency adjustments, properly controlled, would not likely impede progress toward a single market, I would argue that the adoption of a single currency supports free trade and the free movement of labor and capital far more effectively than a regime of pegged but adjustable rates. No one would suggest the erection of artificial, internal barriers to free trade or the free movement of factors within a single country with a single currency. It is much less certain, moreover, that the EC countries would be prepared to continue with a single market if some participants were viewed as engaging unilaterally in competitive devaluations. Few doubt the overall benefits of a single market within the EC, but there is reason to doubt that a single market, with no exchange controls, and with free movement of factors, will be compatible with the ability of its constituent members to vary exchange rates autonomously and sharply. If exchange rates can be shifted independently of the desires and welfare of the other members, the continued cohesion of the single market, as well as other joint federal activities, may be threatened. The political response in France, for example, to Hoover's move from Dijon to Scotland, suggests that the combination of a single market and floating exchange rates is untenable.

If it is also accepted that pegged but adjustable exchange rates are fragile in the face of political unwillingness to realign promptly, and unstable in the face of speculative attacks on currencies seen as realignment candidates, the only way to guarantee the continued success of the single market may be to move rapidly on to EMU. The recent disturbances in the ERM have led to many proposals for accelerating the transition, at least for the core countries that more or less meet the convergence criteria (Broder, 1992; de Largentaye, 1992; Levitt, 1992a; Malo de Molina, 1992; Steinherr, 1992).

The same analysis can be applied to the FSU. The monetary arrangements adopted by the former republics will have a large influence on trade policy among them (Havrylyshyn and Williamson, 1991; Williamson, 1992b). Maintaining a ruble zone does not guarantee, indeed, has not guaranteed, the continuation of free trade between the participating republics. Neither does the adoption of separate currencies and autonomous monetary policies necessarily lead to the abandonment of a single market or of free trade and unimpeded factor movements within that market. Nevertheless, Havrylyshyn and Williamson (1991, p. 74) note that "it is also a worry that in establishing its own currency each republic will feel compelled to control, if not close, its borders, thereby unleashing a damaging beggar-thy-neighbor trade war." Certainly, one of the crucial issues concerning advisers on currency reform in the FSU was whether a move to separate currencies and adjustable or floating exchange rates vis-à-vis the Russian ruble would or would not result in policy measures that would seriously impede trade among the former republics (Bofinger and Gros, 1991; Gros, 1991, 1993; de Largentaye, 1992; Odling-Smee, 1992; Williamson, 1992b).

In a note in the *Financial Times* ("Time for West to Help Russia's Transformation," March 1, 1993), Leyla Boulton reported two developments that are not entirely unrelated: (1) "The [Russian] government is also finally forcing other former Soviet republics to drop the ruble as their currency unless they coordinate monetary and credit policy with it," and (2) "The country is now even building proper borders with other republics which should help it implement foreign exchange controls." Boughton (1993, pp. 101–102), analyzing the success of the CFA franc zone, notes that "the positive factor . . . is that membership in the zone has given these countries access to France and to Europe. . . . First, and foremost, it has generated a great deal of trade. . . . Access to Europe has enabled the countries in the zone to maintain currency convertibility and open capital movements, which has further promoted the growth of trade and output."

The experience of the formerly socialist countries, especially those of the FSU, exemplifies many of the disadvantages of independent floating currencies. Leaving the value of a currency to market forces does not prevent misalignment, as was evident with respect to the U.S. dollar in the mid-1980s. Because it is so difficult and contentious to fix the value of a currency, the measurement of misalignment cannot be made clearly and objectively. Even so, it is arguable that the misalignments occurring under the comparatively free float from 1979 to 1985 were as pronounced as any under the various pegged but adjustable systems. The current misalignment of the Russian ruble, relative to fundamentals, is extreme, however, and values the labor of a Russian worker at a ridiculously low dollar level (Boone, 1993, table 4).

Moreover, a currency that is neither supported by sizable reserves nor based in an economic system run on a known and credible set of economic policy rules, is subject to extreme and volatile movements that may reinforce domestic inflationary pressures and relative price distortions. It is no accident that the most successful independent new currency in the FSU is the Estonian kroon, which is controlled by a currency-board mechanism supported by Estonia's restored prewar gold hoard. Even so, Estonia had a price increase of about 75 percent between June and December of 1992. Although this was comparatively low by FSU standards, it underlines the problems of trying to maintain a currency-board mechanism under such difficult circumstances.

What, then, are countries such as Ukraine and the other non-Russian FSU states to do, with virtually no foreign-exchange reserves and no real prospect of a counterinflationary nominal anchor? The prospects of trying to maintain a unified currency with Russia are slight. Russia itself has few reserves, has a central bank that is sufficiently independent from the executive branch of the government to reverse all the established correlations between independence and price stability, and has severe problems of credit control (with respect to both monopolistic state enterprises and the central government).[10] The probability of hyperinflation in Russia is high (Skorov, 1992–93), but the economic prospects of monetary and economic independence may be even worse, espe-

---

[10] Boulton (*Financial Times*, 1993) reported that the Central Bank of Russia proposed what must be the world's highest monetary target, "20 per cent a month."

cially when Russia acts antagonistically, for example, by withholding oil and gas supplies from its neighbors.[11]

The existing ruble zone has virtually broken up, with local central banks issuing their own rubles to finance their newly national governments. In order to prevent even worse inflationary pressures from unchecked local seigniorage spilling across borders, cross-border payments in, say, Georgian rubles, are not being accepted by shippers of goods in, for example, Kazakhstan. Instead, the so-called ruble area has degenerated into a barter system. In this context, the adoption of new national currencies may be no more than a *de jure* confirmation of a *de facto* breakdown (Williamson, 1992a, 1992b; Sachs and Lipton, 1993).

If separate currencies were to be introduced by regions within a sovereign nation, would trade barriers develop? Would federal nationalism give way to regional nationalism? This is a controversial question. In theory, the existence of flexible exchange rates among regions could facilitate the removal of trade barriers, because it would provide a market means of adjustment to imbalances. Indeed, Anglo-Saxon economists often take the line that an open single market with common minimum standards is perfectly consistent with flexible exchange rates (Wood, 1990; Feldstein, 1992). Continental European economists generally disagree (Giovannini, 1992a; Masera, 1992). Gros and Thygesen (1992 p. 3) quote the dictum attributed to Jacques Rueff: "L'Europe se fera par la monnaie ou elle ne se fera pas."[12] The Association for the Monetary Union of Europe (1992, p. 3) flatly asserts that "so long as the possibility remains that exchange rates within the European Community will change, barriers to trade will not be eliminated."

The Anglo-Saxon argument is further supported by reference to the North American Free Trade Agreement (NAFTA), an agreement that includes no mutual surveillance of exchange rates. This would seem to counter the European claim that a single market requires a single currency. But there are differences between NAFTA and the EC. Recall the argument in Cohen (1993a) that the existence of a hegemon reinforces international agreements. The United States is so large relative to Canada and Mexico that it may be

---

11 Ukraine's oil quota this year is 1 million tons less than Russia has promised Belarus, which is one-fifth the size of Ukraine but which has acceded to all of Russia's political and military demands. Russia's deputy prime minister, Viktor Shokhin, said in February 1993 that Russia will tie the continued supply of fuel to military and political conditions, including the stationing of Russian military bases in Ukraine. "I cannot understand the Russian position," Kuchma said. "It can only be seen as pressure on Ukraine, motivated by something beyond economic considerations. This is a conflict in which there can be no victors" ("Reform Club's New Member," *Financial Times*, February 23, 1993).

12 David Marsh, in a note on "'Franc fort' Set to Survive French Poll," quotes a top French official as stating that if the franc had to float, "this would mean the end of the EMS, of the Maastricht Treaty, of the single market and the Treaty of Rome itself" (*Financial Times*, March 18, 1993).

able to play the role of Stackelberg leader. There is no such hegemon in the EC. We must wait to see, moreover, what complaints there will be under NAFTA if there is great volatility in the exchange rates of its members.

NAFTA and the EC differ in yet another respect. European commentators concerned with the effect of floating exchange rates on the single market assume that the current account, national competitiveness, and employment will be variables influencing the monetary authorities' policy decisions; national interest rates or monetary growth rates may be used to bring about short-term effects on trade and output. The pure theory of international trade usually assumes that the money stock is exogenously given or influenced by some rule that does not involve a feedback link to the current account. In North America, by contrast, the central banks of both Canada and Mexico have been focusing more on achieving price stability in recent years than on maintaining competitiveness. Indeed, the obligation to achieve price stability will be included in the proposed statute that will grant independence to the Central Bank of Mexico. Whether or not floating exchange rates are compatible with a single market may therefore depend on the policies and rules adopted by the monetary authorities in the countries involved.

The apparent reluctance of national authorities to accept constraints on the conduct of domestic monetary policy raises questions about the path to a single currency proposed by the Delors Report and Maastricht Treaty. Might there be a different way of making the transition? Before turning to that question, we can summarize the discussion in Table 12.3. The benefits of a single currency for the EC seem to be clear. It is these, I claim, rather than OCA analysis, that provide the drive toward EMU.

5 The Transition to Monetary Union

The Intermediate Stages

Most of the plans for, and studies on, EMU have assumed that monetary union would be reached through a series of stages progressing closer to union. Thus,

TABLE 12.3
Properties of Alternative Exchange-Rate Regimes

Exchange Rate	Stable without Exchange Controls	Consistent with a Federal Fiscal System	Consistent with a Single Market
Free float	Yes	No	Doubtful
Pegged but adjustable	No	Doubtful	Yes
Single currency	Yes	Yes	Yes

the EMS began with an ERM with frequent realignments (1979 to 1983), which progressed to occasional realignments (1983 to 1987), and then to virtually fixed rates (1987 to 1992). From that point, the system was to have moved in 1994 to Stage 2 of the Delors process, with all EMS countries in the narrow band, to the irrevocable fixing of parities by 1999 at the latest, and, finally, to a single currency.

Advocates of monetary union saw a number of advantages in this phased plan. It not only made each step appear less radical, but it also enabled supporters to compare monetary union, an end point that had many economic and political advantages, to the ERM, a middle stage that shared most of the economic costs of EMU and few of its economic advantages. Thus, the peripheral members of the ERM largely gave up monetary autonomy and independence, so long as they sought to maintain their peg to the deutsche mark anchor; they could adjust their exchange rates only on infrequent occasions, either by a realignment or a temporary float, both of which would severely strain the ordered conduct of macroeconomic policy. In addition, they had to guard against the possibility of future devaluation or float by maintaining their nominal interest rates at a significant premium over those in Germany. Given asymmetric shocks, most notably German reunification, the level and structure of interest rates appropriate for German conditions would not necessarily be suitable for the rest of the EMS.

Those pressing for monetary union therefore claimed that its main cost, the loss of monetary sovereignty, had largely been incurred in the early stages of the ERM, whereas the benefits to the peripheral members would only accrue at the final stage of EMU, when the devaluation- and inflation-risk premia on interest rates would end and monetary policy would be set on an EMS-centered, rather than a German-centered, basis. This argument, which was central to much of the Commission's reasoning, was largely valid within the context of its own assumptions, but it had a number of weaknesses. First, none of the arguments held for Germany. As the anchor country, with the highest credibility, Germany's loss of monetary sovereignty was, as yet, negligible, even under the 1987 Basle-Nyborg rules governing intervention in the ERM; Germany suffered no interest-rate premium (rather the reverse), and the ERM tended to make German exports supercompetitive within Europe (Melitz, 1988). The transfer of power to an ESCB, however, would result in a potentially serious loss of sovereignty to Germany and, in particular, to the Bundesbank.

What, then, has been the German response to EMU? First, the Bundesbank has been one of the main centers of Euroskepticism. Second, the bank, and most Germans, have insisted that the transfer of control over monetary policy to the ESCB must not impose any serious losses on Germany. To this end, they have tried to ensure that the ESCB should perform for the larger community exactly as the Bundesbank does for Germany. This would be achieved by drafting the constitution of the ESCB along the lines of, or more rigidly than, that of the Bundesbank with respect to independence, the overriding priority of price stability, and the absence of significant responsibility for the stability of the banking system. In addition, they have favored strict criteria to prevent EMS countries from joining the ESCB until they have achieved economic convergence with Germany. Even so, Germans would feel much happier about EMU if there were clearer indications, even if largely symbolic, of continuing German sovereignty: if, for example, Germany were host to the European Monetary Institute (EMI) and, subsequently, the European Central Bank (ECB), and if the common currency were given a Germanic, rather than Francophone, name (Waigel, 1992).

What benefits do Germans see in proceeding with EMU? The arguments are largely political and suggest a conscious, and preferred, shifting of political and economic powers to a federal center in order to prevent a rerun of the political and economic disasters of the last two centuries. A move to a single monetary and currency system to reinforce the European single market and a transfer of political and fiscal powers to the center would be important manifestations of such a shift. It has also been argued that Germany stands to benefit more than other members of the EC from both the single market and the enlargement of the EC to incorporate East European countries (Collins and Rodrik, 1991; De Benedictis and Padoan, 1991; Padoan and Pericoli, 1992). Insofar as the single market and its expansion may be conditional on the successful achievement of EMU, Germany would then have an incentive to accept the package as a whole (Martin, 1993).

With the benefit of hindsight, it can be seen that the main weakness of the Commission's arguments, and of the proposed path through various stages, is that they assumed the successful continuation of pegged but adjustable exchange rates, a system known to be susceptible to, and fragile in the face of, speculative attack. This is what occurred in the second half of 1992.

Whether and how the ERM will continue remains now uncertain. One widely drawn conclusion is that the phased route to EMU may have been misdesigned. If the German coronation thesis is correct, countries should seek, instead, to achieve sufficient convergence while retaining residual exchange-rate flexibility. Once such convergence has been achieved, a sudden, complete step to immediate monetary union might then be taken. Stage 2 is not only superfluous and otiose; it is positively dangerous. In this sense, the events of 1992 can be held to represent a defeat for the view shared by France, Italy, and the Commission that increasingly fixed exchange rates will generate the convergence required by the German view. This conclusion, however, has a number of implications for the balance of the argument. It means that the alternative to full monetary union can no longer be taken to be the halfway house of a rigid ERM, in which monetary sovereignty has already been partly relinquished. It needs to be compared, instead, with floating exchange rates or a much more flexible ERM, perhaps like that of the 1979–83 period. In this latter case, national authorities would maintain much more control over domestic monetary policies.

Given the possibility that national governments will pursue time-inconsistent policies, what then would provide the nominal anchor, and what guarantee, if any, would there be of a convergence that might allow a subsequent jump to full monetary union? A plan proposed by Fratianni, von Hagen, and Waller (1992), Begg et al. (1991), and Giovannini (1991) would be, first, to transfer the power to determine national monetary policies to independent national central banks that would be required by statute to achieve price stability (see also Hughes Hallett and Vines, 1993). Kenen (1992b, p. 59) makes a somewhat similar suggestion that the monetary policies of EC countries should be coordinated during the transition by the EMI, which would bring about convergence and show "the skeptics, especially in Germany, that a common monetary policy for Europe does not jeopardize price stability." Convergence would thus be compatible with exchange-rate flexibility for an interim period. France, Italy, and Spain have introduced legislation to provide more independence to their central banks, but, in the United Kingdom, the prime minister and chancellor took advantage of the appointment of the next governor of the Bank of England to reaffirm the bank's political subservience.

When I have argued the case for some such alternative transitional sequence, the most forceful counterargument has been that experience with floating exchange rates since 1973 suggests that they are not solely, or even primarily, determined by the economic fundamentals of relative prices and monetary policies. Thus, even if independent central banks were to deliver price stability to a common degree in each EC country, there would be no guarantee either of relatively stable exchange rates or of properly aligned exchange rates. The critics of this alternative approach therefore argue that some official intervention in the exchange market is a necessary precondition for moving to Stage 3.

We are left with a dilemma. It may be extremely difficult to move directly from a float to irrevocably fixed rates, and it may be equally difficult in the face of speculative attack to operate a system of pegged rates for any length of time. This would seem to suggest that, whenever the political will to move to a single currency is present, the step should be taken as quickly as possible, from whatever the initial starting point may be. The crucial factor may well be the time interval involved, not the precise nature of the intermediate steps. It should be noted, however, that any sudden, unannounced move to monetary union could cause large capital gains and losses to borrowers and lenders. This would be not only unfair, but, because of asymmetries, probably deflationary. A second problem, that of a "two-speed Europe," in which only a subset of EC countries will have met the minimum convergence requirements and desire to move quickly to a single currency, raises issues that must await another discussion.

The problem that I shall tackle now is that there may have to be a long interval between the irrevocable locking of parities (Stage 3A) and the general adoption of a single currency (Stage 3B). It would be relatively simple during this interval for countries to withdraw from EMU. In addition, even though the ECB would begin operations at the start of Stage 3A, continued use of separate currencies for domestic retail purposes could complicate the operations of the emerging monetary union. For both of these reasons, there may be some concern about the viability of Stage 3A, which could continue to exhibit at least part of the fragility of pegged but adjustable rates.

The Costs of Changing Currencies: Dissolution and Unification

Most studies of the benefits and costs of monetary independence or union have focused on the static, steady-state alternatives. This is certainly true of the Commission's "One Market, One Money" (1990). There are, however, significant transitional costs in moving from one currency to another.

The disturbance to information sets is one of the main costs in changing currencies, whether in unifying multiple currencies or in dissolving single-currency systems. In many historical, and current, examples of currency-area dissolution, separation has occurred when some event has already diminished the information value of the shared currency within the separating region or state. Hostilities between regions are one such factor. The inhabitants of the region without control of the single central bank may query the future acceptability of the unified currency in their own region and may seek to substitute into a more highly regarded store of value.

Separation can also occur when the unified currency has become so inflationary that it cannot act as a reasonable nominal anchor. This is clearly the case in both the former Yugoslavia and the FSU (Skorov, 1992–93). At the introduction to the EBRD's first annual economic review, Jacques Attali said, with regard to the FSU, that "establishing separate national currencies or smaller currency zones could improve the prospects for production and trade among the republics. . . . The EBRD said the ruble zone had been undermined by inadequate control of credit and cash creation which had brought its members to the brink of hyperinflation. [It] suggested that some republics, once outside the zone, would opt for more prudent fiscal and monetary policies" (*Financial Times*, February 12, 1993; see also Williamson, 1992b; Gros, 1993; Hansson, 1993). If a monetary system is primarily a device for organizing information, the value of any unified system will depend on whether it is undertaking this function satisfactorily. Under conditions of civil war or hyperinflation, it cannot do so, and the cost of monetary separation will therefore be lessened.

Even apart from informational disturbances, there will be the transitional costs of establishing a new central bank, of designing and printing new notes, of establishing a mint or buying in new coins, and of adapting to the new currency. Many of the larger costs of introducing new currencies, such as altering coin-operated vending machines, changing bank software, and revising automated payment systems, will be much the same whether one is separating from, or moving to, a unified system. These costs are discussed below.

A common problem in cases of amicable currency dissolution[13] is how to divide up the fiscal and monetary assets and liabilities of the previous unit. This is not a problem in hostile conditions; the separating state will renounce responsibility for all liabilities and grab any assets it can. But, what should be the responsibility, if any, of an Armenian government with a separate currency for the liabilities of the former Soviet Union (Williamson, 1992b; Armendariz de Aghion and Williamson, 1993)? If Quebec were to secede and to establish a separate central bank and currency, what share should it take of Canadian federal assets and liabilities? In practice, as occurred in the FSU, formulas can be negotiated for such divisions, given a modicum of good will.

When the information content of an existing monetary system has not already been severely diminished, the transitional cost of replacing it is perceived to be quite large. This is borne out by the reluctance of several countries to reform low-value currency units simply by knocking off several zeros.[14] The benefits of such reforms seem obvious. Entering fewer digits at each transaction would lessen the chance of decimal-point errors. Informational efficiency would clearly be enhanced, and the transitional costs of a decimal change would be much lower than for any other redenomination. Yet even so simple a reform is rarely made in the absence of prior hyperinflation. The last instance I can recall in a Western industrialized country, is de Gaulle's replacement of the old franc with the new franc in 1958.

There are, nevertheless, immediate transitional costs that may be perceived to outweigh the long-run, steady-state benefits. The physical costs of printing and substituting new notes would not be very large. More serious could be fears that such a substitution would be used by a government as a device either for refusing to exchange high-value hoards of old currency (a wealth tax on currency hoarders) or for asking questions about fiscal or possible criminal activity that may have led to the accumulation of such hoards. And time-inconsistency problems could also arise. A good example of this occurred in the Soviet Union in January 1991 (Havrylshyn and Williamson, 1991).

Even such simple reforms as knocking zeros off currency units could cause costly problems. All written contracts, financial arrangements, wills, and electronic software programs dealing with payments would have to be changed. Suppose that the lira is rebased by a factor of 1,000 to 1. Your granny wrote a

[13] A close observer of the Czech-Slovak breakup comments that he is "not sure that an amicable currency dissolution is actually possible."

[14] For example, Portuguese, Spanish, and Italian currency exchange rates against the U.S. dollar in February 1993 were 214 escudos, 167 pesetas, and 2,200 lire.

will before the reform giving you a bequest of 15,000 lire. She dies two days after the reform. Is your bequest valid in law for new or old lire? There are, of course, ways of dealing with such problems, but the change will inevitably cause confusion and legal complexity. For all these reasons, the program for currency reform in Italy is moving very slowly, even though it is widely accepted (De Vecchis, 1990).

Another sort of currency reform is the 1967–71 British shift from nondecimal to decimal coinage (from 20 shillings to the pound, 12 pence to the shilling, and so forth, to 100 new pence to the pound). Not only did the main unit (the pound) remain unchanged, but several of the subsidiary coins continued in use; thus, the previous florin (2 shillings) became 10 new pennies, and the existing shilling, 5 new pennies. The value of the reform is clear to those of us who spent our early childhood years doing sums such as, "You have two pounds, six shillings, and fourpence in your pocket. Chocolate bars cost three shillings and sixpence halfpenny each. How many can you buy?" Yet more than five years were taken in planning and executing the reform; the costs of adjusting vending machines, and so forth, were large; and the public outcry was great.

Economists use the concept of menu costs. A change in subsidiary coinage involves the simultaneous imposition of the required menu cost on every single pricing arrangement involving coins. One reason for the public outcry in England was that the reform required a rounding up or down of all menu prices previously set at a level not immediately translatable into new-penny integers. Not only did most people claim that prices were more frequently rounded up than down, but many accused sales outlets of using the conversion to raise prices surreptitiously. Although I know of no rigorous academic support, a widely held hypothesis at the time was that the introduction of coin decimalization caused an upward blip in inflation. The idea that a currency reform will leave all relative prices unchanged is untenable. The confusion provides a perfect cover for sellers to raise prices, and consumers will expect them to do just that.

The costs of U.K. decimalization would be dwarfed by the costs of changing to an ECU system. Yet these costs have hardly begun to be considered with respect to EMU. There is virtually nothing about such problems in the studies of the Commission, and, among academics, only Giovannini (1991) and Melitz (1991a, 1993b) have yet commented on them. The best and most complete treatment is in Mazzaferro's (1992) San Paolo Bank report. Various working groups of central-bank governors are now addressing these issues, but little has been revealed publicly;[15] some of the studies and options under consideration are, however, outlined in the annual report for 1992 of the Committee of EC Central Bank Governors (1993).

[15] I understand that, among the subcommittees established to prepare for Stage 3, there is one, set up in May 1992, "to supervise technical preparation of Ecu bank notes."

Compare the switch to the ECU with the 1958 French rebasing. Under rebasing, the new franc was worth 100 old francs, and information sets could adjust relatively easily. Assume, for the moment, that the ECU replaces the French franc at the franc's February 1993 ECU parity. Each new ECU is then worth 6.54988 previous francs; each prior franc, worth 0.1526746 ECU. Apart from the enforced need to change all contracts, payment systems, and software programs involving money, consider the shock to our information systems (Clifford Chance, Inc. 1992).

Again, compare ECU unification to British decimalization. In the British case, several coins were common to both regimes, so both the real cost and informational loss were reduced. The proposed ECU, however, does not equal a round number of any national unit and is commonly expressed to the nearest six figures. If we were to switch on the present basis to a unified ECU system, all coins in all currencies participating in EMU would have to be replaced by completely new, totally unfamiliar subsidiary coins. Menu costs may sometimes seem small, but not these.

At least three proposals have been put forward to reduce some of these costs. The first is that the value of the new common currency should be made equal to that of the most widely held existing currency. In this case, 1 ECU would be made equal to 1 deutsche mark, and the subsidiary coin (a pecu?) would be equal to a pfennig. This would eliminate any transitional cost in Germany (Giovannini, 1991; Lehment and Scheide, 1992). Lord Cobbold has recently proposed a variant, whereby an ECU would be valued at exactly 2 deutsche marks, rather than its current rate of 1.953 deutsche marks ("How to Make the ECU User-Friendly," *Financial Times*, May 12, 1993). Because many businesses would be more familiar initially with the deutsche mark than with the ECU, this adjustment would reduce information costs outside Germany. Because the deutsche mark also has the greatest credibility among existing EC currencies as a store of value, its close link to the ECU would launch the new currency in the best possible manner. The economic arguments for this method seem incontrovertible. Nevertheless, it will probably not happen. The French may block it on purely political grounds, and the British, and others, may block it on commercial grounds. Mazzaferro (1992, p. 71) notes that this technique would be illegal under Article 109J of the Maastricht Treaty, but, more important, "that the German financial system will have been offered a lead which it will never lose." For this reason, he states, other countries will not accept it.

A second way to reduce transitional costs would be to have one final realignment to shift the ECU value of each participating EC currency onto a user-friendly fraction. Giovannini (1991) suggests one such realignment (see also Neumann [1992]). There are two problems with this method. The first is that a final realignment might not be consistent with the Maastricht convergence criteria, unless it were done more than two years before Stage 3, when currency parities are to be irrevocably fixed. The conflict might be avoided, however, if the realignments were made on the initiative of the EC, rather than that of the member states. Second, Articles 109g and 109l, 4, of the Maastricht Treaty state that "from the start of the third stage, the value of the ECU shall be irrevocably fixed." There could well be a small window of opportunity for realignment between the end of the two-year convergence period and the start of Stage 3, but any such opportunity would be perceived by the markets, which would react in advance with speculation.

A third proposal to reduce information costs would be to phase in gradual stages the replacement of national currencies by the ECU (Spahn, 1992). To this end, Mrs. Thatcher proposed that a "hard ECU" might be introduced and adopted by private agents in an evolutionary manner (H.M. Treasury, 1989; Richards, 1990). But this might not have led to any appreciable currency unification; indeed, many feel that its expected failure to do so was exactly what some of its antifederalist British proponents wanted.

A similar proposal would be to introduce actual ECU notes in three stages. In the first stage, the round number of the national currency would be on one side, and the equivalent ECU value, on the other. Such notes would be legal tender in all participating countries, but the information costs of making change could still lead holders to acquire the host country's notes when traveling abroad. In the second stage, notes in round numbers of ECUs would be introduced, with the equivalent national value on the reverse side. At first, both sets of notes (national round-number notes and ECU round-number notes) would circulate side by side; subsequently, national round-number notes would be withdrawn. In the final stage, the preunification national equivalent on the reverse side would be omitted, although it would still remain possible to design notes displaying national features for initial issuance in a particular country. Thus, ECU notes issued in England would have the Queen's head on them, although Dutch notes with Queen Beatrix would be just as good for payment purposes. Even so, would the Spanish find it acceptable to have a large part of their note circulation in "British" and "German" ECU after every tourist season? If not, they would have to find means for sorting perhaps seven or eight different denominations of banknotes from seven or more countries, and either destroying or repatriating "nonlocal" notes, a complex and expensive task.

Such dual-valuation printing of notes has occurred in the past.[16] Whether

---

[16] The *Financial Times* (September 9, 1992) noted that, "Lord Younger, the Royal Bank chairman, has been dipping into the history books to make a separate point about the design of European banknotes if Emu one day became a reality. For about a century after political and monetary union between England and Scotland in 1707, one pound sterling banknotes north of the border carried the inscription that they were equivalent to 12 pounds Scots. Lord Younger has been presenting EC Commissioners with facsimiles of 200-year-old Scottish banknotes to show how future European notes could carry the names both of the prospective single European currency and of the old national units. If the Community really wanted to ease popular misgivings about the abandonment of francs, pounds and D-Marks then, the Royal Bank chairman suggests, it could copy this ancient example."

an accompanying procedure could be achieved for subsidiary coins, however, is another question. Subject to possible rounding to a user-friendly fraction, the reverse-side stamping of coins (initially ECU, subsequently national) would presumably have to be an approximation, for, as Mazzaferro (1992, p. 12) notes, "national coins will be non-decimal multiples and submultiples of the Ecu." A fine calculation would have to be made to balance the need for informational simplicity against the opportunities for arbitrage (Gresham's law). If a graduated process for subsidiary coins is not possible, however, and the changeover had to be done on a single big-bang day, the arguments for phasing in notes would become much weaker.[17]

One argument for having a single changeover day is that until national currencies are completely replaced by the ECU, the costs of reneging on the Maastricht commitment will not be perceived as prohibitive (Mazzaferro, 1992); devaluation premia in nominal national interest rates may remain, increasing the temptation for national politicians to withdraw. Those who favor unification therefore want to complete it as quickly as possible once Stage 3 has begun. Moreover, it is arguable that if such a major break is to be made, it is better to make it cleanly and quickly on a chosen day for which everyone can be prepared in advance. The chaos on, and immediately after, changeover day will be indescribable, but the present discounted value of the costs may be less than if the changeover is organized in stages, with some businesses and accountants operating on a national-currency basis while others have shifted to the ECU. Levitt (1992a, p. 32–33), for example, claims that "a parallel currency, favored by some politicians and experts, would add to the problems" and would double some of the costs facing banks. It is, however, quite possible, perhaps probable, that monetary operations in Stage 3A will require the banking systems in the EC to combine a wholesale system denominated in ECUs with a retail system in national currencies. If so, banks may be unable to avoid running two sets of books, at least for the transitional period.

Insufficient appreciation has been given to the length of time required to prepare for the changeover day, and there has been little discussion of the time that is likely to elapse between the start of Stage 3A, with an irrevocable fixing of parities, and the subsequent achievement of a single currency among the participating counties (Stage 3B). It is also unclear which countries will participate and when Stage 3A will begin, although we have a *terminus ad quem* of January 1, 1999. People will consequently be disinclined to spend much time, or to incur many preparatory costs, in advance of an event that might not happen to them at all.

---

[17] The problem of dealing with coins may well turn out to be even more troublesome than harmonizing bank notes. Mazzaferro (1992, p. 9) notes that "the second paragraph of Article 105 underlines that a series of measures *may* be adopted in order to 'harmonize the denominations and technical specifications. . . .' The adoption of such measures is optional . . . ; this might therefore lead to a situation in which coinage was not standardized."(!)

In light of the British experience with decimalization, my guess is that Stage 3A will have to continue for at least three years and may, as all the complexities become apparent, need to last for up to six years. Assuming that Stage 3A begins on January 1, 1999, this would put the changeover day somewhere between January 1, 2002, and January 1, 2005.

Is there not an inconsistency here? It is commonly suggested that the transitional costs of monetary dissolution are much greater than those of monetary union; yet the monetary unions of the former Yugoslavia and the FSU are breaking up rapidly. Although their dissolution has involved much disturbance, it does not seem to have been on the same scale as the dislocation suggested for the changeover to the ECU. The answer to this apparent paradox is threefold. First, the political imperative for dissolution in Eastern Europe has been greater than the public and political enthusiasm for currency union in Western Europe. Second, the monetary system, and the associated hardware and software, is technically much more rudimentary in Eastern Europe than in Western Europe, so there has been less to change and it has been easier so to do. Third, the information function and nominal stability provided by the dinar and the ruble had already been dissipated.

The Interregnum between Currency Regimes: From National Currencies to EMU

The Delors Report originally envisaged Stage 2 as a transitional step en route to a single currency. Under the Maastricht Treaty, however, domestic monetary arrangements are to remain effectively unchanged during Stage 2 and under the sole control of national central banks. Although the convergence criteria, subject to any amendments, revisions, or reinterpretations that may be introduced, will exert an influence over the economies of EC members during Stage 2, the monetary regime will remain essentially unchanged until Stage 3. There will be nearly no shift to ECU usage, no significant currency substitution at the domestic level, and possibly very little substitutability at the wholesale level. Currency usage, payment and settlement systems between and within EC countries, structures of financial markets and central-bank operations are likely to look much the same at the end of Stage 2 as they look now. Although these assertions may appear to be incidental, substantive changes to market structures, payment mechanisms, and so forth, take years to plan and bring into effect. If they are to occur before the start of Stage 3, due by 1999 at the latest, where are the present plans for them? What evidence is there of growing currency substitution, or greater ECU usage, especially after the setback in 1992?

By much the same token, we can imagine relatively easily what the single European currency regime, Stage 3B, will look like when it is fully operational. There are several problems to resolve. How will the ECB and the national central banks balance their operations in money markets to bring into effect the single European monetary policy and to ensure systemic stability in the European payment mechanisms and financial system? Financial markets and payment systems within EC countries currently function on the basis of differing technical systems, for example, gross versus net payment systems. How much harmonization will be necessary or desirable for Stage 3B?

We can nevertheless characterize the larger picture. All transactions within and between EC countries will be undertaken in ECUs, all asset prices, including the various government bonds, will be denominated in ECUs, a single ECU interest-rate structure will obtain, and so on. The question then arises, how do we get from here to there? In practice, this transition will occur during Stage 3A, at which point currencies will be separate but irrevocably fixed. As noted above, this stage is more important and will take much longer than is generally realized.

During the Maastricht negotiations, the transition to the ECU was shifted from Stage 2 to Stage 3A, and the details of the transition were relegated to the various committees established by the EC central-bank governors and, once the EMI was in place, to that institution (Treaty, Article 109f, and Protocol on the EMI Statute). The EMI's main function, in fact, will be to plan the transition. Thus, the transitional arrangements have become the province of a few financial experts drawn primarily from the national central banks and monitored where possible and advised and criticized by a limited group of outside academics (Kenen, 1992a; Melitz, 1993b) and practitioners (Levitt, 1992a, 1992b).

The key features of Stage 3A are that, from day one, the parities between the separate national currencies and the ECU must be absolutely exactly fixed, and that there will be a single monetary policy across all the member countries. As Monticelli and Viñals (1993, p. 12) state, "[A] necessary condition for the conduct of monetary policy in Stage Three is the establishment of an integrated market for central bank money." If the market is to be integrated, its business will have to be conducted from the start in the single currency, the ECU. In order to participate in the ECU funds market, the participating banks will need to be able to exchange ECUs for their domestic currencies without limit at par with their national central banks. A wholesale payment and settlement system in ECUs will need to be in place from the start to settle such transactions in the ECU funds market. Finally, in order to hedge and adjust their ECU positions, banks will need to be able to transact in large, liquid ECU financial markets; these can best be provided, perhaps, if the central governments of the participating countries irrevocably guarantee from the start the ECU value of some portion of their debt (both interest and principal). Note that this guarantee would also represent a strong precommitment to moving on to Stage 3B.

Kenen (1992a, p. 34) sets out six proposed requirements for day one: (1) The balance sheets of the ECB and the national central banks are denominated in ECUs. (2) Credit institutions hold ECU balances with their national central banks. They may or may not be *required* to hold them. (3) An ECB funds market is in place, in which credit institutions can make or take interbank loans and thus lend or borrow ECU cash balances held at the national central banks. (4) Governments have attached "ECU endorsements" to all of their marketable obligations, guaranteeing to redeem them in ECUs; similar endorsements are attached to all other instruments used in open-market operations. (5) A unified market for all securities bearing ECU endorsements is in place, in which interest rates on individual issues differ only insofar as the issues themselves differ in default risk, liquidity, and taxability. (6) Firms and individuals hold and deal in securities with ECU endorsements, although they also use their own national currencies. Because national central banks will still have national note issues as their main liabilities, it may be decided that all national central-bank assets need not be denominated in ECUs, but, given an ECU endorsement to central-government debt, this is a minor issue.

Commercial banks will need to operate simultaneously in two currencies during Stage 3A, in ECUs for wholesale transactions and in national currencies for retail transactions. Various working parties are studying the technical forms of the ECU wholesale payment and settlement systems and the links with the continuing national retail systems, which will still be denominated in national currencies during Stage 3A. A number of papers are becoming available by, for example, the Commission (1992a, 1992b, 1992c), the Committee of Governors (1992), Giovannini (1992a), and the CEPS Working Party (1994).

Monticelli and Viñals (1993, p. 13) suggest that the achievement of same-day ECU payments and settlements

> does not require the centralization of payment and settlement systems at the EC level. . . . the examples of the United States and Germany show that decentralized systems are compatible with a single monetary policy. What is required instead is the linking of national payment systems to ensure that interbank funds can be transferred across borders and, once transferred, can be used for final settlements within the same day. To achieve this result, some harmonization of central-bank practices in the operation of payment systems is needed; in particular, common technical standards on operational reliability and compatibility must be defined together with an agreement on the time of the final clearing. These measures are sufficient to create an integrated interbank market and thus permit the conduct of a single monetary policy. Unfortunately, they do not ensure the safety of the interbank payment and settlement systems. Safety requires measures to reduce liquidity, credit, and systemic risks (such as collateral requirements, caps on exposure, the definition of the conditions of access to the system), as well as common legal provisions regulat-

ing the finality of payments (bankruptcy laws, "zero-hour" clauses) and the revocability of payment instructions.

Unification will also require, even at the outset of Stage 3A, the establishment of a single interest rate (at each maturity on instruments of identical character) throughout the participating countries in the EC. The present structures and types of money markets, however, and the operational mechanisms of central banks, are different in the various countries (see Schnadt [1994] on money markets in London, Frankfurt, Paris, and New York). There could, therefore, be a conflict between the desire for subsidiarity and national continuity enshrined in the Maastricht Treaty (Protocol on the ESCB Statute, Article 12.1, indent 3) and the need for integration and central control (Melitz, 1993b).

The Treaty (Protocol on the ESCB Statute, Article 12.1) states that "to the extent deemed possible and appropriate, . . . the ECB shall have recourse to the national central banks to carry out operations which form part of the tasks of the ESCB." Among those tasks would be open-market operations to achieve a common European interest rate and monetary growth rate. But central banks currently intervene in different ways at different times and frequencies and leave different degrees of latitude to market forces. Might there not be a likelihood of dissonance and financial turmoil among markets, and even of noncooperative behavior deteriorating possibly into disguised discord, between national money markets and the national central banks that back them. Melitz (1993b) is concerned about this. How far the structure of national money markets and the technical mechanisms of central-bank money-market operations will need to be harmonized has not yet been fully assessed and agreed.

Finally, the Maastricht limitations (Treaty, Article 104, and Protocol on the ESCB Statute, Article 21) on direct finance of governments by central banks suggest that certain existing financial arrangements between government bodies, especially the central government and the central bank, will have to be changed. If government bodies should continue to want access to short-term bank finance (overdrafts, ways and means advances), they would need, under these circumstances, to approach commercial banks, not their central banks (Goodhart, 1992a). This may have to occur in advance of Stage 3 for all countries except the United Kingdom, which has been granted an opt-out; for the others, the prohibition on central-bank financing will take effect at the beginning of Stage 2 (Committee of Governors, 1993, p. 58).

This short summary suggests that the following prerequisites will need to be in place and ready to operate on day one for those countries participating in Stage 3: Each national government will have to guarantee the ECU value of a significant proportion of its outstanding debt and to negotiate any desired loan facilities with commercial banks. Commercial banks will have to be prepared to operate simultaneously in ECU wholesale markets and domestic-currency retail markets. The EMI, ECB, and national central banks will have to establish wholesale payment and settlement systems in ECUs and link them with domestic-currency payment systems; to agree on the prudential supervision and regulation of such systems, particularly responsibility for the proper working of the wholesale payment system; and to decide on the modus operandi for central-bank operations in money markets. They must be able and ready to put into place such structural changes as may be required to achieve the minimum harmonization needed for these purposes.

6 Conclusions

My objectives in this discussion have been to probe the political and economic issues linking independent countries with separate currencies. This is particularly important in the context of EMU, for EMU represents a potential counterexample to the one country, one currency format. What considerations that normally make nations want to have separate currencies may now induce EC countries voluntarily to move toward a single currency?

First is the connection between autonomous currencies and international constraints on the flows of goods, capital, and other factors of production. Does the maintenance of a single market require either a single currency or, at least, strict limitations on the autonomous use of national monetary policies among the partner countries? Could the European single market survive a reversion to floating exchange rates? Will the breakup of the ruble area be followed by the building of barriers to interstate trade? How much sovereignty over national monetary policies must be relinquished to gain the benefits of a single market? In theory, a single market is possible among countries with separate currencies, autonomous monetary policies, and floating exchange rates, but would such a market work, given the tendency of governments to manipulate their monetary and exchange-rate policies to achieve competitive trading advantages?

A second consideration is the form and nature of the relations between monetary and fiscal policies. Is it practicable and feasible to carry out the fiscal functions necessary for the existence of a sovereign state without having a single currency over the whole of that state? If not, one can understand why nations do not consider having several currencies within their boundaries. If the autonomous republics within Russia should insist on having their own currencies, would that presage the further dismemberment of Russia's sovereignty? Can sovereignty and fiscal functions remain largely at the national level within EMU, while a single currency is shared with the other EC nations, decisions on monetary policy are taken independently of national governments, and decisions on exchange-rate policy are taken jointly among governments?

I have grave doubts whether this can work. Fiscal-policy decisions at the

EC level will be subject to nationalistic haggling, and central cooperation and coordination will be limited by each country's desire to avoid a net loss nationally. Fiscal policy at the national level, which already faces many constraints, will be further shackled by the fiscal limits set by the Maastricht Treaty. Monetary autonomy will have been abandoned. Consequently, the inhabitants of each member nation are likely to suffer a reduction in their ability to control their own economic destinies. At times of pressure and cyclical downturn, they might perceive this loss as greater than the gain from preserving the single market by remaining within the monetary system.

Economists have become used to the concept of choosing the appropriate *sequence* of steps to achieve a major regime change, most notably in moving from socialist to market regimes in Eastern Europe. What is needed is a similar analysis of the best sequence for moving toward a federal Europe. Whether it is sensible in this context to push monetary union so far ahead of fiscal and political union is, perhaps, the final and most crucial question.

References

Adonis, Andrew, and Andrew Tyrie, "Subsidiarity, as History and Policy," London, Institute of Economic Affairs, December 1990, pamphlet.

Aghion, Philippe, and Patrick Bolton, "Government Domestic Debt and the Risk of Default: A Political-Economic Model of the Strategic Role of Debt," in Rudiger Dornbusch and Mario Draghi, eds., *Public Debt Management: Theory and History*, Cambridge and New York, Cambridge University Press, 1990, pp. 315–344.

Alesina, Alberto, "Politics and Business Cycles in Industrial Democracies," *Economic Policy*, 8 (April 1989), pp. 55–98.

Alogoskoufis, George, and Richard Portes, "International Costs and Benefits from EMU," *European Economy*, Special Issue No. 1 (1991), pp. 231–245.

Armendariz de Aghion, Beatriz, and John Williamson, *The G-7's Joint-and-Several Blunder*, Essays in International Finance No. 189, Princeton, N.J., Princeton University, International Finance Section, April 1993.

Artis, Michael J., "One Market, One Money: An Evaluation of the Potential Benefits and Costs of Forming an Economic and Monetary Union," *Open Economies Review*, 2 (1991), pp. 315–321.

Association for the Monetary Union of Europe, "Questions and Answers about Monetary Union in Europe," Paris, Association for the Monetary Union of Europe, 1992, processed.

Atkeson, Andrew, and Tamim A. Bayoumi, "Private Capital Markets and Adjustment in a Currency Union: Evidence from the United States," in Masson and Taylor, *Policy Issues in the Operation of Currency Unions*, 1993, pp. 75–95.

Attanasio, Orazio P., and Fiorella Padoa-Schioppa, "Regional Inequalities, Migration and Mismatch in Italy, 1960–86," in Fiorella Padoa-Schioppa, ed., *Mismatch and Labour Mobility*, Cambridge and New York, Cambridge University Press, 1991, pp. 237–321.

Baldwin, Richard E., "On the Microeconomics of the European Monetary Union," *European Economy*, Special Issue No. 1 (1991), pp. 21–35.

Bayoumi, Tamim A., and Barry Eichengreen, "Shocking Aspects of European Monetary Integration," in Francisco Torres and Francesco Giavazzi, eds., *Adjustment and Growth in the European Monetary Union*, Cambridge and New York, Cambridge University Press, 1993, pp. 193–229.

Bayoumi, Tamim A., and Paul R. Masson, "Fiscal Flows in the United States and Canada: Lessons for Monetary Union in Europe," Washington, D.C., International Monetary Fund, November 1991, processed.

Bayoumi, Tamim A., and Andrew K. Rose, "Domestic Savings and Intra-National Capital Flows," *European Economic Review*, 37 (August 1993), pp. 1197–1202.

Bean, Charles, R., "Economic and Monetary Union in Europe," *Journal of Economic Perspectives*, 6 (Fall 1992), pp. 31–52.

Bean, Charles R., Daniel Cohen, Francesco Giavazzi, Alberto Giovannini, Xavier Vives, and Charles Wyplosz, "European Monetary Union under Attack," manifesto published in major European newspapers, 1992.

Begg, David, Pierre-André Chiappori, Francesco Giavazzi, Colin Mayer, Damien Neven, Luigi Spaventa, Xavier Vives, Charles Wyplosz, *Monitoring European Integration: The Making of Monetary Union*, London, Centre for Economic Policy Research, 1991.

Bini-Smaghi, Lorenzo, Tommaso Padoa-Schioppa, and Francesco Papadia, "The Policy History of the Maastricht Treaty: The Transition to the Final Stage of EMU," in Guillermo de la Dehesa, Alberto Giovannini, Manuel Guitián, and Richard Portes, eds., *The Monetary Future of Europe*, London, Centre for Economic Policy Research, 1993.

Bini-Smaghi, Lorenzo, and Silvia Vori, "Rating the EC as an Optimal Currency Area: Is It Worse Than the US?" in Richard O'Brien, ed., *Finance and the International Economy*, Amex Bank Review Prize Essays, Vol. 6, Oxford, Oxford University Press, 1992, pp. 78–104.

Blanchard, Olivier, and Lawrence Katz, "Regional Evolutions," *Brookings Papers on Economic Activity*, No. 1 (1992), pp. 1–61.

Bofinger, Peter, and Daniel Gros, "A Multilateral Payments Union of the Republics of the Soviet Union," Brussels, Centre for European Policy Studies, November 1991, processed.

Boone, Peter, "Russia's Balance of Payments Prospects," in Anders Åslund and Richard Layard, eds., *Changing the Economic System in Russia*, London, Pinter, 1993, pp. 210–229.

Boughton, James M., "The Economics of the CFA Franc Zone," in Masson and Taylor, *Policy Issues in the Operation of Currency Unions*, 1993, pp. 96–107.

Broder, Ernst-Gunther, "EMU—Acceleration or Collapse? Honorary President's Opening Address," *The European Finance Convention and Ecu Week*, Special Issue (1992), pp. 9–13.

Bruno, Michael, and Jeffrey D. Sachs, *Economics of Worldwide Stagflation*, Cambridge, Mass., Harvard University Press; Oxford, Blackwell, 1985.

Buiter, Willem H., "Should We Worry About the Fiscal Numerology of Maastricht," CEPR Discussion Paper No. 668, London, Centre for Economic Policy Research, June 1992.

Buiter, Willem H., and Kenneth M. Kletzer, "Fiscal Implications of a Common Currency," in Alberto Giovannini and Colin Mayer, eds., *European Financial Integration*, Cambridge and New York, Cambridge University Press, 1991. pp. 221–244.

Centre for European Policy Studies (CEPS), "European Payment Systems and EMU," CEPS Working Party Report No. 11, Brussels, Centre for European Policy Studies, April 1994.

Chown, John, and Geoffrey Wood, "Russia's Currency—How the West can Help," *Central Banking*, 3 (Winter 1992–93), pp. 39–46.

Clifford Chance, Inc. "Legal Aspects of the ECU as a Single Currency for Europe," London, Clifford Chance, Inc., October 1992, processed.

Cohen, Benjamin J., "Beyond EMU: The Problem of Sustainability," *Economics and Politics*, 5 (July 1993a), pp. 187–203.

———, "The Triad and the Unholy Trinity: Lessons for the Pacific Region," in Richard A. Higgott, Richard Leaver, and John Ravenhill, eds., *Pacific Economic Relations in the 1990's: Conflict or Cooperation*, Sydney, Allen and Unwin, 1993b, pp. 133–158.

Cohen, Daniel, and Charles Wyplosz, "The European Monetary Union: An Agnostic Evaluation," in Ralph C. Bryant, David A. Currie, Jacob A. Frenkel, Paul R. Masson, and Richard Portes, eds., *Macroeconomic Policies in an Interdependent World*, Washington D.C., Brookings Institution, Centre for Economic Policy Research, and International Monetary Fund, 1989, pp. 311–337.

Collins, Susan M., and Dani Rodrik, *Eastern Europe and the Soviet Union in the World Economy*, Policy Analyses in International Economics No. 32, Washington, D.C., Institute for International Economics, May 1991.

Commission of the European Communities, *Report of the Study Group on the Role of Public Finance in European Integration* [MacDougall Report], Luxembourg, Office for Official Publications of the European Communities, 1977.

———, "One Market, One Money: An Evaluation of the Potential Benefits and Costs of Forming an Economic and Monetary Union," *European Economy*, No. 44 (1990).

———, "Easier Cross-Border Payment, Breaking Down the Barriers," Commission Working Document, March 1992a.

———, Directorate-General Financial Institutions and Company Law, "Report of the Payment Systems Users Liaison Group to Sir Leon Brittan," February 14, 1992b.

———, Directorate-General Financial Institutions and Company Law, "Report of the Payment Systems Technical Development Group to Sir Leon Brittan," February 20, 1992c.

———, Directorate-General for Economic and Financial Affairs, "Stable Money—Sound Finances," *European Economy*, No. 53 (1993).

Committee for the Study of Economic and Monetary Union, *Report on Economic and Monetary Union in the European Community* [Delors Report], Luxembourg, Office for Official Publications of the European Communities, 1989.

Committee of Governors of the Central Banks of the Member States of the European Economic Community, "Issues of Common Concern to EC Central Banks in the Field of Payments," Report of the Ad Hoc Working Group on EC Payment Systems [the Padoa-Schioppa Group], September 1992.

———, *Annual Report 1992*, Basle, April 1993.

Council of the European Communities, *Report to the Council and the Commission on the Realisation by Stages of Economic and Monetary Union in the Community* [Werner Report], Supplement to Bulletin II-1970 of the European Communities, Luxembourg, Office for Official Publications of the European Communities, 1970.

Council of the European Communities and Commission of the European Communities, *Treaty on European Union* [Maastricht Treaty], Luxembourg, Office for Official Publications of the European Communities, 1992.

Courchene, Thomas J., "Reflections on Canadian Federation: Are There Implications for European Economic and Monetary Union?" paper presented at Conference on Public Finance and the Future of Europe, London School of Economics, September 21, 1992, processed.

Currie, David A., "European Monetary Union: Institutional Structure and Economic Performance," *Economic Journal* (London), 102 (March 1992), pp. 248–264.

De Benedictis, Luca, and Pier Carlo Padoan, "The Integration of Eastern Europe into the EC: A Club Theory-Interest Groups Approach," CIDEI Working Paper No. 9, Università di Roma, "La Sapienza," November 1991; forthcoming in Siro Lombardini and Pier Carlo Padoan, eds., *Europe between East and South*, Aldershot, Kluwer, 1994.

De Grauwe, Paul, and Hilde Heens, "Real Exchange Rate Variability in Monetary Unions," *Recherches Economiques de Louvain*, 59 (No. 1–2, 1993), pp. 105–117.

De Grauwe, Paul, and Wim Vanhaverbeke, "Is Europe an Optimum Currency Area? Evidence from Regional Data," in Masson and Taylor, *Policy Issues in the Operation of Currency Unions*, 1993, pp. 111–129.

de Largentaye, Bertrand R., "In the Light of the Disquieting Experiences of September and October 1992, Can the ECU Zone Still Be Said to Hold Some Lessons for the Countries of the Former Soviet Union?" *The European Finance Convention and Ecu Week*, Special Issue (1992), pp. 122–124.

De Nardis, Sergio, and Stefano Micossi, "Disinflation and Re-inflation in Italy and the Implications for Transition to Monetary Union," *Banca Nazionale del Lavoro Quarterly Review*, 177 (June 1991), pp. 165–196.

De Vecchis, Pietro, "Moneta e carta valori. Profili generale e divitto privato," *Enciclopedia Giuridica Treccani*, 1990.

Dornbusch, Rudiger, "The European Monetary System, the Dollar and the Yen," in Giavazzi, Micossi, and Miller, *The European Monetary System*, 1988, pp. 23–41.

Doyle, Maurice F., "Regional Policy and European Economic Integration," in Committee for the Study of Economic and Monetary Union, *Report on Economic and Monetary Union in the European Community*, Collection of Papers, Luxembourg, Office for Official Publications of the European Communities, 1989, pp. 69–80.

Drèze, Jacques, and Charles R. Bean, "European Unemployment: Lessons from a Multicountry Econometric Study," *Scandinavian Journal of Economics*, 92 (No. 2, 1990), pp. 135–165.

Eichengreen, Barry, "Costs and Benefits of European Monetary Unification," CEPR Discussion Paper No. 453, London, Centre for Economic Policy Research, September 1990.

———, *Golden Fetters: The Gold Standard and the Great Depression, 1919–1939*, New York, Oxford University Press, 1992a.

———, "Is Europe an Optimum Currency Area?" in Silvio Borner and Herbert

Grubel, eds., *The European Community after 1992: Perspectives from the Outside*, Basingstoke, Hampshire, Macmillan, 1992b, pp. 138–161.

———, *Should the Maastricht Treaty Be Saved?* Princeton Studies in International Finance No. 74, Princeton, N.J., Princeton University, International Finance Section, December 1992c.

———, "Labor Markets and European Monetary Unification," in Masson and Taylor, *Policy Issues in the Operation of Currency Unions*, 1993, pp. 130–162.

Feldstein, Martin, "Europe's Monetary Union: The Case against EMU," *The Economist*, June 13–19, 1992, pp. 19–22.

Fischer, Stanley, "Seigniorage and the Case for a National Money," *Journal of Political Economy*, 90 (April 1982), pp. 295–313.

Forte, Francesco, "Principles for the Assignment of Public Economic Functions in a Setting of Multi-Layer Government," in Commission of the European Communities, *Report of the Study Group on the Role of Public Finance in European Integration*, Vol. 2, Luxembourg, Office for Official Publications of the European Communities, 1977.

Fraser, Patricia, and Ronald MacDonald, "European Excess Stock Returns and Capital Market Integration: An Empirical Perspective," in Masson and Taylor, *Policy Issues in the Operation of Currency Unions*, 1993, pp. 163–211.

Fratianni, Michele, and Jürgen von Hagen, "Public Choice Aspects of European Monetary Unification," *Cato Journal*, 10 (Fall 1990), pp. 389–411.

Fratianni Michele, Jürgen von Hagen, and Christopher Waller, *The Maastricht Way to EMU*, Essays in International Finance No. 187, Princeton, N.J., Princeton University, International Finance Section, June 1992.

Giavazzi, Francesco, "The Exchange Rate Question in Europe," in Ralph C. Bryant, David A. Currie, Jacob A. Frenkel, Paul R. Masson, and Richard Portes, eds., *Macroeconomic Policies in an Interdependent World*, Washington D.C., Brookings Institution, Centre for Economic Policy Research, and International Monetary Fund, 1989, pp. 283–304.

Giavazzi, Francesco, and Alberto Giovannini, *Limiting Exchange Rate Flexibility: The European Monetary System*, Cambridge, Mass., MIT Press, 1989.

Giavazzi, Francesco, Stefano Micossi, and Marcus H. Miller, eds., *The European Monetary System*, Cambridge and New York, Cambridge University Press, 1988.

Giersch, Herbert et al., "Manifesto against EMU," open letter to the *Frankfurter Allgemeine Zeitung*, June 11, 1992.

Giovannini, Alberto, "The Currency Reform as the Last Stage of Economic and Monetary Union, Some Policy Questions," CEPR Discussion Paper No. 591, London, Centre for Economic Policy Research, October 1991.

———, "Central Banking in a Monetary Union: Reflections on the Proposed Statute of the European Central Bank," *Carnegie-Rochester Conference Series on Public Policy*, 38 (Spring 1992a).

———, "Desirable EMU," letter to *The Economist*, July 11–17, 1992b, p. 6.

———, "Comments on Goodhart and Bryant," prepared for the Conference on The International Monetary System: What We Know and Need to Know, Princeton University, April 15–16, 1993, processed.

Glasner, David, *Free Banking and Monetary Reform*, Cambridge and New York, Cambridge University Press, 1989.

Goodhart, Charles A. E., "The ESCB after Maastricht," in Charles A. E. Goodhart, ed., *EMU and ESCB after Maastricht*, London School of Economics, Financial Markets Group, 1992a, pp. 180–215.

———, "The External Dimension of EMU," *Recherches Economique de Louvain*, 59 (No. 1–2, 1993), pp. 65–80; also in Goodhart, *EMU and ESCB after Maastricht*, 1992b, pp. 315–335.

Goodhart, Charles A. E., and Stephen Smith, "Stabilisation," *European Economy*, Reports and Studies, No. 5 (1993), pp. 417–455.

Griffiths, Mark, "Monetary Union in Europe: Lessons from the Nineteenth Century— An Assessment of the Latin Monetary Union," 1992, processed (cited in Cohen, 1993a).

Grilli, Vittorio, "Seigniorage in Europe," in Marcello de Cecco and Alberto Giovannini, eds., *A European Central Bank? Perspectives on Monetary Unification After Ten Years of the EMS*, Cambridge and New York, Cambridge University Press, 1989, pp. 53–79.

Gros, Daniel, "A Soviet Payments Union?" Brussels, Centre for European Policy Studies, October 1991, processed.

———, "Costs and Benefits of Economic and Monetary Union: An Application to the Former Soviet Union," in Masson and Taylor, *Policy Issues in the Operation of Currency Unions*, 1993, pp. 55–74.

Gros, Daniel, and Niels Thygesen, *European Monetary Integration: From the European Monetary System to European Monetary Union*, London, Longman; New York, St. Martin's, 1992.

Hanke, Steve H., and Kurt Schuler, "Keynes and Currency Reform: Some Lessons for Eastern Europe," *Journal of Economic Growth*, 4 (No. 2, 1990), pp. 10–16.

———, "Currency Boards for Eastern Europe," *The Heritage Lectures*, No. 355, Washington, D.C., Heritage Foundation, 1991.

Hanke, Steve H., Lars Jonung, and Kurt Schuler, *Russian Currency and Finance: A Currency Board Approach to Reform*, London and New York, Routledge, 1993.

Hansson, Ardo H., "The Trouble with the Ruble: Monetary Reform in the Former Soviet Union," in Anders Åslund and Richard Layard, eds., *Changing the Economic System in Russia*, London, Pinter, 1993, pp. 163–182.

Havrylyshyn, Oleh, and John Williamson, *From Soviet DisUnion to Eastern Economic Community*, Policy Analyses in International Economics No. 35, Washington, D.C., Institute for International Economics, October 1991.

H.M. Treasury, *An Evolutionary Approach to Economic and Monetary Union*, London, Her Majesty's Stationary Office, November 1989.

Holtfrerich, Carl-Ludwig, "The Monetary Unification Process in Nineteenth-Century Germany, Relevance and Lessons for Europe Today," in Marcello de Cecco and Alberto Giovannini, eds., *A European Central Bank? Perspectives on Monetary Unification After Ten Years of the EMS*, Cambridge, Cambridge University Press, 1988, pp. 216–243.

———, "Did Monetary Unification Precede or Follow Political Unification of Germany in the 19th Century?" paper presented at the European Economic Association Conference, Dublin, August 1992.

Horn, Gustav A., and Rudolph Zwiener, "Wage Regimes in a United Europe: A Simulation Study on QUEST," in Ray Barrell and John Whitley, eds., *Macroeconomic Policy Coordination in Europe*, London, Sage, 1992, pp. 83–101.

Hughes Hallett, Andrew, and David Vines, "On the Possible Costs of European Monetary Union," *Manchester School Journal*, 61 (March 1993), pp. 35–64.

Italianer, Alexander, and Marc Vanheukelen, "Proposals for Community Stabilisation Mechanisms: Some Historical Applications," paper presented at the Conference on Public Finance and the Future of Europe, London School of Economics, September 21, 1992, processed.

Kenen, Peter B., "The Theory of Optimum Currency Areas: An Eclectic View," in Robert A. Mundell and Alexander K. Swoboda, eds., *Monetary Problems of the International Economy*, Chicago and London, University of Chicago Press, 1969, pp. 41–60.

———, *EMU After Maastricht*, Washington, D.C., Group of Thirty, 1992a.

———, "Rescue 911: Is There an EMU Doctor in the House?," *International Economy*, November-December 1992b, pp. 57–59.

———, "EMU, Exchange Rates, and the International Monetary System," *Recherches Economiques de Louvain*, 59 (No. 1–2, 1993), pp. 257–281.

Keohane, Robert O., *After Hegemony: Cooperation and Discord in the World Political Economy*, Princeton, N.J., Princeton University Press, 1984.

Knoester, Anthonie, André Kolodziejak, and Guus Muijzers, "Economic Policy and European Integration," Research Memorandum 9001, Department of Applied Economics, Nijmegen, Netherlands, 1990; reprinted in Ernst Baltensperger and Hans-Werner Sinn, eds., *Exchange Rate Regimes and Currency Unions*, New York, St. Martin's, 1992, pp. 248–184.

Krugman, Paul R., "Lessons of Massachusetts for EMU," in Francisco Torres and Francesco Giavazzi, eds., *Adjustment and Growth in the European Monetary Union*, Cambridge and New York, Cambridge University Press, 1993, pp. 241–269.

Layard, Richard, Stephen Nickell, and Richard Jackman, *Unemployment: Macroeconomic Performance and the Labour Market*, Oxford and New York, Oxford University Press, 1991.

Lehment, Harmen, and Joachim Scheide, "Die europäische Wirtschafts—und Währungsunion: Probleme des Übergangs," *Die Weltwirtschaft*, No. 1 (March 1992), pp. 50–67.

Leijonhufvud, Axel, "High Inflations and Contemporary Monetary Theory," *Economic Notes* (Monte dei Paschi di Siena), 21 (1992), pp. 211–224.

Levitt, Malcolm, "EMU—the Next Steps," *The European Finance Convention and Ecu Week*, Special Issue (1992a), pp. 27–33.

———, ed., "How to Prepare Companies for European Monetary Union," *De Pecunia* (Report of the Association for Monetary Union of Europe), Special Issue (June 1992b), pp. 1–72.

Maastricht Treaty, see Council, 1992.

McKinnon, Ronald I., "Optimum Currency Areas," *American Economic Review*, 53 (September 1963), pp. 717–724.

Malo de Molina, Jose L., "The Peripheral Countries in the Face of European Monetary Union," *The European Finance Convention and Ecu Week*, Special Issue (1992), pp. 21–26.

Martin, Lisa L., "International and Domestic Institutions in the EMU Process," *Economics and Politics*, 5 (July 1993), pp. 125–144.

Masera, Rainer S., "Single Market, Exchange Rates and Monetary Unification,"

503

Osservatorio e Centro di Studi Monetari, Quaderni di Ricerca, No. 25, Rome, Libera Università Internazionale degli Studi Sociali (LUISS), December 1992.

Masson, Paul R., and Mark P. Taylor, "Currency Unions: A Survey of the Issues," in Paul R. Masson and Mark P. Taylor, eds., *Policy Issues in the Operation of Currency Unions*, Cambridge and New York, Cambridge University Press, 1993, pp. 3–51.

Mazzaferro, Francesco, "Unity through Diversity: Bank Notes and Coins in the European Monetary Union," San Paolo, San Paolo Bank Holding, Research and Strategies Unit, 1992, processed.

Melitz, Jacques, "Monetary Discipline and Cooperation in the European Monetary System: A Synthesis," in Giavazzi, Micossi, and Miller, *The European Monetary System*, 1988, pp. 51–79.

———, "Brussels on a Single Money," *Open Economies Review*, 2 (1991a), pp. 323–336.

———, "A Suggested Reformulation of the Theory of Optimal Currency Areas," CEPR Discussion Paper No. 590, London, Centre for Economic Policy Research, October 1991b.

———, "A Multilateral Approach to the Theory of Optimal Currency Areas," INSEE Working Paper No. 9305, Paris, Institut National de la Statistique at des Etudes Economiques, February 1993a.

———, "Reflections on the Emergence of a Single Market for Bank Reserves in a European Monetary Union," CEPR Discussion Paper No. 818, London, Centre for Economic Policy Research, July 1993b.

Melitz, Jacques, and Silvia Vori, "National Insurance against Unevenly Distributed Shocks in a European Monetary Union," paper presented at the Conference on Public Finance and the Future of Europe, London School of Economics, September 21, 1992, processed.

Micossi, Stefano, and Giuseppe Tullio, "Fiscal Imbalances, Economic Distortions, and the Long-Run Performance of the Italian Economy," paper prepared for the International Workshop on Global Macroeconomic Perspectives, Rome, May 29–30, 1991, processed.

Monticelli, Carlo, and José Viñals, "European Monetary Policy in Stage Three: What Are the Issues?" CEPR Occasional Paper No. 12, London, Centre for Economic Policy Research, March 1993.

Mundell, Robert A., "A Theory of Optimum Currency Areas," *American Economic Review*, 51 (September 1961), pp. 657–664.

Neumann, J. Manfred, "In die Ära der Euro-Mark," *Frankfurter Allgemeine Zeitung*, December 25, 1992.

Newlyn, Walter T., and David C. Rowan, *Money and Banking in British Colonial Africa: A Study of the Monetary and Banking Systems of Eight British African Territories*, Oxford, Clarendon, 1954.

Oates, Wallace E., *Fiscal Federalism*, New York, Harcourt Brace Jovanovich, 1972.

Odling-Smee, John, Grant H. Spencer, and Paul S. Ross, "Common Issues and Interrepublic Relations in the Former U.S.S.R.," *Economic Review*, Washington, D.C., International Monetary Fund, April 1992.

Padoan, Pier C., and Marcello Pericoli, "Single Market EMU and Widening: Responses to Three Institutional Shocks in the European Community," Discussion Paper No. 8, Department of Economics, Università degli Studi di Trento, December 1992.

Panić, Milivoje, *European Monetary Union: Lessons from the Classical Gold Standard*, New York, St. Martin's; London, Macmillan, 1992.

Persson, Torsten, and Guido Tabellini, "Federal Fiscal Constitutions. Part 1. Risk Sharing and Moral Hazard," CEPR Discussion Paper No. 728, London, Centre for Economic Policy Research, October 1992a.

———, "The Politics of 1992: Fiscal Policy and European Integration," *Review of Economic Studies*, 59 (October 1992b), pp. 689–702.

Pisani-Ferry, Jean, Alexander Italianer, and Roland Lescure, "Stabilization Properties of Budgetary Systems: A Simulation Analysis," *European Economy*, Reports and Studies, No. 5 (1993), pp. 511–538.

Pissarides, Christopher, and Ian McMaster, "Regional Migration, Wages and Unemployment: Empirical Evidence and Implications for Policy," *Oxford Economic Papers*, 42 (October 1990), pp. 812–831.

Poloz, Stephen S., "Real Exchange Rate Adjustment between Regions in a Common Currency Area," in Victor Argy and Paul De Grauwe, eds., *Choosing an Exchange Rate Regime: The Challenge for Smaller Industrial Countries*, Washington, D.C., International Monetary Fund, 1990, pp. 374–377.

Prud'homme, Rémy, "The Potential Role of the EC Budget in the Reduction of Spatial Disparities in a European Economic and Monetary Union," *European Economy*, Reports and Studies, No. 5 (1993), pp. 317–351.

Richards, O. Paul, "The Case for an Evolutionary Stage 2," London, Samuel Montagu, July 1990, processed.

Sachs, Jeffrey D., and David Lipton, "Remaining Steps to a Market-Based Monetary System in Russia," in Anders Åslund and Richard Layard, eds., *Changing the Economic System in Russia*, London, Pinter, 1993, pp. 127–162.

Sala-i-Martin, Xavier, and Jeffrey D. Sachs, "Fiscal Federalism and Optimum Currency Areas: Evidence for Europe from the United States," in Matthew B. Canzoneri, Vittorio Grilli, and Paul R. Masson, eds., *Establishing a Central Bank: Issues in Europe and Lessons from the US*, Cambridge and New York, Cambridge University Press, 1992, pp. 195–219.

Schnadt, Norbert, The Domestic Money Markets of the U.K., France, Germany and the U.S., Subject Report No. 7, Paper 1, City Research Project, London Business School, January 1994.

Schneider, Friedrich, "The Federal and Fiscal Structures of Representative and Direct Democracies as a Model for European Federal Union," *European Economy*, Reports and Studies, No. 5 (1993), pp. 191–212.

Sentana, Enrique, Mushtaq Shah, and Sushil Wadhwani, "Has the EMS Reduced the Cost of Capital?" Discussion Paper No. 134, London School of Economics, Financial Markets Group, March 1992.

Skorov, Georgy, "From Economic Reform to Hyperinflation," *Central Banking*, 3 (Winter 1992–93), pp. 28–38.

Spahn, P. Bernd, "The Case for EMU: A European View," Working Paper No. 29, Faculty of Economics, Johann Wolfgang Goethe Universität, Frankfurt, August 1992.

Steinherr, Alfred, "The Role of the ECU on the Way to EMU," *The European Finance Convention and Ecu Week*, Special Issue (1992), pp. 54–60.

Tresch, Richard, *Public Finance: A Normative Theory*, Plano, Tex., Business Publications, 1981.

van der Ploeg, Frederick, "Macroeconomic Policy Coordination Issues during the Various Phases of Economic and Monetary Integration in Europe," *European Economy*, Special Issue No. 1 (1991), pp. 136–164.

Van Rompuy, Paul, Filip Abraham, and Dirk Heremans, "Economic Federalism and the EMU," *European Economy*, Special Issue No. 1 (1991), pp. 109–135.

von Hagen, Jürgen, "Fiscal Arrangements in a Monetary Union—Evidence from the US," in Donald E. Fair and Christian de Boissieu, eds., *Fiscal Policy, Taxation and the Financial System in an Increasingly Integrated Europe*, Dordrecht and Boston, Kluwer, 1992, pp. 337–359.

————, "Monetary Union and Fiscal Union: A Perspective from Fiscal Federalism," in Masson and Taylor, *Policy Issues in the Operation of Currency Unions*, 1993, pp. 264–296.

Waigel, Theo, "Kein Esperanto Geld—EZB sollte nach Deutschland," *Handelsblatt*, March 24, 1992.

Walsh, Brendan, "The Irish Pound and the ERM: Lessons from the September Crisis and Its Aftermath," paper prepared for the Academic Working Group of the Association for the Monetary Union of Europe, London, April/May 1993, processed.

Walsh, Cliff, "Fiscal Federalism: An Overview of Issues and a Discussion of Their Relevance to the European Community," paper presented at the Conference on Public Finance and the Future of Europe, London School of Economics, September 21, 1992, processed.

Walters, Alan A., and Steve H. Hanke, "Currency Boards," in Peter Newman, Murray Milgate, and John Eatwell, eds., *The New Palgrave Dictionary of Money and Finance*, London, Macmillan; New York, Stockton, 1992, pp. 558–561.

Williamson, John, ed., *The Economic Consequences of Soviet Disintegration*, Washington, D.C., Institute for International Economics, 1992a.

————, *Trade and Payments after Soviet Disintegration*, Policy Analyses in International Economics No. 37, Washington, D.C., Institute for International Economics, June 1992b.

Wolf, Holger C., "Economic Disintegration: Are There Cures?," in Richard O'Brien, ed., *Finance and the International Economy*, Amex Bank Review Prize Essays, Vol. 6, Oxford, Oxford University Press, 1992, pp. 46–60.

Wood, Geoffrey E., "One Money for Europe?," *Journal of Monetary Economics*, 25 March 1990), pp. 313–322.

VI

CONCLUSION

13

What Do We Need to Know about the International Monetary System?

PAUL R. KRUGMAN

1 Introduction

Frank Graham is today best known for his work in the pure, that is, nonmonetary, theory of international trade. His most famous paper is surely "Some Aspects of Protection Further Considered" (Graham 1923). This paper anticipated many of the themes that I and others have pursued under the unfortunate name of the "new trade theory," and it did so with such insight that reading it makes one wonder whether the rest of us were necessary.

Yet Graham knew that trade takes place in a monetary world, and, unlike many real-trade theorists, he did not retreat from confronting the messier and less secure terrain of international monetary affairs. It is surely appropriate that, at a conference honoring the fiftieth anniversary of Essays in International Finance, I should commend to you Essay No. 2, Graham's (1943) thoughtful discussion of the troubled choice between fixed and floating exchange rates—an issue that I shall argue remains at the heart of what we need to know in international monetary economics.

It is especially fitting for me to refer to the great Graham tradition in international economics, for I shall have a lot to say during this lecture about the virtues of traditional insights and approaches to international monetary economics. I shall not merely celebrate the past, however, but shall begin with a very recent event: the crisis that gripped the European Monetary System (EMS) only eight months ago, in September 1992.

2 Silver Linings in a European Cloud

A few days after a massive speculative attack forced the United Kingdom to pull the pound out of the Exchange Rate Mechanism (ERM) of the EMS,

This chapter is a slightly adjusted version of a monograph by the same title published as Essays in International Finance No. 190, July 1993, copyright © 1993, by the International Finance Section at Princeton University.

Chancellor of the Exchequer Norman Lamont denied that the events represented a policy defeat. He claimed that he had always regarded the defense of a fixed parity as a mistake (although, right up to the day of the debacle, he had asserted Britain's absolute commitment to the ERM), and he went so far as to say that after the pound was freed from its peg to the mark, he had been "singing in the bath" with relief.

I don't know whether the chancellor was actually singing in the bath or whether he was doing so more than usual. I can say, however, that, in late September of 1992, I myself was feeling pretty cheerful. Not that I wished the EMS harm; but the way the events of Black September unfolded encouraged me in my belief that we international macroeconomists do in fact know a thing or two.

It is a slightly shameful but true observation that economists interested in policy find themselves pleasantly stimulated by economic crisis, just as professional military men are somewhat cheered by the prospect of war. This is particularly true when the events are dramatic without being too threatening in a personal sense: I have never seen as many happy people at the National Bureau of Economic Research as I did during the first few days after the 1987 stock market crash. There is extra satisfaction when the crisis is one that you and your friends think you understand, and to be around when a crisis that you have predicted actually comes to pass is very heaven.

The ERM crisis of September was one that many of us thought we understood quite well indeed, and one that at least some of us had predicted well in advance. (For the record: I wrote a column in *U.S. News and World Report* in February 1991, predicting that the fiscal consequences of German reunification would create strains on the EMS and force a realignment; of course I won't tell you about all the crises I predicted that *didn't* materialize). The story of the rise and partial fall of the EMS is deeply satisfying to tell, because it fits so well into the standard, workhorse models that most of us use to discuss international macroeconomic policy. The whole episode seems like a kind of textbook exercise designed to lead the student through the workings of a basic model of exchange rates, interest rates, and policy interdependence. (Indeed, I can guarantee that for a while, at least, the troubles of the EMS will be viewed as precisely such a textbook case; after all, Obstfeld and I [1991] write the textbook!)

The events of September, then, confirmed me in the view that we do, in fact, know quite a lot about the international monetary system. To be sure, our quantitative accuracy is limited. But, in a basic sense, we do know how monetary and fiscal policy work in open economies, and we know how they are transmitted internationally under fixed and floating exchange rates. This knowledge was enough to enable us to predict correctly that the combination of fiscal expansion and tight money in Europe's key currency nation would create a recession in the rest of the continent. And we knew enough about the behavior of exchange markets to anticipate correctly that the breakdown of the system under these strains would be attended by massive speculative attacks (a point that gives me extra pleasure, for I have some personal intellectual property rights in such attacks).

So the policy debacle of 1992 was intellectually reassuring. I was certainly not the only economist who, behind his serious expressions of concern, was thinking "Ha! Told you so!" And yet, even the intellectual satisfaction was not unalloyed. We may know a lot about the international monetary system, but we cannot rest easy with that knowledge. Indeed, hardly anyone is pleased with the state of our field.

One reason for our discontent is that the standard model that so nicely explains the ERM crisis works better in practice than it does in theory. It is essentially a slightly updated version of the Mundell-Fleming model, which is rooted in the kind of old-fashioned, *ad hoc* macroeconomics that nobody respects anymore. It is a short-run model that has never been clearly linked to the long-run stories we use to explain both trade and capital flows. And it is ugly. In Stephen Weinberg's book, *Dreams of a Final Theory* (1992), Weinberg asserts that theories should be beautiful, and that a theory is beautiful if it seems "inevitable," that is, if none of its assumptions can be changed without compromising its entire conceptual basis. By this measure, the standard model of international macroeconomics is exceedingly homely. It involves a set of plausible, but by no means overwhelmingly compelling, assumptions; indeed, some key parameters of the model do not seem to be tied down by any deep economic logic. It is better to use an ugly model that seems to work than to insist on beautiful falsehoods, but modified Mundell-Fleming does not comfort the economist's soul.

Worse yet, the standard model leaves some crucial questions unanswered. We understand pretty well what Britain gained by dropping out of the ERM. We can even hope to make a rough quantitative estimate of the value of the monetary autonomy obtained by abandoning the fixed parity. But what did Britain lose by letting its rate float? What would it be worth to Europe if, despite the odds, the Maastricht Treaty were somehow to succeed in producing a unified European currency? We have some suggestive phrases—reduced transactions costs, improvement in the quality of the unit of account—to describe what we think are the benefits of fixed rates and common currencies. We even have a loose-jointed theory of optimum currency areas that stresses the tension between these hypothesized benefits of fixity and the more measurable costs of lost monetary autonomy. What we do not have, however, is anything we can properly call a model of the benefits of fixed rates and common currencies.

This is an unsatisfactory situation. I would suggest that the issue of optimum currency areas, or, more broadly, that of choosing an exchange regime, should be regarded as the central intellectual question of international monetary economics. We have formulated this question well enough to agree that it is a matter of trading off macroeconomic flexibility against microeconomic efficiency. Unfortunately, we are not completely happy with the way we model the macroeconomic side, and we have no way at all at present to model the microeconomics.

I shall eventually argue in this lecture that developing some kind of model of the microeconomics of international money ought to be our top research priority. Most of the lecture, however, will be spent on a different issue: that of defining what it is that we actually do know about the international monetary system. Unfortunately, macroeconomics in general, and international economics in particular, is a field marked by deep ideological divisions and much mutual incomprehension. It is hard to hold on to the things that we actually do know, let alone expand our territory. My initial task will therefore be to try to make a map, to sketch out the border between what I think we know and what I am sure we do not know about the international monetary system.

3 What I Think We Know

In a recent essay (1991), I used the term "Mass. Ave. model" to describe the slightly updated version of the Mundell-Fleming model that is the workhorse of international-policy analysis. Let me use a different term here and call it "modified-Mundell-Fleming," or "MMF" for short. (I guess that's pronounced "mmph.") A typical version of MMF looks something like the following:

First, we assume a Keynesian demand-side determination of output, in which real output y (in terms of some composite domestic good) is the sum of domestic absorption A and net exports NX:

$$y = A(y, i - \pi) + NX , \qquad (1)$$

where i is the interest rate and π is the expected rate of inflation.

We also assume a standard LM curve:

$$M/P = L(y, i) , \qquad (2)$$

where M is the money supply and P the domestic price level.

Prices are assumed to be sticky. In the original Mundell-Fleming model, they were simply taken as given; in the MMF model, inflation is determined by the difference between real output and the "natural" level y^N, and on the expected inflation rate π:

$$\dot{P}/P = \phi(y - y^N) + \pi , \qquad (3)$$

and expected inflation is assumed to adjust only slowly in response to actual inflation:

$$\dot{\pi} = \lambda(\dot{P}/P - \pi) . \tag{4}$$

All of this is just standard early 1970s macroeconomics. The specifically international side of the model comes in the determination of net exports and the exchange rate. We assume export and import equations that depend on incomes and relative prices, so that the net-export equation looks something like this:

$$NX = NX(y, y^*, EP^*/P) , \tag{5}$$

where y^* is foreign output, E is the exchange rate, and P^* is the foreign price level.

In the original Mundell-Fleming model, international arbitrage was assumed to equalize interest rates. In MMF, we need something that is not so obviously untrue. A typical assumption is that markets expect the real exchange rate to revert toward some "normal" level, e^E, and that they set the expected return on domestic and foreign interest-bearing assets as equal:

$$i = i^* + \pi - \pi^* + \gamma[\ln(e^E) - \ln(EP^*/P)] . \tag{6}$$

I am not going to do anything with these equations. I put them here just to give some concreteness to what I mean when I talk about the standard model of international macroeconomics. I think it is fair to say that something like this model underlies most informed policy discussion of exchange rates, macroeconomic interdependence, balance-of-payments adjustment, and so on.

Of course, each of us would like to make a few changes in the details. The aggregate-demand equation is far too simple: all sorts of other factors should be included as determinants of expenditure. The LM curve is nastier than I have written it, especially given the problem of defining a useful monetary aggregate. The net-export equation definitely needs some lagged effects for the real exchange rate, and it should probably be so constructed as to yield a J-curve. Some people would want to include risk premia in the exchange-rate equation, so as to allow some scope for the effectiveness of sterilized intervention. More broadly, the assumption of perfect capital mobility is questionable. As Obstfeld points out in Chapter 6, there are substantial questions about the degree of long-run capital mobility even for advanced countries. Dooley's paper (Chapter 7) is a reminder that many developing countries were simply shut out of international capital markets for a decade. These are all, however, technical adjustments; they do not challenge the fundamental conceptual basis of the model.

There are many economists—although few of them actually engaged in making policy recommendations—who *would* challenge the fundamental conception. Indeed, a substantial number of economists regard the MMF model as pure nonsense. I shall get to those criticisms in a little while. First, however, I want to spend some time pointing out that the most controversial aspects of the MMF model have actually held up rather well in the face of recent experience.

In terms of the philosophical underpinnings, the most troublesome aspect of the MMF model has nothing to do with international economics. It is the assumption of gradual price adjustment. Indeed, by the early 1980s, after years of relentless criticism from Lucas and his followers, it had become inadvisable to write down anything like my equations (3) and (4) in a paper intended for a refereed journal. Yet this old-fashioned, *ad hoc* approach to aggregate supply has in fact fared rather well in the face of the actual experience of price behavior since 1980. We can see this in two ways.

First, "adaptive-expectations" Phillips curves do not do badly in fitting the actual interplay between the business cycle and inflation. Figure 13.1 shows a crude illustration of this point. It compares the U.S. rate of unemployment on an annual basis with the *change* in the inflation rate (measured by the GDP deflator) since 1973. The relation is far from perfect—I could no doubt do much better by playing with lag structures and demographically corrected unemployment rates—but two things are unmistakable: there is a negative correlation between the rate of unemployment and the change in the inflation rate, and the slope is not all that steep. That is, the picture is broadly consistent with the idea that there is a fairly flat short-run tradeoff between inflation and unemployment, but a vertical tradeoff in the long run. The important point is that this picture, some version of which has been appearing in textbooks since the late 1970s, still looks pretty good after all these years.

A second, crisper test of the idea of sluggish price adjustment comes from the relation between nominal and real exchange rates. During the 1970s, at the same time that new classical macroeconomic theorists were challenging the legitimacy of assuming nominal rigidities in domestic macroeconomics, "monetary-approach" international economists were asserting that it was unacceptable to assume that nominal-exchange-rate changes had any real effect: the exchange rate was the relative price of two moneys, not of two goods. In fact, however, the experience of the post-1980 period has been one of extremely high correlation between nominal and real exchange rates. Figure 13.2 makes the point for the United States: the nominal- and real-exchange-rate indexes have moved almost perfectly together.

The other highly controversial part of the MMF model is the assumed linkage between the real exchange rate and net exports. This relation has been questioned from at least two sides. On one side are those whom I have elsewhere called "structuralists," usually noneconomists who insist that trade def-

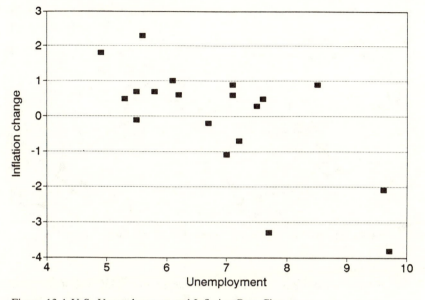

Figure 13.1 U.S. Unemployment and Inflation-Rate Change

icits are rooted in structural causes and cannot be cured by depreciation. On the other are those who like to think of trade imbalances as the result of an intertemporal maximization and who find the assertion of a simple partial-equilibrium relation between real exchange rates and the trade balance unacceptable. I shall not bother with the structuralists in this lecture but shall take the intertemporal approach more seriously. For now, let me simply point out that, in a gross, crude way, U.S. external adjustment since 1980 has seemed to confirm the idea that real exchange rates work the way that the standard model says they should. Figure 13.3 makes the point by comparing U.S. export growth with that of Japan and Germany over the 1982–87 and 1987–91 periods. (In each case, we begin the period two years after the trough and peak in the dollar, to allow for lags in adjustment). During the first, strong-dollar, period, U.S. exports stagnated; during the second, weak-dollar, period, they soared. Of course, one can offer other explanations, but, on the face of it, dollar depreciation seems to have done just what it is supposed to do.

My point, then, is that a framework something like the model described in equations (1) through (6) seems quite useful. Or, to put it another way, what we know about the international monetary system is that we seem to be able to track its performance and predict the outcomes of policy fairly well using a framework similar to the one I have described here. That does not mean that the framework is the last word. In fact, it is far too ugly and *ad hoc* to be our final theory on the subject. Still, when it comes to the issue that this framework addresses, we do seem to know quite a lot.

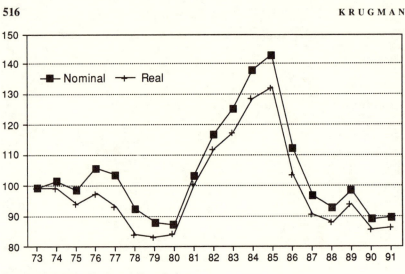

Figure 13.2 U.S. Exchange-Rate Indexes

Nonetheless, the MMF model has been subject to a great deal of criticism and even outright rejection over the years, largely because it seems to fail to connect with other parts of economic theory about which many of us also have strong ideas. So let me now turn to the problems of linking the MMF model with several apparently competing economic doctrines.

Linkage Problem 1: Trade Theory

The problem of joining international macroeconomics with trade theory has not been at the top of many people's agenda in recent years. Nonetheless, it is a glaring gap in our understanding, and I believe that the absence of a well-explained link between trade and finance has been a major source of analytical and even policy confusion.

The nature of the problem should be obvious. In international trade theory, we are concerned with explaining the pattern of production and trade in a many-good, many-factor world. The model described above, however, seems to be one in which each country is simply assumed to produce a single good that is not a perfect substitute for goods produced abroad and in which there is nothing interesting going on in factor markets. Where are the trade-theoretic underpinnings of the macroeconomic model?

In a way, it is remarkable that economists have made so little effort to integrate international trade and monetary economics. The difficulty has been apparent at least since Ricardo's time: there is no room in Ricardo's model, or certainly in the formalization of that model by John Stuart Mill, for the kind of price movements envisioned in Hume's story of balance-of-payments adjust-

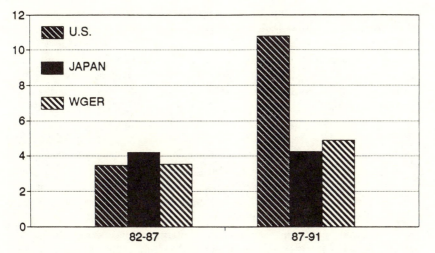

Figure 13.3 Rates of Export Growth

ment. Robert Mundell developed his macroeconomic analysis of exchange-rate regimes only a few years after making major contributions to real-trade theory; yet the two analyses seem to be referring to completely different worlds.

In fact, I can think of only one well-known paper that seriously tries to build a bridge between international trade and international money: the Ricardian model of Dornbusch, Fischer, and Samuelson (1977). That paper struck me like a bolt of lightning when I first read it—it seemed to me to legitimize international macroeconomics and to make sense of some of its characteristic assumptions in a way that had not been possible before. Not everyone appreciates what these three accomplished, however, so let me review briefly their argument, before I talk about what is missing.

The Dornbusch-Fischer-Samuelson approach envisages a world in which each country has only a single factor of production, which it can use to produce a large number of traded goods and perhaps a range of nontraded goods as well. It begins with a pure, static, real-trade model. With a little *ad hockery*, however—simply assuming domestic nominal expenditure proportional to the domestic money supply—the model becomes dynamic and monetary. With a little more *ad hockery*—assuming rigid nominal wages—the model becomes Keynesian as well.

The model immediately suggests answers to several major historical debates in international economics; indeed, it suggests that they are all really about the same thing. It offers a startlingly neat solution to the Keynes-Ohlin debate over the transfer problem: Ohlin is right in principle, but Keynes is right in practice if a large fraction of expenditure falls on nontraded goods. The model also offers a quick integration of trade theory with Hume's adjustment mechanism: allowing money to flow automatically generates a specie-flow mechanism; if nontraded goods are important, this then becomes a *price*-specie-flow mechanism in which a trade deficit is associated with an unusually high relative wage rate and domestic price level. In other words, the question of whether the price component of Hume's story is essential is the same as the answer to the transfer problem. Finally, when we turn to devaluation, we see that the debate between the absorption and elasticity approaches comes down to the same thing: relative price changes are an essential part of the adjustment process if, and only if, conventional wisdom on the transfer problem is right.

The model also shows that the conventional wisdom that exchange-rate adjustment helps reconcile balance-of-payments targets with employment targets is justified in the presence of sticky nominal wages. In so doing, it basically integrates Ricardo's trade theory not only with Hume's earlier monetary story, but with the external-and-internal-balance stories that Swan (1963), Johnson (1958), and others put at the heart of international macroeconomic analysis 140 years later.

All of this is wonderful. I have used what I learned from Dornbusch, Fischer, and Samuelson as an underpinning for a lot of work and, indeed, for some serious policy arguments. With its remarkable encapsulation of two hundred years of thought into seventeen pages of text, it is one of my favorite papers.

There is only one problem. Nobody thinks that the Ricardian model is an adequate representation of the forces driving international trade. And, unfortunately, the integration of trade and monetary theory achieved by Dornbusch, Fischer, and Samuelson does not easily survive introduction of a more complex trade model. To see the problem, let us simply imagine replacing the Ricardian setting with a standard two-factor model of trade and see what happens to the results.

In the Ricardian model, introducing nontraded goods is enough to give us the conventional presumption on the transfer problem. If country A transfers income to country B, the transfer will raise the demand for nontraded goods in B and lower it in A, even if they have the same expenditure patterns on the margin. Because nontraded goods are produced with domestic labor, the effect is to shift world relative demand for the two countries' labor, and thus to push up B's relative wage rate. This shift in the double-factorial terms of trade will produce a corresponding change in just about any measure of the real exchange rate.

It is easy to show, however, that, in a two-or-more-factor world, this need not happen. Suppose, for example, that there are two traded goods and one nontraded good, produced with two factors. And suppose that each country produces at least some of both traded goods. A transfer will then lead to a complicated reshuffle of resources within each country, with the nontraded sector releasing resources to traded-goods production in one country and absorbing them in the other, generating Rybczinski effects all over the place. If technologies and tastes are the same, however, the end result of the shuffle will be to allow the world to accommodate the shift in the location of consumption of nontraded goods without any change in relative prices or factor returns. The simple association of a large nontraded sector with a Keynesian view on the transfer problem is broken.

Worse yet, when there are multiple factors of production, one cannot introduce a Keynesian story about unemployment simply by assuming a rigid nominal wage rate. Fixed wage rates in two-factor models do weird things, leading to abrupt changes in specialization when the relative wage rates shift a little. Obviously, that doesn't happen in practice, and the reason why is clear: steel mills cannot be turned into textile mills over the course of a few months. What we learn, however, is that, once we try to get the realistic trade-off between internal and external balance into anything more complex than a Ricardian model, we are immediately faced with the need to get into a lot of messy stuff. We cannot just assume sticky wages; we need to start worrying about things like the dynamic adjustment of sector-specific capital stocks. The simplicity of both the Mundell-Fleming model and the Dornbusch-Fischer-Samuelson model seems to get buried under a welter of detail.

How, as economists, do we deal with the glaring inconsistency between the models we use to think about macroeconomic and trade issues? One answer is simply to specialize: many trade economists profess a total lack of understanding of, or faith in, macroeconomic analysis, and many macroeconomists simply lack interest in trade. The world wants answers, however, and some of us try to keep abreast in both areas. How do we manage the cognitive dissonance? We do so largely, I believe, by telling ourselves that the MMF model is a short-run story, whereas modern trade theory is a long-run story. In fact, however, nobody other than Dornbusch, Fischer, and Samuelson has succeeded in making anything like MMF emerge as the short run of a long-run model.

Matters get even worse when we introduce the concerns of the "new trade theory," increasing returns and imperfect competition. I have personally made a small stab at integrating monetary factors into a new-trade-theory model (Krugman 1987), using a framework shamelessly plagiarized from Dornbusch, Fischer, and Samuelson. That exercise suggested that, in a world of increasing returns, we may not even be able to assume that the long run is exempt from monetary influences: a large short-run overvaluation or undervaluation may permanently change the pattern of dynamic comparative advantage.

What I have argued, then, is that there is a glaring lack of consistency between the stories we tell about international trade and the way that we model trading economies when we want to talk about macroeconomics. One reaction to this inconsistency would be to dismiss the macroeconomic analysis. After all, the trade stories have coherent microeconomic bases, and the MMF model does not. That is not, however, my reaction. The fact is that the MMF analysis seems to be extremely useful—it appears to work in practice much better than it ought to work in the light of trade theory. The question is why.

So here is a research challenge: let us try to build a link between the trade analysis that works in theory and the macroeconomic analysis that seems to work in practice.

Linkage Problem 2: Intertemporal Analysis

A number of years ago, when I was on the staff of the Council of Economic Advisers, I found myself obliged to defend the CEA free-trade position in a meeting in which most people were much more senior than I. Among them was the then U.S. trade representative. At one point, I tried to emphasize the domestic origins of the U.S. trade deficit by referring to the point that the trade balance equals the difference between domestic saving and domestic investment. Ambassador Brock was polite. "That's an interesting theory," he said.

Of course, the identity $X - M = S - I$ is not a theory. It is one of the few things in international economics about which we are absolutely sure. So one might think that an "intertemporal" approach to the balance of payments, one that treats current accounts as the outcome of long-run savings and investment decisions, would be at the core of the way we do open-economy macroeconomics. And we all invoke such an approach, at least informally, when we try to discuss enduring patterns in international capital flows, such as the persistent current-account surpluses of Japan and prereunification West Germany. There is also a growing formal literature on international economic models based on intertemporal optimization models. This is nicely surveyed by Razin in Chapter 5.

What seems striking to me, however, is that there has been very little contact between the world of more or less practical policy analysis and the intertemporal approach. If anyone has tried to discuss the travails of the EMS in terms of intertemporal optimization, I am not aware of it.

Why do we seem unable to make any use of these models? It could be that the policy-relevant types are simply too old-fashioned to be willing to use modern analysis—but I don't think that's a fair judgment. The real reason, I think, is that the intertemporal approach doesn't seem to accord with what we think we know about what actually happens.

Let me start at the shallow end. The thing I find most striking about the predictions from intertemporal maximizing models is how complicated they are compared with the fairly simple stories told by the MMF model. Suppose I ask how an extra percentage point of U.S. economic growth next year will affect U.S. trade. Even a very simple intertemporal model will respond with a request for more information. Is the shock temporary or permanent? Is the shock in traded or nontraded goods? Or what about the relation between the trade balance and the real exchange rate? The answer again seems to depend on a variety of questions about the source and persistence of shocks. The peculiar thing is that, although things are complicated and messy in theory, they are fairly simple in practice: the trade equations described by Hooper and Marquez (Chapter 4), equations that work rather well, tell us that 1 percent on U.S. GDP means imports rise by 2 percent; 10 percent on the real exchange rate means net exports decline by 1 percent of GDP—end of story. It is hard to sell a practical policy economist on a theoretical framework that seems to require her to throw away simple tools that have proved useful and to replace them with complicated ones that seem to give no answers at all.

A deeper problem with the intertemporal approach is that it may be rigorous but wrong. It assumes that people have a very high degree of rationality about the effects of shocks on their future income, to a degree that one can reasonably argue would actually require irrational expenditures of resources on gathering and processing information.

Consider, for example, what the intertemporal approach says about one of the issues surrounding the troubles of the EMS. Should Germany have tried to finance the rebuilding of the east with higher taxes rather than accept large fiscal deficits? Many economists believe that with a different fiscal stance by Germany, the strains that led to Black Wednesday could have been avoided. According to the standard intertemporal approach, however, it would have made no difference. Robert Barro became famous for arguing that long-lived households should decide on their consumption based on what they expect the government to spend, not on the particular time path of the taxes it plans to collect to pay for that spending.

The point, of course, is that this story requires that ordinary West German households sit down over their evening meal and estimate the impact of likely subsidies to the east on their future tax liabilities. Is this plausible? Would the improvement in expected utility from doing so actually be worth the time and effort for the typical German family? I doubt it. Surely it is far more likely that people use reasonable, but not hyperrational, rules of thumb to decide on their consumption, rules that are not likely to provide an automatic offset to changes in taxes unmatched by changes in spending plans.

We might note as an aside that many intertemporal models make the high rationality required seem more plausible by assuming an ergodic structure of recurrent random shocks. The idea is that, through long experience, households develop rules of thumb that approximate optimal behavior given the shocks they typically face. Unfortunately, the times when we really need our models are when *atypical* shocks come along; German reunification is not something that happens on a regular basis.

Finally, let me note the obvious point that the MMF model focuses crucially on the role of sluggish price adjustment, and that this focus seems to be correct. The intertemporal models currently available, however, are full-employment models in which there is no natural way to introduce the nominal rigidities that remain so critical to understanding the real issues that confront us.

Yet one cannot simply dismiss an intertemporal approach as useless. The present is linked to the future by saving and investment; what we do now matters for what we expect to happen in the future, and vice versa. We cannot ultimately rest easy with any short-run model that is not at least approximately embedded in some kind of intertemporal framework. The MMF model, once again, does not meet that criterion; it respects the accounting identities, but that's about it.

So here is another research challenge: let us try to build an intertemporal approach in which the balance of payments is determined by forward-looking (if not necessarily hyperrational) saving and investment decisions, yet which remains able to discuss the kind of issue that the MMF model seems to handle acceptably.

Linkage Problem 3: Rational Expectations

During the 1970s, the rational-expectations revolution swept all before it in macroeconomics. It became completely unacceptable in polite circles to make *ad hoc* assumptions about expectations or dynamic adjustment processes. Everything, from asset pricing to aggregate supply, was supposed to be grounded in rational behavior, albeit in the presence of incomplete information. At the core of the revolution was what we may call the Lucas Project, the effort to build business-cycle theory on maximizing microfoundations.

The initial effect of this revolution was exhilarating; its eventual effect was devastating. Traditional Keynesian macroeconomics was, as a matter of theory, completely vanquished, as were the various *ad hoc* models of asset markets that had been common ingredients of macroeconomic analysis up to that point. The ramshackle, *ad hoc* intellectual structures of the 1950s and 60s were ruthlessly cleared away, making room for the erection of a new structure to be based on secure microfoundations. Unfortunately, that structure never got built.

The fact is that the Lucas Project succeeded in destroying the old regime but failed to create a workable new macroeconomics. The effort to explain the business cycle in terms of rational confusion over which shocks were nominal and which were real was, in the end, a failure: economic agents have too much information, and business cycles are too persistent. The true believers in equilibrium business cycles shifted to real-business-cycle theory (to which the intertemporal models of the balance of payments are related), while most theorists simply abandoned the subject of business cycles altogether. Meanwhile, forecasts and policy assessments had to be made. So, practical economists continued to use the old-fashioned models, like Cuban drivers stranded by the U.S. embargo doing the best they can with lovingly maintained 1959 Chevys.

The theoretical devastation wreaked by the rational-expectations revolution was perhaps most severe in international macroeconomics, for two reasons.

First, in international even more than domestic economics, the evidence for some kind of nominal rigidity is overwhelming. Domestic macroeconomists can point to the lack of clear correlation between any particular monetary aggregate and real output and deny that nominal variables have real effects; or they can claim that such correlation as there is represents reverse causation from real shocks to an endogenous Federal Reserve. International macroeconomists must face up to much stronger evidence, the nearly perfect correlation between nominal and real exchange rates in industrial countries since 1980. There are a few who try to make the reverse causation argument—but they must then confront the question of why the "real" shocks seem to change so much when the nominal regime shifts. Real exchange rates were far more volatile after 1973 than before; the formation of the EMS was associated with a sharp reduction in real-exchange-rate movement within the currency bloc. An extremist might dismiss even this evidence on the grounds that the changes in exchange-rate regime were endogenous. This is certainly true: physicists tell us that only a few basic constants are truly exogenous, and the rest is all quantum mechanics. But, as Eichengreen (Chapter 1) shows, the factors determining changes in exchange regime are far too subtle to produce such a raw, striking correlation. And one must, in the end, also confront such facts as the change in Ireland's real-exchange-rate behavior from close correlation with the United Kingdom before its entry into the ERM to close correlation with Germany afterward. I personally think that the effort to explain away the apparent real effects of nominal shocks is silly, even if one restricts oneself to domestic evidence. Once one confronts international evidence, however, it becomes an act of almost pathological denial.

The problem, of course, is that Lucas made us all painfully aware that we lack good microfoundations for assuming any sort of nominal rigidities. This leaves international macroeconomics with a painful dilemma: to write a macroeconomic model with sticky prices is professionally dangerous, but to write one without such rigidities is empirically ridiculous. The result is a considerable degree of intellectual paralysis.

The situation is made worse by the second problem of international macro-economics: the apparent failure of rational expectations even in the place where one might hope it would work, international asset markets.

For a number of years, there was a sort of academic industry that focused on testing the speculative efficiency of the forward exchange rate. A few early papers claimed to confirm that the forward rate was an efficient predictor of the subsequent change in the exchange rate (or more accurately, failed to reject the null hypothesis that it was an efficient predictor). Since the crucial paper by Hansen and Hodrick (1980), however, it has been obvious that this is not the case. Indeed, if anything, the correlation is negative. Now, this need not imply a rejection of efficiency if there are risk premia, especially shifting ones—although nobody thought large shifting risk premia were likely to be important until the devastating failure of simple efficiency ideas became apparent. In the end, however, it just won't wash. Taylor (Chapter 2) summarizes the huge and dispiriting literature on foreign-exchange-market efficiency: after more than a decade of work, it seems clear that nobody has found any reasonable way to "save" the speculative-efficiency hypothesis within the data. This is devastating in its impact on our research. What we know how to model are efficient markets; what we apparently confront are inefficient ones. Nor can we, in international macroeconomics, tacitly put speculative behavior on one side. Under floating exchange rates, the role of market expectations is crucial to every aspect of policy analysis.

What practical policy analysts do, of course, is apply *ad hoc* rules about expectation formation, such as the rule embedded in equation (6) in my exposition of the MMF. These rules are clearly wrong as a full description of how markets behave, yet they contain enough truth to give some guidance, and they at least allow the model to be completed. This kind of brutal expediency, however, encourages the slightly disreputable reputation that international macroeconomics has among smart young economists.

In my last two linkage discussions, I have suggested that there is room for some research on trying to put what we think we know about international monetary economics together with what we think we know about related fields. Here, I have no such optimistic suggestion. It seems to me that macroeconomics is in a terrible state independent of its international aspects. Until we find some resolution of its difficulties, which I suspect will involve facing up to deep issues, such as the role of bounded rationality, there is little that can be done on the international front. Perhaps a slender bridge can be constructed between international macroeconomics and "new Keynesian" macroeconomics à la Mankiw (1992; Mankiw and Romer, 1991), but I guess I wouldn't expect more from that than a bit of rationalization for continuing to use the MMF model.

4 What We Need to Know

Up to this point, I have described a series of problems with the MMF model of international macroeconomics. I have pointed out that it is an *ad hoc* model that is poorly linked with the models that we use to explain international trade, even though an open macroeconomy is necessarily also a trading economy. I have pointed out further that the MMF model does not link up at all well with our best models of saving and investment decisions, even though it is a basic identity that the current account equals the savings-investment balance. And I have pointed out that the MMF model, along with virtually all relevant short-run macroeconomics, has been intellectually stranded by the way the rational-expectations macroeconomics first vanquished Keynesianism, then collapsed in the face of its own internal contradictions.

And yet, despite all of these problems, when it comes to making sense of the international monetary system, the macroeconomic side is not the biggest obstacle. The MMF model is crude, *ad hoc*, and in huge need of improvement. Nonetheless, it is a workable guide. If you ask me what will happen if, say, Mexico emulates Argentina and adopts a "currency-board" system that pegs the peso to the dollar; if you ask me what will happen if France gives up the *franc fort*, or Germany decides to slash public spending; if you ask what the consequences have been of Canada's determination to achieve price stability, I think, in all of these cases, I know how to answer—and maybe even to produce a rough quantitative assessment—using something along the lines of the MMF model.

But now, suppose you ask me some related questions, to which policy-makers would very much like to know the answers. What will be the impact on European trade and, beyond that, on the efficiency of the European economy if the European Community (EC) actually adopts a common currency? What will be the effect on North American trade if Canada and Mexico permanently peg their currencies to the U.S. dollar? I can talk a good game on these questions when pressed, but I know, even if my listeners do not, that I do not have a model nearly as well developed as the MMF model to back up my assertions. What I have is only a set of nice words, backed by vague images. In particular, I have no real way of quantifying the forces to which I can allude. To put it briefly, we have a workable, if not beautiful, model of international macroeconomics; we have no real model of the microeconomics of international money.

The same is, of course, true for domestic macroeconomics. The truth is that there is no even halfway adequate model of the microeconomics of money, at least in the sense of a model that addresses the issues that everyone thinks really matter. The case in point is the welfare costs of inflation: existing models only let us get at the "shoe-leather" costs that arise from the use of non-interest-bearing money as a medium of exchange. These costs are small at anything short of hyperinflation. Most economists who worry about the issue believe, however, that the main costs of inflation lie, not in the degraded role of money as medium of exchange, but in its damaged role as unit of account—for which we have no model.

Nonetheless, in domestic macroeconomics, we do not usually find that our microeconomic ignorance is crucial. The consensus that there is no long-run trade-off between unemployment and inflation, but that the short-run trade-off is quite flat, has allowed the emergence of a policy consensus that inflation should be kept at its current fairly low levels, but that it is not worth a costly push to full price stability. To put it another way, the central issues in domestic monetary policy do not, at present, seem to require reaching a judgment about the microeconomic side of the equation. (Strictly, this is true only for advanced countries with low inflation. The relation between inflation and long-run growth is much more central for the kind of stabilization problems discussed by Bruno in Chapter 9).

In international monetary affairs, however, I think it is fair to say that the central, canonical issue is that of choosing an exchange regime. Of course, there are always problems of policy management within an exchange regime: Chancellor Lamont still needs all the advice he can get, and better open-economy macroeconomic models remain essential to many real policy issues, such as the coordination problems discussed by Bryant (Chapter 11). Still, the big issues involve fundamental regime choice. Should Mexico contemplate devaluation to restore some of its industrial competitiveness, or should it lock in its gains against inflation by permanently pegging to the dollar (or even adopting the dollar as its currency)? Should Sweden (Poland? Slovakia?) join EMU, if such a thing happens? These are all questions that are, in effect, variants of the optimum-currency-area problem.

Now, Mundell (1961), McKinnon (1963), and Kenen (1969) gave us a very nice intellectual structure for thinking about the problem of defining an optimum currency area. In all cases, we think of a country as asking whether it prefers the macroeconomic independence that comes with an independent currency and perhaps a floating rate, or whether it prefers the microeconomic benefits of stable rates and perhaps a common currency. We have a fairly good idea of what the macroeconomic trade-off is: we know that fixed rates cost least when trade is large, when labor mobility is high, when shocks are symmetric, and when there are compensating fiscal transfers. Knowing this, we guess that some index based on these criteria will indicate when and if a country should join a currency area.

In fact, however, we know almost nothing about the other side of the comparison. To repeat: what we say about the microeconomics is a matter of metaphor and slogans rather than worked-out models. I am sure that a common European currency would save the transaction expenses now incurred in changing currencies—London and Paris could get by with far fewer foreign-exchange kiosks. Beyond that, we really don't know. Does confusion over fluctuation in units of account significantly inhibit the ability of European businesspeople to reach mutually beneficial deals? To the extent that it does, how large are the costs? I don't think we even have an idea of the order of magnitude.

Of course, we must make judgments anyway. I would identify three different strategies that have been used to try to deal with, or perhaps to paper over, our almost total ignorance about the crucial microeconomic trade-offs involved in the formation of monetary areas.

First, we seem to be able to resolve the issue in many cases by pointing to overriding political concerns, often involving seigniorage, that force monetary areas to coincide with nations. Goodhart (Chapter 12) makes this point effectively, and it is surely often valid. Yet I cannot help noticing the relief with which economists seize upon discussions of seigniorage as a way to avoid the really difficult issues. After all, seigniorage is something we understand; we slip away from the optimum-currency-area argument into a discussion of inflation taxes with something like the attitude of a man changing from his business shoes into a pair of comfortable old slippers. Unfortunately, comfortable as we may be with this kind of argument, it will only sometimes be enough.

Second, quite a few economists have tried to assert that there are no macroeconomic benefits to independent currencies, so we don't have to worry about how big the microeconomic costs are. This line of argument usually rests on rational-expectations macroeconomics, which seems to suggest that highly visible nominal policies such as currency depreciation should have, at most, very transitory real effects. Indeed, with some time-consistency stories thrown in, one may argue that a country with a propensity to inflationary policies is actually better off pegging its currency to a more disciplined partner, because this commitment will gain it credibility that actually improves the *ex post* trade-off between inflation and unemployment. If fixed rates are a macroeconomic plus, then any microeconomic gains are icing on the cake; our ignorance about their size doesn't matter for policy purposes.

Unfortunately, this neat solution to our conundrum is just too neat. There was a time when it seemed reasonably plausible for non-German Europe: as long as the United Kingdom, Italy, and even France were preoccupied with regaining credibility in their fight against inflation, one could argue that pegging to the mark was an unambiguous good. But that was a special contingent circumstance. In the world of 1993, when inflation is nobody's top priority and recession is a big problem, when the vices of German fiscal policy have upstaged the virtues of German monetary policy, it becomes clear that the old-fashioned view that pegging one's currency will impose macroeconomic costs is once again the sensible one. For most of 1992, no European policymaker was willing to say as much, but, despite their protestations that they would never contemplate abandoning the ERM, it was obvious to everyone, speculators especially, that the non-trade-off view was no longer viable. This is not to say that arguments about credibility may not be useful in their place, as in Rodrik's discussion (Chapter 8) of the problems of sequencing of reform. We are kidding ourselves, however, if we think that they can settle the optimum-currency-area problem.

Finally, we often try to deal with our microeconomic ignorance by leaning on analogies. In particular, the Great Analogy of international monetary discussion in the late 1980s and early 1990s has turned out to be between potential currency blocs and the United States. Initially, this analogy was used to justify Europe's lunge toward monetary union. After all, the United States is a continent-sized monetary union that works pretty well, so why shouldn't the same be true for the EC? Subsequent research has driven home just how different Europe is from the United States on at least two of the dimensions of the optimum-currency-area argument—labor mobility and fiscal integration—and the comparison with the United States is now mostly used as a critique of monetary union.

The U.S.-Europe comparison is a useful intellectual strategy. It has led to a lot of very interesting economic research and has clearly raised the tone of the discussion of international monetary reform. I have used it as an effective debating tool myself. Yet it is clear if we are honest with ourselves that it is a bit of an intellectual scam. We can compare Europe (or the North American Free Trade Area, or any other proposed currency bloc) with the United States. But we have no reason to suppose that the United States defines an optimum currency area. Conceivably, the United States would be better off with a half-dozen regional currencies. Equally conceivably, the hidden microeconomic benefits of a common currency are so overwhelming in the United States that Europe should follow suit even though the macroeconomic costs would be much greater. We just don't know. It is not that there are conflicts among the estimates. There are simply no estimates at all. At this point, you may ask me how I propose to remedy this gap. The short answer is that I don't know. All I can do is assert that, if there is one crucial priority in international monetary economics, it is putting some analytical flesh on the microeconomic side of the optimum-currency-area argument.

This lecture is entitled "What Do We Need to Know about the International Monetary System?" Much of it, however, has dealt with things I would *like* to know. I would like to know how the macroeconomic model that I more or less believe can be reconciled with the trade models that I also more or less believe. I would like to know how to build a bridge between an intertemporal story about savings and investment and that macroeconomic model. And I would very much like to be able to rebuild a macroeconomic structure that I can believe in the desolation that rational expectations left behind. For many

purposes, however, including the giving of policy advice, the existing macroeconomic model is good enough to serve for the time being. What we *need* to
know is how to evaluate the microeconomics of international monetary systems. Until we can do that, we are making policy advice by the seat of our
pants.

References

Dornbusch, Rudiger, Stanley Fischer, and Paul A. Samuelson, "Comparative Advantage, Trade, and Payments in a Ricardian Model with a Continuum of Goods,"
American Economic Review, 67 (December 1977), pp. 823–839.

Graham, Frank D., "Some Aspects of Protection Further Considered," *Quarterly Journal of Economics*, 37 (February 1923), pp. 199–227.

———, *Fundamentals of International Monetary Policy*, Essays in International Finance No. 2, Princeton, N.J., Princeton University, International Finance Section,
Autumn 1943.

Hansen, Lars P., and Robert J. Hodrick, "Forward Exchange Rates as Optimal Predictors of Future Spot Rates: An Econometric Analysis," *Journal of Political Economy*,
88 (October 1980), pp. 829–853.

Johnson, Harry G., "Towards a General Theory of the Balance of Payments," in Harry
G. Johnson, *International Trade and Economic Growth*, London and New York,
Allen and Unwin, 1958, pp. 153–168.

Kenen, Peter B., "The Theory of Optimum Currency Areas: An Eclectic View," in
Robert A. Mundell and Alexander K. Swoboda, eds., *Monetary Problems of the
International Economy*, Chicago, University of Chicago Press, 1969, pp. 41–60;
reprinted in Peter B. Kenen, *Essays in International Economics*, Princeton, N.J.,
Princeton University Press, 1980, pp. 163–182.

Krugman, Paul R., "The Narrow Moving Band, the Dutch Disease, and the Competitive Consequences of Mrs. Thatcher: Notes on Trade in the Presence of Dynamic
Scale Economies," *Journal of Development Economics*, 27 (October 1987), pp. 41–
55.

———, *Has the Adjustment Process Worked?* Washington, D.C., Institute for International Economics, 1991.

Krugman, Paul R., and Maurice Obstfeld, *International Economics: Theory and Policy*, 2d ed., New York, Harper Collins, 1991.

McKinnon, Ronald I., "Optimum Currency Areas," *American Economic Review*, 53
(September 1963), pp. 717–724.

Mankiw, N. Gregory, *Macroeconomics*, New York, Worth, 1992.

Mankiw, N. Gregory, and David Romer, eds., *New Keynesian Economics*, Cambridge,
Mass., MIT Press, 1991.

Mundell, Robert A., "A Theory of Optimum Currency Areas," *American Economic
Review*, 51 (September 1961), pp. 657–664.

Swan, Trevor W., "Longer-Run Problems of the Balance of Payments," in Heinz W.
Arndt and W. Max Corden, eds., *The Australian Economy: A Volume of Readings*,
Melbourne, Cheshire, 1963.

Weinberg, Stephen, *Dreams of a Final Theory*, New York, Pantheon, 1992.

Conference Participants _____

(Authors of chapters in this volume are indicated by an asterisk)

Polly Reynolds Allen
Professor of Economics
University of Connecticut

Stanley W. Black
Lurey Professor of Economics
University of North Carolina at Chapel Hill

William H. Branson
John Foster Dulles Professor of International Affairs
Princeton University

*Michael Bruno
Professor of Economics
The Hebrew University

*Ralph C. Bryant
Senior Fellow, Economic Studies
The Brookings Institution

Willem H. Buiter
Juan Trippe Professor of Economics
Yale University

Benjamin Jerry Cohen
Louis G. Lancaster Professor of International Political Economy
University of California at Santa Barbara

Professor Susan Collins
Senior Fellow
The Brookings Institution
Associate Professor
Georgetown University

*Richard N. Cooper
Maurits C. Boas Professor of International Economics
Harvard University

W. Max Corden
Professor of International Economics
The Paul H. Nitze School of Advanced International Studies
The Johns Hopkins University

*Michael P. Dooley
Professor of Economics
University of California at Santa Cruz

Rudiger Dornbusch
Ford International Professor of Economics
Massachusetts Institute of Technology

*Barry Eichengreen
Professor of Economics
University of California at Berkeley

*Stanley Fischer
Professor of Economics
Massachusetts Institute of Technology

Jacob Frenkel
Governor
Bank of Israel

Kenneth A. Froot
Professor of Business Administration
Harvard University Graduate School of Business

Alberto Giovannini
Jerome A. Chazen Professor of International Business
Graduate School of Business
Columbia University

Morris Goldstein
Deputy Director, Research Department
International Monetary Fund

*Charles A. E. Goodhart
Norman Sosnow Professor of Banking and Finance
London School of Economics

*Peter Hooper
Assistant Director
Board of Governors of the Federal Reserve System

Andrew Hughes Hallett
Professor of Macroeconomics
University of Strathclyde and Princeton University

Charles P. Kindleberger
Ford International Professor of Economics, Emeritus
Massachusetts Institute of Technology

*Paul R. Krugman
Professor of Economics
Massachusetts Institute of Technology

*Ronald I. McKinnon
Professor of Economics
Stanford University

*Jaime Marquez
Senior Economist
Board of Governors of the Federal Reserve System

Richard C. Marston
Professor of Finance and Economics
The Wharton School
University of Pennsylvania

*Michael Mussa
Economic Counsellor and Director of Research
International Monetary Fund

*Maurice Obstfeld
Professor of Economics
University of California at Berkeley

*John Odling-Smee
Director, European Department II
International Monetary Fund

Gardner Patterson
Washington, D.C.

*Assaf Razin
Professor of Economics and Vice Rector
Tel Aviv University

*Dani Rodrik
Professor of Economics and International Affairs
Columbia University

Kenneth S. Rogoff
Professor of Economics and International Affairs
Woodrow Wilson School
Princeton University

*Mark P. Taylor
Senior Economist
International Monetary Fund

Paul A. Volcker
Frederick H. Schultz Class of 1951 Professor of International Economic Policy
Woodrow Wilson School
Princeton University

*John Williamson
Senior Fellow
Institute of International Economics

Thomas A. Wolf
Chief, Russia Division
European Department II
International Monetary Fund

Author Index

Subject Index

aid. *See* economic assistance

Albania, 385

arbitrage: in basic target-zone model, 66–68; in foreign-exchange market efficiency, 54–60

Argentina: private investment link to real-exchange-rate anchor, 308–9; stabilization success, 356; trade liberalization, 295, 299–300

Baker Plan (1985), 274–75

balance of payments: conventional model of real, 109–11; crises under gold standard, 8–9; current-account intertemporal optimizing model, 170; current-account theory, 171–78; intertemporal analysis, 520–21; intertemporal approach to current account, 170–71, 180–89; Marshall-Lerner condition, 112–13; model with nontraded goods, 111–12; partial-equilibrium model defined, 141; partial U.S./Japanese trade-balance performance, 148–57; real partial equilibrium, 141–57; static-model approach to current account, 169–70; static model of open-economy current account, 169–70; trade-balance J-curve path, 113

banking system: financial intermediation to developing countries, 263–69; role in creation of and solution to debt crisis, 269–82; Russia, 373

Baring Crisis (1890), 8–9

Bolivia: stabilization success, 352–53, 356; trade liberalization, 295, 296–97

Brady Plan, 262, 279–83

Brazil: trade liberalization, 295, 300–301

Bretton Woods: effect on exchange rates, 14–19; exchange-rate system under, 34; limitations of, 100–101; monetary cooperation under, 10

Bulgaria: economic growth, 385; stabilization, 377

CAP. *See* Common Agricultural Policy (CAP)

capital flows: capital flight during external-debt buildup, 267–68; controls as stabiliza-tion policy instrument, 191–93; inflows into Brady Plan countries, 282–83; resurgence to developing countries of private, 262

capital formation: impact of economic growth and inflation, 337–42

capital markets, international: allocation function, 234; diversification of consumption risk, 217–34; insurance function, 204–6; risk sharing, 225–32

capital mobility: benefits of international, 201; to capital-poor countries, 234–36; cross-sectional saving-investment relation to, 250–55; definition in multicountry context, 202; free, 192; with intertemporal substitution, 170–71; law of one price with perfect, 202–4; measurement of (Feldstein-Horioka), 236–44; perfect and imperfect, 171–78, 202–17, 237–38; regional and international risk sharing, 217–34; saving and investment equality with international, 189–93; volume and rate of, 255

central banks: role in Russia, 370–73; role of national, 95–97; role under gold standard, 8–9; in U.S. financial crisis (1907), 9–10. *See also* European Central Bank (ECB), proposed; European System of Central Banks (ESCB)

Chile: private investment link to real-exchange-rate anchor, 307–9; stabilization success, 352–53; trade liberalization, 295–97

Common Agricultural Policy (CAP), 469

common currency. *See* currency, common; single-currency area

competition, intergovernmental, 424–25

consumption correlations: international, 217–25; regional, 225–29

consumption risks: diversification of international, 217–34; international allocation of, 204–6

cooperation, international: among national governments, 400–404; arguments against, 423–25, 430–31; circumstances for, 419; conditions for counterproductive, 424; harmonization, 408; for international monetary sta-